R 810.9
W399

CHANEY BRANCH LIBRARY

W9-CEC-449
3 5674 02898704 9

REFERENCE

DETROIT PUBLIC LIBRARY

CHANEY BRANCH LIBRARY
16101 GRAND RIVER
DETROIT, MI 48227

DATE DUE

REFERENCE	REFERENCE
REFERENCE	REFERENCE
REFERENCE	REFERENCE

BC-3

AGP3839-1

CY   JUL - - 1999
Ref

Webster's
Dictionary of
American Authors

Webster's

Dictionary of
American Authors

Created in Cooperation with the Editors of

MERRIAM-WEBSTER

SMITHMARK
REFERENCE

Based on Merriam-Webster's Encyclopedia of Literature.
© *1995 by Merriam-Webster Incorporated.*
Philippines © *1995 by Merriam-Webster, Incorporated.*

All rights reserved. No part of this book covered by the copyrights hereon
may be reproduced or copied in any form or by any means—graphic,
electronic, or mechanical, including photocopying, taping, or information
storage and retrieval systems—without written permission of the publisher.

This edition published in 1996 by
SMITHMARK Publishers,
a division of US Media Holdings Inc.
16 East 32nd Street,
New York, NY 10016.

SMITHMARK books are available for bulk purchase for sales promotion
and premium use. For details, write or call the manager of special sales,
SMITHMARK Publishers, 16 East 32nd Street, New York, NY 10016;
(212) 532-6600.

Library of Congress Cataloging-in-Publication Data

Webster's dictionary of American authors / created in cooperation with the
    editors of Merriam-Webster.
            p.   cm.
        "Based on the Merriam-Webster's encyclopedia of literature"—T.p.
verso.
    Includes index.
    ISBN: 0-8317-7158-5
        1. American literature—Bio-bibliography—Dictionaries.   2. Authors,
American—Biography—Dictionaries.   I. Merriam-Webster Inc.
II. Merriam-Webster's encyclopedia of literature.
PS21.W43   1996
810.9'0003—dc20   95-48311
[B]   CIP

Printed in the United States of America.

98   97   96   5   4   3   2   1

Contents

Preface

"It is civilization they are building, a history they are compiling, a way of looking at the world and humanity's place in it."

This is how author Wallace Stegner described the role of writers in the introduction to his book *Where the Bluebird Sings to the Lemonade Springs*. Stegner, no mean writer himself, was speaking of writers of the American West, but his notion that writers are builders of civilization aptly applies to all writers, particularly those who make up the American literary tradition.

Like America itself, American literature is best imagined as a rich and spicy stew of ethnic varieties, regional diversities, political passions, and creative extremes. From philosophies by New England WASPs (Emerson and Hawthorne) to novels by urban Jews (I.B. Singer and Saul Bellow) and tales of the American experience by those of Asian (Amy Tan), Irish (John O'Hara and Eugene O'Neill), Italian (Gay Talese), or African-American (Malcolm X, Langston Hughes) descent, it is clear that ethnic variety contributes greatly to America's literary richness.

Yet America's regional differences are as remarkable as her ethnic ones. The contrast between the poems of New England farmer Robert Frost and those of native Georgia son James Dickey is profound. Each poet's surroundings dominate and mold their use of the tools of their trade.

To make the differences even more complex, the American regional diversities are often defined by the ethnic ones. The Scandinavian settlers of Willa Cather's novels of the American Plains, for example, are quintessential American literary characters. Even as newcomers to this land, they reflect the Western experience not simply as Scandinavians, but as Americans. Furthermore, some American writers (including Ernest Hemingway, F. Scott Fitzgerald, T.S. Eliot, and Edith Wharton) had to leave the North American continent in order to understand and write about the society. The often difficult experiences of these American expatriates nurtured some of the finest accomplishments of any novelists, poets, or even historians in conveying the truth about American culture.

As with most art forms, American literature requires a lifetime of study to truly know it. As most of us cannot be monks or university dons, we instead accept that we can only be enlightened amateurs. We love literature, we love learning about it, and we need to find a way to collect and explain all of the information.

Webster's Dictionary of American Authors is one highly efficient means of organizing what we know. It offers comprehensive guidance through the factors that created and influenced North America's literary tradition. The first section, which forms the heart of the book, is an encyclopedic listing of almost one thousand of the most influential writers in American literary history. The biographies span from writers such as Jonathan Edwards who emerged at the beginning of the American experience through America's literary history to contemporary giants such as Nobel Laureate Toni Morrison.

All of the great North American novelists (Herman Melville, Henry James, and Margaret Atwood are but a few examples), short story writers (F. Scott Fitzgerald and Alice Munro), poets (Emily Dickinson, Ezra Pound, and Sylvia Plath), dramatists (Eugene O'Neill, Arthur Miller, and Edward Albee) are present. Included, too, are many less famous writers who nevertheless have had a profound effect on North American literary history. Each entry includes the writer's salient biographical details, descriptions of the author's most important works, and, often, a brief commentary on the writer's particular influence.

The book's second section, entitled "Major Works of American Literature," highlights over 750 of the most important novels, plays, poems, biographies, critiques, and other works of non-fiction that make up America's literary tradition. Each entry outlines the content of a particular work, provides the name of its author and its publication date, acknowledges any prizes it has received, and comments briefly on its significance.

The final section lists over 100 of the groups, movements, and periodicals that have helped to shape the character of American literature. In a sense, what we know about these groups (the Algonquin Round Table, American Romanticism, Transcendentalism, or the Harlem Renaissance) and periodicals (*Harper's Illustrated* to *The New Yorker*) is almost as important as the works of art. Because these factors of America's literary tradition reveal so much about America's history, each group is described, and the personalities who participated or influenced the group, movement, or periodical are critiqued.

Writing is the lifeline that connects the past, the present, and, ultimately, the future. Writing—in all its forms—keeps the life of a society known. As Wallace Stegner said, writers are the builders of the civilization. With *Webster's Dictionary of American Authors* as a guide to those builders, we can better understand American civilization as a whole.

Explanatory Notes

This section details some of the editorial decisions that were made in order to present a coherent, well-organized body of work.

Biographical Entries

In general, the biographical entries are listed alphabetically under the family name of the author. Names beginning with M', Mac, or Mc are alphabetized according to their spelling. Writers who are better known to readers by a pseudonym or single name are listed under their pseudonym. Thus, the writer Samuel Clemens, better known to readers by his pseudonym, is listed under **Twain, Mark.**

Other Entries

In this book, entry order is determined by ordinary rules of alphabetization applied to the boldface entry names. For ease of use, titles of works or names of movements that are given individual treatment are usually entered at a shortened form of the title. A conspicuous example is Mark Twain's *Pudd'nhead Wilson,* the full title being *The Tragedy of Pudd'nhead Wilson, and the Comedy of Those Extraordinary Twins.*

Cross-References

Cross-references within an entry are indicated by small capitals. Because a one-volume work of this type affords the reader easy access to any entry, cross-references have been used sparingly. Biographies of writers known for their participation in a movement will include mention of this detail, but often will not contain a cross-reference to the movement. It is assumed that the reader who desires more information about the movement will do so without reminder.

The cross-references in this book are employed to lead the reader to further information on his or her subject of immediate inquiry. For example, in a biographical entry, six works by a particular author may be mentioned, but only one is given full-entry treatment in the "Major Works of American

Literature" section. In this case, the title of that work would be written in small capitals, indicating to the reader that more information can be found there. On the other hand, although the book may include a full entry on a particular subject (the Harlem Renaissance, for example) and the movement is mentioned in another entry (such as the entry for "Zora Neale Hurston,") the Harlem Renaissance entry—because it gives no new information on Hurston—will not be mentioned in small capitals in the Hurston entry.

Dates

In general, the dates following the titles of works indicate the date of first publication. With regard to plays, the date following the title of a play refers to the dates of the original publication unless otherwise indicated. The Edward Albee entry, for example, lists *Who's Afraid of Virginia Woolf?* (1962) and *Three Tall Women* (produced 1991).

Webster's Dictionary of American Authors merges the lexical work for which Merriam-Webster dictionaries have long been known—definition, pronunciation, and etymology—with the extensive and varied, yet rigorously edited and verified information that typifies *The Encyclopaedia Britannica.* Members of both organizations teamed together to create this remarkable reference work.

Dictionary of American Authors

Abbey, Edward (b. Jan. 29, 1927, Home, Pa., U.S.—d. March 14, 1989, Oracle, Ariz.) American writer whose works, set primarily in the southwestern United States, reflect an uncompromising environmentalist philosophy.

The son of a Pennsylvania farmer, Abbey earned bachelor's and master's degrees at the University of New Mexico in the 1950s. He subsequently worked as a park ranger and fire lookout for the National Park Service in the Southwest. Central to this experience was the perspective it afforded on the human presence in the environment. Abbey observed both the remnants of ancient Indian cultures and the encroachment of consumer civilization. His book *Desert Solitaire* (1968) is an extended meditation on the sublime and forbidding wilderness of southeastern Utah and the human incursions upon it. This work, along with the novel *The Monkey Wrench Gang* (1975), which recounts the exploits of a band of guerrilla environmentalists, became virtual handbooks of the environmental movement. The strain of cynicism that runs through much of Abbey's writing is leavened by a bracing prose style and mischievous wit. His numerous other works include *The Brave Cowboy* (1958), *Slickrock* (1971), *Abbey's Road* (1979), and *The Fool's Progress* (1988). *Hayduke Lives!*, a sequel to *The Monkey Wrench Gang*, was published posthumously in 1990.

Abbott, Jacob (b. Nov. 14, 1803, Hallowell, Maine, U.S.—d. Oct. 31, 1879, Farmington, Maine) American clergyman, teacher, and writer, best known as a writer of children's books.

Abbott attended Bowdoin College and studied at Andover Newton Theological School. He taught at Amherst College, moving in 1829 to Boston, where he founded and was the first principal of the Mount Vernon School, a secondary school for girls. Abbott was sole author of 180 books and coauthor or editor of 31 others, notably the 28-volume, instructive "Rollo" series. Although now they are chiefly noted for their picture of 19th-century rural American life, Abbott intended them to entertain, to edify, to make children think, and to help them learn to read. Abbott also wrote 22 volumes of biographical histories and the *Franconia Stories* (10 vol.).

Abish, Walter (b. Dec. 24, 1931, Vienna, Austria) American writer of experimental novels and short stories whose fiction took as its subject language itself.

Abish spent his childhood in Shanghai, China, where his family were refugees from Nazi-occupied Europe. In 1949 they moved to Israel, where Abish served in the army and developed strong interests in architecture and writing. He moved to the United States in 1957 and became a citizen in 1960. From 1975 Abish taught English at several eastern colleges and universities.

In *Alphabetical Africa* (1974), the first of the 52 chapters (twice 26) consists solely of words beginning with "A," the second chapter adds words beginning with "B," and so forth through the alphabet and back again. *Minds Meet* (1975) contains short stories in which language is used symbolically rather than to relay specific information. *In the Future Perfect* (1977) features experimental short stories in which words are juxtaposed in unusual patterns. *How German Is It/Wie Deutsch ist es* (1980), often considered Abish's best work, is a multilayered novel about postwar Germany and its past. Other works include a collection of poems, *Duel Site* (1970); *99: The New Meaning* (1990), a group of narratives; and the novel *Eclipse Fever* (1993).

Abrams, M.H., *in full* Meyer Howard (b. July 23, 1912, Long Branch, N.J., U.S.) American literary critic known for his analysis of the Romantic period in English literature.

Following his graduation from Harvard in 1934, Abrams studied for a year at the University of Cambridge before returning to his alma mater for master's and doctoral degrees. He joined the faculty of Cornell University, Ithaca, N.Y., in 1945, becoming professor emeritus in 1983.

Abrams wrote his first book, *The Milk of Paradise: The Effects of Opium Visions on the Works of De Quincey, Crabbe, Francis Thompson, and Coleridge* (1934), while an undergraduate. With his second work, *The Mirror and the Lamp: Romantic Theory and the Critical Tradition* (1953), he joined the front rank of scholars of Romantic literature. The book's title denotes the two metaphors by which Abrams characterized 18th- and 19th-century English literature, respectively—the former as a cool, intellectual reflection of outward reality and the latter as an illumination shed by artists upon their inner and outer worlds. His later work *Natural Supernaturalism* (1971) explores a broader reach of the Romantic sensibility, including its religious implications and its influence on modern literature. Critical essays by Abrams were collected in *The Correspondent Breeze* (1984) and *Doing Things with Texts* (1989).

Acker, Kathy (b. 1948) American novelist whose writing style and subject matter reflect the so-called punk sensibility that emerged in youth culture in the 1970s.

Acker studied classics at Brandeis University and the University of California at San Diego. Her early employment ranged from clerical work to performing in pornographic films. In 1972 she began publishing willfully crude, disjointed prose that drew heavily from her personal experience and constituted a literary analog to contemporary developments in music, fashion, and the visual arts. From the outset, Acker blatantly lifted material from other writers, manipulating it for her own often unsettling purposes. In the early novel *The Childlike Life of the Black Tarantula* (1973), this process of appropriation is central to the narrator's quest for identity. The book's themes of alienation and objectified sexuality recur in such later novels as *Great Expectations* (1982), *Don Quixote* (1986), and *Empire of the Senseless* (1988). In 1993 *My Mother: Demonology*, which consists of seven love stories, was published.

Ackerman, Diane, *original surname* Fink (b. Oct. 7, 1948, Waukegan, Ill., U.S.) American writer whose works often reflected her interest in natural science.

Ackerman was educated at Pennsylvania State University (B.A., 1970) and Cornell University, Ithaca, N.Y. (M.F.A., 1973; M.A., 1976; Ph.D., 1978). From 1980 to 1983 she taught English at the University of Pittsburgh and from 1984 to 1986 directed the writers' program and was writer-in-residence at Washington University, St. Louis, Mo. From 1988 she was a staff writer at *The New Yorker* magazine.

Ackerman's memoir *On Extended Wings* (1985) was adapted for the stage in 1987. Her later books include *A Natural History of the Senses* (1990), *The Moon By Whale Light, and Other Adventures Among Bats, Penguins, Crocodilians, and Whales* (1991), and *A Natural History of Love* (1994).

Ackerman considered such matters as amino acids, viruses, quasars, and corpuscles to be as much in the realm of poetic experience as anything else in the universe. Her published poetry includes *The Planets: A Cosmic Pastoral* (1976), *Wife of Light* (1978), *Lady Faustus* (1983), and *Jaguar of Sweet Laughter: New and Selected Poems* (1991). Ackerman wrote a series of nine radio programs for the Canadian Broadcasting Corporation under the title "Ideas into the Universe" (1975). She also wrote *Twilight of the Tenderfoot: A Western Memoir* (1980) and the play *Reverse Thunder* (1988).

Adamic, Louis (b. March 23, 1899, Blato, Slovenia, Austria-Hungary— d. Sept. 4, 1951, near Riegelsville, N.J., U.S.) Novelist and journalist who wrote about the experiences of American minorities, especially immigrants, in the early 1900s.

Adamic immigrated to the United States from Carniola (now in Slovenia) at age 14 and was naturalized in 1918. He wrote about what he called the failure of the American melting pot in *Laughing in the Jungle* (1932). He returned to Slovenia on a Guggenheim Fellowship and used that journey as the basis for *The Native's Return* (1934). Two successful sequels, *Grandsons* (1935) and *Cradle of Life* (1936), were followed by publication of his first novel, *The House in Antigua* (1937). His next book, *My America* (1938), a mixture of memoir and social philosophy, outlines his dream of a unified American people.

An intensely political man, Adamic suffered greatly because of the fragmentation of what was then unified Yugoslavia. He eventually committed suicide.

Adams, Abigail, *original surname* Smith (b. Nov. 11 [Nov. 22, New Style], 1744, Weymouth, Mass.—d. Oct. 28, 1818, Quincy, Mass., U.S.) Prolific letter writer whose correspondence gives an intimate and vivid portrayal of life in the young American republic.

Although her formal education was meager, Abigail Smith was an avid reader of history. Several enforced separations from her husband, John Adams—including a 10-year period when he was at the Continental Congress in Philadelphia—prompted streams of letters, and the development of Mrs. Adams' genius as a correspondent. Her artless spontaneity brings the times to life with a charming blend of comments on minutiae of the day with observations on the momentous events of the Revolutionary period.

Following the peace treaty of 1783, Mrs. Adams joined her husband abroad in Paris, The Hague, and London. Her letters to friends and family at home again provide a colorful commentary on manners and customs, and her correspondence continued when they returned to the United States. Successive printings of Mrs. Adams' letters (1840, 1876, 1947, 1963, 1977) periodically revived public appreciation of her contribution to the original source material of the early American period.

Adams, Charles Follen (b. April 21, 1842, Dorchester, Mass., U.S.—d. March 8, 1918, Roxbury, Mass.) American regional poet, best known for his humorous Pennsylvania German dialect poems.

As a teenager, Adams was employed by a dry-goods firm. After serving in the army during the American Civil War, he returned to Boston, where he established himself as a "dealer in dry and fancy goods." In 1872 he began writing humorous verses for periodicals and newspapers in a Pennsylvania German dialect. Collections of his verse are *Leedle Yawcob Strauss, and Other Poems* (1877) and *Dialect Ballads* (1888). His complete poetical writings, *Yawcob Strauss, and Other Poems*, with illustrations by "Boz," were published in 1910.

Adams, Franklin Pierce, *byname* F.P.A. (b. Nov. 15, 1881, Chicago, Ill., U.S.—d. March 23, 1960, New York, N.Y.) American newspaper columnist, translator, poet, and radio personality whose humorous syndicated column earned him the reputation of godfather of the contemporary newspaper column.

Adams' newspaper career began in 1903, with the *Chicago Journal*. The next year he went to New York, where he wrote for several newspapers. His column "The Conning Tower" appeared in the *Herald Tribune* and several other New York newspapers from 1913 to 1937, with two major interruptions: during the years of World War I, when Adams wrote a column for *Stars and Stripes*, and from 1923 to 1931, when he worked for the New York *World* until it ceased publication. Witty and well-written, his columns consisted of informal yet careful critiques of the contemporary U.S. scene. His Saturday columns imitated the language and style of Samuel Pepys' diary, and Adams is credited with a renewal of interest in Pepys. Reprints were collected in *The Diary of Our Own Samuel Pepys* (1935).

Adams' poetry is light and conventionally rhymed. It is collected in 10 volumes, beginning with *Tobogganning on Parnassus* (1911); the final volume, *The Melancholy Lute* (1936), is Adams' selection from 30 years of his writing. In 1938 Adams became one of the panel of experts on the radio show "Information, Please."

Adams, Henry (Brooks) (b. Feb. 16, 1838, Boston, Mass., U.S.—d. March 27, 1918, Washington, D.C.) American historian, man of letters, and author of one of the outstanding autobiographies of Western literature, THE EDUCATION OF HENRY ADAMS (1918).

Henry Adams

Adams was the great-grandson of John Adams and the grandson of John Quincy Adams, both presidents of the United States. He graduated from Harvard in 1858 and embarked upon a grand tour of Europe. In 1861 he went to London with his father (who had been appointed U.S. minister to England), and acted as his private secretary until 1868.

Returning to the United States, Adams traveled to Washington, D.C., as a newspaper correspondent for *The Nation* and other leading journals. He wrote numerous essays exposing political corruption and continued his reformist activities as editor of the *North American Review* (1870–76). But after the failure of Horace Greeley's campaign for the presidency, Adams grew disillusioned. His anonymously published novel *Democracy, an American Novel* (1880) reflected his loss of faith in Americans.

In 1870 Adams was appointed professor of medieval history at Harvard, where he was the first American to employ the seminar—as contrasted with the lecture—method in teaching history. In 1877 he resigned and soon completed two biographies, *The Life of Albert Gallatin* (1879) and *John Randolph* (1882). His study of American democracy culminated in his nine-volume *History of the United States of America* (1889–91), a scholarly work that received immediate acclaim. In 1884 Adams wrote another novel, *Esther*, which he published under a pseudonym. The following year his wife of 13 years, Marian Hooper (known as Clover), committed suicide.

From the 1870s until his last years, intellectuals gravitated to his home to discuss art, science, politics, and literature. His closest friends were the geologist Clarence King and the diplomat John Hay. Adams and King were inseparable. Their letters remain a rich source of information on everything from gossip to the most current trends of thought.

On several trips to France, Adams examined medieval Christendom, and in MONT-SAINT-MICHEL AND CHARTRES (1913) he described the medieval worldview as reflected in its cathedrals. *The Education of Henry Adams*, a companion volume to *Chartres*, remains Adams' best-known work and one of the most distinguished of all autobiographies. In 1908 Adams edited the letters and diary of his friend John Hay, secretary of state from 1898 to 1905. His last book, *The Life of George Cabot Lodge*, was published in 1911.

Adams, Léonie (Fuller) (b. Dec. 9, 1899, Brooklyn, N.Y., U.S.—d. June 27, 1988, New Milford, Conn.) American lyrical poet and educator whose verse interprets emotions and nature with an almost mystical vision.

After graduating from Barnard College (A.B., 1922), she became editor of *The Measure,* a literary publication, in 1924. She was persuaded to publish a volume of poetry, *Those Not Elect*, in 1925. She spent two years (1928–30) in France, and her second collection of poetry, *High Falcon & Other Poems*, was published during that period. She began to teach the writing of poetry in New York City and in 1932 edited *Lyrics of François Villon*. She published rarely after 1933, but she lectured at various American colleges and universities over the years and served as poetry consultant for the Library of Congress (1948–49). Her *Poems, a Selection* (1954) won the Bollingen Prize for Poetry in 1955.

Adams, Samuel Hopkins (b. Jan. 26, 1871, Dunkirk, N.Y., U.S.—d. Nov. 15, 1958, Beaufort, S.C.) American journalist and author of more than 50 books of fiction, biography, and exposé.

Adams graduated from Hamilton College in 1891 and worked for the *New York Sun* until 1900. From 1901 to 1905 he was associated in various capacities with McClure's syndicate and *McClure's Magazine*. One of the so-called muckrakers of the period, Adams contributed to *Collier's, the National Weekly* in 1905 a series of articles exposing quack patent medicines, followed by *The Great American Fraud* (1906), which furthered the passage of the Pure Food and Drug Act in 1906. In articles appearing in 1915–16 in the *New York Tribune*, he exposed dishonorable practices in advertising. The novel *Revelry* (1926) and a biography of Warren G. Harding, *Incredible Era* (1939), set forth the scandals of the Harding administration. Adams also wrote biographies of Daniel Webster (*The Godlike Daniel*, 1930) and Alexander Woollcott (1945).

Adams, William Taylor, *pseudonym* Oliver Optic (b. July 30, 1822, Medway, Mass., U.S.—d. March 27, 1897, Boston, Mass.) American teacher and author best known for his children's magazine and the series of adventure books that he wrote under his pseudonym.

Although he never graduated from college, Adams was a teacher and principal in Boston elementary schools for more than 20 years. Under the pen name Oliver Optic, he wrote stories for boys, and in 1865 he resigned his position as a principal to pursue his writing full-time. Soon after that he began *Oliver Optic's Magazine for Boys and Girls* (1867–75), which enjoyed great popularity.

Adams was a prolific writer, producing about a thousand magazine and newspaper stories and well over a hundred full-length books. His books are written in series and take young heroes through exotic and educational adventures. His characters travel much and are athletic and patriotic, and the stories are laced with a strong moral. A significant rival for the readership attracted by Horatio Alger, Adams, too, wrote on the level of the dime novel; libraries occasionally banned his books because of their sensationalism.

Ade, George (b. Feb. 9, 1866, Kentland, Ind., U.S.—d. May 16, 1944, Brook, Ind.) American playwright and humorist known for his *Fables in Slang*.

After graduating from Purdue University, Ade joined the staff of the *Chicago Record* newspaper from 1890 to 1900. Characters introduced in his widely acclaimed editorial-page column, "Stories of the Streets and of the Town," became the subjects of his early books, *Artie* (1896), *Pink Marsh* (1897), and *Doc Horne* (1899). His greatest recognition came with *Fables in Slang* (1899), a national best-seller that was followed by a weekly syndicated fable and by 11 other books of fables. The fables, which contained only a little slang, were, rather, examples of the vernacular.

In 1902 Ade's light opera *The Sultan of Sulu* began a long run in New York, followed by such successful comedies as *The County Chairman* (1903) and *The College Widow* (1904). He was recognized as one of the most successful playwrights of his time. He also wrote many motion-picture scripts and, during the Prohibition era, what many called one of his most amusing books, *The Old Time Saloon* (1931).

Adler, Renata (b. Oct. 19, 1938, Milan, Italy) Italian-born American journalist, experimental novelist, and film critic best known for her analytical essays and reviews.

Adler was educated at Bryn Mawr College (Pa.), the Sorbonne, and Harvard University. From 1962 to 1968 and from 1970 to 1982 she was a staff writer-reporter for *The New Yorker*. Essays and reviews she wrote there were collected and published as *Toward a Radical Middle: Fourteen Pieces of Reporting and Criticism* (1969). From her controversial single-year tenure as film critic for the *New York Times* came a collection of reviews that was published as *A Year in the Dark: Journal of a Film Critic, 1968–69* (1970). Adler then turned to writing short stories, some of which were published under the pseudonym Brett Daniels.

Adler reworked previously published short fiction into *Speedboat* (1976), her first novel. Set mainly in New York City, *Speedboat* consists mainly of a series of disparate sketches and vignettes. Like *Speedboat*, Adler's second novel, *Pitch Dark* (1983), is episodic and nonlinear; critical response to both was mixed.

Adler also wrote the nonfiction work *Reckless Disregard* (1986), an investigation into libel suits brought by American and Israeli generals against major American news organizations. In 1988 she published *Politics and Media*, a collection of essays.

James Agee

Agee, James (b. Nov. 27, 1909, Knoxville, Tenn., U.S.—d. May 16, 1955, New York, N.Y.) American poet, novelist, and one of the most influential American film critics in the 1930s and '40s.

Agee grew up in Tennessee's Cumberland Mountain area, attended Harvard University, and wrote for *Fortune* and *Time* after he graduated in 1932. *Permit Me Voyage*, a volume of poems, appeared in 1934. For a proposed article in *Fortune*, Agee and the photographer Walker Evans lived for about six weeks among poverty-stricken sharecroppers in Alabama in 1936. The article never appeared, but the material they gathered became the lyrical LET US NOW PRAISE FAMOUS MEN (1941).

From 1948 until his death, Agee worked mainly as a film scriptwriter, notably for *The African Queen* (1951) and *The Night of the Hunter* (1955). The novel A DEATH IN THE FAMILY (1957) and his novella *The Morning Watch* (1951), on the religious experiences of a 12-year-old boy, are both autobiographical.

Conrad Aiken

Aiken, Conrad Potter (b. Aug. 5, 1889, Savannah, Ga., U.S.—d. Aug. 17, 1973, Savannah) Poet, short-story writer, novelist, and critic whose works, influenced by early psychoanalytic theory, are concerned largely with the human need for self-awareness.

Aiken himself confronted considerable childhood trauma caused by finding the bodies of his parents after his father had killed his mother and committed suicide. Educated at private schools and at Harvard, where he was a friend and contemporary of T.S. Eliot (whose poetry was to influence his own), Aiken divided his life almost equally between England and the United

States until 1947, when he settled in Massachusetts. He played a significant role in introducing American poets to the British.

After three early collections of verse, he wrote five "symphonies" between 1915 and 1920 in an effort to create poetry that would resemble music in its ability to express several levels of meaning simultaneously. Then came a period of narrative poems, volumes of lyrics and meditations, and, after World War II, a return to musical form but with richer philosophical and psychological overtones. The best of his poetry is contained in *Collected Poems* (1953), including a long sequence "Preludes to Definition," which some critics consider his masterwork, and the frequently anthologized "Morning Song of Senlin."

Most of his fiction was written in the 1920s and '30s. Generally more successful than his novels of this period were his short stories, notably "Strange Moonlight" from *Bring! Bring!* (1925) and "Silent Snow, Secret Snow" and "Mr. Arcularis" from *Among the Lost People* (1934). *The Short Stories of Conrad Aiken* was published in 1950 and his autobiography, *Ushant*, in 1952.

Albee, Edward (Franklin) (b. March 12, 1928, Virginia, U.S.) American dramatist and theatrical producer, best known for WHO'S AFRAID OF VIRGINIA WOOLF? (1962), which examined illusion and reality with slashing insight and witty dialogue in its gruesome portrayal of married life.

Albee was an adopted child, and he grew up in New York City and nearby Westchester County. He was educated at Choate School (graduated 1946) and Trinity College, Hartford, Conn. (1946–47). He began writing plays in the late 1950s. Among his early one-act plays, THE ZOO STORY, THE AMERICAN DREAM, and THE SANDBOX (all published 1959) were the most successful; they established Albee as an astute critic of American values and of human interaction. Many critics, however, consider his first full-length play, *Who's Afraid of Virginia Woolf?* (film, 1966), to be his most important work. It was followed by a number of full-length works—including *Tiny Alice* (1964), A DELICATE BALANCE (1966); winner of a Pulitzer Prize), SEASCAPE (1975); winner of a Pulitzer Prize), and *The Man Who Had Three Arms* (1982). His play *Three Tall Women* (produced 1991) won him a third Pulitzer.

Alcott, Bronson, *in full* Amos Bronson Alcott (b. Nov. 29, 1799, Wolcott, Conn., U.S.—d. March 4, 1888, Concord, Mass.) American philosopher, teacher, reformer, and member of the New England Transcendentalist group.

The self-educated son of a poor farmer, Alcott traveled in the South as a peddler before establishing a series of schools for children. His aim as an educator was to stimulate thought and "awaken the soul." His innovations were not widely accepted, however, and before he was 40 he was forced to close his last school, the famous Temple School in Boston. In 1842 with money from Ralph Waldo Emerson he visited England, where a similar school founded near London was named Alcott House in his honor. He returned from England with a kindred spirit, the mystic Charles Lane, and together they founded a short-lived utopian community, Fruitlands, in Massachusetts. Always poor or in debt, Alcott was not financially secure until his second daughter, Louisa May Alcott, established herself as a writer.

Louisa May Alcott

Alcott, Louisa May (b. Nov. 29, 1832, Germantown, Pa., U.S.—d. March 6, 1888, Boston, Mass.) American author known for her children's books, especially LITTLE WOMEN.

Alcott spent most of her life in Boston and Concord, Mass., where she grew up in the company of Ralph Waldo Emerson, Theodore Parker, and Henry David Thoreau. She soon came to understand that her Transcendentalist father was too impractical to provide for his wife and four daughters; after the failure of Fruitlands, a utopian community that he had founded, Louisa's lifelong concern for the welfare of her family began. In order to earn money she taught briefly, worked as a domestic, and finally began to write, producing potboilers at first, and eventually more serious works. An ardent abolitionist, Alcott volunteered as a nurse during the American Civil War. She contracted typhoid from unsanitary hospital conditions, however, and was sent home. She was never completely well again, but the publication of her letters in book form, *Hospital Sketches* (1863), brought her the first taste of fame.

Alcott's stories then began to appear in *The Atlantic Monthly* (now *The Atlantic*). She wrote the autobiographical *Little Women* (1868–69) under the pressure of serious financial need. The book was an immediate success, and in 1869 Alcott was able to write in her journal: "Paid up all the debts . . . thank the Lord!" Other books for which Alcott drew from her early experiences included *An Old-Fashioned Girl* (1870); *Aunt Jo's Scrap Bag*, 6 vol. (1872–82); *Little Men: Life at Plumfield with Jo's Boys* (1871); *Eight Cousins* (1875); and *Jo's Boys and How They Turned Out* (1886).

Exhausted and in constant pain, she spent the last years of her life shadowed by the deaths of her mother and her youngest sister, May, who left behind a little daughter for Alcott to rear.

Aldrich, Thomas Bailey (b. Nov. 11, 1836, Portsmouth, N.H., U.S.—d. March 19, 1907, Boston, Mass.) Poet, short-story writer, and editor whose use of the surprise ending influenced the development of the short story in America. He drew upon his childhood experiences in New Hampshire in his popular classic THE STORY OF A BAD BOY (1870).

Aldrich left school at 13 to work as a merchant's clerk in New York City and soon began to contribute to various newspapers and magazines. After publication of his first book of verse, *The Bells* (1855), he became junior literary critic on the *New York Evening Mirror* and later an editor of the *Home Journal*. From 1881 to 1890 he was editor of *The Atlantic Monthly* (now *The Atlantic*).

His poems, which reflect the cultural atmosphere of New England and his frequent European tours, were published in such volumes as *Cloth of Gold* (1874), *Flower and Thorn* (1877), *Mercedes and Later Lyrics* (1884), and *Windham Towers* (1890). His best-known prose is *Marjorie Daw and Other People* (1873), a collection of short stories.

Alger, Horatio, Jr. (b. Jan. 13, 1832, Chelsea, Mass., U.S.—d. July 18, 1899, Natick, Mass.) One of the most popular late 19th-century American authors and perhaps the most socially influential American writer of his generation.

Alger was the son of a Unitarian minister. The young Alger showed an interest in writing, and at Harvard University he distinguished himself in the classics and graduated with Phi Beta Kappa honors in 1852. After leaving Harvard, Alger worked as a schoolteacher and contributed to magazines. In 1857 he enrolled in the Harvard Divinity School, from which he took his degree in 1860.

In 1864 Alger was ordained and accepted the pulpit of a church in Brewster, Mass., but was forced to leave in 1866 following allegations of sexual activities with local boys. In that year he moved to New York City, and with the publication and sensational success of RAGGED DICK (1868), the story of a poor shoeshine boy who rises to wealth, Alger found the vein in which he was to write more than 100 volumes.

In a steady succession of books that are almost alike except for the names of their characters, he preached that by honesty, cheerful perseverance, and hard work, the poor but virtuous lad would have his just reward—though the reward was almost always precipitated by a stroke of good luck. Alger's most popular books were the Ragged Dick, Luck and Pluck, and Tattered Tom series. His books sold more than 20,000,000 copies despite the fact that their plots, characterizations, and dialogue were consistently and even outrageously bad.

Algren, Nelson, *original name* Nelson Ahlgren Abraham (b. March 28, 1909, Detroit, Mich., U.S.—d. May 9, 1981, Sag Harbor, N.Y.) Writer whose novels of the poor are lifted from routine naturalism by his vision of their pride, humor, and unquenchable yearnings. He also captures with uncommon skill the mood of the city's underside.

The son of a machinist, Algren grew up in Chicago, where his parents moved when he was three. He worked his way through the University of

Nelson Algren

Illinois, graduating in journalism in the depth of the Depression. He held a variety of jobs. During this period he edited a periodical, *The New Anvil*, with the proletarian writer Jack Conroy.

Somebody in Boots (1935), his first novel, relates the driftings during the Depression of a young, poor white Texan who ends up among the down-and-outs of Chicago. *Never Come Morning* (1942) tells of a Polish petty criminal who dreams of escaping from his squalid Northwest Side Chicago environment by becoming a prizefighter. Algren served as a U.S. Army medical corpsman during World War II, then published the short-story collection *The Neon Wilderness* (1947), which contains some of his best writing.

Algren's first popular success was THE MAN WITH THE GOLDEN ARM (1949; film, 1956), which won the National Book Award. Its hero is Frankie Machine, whose golden arm as a poker dealer is threatened by shakiness connected with his drug addiction. In A WALK ON THE WILD SIDE (1956; film, 1962) Algren returned to the 1930s in a picaresque novel of New Orleans bohemian life.

His nonfiction includes the prose poem *Chicago, City on the Make* (1951) and sketches collected as *Who Lost an American?* (1963) and *Notes from a Sea Diary: Hemingway All the Way* (1965).

Allen, Hervey, *in full* William Hervey Allen, Jr. (b. Dec. 8, 1889, Pittsburgh, Pa., U.S.—d. Dec. 28, 1949, Coconut Grove, Fla.) American poet, biographer, and novelist who had a great impact on popular literature with his historical novel ANTHONY ADVERSE.

Allen's first published work was a book of poetry, *Ballads of the Border* (1916). During the 1920s he established a reputation as a poet, publishing several more volumes of verse. He had been wounded in World War I, and his novel *Toward the Flame* (1926) came out of his wartime experience. That same year his authoritative biography *Israfel: The Life and Times of Edgar Allan Poe* was published.

In 1933, after five years of work, Allen published *Anthony Adverse*, which was a huge success. The book's considerable length and its undisguised passages about sex introduced a new standard for popular fiction. Allen's later novels were less successful.

Ammons, A.R., *in full* Archie Randolph (b. Feb. 18, 1926, Whiteville, N.C., U.S.) American poet, one of the leading late 20th-century exponents of the Transcendentalist tradition.

A 1949 graduate of Wake Forest College (now University), Ammons worked as an elementary school principal and as a glass company executive before turning his full attention to literature. From 1964 he taught creative writing at Cornell University. In his first collection of poems, *Ommateum:*

With Doxology (1955), Ammons wrote about nature and the self, themes that remained the central focus of his work. Subsequent books, such as *Expressions of Sea Level* (1963), *Tape for the Turn of the Year* (1965); composed on adding-machine tape), and *Uplands* (1970), continued the poet's investigation into the relationship between the knowable and the unknowable. Ammons' style is both cerebral and conversational, embodying the often lofty meditations of one well-rooted in the mundane. Among the clearest influences on his work were Robert Frost, Wallace Stevens, and William Carlos Williams. His later work—notably *A Coast of Trees* (1981), which won a National Book Critics Circle Award, and *Sumerian Vistas* (1988)—exhibit a mature command of imagery and ideas, balancing the scientific approach to the universe with a subjective, even romantic one. *Garbage* (1993), Ammons' book-length poem, received a National Book Award in 1993.

Anaya, Rudolfo A., *in full* Alfonso (b. Oct. 30, 1937, Pastura, New Mexico, U.S.) American novelist and educator whose fiction expressed his Mexican-American heritage, the tradition of folklore and oral storytelling in Spanish, and the Jungian mythic perspective.

Anaya graduated from the University of New Mexico and worked as a public school teacher from 1963 to 1970. He then became director of counseling at the University of Albuquerque. From 1974 he taught at the University of New Mexico.

Bless Me, Ultima (1972), Anaya's acclaimed first novel, concerns a young boy growing up in New Mexico in the late 1940s. *Heart of Aztlán* (1976) follows a family's move from rural to urban surroundings and confronts some of the problems of Chicano laborers. In *Tortuga* (1979), a boy encased in a body cast stays at a hospital for paralyzed children. These three novels make up a trilogy about Hispanic children in the United States. The novel *The Legend of La Llorona* (1984) is about La Malinche, an Indian slave who became the consort of the conquistador Hernán Cortés. Anaya's other works include *The Adventures of Juan Chicaspatas* (1985) and his nonfiction *A Chicano in China* (1986).

Anderson, Margaret (Caroline) (b. Nov. 24, 1886?, Indianapolis, Ind., U.S.—d. Oct. 18, 1973, Le Cannet, Fr.) Founder and editor of the LITTLE REVIEW magazine, in which she introduced works by many of the best-known American and English writers of the 20th century.

Raised in a conventional Midwestern home and educated at Western College for Women, Oxford, Ohio, Anderson renounced the "bourgeois" values of her background at an early age and moved to Chicago. There she joined the staff of *The Dial*, a literary review. In 1914 she founded the *Little*

Review, a magazine that reflected her interest in avant-garde art, philosophy, feminism, and psychoanalysis, among other subjects. Ezra Pound, whom she engaged as her European editor, attracted expatriate American and European writers to the magazine. For six months in 1914, after her financial backers abandoned the *Little Review*, she lost her home and offices and camped with family and staff members on the shores of Lake Michigan.

When Anderson began serializing James Joyce's *Ulysses* in the *Little Review* in 1918, the U.S. Post Office seized and burned four issues of the magazine and then convicted Anderson and the associate editor, Jane Heap, on obscenity charges; each was fined $50. Nevertheless Anderson continued to publish for another 11 years. Among her subsequent writings were her three-volume autobiography, consisting of *My Thirty Years' War* (1930), *The Fiery Fountains* (1951), and *The Strange Necessity* (1962).

Anderson, Maxwell (b. Dec. 15, 1888, Atlantic, Pa., U.S.—d. Feb. 28, 1959, Stamford, Conn.) American playwright who attempted to popularize verse tragedy.

Anderson was educated at the University of North Dakota and Stanford University. He collaborated with Laurence Stallings in the comedy *What Price Glory?* (1924), his first hit, a realistically ribald and profane view of World War I. He then composed two ambitious historical dramas in verse— *Elizabeth the Queen* (1930) and *Mary of Scotland* (1933)—and his humorous Pulitzer Prize-winning prose satire, *Both Your Houses* (1933), an attack on venality in the U.S. Congress. He reached the peak of his career with *Winterset* (1935), a poetic drama inspired by the Sacco and Vanzetti case of the 1920s and set in the urban slums. Collaborating with the German refugee composer Kurt Weill (1900–50), Anderson also wrote for the musical theater a play based on early New York history, *Knickerbocker Holiday* (1938), and *Lost in the Stars* (1949), a dramatization of Alan Paton's South African novel *Cry, the Beloved Country*.

Anderson, Patrick John MacAllister (b. Aug. 4, 1915, Ashtead, Surrey, Eng.—d. March 17, 1979, Halstead, Essex) English-born Canadian poet whose writings are characterized by a rapid juxtaposition of contrasting images.

Educated at Oxford and Columbia universities, Anderson settled in Montreal as a teacher and professor and taught at McGill University from 1940 to 1950. He was instrumental in establishing the literary magazine *Preview*; he also wrote sensuous descriptions of nature that revitalized traditional lyrical praise of the Canadian landscape. The collections *A Tent for April* (1945) and *The White Centre* (1946) were followed by *The Colour as Naked* (1953), the autobiographical *Search Me* (1957), and his study *Over the Alps: Reflections on Travel and Travel Writing* (1969). Anderson's last published work was *Return to Canada: Selected Poems* (1977).

Anderson, Poul (William) (b. Nov. 25, 1926, Bristol, Pa., U.S.) Prolific American writer of science fiction and fantasy often praised for his scrupulous attention to scientific detail.

Anderson published his first science-fiction story while an undergraduate at the University of Minnesota and became a freelance writer following his graduation with a degree in physics in 1948. He published his first novel, *Vault of the Ages*, in 1952 and thereafter worked at the rate of several books per year. A number of his works concern the "future history" of what he calls the Technic Civilization, an age of human history lasting from the years 2100 to 7100. Much of the sociological, political, and economic content of these books, such as *Agent of the Terran Empire* (1965), derives from patterns associated with the European Age of Exploration. In *Tau Zero* (1970), considered by some to be his best work, Anderson turns from the broad canvas of future history to the confines of a spaceship, the speed of which is approaching the speed of light. Inside, the travelers experience time as they have always known it while witnessing through the portholes the collapse and rebirth of the universe.

Anderson's interest in Scandinavian languages and literatures informs many of his fantasy novels. *The Merman's Children* (1979), for example, portrays the plight of a surviving species of mermen within human society, a theme found in medieval Danish balladry.

Anderson, Regina M., *married name* Andrews, *pseudonym* Ursala (Ursula) Trelling (b. May 21, 1901, Chicago, Ill., U.S.) Librarian, playwright, and patron of the arts whose New York City home was a salon for Harlem Renaissance writers and artists.

Anderson attended several colleges and worked as a librarian in the New York Public Library System, for which she produced lecture and drama series and arts exhibitions, from the early 1920s to 1967. The Harlem apartment she shared with two other women became an important meeting place for African-American artists and intellectuals in the early 1920s. In 1924 Anderson helped organize a dinner at the Civic Club, attended by such notable authors as W.E.B. Du Bois, Jean Toomer, Countee Cullen, and Langston Hughes, that helped launch the Harlem Renaissance. Later that year she helped Du Bois found the Krigwa Players, a company of black actors performing plays by black authors; it was based at the 135th Street Public Library, where Anderson worked.

The Krigwa Players evolved into the Negro Experimental Theatre (also known as the Harlem Experimental Theatre), which in 1931 produced

Anderson's one-act play *Climbing Jacob's Ladder*, about a lynching that happened while people prayed in church. The next year the theater produced her one-act play *Underground*, about the Underground Railroad. Both plays were written under her pseudonym. The Negro Experimental Theatre served as an inspiration to little theater groups around the country, and it was especially influential in the encouragement of serious black theater and of black playwrights. Anderson also coedited the *Chronology of African-Americans in New York, 1621–1966* (1971); with Ethel Ray Nance.

Sherwood Anderson

Anderson, Sherwood (b. Sept. 13, 1876, Camden, Ohio, U.S.—d. March 8, 1941, Colón, Pan.) Author who strongly influenced American short-story writing between World Wars I and II. His prose style, based on everyday speech and derived from the experimental writing of Gertrude Stein, was markedly influential on Ernest Hemingway.

Anderson held a variety of jobs while writing fiction in his spare time. Eventually he began to earn enough from his published work to quit the business world. Encouraged by several literary men, he began to contribute experimental verse and short fiction to little magazines. His first novels, *Windy McPherson's Son* (1916; rev. ed., 1921) and *Marching Men* (1917), were written while he was still a manufacturer. *Winesburg, Ohio* (1919) was his first mature book and made his reputation. Its related short sketches and tales are told by a newspaper reporter-narrator who is as emotionally limited in some ways as the people he describes. His novels include *Many Marriages* (1923), which stresses the need for sexual fulfillment; *Dark Laughter* (1925), which values the "primitive" over the civilized; and *Beyond Desire* (1932), a novel of Southern textile mill labor struggles. His best work is generally thought to be in his short stories, collected in *The Triumph of the Egg* (1921), *Horses and Men* (1923), *Death in the Woods* (1933), and the previously mentioned *Winesburg, Ohio*.

JILL KREMENTZ

A. Maya Angelou

Angelou, Maya (Annie), *original name* Marguerite Johnson (b. April 4, 1928, St. Louis, Mo., U.S.) African-American poet whose several volumes of autobiography explore the themes of economic, racial, and sexual oppression.

Raped at the age of eight by her mother's boyfriend, Angelou went through an extended period of muteness. Her early life is the focus of Angelou's first autobiographical work, *I Know Why the Caged Bird Sings* (1970). Her subsequent volumes include *Gather Together in My Name* (1974), *The Heart of a Woman* (1981), and *All God's Children Need Traveling Shoes* (1986).

Angelou's poetry, collected in such volumes as *Just Give Me a Cool Drink of Water 'fore I Diiie* (1971) and *And Still I Rise* (1978), draws heavily on her personal history but employs the points of view of various personae. In 1981 she received a lifetime appointment as Reynolds Professor of American Studies at Wake Forest University, Winston-Salem, N.C. Among numerous other honors was her invitation to compose and deliver a poem for the inauguration of President Bill Clinton in 1993.

Anthony, Katharine (Susan) (b. Nov. 27, 1877, Roseville, Ark., U.S.—d. Nov. 20, 1965, New York, N.Y.) American biographer who is best known for *The Lambs* (1945), a controversial study of the British writers Charles and Mary Lamb.

Anthony was deeply interested in psychiatry. Eventually this interest came to shape her approach to biography, and her books centered increasingly on the psychological development and motivation of her subjects. Some of these works include *Margaret Fuller, A Psychological Biography* (1920); *Catherine the Great* (1925); *Louisa May Alcott* (1938); *Dolly Madison, Her Life and Times* (1949); and *Susan B. Anthony, Her Personal History and Her Era* (1954). Anthony's readers were scandalized by *The Lambs*, subtitled *A Story of Pre-Victorian England*, in which she theorized that incestuous feelings within the Lamb family were reflected in the lives and literary collaborations of Charles Lamb and his sister, Mary.

Antin, David (b. Feb. 1, 1932, New York, N.Y., U.S.) American poet, translator, and art critic who championed primitive art and poetry and the use of clichés and pop vernacular. He became perhaps best known for his improvisational "talk poems," first published in *Talking* (1972).

Antin was educated at the City College of New York (B.A., 1955) and New York University (M.A., 1966). He first worked as an editor, translator, and researcher. He was curator of the Institute of Contemporary Art (1967) in Boston and from 1968 taught visual arts at the University of California at San Diego.

His poetry collections include *Definitions* (1967), *Code of Flag Behavior* (1968), *After the War (A Long Novel with Few Words)* (1973), *Talking at the Boundaries* (1976), and *Tuning* (1984). Antin improvised his talk poems in public places, tape-recording his performances. Considering the resulting poems to be "adapted notations" of his performances, he later published those he thought had merit. His subsequent works include *Selected Poems: 1963–73* (1991) and *What It Means to Be Avant Garde* (1993).

Antin, Mary (b. 1881, Polotsk, Russia—d. May 15, 1949, Suffern, N.Y., U.S.) Author of the autobiographical *Promised Land* and other books on immigrant life in the United States.

Antin immigrated to the United States in 1894 and attended Teachers College of Columbia University and Barnard College, New York City,

1901–04. She wrote (in Yiddish) about her voyage to the United States in her first book, *From Polotsk to Boston* (Eng. trans., 1899). Her widely acclaimed *The Promised Land* (1912), narrates the experiences of European Jews and the contrast with Jewish immigrant experience in the United States. After its publication she toured the United States as a lecturer. Her third book on immigrants, *They Who Knock at Our Gates*, was published in 1914.

Apple, Max (Isaac) (b. Oct. 22, 1941, Grand Rapids, Mich., U.S.) American writer known for the comic intelligence of his stories, which chronicle pop culture and other aspects of American life.

Educated at the University of Michigan (B.A., 1963; Ph.D., 1970), Apple taught at Reed College, Portland, Ore., from 1970 to 1971 and at Rice University, Houston, Tex., from 1972.

Apple's satire is distinguished by its gentle spoofing. His cast of characters often includes a mix of historical figures and fictional creations, as in *The Oranging of America* (1976), with its stories about materialism that feature such historical figures as C.W. Post, Howard Johnson, and Norman Mailer. In *Zip: A Novel of the Left and the Right* (1978), brief appearances are made by J. Edgar Hoover, Fidel Castro, and Jane Fonda. His later works include *Free Agents* (1984), *The Propheteers* (1987), and *Roommates: My Grandfather's Story* (1994).

Asch or **Ash, Sholem, Sholem** *also spelled* Shalom *or* Sholom (b. Nov. 1, 1880, Kutno, Poland, Russian Empire—d. Aug. 10, 1957, London, Eng.) Polish-born American novelist and playwright, one of the most widely known writers in modern Yiddish literature.

Asch was educated at Kutno's Hebrew school. In 1899 he went to Warsaw, and in 1900 published his highly praised first story—written, as was a cycle that followed, in Hebrew. On the advice of the Yiddish writer and leader I.L. Peretz, he subsequently decided to write only in Yiddish, and with *Dos Shtetl* (1904); *The Little Town*) he began a career outstanding for both output and impact.

Asch's work falls into three periods. In his first, he describes the tragicomedy of life in small eastern European Jewish villages torn between devotion to Orthodox Jewry and the urge toward emancipation. To this period belong the novels *Kidesh hashem* (1919) and *Motke ganef* (1916); *Mottke the Thief*) and the play *Got fun nekome* (1907); *The God of Vengeance*). To the American period (he visited the United States in 1910, returned in 1914, and was naturalized in 1920) belong *Onkl Mozes* (1918); *Uncle Moses*), *Khayim Lederers tsurikkumen* (1927); *Chaim Lederer's Return*), and *Toyt urteyl* (1926); *Judge Not*). These novels describe the cultural and economic conflicts experienced by eastern European Jewish immigrants in America. In his last, most controversial period he attempted to unite Judaism and Christianity through emphasis upon their historical and theological-ethical connections.

Ashbery, John (Lawrence) (b. July 28, 1927, Rochester, N.Y., U.S.) American poet noted for the elegance, originality, and obscurity of his poetry.

Ashbery graduated from Harvard University in 1949 and received a master's degree from Columbia University (N.Y.) in 1951. After working as a copywriter in New York City (1951–55), he worked as an art critic in Paris until 1965. Returning to New York, he served as executive editor of *Art News* from 1965 to 1972 and then took a teaching post at Brooklyn College.

Ashbery's first published book, *Turandot and Other Poems* (1953), was followed by *Some Trees* (1956), *The Tennis Court Oath* (1962), *Rivers and Mountains* (1966), and *The Double Dream of Spring* (1970). His collection entitled *Self-Portrait in a Convex Mirror* (1975) won several awards, including the Pulitzer Prize for poetry. His subsequent poetry volumes include *Houseboat Days* (1977), *A Wave* (1984), *April Galleons* (1987), and *Flow Chart* (1991).

Ashbery's poetry was initially greeted with puzzlement and even hostility owing to its extreme difficulty. His poems are characterized by arresting images and exquisite rhythms, an intricate form, and sudden shifts in tone and subject that produce curious effects of fragmentation and obscurity.

Asimov, Isaac (b. Jan. 2, 1920, Petrovichi, Russia—d. April 6, 1992, New York, N.Y., U.S.) American author and biochemist, a highly successful and prolific writer of science fiction and of science books for lay readers. He published more than 300 volumes.

Asimov was taken to the United States at the age of three. He grew up in Brooklyn, N.Y., graduating from Columbia University in 1939 and taking a Ph.D. there in 1948. He then joined the faculty of Boston University, with which he was associated thereafter.

Isaac Asimov

He began contributing stories to science-fiction magazines in 1939 and in 1950 published his first book, *Pebble in the Sky*. His trilogy, *Foundation, Foundation and Empire*, and *Second Foundation* (1951–53), which recounts the collapse of an empire in the universe of the future, won a Hugo Award in science fiction. Other novels and collections of stories include *I, Robot* (1950), *The Stars Like Dust* (1951), *The Currents of Space* (1952), *The Caves of Steel* (1954), *The Naked Sun* (1957), *Earth Is Room Enough* (1957), *Foundation's Edge* (1982), *The Robots of Dawn* (1983), *Prelude to Foundation* (1988), and the posthumously published *Forward the Foundation* (1993). His "Nightfall" (1941) is thought by many to be the finest science-fiction short story ever written. Asimov's books on various topics in science are written with lucidity and humor. These include *The Chemicals of Life* (1954), *Inside the Atom* (1956), *The Human Brain* (1964), and *Views of the Universe* (1981).

Asimov also wrote two volumes of autobiography: *In Memory Yet Green: The Autobiography of Isaac Asimov, 1920–1954* (1979) and *In Joy Still Felt: The Autobiography of Isaac Asimov, 1954–1978* (1980).

Atherton, Gertrude Franklin, *original surname* Horn (b. Oct. 30, 1857, San Francisco, Calif., U.S.—d. June 14, 1948, San Francisco) American novelist who was noted as an author of fictional biography and history.

Atherton began her prolific writing career to escape the restrictions of a stifling marriage. Her first work, *The Randolphs of Redwoods* (*c.* 1882), was published anonymously in *The Argonaut* (republished 1899 as a book, *A Daughter of the Vine*). It was based on a local story of a well-bred girl turned alcoholic, and its publication offended her husband's prominent family.

After her husband's death Atherton traveled extensively, and the information she thus accumulated lent vividness to her writing. Her work generally drew mixed reviews, with the notable exception of *The Conqueror* (1902), a novelized account of the life of Alexander Hamilton. Her controversial novel *Black Oxen* (1923), the story of a woman revitalized by hormone treatments and based on Atherton's own experience, was her biggest popular success. Atherton wrote more than 40 novels and many nonfiction works in her long career. Her work is uneven in quality, but it displays a talent for vivid description.

Atwood, Margaret (Eleanor) (b. Nov. 18, 1939, Ottawa, Ont., Can.) Canadian poet, novelist, and critic, noted for her Canadian nationalism and her feminism.

Atwood attended the University of Toronto (B.A., 1961) and Radcliffe College, Cambridge, Mass. (M.A., 1962), continuing her studies at Harvard University (1962–63, 1965–67). She later taught literature at several Canadian universities.

Atwood was a published poet at age 19; her first book of poetry, *Double Persephone*, was published in 1961. Another early collection, *The Circle Game* (1964, revised in 1966), received the Canadian Governor General's Award for Poetry in 1966. In these and other early poetic works, Atwood pondered human behavior, celebrated the natural world, and condemned materialism. One of her many later volumes of poetry, *Power Politics* (1971), examined the use and meaning of power in personal relationships.

Atwood also wrote a number of novels, beginning with *The Edible Woman* (1969), an early feminist treatise. With mordant wit, she used her novels to examine aspects of a woman's role and her shifting relationship to the world

GRAEME GIBSON

Margaret Atwood

and the individuals around her. Her later novels include *Surfacing* (1972), *Lady Oracle* (1976), *Life Before Man* (1979), *Bodily Harm* (1981), *The Handmaid's Tale* (1985); winner of the Governor General's Award for Fiction in 1986), *Cat's Eye* (1988), and *The Robber Bride* (1993). She also wrote short fiction (such as that in *Bluebeard's Egg* [1983]), critical prose (such as that in *Survival* [1972] and *Second Words* [1982]), and children's books.

Auchincloss, Louis (Stanton) (b. Sept. 27, 1917, Lawrence, N.Y., U.S.) American novelist, short-story writer, and critic best known for his novels of manners set in the world of contemporary upper-class New York City.

Auchincloss studied at Yale University from 1935 to 1939 and graduated from the University of Virginia Law School in 1941. He was admitted to the New York State bar that same year and began a legal career that would last until 1986.

For his first novel, *The Indifferent Children* (1947), Auchincloss used the pseudonym Andrew Lee, but by 1950 he was publishing stories under his own name. Noted for his stylistic clarity and skill at characterization, he became the prolific chronicler of life in the rarefied world of corporate boardrooms and brownstone mansions. His interests as a novelist privy to this world lay not so much in the excesses and intrigues of its inhabitants as in their formative influences and personal limitations.

Several of his best novels, including *The House of Five Talents* (1960) and *Portrait in Brownstone* (1962), examine family relationships over a period of decades. Others, notably *The Rector of Justin* (1964) and *Diary of a Yuppie* (1987), are studies of a single character, often from many points of view. Auchincloss frequently employed thematic or geographic linkage in his collections of short stories. *Tales of Manhattan* (1967) and *Skinny Island* (1987), for example, comprise tales set in Manhattan. In addition to his fiction, Auchincloss published critical works on Edith Wharton and Henry James, among other writers.

Auster, Paul (b. Feb. 3, 1947, Newark, N.J., U.S.) American novelist, essayist, translator, and poet whose complex mystery novels are often concerned with the search for identity and personal meaning.

After graduating from Columbia University, Auster moved to France, where he began translating the works of French writers and publishing his own work in American journals. He gained renown for a series of experimental detective stories published collectively as *The New York Trilogy* (1987). It comprises *City of Glass* (1985), about a crime novelist who becomes entangled in a mystery that causes him to assume various identities; *Ghosts* (1986), about a private eye known as Blue who is investigating a man named Black for a client named White; and *The Locked Room* (1986), the story of an author who, while researching the life of a missing writer for a biography, gradually assumes the identity of that writer.

Other books that feature protagonists who are obsessed with chronicling someone else's life are the novels *Moon Palace* (1989) and *Leviathan* (1992). *The Invention of Solitude* (1982) is both a memoir about the death of his father and a meditation on the act of writing. Auster's other writings include the verse volumes *Unearth* (1974) and *Wall Writing* (1976), the essay collections *White Spaces* (1980) and *The Art of Hunger* (1982), and the novels *The Music of Chance* (1990) and *Mr. Vertigo* (1994).

Austin, Mary, *original surname* Hunter (b. Sept. 9, 1868, Carlinville, Ill., U.S.—d. Aug. 13, 1934, Santa Fe, N.M.) Novelist and essayist who wrote on Native American culture and social problems.

Austin graduated from Blackburn College, Carlinville, Ill., in 1888, taught for a time, and then moved to California, where she became the friend and chronicler of nearby Native Americans. Her first book, *The Land of Little Rain* (1903), a description of desert life in the West, won her immediate fame, and was followed by two collections of short stories, *The Basket Woman* (1904) and *Lost Borders* (1909), and a play, *The Arrow Maker* (1911).

A prolific writer, she published 32 volumes and about 200 articles in her lifetime. Her "problem" novels include *A Woman of Genius* (1912). In her essays she discussed such issues as socialism and feminism.

Avison, Margaret (b. April 23, 1918, Galt, Ont., Can.) Canadian poet who revealed the progress of an interior spiritual journey in her three successive volumes of poetry.

The daughter of a Methodist minister, Avison attended the University of Toronto (B.A., 1940; M.A., 1964) and worked as a librarian, editor, lecturer, and social worker at church missions in Toronto. Her poems began to appear in magazines as early as 1939. She began writing the poems of *Winter Sun* (1960), her first collection, in 1956, while living in Chicago as a Guggenheim fellow. The introspective poems of this collection are concerned with belief and moral knowledge, and for the most part they are written in free verse.

In the early 1960s Avison experienced a religious awakening that confirmed her Christian beliefs, an experience she told about in the title poem of her second collection, *The Dumbfounding* (1966). Less introspective and more direct, these poems recall 17th-century Metaphysical poetry, as they present images of spiritual vitality in everyday life. Many of her poems in *Sunblue* (1978) are based on biblical stories; the poems further investigate her Christian beliefs, and she takes nature as a metaphor for spiritual realities. In 1991 she published a fourth collection, *Selected Poems*.

Babbitt, Irving (b. Aug. 2, 1865, Dayton, Ohio, U.S.—d. July 15, 1933, Cambridge, Mass.) American critic and teacher, leader of the movement in literary criticism known as NEW HUMANISM, or Neohumanism.

Babbitt was educated at Harvard University and at the Sorbonne and taught at Harvard from 1894 until his death. A vigorous teacher, lecturer, and essayist, Babbitt was the unrestrained foe of Romanticism and its offshoots, realism and naturalism; instead, he championed the classical virtues of restraint and moderation. His early followers included T.S. Eliot and George Santayana, who later criticized him; his major opponent was H.L. Mencken.

Babbitt extended his views beyond literary criticism: *Literature and the American College* (1908) calls for a return to the study of classical literatures; *The New Laokoön* (1910) deplores the confusion in the arts created by Romanticism; *Rousseau and Romanticism* (1919) criticizes the effects of Jean-Jacques Rousseau's thought in the 20th century; *On Being Creative* (1932) compares the Romantic concept of spontaneity adversely with classic theories of imitation.

Bacheller, Irving (Addison) (b. Sept. 26, 1859, Pierpont, N.Y., U.S.—d. Feb. 24, 1950, White Plains, N.Y.) Journalist and novelist whose books, generally set in upper New York state, are humorous and full of penetrating character delineations.

Bacheller began his career as a journalist. In 1883 in Brooklyn, N.Y., he founded the first modern newspaper syndicate and through its services distributed fiction by such writers as Joseph Conrad, Rudyard Kipling, and Stephen Crane, as well as nonfiction material. From 1898 to 1900 he was editor of the *New York World*.

Bacheller's novel *Eben Holden: A Tale of the North Country* (1900) sold more than 1,000,000 copies. It gives an authentic picture of 19th-century farm life and character in upper New York state. *D'ri and I* (1901), a novel about the Battle of Lake Erie in the War of 1812, was also popular. Bacheller's own favorites were *The Light in the Clearing* (1917) and *A Man for the Ages: A Story of the Builders of Democracy* (1919), the latter a story of Abraham Lincoln. *Opinions of a Cheerful Yankee* (1926); *Coming up the Road, Memories of a North Country Boyhood* (1928); and *From Stores of Memory* (1938) were autobiographical.

Baker, Carlos (Heard) (b. May 5, 1909, Biddeford, Maine, U.S.—d. April 18, 1987, Princeton, N.J.) American teacher, novelist, and critic known for his definitive biographies of Ernest Hemingway and Percy Bysshe Shelley.

Baker taught at Princeton University from 1951. His book *Shelley's Major Poetry: The Fabric of a Vision* (1948) dwells on Shelley's inner self as visible in his poetry and largely ignores the exterior circumstances of the poet's life.

His widely acclaimed *Hemingway: The Writer as Artist* (1952), regarded as one of the definitive works on the writer, provides a portrait of an artist and his generation and a critique of Hemingway's novels in moral and aesthetic terms. Baker's *Ernest Hemingway: A Life Story* (1969) is an authoritative biography of the writer.

Baker, George Pierce (b. April 4, 1866, Providence, R.I., U.S.—d. Jan. 6, 1935, New York, N.Y.) Teacher of some of the most notable American dramatists, among them Eugene O'Neill, Philip Barry, Sidney Howard, and S.N. Behrman. The critic John Mason Brown and the novelists John Dos Passos and Thomas Wolfe also studied under Baker, who appears as Professor Hatcher in Wolfe's autobiographical novel *Of Time and the River*.

Baker, who graduated from Harvard University in 1887, remained there to teach. In 1905 he started his class for playwrights, 47 Workshop (named after its course number), the first of its kind to be part of a university curriculum. He concerned himself not only with writing but also with stage design, lighting, costuming, and dramatic criticism. Baker's annual lecture tours introduced many Americans to European ideas of theater art. His university productions pioneered advanced staging techniques in the United States.

From 1925 until he retired in 1933, Baker was professor of the history and technique of drama at Yale University, founding a drama department there and directing the university theater. Of his writings, the best known are *The Development of Shakespeare as a Dramatist* (1907) and *Dramatic Technique* (1919).

Baker, Houston A., Jr., *in full* Houston Alfred Baker, Jr. (b. March 22, 1943, Louisville, Ky., U.S.) African-American educator and critic who proposed new standards, based on African-American culture and values, for the interpretation and evaluation of literature.

Baker attended Howard University (B.A, 1965), the University of Edinburgh, and the University of California at Los Angeles (M.A., 1966; Ph.D., 1968) and taught at Yale and Cornell universities, Haverford College, and the University of Virginia. From 1974 to 1977 he directed the Afro-American studies program at the University of Pennsylvania. Besides editing collections of poetry and essays, he wrote the studies *Long Black Song* (1972), *Singers of Daybreak* (1974), *The Journey Back* (1980), and *Modernism and the Harlem Renaissance* (1987).

The works of Frederick Douglass, W.E.B. Du Bois, Booker T. Washington, Richard Wright, and Ralph Ellison figure prominently in Baker's studies.

Baker, Ray Stannard, *pseudonym* David Grayson (b. April 17, 1870, Lansing, Mich., U.S.—d. July 12, 1946, Amherst, Mass.) American journalist, popular essayist, literary crusader for the League of Nations, and authorized biographer of Woodrow Wilson.

A reporter for the *Chicago Record* from 1892 to 1898, Baker became associated with *Outlook*, *McClure's*, and other magazines. In 1906 he helped establish and edit the "muckraker" *American Magazine*. He explored the situation of black Americans in *Following the Color Line* (1908), a field report on race relations in America. As David Grayson he published *Adventures in Contentment* (1907), the first of his several collections of widely read essays. From 1910, when he first met Woodrow Wilson, Baker became an increasingly fervent admirer. At Wilson's request, Baker served as head of the American Press Bureau at the Paris Peace Conference (1919–20), where the two were in close and constant association. Despite prolonged ill health, Baker wrote *Woodrow Wilson: Life and Letters*, 8 vol. (1927–39). He was awarded the Pulitzer Prize for the work in 1940.

Baker, Russell (Wayne) (b. Aug. 14, 1925, Loudoun county, Va., U.S.) American newspaper columnist, author, humorist, and political satirist, who used good-natured humor to comment slyly and trenchantly on a wide range of social and political matters.

After graduating from Johns Hopkins University in 1947, Baker worked as a journalist for the *Baltimore Sun* (1947–54). He also wrote a lively weekly column, "From a Window on Fleet Street." At the Washington bureau of the *New York Times* (1954–62), he covered the White House, the State Department, and the Congress. In the early 1960s he began writing the "Observer" column on the paper's editorial page. In this syndicated humor column he initially concentrated on political satire. Moving to New York City in 1974, he found other subjects to skewer, and in 1979 he won the Pulitzer Prize for commentary. His topics included tax reform, Norman Rockwell, inflation, and fear.

Baker's *Growing Up* (1982), which recalled his peripatetic childhood, won the 1983 Pulitzer Prize for autobiography. A sequel, *The Good Times*, was published in 1989. Other works include *American in Washington* (1961), *No Cause for Panic* (1964), *Poor Russell's Almanac* (1972), and other collections of his columns. In 1993 he succeeded Alistair Cooke as host of the television program *Masterpiece Theatre*.

Baldwin, James (Arthur) (b. Aug. 2, 1924, New York, N.Y., U.S.—d. Dec. 1, 1987, Saint-Paul, Fr.) American essayist, novelist, and playwright noted for his eloquence and passion on the subject of race in America.

Baldwin grew up in poverty in Harlem in New York City. From 14 to 16 he was active during out-of-school hours as a preacher in a small revivalist church, a period he wrote about in his semiautobiographical first and finest

James Baldwin

novel, *Go Tell it on the Mountain* (1953), and in his play about a woman evangelist, *The Amen Corner* (performed 1965).

After graduation from high school, he began a restless period of ill-paid jobs, self-study, and literary apprenticeship in New York City. He left in 1948 for Paris, where he lived for the next eight years and wrote a collection of essays, *Notes of a Native Son* (1955), and his second novel, GIOVANNI'S ROOM (1956), which concerns an American in Paris torn between his love for a man and his love for a woman. From 1969, Baldwin commuted between the south of France, New York, and New England.

In 1957 Baldwin became an active participant in the U.S. civil-rights struggle. A book of essays, *Nobody Knows My Name* (1961), explores black-white relations in the United States. This theme also was central to his novel ANOTHER COUNTRY (1962), which examines sexual as well as racial issues. The separatist Black Muslim (Nation of Islam) group and other aspects of the civil-rights struggle are the subject of THE FIRE NEXT TIME (1963). Baldwin also wrote a bitter play about racist oppression, BLUES FOR MISTER CHARLIE (produced 1964). Though Baldwin continued to write until his death, none of his later works achieved the popular and critical success of his early work.

Bambara, Toni Cade, *original name* Toni Cade (b. March 25, 1939, New York, N.Y., U.S.—d. Dec. 9, 1995, Philadelphia, Pa.) American writer, civil-rights activist, and teacher who wrote about the concerns of the African-American community.

Bambara (a surname she adopted in 1970) was educated at Queens College and City College of the City University of New York. She was a frequent lecturer and teacher at universities and a political activist.

Bambara's fiction, which was set in the rural South as well as the urban North, was written in black street dialect and presented sharply drawn characters whom she portrayed with affection. She published the short-story collections *Gorilla, My Love* (1972) and *The Sea Birds Are Still Alive* (1977), as well as the novels *The Salt Eaters* (1980) and *If Blessing Comes* (1987). She edited and contributed to *The Black Woman: An Anthology* (1970) and to *Tales and Stories for Black Folks* (1971).

Banks, Russell (b. March 28, 1940, Newton, Mass.) American novelist known for his portrayals of the interior lives of characters at odds with economic and social forces.

Banks was educated at Colgate University, Hamilton, N.Y., and the University of North Carolina. From 1966 he was associated with Lillabulero Press, initially as editor and publisher. The press issued his first novel, *Waiting to Freeze*, in 1967. Other early works included *Snow* (1975), *Family Life* (1975), and a collection of stories entitled *The New World* (1978). The novel *Hamilton Stark* (1978) was notable for its vividly rendered hardscrabble New Hampshire setting. The story collection *Trailerpark* (1981) explores the same locale. Banks's interest in the Caribbean, which led to his residence in Jamaica for an interval, shaped two of his novels, *The Book of Jamaica* (1980) and *Continental Drift* (1985), the latter being generally considered his best work. Later novels include *Affliction* (1989) and *The Sweet Hereafter* (1991).

Baraka, Amiri, *also called* Imamu Amiri Baraka, *original name* (until 1968) (Everett) LeRoi Jones (b. Oct. 7, 1934, Newark, N.J., U.S.) Playwright, poet, novelist, and essayist who wrote of the experiences and anger of African-Americans with an affirmation of black life.

A graduate of Howard University, Baraka published his first major collection of poetry, *Preface to a Twenty Volume Suicide Note*, in 1961, followed by THE DEAD LECTURER (1964), *Black Art* (1966), and *Black Magic* (1969). His later collections included *It's Nation Time* (1970), *Spirit Reach* (1972), *Hard Facts* (1977), and *AM/TRAK* (1979). His poems reflected an interest in music that is also evident in the many books he wrote on the subject.

In 1964 Baraka's play DUTCHMAN appeared off-Broadway and won critical acclaim. Later that year his plays THE SLAVE and *The Toilet* were also produced. Baraka wrote many other plays in addition to an autobiographical novel, *The System of Dante's Hell* (1965); a collection of short stories, *Tales* (1967); several collections of essays, including *Home: Social Essays* (1966), *Black Music* (1967), and *Daggers and Javelins* (1984); and *The Autobiography of LeRoi Jones/Amiri Baraka* (1984).

Baraka founded the Black Arts Repertory Theatre in Harlem in 1965. In 1968 he founded the Black Community Development and Defense Organization, a Muslim group committed to affirming black culture and to gaining political power for blacks. He taught at several American universities.

Barlow, Joel (b. March 24, 1754, Redding, Connecticut Colony [U.S.]— d. Dec. 24, 1812, Zarnowiec, Pol.) Writer and poet primarily remembered for the mock-heroic poem *The Hasty Pudding* (1796).

Barlow was a chaplain for three years in the Revolutionary Army. In July 1784 he established a weekly paper, the *American Mercury*, at Hartford, Conn. He was a member of the group of young writers known as the Hartford (or Connecticut) wits, whose patriotism led them to attempt to create a national literature. Barlow's *Vision of Columbus* (1787), a poetic paean to America in nine books, brought the author immediate fame.

In 1788 Barlow went to France, where he lived periodically for the next 17 years. He returned to the United States in 1805 and lived there until 1811, when he became U.S. plenipotentiary to France.

In addition to religious verse and political writings, Barlow published an enlarged edition of his *Vision of Columbus* entitled *The Columbiad* (1807). His literary reputation now rests primarily on *The Hasty Pudding*, a pleasant and humorous mock epic inspired by homesickness for New England and containing vivid descriptions of rural scenes.

Barnes, Djuna (b. June 12, 1892, Cornwall-on-Hudson, N.Y., U.S.—d. June 18?, 1982, New York, N.Y.) Avant-garde American writer who was a well-known figure in the Parisian literary scene of the 1920s and '30s.

Barnes attended the Pratt Institute and Art Students League and worked as an artist and journalist. She published an eccentric chapbook entitled *The Book of Repulsive Women: 8 Rhythms and 5 Drawings* in 1915; four years later three of her plays were produced by the Provincetown Players. She went to Paris in 1920 where she interviewed expatriate writers and artists for several magazines, and soon herself became an established figure. She wrote and illustrated a collection of plays, short stories, and poems titled *A Book* (1923); expanded as *A Night Among the Horses*, 1929; revised as *Spillway*, 1962); *Ladies Almanack* (1928); and the novel *Ryder* (1928), which Barnes called the story of "a female *Tom Jones*." Her second novel, *Nightwood* (1936), is her masterpiece, about the doomed homosexual and heterosexual loves of five extraordinary, even grotesque, people. Barnes also wrote a verse drama, *The Antiphon* (1958).

Barry, Philip (b. June 18, 1896, Rochester, N.Y., U.S.—d. Dec. 3, 1949, New York, N.Y.) American dramatist best known for his comedies of life and manners among the socially privileged.

Barry was educated at Yale and in 1919 entered George Pierce Baker's 47 Workshop at Harvard. His *A Punch for Judy* was produced by the workshop in 1920. *You and I*, also written while Barry was a student, played 170 performances on Broadway in 1923. Over the next 20 years, a succession of plays included such comedies as *Paris Bound* (1927), *Holiday* (1928), *The Animal Kingdom* (1932), and *The Philadelphia Story* (1939). They are characterized by witty and graceful dialogue and humorous contrasts of character or situation.

Barry's thoughtful approach to life is apparent in *White Wings* (1926), a fantasy considered by some critics Barry's best play; *John* (1927), a drama about John the Baptist; *Hotel Universe* (1930); *Here Come the Clowns* (1938), an allegory of good and evil; and his final play, *Second Threshold* (1951).

Barthelme, Donald (b. April 7, 1931, Philadelphia, Pa., U.S.—d. July 23, 1989, Houston, Texas) American short-story writer known for modernist "collages" that were marked by melancholy gaiety.

A one-time journalist, Barthelme was managing editor of *Location*, an art and literature review, and director, from 1961 to 1962, of the Contemporary Arts Museum in Houston, Texas. In 1964 he published his first collection of short stories, *Come Back, Dr. Caligari*. His first novel, *Snow White* (1967), initially was published in *The New Yorker*. Other collections of stories include *City Life* (1970), *Sadness* (1972), *Sixty Stories* (1981), and *Overnight to Many Distant Cities* (1983). He wrote three additional novels: *The Dead Father* (1975), *Paradise* (1986), and *The King* (1990).

Barthelme, Frederick (b. Oct. 10, 1943, Houston, Texas, U.S.) American writer of short stories and novels featuring characters who are shaped by the impersonal suburban environments in which they live.

Brother of writer Donald Barthelme, Frederick attended Tulane University, the University of Houston, and Johns Hopkins University. *Rangoon*, a collection of his surreal short fiction, drawings, and photographs, was published in 1970. This was soon followed by his novel *War & War* (1971). With the short stories of *Moon Deluxe* (1983), written in the present tense and almost all in the first person, he attracted wide notice. The protagonist of his humorous novel *Second Marriage* (1984) is a man whose wife kicks him out of their home in order to make room for his first wife. His subsequent works include the short-story collection *Chroma* (1987) and the novels *Two Against One* (1988), *Natural Selection* (1990), and *Breakers* (1993).

Barth, John, *in full* John Simmons Barth, Jr. (b. May 27, 1930, Cambridge, Md., U.S.) American writer best known for novels that combine philosophical depth with biting satire and boisterous, often bawdy humor.

Barth studied at Johns Hopkins University in Baltimore and taught at various universities, including Johns Hopkins. His first two novels, *The Floating Opera* (1956) and *The End of the Road* (1958), describe characters burdened by a sense of futility. THE SOT-WEED FACTOR (1960) is a picaresque tale that burlesques the early history of Maryland, and GILES GOAT-BOY (1966) is a bizarre tale of the career of a mythical hero and religious prophet. His work *Lost in the Funhouse* (1968) consists of short experimental pieces interspersed with stories based on his childhood. It was followed by *Chimera* (1972), a volume of three novellas, and *Letters* (1979), an experimental novel. The novels *Sabbatical* (1982) and *The Tidewater Tales* (1987) are more traditional narratives.

Bates, Katharine Lee (b. Aug. 12, 1859, Falmouth, Mass., U.S.—d. March 28, 1929, Wellesley, Mass.) Author and educator who wrote the text of the national hymn "America the Beautiful." Bates was educated at Wellesley College, Wellesley, Mass., where she taught English literature from 1885 to

1925. Among her many works are *The College Beautiful and Other Poems* (1887), *English Religious Drama* (1893), and *The Pilgrim Ship* (1926). Her *America the Beautiful and Other Poems* was published in 1911.

Bate, W. Jackson, *in full* Walter Jackson Bate (b. May 23, 1918, Mankato, Minn., U.S.) American author and literary biographer known for his studies of the English writers John Keats and Samuel Johnson.

Educated at Harvard University, Bate taught history and literature there from 1946. In 1945 the Modern Language Association published Bate's *Stylistic Development of Keats.* His *John Keats* (1963) was awarded the Pulitzer Prize for biography in 1964. *Samuel Johnson* (1977) won the acclaim of scholars and critics and was awarded the 1978 Pulitzer Prize and the National Book Award. Bate's other works include *From Classic to Romantic* (1946), *The Achievement of Samuel Johnson* (1955), and *Coleridge* (1968).

L. Frank Baum

Baum, L. Frank, *in full* Lyman (b. May 15, 1856, Chittenango, N.Y., U.S.— d. May 6, 1919, Hollywood, Calif.) American writer known for his series of books for children about the imaginary Land of Oz.

Baum began his career as a journalist. His first book, *Father Goose* (1899), was a commercial success, and he followed it the next year with the even more popular *Wonderful Wizard of Oz.* Baum wrote 13 more Oz books, and the series was continued by another author after his death.

Baum, Vicki, *original name* Hedwig Baum (b. Jan. 24, 1888, Vienna, Austria-Hungary [now in Austria]—d. Aug. 29, 1960, Hollywood, Calif., U.S.) Novelist whose *Menschen im Hotel* (1929); "People at the Hotel"; *Grand Hotel* became a best-seller and was adapted as an Academy Award-winning film in 1932.

By the time that Baum took a job at the magazine *Berliner Illustrierte Zeitung*, she had already finished *Menschen im Hotel*, and it first appeared serially in the magazine. It achieved immediate success in Germany. She rewrote it as a play, and it was a great success in translation as *Grand Hotel* on Broadway. She moved to the United States, becoming a screenwriter in Hollywood in 1932, and in 1938 she became an American citizen.

Her later novels include *Men Never Know* (1935), *Shanghai '37* (1939), *Grand Opera* (1942), *Hotel Berlin '43* (1944), *Mortgage on Life* (1946), *Danger from Deer* (1951), *The Mustard Seed* (1953), *Written on Water* (1956), and *Theme for Ballet* (1958).

Beattie, Ann (b. Sept. 8, 1947, Washington, D.C., U.S.) American writer of short stories and novels whose characters, having come of age in the 1960s, often have difficulties adjusting to the cultural values of later generations.

Beattie graduated from the American University in Washington, D.C., in

1969 and received a Master of Arts degree from the University of Connecticut in 1970. She had short stories published in *The New Yorker* and other literary magazines beginning in the early 1970s. Her first collection of stories, *Distortions*, and her first novel, *Chilly Scenes of Winter*, were both published in 1976.

Beattie's characters are usually passive, alienated people who cannot extricate themselves from unsatisfying careers and lives. In detached, unemotional prose Beattie chronicles their unfulfilling lives and catalogues their possessions and favorite songs. There is little examination of motivation, and historical background is usually absent.

Later collections of her stories include *Secrets and Surprises* (1978), *The Burning House* (1982), and *Where You'll Find Me and Other Stories* (1986). Novels include *Falling in Place* (1980) and *Picturing Will* (1989).

Behrman, S.N., *in full* Samuel Nathaniel (b. June 9, 1893, Worcester, Mass., U.S.—d. Sept. 9, 1973, New York, N.Y.) American short-story writer and playwright best known for popular Broadway plays that commented on volatile and usually complicated contemporary moral issues. Behrman wrote about the wealthy, intellectual sector of society, and he is notable for endowing his characters with eloquence and intelligence.

As a young man, Behrman contributed to several leading newspapers and magazines, including *New Republic* and *The New Yorker*, and studied drama at Harvard and Columbia University, N.Y. His play *The Second Man* (1927) was the first in a string of successes that included *Meteor* (1929), *Brief Moment* (1931), and *Biography* (1932). He tackled the subject of fascism in *Rain from Heaven* (1934). Criticized for not making his personal viewpoint known, but instead letting his characters speak for him, Behrman wrote *No Time for Comedy* (1939), in which the protagonist, an author of light comedy, criticizes himself for his failure to address effectively serious contemporary problems.

Behrman wrote more than two dozen comedies during his 40-year career, and nearly every one of them was a hit. He also wrote many short stories, two biographies, and a number of screenplays.

Bellamy, Edward (b. March 26, 1850, Chicopee Falls, Mass., U.S.—d. May 22, 1898, Chicopee Falls) American writer known chiefly for his utopian novel *Looking Backward, 2000–1887.*

Bellamy first became aware of the plight of the urban poor at 18 while studying in Germany. He studied law and was admitted to the bar in 1871, but he soon turned to journalism, first as an associate editor for the *Springfield Union* (Massachusetts) and then as an editorial writer for the *New York Evening Post.*

In *Looking Backward* (1888), set in Boston in the year 2000, he described the United States under an ideal socialist system that featured cooperation, brotherhood, and an industry geared to human need. Bellamy became an active propagandist for the nationalization of public services, and his ideas encouraged the foundation of nationalist clubs. Political groups inspired by Bellamy's works also appeared in Europe. Bellamy's sequel to *Looking Backward*, entitled *Equality* (1897), was less successful. Additional writings were published in *Edward Bellamy Speaks Again!* (1937) and as *Talks on Nationalism* (1938).

Saul Bellow

Bellow, Saul (b. June 10, 1915, Lachine, near Montreal, Que., Can.) American novelist whose characterizations of the modern urban dweller, disaffected by society but not destroyed in spirit, earned him the Nobel Prize for Literature in 1976. Brought up in a Jewish household and fluent in Yiddish, he was representative of the Jewish-American writers whose works became central to American literature after World War II.

Bellow's parents emigrated in 1913 from Russia to Montreal. When he was nine they moved to Chicago. He attended the University of Chicago and Northwestern University, from which he graduated (B.S.) in 1937, and afterward combined writing with a teaching career at various universities.

He won a reputation among a small group of readers with his first two novels, *Dangling Man* (1944) and *The Victim* (1947). THE ADVENTURES OF AUGIE MARCH (1953) brought wider acclaim. In this novel Bellow employed for the first time a loose, breezy style in conscious revolt against the preoccupation of writers of that time with perfection of form. HENDERSON THE RAIN KING (1959) continued the picaresque approach in its tale of an eccentric American millionaire on a quest in Africa. SEIZE THE DAY (1956), a novella, deals with a man who is a failure in a society where the only success is success. He also wrote a volume of short stories, *Mosby's Memoirs* (1968), and *To Jerusalem and Back* (1976), a nonfiction account of trip to Israel.

In his later novels and novellas—HERZOG (1964); National Book Award, 1965), MR. SAMMLER'S PLANET (1970); National Book Award, 1971), HUMBOLDT'S GIFT (1975); Pulitzer Prize, 1976), *The Dean's December* (1982), *More Die of Heartbreak* (1987), *A Theft* (1989), and *The Bellarosa Connection* (1989)—Bellow perfected the combination of cultural sophistication and the wisdom of the streets that constitutes his greatest originality.

Benchley, Robert (Charles) (b. Sept. 15, 1889, Worcester, Mass., U.S.— d. Nov. 21, 1945, New York City) American drama critic, actor, and humorist noted for his motion-picture short subjects and humorous essays.

A graduate of Harvard University (1912), Benchley joined the staff of *Life* magazine in 1920 as drama critic. He was a regular member of the Algonquin

Round Table. His monologue "The Treasurer's Report," delivered as a skit in an amateur revue in 1922, was the basis for one of the first all-talking short subjects. He subsequently wrote and acted in 46 shorts, his *How to Sleep* winning an Academy Award in 1935.

Benchley's essays were illustrated by Gluyas Williams' caricatures and collected in more than ten books, including *My Ten Years in a Quandary, and How They Grew* (1936) and *Benchley Beside Himself* (1943). His writing is characterized by its warmth and the non sequitur quality of its humor; his satire, although sharp, was never cruel. Benchley was drama critic for *The New Yorker* (1929–40), for which he also wrote "The Wayward Press" column under the pseudonym Guy Fawkes. *The Benchley Roundup* (1954) was a selection from his writings edited by his son Nathaniel, who also wrote his biography (1955).

Benét, Stephen Vincent (b. July 22, 1898, Bethlehem, Pa., U.S.—d. March 13, 1943, New York, N.Y.) Poet, novelist, and writer of short stories, best known for JOHN BROWN'S BODY (1928), a long narrative poem on the Civil War.

Benét published his first book at the age of 17. Civilian service during World War I interrupted his education at Yale. He received his M.A. degree after the war, submitting his third volume of poems instead of a thesis.

After publishing the much-admired *Ballad of William Sycamore 1790–1880* (1923), three novels, and a number of short stories, he went to France, where he wrote *John Brown's Body*. Dramatized by Charles Laughton in 1953, it was performed across the United States.

A Book of Americans (1933), poems written with his wife, the former Rosemary Carr, brought many historical characters to life for American schoolchildren. Benét's preoccupation with historical themes was also the basis for *Western Star*, an ambitious story of America left uncompleted at the time of his death. Book I, complete in itself, was published posthumously. Benét's best-known short story, THE DEVIL AND DANIEL WEBSTER (1937), was the basis for a play, an opera by Douglas Moore, and a motion picture.

Bennett, Gwendolyn B. (b. July 8, 1902, Giddings, Tex., U.S.—d. May 30, 1981, Reading, Pa.) African-American poet, essayist, short-story writer, and artist who was a vital figure in the Harlem Renaissance.

Bennett, the daughter of teachers, grew up on a Nevada Indian reservation, in Washington, D.C., and in Brooklyn, N.Y. She attended Columbia University and Pratt Institute, then studied art in Paris in 1925–26. She wrote articles and created covers for *The Crisis* and *Opportunity* magazines. Her close friendships with fellow Harlem-based writers resulted in her becoming an *Opportunity* editor and writing its popular literary news column

(1926–28). Most of her published work, including two short stories, appeared in 1923–28, and though it is often anthologized, it has not been collected. Her ballads, odes, sonnets, and protest poems are notable for their visual imagery; the best known is the sensual "To a Dark Girl."

Berger, Thomas (Louis) (b. July 20, 1924, Cincinnati, Ohio, U.S.) American novelist whose darkly comic fiction probed and satirized the American experience.

Berger graduated from the University of Cincinnati in 1948. His first novel, *Crazy in Berlin* (1958), inaugurated a tetralogy about Carlo Reinhart, who in the first novel is an adolescent American soldier in Germany. His story is continued in *Reinhart in Love* (1962), *Vital Parts* (1970), and *Reinhart's Women* (1981). In *Little Big Man* (1964; film, 1970), the only white survivor of the Battle of the Little Big Horn, the 111-year-old Jack Crabb, tells his life story.

Berger's other novels include *Killing Time* (1967), *Regiment of Women* (1973), *Who Is Teddy Villanova?* (1977), *Arthur Rex: A Legendary Novel* (1978), *Neighbors* (1980), *The Houseguest* (1988), *Changing the Past* (1989), and *Orrie's Story* (1990).

Berrigan, Daniel (b. May 9, 1921, Virginia, Minn., U.S.) Roman Catholic priest whose poems and essays reflected his deep commitment to social, political, and economic change in American society.

Berrigan grew up in Syracuse, N.Y., and taught at a preparatory school in New Jersey before being ordained a Roman Catholic priest in 1952. He later served in various ministries and taught or lectured at a series of colleges, including Cornell and Yale universities. Berrigan's political activism was closely linked to his vision of the responsibilities of Christianity. His poetry was a vehicle for social protest, yet it retained its artistic integrity.

Influenced by his brother Philip (also a priest), Berrigan became active in the antiwar movement during the Vietnam War period. His one-act play *The Trial of the Catonsville Nine* (1970) is a courtroom drama based on his conviction in a federal court for destroying draft records taken from a Maryland draft board. Some of his most eloquent poetry was published in *Prison Poems* (1973).

We Die Before We Live: Talking with the Very Ill (1980) was based in his experiences working in a cancer ward. In 1987 he published his autobiography, *To Dwell in Peace*, and in 1988 selections of his work were collected in *Daniel Berrigan: Poetry, Drama, Prose*.

Berryman, John (b. Oct. 25, 1914, McAlester, Okla., U.S.—d. Jan. 7, 1972, Minneapolis, Minn.) American poet noted for his confessional poetry laced with humor.

Berryman graduated from Columbia University, where he was influenced by his teacher, the poet Mark Van Doren. After study at the University of Cambridge in 1938, he returned to the U.S. to teach at Wayne State University, Detroit, beginning a career that included posts at Harvard, Princeton, and the University of Minnesota.

Five Young American Poets (1940) contained 20 of his poems. Two volumes of poetry—*Poems* (1942) and *The Dispossessed* (1948)—followed. A richly erotic autobiographical sequence about a love affair, *Berryman's Sonnets*, appeared in 1967. He also wrote short fiction: "The Lovers" appeared in *The Best American Short Stories of 1946*, and his story "The Imaginary Jew" (1945) is often anthologized.

John Berryman

HOMAGE TO MISTRESS BRADSTREET (1956) was one of Berryman's first experimental poems. His new technical daring was also evident in 77 DREAM SONGS (1964), augmented to form a sequence of 385 "Dream Songs" by *His Toy, His Dream, His Rest* (1968). The confessional nature of much of Berryman's poetry continued in *Love & Fame* (1970).

Berryman committed suicide by jumping from a bridge onto the ice of the Mississippi River. *Recovery*, an account of his struggle against alcoholism, was published in 1973.

Berry, Wendell (Erdman) (b. Aug. 5, 1934, Port Royal, Ky., U.S.) American author whose nature poetry, novels of America's rural past, and essays on ecological responsibility grew from his experiences as a farmer.

Berry was educated at the University of Kentucky (B.A., 1956; M.A., 1957). He later taught at Stanford and New York universities and spent a year in Italy. In 1964 he returned to the University of Kentucky to teach and settled on a farm near his birthplace. He left the university in 1977 to concentrate on writing and farming.

Berry's poetry, from his first collection, *The Broken Ground* (1964), to *Sabbaths* (1987), revealed a steadily growing concern with the abuse of the land and with the need to restore the balance of nature. The theme of human responsibility to the earth was also present in his novels, including *The Memory of Old Jack* (1974). Among Berry's nonfiction prose works, *The Hidden Wound* (1970; reprinted 1989) explored racism while *The Unsettling of America* (1977) discussed the late 20th-century crises of culture and morality. His essays in *The Long-Legged House* (1969), *The Unforeseen Wilderness: An Essay on Kentucky's Red River Gorge* (1971), *The Gift of Good Land* (1981), *Standing by Words* (1985), *Home Economics* (1987), *What Are People For?* (1990), and *Sex, Economy, Freedom, and Community* (1993) expanded on his themes of ecology and human responsibility.

Bester, Alfred (b. Dec. 18, 1913, New York, N.Y., U.S.—d. Oct. 20?, 1987, Doylestown, Pa.) Innovative American writer of science fiction whose output was small but highly influential.

Bester attended the University of Pennsylvania (B.A., 1935). From 1939 to 1942 he published 14 short stories in science-fiction magazines, including "Hell Is Forever" (1942), which in its fast pacing and obsessive characters anticipated the style of his major novels. He then wrote scenarios for superhero comic books and scripts for radio and television, and he created English-language librettos for operas by Giuseppe Verdi and Modest Moussorgsky. His first novel was the satirical, non-science-fiction work *Who He?* (1953).

Bester's first major work, the novel *The Demolished Man* (1953), was followed by *Tiger! Tiger!* (1955); U.S. title, *The Stars My Destination*). Bester's fiction often employed narrative techniques—such as interior monologue—that were new to science fiction. He published several short-story collections, including *Starburst* (1958) and *The Dark Side of the Earth* (1964). Later works included *The Computer Connection* (1975); also published as *Extro*), followed by *Golem*[100] (1980) and *The Deceivers* (1982), all of which were experimental and thus less accessible than his early work.

Bibaud, Michel (b. Jan. 19, 1782, Côte des Neiges, near Montreal [now in Quebec, Can.]—d. Aug. 3, 1857, Montreal) Author of French Canada's first volume of poetry and of the first substantial history of Canada.

Educated at the Collège Saint-Raphael, he became a teacher and journalist. Bibaud edited periodicals, of which *La Bibliothèque canadienne*, containing his own historical writing, was the best known. His first historical work, *Histoire du Canada, sous la domination française* (1837), covers the period from the founding of Canada to 1731; a second volume (1844) brings the story to 1830. (A third volume, treating events from 1830 to 1837, was published by his son.) Bibaud's volume of didactic poetry, *Épîtres, satires, chansons, épigrammes, et autres pièces de vers* (1830), contains four satires on ignorance, avarice, laziness, and envy.

Bidart, Frank (b. 1939, California) American poet whose introspective verse, notably dramatic monologues by troubled characters, dealt with personal guilt, family life, and madness. His unconventional punctuation and typography gave his colloquial and economical style an added emphasis.

Bidart graduated from the University of California, Riverside, and later studied at Harvard University. His first volume of verse was *Golden State* (1973). It contains "Golden State," an autobiographical account of a father-and-son relationship, and "Herbert White," the lurid musings of a psychopathic pedophile. *The Book of the Body* (1977) features the dramatic monologues of an amputee and of a suicidal anorexic.

Critical acclaim attended Bidart's publication of *The Sacrifice* (1983), a collection of five long poems about guilt. *In the Western Night: Collected Poems 1965–90* was published in 1990.

Bierce, Ambrose (Gwinnett) (b. June 24, 1842, Meigs county, Ohio, U.S.— d. 1914, Mexico?) American newspaperman, wit, satirist, and author of sardonic short stories based on themes of death and horror.

Reared in Indiana, Bierce became printer's devil (apprentice) on a local paper after about a year of high school. In 1861 he enlisted in the army and fought in a number of American Civil War battles. Seriously wounded in 1864, he served until 1865.

Resettling in San Francisco, Bierce began contributing to periodicals, particularly the *News Letter*, of which he became editor in 1868. He was soon the literary arbiter of the West Coast. "The Haunted Valley" (1871) was his first story. From 1872 to 1875 he lived in England, where he wrote for London magazines, edited the *Lantern*, and published three books: *The Fiend's Delight* (1872), *Nuggets and Dust Panned Out in California* (1872), and *Cobwebs from an Empty Skull* (1874).

In 1877 he became associate editor of the San Francisco *Argonaut* but left it in 1879–80 for an unsuccessful try at mining in the Dakota Territory. There-after he was editor of the San Francisco *Wasp* for five years. In 1887 he joined the staff of the *San Francisco Examiner*, for which he wrote the "Prattler" column. In 1896 Bierce moved to Washington, D.C., and there continued newspaper and magazine writing. In 1913 he went to Mexico, then in the middle of a revolution led by Pancho Villa. His end is a mystery, but a reasonable conjecture is that he was killed in the siege of Ojinaga in January 1914.

As a newspaper columnist, Bierce specialized in attacks on frauds of all sorts. His principal books were *Tales of Soldiers and Civilians* (1891; revised as *In the Midst of Life*), which included some of his finest stories, such as AN OCCURRENCE AT OWL CREEK BRIDGE, "The Eyes of the Panther," and "The Boarded Window"; *Can Such Things Be?* (1893), which included "The Damned Thing" and "Moxon's Master"; and THE DEVIL'S DICTIONARY (originally published in 1906 as *The Cynic's Word Book*), a volume of ironic, even bitter, definitions, which has been often reprinted.

Biggers, Earl Derr (b. Aug. 26, 1884, Warren, Ohio, U.S.—d. April 5, 1933, Pasadena, Calif.) American novelist and journalist best remembered for the popular literary creation Charlie Chan. A wise Chinese-American detective on the Honolulu police force, Charlie Chan is the protagonist of a series of mystery detective novels that spawned popular feature films, radio dramas, and comic strips.

Biggers attended Harvard University (B.A., 1907) and became a journalist for the Boston *Traveler*. His successful mystery novel *Seven Keys to Baldpate* (1913) was adapted into a well-received play and a film. The six novels that feature Chan were all initially serialized in *The Saturday Evening Post*.

Billings, Josh, *pseudonym of* Henry Wheeler Shaw (b. April 21, 1818, Lanesboro, Mass., U.S.—d. Oct. 14, 1885, Monterey, Calif.) American humorist whose philosophical comments in plain language were widely popular after the American Civil War through his newspaper pieces, books, and comic lectures. He employed the misspellings, fractured grammar, and hopeless logic then current among comic writers. His special contributions were his rustic aphorisms and droll delineations of animal life.

Expelled from Hamilton College, Clinton, N.Y., because of a prank, he spent some years in the West and Midwest before settling in Poughkeepsie, N.Y., in 1858 as an auctioneer and land dealer. He began writing when he was 45, but became successful only when he adopted the misspelling vogue. His "Essa on the Muel" made him famous, and after joining the *New York Weekly* in 1867 he became a national idol. Some of his best work is in the 10-year series *Josh Billings' Farmer's Allminax*, which he started in 1869 as a burlesque of *The Old Farmer's Almanac*. His other books were hasty collections of his newspaper writings, the most comprehensive being *Everybody's Friend* (1874).

Bird, Robert Montgomery (b. Feb. 5, 1806, New Castle, Del., U.S.—d. Jan. 23, 1854, Philadelphia, Pa.) Novelist and dramatist whose work epitomizes the nascent American literature of the first half of the 19th century. Although immensely popular in his day, his writings are principally of interest in the 20th century to the literary historian.

Bird graduated with a medical degree from the University of Pennsylvania in 1827 but practiced for only a year. He wrote poetry, some of it published in periodicals, and several unproduced plays. His first drama to be staged was *The Gladiator* (1831), which dealt with a slave revolt in the Rome of 73 BC and by implication attacked the institution of slavery in the United States. Other plays included *Oralloossa* (1832), a romantic tragedy of Peru at the time of the Spanish conquest, and *The Broker of Bogota* (1834), a domestic drama set in 18th-century Colombia and considered his best by many critics.

Bird then turned to writing novels, beginning with *Calavar* (1834), a tale of the Spanish conquistadors in Mexico, and its sequel, *The Infidel* (1835). His remaining novels were frontier stories, the most popular of which was *Nick of the Woods* (1837).

Unable to make a living from his writing, Bird taught briefly at Pennsylvania Medical College in Philadelphia and tried his hand at farming. At the time of his death he was literary editor and part owner of a newspaper, the Philadelphia *North American*.

Birney, Earle, *in full* Alfred Earle Birney (b. May 13, 1904, Calgary, Alta. [Canada]) Writer and educator whose contributions to Canadian letters reveal a deep and abiding love of language.

Birney received a Ph.D. from the University of Toronto (1936), and his first collection of poetry, *David and Other Poems* (1942), was published during his tenure there (1936–42). After serving in the army, he held a number of teaching and editorial positions.

Birney's other verse collections include *Now Is Time* (1945), *The Strait of Anian* (1948), and *Near False Creek Mouth* (1964). Most of his later poems are experimental. His verse drama, *Trial of a City* (1952); later revised as a stage play, *The Damnation of Vancouver*), is an indictment of modern Vancouver by heroes from Vancouver's past. Birney also wrote two novels: *Turvey* (1949), a picaresque novel of World War II, and *Down the Long Table* (1955), which is semiautobiographical. Also an essayist and critic, he edited *Twentieth-Century Canadian Poetry* (1953). His *Collected Poems* appeared in 1975. Later works include two collections of verse and several radio plays.

Bishop, Elizabeth (b. Feb. 8, 1911, Worcester, Mass., U.S.—d. Oct. 6, 1979, Boston, Mass.) American poet known for her polished, witty descriptive verse. Her work appeared in *The New Yorker* and other magazines.

After graduating from Vassar College in 1934, Bishop traveled often, living for a time in Key West, Fla., and Mexico. During most of the 1950s and '60s she lived in Petrópolis, near the city of Rio de Janeiro, Braz., later dividing her time between Petrópolis and San Francisco. Her first book of poems, NORTH & SOUTH (1946), which contrasts her New England origins and her love of hot climates, was reprinted (1955) with additions as *North & South: A Cold Spring*. Bishop's *The Complete Poems* was published in 1969, and her GEOGRAPHY III appeared in 1976. She taught writing at Harvard University from 1970 to 1977. Posthumously published volumes include *The Complete Poems, 1927–1979* (1983) and *The Collected Prose* (1984). Bishop wrote a travel book, *Brazil* (1962), and translated from the Portuguese Alice Brant's Brazilian classic *The Diary of Helena Morley* (1957). She also edited and translated *An Anthology of Twentieth-Century Brazilian Poetry* (1972).

Elizabeth Bishop

Bishop, John Peale (b. May 21, 1892, Charles Town, W.Va., U.S.—d. April 4, 1944, Hyannis, Mass.) American poet, novelist, and critic, a close associate of American expatriate writers in Paris in the 1920s.

At Princeton University Bishop formed lifelong friendships with Edmund Wilson, the future critic, and with the novelist F. Scott Fitzgerald, who depicted Bishop as the highbrow writer Tom D'Invilliers in *This Side of Paradise*. Bishop published his first volume of verse, *Green Fruit*, in 1917. After military service in World War I, he was an editor at *Vanity Fair* magazine in New York City from 1920 to 1922. He married into wealth and traveled throughout Europe. From 1926 to 1933 he lived in France and acquired a deep admiration for French culture. His collection of stories about his native South, *Many Thousands Gone* (1931), was followed with a volume of poetry, *Now with His Love* (1933). *Act of Darkness*, a novel tracing the coming of age of a young man, and *Minute Particulars*, a collection of verse, both appeared in 1935. He became chief poetry reviewer for *The Nation* magazine in 1940. That year he published perhaps his finest poem, "The Hours," an elegy on the death of Fitzgerald. His *Collected Poems* and *Collected Essays* were published in 1948.

Bissell, Richard (Pike) (b. June 27, 1913, Dubuque, Iowa, U.S.—d. May 4, 1977, Dubuque) American novelist and playwright whose works provide fresh and witty images of Midwestern speech and folkways.

Bissell graduated from Harvard. From his experiences as a river pilot came the novels *A Stretch on the River* (1950) and *The Monongahela* (1952). His first successful novel was *7½ Cents* (1953); U.K. title, *A Gross of Pyjamas*), based on his experiences as a supervisor in a pajama factory in Dubuque. In collaboration with George Abbott, he turned *7½ Cents* into a musical, *The Pajama Game* (1954; film, 1957), which had a long run on Broadway. From his experiences in the theater he produced a novel, *Say, Darling* (1957), which he then wrote as a musical under the same title (1958), in collaboration with his wife, Marian Bissell, and Abe Burrows. Among his later books are the novels *Good Bye, Ava* (1960), *Still Circling Moose Jaw* (1965), and *New Light on 1776 and All That* (1975).

Blais, Marie-Claire (b. Oct. 5, 1939, Quebec, Que., Can.) French-Canadian novelist and poet known for reporting the bleak inner reality and grinding poverty of characters born without hope, their empty lives often played out against a featureless, unnamed landscape.

In two early dreamlike novels, *La Belle Bête* (1959); *Mad Shadows*) and *Tête blanche* (1960), Blais stakes out her territory—lower-class people doomed to unrelieved sorrow and oppression. She moves her characters into a recognizably Canadian world in the novels *Une Saison dans la vie d'Emmanuel* (1965); *A Season in the Life of Emmanuel*); *Manuscrits de Pauline Archange* (1968) and *Vivre! Vivre!* (1969), published together as *The Manuscripts of Pauline Archange* in English in 1970; *Un Joualonais sa joualonie* (1973); *St. Lawrence Blues*); and *Le Sourd dans la ville* (1979); *Deaf to the City*). She also published collections of poetry and several plays. Blais studied at Laval University, Quebec, and was made a Companion of the Order of Canada. In 1966 the French awarded her the Prix Médicis.

Bloom, Harold (b. July 11, 1930, New York, N.Y., U.S.) American literary critic known for his innovative interpretations of literary history and of the creation of literature.

Bloom attended Cornell and Yale universities and began teaching at Yale in 1955. His early books, *The Visionary Company: A Reading of English Romantic Poetry* (1961, rev. ed., 1971) and *The Ringers in the Tower: Studies in Romantic Tradition* (1971), explored the Romantic tradition and its influence on such poets as A.R. Ammons and Allen Ginsburg.

In *The Anxiety of Influence* (1973) and *A Map of Misreading* (1975), Bloom proposed one of his most original theories: that poetry results from poets deliberately misreading the works that influence them. *Figures of Capable Imagination* (1976) expands upon this theme. His most controversial work appeared in his commentary on *The Book of J*, published (1990) with David Rosenberg's translations of selected sections of the Pentateuch. Bloom speculated that the earliest known texts of the Bible were written by a woman who lived during the time of David and Solomon and that the texts were literary rather than religious ones on which later rewriters imposed beliefs of patriarchal Judaism.

Bly, Robert (Elwood) (b. Dec. 23, 1926, Madison, Minn., U.S.) American poet, translator, editor, and author.

Bly studied at St. Olaf College, Northfield, Minn.; Harvard University; and the University of Iowa. In 1958 he cofounded the magazine *The Fifties* (its name changed with the decades), which published other important young poets and Bly's own translations and serene nature poems. In 1966 Bly was a founder of American Writers Against the Vietnam War, and when his collection *The Light Around the Body* won a 1968 National Book Award he donated his prize money to the Resistance, a draft resisters' organization. His later poems and "prose poems," including those in *Sleepers Joining Hands* (1973) and *This Tree Will Be Here for a Thousand Years* (1979), returned to personal and pastoral themes. Throughout Bly's career he translated the work of many poets, ranging from German, Scandinavian, Spanish, and Latin-American writers to the 15th-century Indian mystic Kabīr.

His poems of *The Man in the Black Coat Turns* (1981) explore themes of male grief and the father-son connection. These were among the concerns of his best-selling *Iron John: A Book About Men* (1990), which drew upon myth, legend, folklore, fairy tales, and Jungian psychology.

Bodenheim, Maxwell, *original surname* Bodenheimer (b. May 26, 1893,

Hermanville, Miss., U.S.—d. Feb. 6, 1954, New York, N.Y.) Poet who contributed to the development of the modernist movement in American poetry but is probably best known as a personality in literary bohemia.

Bodenheim appeared in Chicago in about 1913, during the period of the Chicago literary renaissance. He wrote plays with Ben Hecht and helped him edit the short-lived *Chicago Literary Times* (1923–24). Later they conducted a much-publicized feud, featuring each other as characters in their novels.

Bodenheim's poems were first published in *Poetry* magazine in 1914; his earliest collection was *Minna and Myself* (1918). Several other volumes of poetry followed, his *Selected Poems, 1914–44* appearing in 1946. In these works he employed many of the striking visual techniques of the Imagists.

Bodenheim settled in New York's Greenwich Village in the late 1920s. His novels and poetry appeared regularly during that decade and the next, but increasing dissipation had reduced him to peddling his poems in bars when he and his third wife were murdered by a former mental patient in their lodgings. His unfinished autobiography, *My Life and Loves in Greenwich Village*, appeared in 1954, shortly after his death. Among the better of his largely forgotten novels are *Blackguard* (1923), *Crazy Man* (1924), *Georgie May* (1928), *Sixty Seconds* (1929), and *Naked on Roller Skates* (1931).

Bogan, Louise (b. Aug. 11, 1897, Livermore Falls, Maine, U.S.—d. Feb. 4, 1970, New York, N.Y.) Poet and literary critic whose verse resembles that of the English Metaphysical poets in its restrained, intellectual style and use of traditional techniques while remaining essentially modern, both personal and immediate.

Bogan's poems first appeared in the *New Republic*. *Body of This Death* was published in 1923. She later wrote verse and literary criticism for the magazines *The New Yorker*, *Poetry: A Magazine of Verse*, *The Atlantic Monthly*, and *The Nation*. Her *Collected Poems 1923–1953* (1954) received the Bollingen Prize in Poetry. As a critic Bogan became known for fairness and generosity, and she focused on the strengths of authors in such works as the survey *Achievement in American Poetry 1900–1950* (1951) and *Selected Criticism: Prose, Poetry* (1955). Her other works include *The Sleeping Fury* (1937), *The Blue Estuaries: Poems 1923–1968* (1968), and *A Poet's Alphabet* (1970).

Bolton, Guy (Reginald) (b. Nov. 23, 1884, Broxbourne, Hertfordshire, Eng.—d. Sept. 5, 1979, London) American playwright and librettist perhaps best known for his witty and articulate librettos, on which he collaborated with such notables as P.G. Wodehouse, George Middleton, and Fred Thompson.

Bolton's first play appeared on Broadway in 1911. With his collaborators, he turned out scripts that were enhanced with music by composers such as Jerome Kern, George Gershwin, and Cole Porter. Among his finer works are *Oh, Boy!* (1917); with Wodehouse, music by Kern), *Sally* (1920); with music by Kern), *Lady, Be Good!* (1924); with Thompson, music by George and Ira Gershwin), *Oh, Kay!* (1926); with Wodehouse, music by the Gershwins and Howard Dietz), and *Anything Goes* (1934); with Wodehouse, Howard Lindsay, and Russel Crouse, music by Porter).

Bontemps, Arna (Wendell) (b. Oct. 13, 1902, Alexandria, La., U.S.— d. June 4, 1973, Nashville, Tenn.) American writer who depicted the lives and struggles of black Americans.

Bontemps's poetry began to appear in the influential black magazines *Opportunity* and *Crisis* in the mid-1920s. His first novel, *God Sends Sunday* (1931), is considered the final work of the Harlem Renaissance. In collaboration with the poet Countee Cullen, the novel was dramatized as *St. Louis Woman* (1946). Bontemps' next two novels were about slave revolts—in Virginia in BLACK THUNDER (1936) and in Haiti in DRUMS AT DUSK (1939).

Bontemps's nonfiction works, many for younger readers, include *The Story of the Negro* (1948); 4th ed., 1964); *Chariot in the Sky* (1951); *Frederick Douglass: Slave-Fighter-Freeman* (1959); *One Hundred Years of Negro Freedom* (1961); and *Famous Negro Athletes* (1964). Among the anthologies he edited are *The Poetry of the Negro* (1949) and *The Book of Negro Folklore* (1958), both with Langston Hughes; *American Negro Poetry* (1963); and *Great Slave Narratives* (1969).

Booth, Wayne C., *in full* Clayson (b. Feb. 22, 1921, American Fork, Utah, U.S.) American critic and teacher associated with the Chicago school of literary criticism.

Booth attended Brigham Young University, Salt Lake City, Utah (B.A., 1944). He became devoted to Neo-Aristotelian critical methods while studying with R.S. Crane at the University of Chicago (M.A., 1947; Ph.D., 1950). He taught at Haverford College, Haverford, Pa., and Earlham College, Richmond, Ind., and then at the University of Chicago until his retirement in 1992.

In his influential first book, *The Rhetoric of Fiction* (1961); rev. ed., 1983), Booth argued that as a technique rhetoric can enhance communication between author and reader, not merely manipulate the reader's response, and he also offered a critical methodology. In addition to further works of criticism, Booth cofounded (1974) and coedited from 1974 to 1985 the quarterly *Critical Inquiry*. His other books include *Now Don't Try to Reason with Me: Essays and Ironies for a Credulous Age* (1970), *A Rhetoric of Irony* (1974), and *Critical Understanding: The Powers and Limits of Pluralism* (1979).

Boucicault, Dion, *original name* Dionysius Lardner Boursiquot (b. Dec. 26, 1820/22, Dublin, Ire.—d. Sept. 18, 1890, New York, N.Y., U.S.) Irish-born American playwright and actor who exerted a major influence on the form and content of American drama.

Boucicault began acting in 1837. His second play, *London Assurance* (1841), which foreshadowed the modern social drama, was a huge success. Other notable early plays were *Old Heads and Young Hearts* (1844) and *The Corsican Brothers* (1852). In 1853 Boucicault and his second wife, Agnes Robertson, arrived in New York City, where his plays and adaptations were long popular. He led a movement of playwrights that in 1856 produced the first copyright law for drama in the United States. His play *The Poor of New York* had a long run at Wallack's Theatre in 1857 and was adapted for presentation elsewhere (as, for example, *The Poor of Liverpool*). *The Octoroon; or, Life in Louisiana* (1859) caused a sensation with its implied attack on slavery.

Boucicault and his wife joined Laura Keene's theater in 1860 and began a series of his popular Irish plays—*The Colleen Bawn* (1860), *Arrah-na-Pogue* (1864), *The O'Dowd* (1873), and *The Shaughraun* (1874). Returning to London in 1862, he provided Joseph Jefferson with a successful adaptation of *Rip Van Winkle* (1865). About 150 plays are credited to Boucicault, who, as both writer and actor, raised the stage Irishman from caricature to character.

Bourne, Randolph Silliman (b. May 30, 1886, Bloomfield, N.J., U.S.—d. Dec. 22, 1918, New York, N.Y.) American literary critic and essayist whose polemical articles made him a spokesman for young radicals who came of age on the eve of World War I.

He held a variety of odd jobs before winning a scholarship (at age 23) to Columbia University. That same year his *Youth and Life* appeared, essays asserting that the youth of his day would sweep away much that was antiquated and unworthy in American life. After a year in Europe, resulting in 1914 in "Impressions of Europe: 1913–14," he turned his attention to the progressive educational theories of the pragmatist philosopher John Dewey, who had been his teacher at Columbia. The outcome was two books: *The Gary Schools* (1916) and *Education and Living* (1917).

Bourne's early death was brought on by influenza during the epidemic of 1918–19. He left incomplete a group of writings analyzing culture, power, and the modern state, some of which were collected and edited by Olaf Hansen in *The Radical Will: Randolph Bourne, Selected Writings, 1911–1918* (1977). Two posthumous volumes of Bourne's essays appeared: *Untimely Papers* (1919) and *The History of a Literary Radical and Other Essays* (1920).

Bowen, Catherine (Shober), *original surname* Drinker (b. Jan. 1, 1897, Haverford, Pa., U.S.—d. Nov. 1, 1973, Haverford) American historical biographer known for her partly fictionalized biographies. After attending the Peabody Institute and the Juilliard School of Music, she became interested in writing. Not surprisingly, her earliest works were inspired by the lives of musicians.

Her biography of the Elizabethan jurist Sir Edward Coke, *The Lion and the Throne* (1957), won her the National Book Award in 1958. Her many other books include *Beloved Friend* (1937), about the relationship between Tchaikovsky and Nadezhda von Meck; *Yankee from Olympus: Justice Holmes and His Family* (1944); *John Adams and the American Revolution* (1950); and *Miracle at Philadelphia: The Story of the Constitutional Convention, May to September 1787* (1966).

Bowles, Jane (Sydney), *original surname* Auer (b. Feb. 22, 1917, New York, N.Y., U.S.—d. May 4, 1973, Malaga, Spain) American author whose reputation rests on a small body of highly individualistic work that enjoyed an underground reputation even when it was no longer in print.

Auer married composer-author Paul Bowles in 1938. They lived in Costa Rica, France, Mexico, and the United States, where she began writing her only published novel, *Two Serious Ladies* (1943). The couple settled in Tangier, Morocco, in 1952. In December 1953 her play *In the Summer House* was staged in New York. In addition to the novel and the play, she also published seven short stories.

Bowles deliberately constructed *Two Serious Ladies* without a plot. Its title characters, one sinful and victimized, the other virtuous and domineering, meet only twice; their lives are presented alternately, in a style praised for its wit. Her short stories and play also contrast domineering and weak women. Her *Collected Works* was published in 1966; it was expanded after her death and published as *My Sister's Hand in Mine* (1978).

Bowles, Paul (Frederick) (b. Dec. 30, 1910, New York, N.Y., U.S.) American-born composer, translator, and author of novels and short stories in which violent events and psychological collapse are recounted in a detached and elegant style. His protagonists are often Europeans or Americans who are maimed by their contact with powerful traditional cultures.

Bowles began publishing Surrealist poetry in the magazine *transition* at the age of 16. He studied musical composition under Aaron Copland and composed music for more than 30 theatrical productions and films. He became a member of the loose society of literary expatriates in Europe and North Africa. In Tangier, Morocco, his most potent source of inspiration, he wrote his first novel, THE SHELTERING SKY (1948), a harsh tale of death, rape, and sexual obsession.

His later novels include *Let It Come Down* (1952), *The Spider's House* (1955), and *Up Above the World* (1966). Bowles' *Collected Stories, 1939–1976* (1979) and his subsequent short-story collections, which include *Midnight Mass* (1981) and *Call at Corazón* (1988), also depict human depravity amid exotic settings. Bowles recorded Moroccan folk music for the U.S. Library of Congress, wrote travel essays, translated works from several European and Middle Eastern languages into English, and recorded and translated oral tales from Maghrebi Arabic into English. *Without Stopping* (1972) and *Two Years Beside the Strait: Tangier Journal 1987–1989* (1990); U.S. title, *Days*) are autobiographical.

Boyle, Kay (b. Feb. 19, 1902, St. Paul, Minn., U.S.—d. Dec. 27, 1992, Mill Valley, Calif.) American novelist, poet, essayist, and short-story writer noted for her elegant style.

Boyle studied architecture and music and, after meeting and marrying a French student, moved with him to France in 1923, living there and in England and Austria until returning to the United States in 1941. From 1946 to 1953 she served as a foreign correspondent in France and West Germany for *The New Yorker*. She later taught at several colleges and universities in the United States.

Boyle wrote two award-winning short stories, "The White Horses of Vienna" (1935) and "Defeat" (1941). Among her more notable novels are *Plagued by the Nightingale* (1931), *Monday Night* (1938), and *Generation Without Farewell* (1960). Her major short-story collections include *The White Horses of Vienna and Other Stories* (1936), *The Smoking Mountain: Stories of Postwar Germany* (1951), and *Fifty Stories* (1980). Two critically acclaimed verse collections are *Testament for My Students and Other Poems* (1970) and *This Is Not a Letter and Other Poems* (1985). Boyle's early works center on the conflicts and disappointments that individuals encounter in their search for romantic love. Her later fiction usually deals with the need for an individual's commitment to wider political or social causes as a prerequisite to attaining self-knowledge and fulfillment. *Words That Must Somehow Be Said: Selected Essays of Kay Boyle, 1927–1984*, was published in 1985.

Brackenridge, Hugh Henry (b. 1748, Kintyre, near Campbeltown, Argyll, Scot.—d. June 25, 1816, Carlisle, Pa., U.S.) Author of *Modern Chivalry* (1792–1805; final revision, 1819), the first novel portraying frontier life in the United States after the Revolutionary War.

Brackenridge was educated at Princeton, and later he joined George Washington's army as a chaplain. He published two verse dramas on Revolutionary themes, *The Battle of Bunkers-Hill* (1776) and *The Death of General Montgomery at the Siege of Quebec* (1777), and *Six Political Discourses Founded on the Scripture* (1778). In an attempt to promote a national American literature, he established and edited *The United States Magazine* in 1779, but it failed within the year.

Brackenridge became a lawyer and settled in the frontier village of Pittsburgh in 1781, where he helped start *The Pittsburgh Gazette*, the first newspaper in what was then the Far West. After he was elected to the Pennsylvania Assembly in 1786, he obtained funds to found the academy that became the University of Pittsburgh. In 1795 he published *Incidents of the Insurrection in the Western Parts of Pennsylvania in the Year 1794*.

Bradbury, Ray (Douglas) (b. Aug. 22, 1920, Waukegan, Ill., U.S.) American author best known for highly imaginative science-fiction stories and novels that blend social criticism with an awareness of the hazards of runaway technology.

Bradbury's first book of short stories, *Dark Carnival* (1947), was followed by *The Martian Chronicles* (1950; film, 1966), generally considered a science-fiction classic. Bradbury's other important short-story collections include *The Illustrated Man* (1951), *The Golden Apples of the Sun* (1953), *The October Country* (1955), *A Medicine for Melancholy* (1959), *The Machineries of Joy* (1964), and *I Sing the Body Electric!* (1969). His novels include *Fahrenheit 451* (1953), *Dandelion Wine* (1957), *Something Wicked This Way Comes* (1962), and *Death Is a Lonely Business* (1985). He wrote stage plays and several screenplays, including *Moby Dick* (1956); in collaboration with John Huston). From the 1970s Bradbury wrote poetry, children's stories, and crime fiction.

Bradford, Roark (Whitney Wickliffe) (b. Aug. 21, 1896, Lauderdale county, Tenn., U.S.—d. Nov. 13, 1948, New Orleans, La.) American novelist and short-story writer whose works of fiction and folklore were based on his contacts with American blacks.

Bradford had little formal education. He began work as a reporter in 1920 and became reacquainted with the musicians, preachers, and storytellers familiar from his youth on a plantation. These encounters spurred him to write a series of stories for the New York *World*. When collected, the stories became his popular first book, *Ol' Man Adam an' His Chillun* (1928), which consisted of biblical stories as related by unlettered blacks. The stories were adapted by Marc Connelly into the play *Green Pastures*, which won a Pulitzer Prize in 1930. Bradford also wrote novels that showed American blacks in historical perspective, such as *This Side of Jordan* (1929), about the arrival of machines on the plantations.

Bradstreet, Anne, *original surname* Dudley (b. *c.* 1612, Northampton?, Northamptonshire, Eng.—d. Sept. 16, 1672, Andover, Massachusetts Bay Colony [U.S.]) One of the first poets to write English verse in the American colonies. She won critical acceptance in the 20th century, particularly for her sequence of religious poems, "Contemplations," written for her family and not published until the mid-19th century.

Dudley married Simon Bradstreet when she was 16, and two years later they sailed with other Puritans to settle on Massachusetts Bay. She wrote her poems while rearing eight children. Her brother-in-law, without her knowledge, took her poems to England, where they were published as *The Tenth Muse Lately Sprung Up in America* (1650). The first American edition of this work was published in revised and expanded form as *Several Poems Compiled with Great Variety of Wit and Learning* (1678).

Her later poems, written for her family, show her spiritual growth as she came fully to accept the Puritan creed. She also wrote more personal poems about such subjects as her thoughts before childbirth and her response to the death of a grandchild. Her prose works include "Meditations," a collection of succinct and pithy aphorisms.

Brautigan, Richard (Gary) (b. Jan. 30, 1933, Tacoma, Wash., U.S.—d. September?, 1984, Bolinas, Calif.) American Writer of pastoral, whimsical, often surreal fiction and poetry popular among '60s and '70s counterculture readers.

Brautigan's humorous first novel, *A Confederate General from Big Sur*, was published in 1964. His second novel, *Trout Fishing in America* (1967), a commentary on the state of nature in contemporary America, sold two million copies, and its title was adopted as the name of several American communes.

Brautigan's novels feature passive protagonists whose innocence shields them from the moral consequences of their actions. His later novels include *In Watermelon Sugar* (1968), *The Abortion: An Historical Romance, 1966* (1971), *The Hawkline Monster: A Gothic Western* (1974), and *The Tokyo-Montana Express* (1979). Brautigan also published a short-story collection, *Revenge of the Lawn: Stories, 1962–1970* (1971), and several poetry collections before his suicide in 1984.

Brinnin, John Malcolm (b. Sept. 13, 1916, Halifax, N.S., Can.) American poet, editor, and social historian, also known for his biographies of other poets.

Brinnin's first volume of poetry, *The Garden Is Political* (1942), was highly praised. Subsequent collections, which increasingly displayed his interest in and experiments with form, included *The Lincoln Lyrics* (1942), *No Arch, No Triumph* (1945), *The Sorrows of Cold Stone: Poems 1940–1950* (1951), and *Skin Diving in the Virgins* (1970); his *Selected Poems* was published in 1963.

Brinnin accompanied Dylan Thomas on his tours of America in the early 1950s, and after Thomas' death he wrote *Dylan Thomas in America* (1955). He also wrote *William Carlos Williams* (1963), the memoirs collected in *Sextet: T.S. Eliot & Truman Capote & Others* (1981), and *Truman Capote* (1986). Among the books he edited were three anthologies of 20th-century American and British poetry. Brinnin also wrote three histories of North Atlantic steamships.

Brodkey, Harold (Roy), *original surname* Weintraub (b. Oct. 25, 1930, Staunton, Ill., U.S.—d. Jan. 26, 1996, New York, N.Y.) American novelist and short-story writer whose near-autobiographical fiction avoids plot, instead concentrating upon careful, close description of feeling.

SIGRID ESTRADA

Harold Brodkey

Brodkey attended Harvard University and soon began publishing short stories in magazines. His first collection, *First Love and Other Sorrows* (1957), contained stories of youthful romance and marriage, using incidents from his own life. It was about this time that he began writing an autobiographical novel which was to occupy him for most of the next 30 years. The novel, *The Runaway Soul*, was finally published in 1991 to mixed reviews. Excerpts from it were published earlier as *Women and Angels* (1985). Wiley Silenowicz, the protagonist of *The Runaway Soul*, is also featured in 12 of the 18 tales in *Stories in an Almost Classical Mode* (1988). Brodkey in 1994 published another novel—*Profane Friendship*, about a homosexual affair in Venice—shortly after his dramatic announcement in *The New Yorker* that he had AIDS.

Brodsky, Joseph, *original name* Iosip Aleksandrovich Brodsky (b. May 24, 1940, Leningrad [now St. Petersburg], Russia, U.S.S.R.—d. Jan. 28, 1996, New York, N.Y., U.S.) Russian-born poet who was awarded the Nobel Prize for Literature in 1987 for his lyric and elegiac poems.

Brodsky's early poetry had begun to earn him a reputation in the Leningrad literary scene when his independent spirit and his irregular work record led to his being sentenced to five years of hard labor for "social parasitism." The sentence was commuted in 1965 after prominent Soviet literary figures protested. Exiled from the Soviet Union in 1972, Brodsky lived thereafter in the United States. He was a poet-in-residence and visiting professor at several universities. He served as poet laureate of the United States in 1991–92.

Brodsky's poetry treats in a powerful, meditative fashion the universal concerns of life, death, and the meaning of existence. His earlier works include *Stikhotvoreniya i poemy* (1965); "Verses and Poems") and *Ostanovka v pustyne* (1970); "A Halt in the Wasteland"); these and other works were translated by George L. Kline in *Selected Poems* (1973). His important later works include the poetry collections *A Part of Speech* (1980), *History of the Twentieth Century* (1986), and *To Urania* (1988) and the essays collected in *Less Than One* (1986) and *On Grief and Reason* (1996). Notable, too, is his prose reflection *Venice, Fondamenta degli incurabili* (1991; *Watermark*).

Bromfield, Louis (b. Dec. 27, 1896, Mansfield, Ohio, U.S.—d. March 18, 1956, Columbus, Ohio) American novelist and essayist.

Bromfield was decorated for his service in the French army, which he joined at the outbreak of World War I. He went on to serve as a critic for several periodicals, including the *Bookman* and *Time* magazine. In 1923 he moved to France and began to concentrate on writing fiction. During these expatriate years, he produced his most highly acclaimed novels, including *The Green Bay Tree* (1924), *Possession* (1925), *Early Autumn* (1926); Pulitzer Prize), and *A Good Woman* (1927).

With the onset of World War II, Bromfield returned to the United States, where he wrote *Wild Is the River* (1941), *Until the Day Break* (1942), *Mrs. Parkington* (1943), and *What Became of Anna Bolton* (1944).

Brooks, Cleanth (b. Oct. 16, 1906, Murray, Ky., U.S.—d. May 10, 1994, New Haven, Conn.) American teacher and critic whose work was important in establishing the New Criticism, which stressed close reading and structural analysis of literature.

Brooks was educated at Vanderbilt University, Nashville, Tenn., and at Tulane University, New Orleans. From 1932 he taught at several universities, including Louisiana State University, Baton Rouge, and Yale University. From 1935 to 1942, with Charles W. Pipkin and poet and critic Robert Penn Warren, he edited *The Southern Review*, a journal that advanced the New Criticism, as did Brooks's critical works, *Modern Poetry and the Tradition* (1939) and *The Well-Wrought Urn* (1947). Authoritative college texts by Brooks, with others, reinforced the popularity of the New Criticism: *Understanding Poetry* (1938) and *Understanding Fiction* (1943), written with Warren, and *Understanding Drama* (1945), with Robert Heilman.

Brooks's later works include *Literary Criticism: A Short History* (1957); cowritten with William K. Wimsatt); *A Shaping Joy: Studies in the Writer's Craft* (1972); *The Language of the American South* (1985); and several books on William Faulkner.

Brooks, Gwendolyn (Elizabeth) (b. June 7, 1917, Topeka, Kan., U.S.) American poet whose works deal with the everyday life of urban blacks. She was the first black poet to win the Pulitzer Prize (1949).

Brooks's first published collection, *A Street in Bronzeville* (1945), reveals her talent for making the ordinary life of her neighbors extraordinary. *Annie Allen* (1949), for which she won the Pulitzer Prize, is a loosely connected series of poems related to a black girl growing up in Chicago. The same theme was used for Brooks's novel *Maud Martha* (1953).

The Bean Eaters (1960) contains some of her best verse. Her *Selected Poems* (1963) was followed in 1968 by *In the Mecca*, half of which is a long narrative poem about people in the Mecca, a vast, apartment building on the South Side of Chicago. Brooks also wrote a book for children, *Bronzeville Boys and Girls* (1956). The autobiographical *Report from Part One* (1972) was an assemblage of personal memoirs, interviews, and letters. Later works include *Primer for Blacks* (1980), *Young Poets' Primer* (1981), *To Disembark* (1981), *The Near-Johannesburg Boy, and Other Poems* (1986), *Blacks* (1987), *Winnie* (1988), and *Children Coming Home* (1991).

Brooks, Van Wyck (b. Feb. 16, 1886, Plainfield, N.J., U.S.—d. May 2, 1963, Bridgewater, Conn.) American critic, biographer, and literary historian, whose *Finders and Makers* series traces American literary history in rich biographical detail from 1800 to 1915.

In 1908 Brooks published his first book, *The Wine of the Puritans*, in which he blamed the Puritan heritage for America's cultural shortcomings. He explored this theme more thoroughly in his first major work, *America's Coming-of-Age* (1915), with its thesis that the Puritan duality separating the spiritual from the material had resulted in a corresponding split in contemporary American culture between "highbrow" and "lowbrow."

Brooks's book *The Ordeal of Mark Twain* (1920); rev. ed., 1933) was a psychological study attempting to show that Twain had repressed his natural artistic bent for the sake of his Calvinist upbringing. In *The Pilgrimage of Henry James* (1925), Brooks argued that James's writing suffered because of his too-long separation from his native land. In *The Life of Emerson* (1932), Brooks depicted an American writer who he felt had successfully bridged the gap between art and life.

The *Finders and Makers* series began with *The Flowering of New England, 1815–1865* (1936), followed by *New England: Indian Summer, 1865–1915* (1940), *The World of Washington Irving* (1944), *The Times of Melville and Whitman* (1947), and *The Confident Years: 1885–1915* (1952).

Brougham, John (b. May 9, 1814, Dublin, Ire.—d. June 7, 1880, New York, N.Y., U.S.) Irish-born American author of more than 75 popular 19th-century plays, theater manager, and actor who excelled in eccentric comic roles.

Brougham made his acting debut in 1830, playing six parts in *Tom and Jerry*. A year later he wrote his first play, a burlesque, which was followed by a number of other works. In 1840 he became manager of the Lyceum Theatre, writing *Life in the Clouds*, *Love's Livery*, *Enthusiasm*, *Tom Thumb the Second*, and *The Demon Gift* (with Mark Lemon). In 1842 Brougham went to the United States, managing theaters in New York City and writing a number of comedies and dramas until, in 1860, a trip to London led to a five-year stay in England. In 1865 he returned to the United States.

Brown, Charles Brockden (b. Jan. 17, 1771, Philadelphia, Pa. [U.S.]—d. Feb. 22, 1810, Philadelphia) Writer known as the "father of the American novel." His gothic romances in American settings were the first in a tradition adapted by two of the greatest American authors, Edgar Allan Poe and Nathaniel Hawthorne.

Brown was apprenticed to a Philadelphia lawyer in 1787, but his strong interest in writing led him to help found a literary society. In 1793 he gave up the law entirely to pursue a literary career. His first novel, WIELAND (1798), a minor masterpiece in American fiction, shows the ease with which mental balance is lost when the test of common sense is not applied to strange experiences. Brown also wrote *Ormond* (1799), *Edgar Huntly* (1799), and *Arthur Mervyn* (1799–1800), as well as a number of less well-known novels and a book on the rights of women.

Brownell, W.C., *in full* William Crary (b. Aug. 30, 1851, New York, N.Y., U.S.—d. July 22, 1928, Williamstown, Mass.) Critic who sought to expand the scope of American literary criticism.

After graduating from Amherst College, Amherst, Mass., in 1871, Brownell worked as an editor and literary adviser. His first two books, *French Traits* (1889) and *French Art* (1892), established a new and high standard for the American critic, one that Brownell maintained for himself in his succeeding books: *Victorian Prose Masters* (1901), *American Prose Masters* (1909), *Criticism* (1914), *Standards* (1917), *The Genius of Style* (1924), and *Democratic Distinction in America* (1927).

Brown, Sterling (Allen) (b. May 1, 1901, Washington, D.C., U.S.—d. Jan. 17, 1989, Washington, D.C.) Influential African-American teacher and literary critic whose poetry was rooted in folklore sources and black dialect.

Brown was educated at Williams College, Williamstown, Mass., and Harvard University. While teaching at several schools he began collecting folk songs and stories from blacks. In 1929 Brown began a 40-year teaching career at Howard University, and in 1932 his first volume of poetry, *Southern Road*, was published. Ballads, work songs, spirituals, and blues were primary influences on his work.

Though *Southern Road* was widely praised, Brown found no publisher for his second collection, *No Hiding Place*; it eventually was incorporated into his *Collected Poems* (1980). As critic, essayist, and *Opportunity* magazine columnist, he supported realistic writing and harshly attacked literature that distorted black life. In 1937 he published the pioneering studies *Negro Poetry and Drama* and *The Negro in American Fiction*, and in 1941 he was coeditor of *The Negro Caravan*, a major anthology of African-American writing.

Brown, William Hill (b. November 1765, Boston, Mass. [U.S.]—d. Sept. 2, 1793, Murfreesboro, N.C.) Novelist and dramatist whose anonymously published *The Power of Sympathy, or the Triumph of Nature Founded in Truth* (1789) is considered the first American novel. An epistolary novel about tragic, incestuous love, it imitated the sentimental manner developed by Samuel Richardson.

Brown wrote the romantic tale "Harriot, or the Domestic Reconciliation" (1789), which was published in the first issue of *Massachusetts Magazine*, and the play *West Point Preserved* (published posthumously, 1797). He also wrote a series of verse fables, the comedy *Penelope*, essays, and a short second novel about incest and seduction, *Ira and Isabella* (1807).

Brown, William Wells (b. 1814?, near Lexington, Ky., U.S.—d. Nov. 6, 1884, Chelsea, Mass.) American writer who is considered to be the first African-American to publish a novel.

Born into slavery, Brown escaped in 1834 and adopted the name of a Quaker, Wells Brown, who aided him when he was a runaway. In 1847 his popular autobiography *Narrative of William W. Brown, A Fugitive Slave* was published. Having educated himself, Brown began lecturing on abolitionism and temperance reform. His antislavery lectures in Europe inspired *Three Years in Europe* (1852), which was expanded as *The American Fugitive in Europe* (1855).

Brown's only novel, CLOTEL (1853), tells the story of the daughters and granddaughters of President Thomas Jefferson and his slave Currer. His only published play was *The Escape; or, A Leap for Freedom* (1858). Brown's historical writings include *The Black Man* (1863), *The Negro in the American Rebellion* (1867), and *The Rising Son* (1873). His final book, *My Southern Home* (1880), contains miscellanea about slave life, abolitionism, and racism.

Bryant, William Cullen (b. Nov. 3, 1794, Cummington, Mass., U.S.—d. June 12, 1878, New York, N.Y.) Poet of nature, best remembered for THANATOPSIS, and editor for 50 years of the New York *Evening Post*.

Bryant at 16 entered the sophomore class of Williams College. He left without graduating, but he later studied law and at 21 was admitted to the bar. He spent nearly 10 years as an attorney, a calling for which he held a lifelong aversion. In 1825 he moved to New York City to become coeditor of the *New York Review*. He became an editor of the *Evening Post* in 1827; in 1829 he became editor in chief and part owner and continued in this position until his death.

The religious conservatism imposed on Bryant in childhood found expression in pious doggerel; the political conservatism of his father stimulated "The Embargo" (1808), in which the 13-year-old poet demanded the resignation of President Thomas Jefferson. But in "Thanatopsis," which he wrote when he was 17 and which made him famous when it was published in *The North American Review* in 1817, he rejected Puritan dogma for deism; thereafter he was a Unitarian. Turning also from federalism, he joined the Democratic party and made the *Post* an organ of free trade, workers' rights, free speech, and abolition. As a man of letters, Bryant securely established himself at the age of 27 with *Poems* (1821), which included TO A WATERFOWL.

Pearl Buck

Buck, Pearl, *original surname* Sydenstricker, *pseudonym* John Sedges (b. June 26, 1892, Hillsboro, W.Va., U.S.—d. March 6, 1973, Danby, Vt.) American author noted for her novels of life in China and recipient of the Nobel Prize for Literature in 1938.

She spent her youth in China, where her parents were Presbyterian missionaries. She graduated from Randolph-Macon Woman's College, Lynchburg, Va., in 1914, then returned to China and later became a university teacher in Nanjing.

Her stories about Chinese life first appeared in American magazines in 1923, but it was not until 1931 that she reached a wide audience with THE GOOD EARTH, which described the struggle of a Chinese peasant and his slave wife to gain land and position. That novel was followed by *Sons* (1932) and *A House Divided* (1935); the trilogy was published as *The House of Earth* (1935).

She turned to biography with lives of her father, Absalom Sydenstricker, *Fighting Angel* (1936), and her mother, Caroline, *The Exile* (1936). Her later books include *Dragon Seed* (1942) and *Imperial Woman* (1956), novels; *The First Wife and Other Stories* (1933), *Far and Near* (1947), and *The Good Deed* (1969), short stories; *The Child Who Never Grew* (1950), concerning her retarded daughter; and an autobiography, *My Several Worlds* (1954). She also wrote five novels under her pseudonym, John Sedges.

Bukowski, Charles (b. Aug. 16, 1920, Andernach, Ger.—d. March 9, 1994, San Pedro, Calif., U.S.) American author noted for his use of violent images and graphic language in poetry and fiction that depicted survival in a corrupt, blighted society.

Bukowski lived most of his life in Los Angeles. He briefly attended Los Angeles City College (1939–41) and worked at menial jobs while writing short stories, the first of which were published in the mid-1940s. In 1955 he began publishing poetry; beginning with *Flower, Fist and Bestial Wail* (1959), volumes of his poetry appeared almost annually. By 1963, the year he published *It Catches My Heart in Its Hands*—a collection of poetry about alcoholics, prostitutes, losing gamblers, and down-and-out people—Bukowski had a loyal following.

Bukowski's short stories were unsparingly realistic and most often comic. Collections of his stories include *Notes of a Dirty Old Man* (1969), taken from his underground newspaper column of that name, and *Erections, Ejaculations, Exhibitions, and General Tales of Ordinary Madness* (1972). His later works include the novels *Post Office* (1971) and *Factotum* (1975) and the screenplay (published 1984) for the 1987 motion picture *Barfly*, a semiautobiographical comedy about alcoholic lovers on skid row. The filming of *Barfly* was the subject of his novel *Hollywood* (1989). His novel *Pulp* was published posthumously in 1994.

Bullins, Ed (b. July 2, 1935, Philadelphia, Pa., U.S.) American playwright, novelist, poet, and journalist who emerged as one of the leading and most prolific dramatists of black theater in the 1960s.

Bullins made his theatrical debut in August 1965 with the production of three one-act plays: *How Do You Do?*, *Dialect Determinism, or The Rally*, and *Clara's Ole Man*. His first full-length play, *In the Wine Time* (produced 1968), examines the scarcity of options available to the black urban poor. It was the first in a series of plays—called the Twentieth-Century Cycle—that centered on a group of young friends growing up in the 1950s. Other plays in the cycle were *The Corner* (produced 1968), *In New England Winter* (produced 1969), *The Duplex* (produced 1970), *The Fabulous Miss Marie* (produced 1971), *Home Boy* (produced 1976), and *Daddy* (produced 1977). In 1975 he received critical acclaim for *The Taking of Miss Janie*, a play about the failed alliance of an interracial group of political idealists in the 1960s. Sharing the tenets of the black aesthetic movement, his naturalistic plays incorporated elements of black nationalism, "street" lyricism, and interracial tension. His other notable works include the plays *Goin' A Buffalo* (produced 1968) and *Salaam, Huey Newton, Salaam* (produced 1991), as well as the short-story collection *The Hungered One* (1971) and the novel *The Reluctant Rapist* (1973).

Bunner, Henry Cuyler (b. Aug. 3, 1855, Oswego, N.Y., U.S.—d. May 11, 1896, Nutley, N.J.) Poet, novelist, and editor whose verse and fiction primarily depict the scenes and people of New York City.

Educated in New York City, Bunner served on the staff of the *Arcadian*. At 22 he became assistant editor and later editor of *Puck*, a position he held until his death. He developed *Puck* from a new, struggling comic weekly into a powerful social and political organ. Bunner's fiction, particularly *"Made in France"; French Tales Retold with a United States Twist* (1893), reflects the influence of Guy de Maupassant and other French writers.

Bunner published several novels, but these are considered inferior to his stories and sketches. As a playwright he is known chiefly for *Tower of Babel* (1883). Collections of his verse, which has been praised for its technical dexterity, playfulness, and smoothness of finish, include *Airs from Arcady and Elsewhere* (1884), *Rowen* (1892), and *Poems* (1896).

Buntline, Ned. Pseudonym of E.Z.C. JUDSON.

Burgess, Gelett, *in full* Frank Gelett Burgess (b. Jan. 30, 1866, Boston, Mass., U.S.—d. Sept. 17, 1951, Carmel, Calif.) American humorist and illustrator best known for a single, early, whimsical quatrain:

> I never saw a purple cow,
> I never hope to see one;
> But I can tell you, anyhow,
> I'd rather see than be one.

In 1895 Burgess became the founding editor of *Lark*, a humor magazine, and in 1897 he began to publish books of his self-illustrated whimsical writings. Among his best-known works are *Goops and How to Be Them* (1900) and subsequent books on Goops (bad-mannered children). He is credited with adding several words to the English language, including *blurb*. Among his many other works are *Are You a Bromide?* (1906), *Why Men Hate Women* (1927), and *Look Eleven Years Younger* (1937).

Burke, Kenneth (Duva) (b. May 5, 1897, Pittsburgh, Pa., U.S.—d. Nov. 19, 1993, Andover, N.J.) American literary critic best known for his psychologically based analyses of the nature of knowledge and his views of literature as "symbolic action," that is, a symbolic means by which the writer can act out personal psychic conflicts and tensions.

Burke wrote poems, a novel, and short stories and translated the works of many German writers into English. He was the music critic of the *Dial* (1927–29) and of *The Nation* (1934–36). He then turned to literary criticism, lecturing on this subject at the University of Chicago (1938; 1949–50). He also taught at Bennington College (Vermont) and several other schools throughout the United States.

Burke's chief aim as a literary critic was to use sociological, psychological, and anthropological concepts to integrate all human knowledge and experience into a workable system. Among his books are *Counter-Statement* (1931), *The Philosophy of Literary Form* (1941), *Permanence and Change: An Anatomy of Purpose* (1935), *Attitudes Toward History*, 2 vol. (1937), *A Grammar of Motives* (1945), *A Rhetoric of Motives* (1950), and *Language as Symbolic Action* (1966).

Burnett, Frances (Eliza) Hodgson, *original surname* Hodgson (b. Nov. 24, 1849, Manchester, Eng.—d. Oct. 29, 1924, Plandome, N.Y., U.S.) American playwright and author who wrote the popular novel *Little Lord Fauntleroy*.

Burnett first gained recognition for *That Lass o' Lowrie's* (1877), a tale of the Lancashire, England, coal mines. Her novel *Through One Administration* (1883) had as its theme corruption in Washington, D.C. In addition to *Little Lord Fauntleroy* (1886), *Sara Crewe* (1888); dramatized as *A Little Princess* in 1905) and THE SECRET GARDEN (1911) were also written for children. *A Lady of Quality* (1896) has been considered the best of her other plays. These, like most of her 40-odd novels, stress sentimental, romantic themes.

Burroughs, Edgar Rice (b. Sept. 1, 1875, Chicago, Ill., U.S.—d. March 19, 1950, Encino, Calif.) American novelist whose Tarzan stories created a folk hero known around the world.

Burroughs began writing advertising copy and then turned to fiction. His first published piece, "Under the Moons of Mars," appeared in the adventure magazine *All-Story* in 1911 and was so successful that Burroughs began writing full-time. The first Tarzan story appeared in 1912, followed in 1914 by *Tarzan of the Apes*, the first of 25 such books about the son of an English nobleman abandoned in the African jungle during infancy and brought up by apes.

Burroughs continued to write other novels as well, ultimately publishing some 68 titles in all. During World War II he became a correspondent for the *Los Angeles Times* and, at age 66, was the oldest war correspondent covering the South Pacific.

Burroughs, John (b. April 3, 1837, near Roxbury, N.Y., U.S.—d. March 29, 1921, en route from California to New York) American essayist and naturalist who lived and wrote after the manner of Henry David Thoreau, studying and celebrating nature.

In his earlier years Burroughs worked as a teacher and a farmer and for nine years as a clerk in the U.S. Treasury Department in Washington, D.C. In 1867 he paid tribute to his friend Walt Whitman in the book *Notes on Walt Whitman as Poet and Person*. In 1871 *Wake-Robin*, the first of his books on birds, flowers, and rural scenes, was published. Two years later he moved to a farm in the Hudson River valley and, from various retreats, wrote for half a century on nature subjects. His chief books, in addition to *Wake-Robin*, are *Birds and Poets* (1877), *Locusts and Wild Honey* (1879), *Signs and Seasons* (1886), and *Ways of Nature* (1905). He also wrote a volume of poems, *Bird and Bough* (1906). *Winter Sunshine* (1875) and *Fresh Fields* (1884) are sketches of travel in England and France. His *Whitman: A Study* was published in 1896. Other collections of his essays are *Time and Change* (1912),

The Summit of the Years (1913), *The Breath of Life* (1915), *Under the Apple Trees* (1916), and *Field and Study* (1919).

ALLEN GINSBERG

William Burroughs

Burroughs, William Seward (b. Feb. 5, 1914, St. Louis, Mo., U.S.) American writer of experimental novels that evoke, in deliberately erratic prose, a nightmarish, sometimes wildly humorous world. His sexual explicitness (he was an avowed and outspoken homosexual) and the frankness with which he dealt with his own experiences as a drug addict won him a following among writers of the Beat Movement.

Burroughs grew up in St. Louis in comfortable circumstances, graduating from Harvard University in 1936. Becoming addicted to drugs—notably heroin—in New York City in 1944, he moved with his second wife to Mexico, where in 1951 he shot and killed her in an accident. Fleeing Mexico, he wandered through the Amazon region of South America, continuing his experiments with drugs. This period of his life was detailed in *The Yage Letters*, his correspondence with Allen Ginsberg written in 1953 but not published until 1963.

He used the pen name William Lee in his first published book, *Junkie: Confessions of an Unredeemed Drug Addict* (1953, abridged version; 1977, unexpurgated). *The Naked Lunch* (Paris, 1959; U.S. title, *Naked Lunch*, 1962; film, 1991) was completed after his treatment for drug addiction. The grotesqueness of the drug addict's world is vividly satirized in *The Naked Lunch*, which also is much preoccupied with homosexuality and police persecution. In the novels that followed—notably, *The Soft Machine* (1961), *The Ticket That Exploded* (1962), *Nova Express* (1964), *The Last Words of Dutch Schultz* (1970), *The Wild Boys* (1971), *Exterminator!* (1973), *Cities of the Red Night* (1981), *Place of Dead Roads* (1983), *Queer* (1985), and *The Western Lands* (1987)—Burroughs further experimented with the structure of the novel.

Busch, Frederick (Matthew) (b. Aug. 1, 1941, Brooklyn, N.Y., U.S.) American critic, editor, novelist, and short-story writer whose work often examined aspects of family life from diverse points of view.

Busch graduated from Muhlenberg College, Allentown, Pa., in 1962 and received an M.A. in 1967 from Colgate University, Hamilton, N.Y., where he later served as Fairchild professor of literature.

In his second novel, *Manual Labor* (1974), a married couple grapple with the death of their unborn child. They reappear later in *Rounds* (1979), in which their lives are intertwined with those of a doctor and a psychologist. *Domestic Particulars: A Family Chronicle* (1976), a collection of interlinked short stories, catalogs in vivid detail the everyday lives of people caught up in often futile attempts to express love. *The Mutual Friend* (1978), which represented a departure for Busch in terms of subject matter, is an imaginative account of the last years of Charles Dickens as told by his friend George Dolby. In the novella *War Babies* (1989), Busch returned to the subject of family relationships with the story of a man who attempts to rid himself of feelings of guilt over his now-dead father's imprisonment for treason. *Harry and Catherine* (1990) examines the long and often unpleasant relationship of two lovers.

Butler, Octavia E., *in full* Estelle (b. June 22, 1947, Pasadena, Calif., U.S.) African-American author chiefly noted for her award-winning science-fiction novels about future societies and superhuman powers.

Encouraged by Harlan Ellison, Butler began her writing career in 1970. The first of her novels, *Patternmaster* (1976), was the beginning of her five-volume Patternist series about an elite group of mentally linked telepaths. Other novels in the series were *Mind of My Mind* (1977), *Survivor* (1978), *Wild Seed* (1980), and *Clay's Ark* (1984).

In *Kindred* (1979) a contemporary black woman is sent back in time to a pre-Civil War plantation, becomes a slave, and rescues her white, slave-owning ancestor. Butler's short story "Bloodchild" (1984), about human male slaves who incubate their alien masters' eggs, won several awards. Her later novels include the Xenogenesis trilogy—*Dawn: Xenogenesis* (1987), *Adulthood Rites* (1988), and *Imago* (1989)—and *The Parable of the Sower* (1993).

Byrd of Westover, William (b. March 28, 1674, Virginia Colony [U.S.]—d. Aug. 26, 1744, Westover, Va.) Virginia planter, satirist, and diarist who portrayed plantation life in colonial America.

His birthplace was the James River plantation home of his father, also named William Byrd, an Indian trader and slave importer. He studied law in the Middle Temple, London. After he was admitted to the bar in 1695, he returned to Virginia, but two years later was again in London as colonial agent. In 1705, after his father died, Byrd returned to Virginia to manage the large family estate. He spent the years 1715 to 1726 (except for a trip home in 1720–21) in England, part of the time as colonial agent. He then returned to the colony for the last time, to lead the busy life of a planter and a member of Virginia's ruling clique.

His diaries illuminate the domestic economy of the great plantations. His "History of the Dividing Line," a witty, satirical account of a 1728 survey of the North Carolina-Virginia boundary, is among the earliest colonial literary works. His accounts of similar expeditions, "A Journey to the Land of Eden" and "A Progress to the Mines," were published in *The Westover Manuscripts* (1841). He also kept a less literary but more revealing diary in shorthand, published as *The Secret Diary of William Byrd of Westover, 1709–12* (1941).

Cabell, James Branch (b. April 14, 1879, Richmond, Va., U.S.—d. May 5, 1958, Richmond) American writer known chiefly for his novel JURGEN (1919).

Cabell began writing fiction shortly after the turn of the century, but acclaim arrived only after a controversy developed over the morality of *Jurgen*. For a decade or more Cabell was extravagantly praised, especially for the attack in *Jurgen* on American orthodoxies and institutions, in a story replete with sexual symbolism. In the 1930s his mannered style and his philosophy of life and art lost favor.

Along with *Jurgen*, the 18-volume *Works* (1927–30) includes THE CREAM OF THE JEST (1917), *Beyond Life* (1919), *Figures of Earth* (1921), and *The High Place* (1923). Many of his works were allegories, set in the mythical French province of Poictesme, through which Cabell commented on American life and demonstrated his skeptical view of human experience. In the 1940s he published three novels as well as *Let Me Lie* (1947), a collection of essays about Virginia. A volume of autobiographical essays, *Quiet Please*, was published in 1952.

Cable, George Washington (b. Oct. 12, 1844, New Orleans, La., U.S.—d. Jan. 31, 1925, St. Petersburg, Fla.) American author and reformer. His first books—*Old Creole Days* (1879), a collection of stories, and *The Grandissimes* (1880), a novel—marked Creole New Orleans as his literary province and were widely praised. In these works he employed a realism new to Southern fiction.

Although Cable was the son of slaveholders and fought in the Confederate cavalry, he believed that slavery and the attempts to deny freed slaves full public rights were morally wrong. Thus, in his early fiction, his handling of caste and class and sanctioned oppression contained overtones of moral condemnation. In the face of violent abuse in the Southern press, he used essays and public lectures to urge the cause of black rights, and he published two collections of his social essays, *The Silent South* (1885) and *The Negro Question* (1888). In 1885 he settled in Northampton, Mass. He wrote novels, many of which were set in the South, until he was past 70; these later novels, though better constructed, were felt to lack the freshness and charm and also the force of moral conviction that characterized his early books.

George Washington Cable

Cahan, Abraham (b. July 7, 1860, Vilna, Russian Empire [now Vilnius, Lithuania]—d. Aug. 31, 1951, New York, N.Y., U.S.) Journalist, reformer, and novelist who for more than 40 years served as editor of the New York Yiddish-language daily newspaper *Forverts*, known in English as the *Jewish Daily Forward*.

Himself an immigrant, Cahan arrived in the United States in 1882. While working in a cigar factory, he learned enough English in six years to lecture and write. In 1897 he helped found and joined the staff of the *Forverts*. He prompted the paper to become more outspoken politically, causing it to be regarded as one of the most important institutions upholding the interests of immigrants. Intensely political and bitterly anticommunist, Cahan was also active in organizing trade unions, particularly in the garment industries.

Cahan's fiction is largely unremarkable except for *The Rise of David Levinsky* (1917), one of the first books about the Jewish immigrant's experience. Critics agree that the value of the book is historical rather than literary; its strength lies chiefly in its vivid re-creation of life in New York City's Lower East Side. Cahan was more influential as a mentor than as an author, providing for young writers a Yiddish-language forum.

Cain, James M., *in full* Mallahan (b. July 1, 1892, Annapolis, Md., U.S.— d. Oct. 27, 1977, University Park, Md.) Novelist whose violent, sexually obsessed, and relentlessly paced melodramas epitomized the hard-boiled fiction that flourished in the U.S. in the 1930s and '40s. Three of his novels—*The Postman Always Rings Twice* (1934), *Double Indemnity* (1936), and *Mildred Pierce* (1941)—were also made into classics of the American screen.

Cain's first novel, *The Postman Always Rings Twice*, was a spectacular success. Its sordid milieu, its characters who seek to gain their ends through violence, and its taut, fast-paced prose set the pattern for most of his later books. *Serenade* (1937) was daring for its period in its presentation of a bisexual hero. *Three of a Kind* (1943) contained the short novels *Sinful Woman*, *Double Indemnity*, and *The Embezzler*. His books continued to appear after World War II—among them *The Butterfly* (1947), *The Moth* (1948), *The Root of His Evil* (1954), *The Magician's Wife* (1965), and *Rainbow's End* (1975)—but none approached the success of his earlier works.

Caldwell, Erskine (b. Dec. 17, 1903, Coweta County, Ga., U.S.—d. April 11, 1987, Paradise Valley, Ariz.) American author whose unadorned novels and stories about the rural poor of the American South mix violence and sex in grotesque tragicomedy.

Caldwell's father was a home missionary who moved frequently from church to church, and Caldwell acquired a deep familiarity with the impoverished sharecroppers that his father ministered to. He attended Erskine College, Due West, S.C., and the University of Virginia but did not graduate.

Fame arrived with TOBACCO ROAD (1932), a highly controversial novel whose title grew to be a byword for rural squalor and degradation. A dramatization of *Tobacco Road* ran for seven and a half years in the 1930s and early '40s on the New York stage. Caldwell's reputation as a novelist largely rests on *Tobacco Road* and on *God's Little Acre* (1933), another best-selling novel featuring a cast of hopelessly poor and degenerate whites in the rural South. Among his other works are *Trouble in July* (1940); the episodic narrative *Georgia Boy* (1943), a well-told story of boyhood; the literary autobiography *Call It Experience* (1951); and *In Search of Bisco* (1965).

Caldwell provided the text and Margaret Bourke-White (later his wife) provided the photographs for a powerful documentary book about the rural South entitled *You Have Seen Their Faces* (1937). They collaborated on two more such picture-and-text books, one on Czechoslovakia and one on the Soviet Union.

Calisher, Hortense (b. Dec. 20, 1911, New York, N.Y., U.S.) American writer of novels, novellas, and short stories, known for the elegant style and insightful rendering of characters in her short fiction, much of which was published originally in *The New Yorker*.

The daughter of a German immigrant father and an uprooted Southern mother, Calisher had a middle-class upbringing in New York City. She graduated from Barnard College in 1932 and later taught there.

Her short-story collections *In the Absence of Angels* (1951) and *The Collected Stories of Hortense Calisher* (1975), a compilation of previous collections, contain stories featuring Calisher's alter ego, Hester Elkins, a Jewish child living in New York City with her extended family. The recipient of four O. Henry short-story awards, Calisher excelled in well-plotted, psychologically perceptive short fiction peopled by well-drawn characters.

Her collected fiction includes *Tale for the Mirror: A Novella and Other Stories* (1962), *Extreme Magic: A Novella and Other Stories* (1964), and *Saratoga, Hot* (1985). Her first novel, *False Entry* (1961), contains characters who are reintroduced in a radically different setting in *The New Yorkers* (1969), in which a 12-year-old girl kills her father's unfaithful wife. Other novels include *Queenie* (1971), *On Keeping Women* (1977), *Mysteries of Motion* (1983), *Age* (1987), and *In the Palace of the Movie King* (1993).

Callaghan, Morley (Edward) (b. Sept. 22, 1903, Toronto, Ont., Can.—d. Aug. 25, 1990, Toronto) Canadian novelist and short-story writer.

Callaghan attended the University of Toronto (B.A., 1925) and Osgoode Hall Law School (LL.B., 1928). He never practiced law, but he became a full-time writer in 1928 and won critical acclaim for his short stories collected in *A Native Argosy* (1929). Later collections of stories include *Morley Callaghan's Stories* (1959) and *No Man's Meat and The Enchanted Pimp* (1978).

The first of more than 10 novels, *Strange Fugitive* (1928) describes the destruction of a social misfit, a type that recurs in Callaghan's fiction. A second characteristic element in his later works is the emphasis on Christian love as an answer to social injustice, as in *Such Is My Beloved* (1934), *They*

Shall Inherit the Earth (1935), *The Loved and the Lost* (1951), and *A Passion in Rome* (1961). He published little in the 1940s, turning his hand to playwriting and to work with the Canadian Broadcasting Company. Notable among his later works are *That Summer in Paris* (1963), a memoir of Callaghan's days in Paris in 1929 and his friendship with F. Scott Fitzgerald and Ernest Hemingway, and *A Fine and Private Place* (1975), the story of an author who wants artistic recognition in his own country.

Campbell, John W., *in full* John Wood Campbell, Jr. (b. June 8, 1910, Newark, N.J., U.S.—d. July 11, 1971, Mountainside, N.J.) American science-fiction writer, considered the father of modern science fiction.

Campbell began writing science fiction while in college. His first published story, "When the Atoms Failed" (1930), contained one of the earliest depictions of computers in science fiction.

Through the early 1930s Campbell wrote stories of outer space but also began writing a different kind of science fiction under the pseudonym of "Don A. Stuart" (derived from his wife's name, Dona Stuart). In these stories, technology was secondary to the development of characterization and mood. One such story is "Twilight" (1934), in which machines work on incessantly, long after humans are gone. These popular works prompted much imitation.

Campbell's influence on other science fiction writers continued when he turned his attention in 1937 to editing *Astounding Stories*, later titled *Astounding Science Fiction*, then *Analog*. The magazine's contributors, including Isaac Asimov and Robert A. Heinlein, dominated the field in the mid-20th century.

Campbell, Joseph (b. March 26, 1904, New York, N.Y., U.S.—d. Oct. 31, 1987, Honolulu) Prolific American author and editor whose works on comparative mythology examined the universal functions of mythology in various human cultures and examined the mythic figure in a wide range of literatures.

A reader of American Indian folklore as a child, Campbell later revived his interest in the subject while working on a master's degree in English literature. Discovering that many themes in Arthurian legend resembled the basic motifs in American Indian folklore, he pursued the problem of mythological archetypes. In his essay "The Hero," in *Where the Two Came to Their Father* (1969), he compared the concept of the hero in American Indian mythology with that in the mythology of other peoples. *The Hero with a Thousand Faces* (1949) is another work examining the archetype of the hero. Campbell's major work is a vast study of world mythology, *The Masks of God*, 4 vol. (1959–67). Other books by Campbell include *Flight of the Wild Gander*

(1969), a collection of his essays; *Myths to Live By* (1972); *The Mythic Image* (1975); with M.J. Abadie); and *The Way of the Animal Powers*, vol. 1 (1983), a historical atlas of world mythology. He was also the editor of *Myths, Dreams, and Religion* (1971).

Campbell, William Wilfred (b. June 1, 1861, Berlin, Canada West [now Ontario, Canada]—d. Jan. 1, 1918, near Ottawa) Canadian poet, best remembered for his first volume of poetry, *Lake Lyrics and Other Poems* (1889), which celebrates the scenery of the Lake Huron-Georgian Bay country near his home.

Campbell was educated at the University of Toronto, ordained (1885), and, upon retiring from the ministry (1891), employed by the civil service in Ottawa until his death. His works are informed by a missionary zeal for the culture of the British "race" and an interest in primitive mythology uncommon in his day. His other books of verse are *The Dread Voyage* (1893), *Beyond the Hills of Dream* (1889), *The Collected Poems* (1905), and *Sagas of Vaster Britain* (1914). Campbell's output includes verse plays, descriptive studies of Canadian life, and two historical novels. He edited an edition of *The Oxford Book of Canadian Verse* (1913). W.J. Sykes edited his *Poetical Works* (1923).

Canfield, Dorothy. Pen name of Dorothy Canfield FISHER.

THE ESTATE OF CARL VAN VECHTEN

Truman Capote

Capote, Truman, *original name* Truman Streckfus Persons (b. Sept. 30, 1924, New Orleans, La., U.S.—d. Aug. 25, 1984, Los Angeles, Calif.) American novelist, short-story writer, and playwright, whose early writing extended the Southern gothic tradition. He later developed a more journalistic approach, notably with *In Cold Blood* (1966; copyright 1965), an account of a multiple murder committed by two sociopaths in Kansas, which he called a "nonfiction novel."

Capote's first novel, *Other Voices, Other Rooms* (1948), tells of a 13-year-old boy's search for his father and his own identity. Two years earlier he had won an O. Henry award for his story "Shut a Final Door." This and other tales were collected in *A Tree of Night* (1949). *The Grass Harp* (1951) is a story of nonconforming innocents who retire temporarily from life to a tree house. In 1954, with the composer Harold Arlen, Capote wrote *The House of Flowers*, a musical set in a West Indies bordello. He also wrote several screenplays. *Local Color* (1950) is a collection of travel sketches. Capote's travels accompanying a tour of *Porgy and Bess* in the Soviet Union resulted in *The Muses Are Heard* (1956). *Breakfast at Tiffany's* (1958; film, 1961) is a novella about a young, fey Manhattan prostitute.

His increasing preoccupation with journalism—as well as with celebrity— was reflected in *Observations* (1959; photographs by Richard Avedon). *The*

Dogs Bark (1973) consists of collected essays and profiles, while *Music for Chameleons* (1980) includes both fiction and nonfiction. His novel *Answered Prayers* (published posthumously 1986) was left unfinished at his death.

Carman, Bliss, *in full* William Bliss Carman (b. April 15, 1861, Fredericton, N.B. [Canada]—d. June 8, 1929, New Canaan, Conn., U.S.) Canadian regional poet of the Maritime Provinces and the New England region of the United States.

Carman was educated primarily at Fredericton Collegiate and at the University of New Brunswick in Fredericton. In 1890 he went to New York City and for two decades earned a living doing editorial work on various journals. Between 1893 and 1905 he published nearly 20 volumes of verse, including *Low Tide on Grand Pré* (1893); three series of *Songs from Vagabondia* (1894, 1896, 1901), written in collaboration with Richard Hovey, a poet whom he had met at Harvard; and *Sappho* (1904). He also wrote several prose works on nature, art, and the human personality.

Carr, Emily (b. Dec. 13, 1871, Victoria, B.C., Can.—d. March 2, 1945, Victoria) Painter and writer, regarded as a major Canadian artist for her paintings of western coast Indians and landscape.

While teaching art in Vancouver, B.C., Carr made frequent sketching trips to British Columbian Indian villages. After ill health ended her painting trips, she turned to writing, producing six autobiographical books that were enlivened by satiric character studies. Among them are *Klee Wyck* (1941), dealing with the Indians; *The House of All Sorts* (1944), describing her experiences as a boardinghouse owner and dog breeder in Victoria; *Growing Pains* (1946), an autobiography; and *Pause: A Sketch Book* (1953), telling of her stay in an English sanatorium.

Carr, John Dickson, *pseudonyms* Carr Dickson, Carter Dickson, Roger Fairbairn (b. Nov. 30, 1906, Uniontown, Pa., U.S.—d. Feb. 27, 1977, Greenville, S.C.) American writer of detective fiction whose work is considered among the best in the genre.

Carr's first novel, *It Walks by Night* (1930), won favor that endured as Carr continued to create well-researched "locked-room" puzzles of historical England. Among his later works are *The Witch of the Low-Tide: An Edwardian Melodrama* (1961), *Dark of the Moon* (1967), and *The Hungry Goblin* (1972). Fifty of his mysteries feature one of his three detectives—Henri Bencolin, Dr. Gideon Fell, and Sir Henry Merrivale.

Carr's other successful works include *The Life of Sir Arthur Conan Doyle* (1949) and *The Exploits of Sherlock Holmes* (1954), the further deeds of Conan Doyle's famous sleuth cowritten by Carr and Doyle's youngest son, Adrian.

Carruth, Hayden (b. Aug. 3, 1921, Waterbury, Conn., U.S.) American poet and literary critic.

Carruth was educated at the University of North Carolina and the University of Chicago. He worked as an editor for several magazines, including *Poetry*. Much of Carruth's poetry is concerned with sanity and madness. During hospitalization for psychiatric illness and alcoholism in 1953, he began a long poem later published as *The Bloomingdale Papers* (1975). *Brothers, I Loved You All* (1978), considered his best work by some critics, uses imagery from jazz. Other volumes of collected poems include *North Winter* (1964), *For You* (1970), *Almanach du Printemps Vivarois* (1979), *Lighter Than Air Craft* (1985), and *Sonnets* (1989). Books of literary criticism include *After "The Stranger": Imaginary Dialogues with Camus* (1965) and *Effluences from the Sacred Caves: More Selected Essays and Reviews* (1983).

Carver, Raymond, *in full* Raymond Clevie Carver, Jr. (b. May 25, 1938, Clatskanie, Ore., U.S.—d. Aug. 2, 1988, Port Angeles, Wash.) American short-story writer noted for his spare, unadorned tales about the wrenching lives of working-class people.

The son of a sawmill worker, Carver married a year after finishing high school and supported his wife and two children by working as a janitor, gas-station attendant, and delivery boy. He became interested in writing after taking a creative-writing course and went on to study at Humboldt State College in Arcata, Calif.

Carver taught for several years in universities throughout the United States. In 1967 his story "Will You Please Be Quiet, Please?" was published to great critical acclaim. His first collection of short stories, *Put Yourself in My Shoes* (1974), was followed in 1976 by the highly successful *Will You Please Be Quiet, Please?*, which established his reputation. His later collections include *What We Talk About When We Talk About Love* (1981), *Cathedral* (1983), and *Where I'm Calling From* (1988). Carver is credited as a major force in the revitalization of the short story in the late 20th century.

Cary, Alice and **Phoebe** (respectively b. April 26, 1820, Mount Healthy, near Cincinnati, Ohio, U.S.—d. Feb. 12, 1871, New York, N.Y.; b. Sept. 4, 1824, Mount Healthy—d. July 31, 1871, Newport, R.I.) American writers and sisters whose work was both moralistic and idealistic.

Self-educated, the Cary sisters never married and wrote in unbroken companionship throughout their lives. After moving to New York City, they wrote to support themselves. Their poems were first collected in a volume entitled *Poems of Alice and Phoebe Cary* (1849). Alice, much the more voluminous writer of the two, also wrote prose sketches and novels, the best of which treat the difficult lives of the neighbors and friends of her girlhood. Phoebe published only two individual volumes of poems—*Poems and Parodies* (1854) and *Poems of Faith, Hope, and Love* (1868). She is perhaps best known as the author of the hymn "Nearer Home."

Cather, Willa (Sibert) (b. Dec. 7, 1873, Winchester, Va., U.S.—d. April 24, 1947, New York, N.Y.) American novelist noted for her portrayals of frontier life on the American plains.

Willa Cather

In 1883 Cather moved with her family from Virginia to the Nebraska village of Red Cloud. There she grew up among the immigrants from Europe—Swedes, Bohemians, Russians, Germans—who were establishing homesteads on the Great Plains.

After graduating from the University of Nebraska in 1895, she obtained a position in Pittsburgh on a family magazine. Later she worked as copy editor and music and drama editor of the *Pittsburgh Leader*. She turned to teaching in 1901, and in 1903 she published her first book of verses, *April Twilights*. In 1905, after the publication of THE TROLL GARDEN, her first collection of short stories, she was appointed managing editor of *McClure's* (the New York muck-raking monthly). She left in 1912 to devote herself wholly to writing novels.

Cather's first novel, *Alexander's Bridge* (1912), was an artificial story of cosmopolitan life. Under the influence of Sarah Orne Jewett's regionalism, she turned to her familiar Nebraska for material. With O PIONEERS! (1913) and MY ÁNTONIA (1918), which has frequently been judged her finest achievement, she found her characteristic themes—the spirit and courage of the frontier she had known in her youth. ONE OF OURS (1922), which won the Pulitzer Prize, and A LOST LADY (1923) mourned the passing of the pioneer spirit.

In her earlier SONG OF THE LARK (1915), as well as in the tales assembled in YOUTH AND THE BRIGHT MEDUSA (1920), including the much-anthologized PAUL'S CASE, and in *Lucy Gayheart* (1935), Cather reflected the other side of her experience—the struggle of a talent to emerge from the constricting life of the prairies and the stifling effects of small-town life.

A mature statement of both themes can be found in *Obscure Destinies* (1932). With success and middle age, however, Cather experienced a strong disillusionment, which was reflected in THE PROFESSOR'S HOUSE (1925) and her essays *Not Under Forty* (1936).

Her solution was to write of the pioneer spirit of another age, that of the French Catholic missionaries in the Southwest in DEATH COMES FOR THE ARCHBISHOP (1927) and of the French Canadians at Quebec in SHADOWS ON THE ROCK (1931). Her last novel, SAPPHIRA AND THE SLAVE GIRL (1940), marked a return to the Virginia of her ancestors.

Catton, Bruce, *in full* Charles Bruce Catton (b. Oct. 9, 1899, Petoskey, Mich., U.S.—d. Aug. 28, 1978, Frankfort, Mich.) American journalist and historian, noted for his books on the American Civil War.

As a child living in a small town in Michigan, Catton was stimulated by reminiscences of the Civil War by local veterans. While he worked as a reporter for the *Boston American*, the *Cleveland News*, and the *Cleveland Plain Dealer* (1920–26), Catton continued his lifelong study of the Civil War period. In 1954 he joined the staff of *American Heritage* magazine and from 1959 was its senior editor.

A commission to write a centennial history of the Civil War evolved into Catton's celebrated trilogy on the Army of the Potomac: *Mr. Lincoln's Army* (1951), *Glory Road* (1952), and *A Stillness at Appomattox* (1953). The latter earned Catton both a Pulitzer Prize and the National Book Award in 1954. A second trilogy consisted of *The Coming Fury* (1961), *Terrible Swift Sword* (1963), and *Never Call Retreat* (1965).

Catton's brilliance as a historian lay in his ability to bring to historical narrative the immediacy of reportage. Other works by Catton include *The War Lords of Washington* (1948) and *U.S. Grant and the American Military Tradition* (1954).

Chandler, Raymond (Thornton) (b. July 23, 1888, Chicago, Ill., U.S.—d. March 26, 1959, La Jolla, Calif.) American author of detective fiction, creator of the private detective Philip Marlowe. Set in the Los Angeles area, Chandler's novels and short stories are esteemed (especially by European critics) as outstanding examples of regional writing.

Chandler fought in World War I. After the war he returned to California, where he eventually turned to writing for a living. His first published short story appeared in the "pulp" magazine *Black Mask* in 1933. From 1943 he was a Hollywood screenwriter; *Double Indemnity* (1944), *The Blue Dahlia* (1946), and *Strangers on a Train* (1951), the latter written in collaboration with Czenzi Ormonde, are his best-known film scripts.

Chandler completed seven novels, all with Philip Marlowe as hero: *The Big Sleep* (1939), *Farewell, My Lovely* (1940), *The High Window* (1942), *The Lady in the Lake* (1943), *The Little Sister* (1949), *The Long Good-Bye* (1953), and *Playback* (1958). Among his numerous short-story collections are *Five Murderers* (1944) and *The Midnight Raymond Chandler* (1971).

Chapman, John Jay (b. March 2, 1862, New York, N.Y., U.S.—d. Nov. 4, 1933, Poughkeepsie, N.Y.) American poet, dramatist, and critic who attacked the get-rich-quick morality of the post-Civil War "Gilded Age."

Chapman attended Harvard Law School and practiced law for several years. At the same time, he became editor and publisher of the periodical *The*

Political Nursery (1897–1901). His two books *Causes and Consequences* (1898) and *Practical Agitation* (1900) stressed his belief that individuals should take a moral stand on issues troubling the nation. His play *The Treason and Death of Benedict Arnold* appeared in 1910. In 1912, on the first anniversary of a lynching in Coatesville, Pa., Chapman made a speech, burning with indignation, that became a classic and was reprinted in his book of essays *Memories and Milestones* (1915).

Other works include a biography of William Lloyd Garrison (1913), collected *Songs and Poems* (1919), and volumes of criticism such as *Emerson, and Other Essays* (1898), *Greek Genius, and Other Essays* (1915), and *A Glance Toward Shakespeare* (1922).

Charbonneau, Jean (b. 1875, Montreal, Que., Can.—d. Oct. 25, 1960, Saint-Eustache) French-Canadian poet who was the primary force behind the founding of the Montreal Literary School (1895), a group of Symbolists and Aesthetes who reacted against the traditional Canadian themes of patriotism and local color and, following the Parnassians, espoused the principle of art for art's sake. Charbonneau later wrote the only history of the school, *L'École littéraire de Montréal* (1935); "The Literary School of Montreal"). In 1912 Charbonneau wrote *Les Blessures* ("The Wounds"), the first of several volumes of poetry that dealt primarily with philosophical speculation and myth. *Sur la borne pensive* (1952); "On the Bounds of Thought") is characteristic of his mature style.

Charbonneau, Robert (b. Feb. 3, 1911, Montreal, Que., Can.—d. June 26, 1967, Sainte-Jovite, Que.) French Canadian novelist and literary critic, well known for promoting the autonomy of Quebec literature.

During his teens Charbonneau joined Jeune Canada ("Young Canada"), a French nationalist organization, and in 1934 he cofounded *La Relève* (later called *La Nouvelle Relève*, "The New Relief"), a nationalist review of art, literature, and philosophy. Over the years, he also worked as a journalist on various French journals, newspapers, and Radio-Canada.

Charbonneau wrote five novels, the most noted being his first, *Ils posséderont la terre* (1941); "They Shall Possess the Earth"). He also published a collection of poems, *Petits poèmes retrouvés* (1945); "Little Poems Rediscovered"), critical essays and lectures, and radio plays.

Chase, Mary Ellen (b. Feb. 24, 1887, Blue Hill, Maine, U.S.—d. July 28, 1973, Northampton, Mass.) American scholar and writer whose novels are largely concerned with the Maine seacoast and its inhabitants.

Three autobiographical works describe Chase's childhood in Maine: *A Goodly Heritage* (1932), *A Goodly Fellowship* (1939), and *The White Gate:*

Adventures in the Imagination of a Child (1954). She obtained a Ph.D. in English from the University of Minnesota and also studied in England, which she wrote of in a book of essays, *This England* (1936).

Chase began her writing career with books for children such as *The Girl from the Big Horn Country* (1916) and *Mary Christmas* (1926). Her first novel, *Uplands* (1927), was followed by two of her most powerful novels: *Mary Peters* (1934) and *Silas Crockett* (1935). *Dawn in Lyonesse* (1938) is a retelling of the Tristan and Isolde story. She also wrote literary criticism, biblical studies, and essays.

Chayefsky, Paddy, *original name* Sidney Chayefsky (b. Jan. 29, 1923, New York, N.Y., U.S.—d. Aug. 1, 1981, New York City) American playwright and screenwriter.

Chayefsky worked as a printer's apprentice, then began writing radio adaptations and mystery dramas for television series. His first full-length television play was *Holiday Song* (1952). His greatest success was *Marty* (1953; film, 1955). Two other successful television plays were made into motion pictures—*The Bachelor Party* (1954; film, 1957) and *The Catered Affair* (1955; film, 1956). The television drama, *The Middle of the Night* (1954), was Chayefsky's first stage play (1956). His other stage plays include *The Tenth Man* (1959), *Gideon* (1961), *The Passion of Josef D.* (1964), and *The Latent Heterosexual* (published 1967; performed 1968). He also wrote film scripts and scenarios.

Cheever, John (b. May 27, 1912, Quincy, Mass., U.S.—d. June 18, 1982, Ossining, N.Y.) American short-story writer and novelist whose work described, often through fantasy and ironic comedy, the life, manners, and morals of middle-class, suburban America. He is noted for his clear and elegant prose and his careful fashioning of incidents and anecdotes.

A master of the short story, Cheever worked from "the interrupted event," which he considered the prime source of short stories. His first published story appeared in *The New Republic* in 1930. His works also appeared in *The New Yorker*, *Collier's*, *Story*, and *The Atlantic*. Cheever's first collection of short stories, *The Way Some People Live* (1943), was followed by many others, including *The Enormous Radio and Other Stories* (1953) and *The Brigadier and the Golf Widow* (1964). The latter collection included the much anthologized story THE SWIMMER. *The Stories of John Cheever* (1978) won the Pulitzer Prize for fiction. Cheever's first novel, THE WAPSHOT CHRONICLE (1957), earned him the National Book Award. Later novels include *The Wapshot Scandal* (1964), *Falconer* (1977), and *Oh What a Paradise It Seems* (1982). *The Letters of John Cheever*, edited by his son Benjamin Cheever, was published in 1988, and *The Journals of John Cheever* in 1991.

Chesnut, Mary Boykin Miller (b. March 31, 1823, Pleasant Hill, S.C., U.S.—d. Nov. 22, 1886, Camden, S.C.) Author of *A Diary from Dixie*, an insightful view of Southern life and leadership during the American Civil War.

The daughter of a prominent South Carolina political leader, in 1840 Miller married James Chesnut, Jr., who later served as a U.S. senator from South Carolina until he resigned to take an important role in the secession movement and the Confederacy. Accompanying her husband, who was a staff officer, on his military missions during the Civil War, Chesnut began recording her views and observations on Feb. 15, 1861, and closed her diary on Aug. 2, 1865. *A Diary from Dixie* was not published until 1905, long after her death. Although not a day-by-day account, the diary is highly regarded by historians for its perceptive views of Confederate military and political leaders and for its insight into Southern society during the Civil War.

Chesnutt, Charles Waddell (b. June 20, 1858, Cleveland, Ohio, U.S.— d. Nov. 15, 1932, Cleveland) The first important black American novelist.

Chesnutt was the son of free blacks who had left their native North Carolina prior to the American Civil War. Following the war his parents moved back to North Carolina. By the time Chesnutt was 25, he was married and was already a successful school principal, but he became so distressed about the treatment of blacks in the South that he moved his wife and children to Cleveland.

Between 1885 and 1905 Chesnutt published more than 50 tales, short stories, and essays, as well as two collections of short stories, a biography of the antislavery leader Frederick Douglass, and three novels. His "The Goophered Grapevine," the first work by a black accepted by *The Atlantic Monthly* (August 1887), was so subtle in its refutation of the romantic view of plantation life fostered by such writers as Thomas Nelson Page that most readers missed the irony. This and similarly authentic, psychologically realistic stories of folk life among North Carolina blacks were collected in THE CONJURE WOMAN (1899). *The Wife of His Youth and Other Stories of the Color Line* (1899) examines color prejudice among blacks as well as between the races in a manner reminiscent of George W. Cable. *The Colonel's Dream* (1905) deals trenchantly with problems of the freed slave.

Child, Lydia Maria (Francis) (b. Feb. 11, 1802, Medford, Mass., U.S.— d. Oct. 20, 1880, Wayland, Mass.) American author of influential antislavery works.

In the 1820s, Child taught, wrote historical novels, and founded a periodical for children, *Juvenile Miscellany* (1826). After meeting the abolitionist William Lloyd Garrison in 1831, she devoted her life to his cause. Child's best-known work, *An Appeal in Favor of That Class of Americans Called Africans* (1833), recounts the history of slavery and denounces the inequality of education and employment for blacks; it was the first such work published in book form. Although Child was ostracized socially and her magazine failed in 1834, she succeeded in inducing many people to join the abolitionist movement. Child's further abolitionist efforts included editing the *National Anti-Slavery Standard* (1841–43) and later transcribing the recollections of slaves who had been freed. In addition, her home was part of the Underground Railroad that aided escaping slaves.

Child's other work includes once-popular volumes of advice for women, such as *The Frugal Housewife* (1829), and books on behalf of Native Americans.

Childress, Alice (b. Oct. 12, 1916, Charleston, S.C., U.S.—d. Aug. 14, 1994, New York, N.Y.) African-American playwright, novelist, and actress, known for her realistic stories about the enduring optimism of black Americans.

Childress grew up in Harlem, New York City, where she studied drama with the American Negro Theatre in the 1940s. There she wrote, directed, and starred in her first play, *Florence* (produced 1949), about a black woman who, after meeting an insensitive white actress in a railway station, comes to respect her daughter's attempts to pursue an acting career. *Trouble in Mind* (produced 1955; revised and published 1971), *Wedding Band* (produced 1966), *String* (produced 1969), and *Wine in the Wilderness* (produced 1969) all examine racial and social issues. Among Childress' plays that feature music are *Just a Little Simple* (produced 1950; based on Langston Hughes's *Simple Speaks His Mind*), *Gold Through the Trees* (produced 1952), *The African Garden* (produced 1971), *Gullah* (produced 1984; based on her 1977 play *Sea Island Song*), and *Moms* (produced 1987; about the life of comedienne Jackie "Moms" Mabley).

Childress was also a successful writer of children's literature. A HERO AIN'T NOTHIN' BUT A SANDWICH (1973) is a novel for adolescents about a teenage drug addict. Similarly, the novel *Rainbow Jordan* (1981) concerns the struggles of poor black urban youth. Her other novels include *A Short Walk* (1979), *Many Closets* (1987), and *Those Other People* (1989).

Chopin, Kate, *original name* Katherine O'Flaherty (b. Feb. 8, 1851, St. Louis, Mo., U.S.—d. Aug. 22, 1904, St. Louis) American author and local colorist known as an interpreter of New Orleans culture. There was a revival of interest in Chopin in the late 20th century because her concerns about the freedom of women foreshadowed later feminist literary themes.

Chopin lived in Louisiana after her marriage (1870) to Oscar Chopin; after his death she began to write about the Creole and Cajun people she had observed in the South. Her first novel, *At Fault* (1890), was undistinguished, but she was later acclaimed for her finely crafted short stories, of which she wrote more than 100. Two of these stories, DÉSIRÉE'S BABY and "Madame Celestin's Divorce," continue to be widely anthologized.

In 1899 Chopin published THE AWAKENING, a realistic novel about the sexual and artistic awakening of a young mother who abandons her family and eventually commits suicide. This work, roundly condemned in its time because of its sexual frankness, later received critical approval for the beauty of its writing and for its modern sensibility.

Her stories were collected in *Bayou Folk* (1894) and *A Night in Acadie* (1897).

Choquette, Robert Guy (b. April 22, 1905, Manchester, N.H., U.S.) American-born French-Canadian writer whose work was regarded as revolutionary and who influenced an entire younger generation of poets.

Choquette moved to Montreal at the age of eight. His first collection of poetry, *A travers les vents* (1925); "Through the Winds"), won him a reputation based on his disregard of syntax and his freedom of expression. Other books of poetry were *Metropolitan Museum* (1930), *Suite marine* (1953), the influential two-volume *Oeuvres poétiques* (1956); "Poetic Works"), and *Poèmes choisis* (1970); "Select Poems").

La Pension Leblanc (1928), Choquette's first published novel, provided a foundation on which future television and radio series were to be based. A group of recognizable characters from his novels *Le Curé de village* (1936); "The Village Curate") and *Les Velder* (1941) peopled a radio series called *Le Curé de village*. Two other serials, *La Pension Velder* and *Métropole*, followed. Choquette also brought out a collection of prose sketches, *Le Fabuliste La Fontaine à Montréal* (1935); "The Fabulist La Fontaine in Montreal"), *Language and Religion* (1975), and *Moi, Pétrouchka* (1980), as well as a collection of both prose and poetry entitled *Le Choix de Robert Choquette dans l'oeuvre de Robert Choquette* (1981); "The Choice of Robert Choquette in the Work of Robert Choquette").

Choquette was elected to the French-Canadian Academy and Académie Ronsard (Paris), and he served as Canadian consul general to Bordeaux, France (1965–68), and Canadian ambassador to Argentina, Uruguay, and Paraguay (1968–70).

Christian, Barbara (b. Dec. 12, 1943, St. Thomas, U.S. Virgin Islands) Caribbean-American educator and feminist critic who attempted to define an African-American feminist philosophy.

Educated at Marquette (B.A., 1963) and Columbia universities (M.A., 1964; Ph.D., 1970), Christian taught at the City College of the City University of New York (1965–72) and in the department of African-American studies of the University of California at Berkeley (from 1971).

Her published works include *Black Feminist Criticism: Perspectives on Black Women Writers* (1985), a work emphasizing literary, textual analysis of fiction by black women; *Black Women Novelists: The Development of a Tradition* (1980); and *Teaching Guide to Accompany Black Foremothers* (1980). She contributed to *Black Expression* (1969); edited by Addison Gayle) and to the journals *The Black Scholar* and *The Journal of Ethnic Studies*.

Churchill, Winston (b. Nov. 10, 1871, St. Louis, Mo., U.S.—d. March 12, 1947, Winter Park, Fla.) American author of historical novels of wide popularity.

Churchill graduated from the U.S. Naval Academy in 1894, and having private means, he soon devoted himself to writing. His first novel, *The Celebrity*, appeared in 1898. His next, *Richard Carvel* (1899), a novel of Revolutionary Maryland in which the hero serves as a naval officer under John Paul Jones, sold nearly one million copies. Then followed another great success, *The Crisis* (1901), a novel of the American Civil War, in which the heroine is a descendant of Richard Carvel, and *The Crossing* (1904), which tells of Kentucky pioneers during the American Revolution. His later work consisted chiefly of novels dealing with political, religious, or social problems.

Ciardi, John (Anthony) (b. June 24, 1916, Boston, Mass., U.S.—d. March 30, 1986, Edison, N.J.) American poet, critic, and translator who contributed to making poetry accessible to both adults and children.

Educated at Bates College (Lewiston, Maine), Tufts University (A.B., 1938), and the University of Michigan (M.A., 1939), Ciardi served in the U.S. Army Air Corps (1942–45) and then taught at universities until 1961. He served as poetry editor of the *Saturday Review* from 1956 to 1972. He felt that interaction between audience and author was crucial, and he generated continuous controversy with his critical reviews.

Ciardi's first volume of poetry, *Homeward to America*, appeared in 1940. His *How Does a Poem Mean?* (1960); rev. ed., with Miller Williams, 1975) found wide use as a poetry textbook in high schools and colleges. His other books of poetry include *Person to Person* (1964), *The Little That Is All* (1974), and *For Instance* (1979). He also wrote many books of prose and verse for children.

His translation of Dante's *Divine Comedy* was highly acclaimed. Rather than following Dante's rhyme scheme, Ciardi attempted to capture the feeling of the original in a tense and economical modern verse idiom.

His later works include two books written with Isaac Asimov: *Limericks, Too Gross* (1978) and *A Grossery of Limericks* (1981). Ciardi also wrote *A Browser's Dictionary and Native's Guide to the Unknown American Language* (1980) and *A Second Browser's Dictionary and Native's Guide to the Unknown American Language* (1983).

Cisneros, Sandra (b. Dec. 20, 1954, Chicago, Ill., U.S.) Short-story writer and poet best known for her evocation of Mexican-American life in Chicago.

After graduating from Chicago's Loyola University (B.A., 1976), Cisneros attended the University of Iowa Writers' Workshop (M.F.A., 1978). There she developed what was to be the theme of most of her writing, her unique experiences as a Hispanic woman in a largely alien culture.

Cisneros' first book of fiction, *The House on Mango Street* (1983), was a collection of semiautobiographical prose-poems that recall a girlhood spent trying to be a creative writer in an antagonistic environment. *Woman Hollering Creek and Other Stories* (1991) contained tales of beleaguered girls and women who nonetheless feel that they have power over their destinies. Cisneros' volumes of poetry include *Bad Boys* (1980) and *The Rodrigo Poems* (1985). *My Wicked, Wicked Ways* (1987) collected 60 poems on subjects such as her hometown of Chicago, European travels, and sexual guilt.

Clampitt, Amy (b. June 15, 1920, New Providence, Iowa, U.S.—d. Sept. 10, 1994, Lenox, Mass.) American poet whose work won critical acclaim for its evocation of the natural world.

After graduating from Grinnell College, Clampitt worked as a reference librarian and as an editor, publishing her first book of poetry, *Multitudes, Multitudes* (1973), at her own expense. Her first full-length collection was *The Kingfisher* (1983). It was especially noted for its use of elaborate syntax and vocabulary. *What the Light Was Like* (1985), also highly praised, contained several poems about death, including two elegies to her brother, who had died in 1981 and to whom the work was dedicated. Literary critics commented on the ease and certainty with which Clampitt employed literary allusions as well as references to nature and on her ornamented, sometimes eccentric style. Later collections include *Archaic Figure* (1987), *Westward* (1990), and *Silence Opens* (1994).

Clark, Walter van Tilburg (b. Aug. 3, 1909, East Orland, Maine, U.S.—d. Nov. 10, 1971, Reno, Nev.) American novelist and short-story writer whose works, set in the American West, used the familiar regional materials of the cowboy, outdoor, or frontier tale as a starting point for the exploration of philosophical issues.

Clark grew up in Reno, which forms the background for his novel *The City of Trembling Leaves* (1945), the story of a sensitive adolescent boy's development. His best-known work is THE OX-BOW INCIDENT (1940; film, 1943). The story of a lynching in 1885 of three innocent men, it conveys a powerful and dramatic insight into mob psychology. *The Track of the Cat* (1949), a tale of a hunt for a black panther during a blizzard, is also a moral parable. *The Watchful Gods* (1950) is a collection of short stories.

Clemens, Samuel Langhorne. Real name of Mark TWAIN.

Clifton, Lucille, *in full* Thelma Lucille Sayles Clifton (b. June 27, 1936, Depew, N.Y., U.S.) American poet who employed black vernacular in her examinations of family relationships and life in the urban ghetto.

Clifton's work reflected her pride in being a woman, an African-American, and a poet. Her poetry collections include the ironically titled *Good Times* (1969); *Good News About the Earth* (1972); and *An Ordinary Woman* (1974). *Generations: A Memoir* (1976) is a prose piece celebrating her origins, and *Good Woman: Poems and a Memoir: 1969–1980* (1987) collects her previously published verse.

Clifton's many children's books, written with a young African-American audience in mind, include *All Us Come Cross the Water* (1973) and *My Friend Jacob* (1980). She also wrote a series of books chronicling the everyday adventures of a young black boy.

Clurman, Harold (b. Sept. 18, 1901, New York, N.Y., U.S.—d. Sept. 9, 1980, New York City) Influential American theatrical director and drama critic.

Clurman attended Columbia University in New York City, then the University of Paris, where he received a degree in letters in 1923. He made his stage debut the following year as an extra at the Greenwich Village Theatre in New York City. In 1931 Clurman became a founding member of the Group Theatre, an experimental company, for which he directed several plays, notably *Awake and Sing!* (1935) by Clifford Odets. Clurman's achievements as a director range over many categories of drama, including Carson McCullers' *A Member of the Wedding* (1950); Jean Giraudoux's drama of ideas *Tiger at the Gates* (1955); and Jean Anouilh's farce *Waltz of the Toreadors* (1957). He also directed Eugene O'Neill's *Touch of the Poet* (1957) and Arthur Miller's *Incident at Vichy* (1965). Financed by a grant from the U.S. State Department, Clurman directed the Kumo Theatre Company of Japan in O'Neill's *Long Day's Journey into Night* (1965) and *The Iceman Cometh* (1968).

Clurman also became a drama critic, writing for *The New Republic* in

1948–52, then for *The Nation* from 1953 until his death. He also wrote *On Directing* (1972); *The Divine Pastime* (1974), theatrical essays; and his memoirs, *All People Are Famous* (1974).

Cobb, Irvin Shrewsbury (b. June 23, 1876, Paducah, Ky., U.S.—d. March 10, 1944, New York, N.Y.) American journalist and humorist.

Cobb was a staff writer for the *Evening World* and *Sunday World* in New York City. First through syndicated newspaper features and later in magazines, he became widely known for such articles as "Speaking of Operations," which in book form sold more than 500,000 copies, and for short stories.

Cobb's stories about shrewd and kindly Judge Priest first brought him fame. Some of them were collected in *Back Home* (1912) and *Old Judge Priest* (1916). He wrote many books and columns for journals, as well as plays and scenarios for motion pictures.

Coffin, Robert Peter Tristram (b. March 18, 1892, Brunswick, Maine, U.S.—d. Jan. 20, 1955, Portland, Maine) American poet whose works were based on New England farm and seafaring life.

Coffin regarded poetry as a public function that should speak well of life so that people might find inspiration. *Strange Holiness* (1935) won the Pulitzer Prize for poetry in 1936; *Saltwater Farm* (1937) is a collection of poems about Maine.

Coffin also lectured widely and took part in numerous poetry workshops. He taught at Wells College in Aurora, N.Y., and at Bowdoin College in Brunswick, Maine, and was book and poetry editor for *Yankee* magazine. Coffin also wrote the novel *Red Sky in the Morning* (1935); *Kennebec* (1937), part of a historical series on American rivers; and *Maine Doings* (1950), informal essays on New England life.

Cohen, Leonard (Norman) (b. Sept. 21, 1934, Montreal, Que., Can.) Canadian novelist and lyric poet who became a popular singer of his original songs.

Cohen attended McGill University and Columbia University. His second and third poetry collections, *The Spice-Box of Earth* (1961) and *Flowers for Hitler* (1964), established his reputation as a lyrical love poet and also as a writer of surreal imagery. In his partly autobiographical first novel, *The Favorite Game* (1963), a youth discovers sexual freedom and his vocation as a poet. His second novel was *Beautiful Losers* (1966). His later works include the poetry collections *Death of a Lady's Man* (1977), *Book of Mercy* (1984), and *Stranger Music* (1993). After other singers had recorded songs by Cohen, he himself began a recording career in 1968.

Colby, Frank Moore (b. Feb. 10, 1865, Washington, D.C., U.S.—d. March 3, 1925, New York, N.Y.) American encyclopedia editor and essayist.

Early in his career Colby taught history and economics at Columbia University, Amherst (Mass.) College, and New York University. In 1898 he became editor of the *International Year Book* (later the *New International Year Book*). He was editor, with Daniel Colt Gilman and Harry Thurston Peck, of the *New International Encyclopedia* (1900–03) and helped supervise publication of the second edition.

Colby contributed to many magazines, including *Bookman, The New Republic*, and *Vanity Fair*, and his witty essays were widely read. After his death, his popularity rose with the publication of *The Colby Essays* (1926), edited by Clarence Day, Jr.

Connell, Evan S., Jr., *in full* Evan Shelby (b. Aug. 17, 1924, Kansas City, Mo., U.S.) Writer whose works explore philosophical and cultural facets of the American experience.

Connell's first published work, the critically acclaimed *The Anatomy Lesson and Other Stories* (1957), consists of stories set in various parts of the United States and incorporates subject matter ranging from the near-mythic to the mundane. *Mrs. Bridge* (1959), his first novel and the one with which subsequent works were often compared, dissects the life of a conventional upper middle-class Kansas City matron who lacks a sense of purpose and conforms blindly to what is expected of her. Ten years later Connell published *Mr. Bridge* (1969), which relates the same story from the point of view of the husband. *Son of the Morning Star: Custer and the Little Bighorn* (1984), which retells an almost legendary clash of personalities and cultures, was a critical as well as popular success. Among Connell's other works are the novels *The Diary of a Rapist* (1966), *The Connoisseur* (1974), and *The Alchymist's Journal* (1991) and a book-length poem, *Notes from a Bottle Found on the Beach at Carmel* (1963).

Marc Connelly

Connelly, Marc, *byname of* Marcus Cook Connelly (b. Dec. 13, 1890, McKeesport, Pa., U.S.—d. Dec. 21, 1980, New York, N.Y.) American playwright, journalist, teacher, actor, and director, best known for *Green Pastures* (a folk version of the Old Testament dramatized through the lives of blacks of the southern United States) and for the comedies that he wrote with George S. KAUFMAN.

Connelly worked as a reporter in Pittsburgh until 1917, when he joined the *Morning Telegraph* in New York City, covering theatrical news. He then began his collaboration with Kaufman. Their first successful play, *Dulcy* (1921), written as a vehicle for the actress Lynn Fontanne, was followed by

To the Ladies (1922), a vehicle for Helen Hayes. *Beggar on Horseback* (1924), in the style of German Expressionist drama, depicts the threat to art from a society dominated by bourgeois values.

While they collaborated in writing a satire on Hollywood, *Merton of the Movies* (1922), and two musicals, *Helen of Troy, New York* (1923) and *Be Yourself* (1924), Connelly and Kaufman were members of the Algonquin Round Table. Connelly described this phase of his career in *Voices Offstage: A Book of Memoirs* (1968).

Green Pastures, based on Roark Bradford's book *Ol' Man Adam an' His Chillun*, was first performed in 1930 and was extremely popular both on the stage and in its motion-picture version (1936), but when it was revived in 1951 it was criticized for perpetuating unacceptable stereotypes of blacks.

Connelly's last Broadway success, *The Farmer Takes a Wife* (1934; film, 1935), written with Frank Elser, was a comedy about life along the Erie Canal in the 19th century. From 1946 to 1950 he taught playwriting at Yale University. His novel *A Souvenir from Qam* was published in 1965.

Connor, Ralph, *pseudonym of* Charles William Gordon (b. Sept. 13, 1860, Indian Lands, Glengarry County, Ont., Can.—d. Oct. 31, 1937, Winnipeg, Man.) Canadian Presbyterian minister and writer of numerous popular novels that combine religious messages, wholesome sentiment, and adventure.

Ordained in 1890, Gordon became a missionary to mining and lumber camps in the Canadian Rocky Mountains. It was from this experience and memories of his Glengarry childhood that he derived the major background for his fiction. His first books, the missionary adventure tales *Black Rock* (1898) and its sequel, *The Sky Pilot* (1899), met with phenomenal success. His highest literary achievements are considered to be the books dealing with the pioneer traditions of his Ontario boyhood: *The Man from Glengarry* (1901) and *Glengarry School Days* (1902).

Conroy, Jack, *byname of* John Wesley Conroy, *pseudonym* Tim Brennan *or* John Norcross (b. Dec. 5, 1899, near Moberly, Mo., U.S.—d. Feb. 28, 1990, Moberly) Leftist American writer best known for his contributions to "proletarian literature," fiction and nonfiction about the life of American workers during the early decades of the 20th century.

Conroy was a migratory worker in the 1920s. He first became known in 1933 with his critically acclaimed novel *The Disinherited*. This largely autobiographical book depicts the coming of age of a coal miner's son during the Great Depression. From 1931 to 1941 Conroy edited successively the magazines *Rebel Poet*, *Anvil*, and *New Anvil*. He included writings by Erskine Caldwell, Langston Hughes, and William Carlos Williams. Conroy later edited, with Curt Johnson, a collection of these works entitled *Writers in Revolt: The Anvil Anthology* (1973).

In 1938 Conroy began to work on the Federal Writers' Project of the Works Progress Administration (WPA). With Arna Bontemps, Conroy wrote a juvenile book, *The Fast-Sooner Hound* (1942), and *They Seek a City* (1945), a history of black migration and settlement with biographical data on important black figures. A revised and expanded version of the latter book, *Anyplace But Here* (1966), added background on contemporary events such as the Watts riots. A collection of works entitled *The Jack Conroy Reader* was published in 1980.

Conway, Moncure Daniel (b. March 17, 1832, Stafford County, Va., U.S.— d. Nov. 15, 1907, Paris, Fr.) American clergyman, author, and vigorous abolitionist.

Conway was born of slaveholding parents. While serving in the Methodist ministry he was converted to Unitarianism, but because of his outspoken abolitionist views he was dismissed from his first Unitarian pastorate, in Washington, D.C., in 1856. He moved to Cincinnati, Ohio, and became active in abolitionist causes, even settling a colony of fugitive slaves at Yellow Springs, Ohio.

In 1862 he became coeditor in Boston of the *Commonwealth*, an antislavery paper. During the Civil War he went to England to lecture on behalf of the North. Conway contributed to journals in both England and the United States and wrote more than 70 books and pamphlets on a great variety of subjects. His scholarly works include *Life of Thomas Paine*, 2 vols. (1892), and *The Writings of Thomas Paine*, 4 vols. (1894–96). His *Autobiography* (1904) is valuable for sketches of important 19th-century figures.

Cook, George Cram (b. Oct. 7, 1873, Davenport, Iowa, U.S.—d. Jan. 14, 1924, Delphi, Greece) American novelist, poet, and playwright who, with his wife, Susan GLASPELL, established the noncommercial Provincetown Players.

After completing his degree at Harvard, Cook studied at Heidelberg and the University of Geneva. He taught at the University of Iowa and at Stanford University and then worked as a small farmer.

The influence of Friedrich Nietzsche is reflected in Cook's first novel, *Roderick Taliaferro* (1903), a historical romance set in the Mexico of Emperor Maximilian. One of his hired workers, Floyd Dell, who later became a novelist, converted him to socialism (Cook appears as Tom Alden in Dell's *Moon-Calf* [1920]). In Cook's novel *The Chasm* (1911) his protagonist is torn between Nietzschean aristocratic individualism and socialist ideas; the latter eventually win.

Cook worked with Dell at the *Chicago Evening Post* and married the novelist and playwright Susan Glaspell. In 1915 they launched the Provincetown Players in Provincetown, Mass., initially to perform their jointly written one-act play *Suppressed Desires* (1915, published 1920), a satire on psychoanalysis. Cook continued with the group in New York City's Greenwich Village as the Playwrights' Theatre, performing plays written by American authors. From 1921, he lived in Greece, an experience that influenced his poems *Greek Coins* (1925) and his play *The Athenian Women* (1926).

Cooper, James Fenimore (b. Sept. 15, 1789, Burlington, N.J., U.S.— d. Sept. 14, 1851, Cooperstown, N.Y.) First major American novelist, author of the novels of frontier adventure known as THE LEATHER-STOCKING TALES.

James was a year old when his father, a Federalist congressman, moved his family to the frontier settlement (now Cooperstown) that he had founded in upstate New York. Cooper attended Yale and was expelled during his junior year because of a prank. He then joined the navy as a midshipman but became financially independent upon his father's death in 1809.

For 10 years he led the life of a dilettante. His first fiction, reputedly written on a challenge from his wife, was *Precaution* (1820), a plodding imitation of Jane Austen's novels of English gentry manners. His second novel, *The Spy* (1821), was based on Sir Walter Scott's Waverley novels, but in his own narrative Cooper used an American Revolutionary War setting and introduced several distinctively American character types. The book soon brought him international fame and a certain amount of wealth. The latter was very welcome, indeed necessary, since his father's estate had proved less ample than anybody had thought, and, with the deaths of his elder brothers, he had found himself responsible for the entire Cooper family.

The first of the renowned Leather-Stocking Tales, *The Pioneers* (1823), adhered to the successful formula of *The Spy*. No known prototype exists for the novel's principal character—the wilderness scout Natty Bumppo, alias Leather-Stocking. Public fascination with the character led Cooper to write a series of sequels in which the entire life of the frontier scout was gradually unfolded. *The Pioneers* was followed by *The Last of the Mohicans* (1826), *The Prairie* (1827), *The Pathfinder* (1840), and *The Deerslayer* (1841).

Cooper's fourth novel, THE PILOT (1823), inaugurated a series of popular and influential sea novels—especially *The Red Rover* (1827) and *The Sea Lions* (1849). As developed by Cooper, the genre became a powerful vehicle for spiritual as well as moral exploration. Cooper also wrote a meticulously researched, highly readable *History of the Navy of the United States of America* (1839).

Between 1822 and 1826 Cooper lived in New York City and participated in its intellectual life, founding the Bread and Cheese Club, which had many influential members. In the gentlemanly tradition of Thomas Jefferson and others, he attacked the oligarchical Whig Party, which opposed the egalitarian democracy of President Andrew Jackson. The lawsuits, conflict, and unrest provoked by his political stance were hard to bear, especially because he was writing more and earning less as the years went by. And though he wrote some of his best romances—such as *Satanstoe; or, The Littlepage Manuscripts* (1845)—during the last decade of his life, his profits from publishing had so diminished that he gained little benefit from his increased popularity. He was forced to go on writing for income, and some of his later novels, such as *Mercedes of Castile* (1840) and *Jack Tier* (1846–48), were mere hack work.

Coover, Robert (Lowell) (b. Feb. 4, 1932, Charles City, Iowa, U.S.) American writer of avant-garde fiction, plays, poetry, and essays whose use of experimental forms and techniques mixed reality and illusion.

Coover attended Southern Illinois University, Indiana University, and the University of Chicago. He taught at several universities, notably Brown University, Providence, R.I. His first novel, *The Origin of the Brunists* (1966), the most conventional of his fiction, tells of the rise and eventual disintegration of a religious cult. The protagonist of *The Universal Baseball Association, Inc.* (1968) creates an imaginary baseball league in which fictitious players must take charge of their own lives. The stories in *Pricksongs & Descants* (1969) were praised for their "verbal magic." *The Public Burning* (1976) was what Coover called a "factional account" of the trial and execution of Julius and Ethel Rosenberg; using Richard Nixon as the work's narrator, it satirized the national mood of the early 1950s. Among his other works are *Whatever Happened to Gloomy Gus of the Chicago Bears?* (1987) and *Pinocchio in Venice* (1991). Several of Coover's short stories were adapted for theatrical performance, including "The Baby Sitter" and "Spanking the Maid."

Corn, Alfred, *in full* Alfred Dewitt Corn III (b. Aug. 14, 1943, Bainbridge, Ga., U.S.) American poet whose mild-mannered, meditative lyrics belie a considerable sophistication.

Corn attended Emory University and Columbia University and taught at several universities. He earned critical acclaim for his first volume of verse, *All Roads at Once* (1976). The poems in *A Call in the Midst of the Crowd* (1978) are all about New York City, notably the lengthy title poem. *Notes from a Child of Paradise* (1984), one of Corn's best-known works, is a long semiautobiographical poem modeled after the *Paradiso* in Dante's *La divina commedia*. Other verse collections include *The Various Light* (1980), *An Xmas Murder* (1987), *The West Door* (1988), and *Autobiographies* (1992). *The Pith Helmet* (1992) is a book of aphorisms.

Corso, Gregory (Nunzio) (b. March 26, 1930, New York, N.Y., U.S.) American poet, a leading member in the mid-1950s of the Beat movement.

At 17 Corso was sentenced to three years in Clinton Prison in Dannemora, N.Y., for theft. While there, he was introduced to literature. He met the poet Allen Ginsberg in Greenwich Village in 1950 and published his first volume of verse, *The Vestal Lady on Brattle*, in 1955. In 1956 Corso went to San Francisco, where Ginsberg was residing and the Beat movement was gaining momentum.

Corso's poems in the collection *Gasoline* (1958) use the rhythmic, incantatory style effective in spoken verse. In *The Happy Birthday of Death* (1960) he returned to an easier, conversational tone. *Long Live Man* (1962), *Selected Poems* (1962), *The Mutation of the Spirit* (1964), *Elegiac Feelings American* (1970), *Herald of the Autochthonic Spirit* (1981), *Mindfield* (1989), and other books of poetry followed. He also wrote plays and a novel.

Cortez, Jayne (b. May 10, 1936, Arizona, U.S.) African-American poet noted for performing her own poetry, often accompanied by jazz.

Cortez was artistic director of the Watts Repertory Theatre Company from 1964 to 1970. Unfulfilled love, unromantic sex, and jazz greats from Bessie Smith to Cortez's ex-husband Ornette Coleman are subjects of her first collection of poems, *Pissstained Stairs and The Monkey Man's Wares* (1969). With the poems of *Festivals and Funerals* (1971) she turned to larger social issues, including the place of the artist in revolutionary politics. In *Scarifications* (1973) she confronted the Vietnam War and wrote with a newfound romanticism about a journey to Africa.

The frequent cruelty of Cortez's images and their startling juxtapositions often yield surrealistic effects. These elements and the rhythmic cadences of her lines enhance the impact of her poetry readings, as her recordings show, beginning with *Celebrations and Solitudes* (1975). Among her later works are *Coagulations: New and Selected Poems* (1984), *Everywhere Drums* (1990), and *Poetic Magnetic* (1991).

Costain, Thomas Bertram (b. May 8, 1885, Brantford, Ont., Can.—d. Oct. 8, 1965, New York, N.Y., U.S.) Canadian-born American historical novelist.

A journalist for many years on Canadian newspapers and a *Saturday Evening Post* editor from 1920 to 1934, Costain was 57 when he published his first romance, *For My Great Folly* (1942), dealing with the 17th-century rivalry between England and Spain. An immediate success, it was followed almost yearly by historical adventure tales, the best known of which are *The Black Rose* (1945), whose medieval English hero ranges as far as Kublai Khan's China, and *The Silver Chalice* (1952), about the early Christians in Rome.

Cousins, Norman (b. June 24, 1912, Union Hill, N.J., U.S.—d. Nov. 30, 1990, Los Angeles, Calif.) American essayist and editor, long associated with the *Saturday Review*.

Cousins began his editorial career in 1934. From 1942 to 1972 he was editor of the *Saturday Review*; he introduced essays that drew a connection between literature and current events. He felt strongly that a unique potential for greatness existed in America, as he wrote in *The Good Inheritance: The Democratic Chance* (1942). Cousins wrote on a variety of subjects, including a biography of Albert Schweitzer and a book of reflections on humanity in the atomic age, *Modern Man Is Obsolete* (1945). In 1979 *Anatomy of an Illness* appeared; a book based on Cousins' own experience with a life-threatening illness, it explored the healing ability of the human mind. He also wrote *Human Options* (1981), *The Physician in Literature* (1982), and *The Pathology of Power* (1987).

Cowley, Malcolm (b. Aug. 24, 1898, Belsano, Pa., U.S.—d. March 27, 1989, New Milford, Conn.) American literary critic and social historian who chronicled the writers of the Lost Generation of the 1920s and their successors. As literary editor of *The New Republic* from 1929 to 1944, with a generally leftist position on cultural questions, he played a significant part in many of the literary and political battles of the Depression years.

Cowley was educated at Harvard University and in France at the University of Montpellier. He helped to publish the little magazines *Secession* and *Broom* in Paris. His *Exile's Return: A Narrative of Ideas* (1934); rev. ed., *Exile's Return: A Literary Odyssey of the 1920's*, 1951) is an important social and literary history of the expatriate American writers of the period. Cowley revived the literary reputation of William Faulkner with his editing of the anthology *The Portable Faulkner* (1946).

Among Cowley's other works are *The Literary Situation* (1954), a study of the role of the American writer in society, and the collections of criticism and comment *Think Back on Us* (1967) and *A Many-Windowed House* (1970). The correspondence he exchanged with Faulkner appeared in 1966 in *The Faulkner-Cowley File: Letters and Memories, 1944–1962*. Among the many books he edited are *After the Genteel Tradition: American Writers Since 1910* (1937, reprinted 1964) and *Books That Changed Our Minds* (1939). *And I Worked at the Writer's Trade* (1976) combines literary history and autobiography.

Cowl or **Cowles, Jane,** *original name* Grace Bailey (b. Dec. 14, 1883, Boston, Mass., U.S.—d. June 22, 1950, Santa Monica, Calif.) Highly successful American playwright and actress.

Cowl made her acting debut in New York City in 1903 at the theater of her mentor, David Belasco, in *Sweet Kitty Bellairs*. Among her many successful roles were Jeannine in *Lilac Time* (1917) and Moonyean Claire and Kathleen Dungannon in 1,170 performances of *Smilin' Through* (1919–22); both plays were written by Alan Langdon Martin (pseudonym for Cowl and her most frequent collaborator, Jane Murfin) and produced by her husband, Adolph Klauber, drama critic for the *New York Times*. Other successful plays she wrote include *Daybreak* (1917) and *Information Please* (1918), with Murfin; *The Jealous Moon* (1928), with Theodore Charles; and *Hervey House* (1935), with Reginald Lawrence.

Cozzens, James Gould (b. Aug. 19, 1903, Chicago, Ill., U.S.—d. Aug. 9, 1978, Stuart, Fla.) American novelist whose writings dealt with life in middle-class America.

Cozzens grew up on Staten Island, N.Y., graduated from the Kent (Conn.) School in 1922, and attended Harvard University. In a year of teaching in Cuba he accumulated background material for the short novels *Cockpit* (1928) and *The Son of Perdition* (1929). He gained critical attention in 1931 with his novella *S.S. San Pedro*. Thereafter he published increasingly complex novels, most of which focus on professional people. In *The Last Adam* (1933) the protagonist is a doctor; *Men and Brethren* (1936) depicts the life of an Episcopalian minister; *The Just and the Unjust* (1942) and *By Love Possessed* (1957) are about lawyers; and *Guard of Honor* (1948) concerns air force officers and men. *Ask Me Tomorrow* (1940) is an autobiographical novel, and *Children and Others* (1964) is a short-story collection.

Cozzens' works reflect a philosophy of political and social conservatism. He received the Pulitzer Prize for fiction in 1949 for *Guard of Honor* and the Howells Medal of the American Academy of Arts and Letters in 1960 for *By Love Possessed*, his greatest popular success. His later works became increasingly convoluted in plot and style, especially his last novel, *Morning, Noon, and Night* (1968).

Craddock, Charles Egbert, *pseudonym of* Mary Noailles Murfree (b. Jan. 24, 1850, near Murfreesboro, Tenn., U.S.—d. July 31, 1922, Murfreesboro) American writer who depicted Tennessee mountain life in her short stories. She is characterized as a local colorist (a writer who describes the features and peculiarities of a particular region and its inhabitants).

For her stories published in *Appleton's Journal* and *The Atlantic Monthly*, she utilized the pen name Charles Egbert Craddock, and her identity was not disclosed until after the publication of her first volume of short stories, *In the Tennessee Mountains* (1884). Most of her stories present the narrow, stern life of the mountaineers who were left behind in the advance of modern civilization.

Crane, Hart, *in full* Harold Hart Crane (b. July 21, 1899, Garrettsville, Ohio, U.S.—d. April 27, 1932, at sea, Caribbean Sea) American poet who celebrated the richness of life in lyrics of visionary intensity. His most noted work, *The Bridge* (1930), was an attempt to create an epic myth of the American experience. As a coherent epic it has been deemed a failure, but many of its individual lyrics are judged to be among the best American poems of the 20th century.

Crane worked in a variety of jobs in New York City and Cleveland and, as his poetry began to be published in little magazines, eventually settled in New York in 1923. His first published book was *White Buildings* (1926). It contains his long poem "For the Marriage of Faustus and Helen," which he wrote as an answer to what he considered to be the cultural pessimism of *The Waste Land* by T.S. Eliot. In 1930 *The Bridge* was published. Inspired in part by the Brooklyn Bridge and standing for the human creative power uniting the present and the past, the poem has 15 parts and is unified by a structure modeled after that of a symphony.

Crane was granted a Guggenheim Fellowship and went to Mexico City, where he wrote "The Broken Tower" (1932). Despondent over the tensions of his life, on his way back to the United States he jumped from the ship into the Caribbean and was drowned.

Crane's *Collected Poems* appeared in 1933, and in 1966 *The Complete Poems and Selected Letters and Prose*, which incorporated some of his previously uncollected writings, was published.

Crane, R.S., *in full* Ronald Salmon Crane (b. Jan. 5, 1886, Tecumseh, Mich., U.S.—d. July 12, 1967, Chicago, Ill.) American literary critic who was a leading figure of the Neo-Aristotelian Chicago school. His landmark book, *The Languages of Criticism and the Structure of Poetry* (1953), formed the theoretical basis of the group. Although Crane was an outspoken opponent of New Criticism, he argued persuasively for a pluralism that values separate, even contradictory, critical schools.

Crane was educated at the University of Michigan and the University of Pennsylvania. He taught at Northwestern University, Evanston, Ill., and at the University of Chicago. In addition to publishing many journal articles, he edited the influential book *Critics and Criticism: Ancient and Modern* (1952). Much of his writing was collected in *The Idea of the Humanities and Other Essays Critical and Historical* (1967) and *Critical and Historical Principles of Literary History* (1971).

Crane, Stephen (b. Nov. 1, 1871, Newark, N.J., U.S.—d. June 5, 1900, Badenweiler, Baden, Ger.) American author whose first novel was a milestone in the development of literary realism. He later became a proficient short-story writer.

Crane had finished only one full year of college before he moved to New York City, where he wrote his first book, *Maggie: A Girl of the Streets* (1893), a sympathetic, uncompromisingly realistic study of a slum girl's descent into prostitution and eventual suicide. At that time its subject was so shocking that Crane published it under a pseudonym and at his own expense. He struggled as a poor and unknown freelance journalist until he was befriended by Hamlin Garland and the influential critic William Dean Howells. Suddenly, in 1895, the publication of THE RED BADGE OF COURAGE, a subtle, impressionistic study of a young soldier, and of his first book of poems, *The Black Riders*, brought him international fame.

Crane traveled to Greece and then to Cuba as a war correspondent. His first attempt, in 1897, to report on the insurrection in Cuba ended in near disaster; the ship on which he was traveling sank, and Crane—reported drowned—finally rowed into shore in a dinghy with the captain, cook, and oiler. The result was one of the world's great short stories, THE OPEN BOAT.

Crane then went to Greece to report the Greco-Turkish War for the New York *Journal*, and later to Cuba to report on the Spanish-American War, first for the New York *World* and then for the *Journal*. Afterwards he settled in Sussex, England. He died of tuberculosis that was compounded by the recurrent malarial fever he had caught in Cuba.

Crane's mastery of the short story was remarkable. He exploited youthful small-town experiences in *The Monster and Other Stories* (1899) and *Whilomville Stories* (1900); the Bowery in *George's Mother* (1896); an early trip to the Southwest and in Mexico in THE BLUE HOTEL and THE BRIDE COMES TO YELLOW SKY; the Civil War again in *The Little Regiment* (1896); and experiences as a war correspondent in *The Open Boat* (1898) and *Wounds in the Rain* (1900). His last poems are contained in the volume *War Is Kind* (1899).

Crawford, Isabella Valancy (b. Dec. 25, 1850, Dublin, Ire.—d. Feb. 12, 1887, Toronto, Ont., Can.) Major 19th-century Canadian poet. She is especially noted for her vivid descriptions of Canadian landscape.

The daughter of a physician who immigrated to Canada in 1858, Crawford spent most of her girlhood in the picturesque Kawartha Lakes district of Ontario. From 1875 until her death, she and her widowed mother lived in Toronto, meagerly sustained by the sale of her stories and poems to Toronto newspapers and to magazines.

The only book published during her lifetime (at her own expense) was *Old*

Spookses' Pass, Malcolm's Katie, and Other Poems (1884). A later collection of her poems was published in 1905 and reprinted in 1972. Crawford's work was rediscovered in the 1970s. Among the works that have since been published are *Selected Stories of Isabella Valancy Crawford* (1975), *Fairy Tales of Isabella Valancy Crawford* (1977), *Hugh and Ion* (1977); an unfinished narrative poem), *The Halton Boys* (1979), and *Malcolm's Katie: A Love Story* (1987).

Creeley, Robert (White) (b. May 21, 1926, Arlington, Mass., U.S.) American poet and founder of the BLACK MOUNTAIN POETS, a loose group associated during the 1950s with Black Mountain College in North Carolina.

Creeley attended Harvard University, spent a year in India and Burma, then lived on a farm in New Hampshire. He first began to publish his poems in small magazines. He lived in Europe in the early 1950s, and in Majorca, Spain, he started the Divers Press. In 1955, after graduating from Black Mountain College, he joined its faculty and was editor of the *Black Mountain Review* for its first three years. The *Review* published poems by Creeley, as well as works by other faculty members and poets.

In *For Love* (1962), Creeley emerged as a master technician. He followed this with other books of poetry, most notably *Pieces* (1968). Creeley taught poetry in several universities, including the State University of New York at Buffalo. His *Selected Poems* appeared in 1976. Later collections include *Later* (1979), *The Collected Poems of Robert Creeley 1945–1975* (1982), *Memory Gardens* (1986), and *Windows* (1990).

Crémazie, Octave, *byname of* Claude-Joseph-Olivier Crémazie (b. April 16, 1827, Quebec [Canada]—d. Jan. 16, 1879, Le Havre, Fr.) Poet considered the father of French-Canadian poetry. His poems are characterized by a patriotic love of Canada and its landscape.

In 1860 Crémazie helped found the first literary school of Quebec and in 1861 began issuing the magazine *Les Soirées canadiennes* to preserve the folklore of French Canada. He published poems in the *Journal de Québec* from 1854.

Crémazie left Canada in 1862 for France, where he spent the rest of his life in great poverty under the assumed name of Jules Fontaine. In this period he wrote the pessimistic poem "Promenade des trois morts" ("Parade of Three Corpses"), which remained unfinished, and a journal, *Siège de Paris*, that gave an eyewitness account of the siege of 1870. His most famous patriotic poems were "Le Vieux Soldat canadien" (1855); "The Old Canadian Soldier"), celebrating a French naval ship to visit Quebec, and "Le Drapeau de Carillon" (1858); "The Flag of Carillon"), which almost became Canada's national anthem. *Oeuvres complètes* ("Complete Works") was published in 1882.

Crèvecoeur, Michel-Guillaume-Saint-Jean de, *also called* Hector Saint John de Crèvecoeur *or (especially in America)* J. Hector St. John (b. Jan. 31, 1735, Caen, Fr.—d. Nov. 12, 1813, Sarcelles) French-American author and naturalist whose work provided a broad picture of life in the New World.

After studying in Jesuit schools and spending four years as an officer and mapmaker in Canada, Crèvecoeur chose in 1759 to remain in the New World. He wandered the Ohio and Great Lakes region, took out citizenship papers in New York in 1765, became a farmer in Orange county, and was married in 1769. Torn between the two factions in the American Revolution, Crèvecoeur languished for months in an English army prison in New York City before sailing for Europe in 1780, accompanied by one son. In London he arranged for the publication of 12 essays called *Letters from an American Farmer* (1782).

Within two years this book—charmingly written, optimistic, and timely— went through many editions. He was appointed French consul to three of the new American states. Before assuming his consular duties in 1784, Crève- coeur translated and added to the original 12 essays in *Lettres d'un culti- vateur américain*, 2 vol. (1784). When he returned to America, Crèvecoeur found his home burned, his wife dead, and his daughter and second son with strangers in Boston. Reunited with his children, he set about organizing a packet service between the United States and France. During a two-year furlough in Europe he brought out a larger, second edition of the French *Lettres*, 3 vol. (1790). Recalled from his consulship in 1790, Crèvecoeur wrote one other book on America, *Voyage dans la haute Pennsylvanie et dans l'État de New York*, 3 vol. (1801); *Travels in Upper Pennsylvania and New York*). He lived quietly in France and Germany until his death.

Crèvecoeur was for a while the most widely read commentator on Amer- ica. His reputation was further increased in the 1920s when a bundle of his unpublished English essays was discovered in an attic in France. These were brought out as *Sketches of Eighteenth Century America, or More Letters from an American Farmer* (1925).

Crews, Frederick C., *in full* Campbell (b. Feb. 20, 1933, Philadelphia, Pa., U.S.) American literary critic known for his use of psychoanalytic principles.

Crews attended Yale and Princeton universities, and from 1958 he taught at the University of California at Berkeley. He first attracted notice in academic circles with a controversial book of criticism, *The Sins of the Fathers: Hawthorne's Psychological Themes* (1966), in which he claimed that Nathaniel Hawthorne's work has little value unless read on a Freudian level. Crews was probably best known for his satirical send-up of literary criticism, *The Pooh Perplex: A Freshman Casebook* (1963), which contained parodies of scholarly journal articles. In *Out of My System: Psychoanalysis, Ideology, and Critical Method* (1975), Crews presented a witty defense of the psychoanalytic method while acknowledging its shortcomings. Crews also edited several works, including *The Random House Handbook* (1974); 6th edition, 1992), a text on rhetoric and grammar. In his later works, such as *Skeptical Engagements* (1986) he sought to debunk psychoanalysis and to discredit Freud as a scientific thinker. A later work is *The Critics Bear It Away: American Fiction and the Academy* (1992).

Croly, Herbert David (b. Jan. 23, 1869, New York, N.Y., U.S.—d. May 17, 1930, New York City) American author, editor, and political philosopher, founder of the magazine *The New Republic*.

The son of widely known journalists, Croly was educated at Harvard University and spent his early adult years editing or contributing to architectural journals. In 1914 he founded the liberal weekly *The New Republic*, "A Journal of Opinion." In its pages Croly attacked what he viewed as American complacency and argued that democratic institutions must constantly be revised to suit changing situations.

Crosby, Harry, *byname of* Henry Grew Crosby (b. June 4, 1898, Boston, Mass., U.S.—d. Dec. 10, 1929, New York, N.Y.) American poet who, as an expatriate in Paris in the 1920s, established the Black Sun Press.

Crosby was known for his bizarre behavior. After barely escaping death in World War I, he became morbid and rebellious. He settled in Paris in the early 1920s and soon joined the circle of literary expatriates. In 1927 he and his wife, Caresse Crosby (1892–1970), began to publish their own poetry under the imprint Editions Narcisse, later the Black Sun Press. The following year they started printing books by other writers, including Archibald MacLeish, D.H. Lawrence, and James Joyce, for which the press is best remembered.

In his poetry—which has little artistic merit—Crosby unconsciously traced literary tradition from 19th-century Romanticism, in *Sonnets for Caresse* (1925), to automatic writing, in *Sleeping Together* (1929), descriptions of his dreams. His work includes poetry, such as *Chariot of the Sun* (1928); diaries, *Shadows of the Sun* (1928–30); and contributions to the avant-grade magazine *transition* that demonstrate his obsessive, mystical sun worship. Crosby took his own life in 1929.

Crothers, Rachel (b. Dec. 12, 1878, Bloomington, Ill., U.S.—d. July 5, 1958, Danbury, Conn.) American playwright whose works reflected the position of women in American society more accurately than any other dramatist of her time.

Crothers graduated from the Illinois State Normal School (now Illinois State University) in 1892 and then studied dramatic art in Boston and New

York City and acted in New York City. Her career as a playwright began in 1906 with the success of her first full-length play, *The Three of Us*. For the next three decades, until *Susan and God* (1937), Broadway saw an average of one new Crothers play each year, the majority of them popular and critical successes, an achievement unequaled by any other American woman playwright.

Crothers chronicled, sometimes seriously, more often humorously, such timely problems as the double standard (*A Man's World*, 1909), trial marriage (*Young Wisdom*, 1914), the problems of the younger generation (*Nice People*, 1921), Freudianism (*Expressing Willie*, 1924), and divorce (*As Husbands Go*, 1931; *When Ladies Meet*, 1932). These and other successes were marked by simplicity of plot, happy endings, and expert dialogue, which featured shrewdly combined instruction and amusement. Her comedies always advocated rationality and moderation.

Crothers took full responsibility for the entire production of almost all her plays, casting and directing many of the leading stars of the contemporary stage. The best and most instructive statement of her dramatic theory is to be found in her essay "The Construction of a Play," collected in *The Art of Playwriting* (1928).

Crumley, James (b. Oct. 12, 1939, Three Rivers, Texas, U.S.) American writer of violent mystery novels featuring vivid characters and sordid settings.

Crumley attended Georgia Institute of Technology, Texas Arts and Industries University, and the Writers' Workshop at the University of Iowa. His experiences during service in the U.S. Army (1958–61) are reflected in his Vietnam War novel *One to Count Cadence* (1969). After 1969, apart from occasional pieces of journalism and the short stories collected in *The Muddy Fork and Other Things* (1991), he wrote only detective novels.

His down-and-out detectives, Milo Milodragovitch and C.W. Sughrue, and a number of other notable characters work in the fictional mountain city of Meriwether, Montana. Crumley's first detective novel, featuring Milodragovitch, was *The Wrong Case* (1975). Sughrue and an author with writer's block drink their way through the West while hunting a missing pornography actress in *The Last Good Kiss* (1978); Milodragovitch foils an antienvironmentalist conspiracy in *Dancing Bear* (1983); and Sughrue hunts the mother of a vile-tempered drug dealer in the especially violent *The Mexican Tree Duck* (1993). While the plots of Crumley's novels are conventional, the quality of his writing, his recurring comedy, and his emphasis on cataclysmic climaxes are distinctive.

Cullen, Countee (Porter) Countee *also spelled* Countée (b. May 30, 1903,

Louisville, Ky.?, U.S.—d. Jan. 9, 1946, New York, N.Y.) American poet, one of the finest of the HARLEM RENAISSANCE.

Reared by a woman who was probably his paternal grandmother, at age 15 he was unofficially adopted by the Reverend F.A. Cullen, minister of Salem M.E. Church, one of Harlem's largest congregations. During young Cullen's schooling, academic honors came easily to him. He won a citywide poetry contest as a schoolboy and saw his winning stanzas widely reprinted. At New York University he continued to attract critical attention. Major American literary magazines accepted his poems regularly, and his first collection of poems, *Color* (1925)—which includes the powerful YET DO I MARVEL—was published to critical acclaim before he finished college. Cullen attended Harvard and worked as an assistant editor for *Opportunity* magazine. After publication of *The Black Christ and Other Poems* (1929), his reputation as a poet waned. From 1934 until the end of his life he taught in the New York City public schools.

Most notable among Cullen's other works are *Copper Sun* (1927), *The Ballad of the Brown Girl* (1928), and *The Medea and Some Poems* (1935).

Cummings, E.E., *in full* Edward Estlin Cummings (b. Oct. 14, 1894, Cambridge, Mass., U.S.—d. Sept. 3, 1962, North Conway, N.H.) American poet and painter who first attracted attention, in an age of literary experimentation, for his eccentric punctuation and phrasing. The spirit of New England dissent and of Emersonian self-reliance underlies the urbanized Yankee colloquialism of Cummings' verse. The commonly held belief that Cummings had his name legally changed to lowercase letters only is erroneous.

Cummings graduated from Harvard. During World War I he served with an ambulance corps in France, where he was interned for a time in a detention camp because of his friendship with an American who had written letters home that the French censors thought critical of the war effort. This experience deepened his distrust of officialdom and was the basis for his first book, *The Enormous Room* (1922).

In the 1920s and '30s he divided his time between Paris, where he studied art, and New York City. His first book of verse was *Tulips and Chimneys* (1923), followed by *XLI Poems* (1925) and *&* (1925).

In 1927 his play *him* was produced by the Provincetown Players in New York City. During these years he exhibited his paintings and drawings, but they failed to attract as much critical interest as his writings. His experimental prose work *Eimi* (1933) recorded a visit to the Soviet Union that confirmed his repugnance for collectivism. He published his discussions as the Charles Eliot Norton lecturer on poetry at Harvard University under the title *i: six nonlectures* (1953).

In all Cummings wrote 12 volumes of verse, which are assembled in his two-volume *Complete Poems* (1968). His moods in these are alternately satirical and tough or tender and whimsical. His erotic poetry and love lyrics have a childlike candor and freshness.

Cunningham, J.V., *in full* James Vincent (b. Aug. 23, 1911, Cumberland, Md., U.S.—d. March 30, 1985, Waltham, Mass.) American poet and anti-modernist literary critic whose terse, epigrammatic verse is full of sorrow and wit.

Cunningham studied poetry with Yvor Winters at Stanford University. He taught at several universities before settling at Brandeis University in 1953. *The Helmsman* (1942) and *The Judge Is Fury* (1947) offer a mix of his early and mature poetry. In *The Quest of the Opal: A Commentary on "The Helmsman"* (1950) he explains why he came to reject the modernism of his early verse.

In the 1950s Cunningham wrote two volumes of epigrams, *Doctor Drink* (1950) and *Trivial, Vulgar and Exalted* (1957). *To What Strangers, What Welcome* (1964) is a sequence of short poems about his travels through the American West. Among Cunningham's other verse collections are *The Exclusions of a Rhyme* (1960), *Some Salt* (1967), and *The Collected Poems and Epigrams of J.V. Cunningham* (1971). He also published *The Collected Essays of J.V. Cunningham* (1976).

Curtis, George William (b. Feb. 24, 1824, Providence, R.I., U.S.—d. Aug. 31, 1892, Staten Island, N.Y.) American author, editor, and leader in civil-service reform.

Early in life Curtis spent two years at the Brook Farm community and school, later traveling in Europe, Egypt, and Palestine. In 1850 he joined the *New York Tribune*. As a result of his travels, he became a popular lecturer and published *Nile Notes of a Howadji* (1851) and *The Howadji in Syria* (1852). As an associate editor of *Putnam's Monthly Magazine* and author of "The Lounger" column in *Harper's Weekly* and "The Easy Chair" column in *Harper's Magazine*, he wrote prolifically. Many of his essays were collected, chiefly in *The Potiphar Papers* (1853), a satire on fashionable society, and *Prue and I* (1856).

In 1863 Curtis became political editor of *Harper's Weekly*, and from 1871 until his death he led the movement for civil-service reform.

D

Daly, Augustin, *in full* John Augustin Daly (b. July 20, 1838, Plymouth, N.C., U.S.—d. June 7, 1899, Paris, Fr.) American playwright and theatrical manager whose companies were major features of the New York and London stage.

Beginning in 1859, Daly was drama critic for several New York newspapers. *Leah the Forsaken*, adapted from a German play in 1862, was Daly's first success as a playwright. His first important original play, *Under the Gaslight* (1867), was popular for years. In 1869 he formed his own company and later developed such outstanding actresses as Fanny Davenport and Maude Adams. Daly's best play, *Horizon* (1871), drew heavily upon the Western-type characters of Bret Harte and gave impetus to the development of a drama based on American themes and characters rather than European models. *Divorce* (1871), another of his better plays, ran for 200 performances. After opening Daly's Theatre in New York City in 1879, with a company headed by John Drew and Ada Rehan, he confined himself to adaptations and management; in 1893 he opened Daly's Theatre in London.

Dana, Richard Henry (b. Aug. 1, 1815, Cambridge, Mass., U.S.—d. Jan. 6, 1882, Rome, Italy) American lawyer and author of the popular autobiographical narrative *Two Years Before the Mast*.

Dana withdrew from Harvard College when measles weakened his eyesight, and he shipped to California as a sailor in August 1834 to regain his health. After voyaging among California's ports, he rounded Cape Horn, returned home in 1836, and reentered Harvard.

In 1840, the year of his admission to the bar, he published *Two Years Before the Mast*, a personal narrative presenting "the life of a common sailor at sea as it really is" and showing the abuses endured by his fellow sailors. In 1841 he published *The Seaman's Friend* (U.K. title, *The Seaman's Manual*), which became known as an authoritative guide to the legal rights and duties of seamen. Against vigorous opposition in Boston, Dana gave free legal aid to blacks captured under the Fugitive Slave Law. In 1863, while serving as U.S. attorney for Massachusetts, he won before the U.S. Supreme Court the case of the *Amy Warwick*, securing the right of Union forces to blockade Southern ports without giving the Confederate states an international status as belligerents.

His scholarly edition of Henry Wheaton's *Elements of International Law* (1866) precipitated a lawsuit by an earlier editor. The charges of plagiarism that resulted from the suit contributed to Dana's defeat in the congressional election of 1868 and caused the Senate to refuse his confirmation when President Ulysses S. Grant named him minister to Great Britain in 1876. Among Dana's other works are *To Cuba and Back* (1859) and the post-

Richard Henry Dana

humously published *Speeches in Stirring Times* (1910) and *An Auto-biographical Sketch* (1953).

Davenport, Guy, *in full* Guy Mattison Davenport, Jr. (b. Nov. 23, 1927, Anderson, S.C., U.S.) American author and scholar, best known for his short, experimental fiction. He was also an illustrator, an essayist, a translator, and a critic.

Davenport's first, and best received, collection of short fiction, *Tatlin!* (1974), was heavily influenced by the works of the poet Ezra Pound. Davenport's other works include the collections *Da Vinci's Bicycle* (1979), *Eclogues* (1981), *Apples and Pears* (1984), and *A Table of Green Fields* (1993). These and other works reveal the author's great erudition; his writing is filled with literary, classical, and historical allusions conveyed by a variety of avant-garde techniques.

Originally published in various journals, the essays and reviews collected in *The Geography of the Imagination* (1981) cover a wide variety of subjects. *Cities on Hills: A Study of I-XXX of Ezra Pound's Cantos* (1983) and *A Balthus Notebook* (1989) are other works of criticism. Davenport made many translations, including *Sappho: Songs and Fragments* (1965), *Archilochos, Sappho, Alkman* (1980), and *Anakreon: The Extant Fragments* (1991). He also illustrated several books, including poet Hugh Kenner's *The Stoic Comedians* and his own *Apples and Pears*.

Davidson, Donald (Grady) (b. Aug. 18, 1893, Campbellsville, Tenn., U.S.—d. April 25, 1968, Nashville, Tenn.) American poet, essayist, and teacher who warned against technology as indicative of modern spiritual disorder and idealized the agrarian South and its traditions.

While attending Vanderbilt University (B.A., 1917; M.A., 1922) Davidson became one of the Fugitives, a group of Southern writers determined to conserve their region's distinctive literature and rural economy. They published a journal *The Fugitive* (1922–25) and contributed essays to the book *I'll Take My Stand* (1930). In time Davidson's fellow Fugitives—Robert Penn Warren, Allen Tate, and John Crowe Ransom among them—altered their views, but Davidson, who taught for many years at Vanderbilt, remained passionately devoted to his early ideals. In his verse collections, including *The Tall Men* (1927), *Lee in the Mountains, and Other Poems* (1938), and *Poems, 1922–1961* (1966), and in his prose, including *The Attack on Leviathan: Regionalism and Nationalism in the United States* (1938), *Why the Modern South Has a Great Literature* (1951), and *Still Rebels, Still Yankees, and Other Essays* (1957), he praised historic Southern heroes, defended racial segregation, and warned against the evils of industrialism, which he saw as the enemy of spiritual values. His two-volume *The Tennessee* (1946, 1948) is a history of the Tennessee River and its valley.

JERRY BAUER

Robertson Davies

Davies, Robertson, *in full* William Robertson Davies, *pseudonym* Samuel Marchbanks (b. Aug. 28, 1913, Thamesville, Ont., Can.—d. Dec. 2, 1995, Orangeville, Ont., Can.) Playwright and novelist probably best known for THE DEPTFORD TRILOGY, a series of novels (*Fifth Business* [1970], *The Manticore* [1972], and *World of Wonders* [1975]) that examine the intersecting lives of three men from the small Canadian town of Deptford.

Educated in England at Oxford, Davies had training in acting, directing, and stage management as a member of the Old Vic Repertory Company. He also edited the Peterborough *Examiner* (1942–63) and taught English at the University of Toronto (1960–81; emeritus thereafter). Davies wrote plays—such as *Eros at Breakfast* (1949), *At My Heart's Core* (1950), *A Jig for the Gypsy* (1954), and *A Masque of Mr. Punch* (1963)—novels, and nonfiction—*The Diary of Samuel Marchbanks* (1947), *A Voice From the Attic* (1960), and *Samuel Marchbanks' Almanack* (1967) before publishing his masterwork.

The Fifth Business cemented Davies' reputation. Known as a traditional (that is, nonexperimental) storyteller, Davies was a master of imaginative writing and wicked wit. Among his other notable works of fiction are his SALTERTON TRILOGY (*Tempest-Tost* [1951], *Leaven of Malice* [1954], and *A Mixture of Frailties* [1958]), THE REBEL ANGELS (1981), WHAT'S BRED IN THE BONE (1985), and THE LYRE OF ORPHEUS (1988). *Murther & Walking Spirits*, written from the perspective of a dead man, was published in 1991. His later nonfiction includes *The Mirror of Nature* (1983).

Davis, H.L., *in full* Harold Lenoir (b. Oct. 18, 1896, Yoncalla, Ore., U.S.—d. Oct. 31, 1960, San Antonio, Texas) American novelist and poet who wrote realistically about the West, rejecting the stereotype of the cowboy as hero.

Davis worked as a cowboy, a typesetter, and a surveyor among other jobs before being noticed for his writing. He first received recognition for his poems, which were written in imitation of the poetry of Detlev von Liliencron, a 19th-century German poet. Later Davis was encouraged by the critic H.L. Mencken to try prose, and the results appeared in *American Mercury*. In 1932 Davis went to Mexico on a Guggenheim Fellowship, and he stayed there to write *Honey in the Horn* (1935), which won a Pulitzer Prize in 1936. This novel secured Davis' reputation as a novelist of the West whose slow-moving books explore the magic of the landscape, while realistically examining quiet overall portrait of the era when the last pioneers flooded Oregon. Davis mistrusted heroics and instead wrote realistically the problems facing frontier men and women. Davis' later books include *Beulah Land* (1949) and *The Distant Music* (1957).

Davis, Richard Harding (b. April 18, 1864, Philadelphia, Pa., U.S.—

d. April 11, 1916, Mount Kisco, N.Y.) American author of romantic novels and short stories who was also the best-known reporter of his generation.

Davis studied at Lehigh and Johns Hopkins universities and in 1886 became a reporter on the Philadelphia Record. He then worked on various newspapers in Philadelphia and New York and wrote short stories. In 1890 he became managing editor of *Harper's Weekly*. On assignments for *Harper's*, he toured various parts of the globe, recording his impressions of the American West, Europe, and South America in a series of books from 1892 to 1896. He also acted as a war correspondent, reporting on fighting from the Greco-Turkish war of 1897 to World War I. He plunged into what he reported, defying rules in order to join in the battle of San Juan Hill in the Spanish-American War; he was nearly shot by the Germans as a spy in World War I. His early collections of stories achieved immediate success, particularly *Gallegher and Other Stories* (1891), *Van Bibber and Others* (1892), and *Ranson's Folly* (1902). Many of his published works were illustrated by Charles Dana Gibson. He wrote seven popular novels published between 1897 and 1909. Several of his 25 plays were also very successful, notably *Ranson's Folly* (1904); a dramatization of his earlier work by the same name), *The Dictator* (1904), and *Miss Civilization* (1906).

Day, Clarence (Shepard) (b. Nov. 18, 1874, New York, N.Y., U.S.—d. Dec. 28, 1935, New York City) American writer whose greatest popular success was his autobiographical *Life with Father*.

Educated at St. Paul's School, Concord, N.H., and at Yale (A.B., 1896), Day joined his father's brokerage firm as a partner. He enlisted in the U.S. Navy the following year but was stricken by arthritis, which left him an invalid.

In 1920 Day published his first book, *This Simian World*, a collection of humorous essays and illustrations. This was followed by *The Crow's Nest* (1921) and *Thoughts Without Words* (1928). He achieved great success with *God and My Father* (1932), *Life with Father* (1935), and *Life with Mother* (1936). Drawn from his own family experiences, these were pleasant and gently satirical portraits of a late Victorian household dominated by a gruff, opinionated father and a warm, charming mother. Day was a frequent contributor to *The New Yorker* magazine. *Life with Father* was dramatized by Howard Lindsay and Russel Crouse in 1939.

Clarence Day

DeForest, John William (b. May 31, 1826, Humphreysville, Conn., U.S.—d. July 17, 1906, New Haven, Conn.) American writer of realistic fiction, author of a major novel of the American Civil War—*Miss Ravenel's Conversion from Secession to Loyalty* (1867).

DeForest traveled in the Middle East from 1848 to 1849. He returned home to write a scholarly *History of the Indians in Connecticut* (1851) before setting out for Europe, where he lived from 1851 to 1854. Two travel books came out of these experiences abroad: *Oriental Acquaintance* (1856) and *European Acquaintance* (1858).

When the American Civil War broke out, DeForest organized a company of New Haven volunteers and served as captain in the several Union campaigns. After the war, he was district commander of the Freedmen's Bureau in Greenville, S.C. (1866–67). His experiences in war and its aftermath were published posthumously as *A Volunteer's Adventures* (1946) and *A Union Officer in the Reconstruction* (1948).

In addition to *Miss Ravenel's Conversion*, DeForest wrote *Kate Beaumont* (1872), which depicts the social life in South Carolina before the war, and *The Bloody Chasm* (1881), its social life after the war. Two other novels, *Honest John Vane* (1875) and *Playing the Mischief* (1875), deal with corruption during the administration of President Ulysses S. Grant. His last novel, *A Lover's Revolt* (1898), is a romance of the American Revolution.

Deland, Margaret, *byname of* Margaretta Wade Deland, *original surname* Campbell (b. Feb. 23, 1857, Allegheny, Pa., U.S.—d. Jan. 13, 1945, Boston, Mass.) American writer who frequently portrayed small-town life.

In 1886 Deland published *The Old Garden*, a collection of poems. Her first novel, *John Ward, Preacher* (1888), dealt with religious and social questions after the manner of the British writer Mrs. Humphry Ward. Her most popular works were a nostalgic series of stories set in the fictional small town of Old Chester, which was based on the town of Manchester, Pa., where she was raised. These were collected in *Old Chester Tales* (1898), *Dr. Lavendar's People* (1903), *Around Old Chester* (1915), and *New Friends in Old Chester* (1924). Among her other works were several "problem" novels dealing with such issues as divorce, feminism, and adultery. These include *The Awakening of Helena Richie* (1906), *The Iron Woman* (1911), *The Rising Tide* (1916), and *The Vehement Flame* (1922). She also wrote a volume of childhood memories, *If This Be I, As I Suppose It Be* (1935), and an autobiography, *Golden Yesterdays* (1941).

Margaret Deland

Delany, Martin R., *in full* Robinson (b. May 6, 1812, Charles Town, Va. [now W.Va.], U.S.—d. Jan. 24, 1885, Xenia, Ohio) African-American writer and activist whose dedication to the cause of black nationalism in the pre-Civil War era marked him as a thinker ahead of his time.

Born to free parents, Delany was educated illegally during a period when black literacy was prohibited by law. He began the study of medicine in Philadelphia, where he first formed the Pan-Africanist views that confused and angered many of his contemporaries, including fellow blacks. From 1847 until 1849, he was a coeditor with Frederick Douglass of the antislavery newspaper *North Star.*

After the passage of the 1850 Fugitive Slave Act, by which the federal government undertook to help in the search for and return of runaway slaves, Delany wrote his most important work, *The Condition, Elevation, Emigration, and Destiny of the Colored People of the United States* (1852). He urged blacks to be self-reliant both financially and intellectually. *Blake; or, The Huts of America* (partially published 1859; full publication, 1861–62), his only novel, was one of the first novels by a black American to be published in the United States. It is a penetrating examination of slavery and its many ramifications. Although the book received little critical attention at the time of publication, it was revived in the 1960s and hailed as an early model for African-American consciousness and activism.

Delany, Samuel R., *in full* Samuel Ray Delany, Jr. (b. April 1, 1942, New York, N.Y., U.S.) African-American science-fiction novelist and critic whose highly imaginative works address racial and social issues, heroic quests, and the nature of language.

Delany's first novel, *The Jewels of Aptor,* was published in 1962. *Babel-17* (1966), which clinched his reputation, has an artist protagonist and explores the nature of language and its ability to give structure to experience. Similarly, *The Einstein Intersection* (1967) features an artist-outsider and addresses issues of cultural development and sexual identity. *Dhalgren* (1975), considered his most controversial novel, is the story of a young bisexual man searching for identity in a large, decaying city. The main character of *Triton* (1976) undergoes a sex-change operation, and in this novel the author examines bias against women and homosexuals.

Delany's Neveryon series (*Tales of Nevèrÿon* [1979]; *Neveryóna; or, The Tale of Signs and Cities* [1983]; *Flight from Nevèrÿon* [1985]; and *The Bridge of Lost Desire* [1987]) is set in a magical past at the beginning of civilization. His complex *Stars in My Pocket Like Grains of Sand* (1984) is regarded as a stylistic breakthrough for the author. He also wrote the novella "Time Considered as a Helix of Semi-Precious Stones" (1969) and the criticism *The Jewel-Hinged Jaw: Notes on the Language of Science Fiction* (1977). Delany has also written scripts for film, radio, and *Wonder Woman* comic books.

de la Roche, Mazo (b. Jan. 15, 1879, Newmarket, Ont., Can.—d. July 12, 1961, Toronto) Canadian author whose series of novels about the Whiteoak family of Jalna (their estate in Ontario) made her one of the most popular "family saga" novelists of her time.

De la Roche's first success, *Jalna* (1927), ended with the 100th birthday of Grandmother Adeline Whiteoak, a lusty character later celebrated in a long-running play, *Whiteoaks* (1936), and a film, *Jalna* (1935). Though not written in chronological order, the saga continues with 15 other books, covering 100 years of Whiteoak family history. De la Roche's other works include children's stories, travel books, drama, and an autobiography, *Ringing the Changes* (1957).

DeLillo, Don (b. Nov. 20, 1936, New York, N.Y., U.S.) Novelist whose postmodernist works portray the anomie of an America cosseted by material excess and stupefied by empty mass culture and politics.

DeLillo's first novel, *Americana* (1971), is the story of a network television executive in search of the "real" America. It was followed by *End Zone* (1972) and *Great Jones Street* (1973). *Ratner's Star* (1976) attracted critical attention with its baroque comic sense and verbal facility.

Beginning with *Players* (1977), DeLillo's vision turned darker and his characters became more willful in their destructiveness and ignorance. Critics found little to like in the novel's protagonists, but much to admire in DeLillo's elliptic prose. The thrillers *Running Dog* (1978) and *The Names* (1982) followed. *White Noise* (1985), which won the American Book Award for fiction, tells of a professor of Hitler Studies who is exposed to an "airborne toxic event"; he discovers that his wife is taking an experimental substance said to combat the fear of death, and he vows to obtain the drug for himself at any cost. In *Libra* (1988), DeLillo presents a fictional portrayal of Lee Harvey Oswald, the assassin of President John F. Kennedy. *Mao II* (1991) opens with a mass wedding officiated by cult leader Sun Myung Moon. It tells the story of a reclusive writer who becomes enmeshed in a world of political violence.

Dell, Floyd (b. June 28, 1887, Barry, Ill., U.S.—d. July 23, 1969, Bethesda, Md.) Novelist and radical journalist whose fiction examined the changing mores in sex and politics among American bohemians before and after World War I.

Moving to Chicago in 1908, Dell worked as a newspaperman and soon was a leader of the city's literary movement. From 1909 he edited the *Friday Literary Review* of the *Evening Post*, making it one of the most noted American literary supplements. As a critic, he furthered the careers of Sherwood Anderson and Theodore Dreiser.

A socialist from his youth, he moved to New York in 1914 and was associate editor of the left-wing *The Masses* until 1917. He was on the staff of its successor, *The Liberator*, from 1918 to 1924.

Dell's first and best novel, the largely autobiographical *Moon-Calf*, appeared in 1920, and its sequel, *The Briary-Bush*, in 1921. His other novels on life among the unconventional include *Janet March* (1923), *Runaway* (1925), and *Love in Greenwich Village* (1926). His nonfiction includes *Were You Ever a Child?* (1919), on child rearing; the biography *Upton Sinclair: A Study in Social Protest* (1927); *Love in the Machine Age* (1930), which presented his views on sex; and his autobiography, *Homecoming* (1933).

De Mille, James (b. Aug. 23, 1836, Saint John, N.B. [Canada]—d. Jan. 28, 1880, Halifax, N.S.) Canadian author of more than 30 novels with a wide range of appeal who is particularly noted for his wit and humor.

While a student at Acadia College, De Mille traveled extensively in Europe, and scenes of Italy became settings for many of his novels. After an unsuccessful venture as a bookseller, De Mille taught at Acadia College and at Dalhousie University. De Mille's adult fiction includes thrillers, such as *The Cryptogram* (1871); comic adventures, such as *The Dodge Club; or, Italy in 1859* (1860); and historical romances, such as *A Tale of Rome in the First Century* (1867). He appealed to young readers with the "B.O.W.C." ("Brethren of the White Cross") series, the first popular boys' adventure stories produced in Canada. De Mille's most imaginative work is *A Strange Manuscript Found in a Copper Cylinder* (1888), set in a future time when humanity, devoid of inspiring ideas, rejects the drive for achievement and lapses into conformity.

Dennie, Joseph (b. Aug. 30, 1768, Boston, Mass. [U.S.]—d. Jan. 7, 1812, Philadelphia, Pa.) Essayist and editor who was a major American literary figure in the early 19th century.

Dennie graduated from Harvard and together with Royall Tyler formed a literary partnership; under the pseudonyms Colon and Spondee, they began contributing satirical pieces to local newspapers. Between 1792 and 1802 Dennie wrote his "Farrago" essays in various periodicals. He edited the newspaper *Farmer's Weekly Museum* from 1796 to 1798, contributing the series of graceful, moralizing "Lay Preacher" essays that established his literary reputation.

Dennie's pro-Federalist positions secured him an appointment as personal secretary to Secretary of State Timothy Pickering in 1799–1800. With Asbury Dickins, Dennie began in 1801 a politico-literary periodical called *The Port Folio*, which became the most distinguished literary weekly of its time in America. He contributed "Lay Preacher" essays and also commissioned work from other prominent writers. As the founder of the Tuesday Club, Dennie was the center of the aristocratic literary circle in Philadelphia and was for a time the leading literary arbiter in the country. He derided American rusticity and crudity and praised English literature, manners, and sophistication. He also advocated sound critical standards and encouraged talented younger writers, such as Washington Irving.

Desrosiers, Léo-Paul (b. April 11, 1896, Berthier, Que., Can.—d. April 20, 1967, Montreal) French-Canadian writer best known for his historical novels.

In addition to writing fiction, Desrosiers worked as a journalist, an editor, and a librarian. Both *Âmes et paysages* (1922); "People and Landscapes"), a collection of stories, and his first novel, *Nord-Sud* (1931), are set in the Quebec countryside. *Les Engagés du Grand Portage* (1938); *The Making of Nicolas Montour*) depicts the cutthroat behavior exhibited by rival fur companies in the early 19th century. Desrosiers's *L'Ampoule d'or* (1951); "The Gold Phial") is considered a minor masterpiece for its poetic language and imagery. His philosophical trilogy—*Vous qui passez*, *Les Angoisses et les tourments*, and *Rafales sur les cimes* (1958–60); "You Who Pass," "Agony and Torment," and "Squalls on the Summit")—was less successful.

Deutsch, Babette (b. Sept. 22, 1895, New York, N.Y., U.S.—d. Nov. 13, 1982, New York, N.Y.) American poet, critic, translator, and novelist whose volumes of literary criticism, *Poetry in Our Time* (1952) and *Poetry Handbook* (1957), were standard English texts in American universities. With her husband, Avraham Yarmolinsky, Deutsch translated poetry from Russian and German, including *Two Centuries of Russian Verse* (1966).

Deutsch published poems in magazines such as the *North American Review* and the *New Republic* while still a student at Barnard College, New York City. She first attracted critical notice for her poetry with *Banners* (1919), whose title poem celebrated the beginning of the Russian Revolution of 1917. Her literary collaboration with Yarmolinsky produced several acclaimed translations, many of which were the first rendering into English of important works of European literature.

Deutsch's poetry collections include *Honey Out of the Rock* (1925), Imagist verse on marriage, motherhood, and the arts; *Fire for the Night* (1930); *One Part Love* (1939); and *Take Them, Stranger* (1944) and *Animal, Vegetable, Mineral* (1954), both of which contain antiwar poetry. Among her critical studies are a collection of essays on poetry and poets entitled *Potable Gold* (1929), *Heroes of the Kalevala, Finland's Saga* (1940), *Walt Whitman, Builder for America* (1941), and *The Reader's Shakespeare* (1946). Her novels include the semiautobiographical *A Brittle Heaven* (1926); *In Such a Night* (1927); *Mask of Silenus* (1933), a novel about the philosopher Socrates; and *Rogue's Legacy* (1942), about the poet François Villon.

De Voto, Bernard (Augustine) (b. Jan. 11, 1897, Ogden, Utah, U.S.—d. Nov. 13, 1955, New York, N.Y.) American novelist, journalist, historian, and critic, best known for his works on American literature and the history of the western frontier.

After attending the University of Utah and Harvard University, De Voto taught at Northwestern University and Harvard before becoming editor of the *Saturday Review of Literature*. After two years he resigned and returned to Cambridge, Mass., where he lived during the remainder of his life. Although he wrote a number of novels, De Voto probably found his largest audience through his essays in the "Easy Chair" column for *Harper's Magazine*. His combination of sound scholarship and a vigorous, outspoken style made him one of the most widely read critics and historians of his day. His strong opinions and admitted prejudices for American life and culture put him at the center of many critical controversies.

Among the nonfiction works De Voto wrote are *Mark Twain's America* (1932); *Mark Twain at Work* (1942); *Across the Wide Missouri* (1948), for which he won a Pulitzer Prize; *The World of Fiction* (1950); *The Hour* (1951); and *The Course of Empire* (1952). He also edited several books, including *Mark Twain in Eruption* (1940) and *The Journals of Lewis and Clark* (1953). His novels include *The Crooked Mile* (1924) and *Mountain Time* (1947).

De Vries, Peter (b. Feb. 27, 1910, Chicago, Ill., U.S.—d. Sept. 28, 1993, Norwalk, Conn.) American editor and novelist widely known as a satirist, linguist, and comic visionary.

De Vries, the son of Dutch immigrants, was reared in a Calvinist environment. He graduated from Calvin College in Grand Rapids, Mich. After several years as an editor for *Poetry* magazine in Chicago, he joined the editorial staff of *The New Yorker* and thereafter made his home in Westport, Conn.

Peter De Vries

De Vries' first novel, *But Who Wakes the Bugler?* (1940), was most notable for having been illustrated by the cartoonist Charles Addams. Although his next two novels were hardly noticed at all, his first book of short stories, *No But I Saw the Movie* (1952), won critical acclaim, and his subsequent novel, *The Tunnel of Love* (1954), became a best-seller and was successfully adapted both as a play and as a motion picture. Noted for being light on plot and filled with wit, puns, and sardonic humor, De Vries' novels were appreciated for their imaginative wordplay and ironic vision. Among his better novels are *Comfort Me with Apples* (1956), *The Tents of Wickedness* (1959), *Reuben, Reuben* (1964), *Madder Music* (1977), and *Slouching Towards Kalamazoo* (1983).

Dickey, James, *in full* James Lafayette Dickey (b. Feb. 2, 1923, Atlanta, Ga., U.S.) American poet, novelist, and critic best known for his poetry combining themes of nature mysticism, religion, and history and for his powerful novel *Deliverance* (1970).

Dickey served as a fighter-bomber pilot in the U.S. Army Air Forces during

SOUTH CAROLINA ETV

James Dickey

World War II. After the war he earned B.A. (1949) and M.A. (1950) degrees from Vanderbilt University. By his own account, Dickey began writing poetry at the age of 24 with little awareness of formal poetics. After pursuing graduate studies and working for a time in advertising, he published his first book of poems, *Into the Stone*, in 1960. He was a teacher and writer-in-residence at a number of U.S. colleges and universities. From 1966 to 1968 he served as poetry consultant to the Library of Congress.

Dickey's other collections of poetry include *Drowning with Others* (1962), *Helmets* (1964), *Buckdancer's Choice* (1965), *Poems 1957–1967* (1967), *The Zodiac* (1976), and *The Whole Motion* (1992); collected poems 1949–92). Of his works of nonfiction prose, *Babel to Byzantium: Poets & Poetry Now* (1968), the autobiographical *Self-Interviews* (1970), and *Jericho: The South Beheld* (1974) are notable.

His poetry is noted for its lyrical portrayal of a world in conflict—predator with prey, soldier with soldier, the self with itself.

Dickinson, Emily (Elizabeth) (b. Dec. 10, 1830, Amherst, Mass., U.S.— d. May 15, 1886, Amherst) American lyric poet who is noted for her eloquent, concise, and deceptively simple verses.

Dickinson was educated at Amherst Academy and Mount Holyoke Female Seminary. Though she began to write verse around 1850, only a handful of her 1,775 poems can be dated before 1858, when she began to collect them into small, hand-sewn booklets. In the 1850s she began two of her significant correspondences—with Dr. and Mrs. Josiah G. Holland and with Samuel Bowles. The two men were editors of the *Springfield* (Mass.) *Republican*, a paper that took an interest in literary matters.

Dickinson's poems of the 1850s are fairly conventional in sentiment and form, but beginning about 1860 she began to experiment with both language and prosody. Her prevailing poetic form was the quatrain of three iambic feet, but she used many other forms as well, lending complexity to even the simpler hymnbook measures by constantly altering the metrical beat to fit her thought. She broke new ground in her wide use of off-rhymes. In striving for an epigrammatic conciseness, she stripped her language of superfluous words. She tampered freely with syntax and liked to place a familiar word in an extraordinary context.

In 1862 Dickinson wrote to a literary man, Thomas Wentworth Higginson, asking his opinion of her work. Higginson, although he advised Emily not to publish, recognized the originality of her poems and remained her "preceptor" for the rest of her life. After 1862 she resisted all efforts by her friends to put her verse before the public. Only seven poems were published during her lifetime, five of them in the *Springfield Republican*.

In 1864 and 1865 persistent eye trouble caused her to live several months in Cambridge, Mass., where she sought treatment. Once back in Amherst she never traveled again and after the late 1860s never left the boundaries of the family's property. After the Civil War, she sought increasingly to regulate her life by the rules of art. Her letters, some of them equal in artistry to her poems, classicize daily experience in an epigrammatic style. By 1870 she was dressing only in white and saw few of the callers who came to the homestead; her seclusion was fiercely guarded by her devoted sister, Lavinia.

Soon after Dickinson's death Lavinia determined to have Emily's poems published. In 1890 *Poems by Emily Dickinson*, edited by T.W. Higginson and Mabel Loomis Todd, appeared. Other volumes of Dickinson poems, edited chiefly by Mabel Loomis Todd, Martha Dickinson Bianchi (Emily's niece), and Millicent Todd Bingham, were published between 1891 and 1957, and in 1955 Thomas H. Johnson edited all the surviving poems and their variant versions.

Dick, Philip K., *in full* Kindred (b. Dec. 16, 1928, Chicago, Ill., U.S.— d. March 2, 1982, Santa Ana, Calif.) American science-fiction writer whose novels and short stories often depict the psychological struggles of characters trapped in illusory environments.

Dick worked briefly in radio before studying at the University of California at Berkeley for one year. The publication of his first story, "Beyond Lies the Wub," in 1952 launched his full-time writing career. He published his first novel, *Solar Lottery*, three years later. The theme of a reality at variance with what it appears or was intended to be emerged early in Dick's work and remained his central preoccupation. In such novels as *Time Out of Joint* (1959), *The Man in the High Castle* (1962; Hugo Award winner), and *The Three Stigmata of Palmer Eldritch* (1965), the protagonists must determine their own orientation in an "alternate world." Beginning with *The Simulacra* (1964) and culminating in *Do Androids Dream of Electric Sheep?* (1968; adapted for film as *Blade Runner*, 1982), the illusion centers on artificial creatures at large in a real world of the future.

Among Dick's numerous story collections are *A Handful of Darkness* (1955), *The Variable Man and Other Stories* (1957), *The Preserving Machine* (1969), and the posthumously published *I Hope I Shall Arrive Soon* (1985).

Didion, Joan (b. Dec. 5, 1934, Sacramento, Calif., U.S.) American novelist and essayist known for her lucid prose style and incisive depictions of social and psychological fragmentation.

Didion graduated from the University of California at Berkeley in 1956 and then worked for *Vogue* magazine from 1956 to 1963, first as a copywriter and later as an editor. During this period she wrote her first novel, *Run River*

(1963), which examines the disintegration of a California family. While in New York, she met and married the writer John Gregory Dunne, with whom she returned to California in 1964. A collection of magazine columns published as *Slouching Towards Bethlehem* (1968) established Didion's reputation as an essayist and confirmed her preoccupation with the forces of disorder. In a second collection, *The White Album* (1979), Didion continued her analysis of the turbulent 1960s. The inner decay of the Establishment is a major theme of the essays constituting the volume *After Henry* (1992); also published as *Sentimental Journeys*). Didion's fiction, also centering on personal and social unrest, includes the short novels *Play It as It Lays* (1970), *A Book of Common Prayer* (1977), *Democracy* (1984), and the extended essays *Salvador* (1983) and *Miami* (1987).

Dillard, Annie, *original surname* Doak (b. April 30, 1945, Pittsburgh, Pa., U.S.) American writer best known for her meditative essays on the natural world.

Dillard attended Hollins College in Virginia. She was a scholar-in-residence at Western Washington University in Bellingham from 1975 to 1978 and on the faculty of Wesleyan University in Middletown, Conn., from 1979 to 1981.

Dillard's first published book was a collection of poetry, *Tickets for a Prayer Wheel* (1974). It was as an essayist, however, that she earned critical as well as popular acclaim. In her Pulitzer Prize-winning collection *Pilgrim at Tinker Creek* (1974), she distilled from keen observations of her own habitat the essential enigmas of religious mysticism. Critics hailed the work as an American original in the spirit of Henry David Thoreau's *Walden. Holy the Firm* (1977) and *Teaching a Stone to Talk* (1982) explored similar themes. *Living by Fiction* (1982), *Encounters with Chinese Writers* (1984), and *The Writing Life* (1989) present her views of literary craftsmanship and the writer's role in society. She published an autobiographical narrative, *An American Childhood*, in 1987. When her first novel, *The Living*, appeared in 1992, reviewers found in its depictions of the logging culture of the turn-of-the-century Pacific Northwest the same visionary realism that distinguished the author's nonfiction.

Di Prima, Diane (b. Aug. 6, 1934, New York, N.Y., U.S.) American poet, one of the few women of the Beat movement to attain prominence.

After attending Swarthmore College, Di Prima lived in New York City's Greenwich Village, leading the bohemian lifestyle that typified the Beat movement. Her first book of poetry, *This Kind of Bird Flies Backward*, was published in 1958. In 1961 Di Prima and LeRoi Jones (now Amiri Baraka) began a monthly poetry journal, *Floating Bear*, that featured their own poetry and that of other notable Beat writers such as Jack Kerouac and William Burroughs. Di Prima also founded two publishing houses that specialized in works by avant-garde poets—The Poets Press and Eidolon Editions. From 1974 she was an instructor at the Naropa Institute in Boulder, Colo.

Although Di Prima's career reflected the political and social upheaval of the United States during the decades of the 1960s and '70s, her writing was of a more personal nature; poems about her relationships, her children, and the experiences of everyday life figured prominently. Much of Di Prima's later writing reflected her interests in Eastern religions, alchemy, and female archetypes. Her later collections of poetry include *The New Handbook of Heaven* (1963), *Poems for Freddie* (1966); later published as *Freddie Poems*), *Earthsong: Poems 1957–59* (1968), *The Book of Hours* (1970), *Loba, Parts 1–8* (1978), and *Pieces of a Song* (1990). She also wrote a book of short stories published as *Dinners and Nightmares* (1961); rev. ed., 1974), an autobiographical book entitled *Memoirs of a Beatnik* (1969), and a number of plays, collected in *ZipCode* (1992).

Dixon, Thomas (b. Jan. 11, 1864, Shelby, N.C., U.S.—d. April 3, 1946, Raleigh, N.C.) American novelist, dramatist, and legislator who vigorously propagated ideas of white supremacy. He is chiefly remembered for his novel *The Clansman* (1905), which presented a sympathetic picture of the Ku Klux Klan. Dixon's friend, D.W. Griffith, used the novel as the basis for the epic film *The Birth of a Nation* (1915).

Dixon was admitted to the bar in 1886. He spent a year as a member of the North Carolina legislature but resigned to become a Baptist minister, serving in Raleigh, N.C., Boston, and New York City (1889–99). His first novel was *The Leopard's Spots* (1902); with *The Clansman* and *The Traitor* (1907), it forms a trilogy about the South during Reconstruction. He wrote other novels and some plays, and as late as 1939 he wrote yet another fictional account of black-white relations in the United States, *The Flaming Sword*. He also wrote nonfiction.

Dobyns, Stephen (b. Feb. 19, 1941, Orange, N.J., U.S.) American poet and novelist whose works are characterized by a cool realism laced with pungent wit.

Dobyns attended Shimer College in Mount Carroll, Ill., and graduated from Wayne State University and the University of Iowa. He taught English for a year before becoming a reporter for the *Detroit News* in 1969. From 1973, while writing fiction and poetry, he served as visiting lecturer and teacher at several American colleges and universities.

Dobyns' first collection of poetry, *Concurring Beasts*, appeared in 1971. The following year he published the novel *A Man of Little Evils*, and from that point on he alternated between poetry and crime fiction, publishing roughly a book a year. Subsequent poetry volumes included *Griffon* (1976), *Heat Death* (1980), *Black Dog, Red Dog* (1984), *Cemetery Nights* (1987), and *Velocities: New and Selected Poems, 1966–1992* (1994). Among his other novels are *Saratoga Longshot* (1976), *Dancer with One Leg* (1983), *Cold Dog Soup* (1985), *The Two Deaths of Señora Puccini* (1988), *After Shocks—Near Escapes* (1991), and *The Wrestler's Cruel Study* (1993).

Doctorow, E.L., *in full* Edgar Laurence (b. Jan. 6, 1931, New York, N.Y., U.S.) American novelist known for his skillful manipulation of traditional genres.

Doctorow graduated from Kenyon College and later attended Columbia University. In 1959 he joined the editorial staff of New American Library, leaving that post five years later to become editor in chief at Dial Press. He subsequently taught at several colleges and universities, including Sarah Lawrence College and New York University.

Doctorow's first novel, *Welcome to Hard Times* (1960), was a philosophical turn on the western genre. In his next book, *Big As Life* (1966), he used science fiction to explore the human response to crisis. *The Book of Daniel* (1971) is a fictionalized treatment of the execution of Julius and Ethel Rosenberg for espionage in 1953. In *Ragtime* (1975; film, 1981), his most commercially successful work, actual figures of early 20th-century America share the spotlight with emblematic Anglo, Jewish, and African-American characters. The later novels *Loon Lake* (1980), *World's Fair* (1985), and *Billy Bathgate* (1989; film, 1991) examine the milieu of the Great Depression and its aftermath, and *The Waterworks* (1994) concerns life in 19th-century New York. Doctorow also wrote a play and published *Lives of the Poets* (1984), a collection of short fiction.

Dodge, Mary Mapes, *original name* Mary Elizabeth Mapes (b. Jan. 26, 1831, New York, N.Y., U.S.—d. Aug. 21, 1905, Onteora Park, N.Y.) American author of children's books and first editor of *St. Nicholas* magazine.

At the age of 20 Mary Mapes married William Dodge, a lawyer, and they had two sons. To maintain her independence after she was suddenly widowed seven years later, she started writing children's stories. Her first collection, *Irvington Stories* (1864), centered on the American colonial family. The following year Dodge's beloved classic, HANS BRINKER, appeared.

In 1873, in the midst of an economic depression, Dodge was asked to become editor of a new publishing venture, the children's magazine *St. Nicholas*. Its subsequent success stemmed from Dodge's high literary and moral standards. Dodge's editorial excellence enabled *St. Nicholas* to attract such well-known contemporary writers as Mark Twain, Bret Harte, Lucretia

Peabody Hale, Louisa May Alcott, Robert Louis Stevenson, and Rudyard Kipling.

Dodson, Owen (Vincent) (b. Nov. 28, 1914, Brooklyn, N.Y., U.S.—d. June 21, 1983, New York, N.Y.) African-American poet, teacher, director, and playwright, and a leading figure in black theater.

The son of a journalist, Dodson began writing poetry and directing plays while attending Bates College and Yale University. As an enlistee in the U.S. Navy during World War II he wrote naval history plays for black seamen; the verse chorale *The Ballad of Dorie Miller* (1943), about an African-American Navy hero; and the poem "Black Mother Praying in the Summer of 1943," a plea for racial integration. Dodson's black history pageant *New World A-Coming* was performed at New York's Madison Square Garden in 1944. His first poetry collection, *Powerful Long Ladder*, appeared in 1946 and was widely praised. The next year he began teaching at Howard University, where he remained for 23 years. Dodson wrote the novels *Boy at the Window* (1951) and *Come Home Early, Child* (1977), and more than 35 plays and opera librettos; his verse dramas *Divine Comedy* (produced 1938) and *Bayou Legend* (produced 1948) are especially notable. Dodson himself considered *The Confession Stone* (1970), a song cycle written in the voice of Mary about the life of Jesus, which is often performed as an Easter play, to be his masterpiece.

Donleavy, J.P., *in full* James Patrick (b. April 23, 1926, Brooklyn, N.Y., U.S.) American-born author of the lusty comic novel *The Ginger Man* (Paris, 1955; U.S., 1958), which introduced Dangerfield, the coarse, comic antihero. Donleavy is noted for characters who display heroism in the face of a mad universe and remain deeply attached to life despite its flaws.

Donleavy served with the U.S. Navy during World War II, studied microbiology at Trinity College, Dublin, and became an Irish citizen in 1967. *A Singular Man* (1963), *The Saddest Summer of Samuel S.* (1966), *The Beastly Beatitudes of Balthasar B* (1968), and later works continued to develop the prose style of *The Ginger Man*, which is distinguished by alliteration and an original treatment of voice. Action occurs in the third person while thoughts are conveyed in the first, allowing the character to speak both as observer and observed. Later works include *The Onion Eaters* (1971), *A Fairy Tale of New York* (1973), *The Destinies of Darcy Dancer, Gentleman* (1977), *Schultz* (1979), *Leila: Further in the Destinies of Darcy Dancer* (1983), and *Are You Listening Rabbi Löw* (1987).

Donnelly, Ignatius (b. Nov. 3, 1831, Philadelphia, Pa., U.S.—d. Jan. 1, 1901, Minneapolis, Minn.) American novelist, orator, and social reformer; one of the leading advocates of the theory that Francis Bacon was the author of William Shakespeare's plays.

Donnelly grew up in Philadelphia, where he became a lawyer. In 1856 he moved to Minnesota, where, with another ex-Philadelphian, John Nininger, he founded Nininger City, intended as both a cultural and an industrial center. There he edited the erudite *Emigrant Aid Journal*, published in both English and German, to attract settlers. The scheme was briefly successful, but a panic in 1857 caused abandonment of the town, leaving Donnelly as its only resident.

He entered politics and served as lieutenant governor of Minnesota and as a U.S. congressman from 1863 to 1869. His first and most popular book was *Atlantis* (1882), which traced the origin of civilization to the legendary submerged continent of Atlantis. It was followed in 1883 by another work of speculation, *Ragnarok: The Age of Fire and Gravel*, which attempted to relate certain gravel and till deposits to an ancient near-collision of the Earth and a huge comet. In *The Great Cryptogram* (1888) and *The Cipher in the Plays and on the Tombstone* (1899), he attempted to prove that Bacon was the author of the plays attributed to Shakespeare by deciphering a code he discovered in Shakespeare's works. He also ascribed the plays of Christopher Marlowe and the essays of Michel de Montaigne to Bacon. Donnelly's utopian novel *Caesar's Column* (1891), which predicted such developments as radio, television, and poison gas, portrays the United States in 1988 as ruled by a ruthless financial oligarchy and peopled by an abject working class.

Doolittle, Hilda, *byname* H.D. (b. Sept. 10, 1886, Bethlehem, Pa., U.S.— d. Sept. 27, 1961, Zürich, Switz.) American modernist poet, known initially as an Imagist, whose poetry reflected classicism and classical themes. She was also a translator, novelist, playwright, and self-proclaimed "pagan mystic."

Doolittle went to Europe in 1911, and she remained abroad, except for brief visits, for the remainder of her life. William Carlos Williams was an early acquaintance, and, while at Bryn Mawr in 1905–06, she met and, for a brief time, became engaged to Ezra Pound. She was married to Richard Aldington from 1913 to 1938. Her friends included D.H. Lawrence, Marianne Moore, T.S. Eliot, Amy Lowell, the Sitwells, and the poet and novelist Bryher (Annie Winifred Ellerman), with whom she had a lifelong association.

H.D.'s first book of poetry, *Sea Garden* (1916), was followed by *Hymen* (1921), *Heliodora and Other Poems* (1924), *Red Roses for Bronze* (1929), and *Trilogy* (1944–46). She was one of the first Imagists, and she wrote clear, impersonal, and sensuous verse. Her later work was somewhat looser and more passionate, though it remained erudite and symbolic. The *Collected*

Poems of H.D. (1925 and 1940), *Selected Poems of H.D.* (1957), and *Collected Poems 1912–1944* (1983) secured her position as a major 20th-century poet. She won additional acclaim for her translations (*Choruses from the Iphigeneia in Aulis and the Hippolytus of Euripides* [1919] and *Euripides' Ion* [1937]), for her verse drama (*Hippolytus Temporizes* [1927]), and for such prose works as *Palimpsest* (1926), *Hedylus* (1928), and *The Gift* (1982). Several of her books were autobiographical—including *Tribute to Freud* (1956), *Bid Me to Live* (1960), and *End to Torment* (1979).

Dos Passos, John (Roderigo) (b. Jan. 14, 1896, Chicago, Ill., U.S.—d. Sept. 28, 1970, Baltimore, Md.) American writer, one of the major novelists of the post-World War I "lost generation," whose reputation as a social historian and as a radical critic of the quality of American life rests primarily on his trilogy U.S.A.

John Dos Passos

The son of a wealthy lawyer, Dos Passos graduated from Harvard University (1916) and was an ambulance driver in World War I. His early works were basically portraits of the artist recoiling from the shock of his encounter with a brutal world. Extensive travel as a newspaper correspondent in the postwar years enlarged his sense of history, sharpened his social perception, and confirmed his radical sympathies. His writing began to develop a larger and tougher objective realism.

The execution of Nicola Sacco and Bartolomeo Vanzetti in 1927 crystallized for Dos Passos an image of the United States as "two nations"—one of the rich and privileged and one of the poor and powerless. *U.S.A.* is the portrait of these two nations.

U.S.A. was followed by a less ambitious trilogy, *District of Columbia*, which chronicles Dos Passos' disillusion with the labor movement, radical politics, and New Deal liberalism.

Douglass, Frederick, *original name* Frederick Augustus Washington Bailey (b. Feb. 7, 1817, Tuckahoe, Md., U.S.—d. Feb. 20, 1895, Washington, D.C.) African-American who started life as a slave but was thrust by his oratorical and literary brilliance into the forefront of the U.S. abolition movement.

The son of a slave mother (from whom he was early separated) and a white father he never knew, Frederick lived with his grandmother on a Maryland plantation until the age of eight. He worked as a house servant and later as a field hand, and along the way he learned to read and write. In 1838 he managed to flee to New York City and then to New Bedford, Mass., where he worked as a laborer for three years, eluding slave hunters by changing his name to Douglass.

At an antislavery convention in 1841, Douglass was asked to speak extemporaneously about his own experiences; his remarks were so poignant and

Frederick Douglass

naturally eloquent that he was catapulted into a new career as agent for the Massachusetts Anti-Slavery Society. To counter skeptics who doubted that he could ever have been a slave, Douglass wrote his autobiography in 1845, revised and completed in 1882 as *Life and Times of Frederick Douglass*. Douglass' account became a classic of American literature as well as a primary source about slavery from the bondsman's viewpoint. After a two-year speaking tour of Great Britain and Ireland, Douglass returned with funds to purchase his freedom and also to start his own antislavery newspaper, the *North Star* (later *Frederick Douglass's Paper*), which he published from 1847 to 1860 in Rochester, N.Y.

During the American Civil War, Douglass was a consultant to President Abraham Lincoln. Throughout Reconstruction (1865–77), he fought for full civil rights for freedmen and vigorously supported the women's rights movement. After Reconstruction, Douglass held several government positions, including minister and consul general to Haiti from 1889 to 1891.

Dove, Rita (Frances) (b. Aug. 28, 1952, Akron, Ohio) African-American writer and teacher who was named poet laureate of the United States in 1993.

Dove graduated from Miami University in Ohio and studied subsequently at Tübingen University in Germany. She studied creative writing at the University of Iowa and published the first of several chapbooks of her poetry in 1977. From 1981 to 1989 Dove taught at Arizona State University, leaving that post to teach at the University of Virginia. She was writer-in-residence at Tuskegee (Ala.) Institute in 1982.

In her poetry collections, including *The Yellow House on the Corner* (1980) and *Museum* (1983), as well as a volume of short stories entitled *Fifth Sunday* (1985), Dove focused her attention on the particulars of family life and personal struggle, addressing the larger social and political dimensions of black experience primarily by indirection. The Pulitzer Prize-winning *Thomas and Beulah* (1986) is a cycle of poems chronicling the lives of the author's maternal grandparents, born in the Deep South at the turn of the century. Subsequent works include the poetry collections *The Other Side of the House* (1988) and *Grace Notes* (1989) and the novel *Through the Ivory Gate* (1992).

Drake, Joseph Rodman (b. Aug. 7, 1795, New York, N.Y., U.S.—d. Sept. 21, 1820, New York City) Romantic poet who contributed to the beginnings of an American national literature by a few memorable lyrics before his early death.

Drake graduated from medical school in New York in 1816, after which he married an heiress, honeymooned in Europe, and returned to New York to open a pharmacy. While a student, he had become friends with another poet,

Fitz-Greene Halleck, with whom he began collaborating in 1819 on topical satirical verses; the result was the "Croaker Papers," published under a pseudonym in the New York *Evening Post*. These lampoons of public personages appeared in book form in 1860.

Drake died of tuberculosis in 1820. Although he had asked his wife to destroy his unpublished poems after his death, she kept them, and his daughter saw to the publication of 19 of his verses in 1835 as *The Culprit Fay and Other Poems*. The title poem, considered his best, deals with the theme of the fairy lover in a Hudson River setting. The volume also contains two fine nature poems, "Niagara" and "Bronx." These and other poems appeared in his *Life and Works* (1935), edited by F.L. Pleadwell.

Dreiser, Theodore (b. Aug. 27, 1871, Terre Haute, Ind., U.S.—d. Dec. 28, 1945, Hollywood, Calif.) Novelist who was the outstanding American practitioner of naturalism. He led a national literary movement that replaced a Victorian sense of propriety with the unflinching presentation of real-life subject matter.

Theodore Dreiser

Dreiser was born into poverty, and harsh experiences would become dominant themes in his novels. He spent a year at Indiana University before becoming a newspaper reporter. During this period he came to believe that humans are helpless in the grip of instincts and social forces beyond their control.

SISTER CARRIE (1900), Dreiser's first novel concerned the life of a young kept woman whose behavior goes unpunished; the book sold fewer than 500 copies. Within the next nine years Dreiser achieved notable financial success as an editor in chief of several women's magazines. He was forced to resign in 1910, however, because of an office imbroglio involving an assistant's daughter.

In 1911 Dreiser's second novel, JENNIE GERHARDT, was published, followed by the first two volumes of a projected trilogy of novels, based on the life of the American transportation magnate Charles T. Yerkes, THE FINANCIER (1912) and *The Titan* (1914). In his next major novel, *The 'Genius'* (1915), he transformed his own life and numerous love affairs into a sprawling semiautobiographical chronicle that was censured by the New York Society for the Suppression of Vice. Other published works include a short-story collection, *Free and Other Stories* (1918); a book of sketches, *Twelve Men* (1919); philosophical essays, *Hey-Rub-a-Dub-Dub* (1920); a rhapsodic description of New York, *The Color of A Great City* (1923); works of drama, including *Plays of the Natural and Supernatural* (1916) and *The Hand of the Potter* (1918); and the autobiographical works *A Hoosier Holiday* (1916) and *A Book About Myself* (1922).

In 1925 Dreiser published his first novel in a decade, AN AMERICAN TRAGEDY, based on a celebrated murder case. The book brought Dreiser a degree of critical and commercial success he had never before attained and would not thereafter equal. The book's highly critical view of the American legal system made him the adopted champion of social reformers. In the 1930s he published the autobiographical *Dawn* (1931), one of the most candid self-revelations by any major writer. He completed most of *The Stoic*, the long-postponed third volume of his trilogy, in the weeks before his death.

Dr. Seuss. Pseudonym of Theodor Seuss GEISEL.

Drummond, William Henry (b. April 13, 1854, Mohill, County Leitrim, Ire.—d. April 6, 1907, Cobalt, Ont., Can.) Writer of humorous dialect poems conveying a sympathetic but sentimentalized picture of "habitants," or French-Canadian farmers.

Drummond emigrated with his parents to Canada about 1864. He left school at age 15 to help support his family, but at age 30 took a degree in medicine at Bishop's College in Quebec. After four years in country practice he moved to Montreal, where he gave well-received public readings of his poems. His first collection, *The Habitant* (1897), was followed by several others, all of which were published together as *The Poetical Works of William Henry Drummond* (1912).

W.E.B. Du Bois

Du Bois, W.E.B., *in full* William Edward Burghardt (b. Feb. 23, 1868, Great Barrington, Mass., U.S.—d. Aug. 27, 1963, Accra, Ghana) American sociologist, the most important black protest leader in the United States during the first half of the 20th century. He helped create the National Association for the Advancement of Colored People (NAACP) in 1909 and edited *The Crisis*, its magazine, from 1910 to 1934.

Du Bois graduated from Fisk University, Nashville, Tenn., and received a doctorate from Harvard University. For more than a decade he devoted himself to sociological investigations of the condition of blacks in America, producing 16 research monographs published between 1897 and 1914 at Atlanta University, where he was a professor, as well as *The Philadelphia Negro; A Social Study* (1899), the first case study of a black community in the United States.

Du Bois's black nationalism took several forms, including a belief in the importance of cultural nationalism. As the editor of *The Crisis* he encouraged the development of black literature and art and urged his readers to see "Beauty in Black."

He resigned from the editorship and from the NAACP in 1934 because of ideological differences within the organization and returned to Atlanta University to teach and write. In 1940 he founded the magazine *Phylon*, the university's "Review of Race and Culture." During this period he also produced two major books: *Black Reconstruction* (1935), a Marxist interpretation of the post-Civil War era, and *Dusk at Dawn* (1940), in which he viewed his career as an ideological case study illuminating the complexity of black-white conflict.

From 1944 to 1948 Du Bois returned to the NAACP, but following a second bitter quarrel he severed his connection and thereafter moved steadily leftward politically. In 1961 he joined the Communist Party and, moving to Ghana, renounced his American citizenship more than a year later. *The Autobiography of W.E.B. Du Bois* was published in 1968.

du Bois, William Pène (Sherman) (b. May 9, 1916, Nutley, N.J., U.S.— d. Feb. 5, 1993, Nice, Fr.) American author and illustrator of children's books noted for his comic coterie of peculiar characters. In 1948 he was awarded the Newbery Medal for *The Twenty-One Balloons* (1947).

Born into a family of artists, du Bois studied art in France and published books for children from the mid-1930s. He served in World War II as a correspondent for *Yank* and other magazines and became the first art director of *The Paris Review* in 1953. *The Twenty-One Balloons* is about a retired math teacher who refuses to tell anyone but the Western American Explorer's Club about his fantastic journey by hot-air balloon to the volcano of Krakatoa.

In his uncompleted series about the seven deadly sins, du Bois profiled sloth in *Lazy Tommy Pumpkinhead* (1966), pride in *Pretty Pretty Peggy Moffitt* (1968), gluttony in *Porko von Popbutton* (1969), and avarice in *Call Me Bandicoot* (1970). *The Alligator Case* (1965) and *The Horse in the Camel Suit* (1967) parody the detective novels of Raymond Chandler. Several of du Bois's books feature bears, such as *Bear Party* (1951), *Bear Circus* (1971), and the semiautobiographical *Gentleman Bear* (1983). His other works included *The Flying Locomotive* (1941), *Peter Graves* (1950), *Lion* (1956), and *The Forbidden Forest* (1978). He also illustrated editions of books by such notable authors as Edward Lear, Jules Verne, Arthur Conan Doyle, Isaac Bashevis Singer, Roald Dahl, and Mark Strand.

Dubus, Andre (b. Aug. 11, 1936, Lake Charles, La., U.S.) American short-story writer and novelist who was noted as a chronicler of the struggles of contemporary American men whose lives seem inexplicably to have gone wrong.

After graduating from McNeese State College (now University), Lake Charles, La. Dubus served six years in the Marine Corps and then took an M.F.A. degree from the University of Iowa. He taught literature and creative writing at Bradford (Mass.) College from 1966 to 1984. Dubus wrote of the emotional complexities of ordinary people in ordinary settings, who find that the traditional American virtues they assumed would lead to happiness do not do so. Most of his characters suffer compulsions or addictions focused on cigarettes, alcohol, food, coffee, drugs, or even weight lifting. When these fail to provide enough distraction, the male characters often turn to violence.

Dubus' first collection of stories, *Separate Flights* (1975), was praised for its craft, strong sympathy with its characters, and detailed evocation of setting, as was *Adultery and Other Choices* (1977). "Andromache," from the latter collection, was cited as the best of his many stories about the Marine Corps. "The Fat Girl" and "Graduation" (from *Adultery and Other Choices*) and the 1984 novella *Voices from the Moon* are cited as his best attempts to develop the point of view of his female characters. He also wrote *The Times Are Never So Bad* (1983) and *We Don't Live Here Anymore* (1984).

Dudek, Louis (b. Feb. 6, 1918, Montreal, Que., Can.) Canadian poet noted for his support of Canadian small-press publishing and the development of the nonnarrative long poem.

Educated at McGill University (where he later taught) and Columbia University, Dudek was an editor and critic. His poetic output included *East of the City* (1946), *The Transparent Sea* (1956), love poems, and *Laughing Stalks* (1958), a social satire that includes parodies of certain Canadian poets and critics. His *Collected Poems* appeared in 1971. The influence of Ezra Pound is evident in *Europe* (1954), a travelogue poem in 99 cantos inspired by observations of several countries on the European continent, and in other works. Another collection, *Cross-Section* (1980), contains poems written between 1940 and 1980. Dudek's prose works include *The Theory of the Image in Modern Poetry* (1981), *Ideas for Poetry* (1983), and *In Defence of Art* (1988); a collection of critical essays and reviews). Later collections of poetry include *Zembla's Rocks* (1986) and *Small Perfect Things* (1991).

Dudek also cofounded Contact Press, Delta Canada, and D.C. Books (all small presses), *Delta* literary magazine, and the McGill Poetry Series.

Dugan, Alan (b. Feb. 12, 1923, New York, N.Y., U.S.) American poet who wrote with bemused sarcasm about mundane topics, infusing them with an ironic depth. A fully developed style was evident in his first verse collection, *Poems* (1961), which in 1962 won a National Book Award and a Pulitzer Prize.

Dugan served in World War II and attended Queens College in New York and Olivet College in Michigan before graduating from Mexico City College. Propelled by the success of *Poems,* he accepted grants to travel and to continue publishing. He taught at Sarah Lawrence College in Bronxville,

N.Y., from 1967 until 1971, when he joined the faculty at the Fine Arts Work Center in Provincetown, Mass. Among his later books were *Poems 2* (1963), *Poems 3* (1967), *Poems 4* (1974), *Sequence* (1976), and *Poems Six* (1989).

Dugan examined the triviality of war, the bleakness of ordinary life, the ignorance of humanity, and the nature of beauty and love. As a result of his terse cadences, ironic detachment, and colloquial style, his works have an understated humor. His poetry was compiled in *Collected Poems* (1969), *New and Collected Poems 1961–1983* (1983), and *Ten Years of Poems* (1987).

Dumas, Henry (b. July 20, 1934, Sweet Home, Ark., U.S.—d. May 23, 1968, New York, N.Y.) African-American author of poetry and fiction who wrote about the clash between black and white cultures.

Dumas grew up in Arkansas and in New York City's Harlem. While in the U.S. Air Force (1953–57) he won creative-writing awards for his contributions to Air Force periodicals. Religion (especially Christianity), African-American folklore and music, and the civil-rights movement, in which he was active, were important influences on his writing.

The vulnerability of black children amid the Southern white lynch-mob mentality, a young sharecropper encountering a civil-rights worker, and whites experiencing the mystical force of black music are among the subjects Dumas examined in his short stories, many of which were collected in *Ark of Bones* (1970) and *Rope of Wind* (1979). Nature, revolutionary politics, and music are especially frequent subjects of his poetry, which is noted for its faithfulness to the language and cadence of black American speech. *Poetry for My People* (1970); republished as *Play Ebony, Play Ivory*, 1974) is a collection of blues-influenced verse. Dumas, who was murdered, left an unfinished novel, *Jonoah and the Green Stone*, which was published in 1976.

Dunbar Nelson, Alice, *original name in full* Alice Ruth Moore (b. July 19, 1875, New Orleans, La., U.S.—d. Sept. 18, 1935, Philadelphia, Pa.) Novelist, poet, essayist, and critic associated with the early period of the Harlem Renaissance of the 1920s and '30s.

The daughter of a Creole seaman and a black seamstress, Moore completed a two-year teacher-training program at Straight University by age 17. She further studied at Cornell University, the Pennsylvania School of Industrial Art, and the University of Pennsylvania. She taught at the elementary, secondary, and college levels until 1931.

Her first collection of stories, poems, and essays, *Violets, and Other Tales*, was published in 1895. She later moved to New York, where she taught and helped establish the White Rose Mission in Harlem. In 1898 she married the writer Paul Laurence Dunbar.

Her short-story collection *The Goodness of St. Rocque, and Other Stories* was published as a companion piece to her husband's *Poems of Cabin and Field* in 1899. She moved to Delaware after she and Dunbar separated in 1902; he died four years later. She married a fellow teacher in 1910 and divorced him the following year; in 1916 she married the journalist Robert J. Nelson.

While not considered a major figure in the Harlem Renaissance for her own literary contributions, Dunbar Nelson influenced the work of other black writers not only by her own precise, incisive literary style but also through her numerous reviews of such writers as Langston Hughes.

Dunbar, Paul Laurence (b. June 27, 1872, Dayton, Ohio, U.S.—d. Feb. 9, 1906, Dayton) American author whose reputation rests upon his verse and short stories written in black dialect. He was the first black writer in the United States to attempt to support himself by writing and one of the first to attain national prominence.

Both of Dunbar's parents were former slaves; his father escaped to Canada and then returned to the U.S. to fight in the Civil War. Dunbar published his first volume of poetry, *Oak and Ivy* (1893), at his own expense while working as an elevator operator and sold copies to his passengers to pay for the printing. His second volume, *Majors and Minors* (1895), attracted the favorable notice of the novelist and critic William Dean Howells, who also introduced Dunbar's next book, *Lyrics of Lowly Life* (1896), which contained some of the finest verses of the first two volumes.

Dunbar's poems gained a large popular audience, and he read to audiences in the United States and England. He was given a job in the reading room of the Library of Congress in Washington, D.C. (1897–98). In all, he published four collections of short stories and four novels before his early death.

Writing for a largely white readership, Dunbar depicted the pre-Civil War South in pastoral, idyllic tones. Only in a few of his later stories did a suggestion of racial disquiet appear. His first three novels—including *The Uncalled* (1898), which reflected his own spiritual problems—were about white characters. His last novel, sometimes considered his best, was *The Sport of the Gods* (1902), concerning an uprooted black family in the urban North.

Duncan, Robert Edward, *original name* Edward Howard Duncan, *adopted name* Robert Edward Symmes (b. Jan. 7, 1919, Oakland, Calif., U.S.— d. Feb. 3, 1988, San Francisco, Calif.) American poet, a leader of the Black Mountain group of poets in the 1950s.

Duncan attended the University of California at Berkeley in 1936–38 and 1948–50. He edited the *Experimental Review* from 1938 to 1940 and traveled widely thereafter, lecturing on poetry in the United States and Canada throughout the 1950s. He taught at Black Mountain College in North Carolina in 1956. He was a longtime resident of San Francisco and was active in that city's poetry community.

Duncan's poetry is evocative and highly musical and uses a rich fabric of associations and mythic images whose meanings are sometimes obscure. His thematic concerns include strong social and political statements. His collections include *The Years as Catches: First Poems, 1939–1946* (1966) and *Derivations: Selected Poems, 1950–56* (1968). *The Opening of the Field* (1960), *Roots and Branches* (1964), *Bending the Bow* (1968), and *Ground Work* (1984) contain his finest poems. He also wrote plays, including *Medea at Kolchis* (1965).

Dunne, Finley Peter (b. July 10, 1867, Chicago, Ill., U.S.—d. April 24, 1936, New York, N.Y.) American journalist and humorist who created the homely philosopher Mr. Dooley.

Dunne was born of Irish immigrant parents. In 1884 he began working for various Chicago newspapers, specializing eventually in political reporting and editorial writing. In 1892 he began contributing Irish-dialect sketches to the *Chicago Evening Post* and five years later to the *Chicago Journal*. In these Dunne introduced Martin Dooley, a saloonkeeper who commented in a rich Irish brogue on politics and society. Dunne's witty penetration of shams and hypocrisies made Mr. Dooley a force for clear thinking and tolerance in public affairs. Many of Mr. Dooley's remarks, such as "Thrust ivrybody, but cut th' ca-ards," became part of American lore. Dunne wrote more than 700 dialect essays, some of which were republished in eight volumes from 1898 to 1919.

Dunne, John Gregory (b. May 25, 1932, Hartford, Conn., U.S.) American writer who was noted for his works of social satire, personal analysis, and Irish-American life.

After graduating from Princeton University, Dunne briefly served in the military and became a staff writer for *Time* magazine in New York City. He married novelist Joan Didion in 1964 and moved to California, where he wrote screenplays and contributed to numerous magazines—including a joint column with his wife in the *Saturday Evening Post* (1967–69).

Dunne's first book, *Delano: The Story of the California Grape Strike* (1967); rev. ed., 1971), examines the labor and social issues surrounding the grape-pickers' strike of the mid-1960s. *The Studio* (1969) is a telling portrait of the motion-picture industry. *Vegas: A Memoir of a Dark Season* (1974) describes the narrator's nervous breakdown in a story about three colorful inhabitants of Las Vegas. Dunne examined Irish-American communities in a gritty trilogy of novels: *True Confessions* (1977), *Dutch Shea, Jr.* (1982), and

The Red White and Blue (1987). His other works include the autobiographical *Harp* (1988) and two collections of essays, *Quintana & Friends* (1978) and *Crooning* (1990).

Dwight, Timothy (b. May 14, 1752, Northampton, Mass., U.S.—d. Jan. 11, 1817, New Haven, Conn.) American educator, theologian, and poet who had a strong influence on education in his time.

Educated by his mother, a daughter of the preacher Jonathan Edwards, Dwight entered Yale at age 13 and graduated in 1769. He then pursued a variety of occupations—he was a tutor at Yale, a school principal, a Massachusetts legislator, and a chaplain with the Continental Army. In 1783 he began a successful school in Greenfield Hill, Conn., where he became pastor of the Congregational Church and began to write poetry. His works include *Greenfield Hill* (1794), a popular history of and tribute to the village, and epics such as *The Conquest of Canaan* (1785), a biblical allegory of the taking of Connecticut from the British, which some critics regard as the first American epic poem. Dwight's political satire marks him as a Hartford wit. He served as president of Yale from 1795 to 1817.

Eastman, Max (Forrester) (b. Jan. 12, 1883, Canandaigua, N.Y., U.S.—d. March 25, 1969, Bridgetown, Barbados) American poet, editor, and prominent radical before and after World War I.

Eastman was educated at Williams College, Williamstown, Mass. He taught at Columbia University for four years, and he was the founder of the first men's league for woman suffrage in 1910. Eastman edited and published *The Masses*, a radical political and literary periodical. Its editors were brought to trial twice in 1918 because of their editorial opposition to the entry of the United States into World War I, but both trials ended with hung juries. He then edited and published *The Liberator*, a similar magazine, until 1922, when he traveled to Russia to study the Soviet regime. He married Eliena Krylenko, a sister of the Soviet minister of justice, but returned to the United States believing that the original purpose of the October Revolution (1917) had been subverted by corrupt leaders. In the 1920s and '30s he wrote several books attacking developments in the Soviet Union: *Since Lenin Died* (1925), *The End of Socialism in Russia* (1937), and *Stalin's Russia and the Crisis in Socialism* (1939).

From 1941 he was a roving editor for *Reader's Digest*. His many other books include *Enjoyment of Poetry* (23 eds., 1913–48), *Enjoyment of Laughter* (1936), and two autobiographical works, *Enjoyment of Living* (1948) and *Love and Revolution: My Journey Through an Epoch* (1965).

Eberhart, Richard (b. April 5, 1904, Austin, Minn., U.S.) American poet and teacher, a founder of the Poet's Theatre, Cambridge, Mass. (1951).

Educated at Dartmouth College, Cambridge, and Harvard, Eberhart published his first book of poems, *A Bravery of Earth*, in 1930. In the 1930s he also became tutor to the son of King Prajadhipok of Siam (now Thailand) and afterward taught at several U.S. colleges, particularly at Dartmouth (1956–70). He was consultant in poetry at the Library of Congress (1959–61). In 1962 he was cowinner, with John Hall Wheelock, of the Bollingen Prize in Poetry. His *Collected Poems, 1930–1986* was published in 1988 and *Maine Poems* followed in 1989.

Edel, Leon, *in full* Joseph Leon Edel (b. Sept. 9, 1907, Pittsburgh, Pa., U.S.) American literary critic and biographer, notably of Henry James.

Edel grew up in Saskatchewan, Can., and graduated from McGill University. He received a doctorate of letters from the University of Paris. During the 1930s he held a variety of jobs and then served in the U.S. Army from 1943 to 1947. He taught English at New York University and at the University of Hawaii.

Edel edited James's *Complete Tales*, 12 vol. (1963–65), and wrote the definitive biography of James in five volumes (1953–72). He also edited

James's *Complete Plays* (1949) and James's letters, 4 vol. (1974–84). His other books include *Willa Cather: A Critical Biography* (1953), written with E.K. Brown; *The Psychological Novel, 1900–1950* (1955); rev. ed., *The Modern Psychological Novel*, 1964); and *Literary Biography* (1957). His psychological portrait of the Bloomsbury group, entitled *Bloomsbury: A House of Lions*, was published in 1979 and *Writing Lives* in 1984.

Jonathan Edwards

Edwards, Jonathan (b. Oct. 5, 1703, East Windsor, Conn. [U.S.]—d. March 22, 1758, Princeton, N.J.) Greatest theologian and philosopher of Puritanism and stimulator of the religious revival known as the "Great Awakening."

Edwards' father and grandfather were ministers. He graduated from Yale College in 1720 and received an M.A. degree in 1723. In 1727 he became his grandfather's colleague in the Congregational church at Northampton, Mass. At his grandfather's death in 1729, Edwards became sole occupant of the Northampton pulpit. In his first published sermon, entitled *God Glorified in the Work of Redemption, by the Greatness of Man's Dependence upon Him, in the Whole of It*, Edwards blamed New England's moral ills on its assumption of religious and moral self-sufficiency.

Against the prevailing heretical tendencies, Edwards delivered a series of sermons on "Justification by Faith Alone" in November 1734. The result was a great revival in the winter and spring of 1734–35. His subsequent report, *A Faithful Narrative of the Surprising Work of God* (1737), made a profound impression in America and Europe, particularly through his description of the types and stages of conversion experience.

In 1740–42 came the Great Awakening throughout the colonies. Dating from this period is the sermon "Sinners in the Hands of an Angry God" (1741), with its arresting image of the unredeemed, like loathsome insects, deserving to be flung into the fires of hell. In defense and criticism of the Awakening, which produced not only conversions but also excesses and disorders, Edwards wrote *The Distinguishing Marks of a Work of the Spirit of God* (1741), *Some Thoughts Concerning the Present Revival of Religion in New England* (1742), and *A Treatise Concerning Religious Affections* (1746).

Meanwhile, Edwards' relations with his own congregation had become strained because of his narrowing of the requirements for participation in the Eucharist, or Lord's Supper, and he was eventually dismissed. In the course of this controversy he wrote two books, *Qualifications for Communion* (1749) and *Misrepresentations Corrected, and Truth Vindicated, in a Reply to the Rev. Mr. Solomon Williams's Book* (1752).

In 1751 Edwards was sent into virtual exile as pastor of the frontier church at Stockbridge, Mass., and missionary to the Indians there. Hampered by many difficulties, he nevertheless discharged his pastoral duties and found time to write his famous work *Freedom of Will* (1754).

Late in 1757 Edwards accepted the presidency of the College of New Jersey (later Princeton University) and arrived there in January. He had hardly assumed his duties when he contracted smallpox from a primitive attempt at vaccination and died.

Eggleston, Edward (b. Dec. 10, 1837, Vevay, Ind., U.S.—d. Sept. 4, 1902, Lake George, N.Y.) Clergyman, novelist, and historian who realistically portrayed various regions of the United States in such books as THE HOOSIER SCHOOL-MASTER (1871).

By the age of 19, Eggleston had become an itinerant preacher (or "circuit rider"), but the taxing activity broke his health. He held various pastorates, serving from 1874 to 1879 in Brooklyn; he was an editor of the juvenile paper *Little Corporal* (1866–67), the *National Sunday School Teacher* (1867–73), and other periodicals.

In all of his work he sought to write with "photographic exactness" of the real West. The most popular of his books for adults was *The Hoosier School-Master*, a vivid study of backwoods Indiana. His other novels include *The End of the World* (1872), *The Mystery of Metropolisville* (1873), *Roxy* (1878), and *The Graysons* (1888). His later works are considered less significant. After a trip to Europe in 1879 he turned to the writing of history. His *Beginners of a Nation* (1896) and *Transit of Civilization from England to America* (1900) contributed to the growth of the study of social history.

Eliot T.S., *in full* Thomas Stearns (b. Sept. 26, 1888, St. Louis, Mo., U.S.—d. Jan. 4, 1965, London, Eng.) American-English poet, playwright, and literary critic, a leader of the modernist movement in poetry. In 1948 he was awarded the Nobel Prize for Literature.

T.S. Elliot

One of Eliot's ancestors arrived in Boston in 1670. Although by the time of the poet's birth the Eliots had been in Missouri 54 years, they retained their New England political and theological culture. Eliot graduated from Harvard after three years. He spent a year studying in France, and from 1911 to 1914 he was back at Harvard reading Indian philosophy and studying Sanskrit. In 1914 he met Ezra Pound and moved to England.

Eliot's first important publication, and the first masterpiece of modernism in English, was the poem THE LOVE SONG OF J. ALFRED PRUFROCK. From the appearance of Eliot's first volume, *Prufrock and Other Observations*, in 1917, one may date the maturity of the 20th-century poetic revolution. Together Pound and Eliot set about reforming poetic diction.

Eliot taught for a year before he began his brief career as a bank clerk in Lloyds Bank Ltd. in London. Meanwhile he was also a prolific reviewer and essayist. In 1919 he published *Poems*, which contained the unique "Geron-tion," a meditative interior monologue in blank verse.

With the publication in 1922 of THE WASTE LAND, his best-known poem, Eliot won an international reputation. The poem, in five parts, proceeds on a principle of "rhetorical discontinuity" that reflects the fragmented experi-ence of the 20th-century sensibility of the great modern cities of the West.

Eliot's work as a critic is probably best represented by his first critical volume, THE SACRED WOOD (1920). The essays discuss the poet and tradition and introduce two phrases that were much discussed in later critical theory—Objective Correlative (the use of an external object, event, or situation to evoke emotion in the reader) and Dissociation of Sensibility, a phrase he invented to explain the change that came over English poetry after John Donne and Andrew Marvell. Shortly before the publication of his *The Use of Poetry and the Use of Criticism* (1933)—his Charles Eliot Norton lectures at Harvard—his interests had broadened into theology and sociology. Three short books, or long essays, were the result: *Thoughts After Lambeth* (1931), *The Idea of a Christian Society* (1939), and NOTES TOWARDS THE DEFINITION OF CULTURE (1948). These book-essays, along with his *Dante* (1929), pro-posed the view that whether a work is poetry must be decided by literary standards; whether it is great poetry must be decided by standards higher than the literary.

Eliot's masterpiece is THE FOUR QUARTETS, taken as a single work, though each "quartet" is a complete poem. The four parts, published at intervals between 1936 and 1942, were issued as a book in 1943.

His plays, which begin with SWEENEY AGONISTES (1932) and include such poetic dramas as THE COCKTAIL PARTY (1950), are, with the exception of MURDER IN THE CATHEDRAL (1935), inferior to his lyric and meditative poetry. Eliot's career as editor was ancillary to his main interests, but his quarterly review, *The Criterion* (1922–39), was a distinguished international critical journal of the period. He was a "director," or working editor, of the publishing firm of Faber & Faber Ltd. from the early 1920s until his death.

Eliot always kept his private life rigorously in the background. In 1915 he married Vivian Haigh-Wood; after 1933 she was mentally ill, and they lived apart; she died in 1947. In January 1957 he married Valerie Fletcher, with whom he lived happily until his death.

Elkin, Stanley (Lawrence) (b. May 11, 1930, New York, N.Y., U.S.—d. May 31, 1995, St. Louis, Mo.) American writer known for his extraordinary flights of language and imaginative tragicomic explorations of contemporary life.

Elkin grew up in a Jewish family in Chicago. He was educated at the University of Illinois at Champaign-Urbana, completing a dissertation on

William Faulkner. From 1960 he taught at Washington University in St. Louis.

Elkin's first novel, *Boswell, A Modern Comedy* (1964), tells of an ordinary man who founds a club for famous individuals, hoping like his namesake to bask in reflected glory. *Criers and Kibitzers, Kibitzers and Criers* (1966), a collection of comic short stories on Jewish themes and characters, was well received. Elkin further develops the rift between family ties and the lure of assimilation in *A Bad Man* (1967).

The Franchiser (1976), considered one of Elkin's strongest works, tells of Ben Flesh, an orphaned bachelor adopted as an adult into the absurd Finsberg family of 18 twins and triplets, all with rare and incurable diseases. Like Elkin himself, Ben suffers from multiple sclerosis, and he comes to terms with his disease as his brothers and sisters die from theirs. *The Living End* (1979), a collection of three interwoven novellas about heaven, hell, and Minnesota's twin cities of Minneapolis and St. Paul, is perhaps Elkin's best-known work. Baroque in detail, *The Living End* portrays God as a petulant creator who destroys the world because He was misunderstood. Elkin gained further critical acclaim for *Stanley Elkin's The Magic Kingdom* (1985), in which Eddy Bale arranges a trip to Disney World for seven terminally ill British children, in honor of his young son's death. In *The MacGuffin* (1991) Elkin attempted a more conventional narrative structure while maintaining his usual style as he tracks the life of City Commissioner Robert Druff over a period of 48 hours.

Ellison, Harlan (Jay) (b. May 27, 1934, Cleveland, Ohio, U.S.) American writer of short stories, novels, essays, and television and film scripts; he is best known for his science-fiction writing and editing.

Ellison became a prolific contributor of science fiction, crime and sex fiction, and true confessions for genre magazines. After serving in the U.S. Army from 1957 to 1959, he edited *Rogue* magazine from 1959 to 1960 before becoming a successful television scriptwriter.

Ellison's reputation as an important science-fiction writer rests on short stories such as " 'Repent, Harlequin!' Said the Ticktockman" (1965), "A Boy and His Dog" (1969), and those in collections like *I Have No Mouth and I Must Scream* (1967) and *The Beast That Shouted Love at the Heart of the World* (1969). As an editor he published several important anthologies; for each of the stories he commissioned for *Dangerous Visions* (1967) and *Again, Dangerous Visions* (1972) he added a personal introductory essay that revealed as much about himself as it did about the work in question. His other works include *Deathbird Stories: A Pantheon of Modern Gods* (1975), *All the Lies That Are My Life* (1980), and *The Harlan Ellison Hornbook* (1990).

Ellison, Ralph (Waldo) (b. March 1, 1914, Oklahoma City, Okla., U.S.—
d. April 16, 1994, New York, N.Y.) American teacher and writer who won
eminence with his first and only published novel, INVISIBLE MAN (1952),
about race relations in the United States in the 20th century.

Exhibiting an early interest in jazz as well as in writing, Ellison left
Tuskegee Institute (Alabama) in 1936 after three years' study of music and
joined the Federal Writers' Project in New York City. Encouraged by novelist
Richard Wright, in 1939 he began contributing short stories, reviews, and
essays to various periodicals. He served in the Merchant Marines during
World War II, thereafter producing *Invisible Man*, which won the 1953
National Book Award for fiction. After his novel appeared, Ellison published
only two collections of essays, *Shadow and Act* (1964) and *Going to the
Territory* (1986). He lectured widely on black culture, folklore, and creative
writing and taught at various American colleges and universities. His second
novel was left unfinished at his death.

Ellmann, Richard (David) (b. March 15, 1918, Highland Park, Mich.,
U.S.—d. May 13, 1987, Oxford, Oxfordshire, Eng.) American literary critic
and scholar, an expert on the life and works of James Joyce, William Butler
Yeats, Oscar Wilde, and other modern British and Irish writers.

Ellmann graduated from Yale University and taught at Northwestern University, Evanston, Ill., from 1951 to 1968, at Yale University from 1968 to
1970, and at the University of Oxford from 1970 to 1984. His book *Yeats: The
Man and the Masks* (1948) is a study of one of Yeats's intense conflicts, the
dichotomy between the self of everyday life and the self of fantasy. The book
revealed Yeats as a timid and confused man behind a facade of arrogance.
Other books on Yeats included *The Identity of Yeats* (1954), which focused on
his poems, and *Eminent Domain* (1967), on Yeats' relationships with several
contemporary writers. Ellmann's definitive biography *James Joyce* (1959);
new and rev. ed., 1982) explores in detail aspects of the writer's life and
thought; his work on this biography led to his editing Joyce's letters (1966)
and other works on Joyce. He also edited several books, including *The Artist
as Critic: Critical Writings of Oscar Wilde* (1969) and *The New Oxford Book
of American Verse* (1976). Ellmann's biography *Oscar Wilde* appeared posthumously in 1988.

Emerson, Ralph Waldo (b. May 25, 1803, Boston, Mass., U.S.—d. April
27, 1882, Concord) American poet, essayist, and lecturer who was the
leading exponent of New England Transcendentalism.

Emerson graduated from Harvard College in 1821 and was ordained to the
Unitarian ministry in 1829. Although his position seemed secure, he had
begun to question Christian doctrines, and grief over the death of his wife in

1831 drove him to further doubts. He had become acquainted with the new biblical criticism and the doubts that had been cast on the historicity of miracles. Emerson's own sermons, from the first, had been unusually free of traditional doctrine and were instead a personal exploration of the uses of spirit. Indeed, they had divested Christianity of all external or historical supports and made its basis one's private intuition of the universal moral law and its test a life of virtuous accomplishment. Unitarianism ceased to fulfill his needs, and in 1832 he resigned from the ministry.

Emerson helped initiate Transcendentalism by publishing anonymously in Boston in 1836 a little book of 96 pages entitled NATURE. Having found the answers to his spiritual doubts, he formulated his essential philosophy, and almost everything he ever wrote afterward was an extension, amplification, or amendment of the ideas he first affirmed in *Nature*.

Ralph Waldo Emerson

In a lecture entitled "The American Scholar" (Aug. 31, 1837), Emerson described the resources and duties of the new liberated intellectual that he himself had become. The address was in effect a challenge to the Harvard intelligentsia, warning against pedantry, imitation, traditionalism, and scholarship unrelated to life. Emerson's later Harvard lecture, "Address at Divinity College" (1838), was another challenge, this time directed against a lifeless Christian tradition. This address alienated many and resulted in his being ostracized by Harvard for many years. Young disciples, however, joined the informal Transcendental Club (founded in 1836) and encouraged him in his activities.

In 1840 he helped launch *The Dial*, first edited by Margaret Fuller and later by himself, thus providing an outlet for the ideas Transcendentalists were trying to present to America. He continued to lecture, publishing two volumes entitled *Essays* (1841); 1844); these included the well-known SELF-RELIANCE and made Emerson internationally famous.

His *Representative Men* (dated 1850) contains biographies of Plato, Swedenborg, Michel de Montaigne, William Shakespeare, Napoleon, and J.W. von Goethe. *The Conduct of Life* (1860), Emerson's most mature work, reveals a developed humanism together with a full awareness of human limitations. Emerson's collected *Poems* (dated 1847) were supplemented by others in *May-Day* (1867), and the two volumes established his reputation as a major American poet.

Erdrich, Louise, *in full* Karen Louise Erdrich (b. June 7, 1954, Little Falls, Minn., U.S.) American author whose principal subject was the Chippewa Indians in the northern Midwest.

Erdrich grew up in Wahpeton, N.D., where her parents taught at a Bureau of Indian Affairs boarding school, and attended Dartmouth College and

Johns Hopkins University. She married writer Michael Dorris, her collaborator in her novels. Although she published two volumes of poetry, it was her fiction for which she was best known. After her short story "The World's Greatest Fisherman" won the 1982 Nelson Algren fiction prize, it became the basis of her first novel, *Love Medicine* (1984; expanded edition, 1993). *Love Medicine* began a tetralogy that includes *The Beet Queen* (1986), *Tracks* (1988), and *The Bingo Palace* (1994), about the Indian families on and around a North Dakota Chippewa reservation and the whites they encounter.

Erdrich's novels are noted for their depth of characterization; they are inhabited by a variety of characters, some of which reappear in several stories. White culture, which brings such forces as alcohol, Roman Catholicism, and government policies, acts to destroy the Indian community; tradition and loyalty to family and heritage are what work to keep it intact. Erdrich also wrote short stories, and she and Dorris were coauthors of the novel *The Crown of Columbus* (1991).

Erskine, John (b. Oct. 5, 1879, New York, N.Y., U.S.—d. June 2, 1951, New York City) American educator, novelist, and musician noted for energetic, skilled work in several different fields.

Erskine attended Columbia University and taught there from 1909 to 1937, earning a reputation as a learned, witty teacher and lecturer specializing in Elizabethan literature.

In the 1920s Erskine appeared as a piano soloist with the New York Philharmonic, beginning a distinguished career as a concert pianist. He also served as president of the Juilliard School of Music, director of the Juilliard Musical Foundation, and director of the Metropolitan Opera Association.

Erskine wrote more than 45 books. He was particularly successful with his early satirical novels, which are legends retold with updated views on morality and society. These works include *The Private Life of Helen of Troy* (1925) and *Adam and Eve* (1927), the story of how Adam adjusts to life with women (in the novel, first Lilith and then Eve). Erskine also coedited the *Cambridge History of American Literature*, 3 vol. (1917–19). He described various facets of his life in *The Memory of Certain Persons* (1947), *My Life as a Teacher* (1948), and *My Life in Music* (1950).

Evans, Mari (b. July 16, 1923, Toledo, Ohio, U.S.) African-American author of poetry, children's literature, and plays.

Evans attended the University of Toledo and later taught at several schools in the Midwest and East. She began five years of writing, producing, and directing for an Indianapolis television program, "The Black Experience," in 1968, the same year her first poetry collection, *Where Is All the Music?*, was published. With her second collection, *I Am a Black Woman* (1970), she gained acclaim as an important new poet. Her poem "Who Can Be Born Black" was often anthologized.

Her later collections include *Nightstar: 1973–1978* (1981), whose poems praise blues artists and community heroes and heroines, and *A Dark and Splendid Mass* (1992). Evans also wrote works for juvenile readers and several plays, including *River of My Song* (produced 1977) and the musical *Eyes* (produced 1979), an adaptation of Zora Neale Hurston's *Their Eyes Were Watching God*. She edited the anthology *Black Women Writers (1950–1980): A Critical Evaluation* (1984).

Everson, William (Oliver), *byname* Brother Antoninus (b. Sept. 10, 1912, Sacramento, Calif., U.S.—d. June 3, 1994, Santa Cruz, Calif.) American Roman Catholic poet whose works recorded a personal search for religious vision in a violent, corrupt world.

Raised by Christian Scientist parents, Everson became an agnostic in his teens; while attending Fresno (Calif.) State College, he resolved to become a poet. His first book, *These Are the Ravens*, was published in 1935. He was drafted during World War II but served at a work camp for conscientious objectors in Waldport, Oregon, where he cofounded the Untide Press and printed his own poetry. After marrying his second wife, poet Mary Fabilli, he converted to Roman Catholicism and he became a Dominican lay brother in 1951. For the next seven years he lived in monastic withdrawal. His literary silence was broken in 1957 with the composition of his long poem *River-Root* (1976), which depicts sexual love as a form of religious contemplation. He became identified with the San Francisco poetry renaissance of the Beat movement. After 1957 Everson published most of his poetry as Brother Antoninus, until 1969, when he returned to secular life and married for a third time.

William Everson

Emphatic assertions, rugged landscapes, and harsh juxtapositions mark Everson's poetry. He considered his lifetime of work to form a trilogy, which he called *The Crooked Lines of God* and which was composed of *The Residual Years: Poems 1934–1948* (1968), his early nature poetry; *The Veritable Years: Poems 1949–1966* (1978), his religious poetry; and a projected third volume to be entitled *The Integral Years* and intended to contain his post-1966 poetry. In the 1980s he began writing an autobiographical epic, beginning with the cantos of *In Medias Res* (1984). His final collection, *The Blood of the Poet*, was published in 1994.

Fariña, Richard (b. April 30, 1936?, Brooklyn, N.Y., U.S.—d. April 30, 1966, Carmel, Calif.) American folksinger, songwriter, and novelist. He was killed in a motorcycle accident just after the publication of his first novel, *Been Down So Long It Looks Like Up to Me* (1966).

Fariña studied engineering and literature at Cornell University, served with the Irish Republican Army in the mid-1950s, and later served briefly with guerrillas in Cuba.

Among the folk songs he composed were "Pack Up Your Sorrows" and "Hard Lovin' Loser." His first novel was a comic work about the meaning of life, partially set at Cornell during the late 1950s. His novel *Long Time Coming and a Long Time Gone*, with a foreword by the folksinger Joan Baez, was published posthumously in 1969.

Farrell, James Thomas (b. Feb. 27, 1904, Chicago, Ill., U.S.—d. Aug. 22, 1979, New York, N.Y.) American novelist and short-story writer known for his realistic portraits of the lower-middle-class Irish in Chicago, drawn from his own experiences.

Farrell attended the University of Chicago from 1925 to 1929. In 1932 he moved to New York City. That year the first volume of his well-known STUDS LONIGAN trilogy, *Young Lonigan*, was published. It was followed by *The Young Manhood of Studs Lonigan* in 1934 and *Judgment Day* in 1935. Danny O'Neill, a character introduced in *Studs Lonigan*, is the subject of a later series, published between 1936 and 1953, in which he reflects Farrell's acquired faith in humanitarian values and man's power to cope with circumstances. *The Face of Time* (1953) is considered another of Farrell's best works.

After 1958 Farrell worked on what was to be a 25-volume cycle, *A Universe of Time*, of which he completed 10 volumes. His complete works include 25 novels, 17 collections of short stories, and such works of nonfiction as *A Note on Literary Criticism* (1936) and *Reflections at Fifty* (1954), a collection of personal essays.

Faulkner, William (Cuthbert), *original surname* (until 1924) Falkner (b. Sept. 25, 1897, New Albany, Miss., U.S.—d. July 6, 1962, near Oxford, Miss.) American novelist and short-story writer best known for his Yoknapatawpha cycle, developed as a fable of the American South and of human destiny. He won the Nobel Prize for Literature in 1949.

Faulkner dropped out of high school in his second year and later endured a very brief stint at the University of Mississippi. A neighbor put up most of the money for the publication of Faulkner's first book, a cycle of pastoral poems, *The Marble Faun* (1924). His first novel, *Soldier's Pay* (1926), is about the return to Georgia of a fatally wounded aviator. His second novel, *Mosquitoes*

William Faulkner

(1927), is a heavily satirical picture of the New Orleans literary circle. A third novel, *Flags in the Dust*, was refused by the publisher of the other two. Given a new title, SARTORIS, the manuscript was accepted by another publisher, and it appeared in January 1929. THE SOUND AND THE FURY, the first of his masterworks, appeared in October of the same year.

In the years from 1930 to 1942 Faulkner published two collections of stories, a second and last book of poems (*A Green Bough*, 1933), and nine novels—AS I LAY DYING (1930); SANCTUARY (1931); LIGHT IN AUGUST (1932); *Pylon* (1935); ABSALOM, ABSALOM! (1936); *The Unvanquished* (1938); *The Wild Palms* (1939); THE HAMLET (1940); and GO DOWN, MOSES (1942), which includes the story THE BEAR. By 1945, however, his novels were effectively out of print, and Faulkner accepted a contract to write movie scripts in Hollywood. His second period of success began with the publication in 1946 of *The Portable Faulkner*, which presented his Yoknapatawpha legend as a whole. In 1948 Faulkner published another novel, INTRUDER IN THE DUST. *Collected Stories*, published early in 1950, won the National Book Award.

In 1951 a sequel to *Sanctuary* was published; a three-act play, *Requiem for a Nun*, with a narrative prologue to each act, it had the effect of a novel. In 1954 Faulkner's longest novel, *A Fable*, on which he had been working for nearly 10 years, was published. Faulkner rounded out the Yoknapatawpha story with THE TOWN (1957) and THE MANSION (1959).

Fauset, Jesse Redmon, *married name* Harris (b. April 27, 1882, Snow Hill, N.J., U.S.—d. April 30, 1961, Philadelphia, Pa.) African-American novelist, critic, poet, and editor known for her discovery and encouragement of several writers of the Harlem Renaissance.

Jessie Redmon Fauset

Fauset graduated from Cornell University (B.A., 1905), and she later earned a master's degree from the University of Pennsylvania (1919). She taught french in an all-black secondary school in Washington, D.C., for several years. While there she published articles in *The Crisis* magazine, the journal of the National Association for the Advancement of Colored People (NAACP). Its editor, W.E.B. Du Bois, persuaded her to move to New York City to become the magazine's literary editor. In that capacity, from 1919 to 1926, she published the works of such writers as Langston Hughes, Countee Cullen, Claude McKay, and Jean Toomer. She also edited and wrote for *The Brownies' Book*, a short-lived periodical for black children.

In her own work Fauset portrayed mostly middle-class black characters forced to deal with self-hate as well as racial prejudice. In her best-known novel, *Comedy: American Style* (1933), Olivia Carey, the protagonist, is a black woman who longs to be white, while her son and husband take pride in their cultural heritage. Fauset's other novels include *There Is Confusion* (1924), *Plum Bun* (1928), and *The Chinaberry Tree* (1931).

Fearing, Kenneth (Flexner) (b. July 28, 1902, Oak Park, Ill., U.S.—d. June 26, 1961, New York, N.Y.) American poet and novelist who used an array of topical idioms in his satires of urban life.

In 1924 Fearing moved to New York City and worked as a commercial freelance writer for the rest of his life. In his poetry he depicts a mechanized society devoid of belief, faith, and love. His work, acclaimed for its power, vividness, and wit, appeared in *Poetry* magazine and *The New Yorker*. His books include *Stranger at Coney Island* (1948) and *New and Selected Poems* (1956).

During the 1940s Fearing's readership shifted from his poetry to his psycho-thriller fiction. His most successful book, *The Big Clock* (1946; film, 1948), is a satire about a magazine publisher who commits murder and then sets his top reporter to hunt down a suspect, who is the reporter himself.

Edna Ferber

Ferber, Edna (b. Aug. 15, 1887, Kalamazoo, Mich., U.S.—d. April 16, 1968, New York, N.Y.) American novelist and short-story writer who wrote with compassion and curiosity of the middle-class Midwestern American experience.

Ferber began her career at 17 as a reporter in Wisconsin. Her early stories introduced a traveling petticoat saleswoman named Emma McChesney, whose adventures are collected in several books, including *Emma McChesney & Co.* (1915). Although her books are somewhat superficial in their careful attention to exterior detail at the expense of profound ideas, they do offer an accurate, lively portrait of America in the 1920s and '30s. After SO BIG (1924), for which she won a Pulitzer Prize, and SHOW BOAT (1926), which became a popular play, critics hailed her as the greatest woman novelist of the period. Her autobiography, *A Peculiar Treasure* (1939), evinces her genuine and encompassing love for the United States. Her later works include the novel GIANT (1952).

ABRAHAM ARONOW

Lawrence Ferlinghetti

Ferlinghetti, Lawrence (b. March 24, 1920, Yonkers, N.Y., U.S.) American poet, one of the founders of the BEAT MOVEMENT in San Francisco in the mid-1950s. His City Lights bookstore was an early gathering place of the Beats, and the publishing arm of City Lights was the first to print the Beats' books of poetry.

Ferlinghetti was reared by a female relative in France and later on a Long Island, N.Y., estate on which she was employed as a governess. He was a U.S. naval officer during World War II, and he attended the University of North Carolina, Columbia University, and the Sorbonne.

Ferlinghetti composed his poetry mainly to be read aloud. It was popular in coffeehouses and on college campuses, where it struck a responsive chord in disaffected youth. *Pictures of the Gone World* (1955) and *A Coney Island of the Mind* (1958), with its notable verse "Autobiography," were highly popular, as was the long poem *Tentative Description of a Dinner Given to Promote the Impeachment of President Eisenhower* (1958). His later poems continued to be politically oriented, as indicated by such titles as *One Thousand Fearful Words for Fidel Castro* (1961), *Where Is Vietnam?* (1965), *Tyrannus Nix?* (1969), and *Who Are We Now?* (1976). Selected poems were printed in *Endless Love* (1981).

Fiedler, Leslie A., *in full* Aaron (b. March 8, 1917, Newark, N.J., U.S.) American literary critic who applied psychological (chiefly Freudian) and social theories to American literature.

Fiedler attended the University of Wisconsin (M.A., 1939; Ph.D., 1941), and, after service in the U.S. Naval Reserve from 1942 to 1946, he did further research at Harvard University. Thereafter he taught at many universities, chiefly at the State University of New York at Buffalo.

Fiedler propounded many ingenious but controversial theories. He gained considerable notoriety with his essay "Come Back to the Raft Ag'in, Huck Honey!" later republished in *An End to Innocence* (1955). His major work, *Love and Death in the American Novel* (1960), argued that much of American literature embodies themes of innocent (presexual), but often homoerotic, male bonding and escape from a domestic, female-dominated society. This idea is further explored in *Waiting for the End* (1964) and *The Return of the Vanishing American* (1968). His later critical works include *The Inadvertent Epic: From Uncle Tom's Cabin to Roots* (1979) and *Fiedler on the Roof: Essays on Literature and Jewish Identity* (1990), as well as the books *The Stranger in Shakespeare* (1972) and *What Was Literature?: Class, Culture, and Mass Society* (1982).

Field, Eugene (b. Sept. 2, 1850, St. Louis, Mo., U.S.—d. Nov. 4, 1895, Chicago, Ill.) American poet and journalist, best known, to his disgust, as the "poet of childhood."

Field worked for a variety of newspapers, including the *Denver Tribune*. Comic paragraphs from his *Tribune* column, "Odds and Ends," formed his first book, *The Tribune Primer* (1882), journalistic joking in the tradition of Artemus Ward and Josh Billings. These squibs served as apprentice work for his "Sharps and Flats" column in the *Chicago Morning News* (renamed the *Record* in 1890). Here Field satirized the cultural pretensions of Chicago's newly rich. *A Little Book of Western Verse* (1889), drawn in part from his column, included poems in rural dialect, verses for children in an affected Old

English dialect, translations of Horace, and the well-known "Little Boy Blue" and "Dutch Lullaby" ("Wynken, Blynken, and Nod"). Field's collected works in 10 volumes were published the year after his death, and two more volumes were added in 1900.

Finch, Robert (Duer Claydon) (b. May 14, 1900, Freeport, N.Y., U.S.) A leading Canadian lyric poet whose poetry is characterized by metaphysical wit, complex imagery, and a strong sense of form.

Finch's first collection, *Poems* (1946), won a Governor General's Award, as did *Acis in Oxford* (1961), a series of meditations inspired by a performance of G.F. Handel's dramatic oratorio *Acis and Galatea*. *Dover Beach Revisited* (1961), treating the World War II evacuation of Dunkirk and issues of faith, contains 11 variations on Matthew Arnold's poem. In another collection, *Variations and Theme* (1980), Finch describes in 14 variations the fate of a rare pink water lily. His later works include *Has and Is* (1981), *The Grand Duke of Moscow's Favorite Solo* (1983), and *Sail-boat and Lake* (1988).

Findley, Timothy (b. Oct. 30, 1930, Toronto, Can.) Canadian author of novels about people's troubled, often violent, relationships.

At age 17 Findley began a 15-year acting career. He also began writing short stories during the late 1950s. His first two novels, *The Last of the Crazy People* (1967) and *The Butterfly Plague* (1969), are set in southern California.

Findley's two most acclaimed novels were *The Wars* (1977), which features the struggle of a soldier in the midst of World War I as he attempts to save 130 doomed horses, and *Famous Last Words* (1981), narrated by Hugh Selwyn Mauberley, a character created by Ezra Pound. Findley's later novels include *Not Wanted on the Voyage* (1984), *The Telling of Lies* (1986), and *Headhunter* (1993). He also published several radio and television scripts and a number of plays; the short-story collections *Dinner Along the Amazon* (1984), *Stones* (1988), and *Any Time at All* (1993); and *Inside Memory: Pages from a Writer's Workbook* (1990).

Fisher, Dorothy Canfield, *original name* Dorothea Frances Canfield, *pen name* Dorothy Canfield (b. Feb. 17, 1879, Lawrence, Kan., U.S.—d. Nov. 9, 1958, Arlington, Vt.) Prolific author of novels, short stories, children's books, educational works, and memoirs.

Canfield received a Ph.D. in Romance languages from Columbia University in 1904, a rare accomplishment for a woman of her generation. In 1907 she married John Redwood Fisher and published her first novel, *Gunhild*. In the same year she inherited her great-grandfather's farm in Arlington, Vt.; the town appears (often with the skimpiest of literary veils) in many of her works, including *Hillsboro People* (1915), written with poet Sarah N. Cleghorn, and the novel *The Bent Twig* (1915).

In 1912 Fisher met Maria Montessori in Italy and was impressed by the educator's theories. *A Montessori Mother* (1912), *The Montessori Manual* (1913), and *Mothers and Children* (1914) were the results of their friendship. Her experiences in French clinics and war camps resulted in three volumes of short stories, including *Home Fires in France* (1918).

After returning to the United States, Fisher translated Giovanni Papini's *Life of Christ* (1923) and during the 1920s and '30s produced a string of marriage-and-family stories and novels. *Her Son's Wife* (1926) is one of the best-regarded of her longer works. In the 1940s and '50s, Fisher worked for numerous environmental, children's, and educational causes, while writing several historical children's books, including *Paul Revere and the Minute Men* (1950).

Fisher, M.F.K., *original name in full* Mary Frances Kennedy (b. July 3, 1908, Albion, Mich., U.S.—d. June 22, 1992, Glen Ellen, Calif.) Writer whose compelling style, wit, and interest in the gastronomical made her one of the major American writers on the subject of food. In her 15 celebrated books, Fisher created a new genre: the food essay. Seeing food as a cultural metaphor, she proved to be both an insightful philosopher of food and a writer of fine prose.

JILL KREMENTZ

M.F.K. Fisher

Kennedy was reared in Whittier, Calif., and became accomplished in the kitchen. She married in 1929 and moved to Dijon, France, where she reveled in French cooking and culture. Her first book of essays celebrating food, *Serve It Forth*, was published in 1937. Other early works include *Consider the Oyster* (1941) and *How to Cook a Wolf* (1942), in which she encourages readers to make the most of whatever they can afford.

While all of Fisher's books were well received, critics point to *The Gastronomical Me* (1943) as one of her best early efforts. Her 1949 translation of French gastronomist Jean Anthelme Brillat-Savarin's *The Physiology of Taste* is regarded as the definitive English version. *An Alphabet for Gourmets* (1949) is superbly witty, and *A Cordiall Water* (1961), a discourse on folk remedies, became something of a cult classic. Her 1971 memoir, *Among Friends*, details her early years. *Sister Age* (1983) is a meditation on growing older.

Fish, Stanley (Eugene) (b. April 19, 1938, Providence, R.I., U.S.) Literary critic who is particularly associated with reader-response criticism, according to which the meaning of a text is created, rather than discovered, by the reader.

Fish was educated at the University of Pennsylvania and Yale University.

He taught at Johns Hopkins University from 1974 to 1985 and at Duke University thereafter.

In *Surprised by Sin: The Reader in "Paradise Lost"* (1967), Fish suggested that the subject of John Milton's masterpiece is in fact the reader, who is forced to undergo spiritual self-examination when led by Milton down the path taken by Adam, Eve, and Satan. In *Is There a Text in This Class? The Authority of Interpretive Communities* (1980), Fish further developed his theory. The essays in *Doing What Comes Naturally: Change, Rhetoric, and the Practice of Theory in Literary and Legal Studies* (1989) discuss a number of beliefs in literary theory.

Fitch, Clyde, *in full* William Clyde Fitch (b. May 2, 1865, Elmira, N.Y., U.S.—d. Sept. 4, 1909, Châlons-sur-Marne, Fr.) American playwright best known for plays of social satire and character study.

Fitch began writing short stories for magazines in New York City. He was a prolific writer, producing 33 original plays and 22 adaptations. His earlier plays were largely melodramas and historical plays of lesser significance. Among the more important later plays were *Beau Brummel* (1890), written for the actor Richard Mansfield, *The Climbers* (1901), *Captain Jinks of the Horse Marines* (1901), *The Girl with the Green Eyes* (1902), *The Truth* (1907), and *The City* (1909).

Fitts, Dudley (b. April 28, 1903, Boston, Mass., U.S.—d. July 10, 1968, Lawrence, Mass.) American teacher, critic, poet, and translator, best known for his contemporary English versions of classical Greek works.

Fitts began publishing poetry and criticism in periodicals such as *Poetry*, *transition*, and *Atlantic Monthly*. With poet Robert Fitzgerald he translated *The Alcestis of Euripides* (1936; first performed over BBC radio, 1937) and *The Antigone of Sophocles* (1939; first performed over NBC radio, U.S., 1939). The New Directions press, founded by James Laughlin, a former student of Fitts, published his *Poems 1929–1936* (1937) and his translations *One Hundred Poems from the Palatine Anthology* (1938) and *More Poems from the Palatine Anthology in English Paraphrase* (1941).

While Fitts also translated Latin, Spanish, and Latin-American writings into English, his translations of ancient Greek works became particularly noted. He later translated plays of Aristophanes, including *Lysistrata* (1954), *The Frogs* (1955), *The Birds* (1957), and *Ladies' Day* (1959); *Sixty Poems of Martial* (1967); and, with Fitzgerald, Sophocles' *Oedipus Rex* (1949). He also edited anthologies of poetry translations and, in 1960–68, the Yale Series of Younger Poets.

Fitzgerald, F. Scott, *in full* Francis Scott Key Fitzgerald (b. Sept. 24, 1896,

St. Paul, Minn., U.S.—d. Dec. 21, 1940, Hollywood, Calif.) American short-story writer and novelist known for his depictions of the Jazz Age (the 1920s).

F. Scott Fitzgerald

Fitzgerald attended Princeton University, where he nearly realized his dream of brilliant social and literary success, but because of his poor academic record he left in 1917. In November of that year he joined the U.S. Army. In 1918 he met Zelda Sayre, the daughter of an Alabama Supreme Court judge. To prove himself and win her, Fitzgerald rewrote the novel he had begun at Princeton; in 1920 THIS SIDE OF PARADISE was published and Fitzgerald married Zelda.

Publication of the novel gave Fitzgerald an entrée to literary magazines, such as *Scribner's*, and high-paying general magazines, such as *The Saturday Evening Post*. In them he published early stories such as THE DIAMOND AS BIG AS THE RITZ, later collected in TALES OF THE JAZZ AGE (1922). Fame and prosperity were both welcome and frightening; in THE BEAUTIFUL AND DAMNED (1922), Fitzgerald describes the life he and Zelda feared, a descent into ennui and dissipation.

The Fitzgeralds moved in 1924 to the Riviera, where they fell in with a group of American expatriates. Fitzgerald describes this society in his last completed novel, TENDER IS THE NIGHT (1934). Shortly after their arrival in France, Fitzgerald completed THE GREAT GATSBY (1925), the most profoundly American novel of its time. It poignantly captures Fitzgerald's own ambivalence about American life, at once vulgar and dazzlingly promising. Some of Fitzgerald's finest short stories, particularly "The Rich Boy" and "Absolution," appeared in *All the Sad Young Men* (1926).

Fitzgerald soon began to drink excessively, and in 1930 Zelda had a mental breakdown. In 1932 she had another, from which she never fully recovered. Fitzgerald told the story of his downward slide in THE CRACK-UP (1945). By 1937, however, he had become a scriptwriter in Hollywood, where he met Sheilah Graham, a well-known Hollywood gossip columnist with whom he lived for the rest of his life. In 1939 he began a novel about Hollywood, THE LAST TYCOON (1941), but he died before it was finished.

Flanner, Janet, *pseudonym* Genêt (b. March 13, 1892, Indianapolis, Ind., U.S.—d. Nov. 7, 1978, New York City) American writer and Paris correspondent for *The New Yorker* magazine from 1925 to 1975 (except for the war years 1939–44). Hers was some of the most sophisticated, insightful, and cosmopolitan reportage from Paris during the period.

A friend of Harold Ross, Flanner was hired by him in 1925 to write a periodic "Letter from Paris" for his new magazine, *The New Yorker*. Signed by "Genêt," the articles contained observations on politics, art, theater, and the general quality of French life. In the 1930s she also began writing an occasional "Letter from London." Her first novel, *The Cubical City*, appeared in 1926.

Most of her essays were collected in *American in Paris; Profile of an Interlude Between Two Wars* (1940), *Paris Journal, 1944–1965* (1966), *Paris Journal, 1965–1971* (1971), and *Janet Flanner's World: Uncollected Writings 1932–1975* (1979).

Fodor, Eugene (b. Oct. 14, 1905, Léva, Hung. [now Levice, Slovakia.]—d. Feb. 18, 1991, Torrington, Conn., U.S.) Hungarian-born American travel writer who created a series of popular tourist guidebooks that provided historical background and cultural insights into the people and places described, as well as reliable, practical information designed to assist inexperienced travelers.

Fodor studied in Czechoslovakia, France, and Germany. He then worked as an interpreter for a French shipping company, in his spare time writing articles about exotic ports of call and life aboard ship. He was a travel correspondent and editor in Prague (1930–33) and London (1934–38). His first book, *1936—On the Continent*, was a best-seller in Europe and the United States. Fodor became a naturalized U.S. citizen in 1942 and served in the U.S. Army. In 1949 he settled in Paris and founded Fodor's Modern Guides, Inc. He returned to the United States in 1964 and sold his company in 1968.

Foote, Shelby (b. Nov. 17, 1916, Greenville, Miss., U.S.) Historian, novelist, and short-story writer known for his works treating the United States Civil War and the American South.

Foote attended the University of North Carolina for two years, and he served in the U.S. Army during World War II. His first novel, *Tournament*, was published in 1949. Like many of Foote's later novels, it is set in Bristol, Miss., a fictional town modeled on Foote's hometown.

Follow Me Down (1950), considered by many critics to be his best novel, was based on an actual murder trial. *Love in a Dry Season* (1951) was set against the changing fortunes of the South from the 1920s to World War II. *Shiloh* (1952) was Foote's first popular success. It used the monologues of six soldiers to recreate the Civil War battle of the title. Foote next set out to write what proved to be his masterwork, *The Civil War: A Narrative* (1958–74), which consists of three volumes—*Fort Sumter to Perryville* (1958), *Fredericksburg to Meridian* (1963), *Red River to Appomattox* (1974). Considered a masterpiece by many critics, it was also criticized by academics for its lack of footnotes and other scholarly conventions. Foote appeared as narrator and commentator in Ken Burns's 11-hour television documentary *The Civil War* (1990).

Forché, Carolyn (Louise), *original surname* Sidlosky (b. April 28, 1950,

Detroit, Mich., U.S.) American poet whose concern for human rights was reflected in her writing, especially in the collection *The Country Between Us* (1981), which examines events she witnessed in El Salvador.

Forché educated at Michigan State and Bowling Green State universities. Her first collection of poetry, *Gathering the Tribes* (1976), evoked her childhood, her Slovak ancestry, and reflections on sexuality, family, and race.

From 1978 to 1980 Forché was a journalist in El Salvador, where, in addition to her involvement in Amnesty International as a human-rights advocate, she translated works by Salvadoran poets. The later five-part book-length poem *The Angel of History* (1994) is a compelling distillation of Forché's intensely moral sensibility.

In addition to her own writings, she edited several books, including *Against Forgetting: Twentieth-Century Poetry of Witness* (1993). She also translated the poetry of Claribel Alegría.

Ford, Richard (b. Feb. 16, 1944, Jackson, Miss., U.S.) American writer of novels and short stories.

Ford attended Michigan State University, Washington University Law School, and the University of California, Irvine, and subsequently taught English and writing in several American colleges and universities. In his first novel, *A Piece of My Heart* (1976), critics noted the influence of William Faulkner. *The Ultimate Good Luck* (1981) presents an American in Mexico who is drawn reluctantly into violence and murder as he tries to get his girlfriend's brother out of jail. In the early 1980s Ford worked for a sports magazine; the protagonist of his novel *The Sportswriter* (1986) is an alienated, middle-aged sportswriter reflecting on his life.

Ford also wrote short stories about lonely and damaged people, collected in *Rock Springs* (1987). In his fourth novel, *Wildlife* (1990), a teenager in rugged Montana country witnesses the breakup of his parents' marriage. In 1996 Ford received a Pulitzer prize in fiction for his sequel to *The Sportswriter, Independence Day.*

Forrest, Leon (b. Jan. 8, 1937, Chicago, Ill., U.S.) African-American author of large, inventive novels that fuse myth, history, legend, and contemporary realism.

From 1965 to 1973 Forrest worked as a journalist for various papers, including the Nation of Islam's weekly *Muhammad Speaks*. He also published excerpts from his first novel, *There Is a Tree More Ancient than Eden*, which was issued in book form in 1973.

There Is a Tree portrays the tangled relationships between the illegitimate offspring of a onetime slave-owning family; several of the book's distinctive characters reappear in subsequent Forrest novels. Echoes of Greek and Latin mythology are present in *The Bloodworth Orphans* (1977), about the search by three orphaned siblings for roots and understanding amid turmoil. In *Two Wings to Veil My Face* (1983) an ex-slave tells her life story to her great-grandson. Forrest's most ambitious novel, *Divine Days* (1992), concerns the efforts of an African-American playwright to investigate the disappearance of a fellow black. A book of collected essays, *Relocations of the Spirit*, was published in 1994.

Franklin, Benjamin, *pseudonym* Richard Saunders (b. Jan. 6 [Jan. 17, New Style], 1706, Boston [Mass., U.S.]—d. April 17, 1790, Philadelphia, Pa.) American printer and publisher, author, inventor and scientist, and diplomat. Franklin invented the Franklin stove, bifocal spectacles, and the lightning rod and contributed to science with his experiments in electricity.

Franklin ended his formal education at the age of 10, and at 12 he was apprenticed to his brother, a printer. His first enthusiasm was for poetry, but he soon turned to prose. He achieved much of what was to become his characteristic style from imitation of the writing in *The Spectator*, Joseph Addison and Richard Steele's famous periodical of essays. About 1729 Franklin became the printer of paper currency for the colony of Pennsylvania and some of the other colonies. At that time he began publication of the *Pennsylvania Gazette*, a colonial newspaper generally acknowledged as among the best of such publications, and *Poor Richard's* (1732–57), a series of almanacs in which he printed numerous proverbs praising prudence, industry, and honesty. In 1748 he gave up the management of his publications to devote himself to science, but in 1753 he served as deputy postmaster general for the northern colonies. He wrote many additional papers and essays of significance as well as an incomplete autobiography.

Franklin spent the years from 1757 to 1762 in London representing the colony of Pennsylvania in a dispute over the lands held by the Penn family. In 1764 he was sent back to London, and in March 1775, aware that there might be war between the colonies and Great Britain, he left England. Back in Philadelphia he served as a delegate to the Second Continental Congress, in which he helped draft the Declaration of Independence. In 1776 Franklin went to France to seek military and financial aid for the colonies. There he became a hero to the French people, the personification of the unsophisticated nobility of the New World. At the close of the Revolutionary War, Franklin was one of the diplomats chosen to negotiate peace with Great Britain, and he was instrumental in achieving the adoption of the U.S. Constitution.

Fréchette, Louis-Honoré (b. Nov. 16, 1839, Lévis, Que. [Canada]—d. May 31, 1908, Montreal) Preeminent French-Canadian poet of the 19th century, noted for his patriotic poems.

Fréchette studied law at Laval University, Quebec, and was admitted to the bar in 1864. He worked as a journalist until he was discharged for liberal views. During a sojourn in Chicago (1866–71) he wrote *La Voix d'un exilé* (1866–68); "The Voice of an Exile"), a poem attacking the political and clerical dealings in Quebec during the period of Canadian confederation. Returning to Lévis in 1871, Fréchette entered politics, representing that city in the federal House of Commons (1874–78) and serving from 1889 until his death as clerk of the provincial Legislative Council in Quebec City.

In 1880 his *Les Fleurs boréales* (1879); "The Northern Flowers") and *Les Oiseaux de neige* (1879); "The Snow Birds") became the first works by a Canadian to be awarded a prize by the Académie Française. Fréchette then wrote *La Légende d'un peuple* (1887), his famous cycle of poems that are an epic chronicle of Canadian history. Other works include *Poésies choisies* (1908); "Selected Poems"); the prose stories in *Originaux et détraqués* (1892); "Eccentrics and Lunatics") and *Le Noël au Canada* (1899); *Christmas in French Canada*); the dramas *Félix Poutré* (1871), *Papineau* (1880), and *Véronica* (1908); and the polemical *Lettres à Basile* (1872).

Frederic, Harold (b. Aug. 19, 1856, Utica, N.Y., U.S.—d. Oct. 19, 1898, Henley-on-Thames, Oxfordshire, Eng.) American journalist, foreign correspondent, and author of several historical novels.

Frederic became a reporter and by 1882 was editor of the *Albany Evening Journal*. In 1884 he went to London as the correspondent for *The New York Times*. London remained his base for the rest of his life.

His historical novels ranged in setting from the American Revolution (*In the Valley*, 1890) to the American Civil War (*The Copperhead*, 1893, and *Marsena and Other Stories*, 1894). Of his New York State novels, *The Damnation of Theron Ware* (1896); U.K. title, *Illumination*), the story of the decline and fall of a Methodist minister, brought him his greatest fame. Three other novels, *March Hares* (1896), *Gloria Mundi* (1898), and *The Market Place* (1899), are about English life.

Freeman, Douglas Southall (b. May 16, 1886, Lynchburg, Va., U.S.—d. June 13, 1953, Westbourne, Hampton Gardens, near Richmond, Va.) American journalist, educator, and author noted for writings on the Confederacy.

After receiving degrees from Johns Hopkins and Washington and Lee universities, Freeman began a long and distinguished teaching career. From 1936 he was a lecturer at the Army War College. From 1915 to 1949 he also edited the Richmond (Va.) *News Leader*.

In 1935 Freeman won the Pulitzer Prize for his four-volume biography, *R.E. Lee*. His other works include *Virginia—A Gentle Dominion* (1924); *The Last Parade* (1932); *The South to Posterity: An Introduction to the Writings of Confederate History* (1939); *Lee's Lieutenants, A Study in Command*, 3 vol. (1942–44); *John Steward Bryan* (1947); and *George Washington*, 7 vol. (1948–57), the final volume of which was prepared by his assistants after his death—the whole work earning him a second, posthumous Pulitzer Prize in 1958.

Freeman, Mary Eleanor Wilkins (b. Oct. 31, 1852, Randolph, Mass., U.S.—d. March 13, 1930, Metuchen, N.J.) American writer known for her stories and novels of frustrated lives in New England villages.

In 1867 the Wilkins family moved to Brattleboro, Vt. Mary began writing stories and verse for children to help support her family, and she quickly became successful. Returning to Randolph, she did her best writing there in the 1880s and '90s. Although she produced a dozen volumes of short stories and as many novels, Freeman is remembered chiefly for the first two collections of stories, *A Humble Romance and Other Stories* (1887) and *A New England Nun and Other Stories* (1891), and for the novel *Pembroke* (1894).

Freneau, Philip (Morin) (b. Jan. 2, 1752, New York City [U.S.]—d. Dec. 18, 1832, Monmouth County, N.J.) Poet, essayist, and editor, known as the "poet of the American Revolution."

After the outbreak of the Revolution, Freneau began to write vitriolic satire against the British and Tories. He spent two years in the Caribbean islands, where he produced two of his most ambitious poems, "The Beauties of Santa Cruz" and "The House of Night." On his return he became an active participant in the war. Captured and imprisoned by the British in 1780, he bitterly recounted the experience in the poem *The British Prison-Ship* (1781), written after his release.

During the next several years he contributed to the *Freeman's Journal* in Philadelphia. Freneau became a sea captain until 1790, when he again entered partisan journalism, ultimately as editor from 1791 to 1793 of the strongly Republican *National Gazette* in Philadelphia.

Well schooled in the classics and in the Neoclassical English poetry of the period, Freneau strove for a fresh idiom that would be unmistakably American, but, except in a few poems, he failed to achieve it.

Friedman, Bruce Jay (b. April 26, 1930, New York, N.Y., U.S.) American comic author whose dark, mocking humor and social criticism was directed at the concerns and behavior of American Jews.

Friedman worked in publishing for several years before achieving success with his first novel, *Stern* (1962). The title character is a luckless descendent of the biblical Job, unable to assimilate into mainstream American life. Although most of his characters are Jewish by birth, they feel marginal to both Jewish and American culture.

Friedman's works include the novels *A Mother's Kisses* (1964), *The Dick* (1970), *About Harry Towns* (1974), *Tokyo Woes* (1985), *Violencia* (1988), and *The Current Climate* (1989); the short-story collections *Far from the City of Class* (1963), *Black Angels* (1966), and *Let's Hear It for a Beautiful Guy* (1984); essays such as *The Lonely Guy's Book of Life* (1978); the plays *Scuba Duba: A Tense Comedy* (1967) and *Steambath* (1971); and several screenplays.

Frost, Robert (Lee) (b. March 26, 1874, San Francisco, Calif., U.S.—d. Jan. 29, 1963, Boston, Mass.) American poet best known for his use of colloquial language, familiar rhythms, and symbols taken from common life to express the simple values of New England life. Generations of students have been introduced to poetry by the accessible images of poems such as STOPPING BY WOODS ON A SNOWY EVENING, THE ROAD NOT TAKEN, THE DEATH OF THE HIRED MAN, and MENDING WALL.

Robert Frost

Frost briefly attended Dartmouth and Harvard colleges. He settled on a family farm in Derry, N.H., but sold the farm and in 1912 moved to England, where his first collection of poems, *A Boy's Will* (1913), was published. After the outbreak of World War I, Frost returned to the United States and bought a farm in Franconia, N.H.

Frost's poetry reveals his almost mystical attachment to the fields and farms of New England. An ardent naturalist and botanist, he acutely observed the details of rural life and endowed them with universal, even metaphysical, meaning.

Frost's distinguished career as a teacher and poet-in-residence took him to Amherst College, the University of Michigan, Harvard, and Dartmouth. His poetry collections include *Mountain Interval* (1916), *New Hampshire* (1923), *West-Running Brook* (1928), *A Further Range* (1936), *A Witness Tree* (1942), *Steeple Bush* (1947), and *In the Clearing* (1962).

Frye, Northrop, *in full* Herman Northrop Frye (b. July 14, 1912, Sherbrooke, Que., Can.—d. Jan. 23, 1991, Toronto, Ont.) Canadian educator and literary critic, author of influential theories of criticism.

Frye was educated at the University of Toronto, Emmanuel College in Toronto, and Merton College, Oxford. He taught at Victoria College from 1939.

In 1947 he published *Fearful Symmetry: A Study of William Blake*, a sweeping study of Blake's visionary symbolism. In ANATOMY OF CRITICISM (1957), he analyzed various modes of literary criticism and stressed the recurring importance of archetypal symbols in literature. In later works Frye studied T.S. Eliot (1963), John Milton's epics (1965), Shakespearean comedy (1965) and tragedy (1967), and English Romanticism (1968). *The Stubborn*

Structure: Essays on Criticism and Society appeared in 1970, and *The Great Code: The Bible and Literature*, a study of the mythology and structure of the Bible, was published in 1982. Frye's other critical works include *The Well-Tempered Critic* (1963), *The Secular Scripture: A Study of the Structure of Romance* (1976), *Northrop Frye on Shakespeare* (1986), and *Words with Power: Being a Second Study of "The Bible and Literature"* (1990).

Fuller, Charles, *in full* Charles H. Fuller, Jr. (b. March 5, 1939, Philadelphia, Pa., U.S.) American playwright who is best known for A SOLDIER'S PLAY (1981), which won the 1982 Pulitzer Prize for drama.

In 1967 Fuller cofounded the Afro-American Arts Theatre in Philadelphia, and he was codirector from 1967 to 1971. During the 1970s he wrote plays for the Henry Street Settlement theater in New York, and in 1974 the Negro Ensemble Company produced his *In the Deepest Part of Sleep*. He based *The Brownsville Raid* (1975) on an actual incident involving the dishonorable discharge in 1906 of an entire black U.S. Army regiment.

In *Zooman and the Sign* (produced 1980; published 1982) Fuller presented a father's search for the killer of his daughter. *A Soldier's Play* follows the investigation by a black army captain of the murder of a black soldier at a base in Louisiana.

Fuller, Henry Blake (b. Jan. 9, 1857, Chicago, Ill., U.S.—d. July 28, 1929, Chicago) American novelist who wrote about his native city of Chicago.

Fuller came from a prosperous Chicago family. His first two novels—*The Chevalier of Pensieri-Vani* (1890); written under the pseudonym Stanton Page) and *The Chatelaine of La Trinité* (1892)—were gracefully told, brief but unhurried tales about Europe.

Fuller took a decidedly different direction with *The Cliff-Dwellers* (1893), a realistic novel, called the first important American city novel, about people in a Chicago skyscraper. *With the Procession* (1895) was another realistic novel about a wealthy Chicago merchant family. His other fiction set in Chicago includes *Under the Skylights* (1901), short stories about the city's artistic life; *On the Stairs* (1918), a novel about two men, one going up in life, the other down; and *Bertram Cope's Year* (1919), which is about an instructor at the University of Chicago. Fuller continued his European-based fiction with *Waldo Trench and Others* (1908), collected stories about Americans in Italy, and *Gardens of This World* (1929), which extends the tale begun in his first book.

Fuller, Margaret, *in full* Sarah Margaret Fuller, *married name* Marchesa (Marchioness) Ossoli (b. May 23, 1810, Cambridgeport, Mass., U.S.—d. July 19, 1850, at sea) American critic, teacher, and woman of letters whose efforts to civilize the taste and enrich the lives of her contemporaries make her significant in the history of American culture.

Fuller taught in Bronson Alcott's Temple School in Boston, 1836–37, and in Providence, R.I., 1837–39. In 1839 she published a translation of J.P. Eckermann's *Conversations with Goethe*; her most cherished project, never completed, was a biography of J.W. von Goethe. From 1840 to 1842 she was editor of *The Dial*, a magazine launched by the Transcendentalists, for which she wrote poetry, reviews, and critiques.

Margaret Fuller

Woman in the Nineteenth Century (1845) is a tract on feminism that was both a demand for political equality and an ardent plea for the emotional, intellectual, and spiritual fulfillment of women. It was published by Horace Greeley, who had admired her *Summer on the Lakes, in 1843* (1844), a perceptive study of frontier life in Illinois and Wisconsin.

In 1844 Margaret Fuller became literary critic on Greeley's newspaper, the *New York Tribune*. Before she sailed for Europe in 1846, some of her essays appeared as *Papers on Literature and Art*, which assured the cordial welcome she received in English and French circles. America's first woman foreign correspondent, she reported on her travels for the *Tribune*; the "letters" were later published in *At Home and Abroad* (1856). Settling in Italy in 1847, she was caught up in the cause of the Italian revolutionists, led by Guiseppe Mazzini, and was secretly married to Giovanni Angelo, Marchese Ossoli. Following the suppression of the republic she sailed for America with her husband and infant son, Angelo. They perished in a shipwreck off Fire Island (N.Y.), and with them was lost her manuscript history of the revolution.

Gaddis, William (Thomas) (b. Dec. 29, 1922, New York, N.Y., U.S.) American novelist whose long, experimental works portray the contemporary human condition.

Gaddis first gained note as an author with publication of his controversial novel *The Recognitions* (1955). The book, rich in language and imagery, began as a parody of Faust but developed into a multileveled examination of spiritual bankruptcy. Discouraged by the harsh critical reception of his book, Gaddis published nothing for 20 years and instead worked as a free-lance writer for various corporations. His second novel, *JR* (1975), uses long stretches of cacophonous dialogue to depict what its author viewed as the greed, hypocrisy, and banality of the world of American business. Gaddis' third novel, *Carpenter's Gothic* (1985), is even more pessimistic in its depiction of moral chaos in modern American society.

Gaddis' fiction contains long dialogues and monologues related by a minimum of plot and structured by scant punctuation. It shows the influence of the writings of James Joyce and, in turn, influenced the work of Thomas Pynchon.

Gaines, Ernest J., *in full* James (b. Jan. 15, 1933, Oscar, La., U.S.) American writer whose fiction, as exemplified by THE AUTOBIOGRAPHY OF MISS JANE PITTMAN (1971), his most acclaimed work, reflected African-American experience and the oral tradition of his rural Louisiana childhood.

When Gaines was 15, his family moved to California. He graduated from San Francisco State College (now San Francisco State University) in 1957 and attended graduate school at Stanford University. He taught or was writer-in-residence at several schools, including Denison and Stanford universities.

Gaines's novels are set in rural Louisiana, often in a fictional plantation area named Bayonne that by some critics have compared to William Faulkner's imaginary Yoknapatawpha County. In addition to *The Autobiography of Miss Jane Pittman*, his novels include *Catherine Carmier* (1964), *Of Love and Dust* (1967), *In My Father's House* (1978), and *A Gathering of Old Men* (1983).

Gale, Zona (b. Aug. 26, 1874, Portage, Wis., U.S.—d. Dec. 27, 1938, Chicago, Ill.) American novelist and playwright whose *Miss Lulu Bett* (1920) established her as a realistic chronicler of Midwestern village life.

Gale graduated from the University of Wisconsin and worked as a reporter, first for various Milwaukee newspapers and later for the *New York World*. After the publication of her first short story, in 1903, she gave her full time to writing.

Gale's books include *Friendship Village* (1908), *A Daughter of the Morning* (1917), *Birth* (1918), and *Preface to a Life* (1926). Her early writings were sentimental evocations of the virtues of small-town life and fall within the local-color tradition. Her later writings, however, reveal her interest in progressive causes and are increasingly critical of small-town provincialism. The dramatization of *Miss Lulu Bett*, a study of an unmarried woman's attempts at self-assertion in the face of a constricting social environment, won Gale the Pulitzer Prize in 1921.

Gallagher, Tess, *original surname* Bond (b. July 21, 1943, Port Angeles, Wash., U.S.) American poet known for her introspective verses about self-discovery, womanhood, and family life.

Gallagher studied at the Universities of Washington and Iowa. Her first full-length volume of verse, *Instructions to the Double* (1976), is a confessional work about her efforts to synthesize her past life with her future career as a poet.

In 1978 Gallagher published three collections of poems: *Portable Kisses*, *On Your Own*, and *Under Stars*. Several poems in *Willingly* (1984) eulogize her late father, including "Boat Ride" and "3 A.M. Kitchen: My Father Talking." The collections *Amplitude* (1987) and *Moon Crossing Bridge* (1992) focus on her relationship with her third husband, author Raymond Carver. In addition to her poetry and several plays for film and television, she wrote *The Lover of Horses and Other Stories* (1986), a book of short fiction.

Gallant, Mavis, *original name* Mavis de Trafford Young (b. Aug. 11, 1922, Montreal, Can.) Canadian-born writer of essays, novels, plays, and especially short stories. In unsentimental prose and with trenchant wit she delineated the isolation, detachment, and fear that afflict rootless North American and European expatriates.

Following graduation from high school in New York City, Gallant worked in Montreal at the National Film Board and as a newspaper reporter for the *Montreal Standard*.

From 1950 she lived mostly in Europe, eventually settling in France. In the 1950s she became a regular contributor to *The New Yorker* magazine, which through the years published more than 100 of her short stories and much of her nonfiction. Collections of her well-constructed, perceptive, often humorous short stories include *My Heart Is Broken* (1964), *The Pegnitz Junction* (1973), *Home Truths: Selected Canadian Stories* (1981), *Overhead in a Balloon: Stories of Paris* (1985), *In Transit* (1988), and *Across the Bridge* (1993).

Gardner, Erle Stanley (b. July 17, 1889, Malden, Mass., U.S.—d. March 11, 1970, Temecula, Calif.) Prolific American author and lawyer whose best-known works center on the lawyer-detective Perry Mason.

Erle Stanley Gardner

Gardner dropped out of Valparaiso University, Ind., after a brief time and settled in California, where he worked as a typist in a law firm. After three years he was admitted to the California bar.

While practicing trial law in Ventura, Calif., Gardner began writing for the pulp magazines popular at the time, creating accurate courtroom scenes and brilliant legal maneuvers resembling his own legal tactics. With the successful publication of the first Perry Mason detective stories, *The Case of the Velvet Claws* (1933) and *The Case of the Sulky Girl* (1933), he gave up the law. Eighty Perry Mason novels followed. Gardner also wrote two other series of detective stories, one under the pseudonym A.A. Fair.

Gardner, John, *in full* John Champlin Gardner, Jr. (b. July 21, 1933, Batavia, N.Y., U.S.—d. Sept. 14, 1982, near Susquehanna, Pa.) American novelist and poet whose philosophical fiction reveals his characters' inner conflicts.

Gardner attended Washington University, St. Louis and the University of Iowa and then taught at various colleges and universities throughout the United States, including Oberlin College, Ohio; Bennington College, Vermont; and the University of Rochester.

John Gardner

Gardner published two novels, *The Resurrection* (1966) and *The Wreckage of Agathon* (1970), before his reputation was established with the appearance of *Grendel* (1971), a retelling of the Beowulf story from the point of view of the monster. His next novel, *The Sunlight Dialogues* (1972), is an ambitious epic with a large cast of characters. Later novels include *October Light* (1976; National Book Critics Circle Award), *Freddy's Book* (1980), and *Mickelsson's Ghosts* (1982). Gardner was also a gifted poet and a critic who published several books on Old and Middle English poetry. He expressed his views about writing in *On Moral Fiction* (1978), in which he deplored the tendency of many modern writers toward pessimism, believing that the goal of true art is a celebration of life.

Garland, Hamlin, *in full* Hannibal Hamlin Garland (b. Sept. 14, 1860, West Salem, Wis., U.S.—d. March 4, 1940, Hollywood, Calif.) American author perhaps best remembered for his short stories and his autobiographical "Middle Border" series of narratives. He is considered one of the foremost representatives of Midwestern Regionalism.

As his farming family moved progressively westward from Wisconsin, Garland rebelled against the vicissitudes of pioneering and went to Boston in 1884. There he gradually won a place for himself in the literary set of Boston and Cambridge and was influenced by the novelist William Dean Howells. Garland recorded the physical oppression and economic frustrations of pioneer life on the Great Plains in the short stories collected in *Main-Travelled Roads* (1891), one of his best works. The short stories he published in *Prairie*

Folk (1892) and *Wayside Courtships* (1897) were later combined in *Other Main-Travelled Roads* (1910). His novel *Rose of Dutcher's Coolly* (1895) tells the story of a sensitive young woman who rebels against the drudgery of farm life and goes to Chicago to pursue her talent for literature. After producing a series of mediocre novels that were serialized in the popular "slick magazines," Garland wrote the acclaimed autobiographical tale *A Son of the Middle Border* in 1917. Its sequels and his later novels were lesser efforts.

Garneau, Hector de Saint-Denys (b. June 13, 1912, Sainte-Catherine de Fossanbault, Que., Can.—d. Oct. 24, 1943, Sainte-Catherine de Fossanbault) Poet whose intense and introspective verse, filled with images of death and suicide, stood out from the prevailing regionalism of Canadian literature and strongly influenced the poets who followed.

In his early 20s Garneau suffered a heart attack, and he lived thereafter in increasing solitude, writing poetry that reflects the despair he felt over his joyless life. He published only one volume of poetry, *Regards et jeux dans l'espace* (1937); "Glances and Games in Space") in his lifetime. His *Poésies complètes* (1949); "Complete Poetry") and *Journal* (1954), an intimate record of his life between 1935 and 1939, appeared posthumously.

Gaspé, Philippe Aubert de (b. Oct. 30, 1786, Quebec—d. Jan. 29, 1871, Quebec) Author of the first important French-Canadian novel.

Gaspé received a classical education in Quebec, studied law there, and later became sheriff. Bankruptcy forced his withdrawal from public life in his 40s into a quiet life of reading and meditation. When he was 76 years old, he was inspired by a rebirth of Canadian nationalism to write *Les Anciens Canadiens* (1863); *The Canadians of Old*), a romantic historical novel set in Canada at the time of the British conquest (1760). Its themes of idealization of the past, the farmer's loyalty to the soil, and distrust of English Canada influenced the Canadian regionalist school of literature.

Gass, William Howard (b. July 30, 1924, Fargo, N.D., U.S.) American writer and critic noted for his experimentation with stylistic devices.

Gass called his fiction works "experimental constructions," and each of his books contains stylistic innovations. His first novel, *Omensetter's Luck* (1966), concerns a man who is maliciously and falsely connected to a mysterious death. Piecing together various viewpoints without the use of quotation marks to distinguish speakers, Gass creates levels of insight into character and setting. His novella *Willie Masters' Lonesome Wife* (1968) makes use of typographical and other visual devices.

Gass's other work includes *In the Heart of the Heart of the Country* (1968), short stories; *On Being Blue* (1976), imaginative interpretations of the color blue; *China Through a Writer's Eye* (1985), a travel book with text and photos by Gass; and several collections of critical essays.

Gates, Henry Louis, Jr. (b. Sept. 16, 1950, Keyser, W.Va., U.S.) African-American critic and scholar known for his pioneering theories of black literature. He used the term "signifyin' " to represent African and African-American literary history as a continuing reflection and reinterpretation of what has gone before. Gates was at the forefront of the discovery and restoration of many lost works by black writers—such as Harriet E. Wilson's *Our Nig* (1859), the earliest known novel by an African American—and he argued in *Loose Canons* (1992) and elsewhere for the inclusion of African-American literature in the Western canon.

Gates visited Africa while attending Yale University and did advanced studies at Clare College, Cambridge, where his tutor was the Nigerian writer Wole Soyinka. Gates later taught at several American universities, including Yale and Harvard.

Gates's theory of signifyin' traces black Caribbean and American culture back through the "talking book," the central method for recording slave narratives, and the early "signifying monkey" storyteller to Esu, the trickster figure of the West African Yoruba. Black culture, Gates held, maintains an ongoing dialogue, often humorous, insulting, or provocative, with what has preceded it, and all works of black writers must be seen in this context. Gates's fullest exposition of signifyin' was found in *Figures in Black: Words, Signs, and the "Racial" Self* (1987) and *The Signifying Monkey: A Theory of Afro-American Literary Criticism* (1988). He applied his theory to many texts, including those of Soyinka, the slave narratives, Frederick Douglass, and the 18th-century poet Phillis Wheatley.

Geisel, Theodor Seuss, *pseudonym* Dr. Seuss (b. March 2, 1904, Springfield, Mass., U.S.—d. Sept. 24, 1991, La Jolla, Calif.) American writer and illustrator of immensely popular children's books.

Geisel initially worked as a freelance cartoonist, illustrator, and writer for several American publications. The first book he published under his pseudonym was *And To Think That I Saw It on Mulberry Street* (1937). His lively children's books were a major departure from mainstream writing for children. They were peopled with invented creatures and were brimming with nonsense words and humorous situations. In 1957 he published *The Cat in the Hat*, a book specifically designed for beginning readers.

Among his many popular works are *Horton Hatches the Egg* (1940), *How the Grinch Stole Christmas* (1957), *Yertle the Turtle* (1958), *Green Eggs and Ham* (1960), and *Hop on Pop* (1963).

Geisel also designed and produced animated cartoons for television, many of them based on his books.

Gelber, Jack (b. April 12, 1932, Chicago, Ill., U.S.) American playwright and teacher known for *The Connection* (performed 1959, published 1960), and for his association with THE LIVING THEATRE, an innovative, experimental theater group.

After graduating from the University of Illinois, Champaign-Urbana, Gelber began working with the struggling Living Theatre group in New York City. His first play, *The Connection*, is historically important for its disregard of the traditional relationship between audience and actor; it was a breakthrough for The Living Theatre, and both the production and the playwright received wide notice.

Jack Gelber

Set in a slum apartment, the play was staged to suggest a naturalistic scene, with actors already on stage as the audience arrived (as if the audience were seeing life, not a play, in progress). This nontraditional staging was supported by other techniques: by presenting an actor as an audience member; by using the theater aisles as a performance area; and by having the actors (who represented drug addicts) panhandle the audience during the play's intermission. The play was imaginatively and brilliantly produced, though for all its appearance of improvisation, it was tightly structured.

The Apple (1961), Gelber's second play, also was written expressly for The Living Theatre. His later works continued to challenge theatrical conventions, but none matched the popular or critical success of his first play.

Gérin-Lajoie, Antoine (b. Aug. 4, 1824, Yamachiche, Que., Lower Canada—d. Aug. 4, 1882, Ottawa, Ont., Can.) Writer, librarian, and leader in the early literary movement of French Canada.

While a college student, Gérin-Lajoie wrote the first French-Canadian play, *Le Jeune Latour* (1844; "The Young Latour"). He later served as translator to the legislative assembly of Canada (1852–56) and as assistant librarian of Parliament (1856–80).

Gérin-Lajoie was one of the founders of the Institut Canadien of Montreal and of the literary magazines *Les Soirées canadiennes* (1861–65; "Canadian Evenings") and *Le Foyer canadien* (1863–66; "The Canadian Home"). He was the author of *Catechisme politique* (1851; "Political Catechism") and *Dix Ans au Canada, de 1840 à 1850* (1888; "Ten Years in Canada, from 1840 to 1850"), the history of the advent of "responsible government" (with the colonial executive responsible to the Canadian assembly) in the colony. He also wrote a novel in two parts, *Jean Rivard, le défricheur* (1862; "Jean Rivard, the Reclaimer") and *Jean Rivard, l'économiste* (1864; "Jean Rivard, the Economist"), which portrays rural life in French Canada in the mid-19th century.

Gernsback, Hugo (b. Aug. 16, 1884, Luxembourg, Lux.—d. Aug. 19, 1967, New York, N.Y., U.S.) American inventor and publisher who was largely responsible for the establishment of science fiction as an independent literary form.

After receiving a technical education in Luxembourg and Germany, Gernsback traveled to the United States in 1904 to market an improved dry battery that he had invented. He formed a radio supply house, and in 1908 he founded *Modern Electrics* (later absorbed by *Popular Science*), a pioneer magazine for radio enthusiasts.

In 1926 Gernsback began publishing *Amazing Stories*, the first magazine devoted exclusively to what he referred to as "scientifiction." The stories were often crudely written, but the very existence of the magazine and its successors, including *Wonder Stories*, encouraged the development and refinement of the genre. His contribution was later recognized with the establishment of the annual Hugo Award for the best science fiction.

Ghose, Zulfikar (b. March 13, 1935, Sialkot, India [now Pakistan]) Pakistani-American author of novels, poetry, and criticism about cultural alienation.

Ghose grew up a Muslim in Sialkot and in largely Hindu Bombay, then moved with his family to England. He graduated from the University of Keele in 1959 and married an artist, Helena de la Fontaine, from Brazil (later the setting for six of his novels). In 1969 he moved to the United States to teach at the University of Texas.

His first novel, *The Contradictions* (1966), explores differences between Western and Eastern attitudes and ways of life. In *The Murder of Aziz Khan* (1967) a small farmer tries to save his traditional land from greedy developers. Ghose's trilogy *The Incredible Brazilian*, comprising *The Native* (1972), *The Beautiful Empire* (1975), and *A Different World* (1978), presents the picaresque adventures, often violent or sexually perverse, of a man who goes through several reincarnations. Ghose's other novels include *Crump's Terms* (1975), *Hulme's Investigations into the Bogart Script* (1981), *A New History of Torments* (1982), *Don Bueno* (1983), *Figures of Enchantment* (1986), and *The Triple Mirror of the Self* (1992). His poems, from those in *The Loss of India* (1964) to the *Selected Poems* (1991), are often about the travels and memories of a self-aware alien. He also wrote an early autobiography, *Confessions of a Native-Alien* (1965).

Gibran or **Jibran, Khalil** or **Kahlil,** *Arabic name in full* Jubrān Khalīl Jubrān (b. Jan. 6, 1883, Bsharrī, Lebanon—d. April 10, 1931, New York, N.Y., U.S.) Lebanese-American philosophical essayist, novelist, mystic poet, and artist.

Gibran immigrated with his parents to Boston in 1895. After studying in

Beirut, he returned to Boston, and in 1912 he settled in New York City, where he devoted himself to writing essays and short stories, both in Arabic and in English, and to painting.

Gibran's writings are full of lyrical outpourings and are expressive of his deeply religious and mystical nature. His principal works in Arabic are *Dam`ah wa ibtisāmah* (1914; *A Tear and a Smile*), *Al-Arwāḥal-mutamarridah* (1920); *Spirits Rebellious*), *Al-Ajniḥah al-mutakassirah* (1922); *The Broken Wings*), and *Al-Mawākib* (1923; *The Procession*), a collection of poems. His principal works in English are *The Madman* (1918), *The Forerunner* (1920), THE PROPHET (1923), *Sand and Foam* (1926), and *Jesus, the Son of Man* (1928).

Khalil Gibran

Gibson, William (Ford) (b. March 17, 1948, Conway, S.C., U.S.) Writer of science fiction who was the leader of the genre's cyberpunk movement.

Many of Gibson's early stories were published in *Omni* magazine. With the publication of his first novel, *Neuromancer* (1984), Gibson emerged as a leading exponent of "cyberpunk," a new school of science-fiction writing. Gibson's creation of "cyberspace," a computer-simulated reality that shows the nature of information, is considered the author's major contribution to the genre.

Count Zero (1986) was set on the same world as *Neuromancer*, but seven years later. The characters of *Mona Lisa Overdrive* (1988) can "die" into computers, where they may support or sabotage outer reality. After collaborating with writer Bruce Sterling on *The Difference Engine* (1990), a story set in Victorian England, Gibson returned to the subject of cyberspace in *Virtual Light* (1993).

Gilman, Charlotte Perkins, *original name* Charlotte Anna Perkins, *married names* Stetson, Gilman (b. July 3, 1860, Hartford, Conn., U.S.—d. Aug. 17, 1935, Pasadena, Calif.) Leading theorist of the women's movement in the United States.

Gilman began her literary career in the 1890s with the publication of poetry, short stories, and essays of social analysis. She also gained worldwide fame as a lecturer, speaking on topics concerning women, ethics, labor, and society. In *Women and Economics* (1898), the work for which she is best known, she proposed that the sexual and maternal roles of women had been overemphasized to the detriment of their social and economic potential and that only economic independence could bring true freedom.

Gilman's autobiography, *The Living of Charlotte Perkins Gilman*, appeared in 1935. Among her other publications were a frequently anthologized short story, THE YELLOW WALLPAPER (1899), *The Home* (1903), *The Man-Made World* (1911), and *His Religion and Hers* (1923).

Allen Ginsberg

Ginsberg, Allen (b. June 3, 1926, Newark, N.J., U.S.) American poet whose epic poem HOWL (1956) is considered to be one of the most significant products of the BEAT MOVEMENT.

Ginsberg studied at Columbia University, where he became close friends with Jack Kerouac and William Burroughs, who were later to be numbered among the Beats. *Howl*, his first published book, laments what Ginsberg believed to have been the destruction by insanity of the "best minds of [his] generation." *Empty Mirror*, a collection of earlier poems, appeared in 1961 along with *Kaddish and Other Poems*, followed by REALITY SANDWICHES in 1963. KADDISH, a long confessional poem, is one of Ginsberg's most important works. He became an influential guru of the American youth counterculture in the late 1960s.

His later volumes of poetry include *Planet News* (1968); *The Fall of America: Poems of These States, 1965–1971* (1972); *Mind Breaths: Poems 1972–1977* (1978); and *White Shroud: Poems 1980–1985* (1986). His *Collected Poems 1947–1980* appeared in 1984.

Giovanni, Nikki, *byname of* Yolande Cornelia Giovanni, Jr. (b. June 7, 1943, Knoxville, Tenn., U.S.) African-American poet whose writings ranged from calls for violent revolution to poems for children and intimate personal statements.

Giovanni, entered Nashville's Fisk University in 1960. By 1967, when she received her B.A., she was firmly committed to the civil-rights movement and the concept of black power. In her first three collections of poems, *Black Feeling, Black Talk* (1968), *Black Judgement* (1968), and *Re: Creation* (1970), her content is urgently revolutionary and suffused with deliberate interpretation of experience through a black consciousness.

Giovanni's experiences as a single mother then began to influence her poetry. *Spin a Soft Black Song* (1971), *Ego-Tripping* (1973), and *Vacation Time* (1980) were collections of poems for children. She returned to political concerns in *Those Who Ride the Night Winds* (1983), with dedications to African-American heroes and heroines. In *Gemini* (1971) she presents autobiographical reminiscences, and *Sacred Cows . . . and Other Edibles* (1988) is a collection of her essays.

Glasgow, Ellen (Anderson Gholson) (b. April 22, 1873, Richmond, Va., U.S.—d. Nov. 21, 1945, Richmond) Pulitzer Prize-winning American novelist whose realistic depiction of life in her native Virginia helped direct Southern literature away from sentimentality and nostalgia.

Glasgow was irregularly schooled because of delicate health but otherwise lived the life of a Southern belle except for her intense seriousness about becoming a novelist of stature. In *The Voice of the People* (1900) she began a planned social history of Virginia from 1850. The series also included *The Battle-Ground* (1902), *The Deliverance* (1904), *The Romance of a Plain Man* (1909), and *Virginia* (1913).

Glasgow was past the age of 50 when she first gained serious attention from the critics with *Barren Ground* (1925), a story of the Piedmont country-side of Virginia. She then published a trilogy of ironic novels of manners set in Richmond (disguised as "Queenborough"): *The Romantic Comedians* (1926), *They Stooped to Folly* (1929), and *The Sheltered Life* (1932), the last often linked with *Barren Ground* as her best work. Glasgow's memoirs, *The Woman Within* (1954), and her *Letters* (1958) were published after her death. *The Collected Stories* appeared in 1963.

Ellen A. Glasgow

Glaspell, Susan (b. July 1, 1882, Davenport, Iowa, U.S.—d. July 27, 1948, Provincetown, Mass.) American dramatist and novelist who, with her hus-band, George Cram COOK, founded the influential Provincetown Players in 1915.

Glaspell's first novel was *The Glory of the Conquered* (1909), and some of her short stories were collected in *Lifted Masks* (1912). Cook, whom she married in 1913, interested her in socialist ideas, which figured in her next novel, *The Visioning* (1911). While summering in Provincetown in 1915, Glaspell and Cook launched the Provincetown Players, ostensibly to produce their one-act play *Suppressed Desires*, a satire on psychoanalysis. Two of Glaspell's full-length plays—*Inheritors* (1921) and *The Verge* (1922)—were also produced by the Provincetown group.

After Cook's death in 1924, Glaspell settled in Provincetown. In *The Road to the Temple* (1926), she gave a romantic account of her husband's life. Her last play was the Pulitzer Prize-winning *Alison's House* (1931), which is about the impact of a great poet (said to be patterned on Emily Dickinson) on her family 18 years after her death. Her later novels include *The Fugitive's Return* (1929) and *The Morning Is Near Us* (1940).

Glassco, John, *pseudonyms* Sylvia Bayer, George Colman, Jean de Saint-Luc, *and* Miles Underwood (b. Dec. 15, 1909, Montreal, Que., Can.—d. Jan. 29, 1981, Montreal) Canadian author whose poetry, short stories, novels, memoirs, and translations were notable for their versatility and sophistication.

Glassco abandoned his studies at McGill University to join the expatriate community in Paris, an experience he chronicled in the celebrated *Memoirs of Montparnasse* (1970). He earned acclaim for his first published work, the poem "Conan's Fig," which appeared in the international quarterly *transition* in 1928. After contracting tuberculosis, he returned to Quebec in the early 1930s.

While his poetry dealt with the simplicity of rural life in the Eastern Townships of Quebec, his prose, inspired by the Decadents of the 19th century, was heavy with irony and eroticism. He wrote *Under the Hill* (1959), the completion of an unfinished romance by Aubrey Beardsley; the novel *English Governess* (1960); also published as *Harriet Marwood, Governess*), a parody of Victorian pornography; and *The Fatal Woman* (1974), a collection of three novellas that explore the dehumanization of sexual fantasies. His verse collections, elegant and classical, include *The Deficit Made Flesh* (1958), *A Point of Sky* (1964), and *Selected Poems* (1971).

Glück, Louise (Elisabeth) (b. April 22, 1943, New York, N.Y., U.S.) Poet known for her insights into the self and for her severe lyricism. Glück was noted for her willingness to confront in her writing the horrible, the difficult, and the painful.

After attending Sarah Lawrence College and Columbia University, from 1971 Glück taught poetry at numerous colleges and universities. Her first collection of poetry, *Firstborn* (1968), used a variety of first-person personae, all disaffected or angry. The collection's tone disturbed many critics, but Glück's exquisitely controlled language and imaginative use of rhyme and meter delighted others. Although its outlook was equally grim, her collection *The House on Marshland* (1975) showed a greater mastery of voice. Her adoption of different perspectives became increasingly imaginative; for example, in "The Sick Child," from the collection *Descending Figure* (1980), her voice is that of a mother in a museum painting looking out at the bright gallery. The poems in *The Triumph of Achilles* (1985), which won the National Book Critics Circle Award for poetry, address archetypal concerns of classic myth, fairy tales, and the Bible. These concerns are also evident in *Ararat* (1990), which was praised for searing honesty in its examination of the family and the self. *The Wild Iris* was published in 1992; and a volume of essays on poetry, *Proofs and Theories*, was published in 1994.

Godwin, Gail (Kathleen) (b. June 18, 1937, Birmingham, Ala., U.S.) American novelist who wrote about women searching for a personal identity and for meaning in their lives.

After graduating from the University of North Carolina in 1959, Godwin worked as a reporter for the Miami *Herald* and then worked from 1962 to 1965 at the U.S. embassy in London. Returning to the United States, she attended the University of Iowa. She examined the experiences of women smothered by marriage in the violent novel *The Perfectionists* (1970), which was based on her own brief marriage, and in *Glass People* (1972).

The protagonist of Godwin's widely admired *The Odd Woman* (1974) is a college teacher who attempts to come to terms with her family and her married lover. The three principal characters of *A Mother and Two Daughters* (1982) have close relationships with each other, yet grow in separate ways to self-fulfillment. Godwin also wrote the novels *Violet Clay* (1978), *The Finishing School* (1984), *A Southern Family* (1987), *Father Melancholy's Daughter* (1991), and *The Good Husband* (1994).

Goldbarth, Albert (b. Jan. 31, 1948, Chicago, Ill., U.S.) American poet noted for his erudition and wit and whose compulsive wordiness brought comparisons with Walt Whitman.

Educated at the University of Illinois at Chicago, the University of Iowa, and the University of Utah, Goldbarth taught at several schools, notably the University of Texas, Austin, and Wichita State University in Kansas.

Goldbarth often published one or more collections of poems annually. His collections include *Coprolites* (1973), a group of meditations on human leavings; *Opticks* (1974), a long poem about glass, light, and perception; *Comings Back* (1976); *Curve: Overlapping Narratives* (1977); *Different Fleshes* (1979), subtitled "A Novel/Poem"; *Ink, Blood, Semen* (1980); *Faith* (1981); and *Heaven and Earth: A Cosmology* (1991).

Goodrich, Samuel Griswold, *pseudonym* Peter Parley (b. Aug. 19, 1793, Ridgefield, Conn., U.S.—d. May 9, 1860, New York, N.Y.) American publisher and author of children's books.

Goodrich became a bookseller and publisher at Hartford and later in Boston. There, beginning in 1828, he published for 15 years an illustrated annual, the *Token*, to which he was a frequent contributor both of prose and verse. The *Token* contained some of the earliest work of Nathaniel Hawthorne and Henry Wadsworth Longfellow. Goodrich published *Peter Parley's Magazine* (1832–44) and then merged it into his *Merry's Museum*, founded in 1841 and for a time edited by Louisa May Alcott.

Samuel Griswold Goodrich

In 1827 he began, under the name of Peter Parley, his series of books for the young, which embraced geography, biography, history, science, and miscellaneous tales. He was the sole composer of comparatively few of these, but in his *Recollections of a Lifetime*, 2 vol. (1856), he wrote that he was "the author and editor of about 170 volumes," of which some 7,000,000 copies had been sold, and he listed both the works of which he was the author or editor and the spurious works published under his name. He was widely imitated, especially in England.

Gordon, Mary (Catherine) (b. Dec. 8, 1949, Long Island, N.Y.) Writer whose novels and short fiction deal with growing up as a Roman Catholic and with the nature of goodness and piety as expressed within that tradition.

Gordon was educated at Barnard College and Syracuse University. Her first novel, *Final Payments* (1978), was a critical and popular success. The protagonist, Isabel, is 30 before she leaves home, having cared for her domineering father for 11 years until his death. Soon she has friends, a career as a social worker, and several married lovers. Feeling the need to atone for her "self-indulgence," she becomes the caregiver to her father's former housekeeper, a woman she hates.

In *The Company of Women* (1981), Felicitas is nurtured by a large circle of Catholic women. After attending only parochial schools, Felicitas goes to Columbia University, where she becomes sexually involved with a married professor, gives up her studies, and becomes pregnant. She returns to the company of women, gives birth to her baby, and later marries only to provide a father for her child.

Gordon's later works include a collection of short stories, *Temporary Shelter* (1987), and the three novellas in *The Rest of Life* (1993); the novels *Men and Angels* (1985) and *The Other Side* (1989); and three works of nonfiction, *Spiritual Quests: The Art and Craft of Religious Writing* (1988), *Good Boys and Dead Girls and Other Essays* (1991), and *The Shadow Man* (1996).

Gorey, Edward (St. John) (b. Feb. 22, 1925, Chicago, Ill., U.S.) Writer, illustrator, and designer, noted for his arch humor and gothic sensibility. Gorey drew a pen-and-ink world of beady-eyed, blank-faced individuals whose dignified Edwardian demeanor is undercut by silly and often macabre events. His nonsense rhymes recalled those of Edward Lear, and his mock-Victorian prose delighted readers with its ludicrous fustiness. Gorey's work evoked the cosy sensibilities of childhood reading while subverting that feeling with its often grisly humor.

After graduating in 1950 from Harvard, Gorey immersed himself in the New York cultural scene. In 1953 he began writing and illustrating short books. *The Doubtful Guest* (1957), his first book for children, featured a penguinlike creature that moved into a wealthy home: "It came 17 years ago—and to this day/It has shown no intention of going away."

During the 1960s Gorey published under several playful pseudonyms, mostly anagrams such as Ogdred Weary and Mrs. Regera Dowdy. Gorey was fond of illustrated alphabets; his most celebrated was *The Gashlycrumb Tinies* (1962), which disposes of 26 children: "M is for Maud who was swept out to sea / N is for Neville who died of ennui." He illustrated two books by Edward Lear, including *The Dong with a Luminous Nose* (1969). Gorey continued to write his own stories, including *The Hapless Child* (1961), *The Gilded Bat* (1966), and *The Deranged Cousins: or, Whatever* (1969).

From 1970 Gorey concentrated on adult works, although he still wrote children's stories. His anthologies *Amphigorey* (1972), *Amphigorey Too*

(1975), and *Amphigorey Also* (1983) sold well; the first two volumes were the basis for a 1978 musical stage adaptation, *Gorey Stories*.

Graham, Jorie (b. May 9, 1951, New York, N.Y., U.S.) American poet whose abstract, intellectual verse was known for its visual imagery, complex metaphors, and philosophical content.

Graham began publishing poems in 1977. Her first volume of verse, *Hybrids of Plants and of Ghosts* (1980), features compact, intricate poems that explore death, beauty, and change. *Erosion* (1983) examines the connection between the body and the soul in such poems as "Reading Plato," "I Watched a Snake," and "The Sense of an Ending." In *The End of Beauty* (1987), Graham experimented with form, constructing subtle, sometimes inaccessible poems divided into series of short, numbered stanzas with missing words and lively enjambment. *Region of Unlikeness* (1991), which is annotated to explain textual obscurities, furthers her exploration of philosophy and religion in such poems as "The Tree of Knowledge," "The Holy Shroud," and "Chaos." She also published *Materialism* (1993) and contributed to several anthologies. In 1994 Graham received the Pulitzer prize in poetry for *The Dream of the Unified Field; Selected Poems 1974–1994*.

Grandbois, Alain (b. May 25, 1900, Saint-Casimir, Que., Can.—d. March 18, 1975, Quebec) French-Canadian poet whose use of unconventional verse forms, abstract metaphors of voyage and death, and colorful imagery influenced younger experimental poets.

Much of Grandbois's early poetry was originally published in volumes such as *Poèmes* (1934) and *Les Îles de la nuit* (1944); "The Isles of the Night"). Among his later collections are *Poèmes* (1963) and *Selected Poems* (1965), containing both the French originals and English translations. In addition to poetry, he wrote biographies of Louis Jolliet, *Né à Québec* (1948; *Born in Quebec*), and Marco Polo, *Les Voyages de Marco Polo* (1942), as well as a volume of short tales, *Avant le chaos* (1945; "Before the Chaos").

Grau, Shirley Ann (b. July 8, 1929, New Orleans, La., U.S.) American novelist and short-story writer noted for her examinations of evil and isolation among American Southerners.

Grau's first book, *The Black Prince, and Other Stories* (1955), had considerable success. Her first novel, *The Hard Blue Sky* (1958), concerns Cajun fishermen and their families. This was followed by *The House on Coliseum Street* (1961) and *The Keepers of the House* (1964), which won a Pulitzer Prize for fiction. It deals with three generations of the Howland family, a once-mighty Southern dynasty. Among her later novels are *The Condor Passes* (1971), *Evidence of Love* (1977), and *Roadwalkers* (1994). Her other short-story collections include *The Wind Shifting West* (1973) and *Nine Women* (1985).

Green, Anna Katharine (b. Nov. 11, 1846, Brooklyn, N.Y., U.S.—d. April 11, 1935, Buffalo, N.Y.) American writer of detective fiction who helped to make the genre popular in America by creating well-constructed plots based on a good knowledge of criminal law.

Inspired by her father's work as a lawyer, Green began her writing career with the detective story *The Leavenworth Case* (1878), which introduced her detective hero, Ebenezer Gryce, and rapidly became popular. After writing her third detective novel, Green wrote two volumes of poetry. Thereafter she concentrated on detective fiction.

Green's tendency to intersperse romantic characterizations and dialogue in her work sometimes makes her style old-fashioned, but her skillful plotting and technical accuracy are noteworthy. Some of her works are *Lost Man's Lane* (1898), *The Filigree Ball* (1903), *The House of the Whispering Pines* (1910), and *The Step on the Stair* (1923).

Green, Paul (Eliot) (b. March 17, 1894, Lillington, N.C., U.S.—d. May 4, 1981, Chapel Hill, N.C.) American novelist and playwright whose characteristic works deal with North Carolina folklore and regional themes; he was one of the first white playwrights to write perceptively about the problems of Southern blacks.

Green began writing plays for the Carolina Playmakers in 1919. His best-known play, *In Abraham's Bosom*, concerns a man's attempt to establish a school for his fellow blacks; it was awarded the Pulitzer Prize in 1927. During the Great Depression, Green's work took on a stronger note of social protest. Among his plays from this period are *Hymn to the Rising Sun*, about a chain gang, and *Johnny Johnson*, an expressionistic, episodic antiwar play for which Kurt Weill wrote the music; both plays were first performed in 1936. In 1941 Green collaborated with Richard Wright in the dramatization of Wright's novel *Native Son*. Green also wrote more than a dozen symphonic dramas, including *The Stephen Foster Story* (1959), *Trumpet in the Land* (1970), and *The Lone Star* (1977), which won wide popularity.

Gregory, Horace (Victor) (b. April 10, 1898, Milwaukee, Wis., U.S.—d. March 11, 1982, Shelburne Falls, Mass.) American poet, critic, translator, and editor noted for both conventional and experimental writing.

Gregory began to write poetry while studying Latin in college, and he first contributed to periodicals in the early 1920s. Finding formal verse inadequate, he tried to combine the idiom of modern life with literary influences in *Chelsea Rooming House* (1930), his first success. His poetry also appeared in many avant-garde magazines during the 1920s and '30s. A later volume was *Another Look* (1976).

Gregory wrote biographies of Amy Lowell (1958) and James McNeill Whistler (1959). His *Pilgrim of the Apocalypse* (1933; 2nd ed., 1957) was one of the first important critiques of D.H. Lawrence. Gregory edited the works of many writers, and with his wife, Marya Zaturenska, he wrote *A History of American Poetry, 1900–1940* (1946). His essays are collected in *Spirit of Time and Place* (1973), and his translated works include *Love Poems of Ovid* (1964).

Grey, Zane, *original name* Pearl Grey (b. Jan. 31, 1872, Zanesville, Ohio, U.S.—d. Oct. 23, 1939, Altadena, Calif.) Prolific writer whose romantic novels of the American West helped create a new literary genre, the WESTERN.

Zane Grey

Trained as a dentist, Grey practiced in New York City from 1898 to 1904, when he published privately a novel of pioneer life, *Betty Zane*, based on an ancestor's journal. He published several works before he achieved success with *The Heritage of the Desert* (1910). Grey subsequently wrote more than 80 books, a number of which were published posthumously. The novel *Riders of the Purple Sage* (1912) was the most popular; others include *The Lone Star Ranger* (1915), *The U.P. Trail* (1918), *Call of the Canyon* (1924), and *Code of the West* (1934). Prominent among his nonfiction works is *Tales of Fishing* (1925).

Grimké, Angelina Weld (b. Feb. 27, 1880, Boston, Mass., U.S.—d. June 10, 1958, New York, N.Y.) African-American poet and playwright, an important forerunner of the Harlem Renaissance.

Grimké was born into a prominent biracial family of abolitionists and civil-rights activists; the noted abolitionists Angelina and Sarah Grimké were her great-aunts, and her father was the son of a wealthy white aristocrat and a slave. In the early 1900s she began to write articles and poems to express her concern about racism and the plight of blacks in America. Her play *Rachel*, produced in 1916 and published in 1920, concerns a young woman who is so horrified by racism that she vows never to bring children into the world. Although the play is considered to be overly sentimental and was criticized for its defeatism, it was one of the first plays written by a black author about black issues.

Grimké is best known for her small body of poetry, which has been anthologized in *Negro Poets and Their Poems* (1923), *The Poetry of the Negro* (1949; edited by Langston Hughes), and *Caroling Dusk* (1927); edited by Countee Cullen, among others. Her poems are mainly personal lyrics that draw images from nature and express a sense of isolation or a yearning for love.

Grove, Frederick Philip (b. 1871, Russia—d. Aug. 19, 1948, Simcoe, Ont., Can.) Canadian novelist whose fame rests on somber naturalistic works that deal frankly and realistically with pioneer life on the Canadian prairies.

Grove grew up in Sweden, traveled widely in Europe as a youth, and attended European universities. On a visit to Canada in 1892, he was left stranded there by his father's sudden death. He worked as an itinerant farm laborer from 1892 to 1912 and as a teacher in Manitoba from 1912 to 1924. He worked as an editor in Ottawa before retiring to a farm near Simcoe.

Grove's series of prairie novels, *Settlers of the Marsh* (1925), *Our Daily Bread* (1928), *The Yoke of Life* (1930), and *Fruits of the Earth* (1933), were his most successful works. He also wrote two books of essays on prairie life and an autobiography, *In Search of Myself* (1946).

Guare, John (b. Feb. 5, 1938, New York, N.Y., U.S.) American playwright known for his innovative and often absurdist dramas.

Guare was educated at Georgetown and Yale universities. He then began staging short plays, primarily in New York City. His first notable works—*Muzeeka* (1968), about American soldiers of the Vietnam War who have television contracts, and *Cop-Out* (1968)—satirized the American media.

In 1971 Guare earned critical acclaim for *The House of Blue Leaves*, a farce about a zookeeper who murders his insane wife after he fails as a songwriter. *Two Gentlemen of Verona* (1972); with Mel Shapiro), a rock-musical modernization of William Shakespeare's comedy, won the Tony and New York Drama Critics Circle awards for best musical of 1971–72. Guare dealt with such issues as success—in *Marco Polo Sings a Solo* (1977) and *Rich and Famous* (1977)—and parent-child relationships—in *Landscape of the Body* (1978) and *Bosoms and Neglect* (1980). The plays *Lydie Breeze* (1982), *Gardenia* (1982), and *Women and Water* (1990) make up a family saga set in Nantucket, Mass., in the second half of the 19th century. Guare also wrote several screenplays.

Guest, Edgar Albert (b. Aug. 20, 1881, Birmingham, Warwickshire, Eng.—d. Aug. 5, 1959, Detroit, Mich., U.S.) Writer whose sentimental verses were widely read.

Guest's family moved to the United States in 1891. Four years later he went to work for the *Detroit Free Press* as an office boy, eventually becoming a reporter and then a writer of daily rhymes. These became so popular that they were eventually syndicated to newspapers throughout the country and made his name a household word. His first book, *A Heap o'*

Livin' (1916), became a best-seller and was followed by similar collections of his optimistic rhymes on such subjects as home, mother, and the virtue of hard work.

Guèvremont, Germaine, *original name* Marianne-Germaine-Grignon (b. April 16, 1893, Saint-Jérôme, Que., Can.—d. Aug. 21, 1968, Montreal) French-Canadian regional writer, one of the last novelists to skillfully recreate the confined world of rural Quebec.

Grignon published her first article in 1912. She moved to Sorel, Que., with her husband in 1920. She moved to Montreal in 1935 and began to contribute sketches of the rural life she had observed in the region around Sorel for a monthly magazine entitled *Paysana*. Several of these pieces are included in *En Plein Terre* (1942); "On Open Ground"). The same characters and subject matter were presented in novel form in *Le Survenant* (1945); "The Unexpected One"), which inspired a French-Canadian television series, and its sequel, *Marie-Didace* (1947). The two novels were translated and published together as *The Outlander* (1950) in the United States and Canada and as *Monk's Reach* (1950) in the United Kingdom.

Gunn, Thom, *byname of* Thomson William Gunn (b. Aug. 29, 1929, Gravesend, Kent, Eng.) Anglo-American poet whose verse is notable for its adroit, terse language.

Gunn graduated from Trinity College, Cambridge, and later studied and taught at Stanford University in California. He also taught at the University of California at Berkeley.

His first volume of verse was *Fighting Terms* (1954); rev. ed., 1962). *The Sense of Movement* (1957) contains one of his best-known poems, "On the Move," a celebration of black-jacketed motorcyclists. In the late 1950s his poetry became more experimental. A selection of his work from this period was published in *Poems, 1950–1966* (1969). In the 1970s Gunn produced both a euphoric volume, *Moly* (1971), and a collection expressing disenchantment, *Jack Straw's Castle* (1976). *Selected Poems 1950–1975* was published in 1979, and *The Passages of Joy* in 1982. *The Occasion of Poetry* (1982) is a collection of essays. *The Man with Night Sweats* (1992) has AIDS as its subject.

Gustafson, Ralph (Barker) (b. Aug. 16, 1909, Lime Ridge, near Sherbrooke, Que., Can.) Canadian poet whose work shows a development from traditional form and manner to an elliptical style that reflects the influence of Anglo-Saxon verse and the metrical experiments of the 19th-century British poet Gerard Manley Hopkins.

Gustafson attended the University of Oxford and then became a tutor and journalist in London. He settled in New York after World War II but later returned to Canada.

Gustafson's early volumes of verse, such as *The Golden Chalice* (1935), *Lyrics Unromantic* (1942), and *Flight into Darkness* (1944), showed a gradually increasing individuality of style and an evolving vision. The later of his numerous works, which are usually considered his better writings, include *Rivers Among Rocks* (1960), *Sift in an Hourglass* (1966), *Ixion's Wheel* (1969), *Conflicts of Spring* (1981), *Plummets and Other Partialities* and *Winter Prophecies* (both 1987), and *Shadows in the Grass* (1991). Gustafson also produced two volumes of short stories, *The Brazen Tower* (1974) and *The Vivid Air* (1980).

Guthrie, A.B., *in full* Alfred Bertram Guthrie, Jr. (b. Jan. 13, 1901, Bedford, Ind., U.S.—d. April 26, 1991, Choteau, Mont.) American novelist best known for his writing about the American West.

Guthrie earned a degree in journalism from the University of Montana and later went to work for the *Lexington Leader* newspaper in Kentucky, where between 1926 and 1947 he rose from cub reporter to executive editor. His first book, *Murders at Moon Dance*, was published in 1943. Next came his three most famous novels (often designated a trilogy)—*The Big Sky* (1947), *The Way West* (1949), which won a Pulitzer Prize, and *These Thousand Hills* (1956)—all of which realistically depict the lives of Americans settling along the upper Missouri and Columbia rivers. Guthrie returned permanently to Montana in 1953, where he later successfully blended the Western and detective genres in such books as *Wild Pitch* (1973), *The Genuine Article* (1977), and *No Second Wind* (1980). He also published *The Big It* (1960), a collection of short stories; *The Blue Hen's Chick* (1965), an autobiography; and *A Field Guide to Writing Fiction* (1991).

Guy, Rosa (Cuthbert) (b. Sept. 1, 1925/28, Trinidad, West Indies) African-American writer whose fiction for young adults usually concerned family conflicts and the realities of life in the urban American ghetto as well as life in the West Indies.

After immigrating to the United States with her family in 1932, Guy grew up in New York City's Harlem. She became a writer and studied at New York University. In the late 1940s, with other young black writers, she formed the Harlem Writers' Guild.

Her first novel, *Bird at My Window* (1966), was set in Harlem and dealt with social forces that foster the demoralization of black men; the work also examined the relationship between the black mother and her children. *Children of Longing* (1970), which Guy edited, contained accounts of firsthand experiences and of the aspirations of young black people aged 13 to 23. After publication of these works, Guy traveled in the Caribbean, living in Haiti and Trinidad. Her subsequent novels, such as *The Friends* (1973) and *Ruby* (1976), reflect West Indian and Haitian cultures. Still later works include *The Disappearance* (1979), *A Measure of Time* (1983), *New Guys Around the Block* (1983), *Paris, Pee Wee, and Big Dog* (1984), *My Love, My Love; or, The Peasant Girl* (1985), *And I Heard a Bird Sing* (1987), and *The Ups and Downs of Carl David III* (1989).

Edward Everett Hale

Hale, Edward Everett (b. April 3, 1822, Boston, Mass., U.S.—d. June 10, 1909, Roxbury, Mass.) American clergyman and author best remembered for his short story "The Man Without a Country."

Hale trained on his father's newspaper, the *Boston Daily Advertiser*, and early on turned to writing. He wrote for such journals as the *North American Review*, *The Atlantic Monthly*, and *Christian Examiner*. From 1870 to 1875 he published and edited the Unitarian journal *Old and New*. "My Double and How He Undid Me" (1859) established the vein of realistic fantasy that was Hale's forte. It introduced a group of loosely related characters figuring in *If, Yes, and Perhaps* (1868), *The Ingham Papers* (1869), *Sybaris and Other Homes* (1869), *His Level Best* (1872), and other collections. "The Man Without a Country," which appeared first in *The Atlantic Monthly* in 1863, was written to inspire greater patriotism during the Civil War. *East and West* (1892) and *In His Name* (1873) were his most popular novels.

Hale's ministry began in 1846. Many of his 150 books and pamphlets were tracts for such causes as the education of blacks, workers' housing, and world peace. The reminiscent writings of his later years are rich and colorful—*A New England Boyhood* (1893), *James Russell Lowell and His Friends* (1899), and *Memories of a Hundred Years* (1902). His *Works*, in 10 volumes, appeared in 1898–1900.

Hale, Lucretia Peabody (b. Sept. 2, 1820, Boston, Mass., U.S.—d. June 12, 1900, Belmont, Mass.) American novelist and writer of children's books.

Hale produced her first novel, *Struggle for Life*, in 1861. From 1868 to 1883 she wrote about the bumbling but endearing Peterkin family. These tales were eventually gathered into *The Peterkin Papers* (1880), the first American nonsense classic, and *The Last of the Peterkins, with Others of Their Kin* (1886). The success of these stories arose from Hale's skill in combining a realistic depiction of contemporary Bostonian society with a silliness that charmed youngsters.

Hale, Sarah Josepha, *original surname* Buell (b. Oct. 24, 1788, Newport, N.H., U.S.—d. April 30, 1879, Philadelphia, Pa.) American writer who, as the first female editor of a magazine, shaped many of the attitudes and thoughts of women of her period.

Hale turned to writing in 1822 as a widow trying to support her family. Within several years she was invited to edit the *Ladies' Magazine* (1828–37). When the magazine was bought by Louis A. Godey in 1837, Hale was retained as editor for the new magazine entitled *Lady's Book*, later called *Godey's Lady's Book* (1837–77).

One of Hale's more important books is *The Ladies' Wreath* (1837), a collection of poetry by English and American women that sold widely. Her most significant work is *Woman's Record: or, Sketches of All Distinguished Women from "the Beginning" till A.D. 1850* (1853). The 2,500 entries contain valuable, orderly biographical information. Hale is also remembered as the author of the children's verse "Mary Had a Little Lamb" (1830).

Haley, Alex (Palmer) (b. Aug. 11, 1921, Ithaca, N.Y., U.S.—d. Feb. 10, 1992, Seattle, Wash.) American writer whose works of historical fiction and reportage depicted the struggles of American blacks.

Alex Haley

Haley's first major work, THE AUTOBIOGRAPHY OF MALCOLM X (1965; film, 1992), was an authoritative and widely read narrative based on Haley's interviews with the Black Muslim spokesman. The work is recognized as a classic of black American autobiography.

Haley's greatest success was ROOTS (1976). This well-researched genealogy—born of the history recited by one of Haley's grandmothers—covers seven American generations, from the enslavement of Haley's African ancestors to his own genealogical quest. In 1977 Haley won a special Pulitzer Prize. *A Different Kind of Christmas* (1988) is a novella about a plantation owner who rejects slavery.

Haliburton, Thomas Chandler (b. Dec. 17, 1796, Windsor, Nova Scotia [Canada]—d. Aug. 27, 1865, Isleworth, Middlesex, Eng.) Canadian writer best known as the creator of Sam Slick, a resourceful Yankee clock peddler and cracker-barrel philosopher whose encounters with a variety of people illuminated Haliburton's conservative view of human nature.

Haliburton, as a member of the Nova Scotia Legislative Assembly (1826–29), led a popular movement for liberal reform. He later reverted to his early Tory convictions. In 1856 he moved to England, where from 1859 until his death he was a member of Parliament.

The escapades of Sam Slick were first revealed serially in the newspaper *Nova Scotian* (1835) but subsequently published in book form (1836, 1838, 1840) as *The Clockmaker; or, The Sayings and Doings of Samuel Slick of Slickville*. The satirical dialogues between Sam Slick and the squire are enriched by the tremendous vitality of Sam's colloquial speech and by his fund of anecdotes and tall tales. Haliburton's subsequent works were *The Attaché; or, Sam Slick in England*, 4 vol. (1843–44), *Sam Slick's Wise Saws and Modern Instances; or, What He Said, Did, or Invented* (1853), and *Nature and Human Nature* (1855).

Hall, Donald, *in full* Donald Andrew Hall, Jr. (b. Sept. 20, 1928, New Haven, Conn., U.S.) American poet and critic whose poetic style moved from studied formalism to greater emphasis on personal expression.

Hall received bachelor's degrees in literature from both Harvard and

Oxford universities. He was a junior fellow at Harvard from 1954 to 1957. From 1957 to 1975 he taught at the University of Michigan. His first volume of poetry, *Exiles and Marriages* (1955), exhibits the influence of his academic training. In *The Dark Houses* (1958) Hall showed a richer emotional range, presaging the intuitive, often idiosyncratic later work collected in *A Roof of Tiger Lilies* (1964), *The Alligator Bride* (1968), *The Yellow Room* (1971), and *The Town of Hill* (1975). Subsequent volumes include *Kicking the Leaves* (1978), *The One Day: A Poem in Three Parts* (1988), and *Old and New Poems* (1990).

The author's critical views and theories of literature were presented in *Marianne Moore: The Cage and the Animal* (1970), *Writing Well* (1973), *Goatfoot Milktongue Twinbird* (1978), *To Read Literature, Fiction, Poetry, Drama* (1981), and *The Weather for Poetry* (1982), among other works. He also published *String Too Short to Be Saved* (1961; rev. ed., 1979); several books on baseball, notably *Fathers Playing Catch with Sons* (1985); and a biography of the sculptor Henry Moore. He edited *The Oxford Book of American Literary Anecdotes* (1981), *The Oxford Book of Children's Verse in America* (1985), and other anthologies.

Halleck, Fitz-Greene (b. July 8, 1790, Guilford, Conn., U.S.—d. Nov. 19, 1867, Guilford) American poet who was a member of the Knickerbocker school and was known for both his satirical and romantic verse.

In collaboration with Joseph Rodman Drake, Halleck contributed the satirical "Croaker Papers" to the New York *Evening Post* in 1819, and on the death of Drake he wrote the moving tribute beginning "Green be the turf above thee." Other popular works were the feudal romance "Alnwick Castle" (1822), "Burns" (1827), the often recited "Marco Bozzaris" (1825), "Red Jacket" (1828), and "Young America" (1865).

Hall, James (b. Aug. 19, 1793, Philadelphia, Pa., U.S.—d. July 5, 1868, Cincinnati, Ohio) One of the earliest American authors to write of the American frontier.

In 1828 Hall compiled the first western literary annual, the *Western Souvenir*, and he edited the *Illinois Monthly Magazine* (1830–32), which he continued at Cincinnati until 1836 as the *Western Monthly Magazine*.

Hall wrote a travel book, *Letters from the West* (1828); one novel, *The Harpe's Head* (1833); a survey of western exploration, *The Romance of Western History* (1857); and several volumes of short stories. Such tales as "Pete Featherton" and "A Legend of Carondelet" established Hall early on as a short-story writer of distinction. He was particularly successful in sketching life in the French settlements of the Illinois country and in interpreting such authentic figures as the backwoodsman, voyageur, and Indian hater. His best stories appear in *Legends of the West* (1832) and *Tales of the Border* (1835).

Hammett, Dashiell, *in full* Samuel Dashiell Hammett (b. May 27, 1894, St. Mary's county, Md., U.S.—d. Jan. 10, 1961, New York City) American writer who helped to create the hard-boiled school of detective fiction.

Hammett left school at age 13 and worked at a variety of low-paying jobs before working for eight years as a detective for the Pinkerton agency. He began to publish short stories and novelettes in pulp magazines and published two novels—*Red Harvest* and *The Dain Curse* (both 1929)—before writing THE MALTESE FALCON (1930), often considered his finest work. The novel introduced Sam Spade, Hammett's fictional detective, who epitomized the character of the hard-boiled detective. Hammett also wrote *The Glass Key* (1931) and THE THIN MAN (1934), which initiated a series of motion pictures built around his detective couple Nick and Nora Charles. Nora was based on the playwright Lillian Hellman, with whom Hammett formed a romantic alliance in 1930 that lasted until his death.

Hannah, Barry (b. April 23, 1942, Meridian, Miss., U.S.) American author of darkly comic, often violent novels and short stories set in the Deep South.

Hannah was educated at Mississippi College and the University of Arkansas. He subsequently taught writing at numerous schools, including the universities of Alabama, Iowa, Montana, and Mississippi. His first novel, *Geronimo Rex* (1972), was a raucous coming-of-age story addressing the theme of racism. In the less successful *Nightwatchmen* (1973), both a secret killer and a hurricane are unleashed upon a small college town.

Hannah's reputation as a daring stylist was secured with *Airships*, a collection of short stories that appeared in 1978. The book's recurrent motif of American Civil War valor was developed more fully in the short novel *Ray* (1980). Hannah's later works include *The Tennis Handsome* (1983), which portrays the misadventures of a dissipated professional tennis player; *Captain Maximus* (1985), containing short stories and the outline of an original screenplay; the novel *Hey Jack!* (1987); *Never Die* (1991), an offbeat treatment of the western genre; and a collection of stories entitled *Bats Out of Hell* (1993).

Hansberry, Lorraine (b. May 19, 1930, Chicago, Ill., U.S.—d. Jan. 12, 1965, New York, N.Y.) American playwright whose A RAISIN IN THE SUN (1959) was the first drama by a black woman to be produced on Broadway.

A Raisin in the Sun is an insightful study of the stresses that both divide and unite a working-class black family when it is presented with a chance for a better life. It won the New York Drama Critics' Circle Award, and the film

Lorraine Hansberry

version of 1961 received a special award at the Cannes festival. Hansberry's next play, THE SIGN IN SIDNEY BRUSTEIN'S WINDOW, a drama of political questioning and affirmation set in the New York City neighborhood of Greenwich Village, where Hansberry had long made her home, had only a modest run on Broadway in 1964. Her promising career was cut short by her early death from cancer.

TO BE YOUNG, GIFTED AND BLACK, adapted by Robert Nemiroff from her writings, was produced Off-Broadway in 1969 and published in book form in 1970.

Hansen, Joseph (b. July 19, 1923, Aberdeen, S.D., U.S.) American writer, author of a series of crime novels featuring the homosexual insurance investigator and detective Dave Brandstetter.

Hansen, who also wrote under the pseudonyms Rose Brock and James Colton, began his career as editor, novelist, and journalist in the mid-1960s. He taught writing through the University of California extension programs from 1977.

In *Fadeout* (1970), the first novel to feature Brandstetter, the detective falls in love with a man whom he clears of murder charges. *Death Claims* (1973) is about surviving the death of a lover. Brandstetter investigates the murder of the owner of a bar for homosexuals in *Troublemaker* (1975). In *Early Graves* (1987) he comes out of retirement to trace a serial killer who murders men with AIDS. Brandstetter also appears in the several other novels and in *Brandstetter and Others* (1984), a collection of short stories.

In addition to the Brandstetter series, Hansen wrote the novels *A Smile in His Lifetime* (1981), *Backtrack* (1982), and *Job's Year* (1983), as well as the short-story collections *The Dog and Other Stories* (1979), *Bohannon's Book* (1988), and *Bohannon's Country* (1993).

Hardwick, Elizabeth (b. July 27, 1916, Lexington, Ky., U.S.) American novelist, short-story writer, and essayist best known for her eloquent literary and social criticism.

Hardwick attended the University of Kentucky and Columbia University in New York City. Her experience as a young Southern woman in Manhattan provided the backdrop for her somber, introspective first novel, *The Ghostly Lover* (1945). As a frequent contributor to the *Partisan Review* and other liberal intellectual journals, she developed the elegant, incisive analytical voice that became her trademark. Her marriage to the poet Robert Lowell lasted from 1949 to 1972, during which period Hardwick wrote her second novel, *The Simple Truth* (1955), edited *The Selected Letters of William James* (1961), published an essay collection entitled *A View of My Own* (1962), and helped to found *The New York Review of Books* (1963). The latter journal became the principal outlet for her criticism, a second volume of which, *Seduction and Betrayal: Women and Literature*, appeared in 1974. She also edited the multivolume *Rediscovered Fiction by American Women* (1977). The novel *Sleepless Nights* (1979) is a partly autobiographical work.

Harjo, Joy (b. May 9, 1951, Tulsa, Okla., U.S.) American poet, writer, academic, and Native-American activist.

An enrolled member of the Creek tribe, Harjo was the daughter of a Creek father and a Cherokee-French mother. A graduate of the universities of New Mexico and Iowa, she taught at several American colleges and universities.

Harjo used Native-American symbolism, imagery, history, and ideas set within a universal context. Her poetry also dealt with social and personal issues, notably feminism, and with music, particularly jazz. Her poetry collections included *The Last Song* (1975), *What Moon Drove Me to This?* (1979), *She Had Some Horses* (1983), *In Mad Love and War* (1990), and *Fishing* (1993).

Harper, Frances E.W., *in full* Ellen Watkins (b. Sept. 24, 1825, Baltimore, Md., U.S.—d. Feb. 22, 1911, Philadelphia, Pa.) African-American author, orator, and social reformer, notable for her poetry, speeches, and essays on abolitionism, temperance, and woman suffrage.

Harper taught school before becoming a traveling lecturer for abolition and other reform movements. Her lyrical poetry, which she often recited during her lectures, echoed her reformist ideals. Generally written in conventional rhymed quatrains, it was noted for its simple rhythm and biblical imagery. Its narrative voice reflected the storytelling style of the oral tradition. *Forest Leaves* (*c.* 1845) was her first volume of verse.

Harper's most popular verse collection, *Poems on Miscellaneous Subjects* (1854; enlarged 1855 and 1871), contains the antislavery poem "Bury Me in a Free Land." *Moses: A Story of the Nile* (1869) is a blank-verse allegory of the aspirations of black Americans during Reconstruction. *Sketches of Southern Life* (1872) is a series of poems told in black vernacular by Aunt Chloe, a mother and former slave. Her novel *Iola Leroy; or, Shadows Uplifted* was published in 1892. She also wrote three novels serialized in *The Christian Recorder*, a religious periodical: *Minnie's Sacrifice*, *Sowing and Reaping*, and *Trial and Triumph*, all of which were published in book form in 1994. Harper's works were anthologized in *Complete Poems of Frances E.W. Harper* (1988) and *A Brighter Coming Day: A Frances Ellen Watkins Harper Reader* (1990).

Harper, Michael S., *in full* Steven (b. March 18, 1938, New York, N.Y., U.S.) African-American poet whose sensitive, personal verse is concerned with ancestral kinship, jazz and the blues, and the separation of the races in America.

Harper grew up in New York City and in West Los Angeles. He was educated at Los Angeles City College, Los Angeles State College of Applied Arts and Sciences and the Writers' Workshop at the University of Iowa (M.F.A., 1963). He taught at several West Coast colleges before joining the faculty of Brown University in 1971.

Harper's first book, *Dear John, Dear Coltrane* (1970), addresses the theme of redemption in compact poems that are based both on historical events and figures and on his travels and personal relationships. The poetry in *History Is Your Own Heartbeat* (1971) and *Song: I Want a Witness* (1972) stresses the significance of history to the individual, particularly to black Americans. *Nightmare Begins Responsibility* (1974), one of his most acclaimed and complex works, contains portraits of individual courage. In *Healing Song for the Inner Ear* (1985), Harper gives the theme of personal history an international focus. His other works include *Debridement* (1973), *Images of Kin* (1977), and *Rhode Island* (1981). He edited *The Collected Poems of Sterling A. Brown* (1980) and *Every Shut Eye Ain't Asleep* (1994); with Anthony Walton), an anthology of poetry by African-Americans since 1945.

Harris, Frank, *byname of* James Thomas Harris (b. Feb. 14, 1856, County Galway, Ire.—d. Aug. 26, 1931, Nice, Fr.) Irish-born American journalist and man of letters best known for his unreliable autobiography, *My Life and Loves*, 3 vol. (1923–27), the sexual frankness of which was new for its day and created trouble with censors. He was also an editor of fearless talent, which he sometimes abused by turning out scandal sheets.

Harris moved to the United States at age 15. Later he moved to England and edited a series of important journals, notably the *Saturday Review* (1894–98), for which he hired George Bernard Shaw. He returned to the United States to publish a biography, *Oscar Wilde: His Life and Confessions* (1916), which no one in England would publish, and in 1922 he moved to Nice. Among his other works is a biography of Shaw (1931).

Harris, George Washington (b. March 20, 1814, Allegheny City, near Pittsburgh, Pa., U.S.—d. Dec. 11, 1869, on a train en route to Knoxville, Tenn.) American humorist who combined the skill of an oral storyteller with a dramatic imagination.

Harris was a steamboat captain from an early age. From 1843 until his death, Harris wrote humorous tales for the New York *Spirit of the Times* and other publications that were reprinted widely throughout the country. The best of them were published in *Sut Lovingood: Yarns Spun by a "Natural Born Durn'd Fool"* (1867) and, according to a leading critic, surpassed anything before Mark Twain, who himself knew and liked the tales. Harris' tales are introduced by his comic narrator, Sut Lovingood.

Harris, Joel Chandler (b. Dec. 9, 1848, Eatonton, Ga., U.S.—d. July 3, 1908, Atlanta, Ga.) American author and creator of the folk character Uncle Remus.

Joel Chandler Harris

As apprentice on a weekly paper, *The Countryman*, Harris became familiar with the lore and dialects of the plantation slave. He established a reputation as a brilliant humorist and writer of dialect while employed on various Southern newspapers, notably on the *Atlanta Constitution* for 24 years. In 1879 "Tar-Baby" appeared in the *Atlanta Constitution* and created a vogue for a distinctive type of dialect literature. *Uncle Remus: His Songs and His Sayings* was published in book form in 1880, followed by others. Included in a series of children's books were *Little Mr. Thimblefinger and His Queer Country* (1894), *The Story of Aaron* (1896), and *Aaron in the Wildwoods* (1897). *Mingo, and Other Sketches in Black and White* (1884), *Free Joe and Other Georgian Sketches* (1887), *Sister Jane, Her Friends and Acquaintances* (1896), and *Gabriel Tolliver* (1902) reveal Harris' ability to vitalize other Southern types and to delve into issues faced by the South after Reconstruction. From 1907 until his death he edited *Uncle Remus's Magazine*.

Harrison, Jim, *byname of* James Thomas Harrison (b. Dec. 11, 1937, Grayling, Mich., U.S.) American novelist and poet known for his lyrical treatment of the human struggle between nature and domesticity.

Harrison attended Michigan State University, and he taught English at the State University of New York at Stony Brook. He began his writing career as a poet. In *Plain Song* (1965), *Locations* (1968), *Walking* (1967), and *Outlyer and Ghazals* (1969), critics noted a distinctive amalgam of earthy style and philosophical inquiry. Harrison also experimented with poetic forms, as exemplified by his use of the ghazel of ancient Persia.

Harrison's first novel, *Wolf* (1971), concerns the efforts of a disaffected man to view a wolf in the wilderness, an experience that he believes will cause his luck to change. *A Good Day to Die* (1973) treats the issue of the environment more cynically. Quandaries of love and work illumine *Farmer* (1976) but take on increasingly dark and obsessive overtones in *Legends of the Fall* (1979), *Warlock* (1981), and *Sundog* (1984). The novel *Dalva* (1988) and the novella *The Woman Lit by Fireflies* (1990) represent the author's first attempts to create female protagonists. Harrison's later books of poetry include *Letters to Yesenin* (1973), *Returning to Earth* (1977), *Selected and New Poems, 1961–1981* (1982), and *The Theory & Practice of Rivers* (1985).

Bret Harte

Harte, Bret, *original name* Francis Brett Harte (b. Aug. 25, 1836, Albany, N.Y., U.S.—d. May 5, 1902, London, Eng.) American writer who helped create the local-color school in American fiction.

In 1854 Harte left New York for California and went into mining country on a brief trip that legend has expanded into a lengthy participation in, and intimate knowledge of, camp life. In 1857 he was employed by the *Northern Californian*, a weekly paper.

In about 1860 he moved to San Francisco and began to write for the *Golden Era*, which published the first of his *Condensed Novels*, brilliant parodies of James Fenimore Cooper, Charles Dickens, Victor Hugo, and others. He edited the periodical *Californian*, for which he engaged Mark Twain to write weekly articles.

In 1868, after publishing a series of Spanish legends akin to Washington Irving's *The Alhambra*, Harte was named editor of the *Overland Monthly*. For it he wrote THE LUCK OF ROARING CAMP and THE OUTCASTS OF POKER FLAT. Following *The Luck of Roaring Camp, and Other Sketches* (1870), he found himself world famous. He furthered his reputation with the poem "Plain Language from Truthful James" (1870), better known as "The Heathen Chinee." On it he based his best play, *Ah Sin* (1877), a collaboration with Twain.

Flushed with success, Harte in 1871 signed with *The Atlantic Monthly* for $10,000 for 12 stories a year, the highest figure offered an American writer up to that time. Harte moved to the East, where he was greeted as an equal by eminent writers of the day Henry Wadsworth Longfellow, James Russell Lowell, Oliver Wendell Holmes, and William Dean Howells. But his work eventually began to slump, and after several years of indifferent success on the lecture circuit, Harte in 1878 accepted consulships in Crefeld, Ger., and later in Glasgow, Scot. In 1885 he retired to London. He found in England a ready audience for his tales of a past or mythical California long after American readers had tired of the formula. "Ingénue of the Sierras" and "A Protégée of Jack Hamlin's" (both 1893) are perhaps better than his earlier stories.

Hartman, Geoffrey H. (b. Aug. 11, 1929, Frankfurt-am-Main, Ger.) American literary critic and theorist who opposed formalism and championed criticism as a creative act. In his writing, noted for its difficulty, he maintained that the greatest writing is infinitely interpretable.

Hartman came to the United States in 1946 and became a U.S. citizen in that year. After studying at Queens College, New York City, the University of Dijon, France, and Yale University, he embarked on a university teaching career, most of it at Yale University. In his first book, *The Unmediated Vision*

(1954), he argued that poetry mediates between its readers and direct experience, much as religion had done in more religious eras. Romantic poetry especially interested him; he wrote several books on William Wordsworth.

With his essay collection *The Fate of Reading* (1975) Hartman argued that history, like literature, is open to many interpretations, and therefore is also a kind of "critical energy." In *Criticism in the Wilderness* (1980) he called for uniting the studies of literature, history, and philosophy and disputed the common notion of criticism as a form separate from, and inferior to, creative writing. Among his later writings were *Easy Pieces* (1985) and *Minor Prophecies* (1991).

Hart, Moss (b. Oct. 24, 1904, New York City, N.Y., U.S.—d. Dec. 20, 1961, Palm Springs, Calif.) One of the most successful American playwrights of the 20th century.

Hart wrote his first play, which was unsuccessful, at 18. In 1929 he wrote the first draft of *Once in a Lifetime*, a satire on Hollywood that became a hit the following year, after its exuberant humor had been tempered by the sardonic skill of George S. Kaufman. Hart then wrote books for musicals for Irving Berlin and Cole Porter, but until 1941 he continued to work with Kaufman, a collaboration that produced such popular comedies as *You Can't Take It with You* (1936) and *The Man Who Came to Dinner* (1939). His success continued with his musical play *Lady in the Dark*, which he himself directed in 1941. Among other plays he directed was the long-running *My Fair Lady* (1956). In 1959 he published *Act One*, the story of his theatrical apprenticeship.

Hartog, Jan de (b. April 22, 1914, Haarlem, Neth.) Dutch-American novelist and playwright who wrote adventure stories in both Dutch and English.

De Hartog's first major novel, *Hollands glorie: roman van de zeesleepvaart* (1947); *Captain Jan: A Story of Ocean Tugboats*), tells the humorous tale of a young boy's career in the merchant navy. De Hartog later settled in the United States and wrote entertaining novels in English. Among these are *A Sailor's Life* (1956), *The Inspector* (1960), *The Peaceable Kingdom: An American Saga* (1972), *The Lamb's War* (1980), *The Trail of the Serpent* (1983), *Star of Peace* (1984), and *The Centurion* (1990). Of his plays, the most popular is the comedy *The Fourposter*, produced in 1951.

Hawkes, John, *in full* John Clendennin Burne Hawkes, Jr. (b. Aug. 17, 1925, Stamford, Conn.) American author whose novels achieve a dreamlike (often nightmarish) intensity through the suspension of traditional narrative constraints.

Hawkes attended Harvard University; he taught there from 1949 to 1958 and for the next 30 years at Brown University.

Hawkes's first novel, *The Cannibal* (1949), depicts harbingers of a future apocalypse amid the rubble of postwar Germany. *The Beetle Leg* (1951) is a surreal parody of the pulp western. In 1954 he published two novellas, *The Goose on the Grave* and *The Owl*, both set in Italy. With *The Lime Twig* (1961), a dark thriller set in postwar London, Hawkes attracted the critical attention that would place him among the front rank of avant-garde American writers. His next novel, *Second Skin* (1964), is the first-person confessional of a retired naval officer. *The Blood Oranges* (1971), *Death, Sleep, & the Traveler* (1974), and *Travesty* (1976) explore the concepts of marriage and freedom. *The Passion Artist* (1979) and *Virginie: Her Two Lives* (1982) are tales of sexual obsession. Later works include *Adventures in the Alaskan Skin Trade* (1985), *Whistlejacket* (1988), and *Sweet William: A Memoir of Old Horse* (1993). Hawkes also published *The Innocent Party* (1966), a collection of short plays, and *Lunar Landscapes* (1969), a volume of short stories and novellas.

Hawthorne, Nathaniel (b. July 4, 1804, Salem, Mass., U.S.—d. May 19, 1864, Plymouth, N.H.) American novelist and short-story writer who was a master of the allegorical and symbolic tale. One of the greatest fiction writers in American literature, he is best known for THE SCARLET LETTER (1850) and THE HOUSE OF THE SEVEN GABLES (1851).

Hawthorne grew up in Salem and in Raymond, Maine, on the shores of Sebago Lake. He returned to Salem in 1825 after four years at Bowdoin College, in Brunswick, Maine.

His first work was the amateurish novel FANSHAWE, which he published in 1828 at his own expense—only to decide that it was unworthy of him and to try to destroy all copies. He soon found his own voice, style, and subjects, however, in such impressive and distinctive stories as "The Hollow of the Three Hills" and "An Old Woman's Tale." By 1832, MY KINSMAN, MAJOR MOLINEUX and ROGER MALVIN'S BURIAL, two of his greatest tales, had appeared. YOUNG GOODMAN BROWN, perhaps the greatest tale of witchcraft ever written, appeared in 1835.

Even when his first signed book, TWICE-TOLD TALES, was published in 1837, it brought him little financial reward. By 1842, however, Hawthorne's writing was producing a sufficient income to allow him to marry Sophia Peabody; the couple rented the Old Manse in Concord and began a happy three-year period that Hawthorne would later record in his essay "The Old Manse."

Hawthorne welcomed the companionship of his Transcendentalist neighbors—Ralph Waldo Emerson, Henry David Thoreau, Bronson Alcott—but in general he had little confidence in artists and intellectuals. At the Old Manse, Hawthorne continued to write stories, with the same result as

Nathaniel Hawthorne

before: literary success, monetary failure. His short-story collection MOSSES FROM AN OLD MANSE, which included such stories as RAPPACCINI'S DAUGHTER, was published in two volumes in 1846.

A growing family and mounting debts compelled the family's return in 1845 to Salem, where Hawthorne was appointed surveyor of the Custom House. Three years later Hawthorne lost his job, but in a few months of concentrated effort, he produced his masterpiece, *The Scarlet Letter*, which made him famous and which was eventually recognized as one of the greatest American novels.

Hawthorne then moved to Lenox in western Massachusetts. There he began work on *The House of the Seven Gables*, the story of the Pyncheon family, who for generations had lived under a curse until it was removed at last by love. In the autumn of 1851 Hawthorne moved his family to West Newton, near Boston. There he quickly wrote THE BLITHEDALE ROMANCE (1852), based on his disenchantment with Brook Farm, an agricultural cooperative in West Roxbury, Mass., where he had lived in 1841.

In 1853 Hawthorne was appointed to the consulship in Liverpool, England, by his old college friend, President Franklin Pierce. When his position was terminated in 1857, he spent a year and a half sight-seeing in Italy. He then produced THE MARBLE FAUN (1860).

Hayden, Robert (Earl), *original name* Asa Bundy Sheffey (b. Aug. 4, 1913, Detroit, Mich., U.S.—d. Feb. 25, 1980, Ann Arbor, Mich.) African-American poet whose subject matter was most often the black experience.

Robert Hayden

Hayden joined the Federal Writers' Project, researching black folklore and the history of the Underground Railroad in Michigan. His first collection of poems, *Heart-Shape in the Dust*, was published in 1940. He gained a public after his *A Ballad of Remembrance* (1962) won a grand prize at the First World Festival of Negro Arts in 1966 in Dakar, Senegal. In 1976 he became the first African-American to be appointed poetry consultant to the Library of Congress.

Hayden's best-known poem dealing with black history is "Middle Passage," an alternately lyric, narrative, and dramatic view of the slave trade. Hayden's Bahā'ī beliefs were often reflected in his poetry, which confronted the brutality of racism. He also published the poetry collections *Words in the Mourning Time* (1970), including his tribute to Malcolm X; *The Night-Blooming Cereus* (1972), concerned with the meaning of life; *Angle of Ascent: New and Selected Poems* (1975); and *American Journal* (1980).

Hay, John (Milton) (b. Oct. 8, 1838, Salem, Ind., U.S.—d. July 1, 1905, Newbury, N.H.) U.S. secretary of state and author of both fiction and historical works.

Hay studied law in Springfield, Ill., where he met the future president Abraham Lincoln. He served as President Lincoln's private secretary from 1861 to 1865, and under succeeding Republican administrations he held various diplomatic posts in Europe. Following a five-year stint as editorial writer for the *New York Tribune*, Hay returned to government service and was assistant secretary of state from 1879 to 1881. He became nationally prominent with the election of President William McKinley, under whom he served as ambassador to Great Britain (1897–98) and then secretary of state (1898–1905).

Throughout his life Hay found time to exercise his considerable literary talent, and his *Pike County Ballads and Other Pieces* (1871) and his novel *The Bread-Winners* (1883) were well received. In collaboration with John G. Nicolay, he was also responsible for two historical works that remained standard for many years: *Abraham Lincoln: A History* (1890) and an edition of Lincoln's *Complete Works* (1894).

Hayne, Paul Hamilton (b. Jan. 1, 1830, Charleston, S.C., U.S.—d. July 6, 1886, Grovetown, Ga.) American poet and editor, one of the best-known poets of the Confederate cause.

Hayne wrote for the *Charleston Evening News* and the Richmond *Southern Literary Messenger* and was associate editor of the weekly *Southern Literary Gazette*. His first collected poems were published at his own expense in 1855. He was coeditor of the influential *Russell's Magazine* (1857–60). During the American Civil War he contributed verse supporting the Southern cause— notably "The Battle of Charleston Harbor"—to the *Southern Illustrated News* of Richmond. Hayne's published works include *Sonnets and Other Poems* (1857), *Legends and Lyrics* (1872), *The Mountain of the Lovers* (1875), and *The Broken Battalions* (1885).

Hazzard, Shirley (b. Jan. 30, 1931, Sydney, Australia) Australian-born American writer whose novels and short stories were acclaimed for both their literary refinement and their emotional complexity.

Hazzard published her first collection of short stories, *Cliffs of Fall*, in 1963 and won immediate critical praise. Both *The Evening of the Holiday* (1966) and *The Bay of Noon* (1970), her first two novels, are elegiac love stories set in Italy. A collection of character sketches, *People in Glass Houses* (1967), satirizes the intricate, idealistic world of the United Nations, where she had worked from 1952 to 1962. Although Hazzard had long enjoyed critical favor and a modest loyal following, her reputation swelled to fame with the publication of *The Transit of Venus* (1980), an award-winning novel of international scope and rich psychological texture. The book's omniscient narrative voice constitutes by most evaluations a stylistic tour de force.

Hazzard also published *Defeat of an Ideal: A Study of the Self-Destruction of the United Nations* (1973).

H.D. Byname of Hilda DOOLITTLE.

Hearn, Lafcadio, *in full* Patricio Lafcadio Tessima Carlos Hearn, *also called* (from 1895) Koizumi Yakumo (b. June 27, 1850, Levkás, Ionian Islands, Greece—d. Sept. 26, 1904, Ōkubo, Japan) Writer, translator, and teacher who introduced the culture and literature of Japan to the West.

Hearn immigrated to the United States at age 19 and settled in Cincinnati, Ohio, where he worked as a reporter and translated stories by the French authors Théophile Gautier and Gustave Flaubert. In 1877 Hearn went to New Orleans to write a series of articles on Louisiana politics; he also translated French authors and wrote original stories and sketches. Two of his earliest works—*Stray Leaves from Strange Literature* (1884) and *Some Chinese Ghosts* (1887)—were adapted from foreign literature. *Chita* (1889), an adventure novel about the only survivor of a tidal wave, dates from this time.

From 1887 to 1889, Hearn was in the West Indies on assignment for *Harper's Magazine*. This experience resulted in *Two Years in the French West Indies* (1890) and his novel *Youma* (1890), a highly original story of a slave insurrection.

In 1890 Hearn traveled to Japan for Harper's. He soon broke with the magazine and worked as a schoolteacher in Izumo in northern Japan. There he met Koizumi Setsuko, a Japanese woman of high samurai rank, whom he married in 1891. Hearn's articles on Japan began appearing in *The Atlantic Monthly* and were syndicated in several U.S. newspapers. These essays and others, reflecting Hearn's initial captivation with the Japanese, were subsequently collected and published in two volumes as *Glimpses of Unfamiliar Japan* (1894).

In 1891 Hearn transferred to the Government College at Kumamoto, where he remained for three years. In 1895 he became a Japanese subject, taking the name Koizumi Yakumo.

Hearn's most brilliant and prolific period was from 1896 to 1903 as professor of English literature at the Imperial University of Tokyo. In four books written during this time—*Exotics and Retrospective* (1898), *In Ghostly Japan* (1899), *Shadowings* (1900), and *A Japanese Miscellany* (1901)—he is informative about the customs, religion, and literature of Japan. *Kwaidan* (1904) is a collection of stories of the supernatural and translations of haiku poetry.

Hébert, Anne (b. Aug. 1, 1916, Sainte-Catherine-de-Fossambault, Que., Can.) French-Canadian poet, novelist, and playwright, noted for her examination of the lives of the Quebeçois. She wrote about both the brutal and the brutalized and many aspects of violence in modern life.

Hébert began writing poetry in her teens under the tutelage of her father, Maurice-Lang Hébert, a distinguished literary critic, and her cousin, Hector de Saint-Denys-Garneau, a poet. Her early poetry, *Les Songes en équilibre* (1942); "Dreams in Equilibrium") and *Le Tombeau des rois* (1953); *The Tomb of the Kings*), reveals the poet in anguish, trading a child's joy of living for the stifling responsibilities of maturity. *Oeuvre poétique, 1950–1990* was published in 1993.

In the 1950s Hébert moved to Paris. Her first novel, *Les Chambres de bois* (1958); *The Silent Rooms*), and the short stories in *Le Torrent* (1950); *The Torrent*) take place in a world of symbolism and fantasy. She also wrote *Kamouraska* (1970), a suspenseful novel set in 19th-century Quebec, and *Les Enfants du sabbat* (1975); *Children of the Black Sabbath*), a novel of sorcery and demonic possession, which won for Hébert a 1975 Governor General's Award. *Les Fous de bassan* (1982); *In the Shadow of the Wind*; film, 1986) won the Prix Fémina in 1982. Two later outstanding novels are *Le Premier Jardin* (1988); *The First Garden*) and *L'Enfant chargé de songes* (1992); "The Child Burdened with Dreams"). Her plays were collected as *Le Temps sauvage* (1967).

Hecht, Ben (b. Feb. 28, 1894, New York, N.Y., U.S.—d. April 18, 1964, New York City) American journalist, novelist, playwright, and film writer. His play *The Front Page* (1928), written with Charles MacArthur, influenced the public's idea of the newspaper world and the newspaperman's idea of himself.

Hecht was the son of Russian-Jewish immigrants. After attending high school in Racine, Wis., he moved to Chicago and worked as a reporter for the *Chicago Journal* and for the *Chicago Daily News*, which sent him to Berlin during the revolutionary upheaval following World War I. From this experience came some of the material for his first novel, *Erik Dorn* (1921). For the *Daily News* he developed a column that formed the basis of his collection of sketches *A Thousand and One Afternoons in Chicago* (1922).

He was associated in Chicago with the novelist and poet Maxwell Bodenheim. Lively reminiscences of these years are found in his *Gaily, Gaily* (1963), *Letters from Bohemia* (1946), and his autobiography, *A Child of the Century* (1954).

Hecht later divided his time between New York City and Hollywood. *Twentieth Century* (produced 1932) was the first successful stage comedy on which he collaborated with MacArthur. In Hollywood he wrote scripts in the 1930s and 40s, often with MacArthur, for a number of successful motion pictures.

Hecht's last Broadway success was *Ladies and Gentlemen* (produced 1939; also with MacArthur). Columns written for the New York newspaper *PM* appeared as *1001 Afternoons in New York* (1941). Among his other works are *A Guide for the Bedevilled* (1944), an analysis of anti-Semitism; *Collected Stories* (1945); and *Perfidy* (1961).

Heilbrun, Carolyn (Gold), *pseudonym* Amanda Cross (b. Jan. 13, 1926, East Orange, N.J., U.S.) American scholar and feminist literary critic who became known for mystery stories written under her pseudonym.

Heilbrun attended Wellesley College and Columbia University, and in 1960 she joined the faculty of Columbia. Among her scholarly works are *The Garnett Family* (1961), about the British literary family that included noted translator Constance Garnett, and *Christopher Isherwood* (1970). Heilbrun also edited *Lady Ottoline's Album* (1976) and coedited *The Representation of Women in Fiction* (1983). In *Toward a Recognition of Androgyny* (1973) and *Reinventing Womanhood* (1979) she examined the effects of rigid gender roles. *Hamlet's Mother and Other Women* (1990) is a collection of her feminist literary essays.

Not until Heilbrun received tenure from Columbia did she reveal that she was the author of the Amanda Cross mysteries, which feature the literate amateur detective Professor Kate Fansler and are typically set in academic surroundings.

Heinlein, Robert Anson (b. July 7, 1907, Butler, Mo., U.S.—d. May 8, 1988, Carmel, Calif.) Prolific American writer considered to be one of the most sophisticated of science-fiction writers. He did much to develop the genre, producing such novels as *Starship Troopers* (1959), *Stranger in a Strange Land* (1961), *The Moon Is a Harsh Mistress* (1966), and *I Will Fear No Evil* (1970).

Heinlein was an established professional writer from 1939. His first story, "Life-Line," was published in the action-adventure pulp magazine *Astounding Science Fiction*, for which he wrote until 1942, when he began war work as an engineer. Heinlein returned to writing in 1947, with an eye toward a more sophisticated audience. His first book, *Rocket Ship Galileo* (1947), was followed by a large number of novels and story collections, including works for children and young adults. After the 1940s he largely avoided shorter fiction. His popularity probably reached its peak after the publication of his best-known work, *Stranger in a Strange Land*, which attracted a cult audience. Among his more popular books are *The Green Hills of Earth* (1951), *Double Star* (1956), *The Door into Summer* (1957), *Citizen of the Galaxy* (1957), and *Methuselah's Children* (1958). Later works include *Friday* (1982) and *The Cat Who Walks Through Walls: A Comedy of Manners* (1985). Heinlein won an unprecedented four Hugo Awards.

Heller, Joseph (b. May 1, 1923, Brooklyn, N.Y., U.S.) American writer whose novel CATCH-22 (1961) was one of the most significant works of protest literature to appear after World War II. The satirical novel was both a critical and a popular success.

Heller flew 60 combat missions as a bombardier with the U.S. Army Air Forces in Europe. He received an M.A. at Columbia University, New York City, in 1949 and was a Fulbright scholar at Oxford (1949–50). He taught English at Pennsylvania State University (1950–52) and worked as an advertising copywriter for the magazines *Time* (1952–56) and *Look* (1956–58) and as promotion manager for *McCall's* (1958–61), meanwhile writing *Catch-22* in his spare time.

Less successful were his later novels, including *Something Happened* (1974), *Good as Gold* (1979), *God Knows* (1984), and *Closing Time* (1994), a sequel to *Catch-22*. Heller's dramatic work includes the play *We Bombed in New Haven* (1968). The sequel to *Catch-22, Closing Time*, was published in 1994.

Lillian Hellman

Hellman, Lillian (b. June 20, 1905, New Orleans, La., U.S.—d. June 30, 1984, Vineyard Haven, Martha's Vineyard, Mass.) American playwright and motion-picture screenwriter whose dramas bitterly and forcefully attacked injustice, exploitation, and selfishness.

Her marriage (1925–32) to the playwright Arthur Kober ended in divorce. (She had already begun an intimate friendship with the novelist Dashiell Hammett that would continue until his death in 1961.)

Her dramas exposed various forms in which evil appears—a malicious child's lies about two schoolteachers (THE CHILDREN'S HOUR, 1934), a ruthless family's exploitation of fellow townspeople and of one another (THE LITTLE FOXES, 1939, and *Another Part of the Forest*, 1947), and the irresponsible selfishness of the post-World War I generation (WATCH ON THE RHINE, 1941, and *The Searching Wind*, 1944). In the 1950s she showed her skill in handling the more subtle structure of Chekhovian drama (*The Autumn Garden*, 1951) and in translation and adaptation (Jean Anouilh's *The Lark*, 1955, and Voltaire's *Candide*, 1957, in a musical version). Her play *Toys in the Attic* (1960), was followed by another adaptation, *My Mother, My Father, and Me* (1963). She also edited Anton Chekhov's *Selected Letters* (1955) and a collection of stories and short novels, *The Big Knockover* (1966), by Hammett. Her reminiscences, *An Unfinished Woman* (1969), were continued in *Pentimento* (1973) and *Maybe* (1980). Hellman was a longtime supporter of leftist causes, and in *Scoundrel Time* (1976) she detailed her troubles and those of her friends during U.S. Senator Joseph McCarthy's anticommunist witch-hunt of the 1950s. Her *Collected Plays* was published in 1972.

Hemingway, Ernest (Miller) (b. July 21, 1899, Oak Park, Ill., U.S.—d. July 2, 1961, Ketchum, Idaho) American novelist and short-story writer, awarded the Nobel Prize for Literature in 1954. His adventuresome life and four marriages were widely publicized.

Ernest Hemingway

On graduation from high school in 1917, Hemingway became a reporter for the Kansas City *Star*. During World War I he served as an ambulance driver for the American Red Cross. On July 8, 1918, he was injured on the Austro-Italian front and was decorated for heroism.

After recuperating in the United States, Hemingway sailed for France as a foreign correspondent for the *Toronto Star*. In Paris he became part of the coterie of expatriate Americans that included Gertrude Stein, Ezra Pound, and F. Scott Fitzgerald. In 1925 his first important book, a collection of stories called *In Our Time*, was published. The following year he published THE SUN ALSO RISES, the novel with which he scored his first solid success.

Based in Paris, he traveled widely for the skiing, bullfighting, fishing, and hunting that by then formed the background for much of his writing. His position as a master of short fiction was advanced by *Men Without Women* (1927), which included the story HILLS LIKE WHITE ELEPHANTS, and was confirmed by *Winner Take Nothing* (1933), which included A CLEAN, WELL-LIGHTED PLACE. At least in the public view, however, the novel A FAREWELL TO ARMS (1929), with its powerful fusion of love story with war story, overshadowed both.

Hemingway's love of Spain and his passion for bullfighting are evident in *Death in the Afternoon* (1932), a study of a spectacle he saw more as tragic ceremony than as sport. Similarly, an African safari provided the subject for *Green Hills of Africa* (1935). His TO HAVE AND HAVE NOT (1937) reflected his growing concern with social problems.

Acting again as a correspondent, Hemingway made four trips to Spain, then in the throes of civil war. He raised money for the Loyalists and wrote a play called *The Fifth Column*, set in besieged Madrid, that was published with some of his best short stories, including THE SHORT HAPPY LIFE OF FRANCIS MACOMBER and THE SNOWS OF KILIMANJARO, in *The Fifth Column and the First Forty-Nine Stories* (1938). The harvest of his considerable experience of Spain was the novel FOR WHOM THE BELL TOLLS (1940), the best selling of all his books.

After seeing action in World War II, Hemingway returned to his home in Cuba. In 1953, he received the Pulitzer Prize in fiction for the short novel THE OLD MAN AND THE SEA (1952). This book was as enthusiastically praised as his previous novel, *Across the River and into the Trees* (1950), had been damned.

By 1960 Fidel Castro's revolution had driven Hemingway from Cuba. He then moved to Ketchum, Idaho. Anxiety-ridden and depressed, he eventually took his own life, leaving behind many manuscripts. Two of his posthumously published books are *A Moveable Feast* (1964), the memoir of his apprentice days in Paris, and *Islands in the Stream* (1970), three closely related novellas.

Hémon, Louis (b. Oct. 12, 1880, Brest, Fr.—d. July 8, 1913, near Chapleau, Ont., Can.) French author of *Maria Chapdelaine*, the best-known novel of French-Canadian pioneer life.

After a few years in England as a journalist and sportswriter, Hémon went to Canada in 1911 and, while working as a farmhand, completed *Maria Chapdelaine*, a realistic presentation of the struggle of men and women faced with the inhospitable soil and climate of the Lac Saint-Jean area in Quebec. Initially serialized in 1914 in the Paris magazine *Le Temps*, the novel appeared in book form in 1915, went through many editions, and was translated into many languages. Hémon did not live to see its success: he was killed in a train accident before it was published.

Henley, Beth, *in full* Elizabeth Becker Henley (b. May 8, 1952, Jackson, Miss., U.S.) American playwright of regional dramas set in provincial Southern towns, the best known of which, CRIMES OF THE HEART (1982; film, 1986), was awarded the Pulitzer Prize in 1981.

Henley turned from acting to writing as a career because she felt that the theater offered few good contemporary roles for Southern women. Her first play, the one-act *Am I Blue*, was produced while she was still an undergraduate. *Crimes of the Heart*, her first full-length play, was first produced in 1979.

Later plays include the two-act *The Miss Firecracker Contest* (1979; film, 1988), which concerns the attempts of a small-town young woman of dubious reputation to gain respect by winning a beauty contest; *The Wake of Jamey Foster* (1983); *The Lucky Spot* (1986); and *Abundance* (1991).

Henry, O., *pseudonym of* William Sydney Porter (b. Sept. 11, 1862, Greensboro, N.C., U.S.—d. June 5, 1910, New York, N.Y.) American short-story writer whose tales romanticized the commonplace—in particular the life of ordinary people in New York City. His stories expressed the effect of coincidence on character through humor, grim or ironic, and often had surprise endings, a device that became identified with his name and cost him critical favor when its vogue had passed.

Porter began writing sketches about 1887, and in 1894 he started a humorous weekly, *The Rolling Stone*. When the venture failed, Porter joined the *Houston Post* as reporter, columnist, and occasional cartoonist.

Porter was convicted of embezzling bank funds while working as a teller in

Austin, Texas, and in 1898 he entered a penitentiary at Columbus, Ohio. While in prison he wrote to earn money for support of his daughter Margaret. His stories of adventure in the U.S. Southwest and in Central America were immediately popular with magazine readers, and by the time he emerged from prison W.S. Porter had become O. Henry.

In 1902 O. Henry arrived in New York City. From December 1903 to January 1906 he produced a story a week for the New York *World*, writing also for magazines. His first book, *Cabbages and Kings* (1904), depicted fantastic characters against exotic Honduran backgrounds. Both *The Four Million* (1906), which included his well-known stories THE GIFT OF THE MAGI and THE FURNISHED ROOM, and *The Trimmed Lamp* (1907), which included THE LAST LEAF, explored the lives of the multitudes of New York in their daily routines and searchings for romance and adventure. *Heart of the West* (1907) presented accurate and fascinating tales of the Texas range.

O. Henry then published, in rapid succession, *The Voice of the City* (1908), *The Gentle Grafter* (1908), *Roads of Destiny* (1909), *Options* (1909), *Strictly Business* (1910), and *Whirligigs* (1910). *Whirligigs* contains perhaps his funniest story, THE RANSOM OF RED CHIEF.

Despite his popularity, O. Henry's final years were marred by ill health, a desperate financial struggle, and alcoholism. After his death three more collected volumes appeared: *Sixes and Sevens* (1911), *Rolling Stones* (1912), and *Waifs and Strays* (1917).

Herbert, Frank (Patrick) (b. Oct. 8, 1920, Tacoma, Wash., U.S.—d. Feb. 11, 1986, Madison, Wis.) American science-fiction writer noted as the author of the best-selling *Dune* series of futuristic novels, a group of highly complex works that explored such themes as ecology, human evolution, the consequences of genetic manipulation, and mystical and psychic possibilities.

Until 1972, when he began to write full-time, Herbert held a variety of jobs while writing socially engaged science fiction. His reputation was made with the publication of the epic *Dune* (1965), which sold more than 12 million copies, and its sequels, *Dune Messiah* (1969), *Children of Dune* (1976), *God-Emperor of Dune* (1981), and *Chapterhouse: Dune* (1985). Included among his more than two dozen novels are the highly acclaimed *Dragon in the Sea* (1956), *The Green Brain* (1966), *The Santaroga Barrier* (1968), *The Heaven Makers* (1968), *The God Makers* (1972), and *The Dosadi Experiment* (1977).

Hergesheimer, Joseph (b. Feb. 15, 1880, Philadelphia, Pa., U.S.—d. April 25, 1954, Sea Isle City, N.J.) American author whose novels are typically concerned with the decadent and sophisticated milieu of the very wealthy.

After giving up the study of painting, Hergesheimer turned to writing. Beginning with *The Lay Anthony* (1914), he established himself as a popular and prolific writer of novels, short stories, biography, history, and criticism. Of his novels, *The Three Black Pennys* (1917), the story of three generations of the wealthy, mine-owning Penny family; *Java Head* (1919); and *Balisand* (1924) are considered his best. In 1921 a motion picture based on his short story "Tol'able David" was made.

Herne, James A., *original name* James Ahern (b. Feb. 1, 1839, Troy, N.Y., U.S.—d. June 2, 1901, New York City) American playwright who helped bridge the gap between 19th-century melodrama and the 20th-century drama of ideas. He was especially strong in character delineation.

After several years as a traveling actor, Herne scored an impressive success with his first play, *Hearts of Oak* (1879), written with the young David Belasco. Subsequent dramas, *Drifting Apart* (1885), *The Minute Men* (1886), and *Margaret Fleming* (1890), did not achieve the same popularity. *Margaret Fleming*, a drama of marital infidelity, has been judged his major achievement. Herne's most popular play, *Shore Acres*, was first presented in 1892.

Hersey, John (Richard) (b. June 17, 1914, Tianjin, China—d. March 24, 1993, Key West, Fla., U.S.) American novelist and journalist noted for his documentary fiction about catastrophic events in World War II.

Hersey lived in China until the age of 10, at which time his family returned to the United States. He graduated from Yale University in 1936, and he served as a foreign correspondent in the Far East, Italy, and Russia for *Time* and *Life* magazines from 1937 to 1946. His early novel A BELL FOR ADANO (1944), depicting the Allied occupation of a Sicilian town during World War II, won the 1945 Pulitzer Prize. Hersey's next books demonstrated his gift for combining a reporter's skill for relaying facts with imaginative fictionalization. Both THE WALL (1950), about the Warsaw ghetto uprisings, and HIROSHIMA (1946), an objective account of the atomic bomb explosion in that city as experienced by survivors of the blast, are based on fact, but they are also personal stories of survival in Poland and Japan during World War II.

Heyward, DuBose, *in full* Edwin DuBose Heyward (b. Aug. 31, 1885, Charleston, S.C., U.S.—d. June 16, 1940, Tryon, N.C.) American novelist, dramatist, and poet whose first novel, PORGY (1925), was the basis for a highly successful play, an opera, and a motion picture.

At the age of 17 Heyward worked on the waterfront, where he observed the people who were to become the subjects of his writing. His works of poetry include *Carolina Chansons* (1922), a joint publication with Hervey Allen; *Skylines and Horizons* (1924); and *Jasbo Brown* (1931). In addition to *Porgy*, which is set in a Charleston tenement, Heyward wrote the novels *Angel* (1926), about mountain people in North Carolina; *Peter Ashley* (1932), about pre-Civil War Charleston; and *Star-Spangled Virgin* (1939), concerned with the Virgin Islands during the New Deal.

In 1935 the opera *Porgy and Bess* was produced with libretto and words by Heyward and Ira Gershwin and music by George Gershwin. A motion-picture version appeared in 1959.

Hicks, Granville (b. Sept. 9, 1901, Exeter, N.H., U.S.—d. June 18, 1982, Franklin Park, N.J.) Critic, novelist, and teacher who was one of the foremost practitioners of Marxist criticism in American literature.

After graduating from Harvard and studying for two years for the ministry, Hicks joined the Communist Party in 1934. As literary editor of the *New Masses*, he became one of the party's chief cultural spokespersons. His book *The Great Tradition* (1933) evaluated American literature since the Civil War from a Marxist point of view.

Hicks was dismissed from his teaching position at Rensselaer Polytechnic Institute in 1935 and consequently became the center of a storm of controversy over academic freedom in the United States. In 1939 he broke with the communists after the Nazi-Soviet pact, explaining his growing dissatisfaction with the party's uncritical endorsement of Soviet policy in a letter to *The New Republic* magazine. He remained an active writer; *Part of the Truth: An Autobiography* was published in 1965, and *Literary Horizons*, a collection of his book reviews over the preceding 25 years, was published in 1970.

Highsmith, Patricia, *original name* Mary Patricia Plangman (b. Jan. 19, 1921, Fort Worth, Tex., U.S.—d. Feb. 4, 1995, Locarno, Switz.) American novelist and short-story writer who was best known for her psychological thrillers in which she delved into the nature of guilt, innocence, goodness, and evil.

Highsmith graduated from Barnard College in 1942. In 1950 she published *Strangers on a Train*, an intriguing story of two men, one ostensibly good and the other ostensibly evil, who undergo character reversals. *The Talented Mr. Ripley* (1955) was the first of several books featuring the adventures of a likeable murderer, Tom Ripley, who takes on the identities of his victims. Ripley also appears in *Ripley Under Ground* (1970), *Ripley's Game* (1974), *The Boy Who Followed Ripley* (1980), and *Ripley Under Water* (1991). Highsmith's collections of short stories include *The Black House* (1981) and *Tales of Natural and Unnatural Catastrophes* (1987).

In her *Plotting and Writing Suspense Fiction* (1966); revised and enlarged 1981), Highsmith held that "art has nothing to do with morality, convention or moralizing."

ROBERTO KOCH

Oscar Hijuelos

Hijuelos, Oscar (b. Aug. 24, 1951, New York, N.Y., U.S.) Novelist whose writing chronicles the pre-Castro Cuban immigrant experience in the United States, particularly in New York.

Hijuelos was a full-time writer of fiction from 1984. He won critical acclaim for his first novel, *Our House in the Last World* (1983), and was awarded the 1990 Pulitzer Prize for fiction for his second novel, *The Mambo Kings Play Songs of Love* (1989; film, 1992).

Our House in the Last World concerns members of the immigrant Santinio family who try to integrate into their Cuban identity and values the rhythms and culture of life in New York's Spanish Harlem. In the novel Hijuelos employs surreal effects suggestive of Latin-American fiction. *The Mambo Kings Play Songs of Love* also chronicles Cuban immigrants, their quest for the American dream, and their eventual disillusionment. It vividly recreates the musical and social environment of North America in the 1950s. A later novel was *The Fourteen Sisters of Emilio Montez O'Brien* (1993).

Himes, Chester (Bomar) (b. July 29, 1909, Jefferson City, Mo., U.S.— d. Nov. 12, 1984, Moraira, Spain) African-American writer whose novels reflect his encounters with racism.

Himes attended Ohio State University. From 1929 to 1936 he was incarcerated for armed robbery at the Ohio State Penitentiary, and while there he began to write fiction. A number of his stories appeared in *Esquire* and other American magazines. After his release from prison, he joined the Works Progress Administration, eventually serving as a writer with the Ohio Writers' Project. His first two novels, IF HE HOLLERS LET HIM GO (1945) and *Lonely Crusade* (1947), concern racism in the defense industry and the labor movement, respectively. *Cast the First Stone* (1952) portrays prison life, and *The Third Generation* (1954) examines family life.

In the mid-1950s Himes moved to Paris. There he wrote chiefly murder mysteries set in Harlem. These include *The Crazy Kill* (1959), *Cotton Comes to Harlem* (1965; film, 1970), and *Blind Man with a Pistol* (1969; later retitled *Hot Day, Hot Night*). Among his other works are *Run Man, Run* (1966), a thriller; *Pinktoes* (1961), a satirical work of interracial erotica; and *Black on Black* (1973), a collection of stories. He also published two volumes of autobiography, *The Quality of Hurt* (1972) and *My Life as Absurdity* (1976).

Hoagland, Edward (b. Dec. 21, 1932, New York, N.Y., U.S.) American novelist, travel writer, and essayist, noted especially for his writings about nature and wildlife.

Hoagland sold his first novel, *Cat Man* (1956), shortly before graduating from Harvard University. The novels *The Circle Home* (1960), set in a seedy boxing milieu, and *The Peacock's Tail* (1965) were noted for their sympathetic portrayals of impoverished, struggling people. His fourth novel, *Seven Rivers West* (1986), tells of the cultural collision between white railroad builders and Indians in western Canada during the 1880s. He also published the short-story collections *City Tales* (1986) and *The Final Fate of the Alligators* (1992).

Hoagland turned a diary into *Notes from the Century Before: A Journal from British Columbia* (1969); *African Calliope: A Journey to the Sudan* (1979) was a later travel book. Perhaps his best work was his nature essays and editorials, which combined a lifelong fondness for wilderness with his characteristic close observation. His essays were collected in *The Courage of Turtles* (1971), *Walking the Dead Diamond River* (1973), *The Moose on the Wall: Field Notes from the Vermont Wilderness* (1974), *Red Wolves and Black Bears* (1976), *The Edward Hoagland Reader* (1979), and *Balancing Acts* (1992).

Edward Hoagland

Hoban, Russell (Conwell) (b. Feb. 4, 1925, Lansdale, Pa., U.S.) Novelist and children's writer who combined myth, fantasy, humor, and philosophy to explore issues of self-identity.

Hoban attended the Philadelphia Museum School of Industrial Art before beginning his career as an advertising artist and copywriter. He moved to London in 1969. His first book, *What Does It Do and How Does It Work?* (1959), developed from his drawings of construction machinery. He then started writing fiction for children. One of his most enduring creations is the anthropomorphic badger Frances, who is featured with her family and friends in a series of books beginning with *Bedtime for Frances* (1960). Fear and mortality intrude on the fantasy story *The Mouse and His Child* (1967), another of Hoban's best-known books. His other notable works for children include *The Sorely Trying Day* (1964), *Charlie the Tramp* (1967), *Emmet Otter's Jug-Band Christmas* (1971), *How Tom Beat Captain Najork and His Hired Sportsmen* (1974), and *Dinner at Alberta's* (1975).

Among Hoban's adult-oriented novels are *The Lion of Boaz-Jachin and Jachin-Boaz* (1973), *Kleinzeit* (1974), and *Turtle Diary* (1975; film, 1985). *Riddley Walker* (1980), probably Hoban's best-known novel, is set in the future in an England devastated by nuclear war. Events are narrated in a futuristic form of English. Hoban's later writings include the novels *Pilgermann* (1983) and *The Medusa Frequency* (1987).

Hobson, Laura Z., *original name* Laura Kean Zametkin (b. June 18/19, 1900, New York, N.Y., U.S.—d. Feb. 28, 1986, New York City) American novelist and short-story writer noted for her novel *Gentleman's Agreement* (1947; film, 1947), a best-selling study of anti-Semitism.

The daughter of Jewish socialist parents, she was educated at Cornell University, Ithaca, N.Y. In the early 1930s she began writing advertising copy and short stories, and in 1934 she joined the promotional staff of the Henry R. Luce publications (*Time*, *Life*, and *Fortune* magazines). After 1940 she devoted herself entirely to writing, producing a total of nine novels and hundreds of short stories and magazine articles. Hobson is best known for *Gentleman's Agreement*, the story of a journalist who poses as a Jew in order to gain a firsthand experience of anti-Semitism. The book is a scathing depiction of the subtle and insidious manifestations of anti-Semitism in American society at that time. Hobson's other novels include *The Trespassers* (1943) and *Consenting Adult* (1975). The first volume of her autobiography, *Laura Z.: A Life*, was published in 1983. A second volume remained unfinished at her death.

Hoffman, Alice (b. March 16, 1952, New York, N.Y., U.S.) American novelist whose books about women in search of their identities mixed realism and the supernatural.

Hoffman began her professional writing career by contributing short stories to magazines. Her first novel, *Property Of* (1977), which traces the one-year relationship of a suburban girl and a gang leader, is both gritty and romantic. In *The Drowning Season* (1979), she presented a modern fairy tale about a grandmother, Esther the White, and her granddaughter, Esther the Black. *Angel Landing* (1980) is a love story set near a nuclear power plant on Long Island.

Hoffman's *Fortune's Daughter* (1985) relates a sentimental tale about the healing friendship between Rae, a pregnant young woman, and Lila, a middle-aged fortune-teller. *Illumination Night* (1987), the story of a young couple whose marriage is challenged by a teenaged girl, was noted for its subtle characterizations. In *At Risk* (1988) a young girl with AIDS sparks varied reactions from her family and community. *Seventh Heaven* (1990) concerns an unconventional divorcée in a Long Island suburb in 1959–60, while *Turtle Moon* (1992) contemplates the status of single mothers.

Holmes, Oliver Wendell (b. Aug. 29, 1809, Cambridge, Mass., U.S.— d. Oct. 7, 1894, Cambridge) American physician, poet, and humorist chiefly remembered for a few poems and for his "Breakfast-Table" series of essays.

Holmes received a degree from Harvard in 1836. He practiced medicine for 10 years, taught anatomy at Dartmouth College (Hanover, N.H.), and in 1847 became professor of anatomy and physiology at Harvard. He was later made dean of the Harvard Medical School.

Holmes achieved his greatest fame, however, as a humorist and poet. He won national acclaim with the publication of "Old Ironsides" (1830), which

Oliver Wendell
Holmes

aroused public sentiment against destruction of the USS *Constitution*, an American fighting ship from the War of 1812. Beginning in 1857, he contributed his "Breakfast-Table" papers to *The Atlantic Monthly* and subsequently published *The Autocrat of the Breakfast-Table* (1858), *The Professor of the Breakfast-Table* (1860), *The Poet of the Breakfast-Table* (1872), and *Over the Teacups* (1891).

Among his other works are the poems THE CHAMBERED NAUTILUS (1858) and THE WONDERFUL ONE-HOSS SHAY (1858) and the psychological novel *Elsie Venner* (1861).

Hopkins, Pauline (Elizabeth) (b. 1859, Portland, Maine, U.S.—d. Aug. 13, 1930, Cambridge, Mass.) African-American novelist, playwright, journalist, and editor. She was a pioneer in her use of traditional romance novels as a medium for exploring racial and social themes. Her work reflects the influence of W.E.B. Du Bois.

In 1880 Hopkins joined her mother and stepfather in performing her first work, a musical entitled *Slaves' Escape; or, The Underground Railroad* (also called *Peculiar Sam*). She then spent several years touring with her family's singing group, Hopkins' Colored Troubadors. Her second play, *One Scene from the Drama of Early Days*, based on the biblical character Daniel, was also written about this time. The difficulties of blacks amid the racist violence of post-Civil War America provided a theme for her first novel, CONTENDING FORCES (1900). She also wrote short stories and biographical articles for the *Colored American Magazine*, of which she was women's editor and literary editor from approximately 1900 to 1904.

Hopkins' novels include *Hagar's Daughter* (published serially in 1901–02 under the pseudonym Sarah A. Allen), *Winona: A Tale of Negro Life in the South and Southwest* (published serially in 1902), and *Of One Blood; or, The Hidden Self* (published serially in 1902–03). Her final work was the novella *Topsy Templeton* (published serially in 1916).

Hopkins, Sarah Winnemucca, *also known as* Sarah Hopkins Winnemucca, Sally Winnemucca, Thocmectony *or* Tocmectone ("shell flower") (b. *c.* 1844, Humboldt Sink, Mex. [now in Nevada, U.S.]—d. Oct. 16, 1891, Monida, Mont.) Native American educator, lecturer, tribal leader, and writer best known for her book *Life Among the Piutes; Their Wrongs and Claims* (1883). Her writings, valuable for their description of Northern Paiute life and for their insights into the impact of white settlement, are among the few contemporary Native American works.

A granddaughter of Truckee and daughter of Winnemucca, both Northern Paiute chiefs, she was encouraged to learn about whites. She lived with a white family, learned fluent English, and attended a convent school in San

Jose, Calif., until bigotry forced her removal. As an interpreter and scout for the U.S. Army, Hopkins led a group of Paiutes, including her father, to safety during the Bannock War of 1878; she was awarded tribal honors for bravery.

To protest official government policy toward Native Americans, she toured the East in the early 1880s, giving some 300 lectures. To Hopkins, the U.S. military was a fairer and abler manager of Indian matters than the federal Bureau of Indian Affairs, an agency she considered corrupt and self-serving. Hopkins taught Indian children at an army post in Vancouver, Wash.; she later returned to Nevada and founded an Indian school with private donations, but lack of money and ill health ended this endeavor.

Horgan, Paul (b. Aug. 1, 1903, Buffalo, N.Y., U.S.—d. March 8, 1995, Middletown, Conn.) Versatile American author noted especially for histories and historical fiction about the southwestern United States.

Horgan moved with his family to New Mexico in 1915. His career as a novelist began with the publication of the satirical novel *The Fault of Angels* (1933), about a Russian emigré's attempt to bring high culture to an American city. His trilogy *Mountain Standard Time* (1962), consisting of *Main Line West* (1936), *Far From Cibola* (1938), and *The Common Heart* (1942), depicts life in the Southwest in the early 1900s. *A Distant Trumpet* (1960) concerns late-19th-century soldiers who fought the Apaches. His short stories were collected in *The Return of the Weed* (1936), *Figures in a Landscape* (1940), and *The Peach Stone* (1967).

In addition to novels Horgan wrote historical sketches and books that sympathetically depicted the successive Native American, Spanish, Mexican, and Anglo-American frontier cultures of the Southwest. Both his two-volume *Great River: The Rio Grande in North American History* (1954) and the biography *Lamy of Santa Fe* (1975) won Pulitzer Prizes for history. He also produced poetry, drama, and children's books.

Horton, George Moses (b. 1797?, Northampton county, N.C., U.S.—d. 1883?) African-American poet who wrote sentimental love poems and antislavery protests. He was one of the first professional black writers in America.

A slave from birth, Horton was relocated, in 1800, to a plantation near Chapel Hill, seat of the University of North Carolina, where he regularly came into contact with the university students. From the 1820s, they regularly commissioned him to create love poems, including clever acrostic compositions based on the names of their lovers. He received literary training from Caroline Lee Hentz, a student who also published his verse in newspapers and unsuccessfully attempted to engineer his release from slavery.

Horton's first book of poetry, *The Hope of Liberty* (1829); retitled *Poems by a Slave),* includes several love lyrics originally written for students, as well as hopeful poems about freedom from enslavement. Probably because of fears of punishment, *The Poetical Works of George M. Horton, The Colored Bard of North Carolina* (1845) addressed the issue of slavery in a subtle manner. His last and largest volume of verse was *Naked Genius* (1865).

Hovey, Richard (b. May 4, 1864, Normal, Ill., U.S.—d. Feb. 24, 1900, New York, N.Y.) American poet, translator, and dramatist whose works consistently reflected his optimism and his faith in a vital United States.

After graduating in 1885 from Dartmouth, Hovey studied art and theology. In 1887 he met the poet Bliss Carman, with whom he later collaborated. Hovey lectured on aesthetics at the Farmington School of Philosophy in Connecticut and at Columbia University, New York City, where he held a post as professor of English at Barnard College.

Hovey's first major work was *Launcelot and Guenevere: A Poem in Dramas* (1891); it was the first part of a planned three-trilogy scheme—each trilogy to consist of a masque, a tragedy, and a drama. Hovey managed to complete the first trilogy and only the masque, *Taliesin* (1896), of the second trilogy. With his friend Carman he collaborated on a series of books of verse, *Songs from Vagabondia* (1894), *More Songs from Vagabondia* (1896), and *Last Songs from Vagabondia* (1901, published posthumously). Hovey's other works include *Seaward* (1893), an elegy on the poet and Dante scholar Thomas William Parsons, and *Along the Trail* (1898), a book of verse on the Spanish-American War.

Howard, Bronson (Crocker) (b. Oct. 7, 1842, Detroit, Mich., U.S.—d. Aug. 4, 1908, Avon, N.J.) American journalist, dramatist, and founder-president of the first society for playwrights in the United States.

Howard had his first success with *Saratoga,* produced in 1870 at a time when dramas of American life written by Americans were practically nonexistent; its success encouraged other native playwrights. *The Henrietta* (1887), a satire on business, and *Shenandoah* (1889), which established Charles Frohman as a great producer, were also successes. Howard's other plays include *The Banker's Daughter* (1878), first produced in 1873 as *Lillian's Last Love; Wives* (1879); *Young Mrs. Winthrop* (1882); and *One of Our Girls* (1885). He described his craft in *Autobiography of a Play* (1914).

Howard, Richard (b. Oct. 13, 1929, Cleveland, Ohio, U.S.) Poet, critic, and translator who was influential in introducing modern French poetry and experimental novels to American readers and whose own volume of verse, *Untitled Subjects* (1969), won the Pulitzer Prize for poetry in 1970.

Educated at Columbia University and the Sorbonne, Howard worked as a lexicographer before becoming a freelance critic and translator. He also taught comparative literature at the University of Cincinnati and was a fellow at Yale University.

Beginning with his first volume, *Quantities* (1962), much of Howard's poetry was in the form of dramatic monologues in which historic and literary personages address the reader directly. Howard's other volumes of poetry include *Two-Part Inventions* (1974), *Misgivings* (1979), *Lining Up* (1984), *No Traveller* (1989), and *Selected Poems* (1991).

In *Alone with America: Essays on the Art of Poetry in the United States Since 1950* (1969), Howard offers a critical analysis of the work and styles of 41 American. He translated a vast body of work from the French, including works by Simone de Beauvoir, Roland Barthes, Alain Robbe-Grillet, Claude Simon, Jean Genet, and Jean Cocteau. Howard's translation of Charles Baudelaire's *Les Fleurs du Mal: The Complete Text of The Flowers of Evil* won an American Book Award in 1984.

Howard, Sidney (Coe) (b. June 26, 1891, Oakland, Calif., U.S.—d. Aug. 23, 1939, Tyringham, Mass.) American playwright whose works helped to bring psychological as well as theatrical realism to the American stage.

Howard graduated from the University of California, Berkeley, in 1915 and studied under George Pierce Baker at his Harvard 47 Workshop. He was on the editorial staff of the magazine *Life* in 1919–22 and in 1923 was a feature writer for William Randolph Hearst's *International Magazine*.

One of Howard's best-known plays is *They Knew What They Wanted* (1924), the story of an aging Italian immigrant in California and his mail-order bride. The play won the Pulitzer Prize in 1925 and was the basis of Frank Loesser's musical *The Most Happy Fella* (1957). Other well-known plays are *The Silver Cord* (1926) and *Yellow Jack* (1934, in collaboration with Paul de Kruif), a dramatized documentary of the conquest of yellow fever. Howard also wrote *Lute Song* (1930); with Will Irwin), *The Late Christopher Bean* (1932); an adaptation from a French play by René Fauchois), and *Dodsworth* (1934); adapted from Sinclair Lewis' novel). He translated and adapted a number of European dramas, including *Salvation* (1928); with Charles MacArthur).

Howe, E.W., *in full* Edgar Watson (b. May 3, 1853, Treaty, Ind., U.S.—d. Oct. 3, 1937, Atchison, Kan.) American editor, novelist, and essayist known for his iconoclasm and pessimism.

An apprentice printer at age 12, Howe worked at the trade in Missouri, Iowa, Nebraska, and Utah (1867–72). At 19 he was publisher of the *Golden* (Colo.) *Globe* and in 1877 founded the *Atchison* (Kan.) *Daily Globe*, which was made famous by the frequent reprinting throughout the United States of articles and comments he published in it. His first and most successful novel, *The Story of a Country Town* (1883), was the first realistic novel of Midwestern small-town life. He published and edited *Howe's Monthly* (1911–33) and wrote essays, travel books, and an autobiography, *Plain People* (1929). His journalistic writing was collected in *The Indignations of E.W. Howe* (1933) and other books.

Howe, Irving (b. June 11, 1920, New York, N.Y., U.S.—d. May 5, 1993, New York City) American literary and social critic and educator noted for probing into social and political viewpoints in literary criticism.

Howe was educated at the City College of New York. He taught at Brandeis and Stanford universities and the City University of New York at Hunter College. He wrote critical works on Sherwood Anderson (1951), William Faulkner (1952), and Thomas Hardy (1967), and he synthesized his political and literary interests in *Politics and the Novel* (1957) and *A World More Attractive: A View of Modern Literature and Politics* (1963). He edited the works of George Gissing, Edith Wharton, Leon Trotsky, and George Orwell and from 1953 was editor of the periodical *Dissent*. He also edited *Favorite Yiddish Stories* (1974); with Eliezer Greenberg), *The Best of Sholom Aleichem* (1979); with Ruth R. Wisse), and *The Penguin Book of Modern Yiddish Verse* (1987); with Khone Shmeruk and Wisse).

His *World of Our Fathers* (1976) is a sociocultural study of eastern European Jews who immigrated to the United States between 1880 and 1924. *Celebrations and Attacks* (1978) is a collection of his critical articles, and *A Margin of Hope: An Intellectual Biography* (1982) deals with his involvement with culture and politics. *Selected Writings 1950–1990* was published in 1990.

Howe, Julia Ward (b. May 27, 1819, New York, N.Y., U.S.—d. Oct. 17, 1910, Newport, R.I.) American author and lecturer best known for her "Battle Hymn of the Republic." The "Battle Hymn," composed to the rhythm of the folk song "John Brown's Body," was first published in *The Atlantic Monthly* in February 1862. Moved by the economic plight of Civil War widows, Howe worked for equal educational, professional, and business opportunities for women. She was the author of travel books, drama, and verse and composed songs for children.

Howells, William Dean (b. March 1, 1837, Martins Ferry, Ohio, U.S.—d. May 11, 1920, New York City) American novelist and critic, preeminent in late 19th-century American letters.

Howells grew up in various Ohio towns and began work early as a typesetter and later as a reporter. Meanwhile, he taught himself languages, becoming well read in German, Spanish, and English classics, and began contributing poems to *The Atlantic Monthly*. His campaign biography of Abraham Lincoln (1860) financed a trip to New England, where he met the great men of the literary establishment, including Oliver Wendell Holmes, Nathaniel Hawthorne, and Ralph Waldo Emerson. Following Lincoln's victory, Howells received a consulship at Venice (1861–65), which enabled him to marry. On his return to the U.S. he became assistant editor (1866–71) and then editor (1871–81) of *The Atlantic Monthly*, in which he began publishing reviews and articles interpreting American writers. He immediately recognized the worth of Henry James, and he was the first to take Mark Twain seriously as an artist.

Their Wedding Journey (1872) and *A Chance Acquaintance* (1873) were his first realistic novels of uneventful middle-class life. There followed several international novels, contrasting American and European manners. Howells' best work depicts the American scene as it changed from a simple, egalitarian society where luck and pluck were rewarded to one in which social and economic gulfs were becoming unbridgeable. He also wrote *A Modern Instance* (1882), a powerful novel that tells the story of the disintegration of a marriage. His best-known work, THE RISE OF SILAS LAPHAM (1885), deals with a self-made businessman's efforts to fit into Boston society. In 1887 he made a plea for clemency for the condemned Haymarket anarchists, a group of labor leaders who were convicted of murder after a violent riot in Chicago in 1886. He risked both livelihood and reputation in the cause, believing that they had been convicted for their political beliefs. In 1888 he left Boston for New York.

His deeply shaken social faith was reflected in his later novels, such as the strongly pro-labor *Annie Kilburn* (1888) and *A Hazard of New Fortunes* (1890). The latter, generally considered one of his finest works, dramatizes the competitive life of New York, where a representative group of characters try to establish a magazine.

Hubbard, Elbert (Green) (b. June 19, 1856, Bloomington, Ill., U.S.— d. May 7, 1915, at sea off Ireland) American editor, publisher, and author of the moralistic essay "A Message to Garcia" (1899).

A freelance newspaperman and businessman, Hubbard retired in 1892 and founded the Roycroft Press in 1895 at East Aurora, N.Y., based on the model of William Morris' communal Kelmscott Press. Beginning in 1895 he issued the famous monthly "Little Journey" booklets. These were pleasant biographical essays on famous persons, in which fact was interwoven with comment and satire. Hubbard also began publishing *The Philistine*, an avant-garde magazine, which he ultimately wrote single-handedly. "A Message to Garcia," in which the importance of perseverance was drawn as a moral from a Spanish-American War incident, appeared in an 1899 number of *The Philistine*. In 1908 Hubbard began to edit and publish a second monthly, *The Fra*.

Valuable collections of Hubbard's writings are *Little Journeys*, 14 vol. (1915), and *Selected Writings*, 14 vol. (1923). His *Scrap Book* (1923) and *Note Book* (1927) were published posthumously.

Hughes, Langston, *in full* James Mercer Langston Hughes (b. Feb. 1, 1902, Joplin, Mo., U.S.—d. May 22, 1967, New York, N.Y.) African-American poet and writer who became one of the foremost interpreters to the world of the black experience in the United States.

Langston Hughes

Hughes first came to notice when his poem THE NEGRO SPEAKS OF RIVERS, written the summer after his graduation from high school in Cleveland, was published in the African-American journal *Crisis* (1921). After attending Columbia University (1921–22) in New York City, he worked as a steward on a freighter bound for Africa. Upon his return to the United States he took a variety of menial jobs and continued writing.

While working as a busboy in a hotel in Washington, D.C., Hughes put three of his own poems beside the plate of American poet Vachel Lindsay in the dining room. The next day, newspapers around the country reported that Lindsay had discovered a Negro busboy poet. A scholarship to Lincoln University in Pennsylvania followed, and before Hughes received his degree in 1929, his first two books had been published.

The Weary Blues (1926), which includes DREAM VARIATION, was warmly received. *Fine Clothes to the Jew* (1927) was criticized harshly for its title and for its frankness, but Hughes himself felt it represented a step forward. A few months after graduation *Not Without Laughter* (1930), his first prose work, had a cordial reception. In 1931 he collaborated with Zora Neale Hurston on the play MULE BONE. He then traveled widely in the Soviet Union, Haiti, and Japan and served as a newspaper correspondent (1937) in the Spanish Civil War; his poetry of the 1930s was highly political. He published a collection of short stories, *The Ways of White Folks* (1934), and *The Big Sea* (1940), his autobiography up to the age of 28.

Hughes's *Montage of a Dream Deferred*, containing the famous poem HARLEM, was published in 1951. He wrote *A Pictorial History of the Negro in America* (1956) and edited the anthologies *The Poetry of the Negro* (1949) and *The Book of Negro Folklore* (1958; with Arna Bontemps). He also wrote numerous works for the stage, including the lyrics for *Street Scene*, an opera with music by Kurt Weill. A posthumous book of poems, *The Panther and the Lash* (1967), reflected the black anger and militancy of the 1960s. Hughes translated the poetry of Federico García Lorca and Gabriela Mistral. He was also widely known for his comic character Jesse B. Semple, familiarly called Simple, who appeared in Hughes's columns in the *Chicago Defender* and the New York *Post*. Hughes later published a collection entitled *The Best of Simple* (1961).

Humphreys, Josephine (b. Feb. 2, 1945, Charleston, S.C., U.S.) American novelist noted for her sensitive evocations of family life in the southern United States.

Humphreys studied creative writing at Duke University and attended Yale University and the University of Texas. From 1970 to 1977, before beginning her writing career, she taught at Baptist College in Charleston. Her first novel, *Dreams of Sleep* (1983), examines a faltering marriage that is saved by a third party. Her later novels include *Rich in Love* (1987) and *The Fireman's Fair* (1991).

Hunter, Evan, *original name* Salvatore A. Lombino, *pseudonyms* Ed McBain, Curt Cannon, Ezra Hannon, Hunt Collins, *and* Richard Marsten (b. Oct. 15, 1926, New York, N.Y., U.S.) Prolific American writer of best-selling fiction, of which more than 50 books were crime stories published under the pseudonym McBain.

Hunter graduated from Hunter College (1950). His best-known novel was among his earliest: *The Blackboard Jungle* (1954), a story of violence in a New York high school that was the basis of a popular film. After his *Strangers When We Meet* (1958) and *A Matter of Conviction* (1959); U.S. title, *The Young Savages*) became best-sellers, Hunter wrote the screenplays for both (1960–61), as well as for Alfred Hitchcock's *The Birds* (1962) and several later films. Hunter wrote several novels on the theme of family tensions between generations, including *Mothers and Daughters* (1961), *Last Summer* (1968), *Sons* (1969), and *Streets of Gold* (1974).

Hunter was most prolific as a crime novelist. Nearly all of his books using the pseudonym McBain are novels of police procedure, set in a city much like New York. They include *Cop Hater* (1956), *Fuzz* (1968), *Widows* (1991), and *Mischief* (1993). Hunter also wrote children's stories and stage plays.

Hunter, Kristin (b. Sept. 12, 1931, Philadelphia, Pa., U.S.) African-American novelist who examined black life and racial relations in the United States in both children's stories and works for adults.

Hunter began writing for *The Pittsburgh Courier*, an important black newspaper, when she was 14 and continued until the year after she graduated from the University of Pennsylvania (1951). While working as an advertising copywriter, she won a 1955 television contest with her script *Minority of One*, about black-white school integration; fearing controversy, the network rewrote the story to show a French-speaking immigrant entering an all-white school. In Hunter's first and best-known novel, *God Bless the Child* (1964), three generations of women confront choices forced upon them by their skin tones.

Despite harshly realistic settings, Hunter's subsequent fiction tended to optimism. *The Landlord* (1966) presents a misanthropic white landlord transformed by his new black tenants. In *The Survivors* (1975) a lonely, prosperous middle-aged dressmaker befriends a neglected 13-year-old boy despite his involvement with dishonest, sometimes brutal acquaintances. Her first book for young readers, *The Soul Brothers and Sister Lou* (1968), was about a musical group inspired by a group of youths who sang together nightly in the alley below her apartment. Its sequel was *Lou in the Limelight* (1981). She has also written *Boss Cat* (1971) and *Guests in the Promised Land* (1973) for young readers.

Hurst, Fannie (b. Oct. 18, 1889, Hamilton, Ohio, U.S.—d. Feb. 23, 1968, New York City) American novelist, dramatist, and movie scenarist. Hurst's first book of short stories, *Just Around the Corner* (1914), was followed by more than 40 novels and story collections, noted for sympathetic but shallow portrayals of women of various social levels. A number of her books were made into films, some with scripts by her. Her autobiography, *Anatomy of Me*, appeared in 1958.

Fannie Hurst

Hurston, Zora Neale (b. Jan. 7, 1903, Eatonville, Fla., U.S.—d. Jan. 28, 1960, Fort Pierce, Fla.) African-American folklorist and writer who celebrated black culture in the voice of the rural black South.

At age 16, Hurston joined a traveling theatrical company, ending up in New York City during the Harlem Renaissance. She studied anthropology with Franz Boas at Columbia University, taking a scientific approach to ethnicity. As an ethnologist, Hurston traveled to Haiti to study voodoo. She ultimately rejected the conventional viewpoint of the scholar in favor of personal involvement with her heritage. In 1931 she collaborated with Langston Hughes on the play MULE BONE. Her first novel, *Jonah's Gourd Vine* (1934), was well received though some critics considered it uneven. Her second novel, THEIR EYES WERE WATCHING GOD (1937), was both widely acclaimed and highly controversial. It was criticized by blacks because, although Hurston refused to endorse the myth of black inferiority, neither did she portray blacks as victims of this myth.

The tone of Hurston's work is celebratory, rooted in a rural black South reminiscent of her hometown. Her characters act freely within their rich

Zora Neale Hurston

heritage and narrow social position. Hurston influenced such contemporary black authors as Ralph Ellison and Toni Morrison. Her autobiography is titled DUST TRACKS ON A ROAD (1942), and an anthology of her work, *I Love Myself When I Am Laughing and Then Again When I Am Looking Mean and Impressive*, was released in 1979.

Ignatow, David (b. Feb. 7, 1914, Brooklyn, N.Y., U.S.) American poet whose works addressed social as well as personal issues in meditative, vernacular free verse.

Ignatow worked for a time as a journalist with the WPA Federal Writers' Project. His first book of poetry, entitled *Poems* (1948), was followed by *The Gentle Weight Lifter* (1955). Many of the pieces in the latter collection, as well as many in *Say Pardon* (1961) and *Figures of the Human* (1964), are written in the form of parables. From the 1960s, Ignatow taught poetry at several American colleges and universities.

Ignatow's thematic range, as well as his reputation, expanded significantly with *Rescue the Dead* (1968), which explored family, marriage, nature, and society. In *Facing the Tree* (1975), *The Animal in the Bush* (1977), and *Tread the Dark* (1978), he further examined death and the art of poetry. Later collections include *Whisper to the Earth* (1981), *Leaving the Door Open* (1984), and *Shadowing the Ground* (1991). *The Notebooks of David Ignatow* was published in 1973, and he published *The One in the Many: A Poet's Memoirs* in 1988.

Inge, William (Motter) (b. May 3, 1913, Independence, Kan., U.S.—d. June 10, 1973, Hollywood Hills, Calif.) American playwright best known for his plays *Come Back, Little Sheba* (1950; film, 1952); PICNIC (1953; film, 1956), for which he won a Pulitzer Prize; and BUS STOP (1955; film, 1956).

Inge's first play, *Farther Off from Heaven* (1947), was produced with the help of Tennessee Williams; 10 years later it was revised for Broadway as *The Dark at the Top of the Stairs* (film, 1960).

Inge was one of the first American dramatists to deal with the quality of life in the small towns of the Midwest, and he achieved notable success throughout the 1950s. His later plays—*A Loss of Roses* (1960; film, *The Stripper*, 1963), *Natural Affection* (1963), *Where's Daddy?* (1966), and *The Last Pad* (1970)—were less successful. Inge received an Academy Award for his original screenplay *Splendor in the Grass* (1961). His shorter works include *Glory in the Flower* (1958), *To Bobolink, for Her Spirit* (1962), *The Boy in the Basement* (1962), and *Bus Riley's Back in Town* (1962).

Irving, John (Winslow) (b. March 2, 1942, Exeter, N.H., U.S.) American novelist and short-story writer who established his reputation with the novel *The World According to Garp* (1978; film, 1982). Characteristic of his other works, it was noted for its engaging story line, colorful characterizations, macabre humor, and examination of contemporary issues.

After graduating from Phillips Exeter Academy, Irving attended the universities of Pittsburgh, Vienna, New Hampshire, and Iowa. He taught until the late 1970s, when he began to write full-time. His early novels—*Setting*

Free the Bears (1969), *The Water-Method Man* (1972), and *The 158-Pound Marriage* (1974)—did not achieve the success of *The World According to Garp*. Infused with comedy and violence, his breakthrough book chronicles the tragic life and death of the novelist T.S. Garp. Irving's later novels include *The Hotel New Hampshire* (1981), *The Cider House Rules* (1985), *A Prayer for Owen Meany* (1989), and *A Son of the Circus* (1994); his short-story collection *Nowhere Man* was published in 1992.

Irving, Washington (b. April 3, 1783, New York, N.Y., U.S.—d. Nov. 28, 1859, Tarrytown, N.Y.) Writer called the "first American man of letters." He is best known for the short stories THE LEGEND OF SLEEPY HOLLOW and RIP VAN WINKLE.

The favorite and last of 11 children, Irving avoided a college education but intermittently read law. A series of his whimsically satirical essays appeared over the signature of Jonathan Oldstyle, Gent., published in the *Morning Chronicle* during 1802–03.

In 1806 he passed the bar examination and soon set up as a lawyer. In 1807–08, however, his chief occupation was the writing (with his brother William and James K. Paulding) of a series of 20 periodical essays entitled SALMAGUNDI.

Irving next wrote A HISTORY OF NEW YORK, a comic history of the Dutch regime in New York, prefaced by a mock-pedantic account of the world from creation onward. He produced little original work for the next decade, then published THE SKETCH BOOK (1819–20), a collection of stories and essays that mix satire and whimsicality with fact and fiction. Its tremendous success in both England and the United States assured Irving that he could live by his pen. In 1822 he produced *Bracebridge Hall*, a sequel to *The Sketch Book*.

Early in 1826 he accepted an invitation to attach himself to the American legation in Spain, where he wrote *Columbus* (1828), followed by *The Companions of Columbus* (1831). Meanwhile, Irving had become absorbed in the legends of the Moorish past and wrote *A Chronicle of the Conquest of Granada* (1829) and *The Alhambra* (1832), a Spanish counterpart of *The Sketch Book*.

After a 17-year absence, Irving returned to New York in 1832, where he was warmly received. He made a journey west and produced in rapid succession *A Tour of the Prairies* (1835), *Astoria* (1836), and *The Adventures of Captain Bonneville* (1837). Except for four years (1842–46) as minister to Spain, Irving spent the remainder of his life at his home on the Hudson River, "Sunnyside" in Tarrytown, where he devoted his time to literary pursuits.

Isherwood, Christopher, *byname* of Christopher William Bradshaw-Isherwood (b. Aug. 26, 1904, High Lane, Cheshire, Eng.—d. Jan. 4, 1986,

Washington Irving

Santa Monica, Calif., U.S.) Anglo-American novelist and playwright best known for his novels about Berlin in the early 1930s.

Isherwood gained recognition with his first two novels, *All the Conspirators* (1928) and *The Memorial* (1932). During the 1930s he collaborated with W.H. Auden on three verse dramas, including *The Ascent of F6* (1936). Living in Berlin from 1929 to 1933, he observed the decay of the Weimar Republic and the rise of Nazism; his novels about this period—*Mr. Norris Changes Trains* (1935); U.S. title, *The Last of Mr. Norris*) and *Goodbye to Berlin* (1939), which were later published together as THE BERLIN STORIES— established his reputation. In 1938 Isherwood published *Lions and Shadows*, an account of his early life and friendships while a student at the University of Cambridge.

The coming of World War II prompted Isherwood to immigrate to the United States. In 1939 he settled in southern California, where he taught and wrote for Hollywood films. That same year Isherwood turned to pacifism and the self-abnegation of Indian Vedānta, becoming a follower of Swami Prabhavananda. In the following decades, he produced several works on Vedānta and translations with Prabhavananda, including one of the *Bhagavadgita*.

Isherwood was naturalized in 1946. *A Single Man* (1964), a brief but highly regarded novel, presents a single day in the life of a lonely, middle-aged homosexual. His avowedly autobiographical works include a self-revealing memoir of his parents, *Kathleen and Frank* (1971); a retrospective biography of himself in the 1930s, *Christopher and His Kind* (1977); and a study of his relationship with Prabhavananda and Vedānta, *My Guru and His Disciple* (1980).

Jackson, Helen (Maria) Hunt, *original surname* Fiske (b. Oct. 15, 1830, Amherst, Mass., U.S.—d. Aug. 12, 1885, San Francisco, Calif.) American poet and novelist best known for her novel *Ramona* (1884).

She turned to writing after the deaths of her first husband, Captain Edward Hunt, and her two sons. She later married William Jackson and moved to Colorado. A prolific writer, Jackson is remembered primarily for her efforts on behalf of American Indians. *A Century of Dishonor* (1881) arraigned government Indian policy; her subsequent appointment to a federal commission investigating the plight of Indians on missions provided material for *Ramona*. The novel aroused public sentiment but has been admired chiefly for its romantic picture of old California.

Jackson, Shirley (Hardie) (b. Dec. 14, 1916, San Francisco, Calif., U.S.—d. Aug. 8, 1965, North Bennington, Vt.) American novelist and short-story writer best known for her story THE LOTTERY (1948).

Jackson graduated from Syracuse University, N.Y., in 1940 and married the American literary critic Stanley Edgar Hyman. *Life Among the Savages* (1953) and *Raising Demons* (1957) are fictionalized memoirs about their life with their four children. Their light, comic tone contrasts sharply with the dark pessimism of Jackson's other works. "The Lottery," a chilling tale whose meaning has been much debated, provoked widespread public outrage when it was first published in *The New Yorker* in 1948. Jackson's six finished novels, especially *The Haunting of Hill House* (1959) and *We Have Always Lived in the Castle* (1962), further established her reputation as a master of gothic horror and psychological suspense.

James, Henry (b. April 15, 1843, New York, N.Y., U.S.—d. Feb. 28, 1916, London, Eng.) American novelist and, as a naturalized English citizen from 1915, a great figure in transatlantic culture. His fundamental theme was the innocence and exuberance of the New World in conflict with the corruption and wisdom of the Old.

James grew up in Manhattan but also spent much of his childhood abroad. After briefly attending Harvard Law School, he devoted himself to literature, publishing his first story at the age of 21. When William Dean Howells became editor of *The Atlantic Monthly*, James found in him a friend and mentor. Between them, James and Howells inaugurated the era of American realism.

Henry James

James made the first of many trips to Europe as an adult in 1869, and within five years he had decided to live abroad permanently. Thus began his long expatriation, heralded by publication in 1876 of the novel RODERICK HUDSON—his first collection of travel writings—and a collection of tales. During 1875–76 James lived in Paris, writing literary and topical letters for the *New York Tribune* and working on his novel THE AMERICAN (1877). Late in 1876 he crossed to London, where he later was to write the major fiction of his middle years. In 1878 he achieved international renown with his story of an American flirt in Rome, DAISY MILLER (1879), and he further enhanced his prestige with *The Europeans* that same year.

James's reputation was founded on his versatile studies of "the American girl." In a series of witty tales he pictured the "self-made" young woman, the bold and brash American innocent who insists upon American standards in European society. James ended this first phase of his career by producing his masterpiece, THE PORTRAIT OF A LADY (1881).

In the middle phase of his career, James wrote two novels dealing with social reformers and revolutionaries, THE BOSTONIANS (1886) and THE PRINCESS CASAMASSIMA (1886). These were followed by THE TRAGIC MUSE (1890), in which James projected a study of the London and Paris art studios and the stage. After a failed attempt to win success as a playwright, James spent several years seeking to adapt the techniques of drama to his fiction (as evidenced by WASHINGTON SQUARE [1880]). The result was a complete change in his storytelling methods. In THE SPOILS OF POYNTON (1897), WHAT MAISIE KNEW (1897), THE TURN OF THE SCREW (1898), and THE AWKWARD AGE (1899), James began to use the methods of alternating "picture" and dramatic scene, close adherence to a given angle of vision, and a withholding of information from the reader, presenting only that which the characters see.

The experiments of this "transition" phase led to three great novels that represent James's final phase: THE WINGS OF THE DOVE (1902), THE AMBASSADORS (1903), and THE GOLDEN BOWL (1904). James's other major works include the essay THE ART OF FICTION (1884), the novelette THE ASPERN PAPERS (1888), and the short story THE BEAST IN THE JUNGLE (1903).

Jarrell, Randall (b. May 6, 1914, Nashville, Tenn., U.S.—d. Oct. 14, 1965, Chapel Hill, N.C.) American poet, novelist, and critic who is noted for revitalizing the reputations of Robert Frost, Walt Whitman, and William Carlos Williams in the 1950s.

Childhood was one of the major themes of Jarrell's verse, and he wrote about his own extensively in *The Lost World* (1965). In 1942 he joined the U.S. Army Air Forces, and his first book of verse, *Blood for a Stranger*, was published. Many of his best poems appeared in *Little Friend, Little Friend* (1945) and *Losses* (1948), both of which dwell on his wartime experiences.

Jarrell taught at Sarah Lawrence College, Bronxville, N.Y. (1946–47), and his only novel, the sharply satirical *Pictures from an Institution* (1954), is about a similar progressive girls' college. He was a teacher at the University of North Carolina at Greensboro from 1947 until his death.

TED RUSSELL

Randall Jarrell

Jarrell's criticism has been collected in *Poetry and the Age* (1953), *A Sad Heart at the Supermarket* (1962), and *The Third Book of Criticism* (1969). Jarrell's later poetry collections include *The Seven-League Crutches* (1951), *The Woman at the Washington Zoo* (1960), and *The Lost World*. His *Complete Poems* appeared in 1969.

Jeffers, Robinson, *in full* John Robinson Jeffers (b. Jan. 10, 1887, Pittsburgh, Pa., U.S.—d. Jan. 20, 1962, Carmel, Calif.) One of the most controversial American poets of the 20th century, who viewed human life as a frantic, often contemptible struggle within a net of passions.

Educated in English literature, medicine, and forestry, Jeffers inherited money, which allowed him to write poetry. His third book, *Tamar and Other Poems* (1924), which brought him immediate fame, revealed the unique style and eccentric ideas developed in such later volumes as *Cawdor* (1928), *Thurso's Landing* (1932), and *Be Angry at the Sun* (1941). The shorter lyrics as well as his sprawling narrative poems celebrate the coastal scenery near Carmel, where Jeffers and his wife moved in 1916. He made a brilliant adaptation of Euripides' *Medea* that was produced in 1946.

Jewett, Sarah Orne (b. Sept. 3, 1849, South Berwick, Maine, U.S.—d. June 24, 1909, South Berwick) American writer of regional fiction.

Early in her teens Jewett determined to write about the rapidly disappearing traditions of provincial life about her, and by the age of 28 she was an established writer. Outstanding among her 20 volumes are *Deephaven* (1877) and THE COUNTRY OF THE POINTED FIRS (1896), the latter often regarded as her finest achievement. The books contain realistic sketches of aging Maine natives, whose manners, idioms, and pithiness she recorded with pungency and humor, sympathetically but without sentimentality. A disabling accident virtually ended her writing career in 1902.

Johnson, Diane, *in full* Diane Lain Johnson Murray (b. April 28, 1934, Moline, Ill., U.S.) American writer and academic, best known for worldly and satiric novels set in California that portray contemporary women in crisis.

Johnson was educated at Stephens College, the University of Utah, and the University of California. From 1968 she was a professor of English at the University of California at Davis.

The heroine of her first novel, *Fair Game* (1965), conscious of having been exploited by a series of lovers, eventually finds a man who will foster her desire to grow into a more complete person. In *Loving Hands at Home* (1968) a woman leaves her Mormon husband and his family, with whom she feels no spiritual kinship, but fails to succeed on her own in the wider world. *Burning*

(1971) satirizes the southern California way of life. *The Shadow Knows* (1974) concerns a divorced mother whose secure life is shattered when she becomes convinced that she is marked for violence. *Lying Low* (1978) chronicles four days in the lives of three markedly different women. Later novels include *Persian Nights* (1987) and *Health and Happiness* (1990).

Johnson wrote a well-received novelistic biography of writer George Meredith's first wife, *The True History of the First Mrs. Meredith and Other Lesser Lives* (1972), and the biography *Dashiell Hammett: A Life* (1983). She also wrote screenplays (with Stanley Kubrick, *The Shining*, 1980) and a collection of essays, *Terrorists and Novelists* (1982).

Johnson, James Weldon (b. June 17, 1871, Jacksonville, Fla., U.S.—d. June 26, 1938, Wiscasset, Maine) Poet, diplomat, and anthologist of African-American culture.

Johnson graduated from Atlanta (Ga.) University. He later read law, was admitted to the Florida bar in 1897, and began practicing there. During this period, he and his brother, John Rosamond Johnson (1873–1954), a composer, began writing songs, and in 1901 the two went to New York, where they wrote some 200 songs for the Broadway stage.

From 1906 to 1914 he held various diplomatic posts, and he later taught at Fisk University in Nashville, Tenn. His novel AUTOBIOGRAPHY OF AN EX-COLORED MAN (published anonymously, 1912) attracted little attention until it was reissued under his own name in 1927.

Fifty Years and Other Poems (1917) was followed by his pioneering anthology *Book of American Negro Poetry* (1922) and *American Negro Spirituals* (1925, 1926), collaborations with his brother. His best-known work is GOD'S TROMBONES (1927), a group of black dialect sermons in verse. His *Along This Way* (1933) is an autobiography.

Jolas, Eugene and **Maria,** Maria Jolas *née* Maria McDonald (respectively b. Oct. 26, 1894, Union City, N.J., U.S.—d. May 26, 1952, Paris, Fr.; b. January 1893, Louisville, Ky., U.S.—d. March 4, 1987, Paris) American founders, with Elliot Paul, of the revolutionary literary quarterly Transition.

Raised in Lorraine, France, Eugene Jolas worked as a journalist both in the United States and France. Maria McDonald moved to Europe to study voice in 1913. She was in the United States during World War I but then returned to Europe. The two met in the United States and were married in 1926. Soon after the marriage the Jolases moved to Paris, where Eugene sought to provide a forum for international writers with the establishment of the periodical *transition*. In addition to his role as the chief editor, and guiding light Jolas wrote poetry reflecting his beliefs that language should be re-created and should rely upon dreams and the subconscious for inspiration. His best volume was *The Language of Night* (1932).

Maria Jolas's work on *transition* was less visible than her husband's; she was essentially the managing and production editor as well as a translator of the foreign pieces that appeared in the magazine. Her other work included the establishment of the Bilingual School of Neuilly (1932–40) and the translation of 12 novels by Nathalie Sarraute.

Jones, James (b. Nov. 6, 1921, Robinson, Ill., U.S.—d. May 9, 1977, Southampton, Long Island, N.Y.) American novelist best known for *From Here to Eternity* (1951), set in Hawaii just before the Pearl Harbor attack.

The strongest influence on Jones's writing was his service in the U.S. Army from 1939 to 1945. He used his knowledge of day-to-day life in the military in his first novel, *From Here to Eternity*, which describes the experiences of a charismatic serviceman who dies shortly after the outbreak of war in the Pacific. In his second novel, *Some Came Running* (1957), Jones drew on his life in Illinois after the war. His next two novels, *The Pistol* (1958) and *The Thin Red Line* (1962), however, return to his wartime experiences. Jones was an expatriate in Paris from 1958 until 1975, when he returned to the United States. *Whistle*, published posthumously in 1978, is the last in the trilogy that includes *From Here to Eternity* and *The Thin Red Line*.

Jones, LeRoi. Original name of Amiri BARAKA.

Jordan, June, *married surname* Meyer (b. July 9, 1936, New York, N.Y., U.S.) Versatile African-American author who investigated both social and personal concerns through poetry, essays, and drama.

Jordan grew up in Brooklyn, N.Y., and attended Barnard College and the University of Chicago; beginning in 1967 she taught English and literature. She fought for the inclusion of black studies and third world studies in university curricula and advocated acceptance of Black English. Her first poetry collection, *Who Look at Me*, appeared in 1969; among her subsequent collections of poems were *Some Changes* (1971), *Things That I Do in the Dark* (1977), *Living Room* (1985), and *Naming Our Destiny* (1989).

In the 1970s Jordan wrote books for children and young adults, including the novel *His Own Where* (1971) and the biography *Fannie Lou Hamer* (1972). As a journalist and poet Jordan wrote about feminism and the struggles against racism and for freedom of choice and opportunity for minorities. Her essays are collected in the books *Civil Wars* (1981), *On Call* (1985), and *Technical Difficulties: African-American Notes on the State of the Union* (1992).

Josephson, Matthew (b. Feb. 15, 1899, Brooklyn, N.Y., U.S.—d. March 13,

1978, Santa Cruz, Calif.) American biographer whose clear writing was based on sound and thorough scholarship.

As an expatriate in Paris in the 1920s, Josephson was an associate editor of *Broom* (1922–24), which featured both American and European writers, and he later served as an editor for the magazine *transition* (1928–29).

His first book was a well-researched and authoritative biography of Émile Zola, *Zola and His Time: The History of His Martial Career in Letters* (1928). Other highly praised biographies followed. His interest in 19th-century French literature appeared in such works as *Victor Hugo* (1942) and *Stendhal* (1946), which helped to regenerate American interest in Stendhal's work. He addressed another favorite topic, American economics, in what is perhaps his best-known work, *The Robber Barons: The Great American Capitalists, 1861–1901* (1934). The book chronicles the lives of John D. Rockefeller, Andrew Carnegie, and other barons of industry in the late 19th century.

Judson, E.Z.C., *in full* Edward Zane Carroll, *pseudonym* Ned Buntline (b. March 20, 1823, Stamford, N.Y., U.S.—d. July 16, 1886, Stamford) American adventurer and writer, an originator of the so-called dime novels that were popular during the late 19th century.

Judson's earlier stories were based on the exploits of his own picaresque career, which began as a cabin boy in the U.S. Navy. In 1844 he left the navy, reputedly to fight Indians and travel in the West. He contributed stories to the *Knickerbocker Magazine* and in 1844 established the short-lived *Ned Buntline's Magazine* in Cincinnati, Ohio. He later went to Nashville, Tenn., and founded the sensational newspaper *Ned Buntline's Own*. P Judson joined the Union Army during the Civil War but was dishonorably discharged in 1864 for drunkenness. He later met William F. Cody, whom he styled "Buffalo Bill" and portrayed as the hero of a number of his dime novels. He also wrote a play for Cody, *The Scouts of the Plains* (1872); also published as *The Scouts of the Prairies*), patterned on his life.

Judson's hundreds of dime novels and serials were sensational stories of swashbuckling heroes and violence and had such titles as *The Mysteries and Miseries of New York* (1848), *Ned Buntline's Life Yarn* (1848), *Stella Delorme; or, The Comanche's Dream* (1860), Red Ralph: The Ranger (1870), and *Buffalo Bill's First Trial; or, Will Cody, the Pony Express Rider* (1888).

Justice, Donald (Rodney) (b. Aug. 12, 1925, Miami, Fla., U.S.) American poet and editor best known for finely crafted verse that frequently illuminates the pain of loss and the desolation of an unlived life.

Educated at the University of Miami, the University of North Carolina, and the University of Iowa, Justice taught English and writing at several American universities.

Justice's poetry collections include *The Summer Anniversaries* (1960), *Night Light* (1967), *Departures* (1973), and *Selected Poems* (1979), which won a Pulitzer Prize. He also published *Platonic Scripts* (1984), a collection of essays, and *The Sunset Maker: Poems, Stories, A Memoir* (1987). Having considered becoming a composer when he was a young man, Justice retained a lifelong interest in music, writing the libretto for *The Death of Lincoln* (1988), a musical work by A. Thomas Taylor. Among books Justice edited or coedited are *The Collected Poems of Weldon Kees* (1960), *Contemporary French Poetry* (1965), and *Syracuse Poems* (1968). He also translated Eugène Guillevic's *L'Homme qui se ferme* (1973); *The Man Closing Up*) from the French.

Kantor, MacKinlay, *original name* Benjamin McKinlay Kantor (b. Feb. 4, 1904, Webster City, Iowa, U.S.—d. Oct. 11, 1977, Sarasota, Fla.) American author whose more than 30 novels and numerous popular short stories included the highly acclaimed *Andersonville* (1955), a Pulitzer Prize-winning novel about the American Civil War.

After finishing high school, Kantor became a reporter on *The Webster City Daily News,* of which his mother was an editor. He moved to Chicago for a number of years before returning to Iowa as a columnist for the *Des Moines Tribune*. He wrote many short stories and achieved recognition for his first historical novel, *Long Remember* (1934), a story about Gettysburg.

After service in World War II he became a screenwriter in Hollywood, where he adapted *Glory for Me* (1945), his verse novel about three American servicemen returning to civilian life, for the film *The Best Years of Our Lives* (1946).

In his long career Kantor also published nonfiction and several collections of short stories on subjects ranging from Chicago gangsters to life in the Ozarks. His historical novels include *Spirit Lake* (1961) and *Valley Forge* (1975).

Kaplan, Justin (b. Sept. 5, 1925, New York, N.Y., U.S.) American writer, biographer, and book editor, best known for his acclaimed literary biographies of Mark Twain, Lincoln Steffens, and Walt Whitman.

Kaplan graduated from Harvard in 1944. He left graduate school in 1946 and worked for a publishing house, eventually becoming a senior editor. In that capacity he worked with authors such as Bertrand Russell, Will Durant, Níkos Kazantzákis, and the sociologist C. Wright Mills.

Kaplan's his first book, a biography of Mark Twain entitled *Mr. Clemens and Mark Twain* (1966), won both a Pulitzer Prize and a National Book Award. Also well regarded were Kaplan's *Lincoln Steffens, A Biography* (1974), about the prominent journalist and muckraker of the late 19th and early 20th centuries, and *Walt Whitman: A Life* (1980).

Kaplan lectured at Harvard and at Emerson College, Boston, Mass., and was biographer in residence at the Institute for Modern Biography at Griffith University, Brisbane, Australia. He edited several anthologies and was general editor for the 16th edition of *Bartlett's Familiar Quotations* (1992).

Kaufman, Bob, *in full* Robert Garnell Kaufman (b. April 18, 1925, New Orleans, La., U.S.—d. Jan. 12, 1986, San Francisco, Calif.) Innovative African-American poet who became an important figure of the Beat movement.

With a Roman Catholic mother, a German-Jewish father, and a grandmother who believed in voodoo, Kaufman was exposed to a wide variety of religious influences; he eventually adopted the Buddhist religion. After settling in San Francisco in 1958 he became involved in the city's bohemian artistic community and wrote witty, surreal poetry inspired by the rhythms of bebop jazz. Three broadside poems that were published by Kaufman in 1959 were later included in his collection *Solitudes Crowded with Loneliness* (1965). He also was a cofounder of the poetry magazine *Beatitude*.

In the early 1960s Kaufman was one of the most popular American poets among European readers; his second collection, *Golden Sardine*, was published in 1967. After seeing the televised assassination of President John F. Kennedy in 1963, Kaufman took a vow of silence, and he remained silent, neither speaking nor writing, until the end of the Vietnam War. After that he wrote prolifically, producing poems with literary themes that were published with earlier works in *The Ancient Rain: Poems, 1956–1978* (1981). In 1978 he resumed his silence, which he seldom broke for the rest of his life.

Kaufman, George S. *in full* Simon (b. Nov. 16, 1889, Pittsburgh, Pa., U.S.— d. June 2, 1961, New York, N.Y.) American playwright and journalist noted for his collaboration with a number of other authors on some of the most successful plays and musical comedies of the 1920s and '30s.

After attending public school in Pittsburgh and Paterson, N.J., Kaufman worked briefly as a salesman. He contributed to the satirical column of Franklin P. Adams ("F.P.A.") in the New York *Evening Mail* and, in 1912, on Adams' recommendation, was given a column of his own in the *Washington Times*. He was a drama critic for *The New York Times* from 1917 to 1930. During this time he also became a member of the Algonquin Round Table.

His first successful play, written in collaboration with Marc CONNELLY, was *Dulcy* (1921), a comedy based on a central character of Adams' column. *The Butter and Egg Man* (1925), a satire on theatrical production, was the only play Kaufman wrote alone. His plays with Connelly included *Beggar on Horseback* (1924) and *Merton of the Movies* (1922), one of the first satires on Hollywood. Among his other collaborations were *Of Thee I Sing* (1931), with Morrie Ryskind and Ira Gershwin (with music by George Gershwin); *Dinner at Eight* (1932) and *The Land Is Bright* (1941), with Edna Ferber; *The Solid Gold Cadillac* (1953), with Howard Teichmann; and a number of memorable successes with Moss Hart that included *Once in a Lifetime* (1930), *You Can't Take It with You* (1936), and *The Man Who Came to Dinner* (1939).

Kaufman was twice winner of the Pulitzer Prize for plays of which he was coauthor. His range was wide, varying in tone with his collaborators, but brilliant satire and caustic wit were his forte.

Kazin, Alfred (b. June 5, 1915, Brooklyn, N.Y., U.S.) American teacher, editor, and literary critic.

Kazin attended the City College of New York and then worked as a freelance book reviewer for various periodicals. At age 27 he wrote a sweeping historical study of modern American literature, *On Native Grounds* (1942), that won him instant recognition as a perceptive critic with a distinct point of view. The book traced the social and political movements that inspired successive stages of literary development in America.

Many of Kazin's later works dealt with the forces that drive an individual to write. Kazin felt that with increasing technological domination of society, literature had diminished in importance as a vehicle of personal growth and political definition. Kazin's sketches of literary personalities revealed much about both the writers and their eras. His critical and political sensibilities were inextricably intertwined. Among the books he edited were *The Portable Blake* (1946), *The Stature of Theodore Dreiser* (1955), and *The Works of Anne Frank* (1959). His other writings include *Starting Out in the Thirties* (1965), *Bright Book of Life* (1973), *New York Jew* (1978), *An American Procession* (1984), and *A Writer's America* (1988).

Kelly, George (Edward) (b. Jan. 16, 1887, Philadelphia, Pa., U.S.—d. June 18, 1974, Bryn Mawr, Pa.) American playwright, actor, and director whose dramas of the 1920s depict the foibles of the American middle class with a telling accuracy.

Kelly followed his elder brother Walter into vaudeville as an actor, writing his first sketches for his own performance. His first success on Broadway was *The Torchbearers* (performed 1922), a satire on the social and aesthetic pretensions of the little-theater movement then flourishing in the United States. His next play, *The Show-Off* (1924), became an American comedy classic, and was made as a film three times (1926, 1934, 1946). In *Craig's Wife* (1925), a savage drama, Kelly shifted his vision to the upper middle class.

Kelly also wrote film scripts, among them those for the motion-picture versions of his plays, including *Craig's Wife* (1936), remade as *Harriet Craig* (1950).

Kennedy, John Pendleton, *pseudonym* Mark Littleton (b. Oct. 25, 1795, Baltimore, Md., U.S.—d. Aug. 18, 1870, Newport, R.I.) American statesman and writer whose best-remembered work was his historical fiction.

Kennedy was admitted to the Maryland bar in 1816. From 1821 he served two terms in the Maryland House of Delegates and three terms in the U.S. Congress. He was also secretary of the navy in the cabinet of President Millard Fillmore.

Meanwhile, using the pen name of Mark Littleton, Kennedy wrote historical novels, including *Swallow Barn* (1832), sketches of the post revolutionary life of gentlemen on Virginia plantations, and *Rob of the Bowl* (1838), a tale of colonial Maryland.

Kennedy's major work of nonfiction is *Memoirs of the Life of William Wirt* (1849), about an attorney for the prosecution in the trial of Aaron Burr for treason. He also coedited the satirical magazine *Red Book* (1818–19) and wrote political articles for the *National Intelligencer*.

Kennedy, Leo, *in full* John Leo Kennedy (b. Aug. 22, 1907, Liverpool, Eng.) Canadian poet of the modernist Montreal group, which reacted against the traditional and experimented with new techniques and subject matter.

Kennedy's family immigrated to Canada in 1912. Ending his formal education in the sixth grade, he went to work for his father, in the meantime publishing poetry and letters in *The Montreal Star*. By 1928 his poetry had come to the attention of a group of students at McGill University. This association led him to help found and to edit the *Canadian Mercury*, a short-lived experimental literary magazine. The criticism he wrote during this period helped to establish modernism in Canadian poetry. His notable creative work included the mortuary collection, *The Shrouding* (1933).

For the most part Kennedy had stopped publishing verse and other literary works by the 1940s, when he began to work in the United States as a copywriter.

Kennedy, William (b. Jan. 16, 1928, Albany, N.Y., U.S.) American author and journalist whose *Ironweed* (1983) won him the Pulitzer Prize for fiction in 1984.

Kennedy graduated from Siena College, Loudonville, N.Y., in 1949 and worked as a journalist in New York state and in San Juan, Puerto Rico, where he also began writing fiction. In 1963 he returned to Albany, which he considered the source of his literary inspiration. His first novel, *The Ink Truck* (1969), concerns a colorful columnist named Bailey who leads a strike at his newspaper in Albany.

Kennedy combined history, fiction, and black humor in his next novel, *Legs* (1975), about Jack "Legs" Diamond, an Irish-American gangster who was killed in Albany in 1931. *Billy Phelan's Greatest Game* (1978), also set in Albany, chronicles the life of a small-time streetwise hustler who sidesteps the powerful local political machine. *Ironweed*, which brought Kennedy widespread acclaim, tells the story of the hustler's father, Francis Phelan. Also published in 1983, *O Albany!* is a spirited nonfictional account of the politics and history of the city. Kennedy also wrote the novels *Quinn's Book* (1988) and *Very Old Bones* (1992), as well as the screenplays for *The Cotton Club* (1984, with Francis Ford Coppola) and *Ironweed* (1987).

Kennedy, X.J., *pseudonym of* Joseph Charles Kennedy (b. Aug. 21, 1929, Dover, N.J., U.S.) American author of witty verse for children as well as for adults.

Kennedy served in the U.S. Navy and studied at Seton Hall University, Columbia University, and the Sorbonne. He studied and taught at the University of Michigan, served as poetry editor of the *Paris Review*, and wrote and edited several books on literature while teaching at Tufts University.

Beginning with his first collection, *Nude Descending a Staircase: Poems, Song, a Ballad* (1961), and with rare subsequent exceptions, Kennedy's poems are in rhyming stanzas and traditional meters and forms. They exhibit vivid language and frequent humor, including parody and satire. His *Cross Ties: Selected Poems* was published in 1985.

Composing poems and stories for his own children led Kennedy to write *One Winter Night in August and Other Nonsense Jingles* (1975). Children misbehave hilariously and are punished outrageously in his nonsense poems published in *Brats* (1986), *Fresh Brats* (1990), and *Drat These Brats!* (1993); by contrast, *The Kite That Braved Old Orchard Beach: Year-Round Poems for Young People* (1991) includes serious, even poignant verses. With his wife, Dorothy M. Kennedy, he wrote and edited *Knock at a Star: A Child's Introduction to Poetry* (1982) and *Talking Like the Rain: A First Book of Poems* (1992).

Kenner, Hugh, *in full* William Hugh Kenner (b. Jan. 7, 1923, Peterborough, Ont., Can.) Canadian literary critic who wrote several witty and readable books on modernist writers. His criticism was often based on the writer's own literary criteria.

Kenner studied at the University of Toronto and at Yale University. He was a faculty member of the University of California at Santa Barbara from 1950 until 1973, when he began teaching at Johns Hopkins University. In his influential books *The Poetry of Ezra Pound* (1951) and *The Pound Era* (1971), Kenner described Pound as the central figure in modernist literature and helped to reestablish the poet's battered reputation. Of comparable importance were his studies of James Joyce in *Dublin's Joyce* (1955), *Flaubert, Joyce and Beckett: The Stoic Comedians* (1962), *Joyce's Voices* (1978), and *Ulysses* (1980).

His other works include *Gnomon: Essays on Contemporary Literature* (1958), *The Counterfeiters: An Historical Comedy* (1968), *A Homemade World: The American Modernist Writers* (1975), *A Colder Eye: The Modern Irish Writers* (1983), and *A Sinking Island: The Modern English Writers* (1988). In particular, he focused on T.S. Eliot, Samuel Beckett, G.K. Chesterton, Wyndham Lewis, and Desmond Egan.

Kerouac, Jack, *original name* Jean-Louis Kerouac (b. March 12, 1922, Lowell, Mass., U.S.—d. Oct. 21, 1969, St. Petersburg, Fla.) American poet and novelist, leader and spokesman of the BEAT MOVEMENT. Kerouac gave the Beat movement its name and celebrated its code of poverty and freedom in a series of novels, of which the first and best known is ON THE ROAD (1957).

Of French-Canadian descent, Kerouac learned English as a second language as a schoolboy. Discharged from the U.S. Navy during World War II as a schizoid personality, he then served as a merchant seaman. Thereafter he roamed the United States and Mexico before publishing his first novel, *The Town and the City* (1950). Dissatisfied with fictional conventions, Kerouac developed a new, spontaneous, nonstop, unedited method of writing that shocked more polished writers. *On the Road*, written in three weeks, was the first product of the new style.

The book drew the attention of the public to a widespread subterranean culture of poets, folksingers, hipsters, mystics, and eccentrics, including the writers Allen Ginsberg, Gregory Corso, William Burroughs, Gary Snyder, and Philip Whalen, all important contributors to the Beat movement. All of Kerouac's works, including THE DHARMA BUMS (1958), *The Subterraneans* (1958), *Doctor Sax* (1959), *Lonesome Traveler* (1960), and *Desolation Angels* (1965), are autobiographical. The posthumously published *Visions of Cody* (1972) was originally a part of *On the Road*.

BRIAN LANKER

Ken Kesey

Kesey, Ken (Elton) (b. Sept. 17, 1935, La Junta, Colo., U.S.) Writer who was a hero of the countercultural revolution and the hippie movement of the 1960s.

Kesey was educated at the University of Oregon and Stanford University. At a Veterans Administration hospital in Menlo Park, Calif., he was a paid volunteer experimental subject, taking mind-altering drugs and reporting on their effects. This experience and his work as an aide at the hospital served as background for his best-known novel, *One Flew Over the Cuckoo's Nest* (1962; film, 1975), which is set in a mental hospital. He further examined values in conflict in *Sometimes a Great Notion* (1964).

In the nonfiction *Kesey's Garage Sale* (1973), *Demon Box* (1986), and *The Further Inquiry* (1990), Kesey wrote of his travels and psychedelic experiences with the Merry Pranksters, a group that traveled together in a bus during the 1960s. Tom Wolfe recounted many of their adventures in *The Electric Kool-Aid Acid Test* (1968).

In 1988 Kesey published a children's book, *Little Tricker the Squirrel Meets Big Double the Bear*. With 13 of his graduate students in creative writing at the University of Oregon he wrote a mystery novel, *Caverns*

(1990), under the joint pseudonym of O.U. Levon, which read backwards is "novel U.O. (University of Oregon)."

Kilmer, Joyce, *in full* Alfred Joyce Kilmer (b. Dec. 6, 1886, New Brunswick, N.J., U.S.—d. July 30, 1918, near Seringes, Fr.) American poet known chiefly for his 12-line verse entitled "Trees."

Joyce Kilmer

Kilmer's first volume of verse, *Summer of Love* (1911), showed the influence of William Butler Yeats and the Irish poets. After his conversion to Roman Catholicism, Kilmer attempted to model his poetry upon that of Coventry Patmore and the 17th-century Metaphysical poets. "Trees" first appeared in *Poetry* magazine in 1913. His books include *Trees and Other Poems* (1914), *The Circus and Other Essays* (1916), *Main Street and Other Poems* (1917), and *Literature in the Making* (1917). Kilmer joined the staff of *The New York Times* in 1913. In 1917 he edited *Dreams and Images*, an anthology of modern Catholic poetry. Kilmer was killed in action during World War I and was posthumously awarded the Croix de Guerre.

Kingsolver, Barbara (b. April 8, 1955, Annapolis, Md., U.S.) American writer and political activist whose novels concern the strength and endurance of the poor and disenfranchised people of the American Southwest.

Kingsolver grew up in eastern Kentucky, the daughter of a physician who treated the rural poor. After graduating from DePauw University, Greencastle, Ind., she traveled and worked in Europe and then returned to the United States.

Kingsolver's novel *The Bean Trees* (1988) concerns a woman who makes a meaningful life for herself and a young Cherokee girl with whom she moves from rural Kentucky to the Southwest. In *Animal Dreams* (1990) a disconnected woman finds purpose and moral challenges when she returns to live in her small Arizona hometown. *Pigs in Heaven* (1993), a sequel to her first novel, deals with the protagonist's attempts to defend her adoption of her Native American daughter. Kingsolver also wrote the nonfictional *Holding the Line: Women in the Great Arizona Mine Strike of 1983* (1989) and a short-story collection, *Homeland and Other Stories* (1989). Her poetry collection, *Another America (Otra America)* (1991), in English with Spanish translation, concerns the struggles, primarily of impoverished women, against sexual and political abuse, war, and death.

King, Stephen (Edwin) (b. Sept. 21, 1947, Portland, Maine, U.S.) American novelist and short-story writer whose enormously popular books were credited with reviving the genre of horror fiction in the late 20th century.

King graduated from the University of Maine in 1970. His first published novel, *Carrie*, about a tormented teenage girl gifted with telekinetic powers, appeared in 1974 and was an immediate popular success. *Carrie* was the first of many novels in which King blended horror, the macabre, fantasy, and science fiction. Among such works were *Salem's Lot* (1975), *The Shining* (1977), *The Stand* (1978), *The Dead Zone* (1979), *Firestarter* (1980), *Cujo* (1981), *Christine* (1983), *It* (1986), *Misery* (1987), *The Tommyknockers* (1987), and *The Dark Half* (1989). King also wrote the short stories collected in *Night Shift* (1978), as well as several novellas and motion-picture screenplays. Many of his works were made into films.

Kingston, Maxine Hong, *original surname* Hong (b. Oct. 27, 1940, Stockton, Calif., U.S.) Writer whose novels and nonfiction works explore the myths, realities, and cultural identities of Chinese and American families, as well as the role of women in Chinese culture.

The daughter of Chinese immigrants, Kingston was educated at the University of California at Berkeley. She taught at a number of schools, including the University of Hawaii and the University of California at Berkeley.

Kingston's first book, *The Woman Warrior: Memoirs of a Girlhood Among Ghosts* (1976), recalls her own girlhood, blending fact and fantasy in recreating the history of her female relatives in China. In *China Men* (1980), Kingston used biographical, mythological, and fantasy elements to tell the story of her father's life in China and his accommodations to life in America. The protagonist of her novel *Tripmaster Monkey: His Fake Book* (1988) is a young Chinese-American man who lives without regard to consequences.

Kinnell, Galway (b. Feb. 1, 1927, Providence, R.I., U.S.) American poet who examined the primitive bases of existence that are obscured by the overlay of civilization. His poems search for significance in such circumstances as an individual's personal relationship with violence and inevitable death, attempts to hold death at bay, the plight of the urban dispossessed, and the regenerative power of nature.

Educated at Princeton University and the University of Rochester, Kinnell worked for the University of Chicago in the early 1950s. Thereafter he taught and was poet-in-residence or poetry consultant at a number of colleges and universities.

His collections of poetry include *What a Kingdom It Was* (1960), *Flower Herding on Mount Monadnock* (1964), *Body Rags* (1967), *The Avenue Bearing the Initial of Christ into the New World: Poems 1946–64* (1974), *Selected Poems* (1982), for which he won both a National Book Award and a Pulitzer Prize, and *When One Has Lived a Long Time Alone* (1990). Kinnell also wrote a novel, *Black Light* (1966); revised 1980).

Kirby, William (b. Oct. 13, 1817, Kingston upon Hull, Yorkshire, Eng.— d. June 23, 1906, Niagara, Ont., Can.) Writer whose historical novel *The Golden Dog* (1877); authorized version, 1896) is a classic of Canadian literature.

In 1832 Kirby's family moved to the United States and in 1839 to Canada. Kirby eventually settled in Niagara, where he worked as editor of the Niagara *Mail* from 1850 to 1871 and as collector of customs from 1871 to 1895.

Kirby was a fervent Loyalist (favoring retention of Canada as part of the British Empire) and in the 1840s wrote several works intensely pro-British in sentiment. Topical history was the subject of his *Annals of Niagara* (1896) and of his verse epic *The U.E.: A Tale of Upper Canada in XII Cantos* (1859).

His masterpiece, *The Golden Dog*, contains historical information and materials from French-Canadian legend that are fused into a skillful plot dealing with British ascendancy in Quebec at the time of Louis XV.

Kirkland, Joseph (b. Jan. 7, 1830, Geneva, N.Y., U.S.—d. April 29, 1894, Chicago, Ill.) American novelist whose only work, a trilogy of Midwestern pioneer life, contributed to the development of realistic fiction.

Kirkland was influenced by the English realist Thomas Hardy and by his own mother, Caroline Kirkland, whose realistic accounts of the family's life in backwoods Michigan were published in the 1840s. *Zury: The Meanest Man in Spring County* (1887) was the first book of his trilogy. *The McVeys* (1888), depicting village life, and *The Captain of Company K* (1891), about the American Civil War, complete the trilogy.

Kirkwood, James (b. Aug. 22, 1924, Los Angeles, Calif., U.S.—d. April 21, 1989, New York, N.Y.) American librettist, actor, author, and playwright who, together with Nicholas Dante, wrote the text for the Broadway musical *A Chorus Line* (1975), which in 1983 became the longest-running musical in the history of Broadway.

As the son of silent film stars Lila Lee and James Kirkwood, the young Kirkwood appeared on Broadway in *Junior Miss*, *Small Wonder*, and *Welcome Darling* and in such films as *Oh God, Book II* (1980) and *Mommie Dearest* (1981). For *A Chorus Line*, a story about dancers auditioning for a musical, Kirkwood won both a Tony award and a Pulitzer Prize in 1976. Kirkwood also wrote such plays as *U.T.B.U.: Unhealthy To Be Unpleasant* (1966) and the comedy *Legends* (1987). Among his books are *There Must Be a Pony!* (1960), *Good Times/Bad Times* (1968), *P.S. Your Cat Is Dead!* (1972), *Some Kind of Hero* (1975), and *Hit Me with A Rainbow* (1979). His autobiography, *Diary of a Mad Playwright*, was published in 1989.

DAVID LANGFITT

Lincoln Kirstein

Kirstein, Lincoln (b. May 4, 1907, Rochester, N.Y., U.S.—d. Jan. 5, 1996, New York, N.Y., U.S.) American dance authority and writer who collaborated with George Balanchine to found and direct the various ballet companies that eventually became the world-renowned New York City Ballet. He is known to literature for his establishment of HOUND AND HORN, a literary magazine.

While a student at Harvard University, he founded and edited (1927–34) *Hound and Horn*, whose contributors included T.S. Eliot, Ezra Pound, and E.E. Cummings.

Kirstein became involved in ballet when he helped Romola Nijinsky write the biography of her famous husband. In 1933, he persuaded a young member of Diaghilev's Ballets Russes, George Balanchine, to come to the United States. The two founded the School of American Ballet and several companies that had a profound effect on ballet in the United States. Kirstein's books include *Dance* (1935), *The Classic Ballet* (1952); with Muriel Stuart), *Movement and Metaphor* (1970), *The New York City Ballet* (1974), *Nijinsky Dancing* (1975), and *Thirty Years with the New York City Ballet* (1978). From 1942 to 1948 he edited *Dance Index*, a scholarly magazine that published illustrated and annotated monographs on dance.

Kizer, Carolyn (Ashley) (b. Dec. 10, 1925, Spokane, Wash., U.S.) American poet whose work reflected her advocacy of feminism and her concern for human rights. She was awarded the Pulitzer Prize for poetry in 1985 for her collection *Yin: New Poems* (1984).

After attending Sarah Lawrence College, Kizer did graduate work at Columbia University and at the University of Washington. In 1959 she cofounded *Poetry Northwest*, which she also edited from 1959 to 1965. After serving in Pakistan as literary specialist for the U.S. State Department from 1964 to 1965 and from 1966 to 1970, she was the first director of literary programs for the National Endowment for the Arts. Kizer lectured, taught, or was poet-in-residence at several universities.

Her collections included *Poems* (1959), *The Ungrateful Garden* (1961), *Knock upon Silence* (1965), *Midnight Was My Cry* (1971), *Mermaids in the Basement: Poems for Women* (1984), and *The Nearness of You* (1986). "Pro Femina," one of her best-known poems, is a satiric work about women writers.

Klein, A.M., *in full* Abraham Moses (b. 1909, Ratno, Volhynia, Russian Empire [now in Ukraine]—d. Aug. 21, 1972, Montreal, Que., Can.) Canadian poet whose verse reflects his strong involvement with Jewish culture and history. He was a member of the Montreal group, a coterie of poets who advocated a break with traditional picturesque landscape poetry.

Klein practiced law in Montreal and at various times edited the *Canadian*

Jewish Chronicle, lectured at McGill University, and was active in the Co-operative Commonwealth Federation (now the New Democratic Party). Following a nervous breakdown in the mid-1950s, he lived in seclusion until his death.

An ardent supporter of Zionism, Klein made the Jewish experience a vehicle for his artistic expressions. *Hath Not a Jew . . .* (1940), *Poems* (1944), and *The Hitleriad* (1944) deal with persecution of the Jews by the Russians and Nazis. After a visit to Israel he wrote about its creation in *The Second Scroll* (1951), a symbolic novel that carries overtones of the techniques of James Joyce, on whom Klein was an authority. *The Rocking Chair and Other Poems* (1948) describes the change wrought by industrialization on Quebec.

Knight, Etheridge (b. April 19, 1931, Corinth, Miss., U.S.—d. March 10, 1991, Indianapolis, Ind.) African-American poet who emerged as a robust voice of the black aesthetic movement with his first volume of verse, *Poems from Prison* (1968). His poetry combined the energy and bravado of African-American "toasts" (long narrative poems that were recited in a mixture of street slang, specialized argot, and obscenities) with a sensitive concern for freedom from oppression.

Arrested for robbery in 1960, Knight was imprisoned for eight years—an experience that he recounted in verse in *Poems from Prison* and in prose in the anthology *Black Voices from Prison* (1970); originally published two years earlier in Italian as *Voce negre dal carcere*). After his release from prison, Knight taught at various universities and contributed to several magazines. He experimented with rhythmic forms of punctuation in *Belly Song and Other Poems* (1973), which addressed the themes of ancestry, racism, and love. In *Born of a Woman* (1980)—a work that balances personal suffering with affirmation—he introduced the concept of the poet as a "meddler" who forms a trinity with the poem and the reader. Much of his verse was collected in *The Essential Etheridge Knight* (1986).

Knight, Sarah Kemble, *byname* Madame Knight (b. April 19, 1666, Boston, Mass. [U.S.]—d. Sept. 25, 1727, New London, Conn.) American colonial teacher and businesswoman whose vivid and often humorous diary of her unchaperoned journey on horseback from Boston to New York in 1704 is considered one of the most authentic chronicles of 18th-century colonial life in America. *The Journal of Mme Knight* was published posthumously in 1825.

The Journal was one of very few published works of the era not written by a clergyman. It also was a precursor of a type of literature based on regional caricature.

Knowles, John (b. Sept. 16, 1926, Fairmont, W.Va., U.S.) American author who gained prominence for his first published novel, A SEPARATE PEACE (1959; filmed 1972). Most of his novels were psychological examinations of characters caught in conflict between the wild and the pragmatic sides of their personalities.

Knowles contributed articles to various publications during the 1950s before becoming a full-time writer. *A Separate Peace* The book chronicles the competitive friendship of two students at a New England preparatory school during World War II. Its sequel, *Peace Breaks Out* (1981), is viewed from the perspective of a troubled young teacher who has recently returned from World War II.

Other novels include *Indian Summer* (1966), *The Paragon* (1971), *A Vein of Riches* (1978), *Morning in Antibes* (1962), *Spreading Fires* (1974), *A Stolen Past* (1983), and *The Private Life of Axie Reed* (1986). He also wrote the travelogue *Double Vision* (1964) and *Phineas* (1968), a collection of six short stories.

Koch, Kenneth (b. Feb. 27, 1925, Cincinnati, Ohio, U.S.) American teacher and author noted especially for his witty, often surreal, sometimes epic, poetry. He was also an accomplished playwright.

Koch attended Harvard University and Columbia University, where he subsequently taught for many years. With the publication of *Poems* (1953), his first collection, he became one of the leading poets of the so-called New York school, a loose-knit group that included poets Frank O'Hara and John Ashbery. His work was noted for its rather whimsical humor and unusual juxtapositions.

Koch wrote two Byronic epics in ottava rima: *Ko; or, A Season on Earth* (1959), and *The Duplications* (1977). He also composed the long prose poem *The Burning Mystery of Anna in 1951* (1979), as well as many shorter verses, including those collected in *Selected Poems* (1991). Two dozen of his plays, which are often short, and 10 of his screenplays were collected in *A Change of Hearts: Plays, Films, and Other Dramatic Works 1951–1971* (1973). Koch is also noted for teaching poetry writing and appreciation to children and retirees, as described in his books *Wishes, Lies, and Dreams: Teaching Children to Write Poetry* (1970), *Rose, Where Did You Get That Red? Teaching Great Poetry to Children* (1973), and *I Never Told Anybody: Teaching Poetry Writing in a Nursing Home* (1977). He also wrote the novel *The Red Robins* (1975) and the short stories of *Hotel Lambosa* (1993). Koch published two books in 1994, *On the Great Atlantic Rainway: Selected Poems 1950–1988* and *One Train*. He was awarded the Bollingen Prize in 1995.

Kopit, Arthur (Lee) (b. May 10, 1937, New York, N.Y., U.S.) American playwright best known for *Oh Dad, Poor Dad, Mama's Hung You in the*

Closet and I'm Feelin' So Sad (1960). Subtitled "a pseudoclassical tragifarce in a bastard French tradition," the play parodies the Theater of the Absurd and the conventions of avant-garde drama.

Kopit attended Harvard University, where seven of his plays were produced while he was still a student. He later served as playwright-in-residence at Wesleyan University and adjunct professor of playwrighting at Yale University and at City College, New York.

Praised for his ease with language, impressive theatricality, and his skewering of American popular culture, Kopit wrote plays on a range of subjects. Among the works contained in *The Day the Whores Came Out to Play Tennis and Other Plays* (1965) are the one-act title play *Chamber Music*, and *Sing to Me Through Open Windows*. Kopit's other plays include *Indians* (1969), *Wings* (1978), the parodic *The End of the World* (1984), and *The Road to Nirvana* (1991), a racy satire of Hollywood.

Kornbluth, C.M., *original name* Cyril Kornbluth (b. 1923, New York, N.Y., U.S.—d. March 21, 1958, Waverly, N.Y.) American writer whose science-fiction stories reflect a dark, acerbic view of the future.

Kornbluth published science-fiction stories as a teenager. Called the Futurians, he and other young writers, including Isaac Asimov and Frederik Pohl (his frequent coauthor), composed and edited most of the tales in such sci-fi magazines as *Astonishing Stories* and *Super Science Stories*. Kornbluth wrote under almost 20 pseudonyms. After army service during World War II, he attended the University of Chicago.

His well-plotted fiction was acclaimed for its vision and social concerns. Critical of stories in which science was presented as the ultimate savior of humanity, Kornbluth instead examined the dangers of sophisticated technologies allowed to run amok. His essay "The Failure of the Science Fiction Novel as Social Criticism" was published posthumously in 1959. Much of his work was serialized in *Galaxy Science Fiction*. In collaboration with Judith Merril he wrote such works as *Outpost Mars* (1952); revised as *Sin in Space*, 1961) and *Gunner Cade* (1952). Among the books he published with Pohl were *Search the Sky* (1954), and *Gladiator-at-Law* (1955). Kornbluth also wrote *Takeoff* (1952), a science-fiction detective novel about the first space flight, and *The Syndic* (1953), about organized crime in a futuristic United States.

Kosinski, Jerzy (Nikodem) (b. June 14, 1933, Łódź, Pol.—d. May 3, 1991, New York, N.Y., U.S.) Polish-born American writer whose novels were sociological studies of individuals in controlling and bureaucratic societies.

According to Kosinski's own account, at the age of six, upon the outbreak of World War II, he was separated from his parents and wandered through Poland and Russia, living by his wits and under continual suspicion. He became mute and did not regain his speech until 1947. He studied at the University of Łódź, receiving degrees in history and political science, and from 1955 to 1957 he was professor of sociology at the Polish Academy of Sciences. In 1957 he immigrated to the United States (settling in New York), taught himself English, and published two nonfiction works, *The Future Is Ours, Comrade: Conversations with the Russians* (1960) and *No Third Path* (1962), both under the pen name Joseph Novak.

Kosinski then published the novel THE PAINTED BIRD (1965), followed by *Steps* (1968), which won the National Book Award, and *Being There* (1970; film, 1979). Later novels include *The Devil Tree* (1973); revised 1981), *Cockpit* (1975), *Passion Play* (1979), *Pinball* (1981), and *The Hermit of 69th Street* (1988).

A biography of Kosinski published in 1996 revealed that much of Kosinski's autobiography had been fabricated.

Kostelanetz, Richard (Cory) (b. May 14, 1940, New York, N.Y., U.S.) Avant-garde writer, artist, critic, and editor who was productive in many fields.

Kostelanetz attended Brown University, Columbia University, and King's College, London. He served as visiting professor or guest artist at a variety of institutions and lectured widely.

In 1971, employing a radically formalist approach, Kostelanetz produced the novel *In the Beginning*, which consists of the alphabet, in single- and double-letter combinations, unfolding over 30 pages. Most of his other literary work also challenges the reader in unconventional ways.

Among his other works are *Recyclings: A Literary Autobiography* (1974, 1984), *Politics in the African-American Novel* (1991), *Published Encomia, 1967–91* (1991), and *On Innovative Art(ist)s* (1992). He also made films and issued many audio recordings.

Krieger, Murray (b. Nov. 27, 1923, Newark, N.J., U.S.) American literary critic known for his studies of the special nature of the language of imaginative literature.

Krieger attended Rutgers University, the University of Chicago, and Ohio State University. He taught at the universities of Minnesota and Illinois before his appointment to the first American chaired professorship in literary criticism, at the University of Iowa. He also taught in the University of California system, and in 1967 he founded the influential School of Criticism and Theory while he was at the university's Irvine campus.

Krieger believed that poetic language has a unique capacity to reveal vision and meaning, a capacity beyond the scope of everyday language. He set forth his philosophy of literature in *The New Apologists for Poetry* (1956), *The Tragic Vision* (1960), and *The Classic Vision* (1971), which were later published together as *Visions of Extremity in Modern Literature* (1973). Krieger was among the earliest literary critics to insist on the importance of literary theory; he also stated, in *The Play and Place of Criticism* (1967), that language provides order and meaning to human experience. Among his later works are *Theory of Criticism: A Tradition and Its System* (1976), *Poetic Presence and Illusion* (1979), *Arts on the Level* (1981), *Words About Words About Words* (1988), *A Reopening of Closure* (1989), and *Ekphrasis: The Illusion of the Natural Sign* (1992).

Krutch, Joseph Wood (b. Nov. 25, 1893, Knoxville, Tenn., U.S.—d. May 22, 1970, Tucson, Ariz.) American writer, critic, naturalist, and conservationist.

Krutch attended the University of Tennessee and Columbia University, N.Y. He taught at Brooklyn Polytechnic and began to contribute book reviews and essays to periodicals. From 1924 through 1952, during which time he was drama critic for *The Nation*, he taught and lectured at various schools in the New York area and wrote a number of books, including *The Modern Temper* (1929). In the 1940s he wrote two critical biographies, *Samuel Johnson* (1944) and *Henry David Thoreau* (1948), which reflected his growing interest in commonsense philosophy and natural history. His later work included *The Measure of Man* (1954), *The Great Chain of Life* (1956), and his autobiography, *More Lives Than One* (1962).

Kumin, Maxine, *original surname* Winokur (b. June 6, 1925, Philadelphia, Pa., U.S.) Pulitzer Prize-winning poet, novelist, and children's author. Kumin's novels were praised in literary circles, but she was best known for her poetry, written primarily in traditional forms, on loss, fragility, family, and the cycles of life and nature.

After graduating from Radcliffe College, Kumin taught English at several colleges. In the 1950s she met the poet Anne Sexton, who influenced her stylistic development and with whom she collaborated on several children's books. Kumin's first book of poetry, *Halfway*, was published in 1961; *The Privilege* (1965) and *The Nightmare Factory* (1970) address issues of Jewish identity and family and of love between men and women. Kumin's New Hampshire farm was the inspiration for her collection *Up Country: Poems of New England, New and Selected* (1972); Pulitzer Prize, 1973). Critics compared Kumin to Robert Frost and Henry David Thoreau for her precise, unsentimental evocations of rural New England and the rhythms of daily life. The poet's later works include the acclaimed *The Retrieval System* (1978) and *Our Ground Time Here Will Be Brief* (1982).

Kumin's numerous children's books also reflected her love of nature and interest in family, and her short-story collection, *Why Can't We Live Together*

Like Civilized Human Beings? (1982), further explored issues of loss and relationships between men and women. Kumin served as poetry consultant to the Library of Congress from 1981 to 1982.

Kunitz, Stanley (Jasspon) (b. July 29, 1905, Worcester, Mass., U.S.) American poet noted for his subtle craftsmanship and his treatment of complex themes.

Kunitz attended Harvard University. While working as an editor, he contributed poems to magazines, eventually compiling them in his first book, *Intellectual Things* (1930). His collection *Passport to the War* (1944), like his first book, contained meticulously crafted, intellectual verse. Most of the poems from these first two works were reprinted in *Selected Poems 1928–1958* (1958), which won him the Pulitzer Prize in 1959.

With *The Testing-Tree* (1971), Kunitz departed from the formal structure and rational approach of his earlier verse and wrote shorter, looser, and more emotional poetry. Included in the book are "The Illumination" and "King of the River." His later books of poetry include *The Terrible Threshold* (1974), *The Coat Without a Seam* (1974), *The Lincoln Relics* (1978), *The Poems of Stanley Kunitz* (1979), *The Wellfleet Whale and Companion Poems* (1983), and *Next-to-Last Things* (1985), which contains essays as well as verse. In 1995 Kunitz received a National Book Award for *Passing Through the Later Poems, New and Selected*. Kunitz also edited numerous literary anthologies and translated Russian literature. In 1995 Kunitz received a National Book Award for *Passing Through the Later Poems; New and Selected*.

La Farge, Oliver (Hazard Perry) (b. Dec. 19, 1901, New York, N.Y., U.S.—d. Aug. 2, 1963, Albuquerque, N.M.) American anthropologist, short-story writer, and novelist who acted as a spokesman for Native Americans through his political actions and his fiction.

La Farge rejected the popular sentimental image of the Indian in contemporary literature. His first novel, *Laughing Boy* (1929; film, 1934), is a poetic but realistic story of the clash of two cultures; it was awarded the Pulitzer Prize for fiction in 1929. La Farge's autobiography, *Raw Material*, was published in 1945.

Lamontagne-Beauregard, Blanche (b. 1889, Les Escoumains, Que., Can.—d. 1958, Canada) French-Canadian poet who is recognized as the first important female poet of French Canada.

Lamontagne-Beauregard's mature writing extols her homeland, the Gaspé Peninsula, in a robust, emotional style. Her collections of lyric poetry include *Visions Gaspésiennes* (1913); "Views of the Gaspé"), *Par nos champs et nos rives* (1917); "Through Our Fields and Shores"), *Ma Gaspésie* (1928); "My Gaspé"), and *Moisson nouvelle* (1926); "New Harvest").

L'Amour Louis, *original name* Louis Dearborn LaMoore, *pseudonyms* Tex Burns *and* Jim Mayo (b. March 22, 1908, Jamestown, N.D., U.S.—d. June 10, 1988, Los Angeles, Calif.) American writer, prolific and best-selling author of more than 100 books, mostly formula westerns with authentic portrayals of frontier life.

L'Amour began his career as a writer in the 1940s. He stopped using pseudonyms after *Hondo* was published in 1953. More than 30 of his books—including *Kilkenny* (1954), *The Burning Hills* (1956), *Guns of the Timberland* (1955), and *How the West Was Won* (1963)—formed the basis of films. His books sold 200 million copies in 20 languages.

Lampman, Archibald (b. Nov. 17, 1861, Morpeth, Ont. [Canada]—d. Feb. 10, 1899, Ottawa) Important Canadian poet of the Confederation group, whose most characteristic work sensitively records the feelings evoked by scenes and incidents of the outdoors.

Lampman worked for the Canadian civil service from 1883 until his death. He collaborated with two other Ottawa poets in the writing of a weekly column, "At the Mermaid Inn," in the Toronto *Globe* (1892–93).

Repelled by the mechanization of urban life, Lampman wrote nature poems, eventually publishing two volumes of verse, *Among the Millet and Other Poems* (1888) and *Lyrics of Earth* (1893).

Lanier, Sidney (b. Feb. 3, 1842, Macon, Ga., U.S.—d. Sept. 7, 1881, Lynn, N.C.) American musician and poet whose verse often suggests the rhythms and thematic development of music.

In 1867 Lanier published his first book, the novel *Tiger-Lilies*, a mixture of German philosophy, Southern traditional romance, and his own experiences as a soldier in the American Civil War. In 1873 he accepted a position as first flutist in the Peabody Orchestra, Baltimore, Md., and he also played private concerts. With numerous poems already published in magazines, he wrote several potboilers.

"Corn" (1875), a poem treating agricultural conditions in the South, and "The Symphony" (1875), treating industrial conditions in the North, brought national recognition. Adverse criticism of his "Centennial Meditation" in 1876 launched him on an investigation of verse technique that he continued until his death. *The Song of the Chattahoochee*, a volume of poems, was published in 1877. Appointed lecturer in English literature at Johns Hopkins University in 1879, he delivered a series of lectures on verse technique, the early English poets, and the English novel, later published as *The Science of English Verse* (1880), *Shakspere and His Forerunners* (1902), and *The English Novel* (1883; rev. ed., 1897).

Ring Lardner

Lardner, Ring, *in full* Ringgold Wilmer Lardner (b. March 6, 1885, Niles, Mich., U.S.—d. Sept. 25, 1933, East Hampton, N.Y.) American writer, one of the most gifted American satirists and a fine storytellers.

Lardner began his writing career in 1905 as a reporter for the *South Bend* (Ind.) *Times*. He went on to work at newspapers in Chicago, where he established a reputation as a sportswriter specializing in baseball stories. From 1913 to 1919 he wrote a daily column for the *Chicago Tribune* and from 1919 to 1927 a humorous weekly column for the Bell syndicate. Meanwhile, in 1914, he had begun publishing fiction and had won popular success with his comic stories about baseball player Jack Keefe, some of which were collected in *You Know Me Al* (1916).

Lardner moved to New York in 1919, and he first attracted serious critical interest with his collection *How to Write Short Stories* (1924). Some of Lardner's best stories—"My Roomy," "Champion," "The Golden Honeymoon," and "Some Like Them Cold"—appeared in the 1924 collection. Equally good was his next collection, *The Love Nest and Other Stories* (1926). He collaborated on two plays that had Broadway runs: *Elmer the Great* (1928) with George M. Cohan and *June Moon* (1929) with George S. Kaufman. His spoof autobiography, *The Story of a Wonder Man*, appeared in 1927.

Larsen, Nella, *married surname* Imes (b. April 13, 1891, Chicago, Ill., U.S.—d. March 30, 1964, New York, N.Y.) Novelist and short-story writer of the Harlem Renaissance.

Larsen was born to a Danish mother and a West Indian father who died when she was two years old. Her first story was published in 1926. Her first novel, *Quicksand* (1928), concerns a young, headstrong biracial woman who seeks love, acceptance, and a sense of purpose, only to be mired in an emotional morass of her own creation. Her second novel, *Passing* (1929), centers on two light-skinned women, one of whom, Irene, marries a black man and lives in Harlem, while the other, Clare, marries a white man but cannot reject her black cultural ties. In 1930 Larsen became the first black woman to be awarded a Guggenheim fellowship. She never published again.

Lattimore, Richmond (Alexander) (b. May 6, 1906, Baoding prefecture, China—d. Feb. 26, 1984, Rosemont, Pa., U.S.) American poet and translator renowned for his disciplined yet poetic translations of Greek classics.

While in college, Lattimore wrote poetry that touched on Greek, Anglo-Saxon, and Norse tradition. He later focused on composing lyric poetry. His translations include Homer's *Iliad* (1951) and *Odyssey* (1967) and *The Four Gospels and the Revelation* (1979); he coedited, with David Grene, *Complete Greek Tragedies* (1959). His translations of the works of Aeschylus, Euripides, Aristophanes, and Pindar were particularly highly praised. Lattimore's translation of the *Iliad* is also well regarded.

Lattimore was a professor of Greek at Bryn Mawr (Pa.) College from 1935 to 1971. A collection of his poetry, *Poems from Three Decades*, was published in 1972. He also wrote criticism, such as *Story Patterns in Greek Tragedy* (1964).

Laughlin, James (b. Oct. 30, 1914, Pittsburgh, Pa., U.S.) American publisher and poet, founder of the New Directions press.

In the mid-1930s Laughlin lived in Italy with Ezra Pound, a major influence on his life and work; returning to America, he founded New Directions in 1936. Initially he intended to publish writings by ignored yet influential avant-garde writers of the period; Pound's *The Cantos* and William Carlos Williams' *Paterson* were among the works eventually issued by his press. During the 1940s New Directions also republished out-of-print novels by authors such as Henry James and F. Scott Fitzgerald. Laughlin's editions of such authors as Dylan Thomas, Lawrence Ferlinghetti, Tennessee Williams, and Herman Hesse proved very popular. New Directions also produced a large body of English translations of foreign authors. Laughlin himself wrote poetry noted for its warmth and imagination; his volume *Collected Poems* was published in 1992. Among his prose writings are memoirs of Pound, *Random Essays* (1989), and *Random Stories* (1990).

Laurence, Margaret, *original name* Jean Margaret Wemyss (b. July 18, 1926, Neepawa, Man., Can.—d. Jan. 5, 1987, Lakefield, Ont.) Canadian writer best known for her stories and novels depicting the lives of women struggling for self-realization in the male-dominated world of western Canada.

In the 1950s, Laurence lived in Africa; she reflected on her experiences in her first novel, *This Side Jordan* (1960), which deals with the exchange of power between old colonials and native Africans in the emerging nation of Ghana. *The Prophet's Camel Bell* (1963); U.S. title, *New Wind in a Dry Land*) is an account of Laurence's years in Somaliland (now Somalia). *The Tomorrow-Tamer* (1963), also set in Ghana, is a collection of short stories.

Laurence's next three novels—*The Stone Angel* (1964), *A Jest of God* (1966); U.K. title, *Now I Lay Me Down*), and *The Fire-Dwellers* (1959)— were set in the fictional Canadian prairie town of Manawaka. Each is centered on a woman of considerable strength of character. Other stories about Manawaka were collected in *A Bird in the House* (1970) and *The Diviners* (1974). She published her first children's book, *Jason's Quest*, in 1970 and a collection of occasional essays, *Heart of a Stranger,* in 1976. She twice received the Governor General's Award for fiction.

Lawson, John Howard (b. Sept. 25, 1894, New York, N.Y., U.S.—d. Aug. 11, 1977, San Francisco, Calif.) American playwright, screenwriter, and member of the "Hollywood Ten," who was jailed (1948–49) and blacklisted for his refusal to tell the House Committee on Un-American Activities about his political allegiances.

Lawson's early plays, such as *Roger Bloomer* (1923) and *Processional* (1925), are notable examples of Expressionism. He later portrayed problems of the working class: *The International* (1928) depicts a world revolution of the proletariat; *Marching Song* (1937) concerns a sit-down strike. Lawson's plays emphasize ideology and innovation.

During the 1930s and '40s Lawson devoted his time to writing screenplays. He wrote such scripts as *Action in the North Atlantic* (1943) and *Sahara* (1943) and was the cofounder and first president of the Screen Writers Guild. In 1949 he published *Theory and Technique of Playwriting and Screenwriting*, a revised edition of his earlier *Theory and Technique of Playwriting* (1936). Lawson explored American cultural tradition in *The Hidden Heritage: A Rediscovery of the Ideas and Forces That Link the Thought of Our Time with the Culture of the Past* (1950).

Layton, Irving (Peter) (b. March 12, 1912, Neamţ, Rom.) Poet who treated the Jewish-Canadian experience with rebellious vigor.

Layton's family immigrated to Canada in 1913. His poems, lyrical and romantic in tone and classical in form, developed from the early descriptive poetry collected in *Here and Now* (1945) and *Now Is the Place* (1948) into the tough and denunciatory expressions of his hatred of the bourgeoisie contained in *In the Midst of My Fever* (1954) and *The Cold Green Element* (1955). He later turned from social satire to concern for the universal human condition—e.g., *The Swinging Flesh* (1961) and *Europe and Other Bad News* (1981). *A Wild Peculiar Joy: Selected Poems 1945–1989* was published in 1989. He also published volumes of prose, including *Engagements* (1972), *Taking Sides* (1978), and *Wild Gooseberries: The Selected Letters of Irving Layton* (1989).

Lazarus, Emma (b. July 22, 1849, New York, N.Y., U.S.—d. Nov. 19, 1887, New York City) American writer best known for her sonnet "The New Colossus" (1883), written to the Statue of Liberty.

Lazarus' first book, *Poems and Translations* (1866), caught the attention of Ralph Waldo Emerson. At 21 she published *Admetus and Other Poems* (1871). She also wrote a prose romance (*Alide*) based on J.W. von Goethe's autobiography, a tragedy (*The Spagnoletto*), and the translation *Poems and Ballads of Heinrich Heine* (1881). About 1881 she began working for the relief of new immigrants in the United States. "The New Colossus," written to express her faith in America as a refuge for the oppressed, closes with the lines:

> Give me your tired, your poor,
> Your huddled masses, yearning to breathe free,
> The wretched refuse of your teeming shore.
> Send these, the homeless, tempest-tost to me,
> I lift my lamp beside the golden door!

This sonnet was chosen to be inscribed on a bronze plaque inside the base of the statue, which was dedicated in 1886.

Leacock, Stephen (Butler) (b. Dec. 30, 1869, Swanmore, Hampshire, Eng.—d. March 28, 1944, Toronto, Ont., Can.) Canadian humorist, educator, lecturer, and author of many books of lighthearted sketches and essays.

Leacock immigrated to Canada with his parents at the age of six. He was educated at the University of Toronto and the University of Chicago. He taught economics and political science at McGill University in Montreal from 1903 to 1936. Although Leacock wrote extensively on history and political economy, his true calling was humor, both as a lecturer and as an author.

His fame now rests securely on work begun with the beguiling fantasies of *Literary Lapses* (1910) and *Nonsense Novels* (1911). Leacock's humor is typically based on a comic perception of social foibles and the incongruity between appearance and reality in human conduct.

Ursula K. Le Guin

Le Guin, Ursula K., *original surname* Kroeber (b. Oct. 21, 1929, Berkeley, Calif., U.S.) Writer best known for tales of science fiction and fantasy imbued with concern for character development and language.

The daughter of the distinguished anthropologist Alfred L. Kroeber and writer Theodora Kroeber, Le Guin attended Radcliffe College and Columbia University. The methods of anthropology influenced her science-fiction stories, which often featured highly detailed descriptions of alien societies. Her first three novels, *Rocannon's World* (1966), *Planet of Exile* (1966), and *City of Illusions* (1967), introduced beings from the planet Hain, who established human life on habitable planets, including the Earth. Though her Earthsea series—*A Wizard of Earthsea* (1968), *The Tombs of Atuan* (1971), *The Farthest Shore* (1972), and *Tehanu: The Last Book of Earthsea* (1990)—was written for children, it attracted a large adult readership.

Among Le Guin's most important novels are THE LEFT HAND OF DARKNESS (1969), *The Dispossessed* (1974), *The Word for World Is Forest* (1972), and *Always Coming Home* (1985). Le Guin also wrote non-science fiction and essays on fantasy fiction, feminist issues, and other topics, some of them collected in *The Language of the Night* (1979) and *Dancing at the Edge of the World* (1989).

Leiber, Fritz, *in full* Fritz Reuter Leiber, Jr. (b. Dec. 24, 1910, Chicago, Ill., U.S.—d. Sept. 5, 1992, San Francisco, Calif.) American writer noted for his stories of innovation in sword-and-sorcery, contemporary horror, and satiric science fiction.

Leiber's first published story, "Two Sought Adventure," appeared in 1939. The story introduced the characters Grey Mouser and Fahfrd, who were featured in a series of swashbuckling adventure fantasies collected in *The Three of Swords* (1989) and *Swords' Masters* (1990). Leiber was also a pioneer of horror stories with modern urban settings, beginning with "Smoke Ghost" (1941) and continuing in his early novels such as *Gather, Darkness!* (1950) and *Conjure Wife* (1953).

In the early 1950s, the height of McCarthyism, the politically liberal Leiber was noted for his savagely satiric works about a chaotic, crumbling America, including the short story "Coming Attraction" (1950) and the novel *The Green Millennium* (1953). The satire is less harsh in his later fiction, which includes *The Silver Eggheads* (1961) and *A Specter is Haunting Texas* (1969). Leiber's later short stories, which includes "Gonna Roll the Bones" (1967), "Ill Met in Lankhmar" (1970), and "Belsen Express" (1975), are among his most admired works.

Leland, Charles Godfrey (b. Aug. 15, 1824, Philadelphia, Pa., U.S.—d. March 20, 1903, Florence, Italy) American poet and writer of miscellany, best known for the "Hans Breitmann Ballads," which reproduce the dialect and humor of the Philadelphia Germans (also called Pennsylvania Dutch).

Leland studied for two years in Germany, where he became fascinated with German culture. In 1853 he turned to journalism and worked for a number of years on P.T. Barnum's *Illustrated News*, the Philadelphia *Evening Bulletin*, and *Vanity Fair*. He also edited *Graham's Magazine*, where he published the first of his German-English poems, "Hans Breitmann's Barty" (1857). Written in a mixture of German and broken English, the poems were later collected in *The Breitmann Ballads* (complete edition, 1895).

L'Engle, Madeleine, *original surname* Camp, *married name* Franklin (b. Nov. 29, 1918, New York, N.Y., U.S.) American author of imaginative juvenile literature that was often concerned with such themes as the conflict of good and evil, the nature of God, individual responsibility, and family life.

L'Engle pursued a career in the theater before publishing her first book, *The Small Rain* (1945), a novel about an aspiring pianist who chooses her art over her personal relationships. After writing her first children's book, *And Both Were Young* (1949), she began a series of juvenile fictional works about the Austin family—*Meet the Austins* (1960), *The Moon by Night* (1963), *The Twenty-four Days Before Christmas* (1964), *The Young Unicorns* (1968), and *A Ring of Endless Light* (1980).

Madeleine L'Engle

In A WRINKLE IN TIME (1962), L'Engle introduced a group of young children who engage in a cosmic battle against a great evil that abhors individuality. Their story continued in *A Wind in the Door* (1973), *A Swiftly Tilting Planet* (1978), and *Many Waters* (1986). L'Engle also wrote fiction and poetry for adults. She discussed her life and writing career in *A Circle of Quiet* (1972), *The Summer of the Great-Grandmother* (1974), *The Irrational Season* (1977), *Walking on Water* (1980), and *Two Part Invention* (1988), a series of autobiographical books.

Leonard, Elmore, *in full* Elmore John Leonard, Jr. (b. Oct. 11, 1925, New Orleans, La., U.S.) American author of popular crime novels known for his use of local color and his uncanny ear for realistic dialogue.

Leonard served in the U.S. Naval Reserve (1943–46), then graduated from the University of Detroit. While composing scripts for advertising and educational films, he began writing western novels and short stories. The 1957 films *3:10 to Yuma* and *The Tall T* were based on his novelettes, and Leonard's novel *Hombre* (1961) was also adapted for film in 1967. His first crime novel, *The Big Bounce*, was published in 1969.

Leonard followed the latter with a series of novels set primarily in Detroit and Florida. Among his outstanding crime novels of the 1970s are *Fifty-two Pickup* (1974), *Swag* (1976); also published as *Ryan's Rules*), *Unknown Man*

No. 89 (1977), and *The Switch* (1978). His novel *Stick* (1983) became a best-seller. Subsequent novels include *LaBrava* (1983), *Glitz* (1985), *Bandits* (1987), *Freaky Deaky* (1988), and *Rum Punch* (1992).

Le Sueur, Meridel (b. Feb. 22, 1900, Murray, Iowa, U.S.) American author who espoused feminism and social reform in her fiction, journalism, and poetry.

Le Sueur grew up on the Midwestern plains, where she was influenced by her family's heritage of social and political activism and by the stories and poetry she heard from Native American women. She quit high school, acted in silent films, and began writing fiction and working as a journalist in the late 1920s.

The lives of women during the Great Depression was the subject of her first novel, *The Girl*. Although she wrote it in 1939, the novel was not published until 1978. Le Sueur's short stories, including those collected in *Salute to Spring* (1940), were widely admired. *North Star Country* (1945) is a history of the people of the Midwest in the form of an oral history, and *Crusaders* (1955) is a biography of her parents. In the late 1940s and the 1950s, while under FBI surveillance because of her political views, she wrote children's books on American history and folklore. Her other works include the nonfiction *Conquistadores* (1973) and *The Mound Builders* (1974); *Rites of Ancient Ripening* (1975); poetry); *Harvest: Collected Stories* (1977); and *Ripening: Selected Work, 1927–80* (1982).

Levertov, Denise (b. Oct. 24, 1923, Ilford, Essex, Eng.) English-born American poet who wrote deceptively matter-of-fact verse.

Levertov became a civilian nurse during World War II, serving in London throughout the bombings. She settled in New York in 1947 with her husband and was naturalized in 1955.

Her first volume of verse, *The Double Image* (1946), was not successful. *Here and Now* (1957) was quickly followed by *Overland to the Islands* (1958), and five more volumes appeared in the 1960s. She also translated the Buddhist work *In Praise of Krishna: Songs from the Bengali* (1967); with Edward Dimock, Jr.). *Relearning the Alphabet* (1970) discloses her concern with social issues. Opposed to the war in Vietnam, she was active in the War Resisters League and edited for it the collection *Out of the War Shadow* (1967).

In *Footprints* (1972) she reverted to the mystical tone of her earlier works. Levertov's later efforts include essays and prose, as in *The Poet in the World* (1973), and several collections of poetry, including *Candles in Babylon* (1982), *Breathing the Water* (1987), *A Door in the Hive* (1989), and *Evening Train* (1992).

Levine, Philip (b. Jan. 10, 1928, Detroit, Mich., U.S.) American poet of urban working-class life.

Levine studied at Wayne State University, Detroit, Mich., and the University of Iowa. He worked at a series of industrial jobs before he began teaching English and poetry at a number of colleges and universities. In his poetry Levine attempted to speak for those whose intelligence, emotions, and imagination are constrained by tedious and harsh working conditions.

Despite Levine's concern with modern life's brutalities, he also wrote poems of love and joy. His numerous poetry collections include *On the Edge* (1963), *They Feed They Lion* (1972), *Ashes: Poems New and Old* (1979), and *A Walk with Tom Jefferson* (1988). Inspired by a visit to Barcelona, he wrote the poems of *The Names of the Lost* (1976) in honor of the Loyalists who fought in the Spanish Civil War (1936–39). He won the 1991 National Book Award for his collection *What Work Is* and in 1995 received a Pulitzer prize for *Simple Truth*.

Levin, Meyer (b. Oct. 8, 1905, Chicago, Ill., U.S.—d. July 9, 1981, Jerusalem, Israel) American author of novels and nonfiction about the Jewish people and Israel.

Levin first became known with the novel *Yehuda* (1931). One of his most significant works, *The Old Bunch* (1937), traces the lives of several young Chicago Jews from 1921 to 1934. His other notable works are *Citizens* (1940) and *Compulsion* (1956), the latter about the notorious Leopold-Loeb murder case.

Beginning in 1933 Levin worked for *Esquire* magazine, and he was a reporter for the Loyalists in the Spanish Civil War (1936–39). He was also a war correspondent during World War II. After the war he produced a documentary film, *The Illegals* (1948), about the journey of Jewish immigrants from Poland to Israel.

Levin settled in Israel in 1958. His only comic novel, *Gore and Igor*, was published in 1968. His later works on the early settlement of Israel—*The Settlers* (1972) and *The Harvest* (1978)—were not well received. *The Architect*, published posthumously in 1981, was a thinly veiled treatment of the early career of architect Frank Lloyd Wright.

Lewis, Sinclair, *in full* Harry Sinclair Lewis (b. Feb. 7, 1885, Sauk Center, Minn., U.S.—d. Jan. 10, 1951, near Rome, Italy) American novelist and social critic who punctured American complacency with his broadly drawn, widely popular satirical novels. He won the Nobel Prize for Literature in 1930, the first given to an American.

Lewis graduated from Yale University in 1907. His first novel, *Our Mr. Wrenn* (1914), attracted favorable notice but few readers. At the same time, he was writing with ever-increasing success for such popular magazines as

Sinclair Lewis

The Saturday Evening Post and *Cosmopolitan.* The publication of MAIN STREET in 1920 made his literary reputation. *Main Street* was followed by a string of successful novels, including BABBITT (1922), ARROWSMITH (1925), ELMER GANTRY (1927), and DODSWORTH (1929). Lewis' later books were not up to the standards of his work in the 1920s. IT CAN'T HAPPEN HERE (1935) dramatized the possibilities of a fascist takeover of the United States. It was produced as a play by the Federal Theater with 21 companies in 1936. *Kingsblood Royal* (1947) is a novel of race relations.

Lindsay, Howard and **Crouse, Russel** (respectively b. March 29, 1889, Waterford, N.Y., U.S.—d. Feb. 11, 1968, New York, N.Y.; b. Feb. 20, 1893, Findlay, Ohio—d. April 3, 1966, New York, N.Y.) Team of American playwrights and producers who coauthored successful humorous plays and collaborated on theatrical productions.

Lindsay and Crouse first collaborated on *Anything Goes* (1934). Their longest-playing drama was a 1939 production based on Clarence Day's book *Life with Father,* which ran for 7½ years (3,213 performances) and in which Lindsay played Father opposite his real-life wife, Dorothy Stickney. Lindsay and Crouse produced *Arsenic and Old Lace* in 1940, and the result was another success. In 1946 the pair won the Pulitzer Prize in drama for *State of the Union* (1945), which was a satire of American politics. They also wrote the libretto for the play *The Sound of Music* (1959).

Lindsay, Vachel, *in full* Nicholas Vachel Lindsay (b. Nov. 10, 1879, Springfield, Ill., U.S.—d. Dec. 5, 1931, Springfield) American poet who—in an attempt to revive poetry as an oral art form of the common people—wrote and read to audiences compositions with powerful rhythms that had an immediate appeal.

A part-time lecturer, Lindsay wandered throughout the country reciting his poems in return for food and shelter. He first received widespread recognition in 1913 when *Poetry* magazine published his poem "General William Booth Enters into Heaven," about the founder of the Salvation Army. His poems of this kind are studded with vivid imagery and bold rhymes and express both his ardent patriotism and his romantic appreciation of nature.

Vachel Lindsay

Lindsay's best volumes of verse include *Rhymes to Be Traded for Bread* (1912), *General William Booth Enters into Heaven and Other Poems* (1913), *The Congo and Other Poems* (1914), and *The Chinese Nightingale and Other Poems* (1917).

Livesay, Dorothy (Kathleen) (b. Oct. 12, 1909, Winnipeg, Man., Can.) Canadian lyric poet whose works range from angry protest (*Day and Night,* 1944) to intensely personal evocations (*Selected Poems,* 1957).

Livesay's poetry shows the influence of the French Symbolist poets. A second influence was her experience in Montreal as a social worker during the Depression, intensified by an affinity for the social gospel of such liberal poets of the 1930s as C. Day-Lewis, Stephen Spender, and W.H. Auden. Her other collections of poetry include *Poems for People* (1947), *Call My People Home* (1950), *New Poems* (1955), *The Unquiet Bed* (1967), *Ice Age* (1975), and *Phases of Love* (1983). She twice (1944, 1947) received the Governor General's award for poetry, and in 1947 she received the Lorne Pierce Medal, Canada's greatest literary honor. Her *Collected Poems* appeared in 1972 and *Selected Poems: The Self-Completing Tree* in 1986.

Locke, Alain (LeRoy) (b. Sept. 13, 1886, Philadelphia, Pa., U.S.—d. June 9, 1954, New York, N.Y.) American educator, writer, and philosopher, best remembered as a leader and one of the chief interpreters of the HARLEM RENAISSANCE.

Graduated in philosophy from Harvard University(1907), Locke was the first black Rhodes scholar, studying at Oxford (1907–10) and the University of Berlin (1910–11). For almost 40 years, as head of the department of philosophy, he taught at Howard University, Washington, D.C.

Locke encouraged black authors to seek subjects in black life and to set high artistic standards for themselves. He familiarized American readers with the Harlem Renaissance by editing a special Harlem issue for *Survey Graphic* (March 1925), which he expanded into *The New Negro* (1925), an anthology of fiction, poetry, drama, and essays.

Locke edited the *Bronze Booklet* studies of cultural achievements by blacks, and he annually reviewed literature by and about blacks in *Opportunity* and *Phylon*. His many works include *Four Negro Poets* (1927), *Frederick Douglass, a Biography of Anti-Slavery* (1935), *Negro Art—Past and Present* (1936), and *The Negro and His Music* (1936). His unfinished materials for a definitive study of blacks in American culture formed the basis for M.J. Butcher's *The Negro in American Culture* (1956).

Lofting, Hugh (b. Jan. 14, 1886, Maidenhead, Berkshire, Eng.—d. Sept. 26, 1947, Santa Monica, Calif., U.S.) English-born American author and illustrator of a series of children's classics about Doctor Dolittle, a chubby, gentle, eccentric physician to animals.

Lofting lived most of his life in the United States, but the ambience of all his books is English. The character Dr. Dolittle was originally created to entertain Lofting's children in letters he sent from the front during World War I. *The Story of Dr. Dolittle*, the first of his series, appeared in 1920 and won instant success. From 1922 to 1928 he wrote one Dr. Dolittle book a year, and these seven are generally considered the best of the series—certainly the sunniest. *The Voyages of Dr. Dolittle* (1922) won the Newbery Medal as the best children's book of the year. Wearying of his hero, Lofting tried to get rid of him by sending him to the moon (*Dr. Dolittle in the Moon*, 1928), but popular demand compelled him to write *Dr. Dolittle's Return* in 1933. The last book of the series was published posthumously.

Lofting also wrote books in which the doctor did not appear, including *The Story of Mrs. Tubbs* (1923) and its sequel, *Tommy, Tilly, and Mrs. Tubbs* (1934).

Jack London

London, Jack, *original name* John Griffith Chaney (b. Jan. 12, 1876, San Francisco, Calif., U.S.—d. Nov. 22, 1916, Glen Ellen, Calif.) American novelist and short-story writer whose works deal romantically with elemental struggles for survival.

Deserted by his father, a roving astrologer, London was raised in Oakland, Calif., by his spiritualist mother and his stepfather, whose surname, London, he took. He worked as a sailor and saw much of the United States as a hobo riding freight trains and as a member of one of the many protest armies of the unemployed born of the panic of 1893. He was jailed for vagrancy and in 1894 became a militant socialist. London educated himself at public libraries, and at age 19 he crammed a four-year high-school course into one year and entered the University of California at Berkeley. After a year he quit school to unsuccessfully seek a fortune in the Klondike gold rush of 1897.

London studied magazines and then set himself an energetic daily schedule of writing. Within two years, stories of his Alaskan adventures, though often crude, began to win acceptance for their fresh subject matter and virile force. His first book, *The Son of the Wolf* (1900), gained a wide audience. His reputation was further enhanced by publication of the short story TO BUILD A FIRE (1908). During the remainder of his life he produced steadily, completing 50 books of fiction and nonfiction in 17 years. He sailed a ketch to the South Pacific, telling of his adventures in *The Cruise of the Snark* (1911). In 1910 he settled in California, where he built his grandiose Wolf House.

Jack London's hastily written output is of uneven quality. His Alaskan stories—THE CALL OF THE WILD (1903), WHITE FANG (1906), and *Burning Daylight* (1910)—in which he dramatized, in turn, atavism, adaptability, and the appeal of the wilderness are outstanding. His autobiographical novels include *The Road* (1907); *Martin Eden* (1909), perhaps his most enduring work; and *John Barleycorn* (1913). Other important works are THE SEA-WOLF (1904), which features a Nietzschean superman hero, and THE IRON HEEL (1907), a fantasy of the future that is a terrifying anticipation of fascism.

Longfellow, Henry Wadsworth (b. Feb. 27, 1807, Portland, Mass. [now in Maine], U.S.—d. March 24, 1882, Cambridge, Mass.) The most popular American poet of the 19th century.

Longfellow graduated from Bowdoin College (Brunswick, Maine) in 1825. In 1829, after traveling in Europe, he returned to the United States to be a professor and librarian at Bowdoin. When he was offered a professorship at Harvard, with another opportunity to go abroad, he accepted, and in 1835 he settled at Heidelberg, where he fell under the influence of German Romanticism.

In 1836 Longfellow returned to Harvard. In 1839 he published *Hyperion*, a romantic novel, and *Voices of the Night,* containing the poems "The Psalm of Life" and "The Light of the Stars," which became immediately popular. "The Wreck of the Hesperus," included in *Ballads and Other Poems* (1841), swept the nation, as did EVANGELINE (1847), an idyll of the former French colony of Acadia.

After presiding over Harvard's modern-language program for 18 years, Longfellow left teaching in 1854. In 1855 he published HIAWATHA, and its appeal was immediate. He translated Dante's *The Divine Comedy*, 3 vol. (1865–67), producing one of the most notable translations to that time, and wrote six sonnets on Dante that are among his finest poems.

The *Tales of a Wayside Inn*, modeled roughly on Geoffrey Chaucer's *The Canterbury Tales* and published in 1863, reveals Longfellow's narrative gift. The first poem, PAUL REVERE'S RIDE, became a national favorite. In 1872 he published what was intended to be his masterpiece, *Christus: A Mystery*, a trilogy dealing with Christianity from its beginnings, and he followed this work with two fragmentary dramatic poems, "Judas Maccabaeus" and "Michael Angelo." Although his genius was not dramatic, these neglected works were later seen to contain some of his most effective writing.

Lopez, Barry (Holstun) (b. Jan. 6, 1945, Port Chester, N.Y., U.S.) American writer best known for his books on natural history and the environment. In *Of Wolves and Men* (1978) and *Arctic Dreams* (1986), Lopez employed natural history as a metaphor for wider moral issues.

In 1977 Lopez' collection of Native American trickster stories, *Giving Birth to Thunder, Sleeping with His Daughter: Coyote Builds North America,* was published. The critically acclaimed *Of Wolves and Men* combines scientific information, folklore, and essays on the wolf's role in human culture. Lopez' other works include the fictional narratives *Desert Notes: Reflections in the Eye of a Raven* (1976) and *River Notes: The Dance of Herons* (1979); a volume of short fiction, *Winter Count* (1981); and a collection of essays, *Crossing Open Ground* (1988).

Lorde, Audre (Geraldine), *also called* Gamba Adisa (b. Feb. 18, 1934, New York, N.Y., U.S.—d. Nov. 17, 1992, St. Croix, Vir.Is.) African-American poet, essayist, and autobiographer known for her passionate writings on lesbian feminism and racial issues.

Lorde's first volume of poetry, *The First Cities* (1968), focused on personal relationships. *Cables to Rage* (1970) explored her anger at social and personal injustice and contained the first poetic expression of her lesbianism. Her next volumes, *From a Land Where Other People Live* (1973) and *New York Head Shop and Museum* (1974), were more rhetorical and political. Most critics consider *The Black Unicorn* (1978) to be her finest poetic work. In it she turned from the urban themes of her early work, looking instead to Africa, and wrote on her role as mother and daughter, using rich imagery and mythology.

The poet's 14-year battle with cancer is examined in *The Cancer Journals* (1980), in which she recorded her early battle with the disease and gave a feminist critique of the medical profession. *A Burst of Light* (1988), which further detailed her struggle, won a National Book Award in 1989. She also wrote the novel *Zami: A New Spelling of My Name* (1982), noted for its clear, evocative imagery. Her last poetry collection, *Undersong: Chosen Poems Old and New*, was published in 1992.

Lovecraft, H.P., *in full* Howard Phillips (b. Aug. 20, 1890, Providence, R.I., U.S.—d. March 15, 1937, Providence) American author of fantastic and macabre short novels and stories.

Most of Lovecraft's short stories appeared in the magazine *Weird Tales* beginning in 1923. His Cthulhu Mythos series of tales describe ordinary New Englanders' encounters with horrific beings of extraterrestrial origin. His other short stories deal with similar phenomena in which horror and morbid fantasy acquire an unexpected verisimilitude. *The Case of Charles Dexter Ward* (1928), *At the Mountains of Madness* (1931), and *The Shadow Over Innsmouth* (1936) are considered his best short novels. Lovecraft was a master of poetic language, and he attained unusually high literary standards for the genre.

Lowell, Amy (b. Feb. 9, 1874, Brookline, Mass., U.S.—d. May 12, 1925, Brookline) American critic, lecturer, and a leading Imagist poet.

At 28 Lowell began to devote herself seriously to poetry, but she published nothing until 1910. Her first volume, *A Dome of Many-Coloured Glass* (1912), was succeeded by *Sword Blades and Poppy Seed* (1914), which included her first poems in free verse and what she called "polyphonic prose." *A Critical Fable* (1922), an imitation of her kinsman James Russell

Lowell's *A Fable for Critics*, was published anonymously and stirred widespread speculation until she revealed her authorship.

Lowell's vivid and powerful personality and her independence and zest made her conspicuous, as did her scorn of convention. A bold experimenter in form and technique, she remained conservative at the core, retaining conventional verse forms and in her last years severing connections with all radical schools of poetry. Her works include *Six French Poets* (1915); *Tendencies in Modern American Poetry* (1917); *Can Grande's Castle* (1918); a two-volume biography, *John Keats* (1925); *What's O'Clock* (1925); and the posthumously published *East Wind* (1926) and *Ballads for Sale* (1927). *Complete Poetical Works* was published in 1955. She also wrote critical articles for periodicals and frequently lectured.

Lowell, James Russell (b. Feb. 22, 1819, Cambridge, Mass., U.S.—d. Aug. 12, 1891, Cambridge) American poet, critic, essayist, editor, and diplomat whose major significance probably lies in the interest in literature he helped develop in the United States.

James Lowell

Lowell graduated from Harvard in 1838 and in 1840 took his degree in law, which he never practiced. In 1844 he was married to the poet Maria White, who had inspired his poems in *A Year's Life* (1841). Another early work, *Conversations on Some of the Old Poets* (1845), contained a collection of critical essays that included pleas for the abolition of slavery. From 1845 to 1850 he wrote some 50 antislavery articles for periodicals and began serial publication of his BIGLOW PAPERS on the same subject. The year 1848 saw the publication of Lowell's two other most important pieces of writing: THE VISION OF SIR LAUNFAL, an enormously popular long poem extolling the brotherhood of man; and *A Fable for Critics*, a witty verse evaluation of contemporary American authors.

The death of three of Lowell's four children was followed by the death of his wife in 1853. Henceforth his literary production comprised mainly prose essays on topics in literature, history, and politics. In 1855 his lectures on English poets before the Lowell Institute led to his appointment as Smith professor of modern languages at Harvard University, succeeding Henry Wadsworth Longfellow. In 1857 he married Frances Dunlap and began four years as editor of the new *Atlantic Monthly*.

With Charles Eliot Norton, Lowell was editor of *The North American Review* from 1864 to 1872, and during this time he wrote a series of critical essays on major literary figures that were collected with other essays in the two series of *Among My Books* (1870, 1876). He was appointed minister to Spain (1877–80) and ambassador to Great Britain (1880–85). After his second wife died in 1885, Lowell retired from public life.

Lowell, Robert, *in full* Robert Traill Spence, Jr. (b. March 1, 1917, Boston, Mass., U.S.—d. Sept. 12, 1977, New York, N.Y.) American poet noted for his complex, confessional poetry.

Lowell graduated from Kenyon College in Gambier, Ohio, in 1940 and that year married the novelist Jean Stafford. Lowell's first major work, LORD WEARY'S CASTLE (1946), won the Pulitzer Prize in 1947. It contains two of his most praised poems: THE QUAKER GRAVEYARD IN NANTUCKET and "Colloquy in Black Rock," celebrating the feast of Corpus Christi.

After being divorced in 1948, Lowell married the writer and critic Elizabeth Hardwick the next year (divorced 1972). He spent a few years abroad and then settled in Boston in 1954. His LIFE STUDIES (1959), which won the National Book Award for poetry, contains an autobiographical essay, "91 Revere Street," as well as a series of 15 confessional poems. Chief among the poems are "Waking in Blue," which tells of his confinement in a mental hospital, and SKUNK HOUR, which dramatically conveys his mental turmoil.

Lowell's activities in the civil-rights and antiwar campaigns of the 1960s lent a more public note to his next three books of poetry: FOR THE UNION DEAD (1964), *Near the Ocean* (1967), and *Notebook 1967–68* (1969). Lowell's trilogy of plays, *The Old Glory*, which views American culture over the span of history, was published in 1965 (rev. ed., 1968). His later poetry volumes include THE DOLPHIN (1973), which won a second Pulitzer Prize, and *Day by Day* (1977). His translations include *Phaedra* (1963) and *Prometheus Bound* (1969); *Imitations* (1961), free renderings of various European poets; and *The Voyage and Other Versions of Poems by Baudelaire* (1968).

Luce, Clare Boothe, *original name* Ann Clare Boothe (b. March 10, 1903, New York, N.Y., U.S.—d. Oct. 9, 1987, Washington, D.C.) American playwright, politician, and celebrity, noted for her satiric wit and for her role in American politics.

Boothe held editorial positions at *Vogue* magazine and at *Vanity Fair* during the early 1930s. Some of her satiric articles for *Vanity Fair* were collected in *Stuffed Shirts* (1931). In 1935 she married magazine publisher Henry R. Luce.

After an earlier play failed, Luce wrote *The Women* (1936), a comedy that ran for 657 performances on Broadway; *Kiss the Boys Goodbye* (1938), a satire on American life; and *Margin for Error* (1939), an anti-Nazi play. All three were adapted into motion pictures.

Luce was elected to the U.S. House of Representatives (1943–47) as a Republican from Connecticut. She was influential in the Republican Party nationally and served as ambassador to Italy from 1953 to 1956.

Ludwig, Jack (Barry) (b. Aug. 30, 1922, Winnipeg, Manitoba, Can.) Canadian author whose fiction, set in Canada and the United States, urged an enthusiastic approach to life and often reflected his Jewish background.

Ludwig was educated at the University of Manitoba and the University of California at Los Angeles; he later taught in several American colleges and universities.

The issues of Ludwig's partly satirical first novel, *Confusions* (1963), are moral, social, sexual, and racial, as a schizophrenic young Jewish man seeks his identity. The hero of *Above Ground* (1968), after spending most of his youth in hospital rooms, finds rejuvenation in sexual encounters with a series of willing women. At the center of *A Woman of Her Age* (1973) is an 85-year-old former radical whose compassion lends strength to those around her. In addition to novels, Ludwig wrote short stories, essays, adaptations of several classic plays, and several volumes on sports.

Luhan, Mabel Dodge, *original surname* Ganson (b. Feb. 26, 1879, Buffalo, N.Y., U.S.—d. Aug. 13, 1962, Taos, N.M.) American writer whose candid autobiographical volumes, collectively known as *Intimate Memories*, contain much information about well-known Americans of her era.

Luhan's life and writing revolved around the literary, artistic, and political celebrities she gathered about her both in New York City and abroad. She later settled in an artists' colony in Taos, where her home again became a gathering place for celebrated artists and writers. She devoted herself to recording her relationships with such figures as Gertrude Stein, John Reed, and Walter Lippmann, with little regard for propriety or privacy.

The volumes of Luhan's *Intimate Memories* are *Background* (1933), *European Experiences* (1935), *Movers and Shakers* (1936), and *Edge of Taos Desert* (1937).

Lurie, Alison (b. Sept. 3, 1926, Chicago, Ill., U.S.) Writer whose urbane and witty novels usually feature upper-middle-class academics in a university setting.

Lurie graduated from Radcliffe College in 1947 and later taught English and then children's literature at Cornell University. One of her best-known books, *The War Between the Tates* (1974; film, 1977), concerns the manner in which the wife of a professor at mythical Corinth University deals with her husband's infidelity. *Foreign Affairs* (1984), winner of the 1985 Pulitzer Prize for fiction, describes the separate, unexpected sexual and romantic affairs of two academics from Corinth University during a sabbatical semester in England. Lurie's other works, almost all set in academia, included *Love and Friendship* (1962), *The Nowhere City* (1965), *Imaginary Friends* (1967),

Real People (1969), *Only Children* (1979), and *The Truth About Lorin Jones* (1988).

She also wrote books for children, such as *The Heavenly Zoo* (1979), *Clever Gretchen and Other Forgotten Folktales* (1980), and *Fabulous Beasts* (1981), as well as works about children's literature.

MacArthur, Charles (b. Nov. 5, 1895, Scranton, Pa., U.S.—d. April 21, 1956, New York, N.Y.) American journalist, dramatist, and screenwriter, who is remembered for his comedies written with Ben Hecht.

At the age of 17, MacArthur moved to Chicago to begin a career in journalism, working at the *Chicago Tribune* and the *Chicago Herald-Examiner*, before moving to New York City to work for the *New York American* and to begin writing plays.

MacArthur and Hecht began their long partnership and earned critical acclaim with *The Front Page* (1928), a farce about a star reporter who is drawn into his own story. They also achieved success with *Twentieth Century* (produced 1932), a lively satire of the entertainment industry. Later collaborations included *Jumbo* (1934), *Ladies and Gentlemen* (produced 1939), and *Swan Song* (produced 1946). The pair also wrote many successful screenplays in the 1930s, among them *Crime Without Passion*, *The Scoundrel*, which won an Academy Award for best original story, *Soak the Rich*, *Gunga Din*, and *Wuthering Heights*. MacArthur's solo screenplays included *The Sin of Madelon Claudet* (1931), which featured an Academy Award-winning performance by his second wife, Helen Hayes, *Rasputin and the Empress* (1932), and *The Senator Was Indiscreet* (1947).

Macdonald, Cynthia (b. Feb. 2, 1928, New York, N.Y., U.S.) American poet who employed a sardonic tone and used grotesque imagery to comment on the mundane.

Macdonald taught English at Sarah Lawrence College (1970–75) and Johns Hopkins University (1975–78). In 1979 she founded the creative writing program at the University of Houston, serving as codirector.

Amputations (1972), her first published volume of poetry, attracted attention by its startling imagery. Almost all the poems concern freakish people who have undergone amputation—either physical or symbolic—of a body part or who feel amputated from society. Continuing the theme of separateness and alienation, Macdonald places the subjects of her poems in *Transplants* (1976) in threatening environments. *(W)holes* (1980) also focuses on grotesques and incongruous surroundings. Her later works include *Alternate Means of Transport* (1985) and *Living Wills* (1991). She also wrote the libretto for *The Rehearsal* (1978), an opera by Thomas Benjamin.

MacDonald, John D., *in full* Dann (b. July 24, 1916, Sharon, Pa., U.S.—d. Dec. 28, 1986, Milwaukee, Wis.) American author of mystery and science-fiction novels and short stories. who published more than 70 books. He is best remembered for his series of 24 crime novels featuring private investigator Travis McGee.

MacDonald began contributing science-fiction and suspense stories to pulp magazines in the mid-1940s. His first full-length novel was *The Brass Cup-cake* (1950).

In *The Deep Blue Good-By* (1964), MacDonald introduced Travis McGee—a tough, eccentric "salvage consultant." Going beyond the usual formula of sex and violence, the author investigates contemporary social and moral concerns through McGee and his erudite sidekick Meyer. Books in the series include *One Fearful Yellow Eye* (1966), *A Tan and Sandy Silence* (1971), and *Cinnamon Skin* (1982). Among his science-fiction novels are *Wine of the Dreamers* (1951), *Ballroom of the Skies* (1952), and *The Girl, the Gold Watch, and Everything* (1962). MacDonald's other notable works include *The Neon Jungle* (1953), *Condominium* (1977), and *One More Sunday* (1984).

Macdonald, Ross, *pseudonym of* Kenneth Millar, *also called* John Macdonald *or* John Ross Macdonald (b. Dec. 13, 1915, Los Gatos, Calif., U.S.—d. July 11, 1983, Santa Barbara, Calif.) American mystery writer who is credited with elevating the detective novel to the level of literature with his compactly written tales of murder and despair.

Millar, who adopted a wide array of pseudonyms, wrote his first novels under his real name; these include *The Dark Tunnel* (1944), *Trouble Follows Me* (1946), and *The Three Roads* (1948). Under the name John Macdonald he wrote *The Moving Target* (1949); reissued in 1966 as *Harper*), in which he introduced the shrewd private investigator Lew Archer. Macdonald then assumed the pen name John Ross Macdonald for such Lew Archer mysteries as *The Way Some People Die* (1951), *The Ivory Grin* (1952), *Find a Victim* (1954), and *The Name Is Archer* (1955). Under the name Ross Macdonald he wrote *The Barbarous Coast* (1956), *The Doomsters* (1958), and *The Galton Case* (1959). Such later novels as *The Underground Man* (1971) and *Sleeping Beauty* (1973) reflected Macdonald's abiding interest in conservation.

MacInnes, Tom, *byname of* Thomas Robert Edward McInnes (b. Oct. 29, 1867, Dresden, Ont., Can.—d. Feb. 11, 1951, Vancouver, B.C.) Canadian writer whose works range from vigorous, slangy recollections of the Yukon gold rush, as in *Lonesome Bar* (1909), to a translation of and commentary on the philosophy of Laozi (Lao-tzu), irreverently titled *The Teaching of the Old Boy* (1927). His collected poems include *Complete Poems* (1923) and *In the Old of My Age* (1947). *Chinook Days* (1927), a fictionalized autobiography, also contains history and folklore of British Columbia.

MacKaye, Percy (b. March 16, 1875, New York, N.Y., U.S.—d. Aug. 31, 1956, Cornish, N.H.) American poet and playwright whose use of historical and contemporary folk literature furthered the development of the pageant in the United States.

MacKaye was introduced to the theater at an early age by his father, actor Steele MacKaye, with whom he first collaborated. In 1912 he published *The Civic Theatre*, in which he advocated amateur community theatricals. He attempted to bring poetry and drama to large participant groups and to unite the stage arts, music, and poetry by the use of masques and communal chanting. He wrote, among others, the pageants *The Canterbury Pilgrims* (published in 1903) and, as coauthor, *St. Louis: A Civic Masque* (performed 1914 with 7,500 participants).

In 1929 MacKaye became advisory editor to *Folk-Say*, a journal of American folklore. He also conducted research in collaboration with his wife, Marion Morse MacKaye. His most noteworthy contributions to U.S. drama and pageantry are *The Scarecrow* (1908), a historical play; *Caliban* (1916), a pageant-masque; *This Fine Pretty World* (1923), a regional play; and *The Mystery of Hamlet: King of Denmark* (1945), a study of past and present tragedy.

MacKaye, Steele, *in full* James Morrison Steele MacKaye (b. June 6, 1842, Buffalo, N.Y., U.S.—d. Feb. 25, 1894, Timpas, Colo.) American playwright, actor, theater manager, and inventor.

MacKaye was the first American to act Hamlet in London (1873). At Harvard, Cornell, and elsewhere he lectured on the philosophy of aesthetics. In New York City he founded the St. James, Madison Square, and Lyceum theaters. MacKaye wrote 30 plays, including the popular *Hazel Kirke*, *Paul Kauvar*, and *Money Mad*, acting in them in 17 different roles. He organized the first school of acting in the U.S, which later became the American Academy of Dramatic Art, and patented more than 100 theatrical inventions, including folding theater seats.

MacLeish, Archibald (b. May 7, 1892, Glencoe, Ill., U.S.—d. April 20, 1982, Boston, Mass.) American poet, playwright, professor, and public official whose concern for liberal democracy figured in much of his work.

MacLeish was educated at Yale and went to France in 1923 to perfect his poetic craft. The verse he published during his expatriate years—*The Happy Marriage* (1924), *The Pot of Earth* (1925), *Streets in the Moon* (1926), and *The Hamlet of A. MacLeish* (1928)—shows the fashionable influence of Ezra Pound and T.S. Eliot. During this period he wrote his frequently anthologized poem "Ars Poetica" (1926). After returning to the United States in 1928, he published *New Found Land* (1930), which reveals his simple lyric eloquence and includes one of his best-known poems, "You, Andrew Marvell."

In the 1930s MacLeish grew concerned about the menace of fascism. *Conquistador* (1932), about the conquest and exploitation of Mexico, was the first of his "public" poems. Others were collected in *Frescoes for Mr.*

Archibald MacLeish

Rockefeller's City (1933), *Public Speech* (1936), and *America Was Promises* (1939). His radio verse plays include *The Fall of the City* (1937), *Air Raid* (1938), and *The Great American Fourth of July Parade* (1975).

MacLeish served as librarian of Congress (1939–44) and assistant secretary of state (1944–45). He published his *Collected Poems: 1917–1952* in 1952, and his *New and Collected Poems 1917–1976* appeared in 1976. His verse drama *J.B.*, based on the biblical story of Job, was performed on Broadway in 1958. *Riders on the Earth* (1978) is a collection of his essays.

MacLennan, Hugh (b. March 20, 1907, Glace Bay, Cape Breton, Nova Scotia, Can.—d. Nov. 7, 1990, Montreal, Que.) Canadian novelist and essayist whose books offer an incisive critique of Canadian life.

A Rhodes scholar at Oxford, MacLennan studied at Princeton and taught at Lower Canada College, Montreal, and at McGill University. His first novel, *Barometer Rising* (1941), is a moral fable that uses as a background the actual explosion of a munitions ship that partly destroyed the city of Halifax in 1917. His later novels include *Two Solitudes* (1945), *The Precipice* (1948), *The Watch That Ends the Night* (1959), and *Voices in Time* (1980).

Macpherson, Jay, *in full* Jean Jay Macpherson (b. June 13, 1931, London, Eng.) Canadian lyric poet who expressed serious religious and philosophical themes in symbolic verse that was often lyrical or comic.

Macpherson's early works, *Nineteen Poems* (1952) and *O Earth Return* (1954), were followed by *The Boatman and Other Poems* (1957, reissued with additional poems, 1968), a collection that established her reputation as a poet.

Her lyrics, often ironic and epigrammatic and linked by recurrent mythical and legendary symbols, reflect the influences of the modern critical theories of Northrop Frye and Robert Graves, Elizabethan songs, the poetry of William Blake, Anglo-Saxon riddles, and traditional ballads. *Four Ages of Man* (1962) is an illustrated account of classical myths, designed for older children. *Welcoming Disaster* (1974) is a collection of her poems from 1970 to 1974. Her study of the pastoral romance, *The Spirit of Solitude: Conventions and Continuities in Late Romance*, was published in 1982.

Madhubuti, Haki R., *byname of* Don Luther Lee (b. Feb. 23, 1942, Little Rock, Ark., U.S.) African-American author, publisher, and teacher.

Lee attended graduate school at the University of Iowa. He taught at several colleges and universities, in 1984 becoming a faculty member at Chicago State University. His poetry, which began to appear in the 1960s, was written in black dialect and slang. His work is characterized both by anger at social and economic injustice and by rejoicing in African-American culture. The verse collection *Don't Cry, Scream* (1969) includes an introduction by poet Gwendolyn Brooks.

Lee founded the Third World Press in 1967, and he established the Institute of Positive Education in Chicago, a school for black children, in 1969. Among his poetry collections published under the Swahili name Haki R. Madhubuti are *Book of Life* (1973) and *Killing Memory, Seeking Ancestors* (1987). He also wrote *From Plan to Planet—Life Studies: The Need for Afrikan Minds and Institutions* (1973) and an essay collection, *Enemies: The Clash of Races* (1978).

Mailer, Norman (b. Jan. 31, 1923, Long Branch, N.J., U.S.) American novelist who successfully developed a form of journalism that conveys actual events with the subjective richness and imaginative complexity of the novel.

Mailer graduated from Harvard University and was drafted into the army. After his service, he enrolled at the Sorbonne, where he wrote the extraordinarily successful novel THE NAKED AND THE DEAD (1948).

Mailer's second and third novels, *Barbary Shore* (1951) and *The Deer Park* (1955), were greeted with critical hostility and mixed reviews, respectively. His next important work was a long essay, *The White Negro* (1957), a sympathetic study of a marginal social type—the "hipster."

In 1959, Mailer made a bid for attention with *Advertisements for Myself*; the miscellany's naked self-revelation won the admiration of a younger generation. Mailer's subsequent novels, though not critical successes, were widely read as guides to life. *An American Dream* (1965) is about a man who murders his wife, and *Why Are We in Vietnam?* (1967) is about a young man on an Alaskan hunting trip.

A controversial figure whose egotism and belligerence often antagonized both critics and readers, Mailer did not command the same respect for his fiction that he received for his journalism. *The Armies of the Night* (1968), for example, was based on the Washington peace demonstrations of October 1967, during which Mailer was jailed and fined. A similar treatment was given to the Republican and Democratic presidential conventions in *Miami and the Siege of Chicago* (1968) and to the Moon exploration in *Of a Fire on the Moon* (1970).

Among his other works are his essay collections *The Presidential Papers* (1963) and *Cannibals and Christians* (1966); *The Executioner's Song* (1979), a "nonfiction novel" based on the life of convicted murderer Gary Gilmore; *Ancient Evenings* (1983), the first volume of a projected trilogy about Egypt; *Tough Guys Don't Dance* (1984), a contemporary mystery thriller; and the extremely lengthy *Harlot's Ghost* (1991).

Bernard Malamud

Malamud, Bernard (b. April 26, 1914, Brooklyn, N.Y., U.S.—d. March 18, 1986, New York, N.Y.) American novelist and short-story writer who made parables out of Jewish immigrant life.

A son of Russian Jews, Malamud was educated at the City College of New York and Columbia University. His first novel, THE NATURAL (1952), is a fable about a baseball hero who is gifted with miraculous powers. THE ASSISTANT (1957) is about a young Gentile hoodlum and an old Jewish grocer. THE FIXER (1966) won a Pulitzer Prize. His other novels are *A New Life* (1961), *The Tenants* (1971), *Dubin's Lives* (1979), and *God's Grace* (1982).

Malamud's genius is most apparent in his short stories. Though the stories are told in spare, compressed prose, they include bursts of emotional, metaphorical language. Grim city neighborhoods are visited by magical events, and their hardworking residents have glimpses of love and self-sacrifice. Malamud's short-story collections are THE MAGIC BARREL (1958), *Idiots First* (1963), *Pictures of Fidelman* (1969), and *Rembrandt's Hat* (1973).

Malone, Dumas (b. Jan. 10, 1892, Coldwater, Miss., U.S.—d. Dec. 27, 1986, Charlottesville, Va.) American historian, editor, and the author of an authoritative multivolume biography of Thomas Jefferson.

Malone taught at Yale, Columbia, and the University of Virginia, where he was the Thomas Jefferson Foundation Professor of History. He edited the *Dictionary of American Biography* from 1929 to 1936 and the *Political Science Quarterly* from 1953 to 1958, and he served as director of the Harvard University Press from 1936 to 1943. Malone's masterwork is *Jefferson and His Time*, consisting of *Jefferson the Virginian* (1948), *Jefferson and the Rights of Man* (1951), *Jefferson and the Ordeal of Liberty* (1962), *Jefferson the President: First Term, 1801–1805* (1970), *Jefferson the President: Second Term, 1805–1809* (1974), and *The Sage of Monticello* (1981).

Malone's other writings include *The Public Life of Thomas Cooper* (1926), *Saints in Action* (1939), and *Empire for Liberty*, 2 vol. (1960, with Basil Rauch).

Mamet, David (Alan) (b. Nov. 30, 1947, Chicago, Ill., U.S.) Playwright, director, and screenwriter noted for his often desperate working-class characters and for his distinctive and colloquial dialogue that is frequently profane.

Mamet began writing plays at Goddard College, Plainfield, Vt. Returning to Chicago, he worked at various factory jobs, at a real estate agency, and as a taxi driver; all these experiences provided background for his plays. In 1973 he cofounded a theater company in Chicago.

Mamet's plays include *Duck Variations* (produced 1972), *Sexual Perversity in Chicago* (produced 1974; filmed as *About Last Night . . .* [1986]),

AMERICAN BUFFALO (1976), *A Life in the Theatre* (1977), *The Water Engine* (1978), and *Speed-the-Plow* (1987). GLENGARRY GLEN ROSS (1983; film, 1992) won the 1984 Pulitzer Prize for drama.

Mamet wrote fiction, plays for children, and a number of screenplays. He both wrote and directed the motion pictures *House of Games* (1987) and *Homicide* (1991).

Markham, Edwin, *original name* Charles Edward Anson Markham (b. April 23, 1852, Oregon City, Ore., U.S.—d. March 7, 1940, New York, N.Y.) American poet and lecturer, best known for a poem of social protest, "The Man with the Hoe."

Edwin Markham

Markham grew up on an isolated ranch in central California. In 1899 he gained national fame with the publication in the *San Francisco Examiner* of "The Man with the Hoe." Inspired by Jean-François Millet's painting, Markham made the French peasant the symbol of the exploited classes throughout the world. Its success enabled Markham to devote himself to writing and lecturing.

His first book of verse, *The Man with the Hoe and Other Poems* (1899), was followed in 1901 by *Lincoln and Other Poems*. Succeeding volumes—*Shoes of Happiness* (1915), *Gates of Paradise* (1920), *New Poems: Eighty Songs at Eighty* (1932), and *The Star of Araby* (1937)—have the commanding rhetoric but lack the passion of the early works.

Marquand, J.P., *in full* John Phillips (b. Nov. 10, 1893, Wilmington, Del., U.S.—d. July 16, 1960, Newburyport, Mass.) American novelist who recorded the shifting patterns of middle- and upper-class American society in the mid-20th century.

Marquand grew up in comfortable circumstances until his father's business failure, when he was sent to live with relatives in Newburyport. This experience of reduced status and security made him acutely conscious of social gradations and their psychological corollaries.

Marquand devoted some 15 years to writing popular fiction, including the widely read adventures of the Japanese intelligence agent Mr. Moto. He then produced his three most characteristic novels, satirical but sympathetic studies of a crumbling New England gentility: *The Late George Apley* (1937), *Wickford Point* (1939), and *H.M. Pulham, Esquire* (1941). He wrote three novels dealing with the dislocations of wartime America—*So Little Time* (1943), *Repent in Haste* (1945), and *B.F.'s Daughter* (1946)—but in these his social perceptions were somewhat less keen. He came back to his most able level of writing in his next novel, *Point of No Return* (1949), a painstakingly accurate social study of a New England town. Two social types particularly important in the 1950s were depicted in *Melville Goodwin, U.S.A.* (1951), about a professional soldier, and *Sincerely, Willis Wayde* (1955), a sharply satiric portrait of a big-business promoter. His last important novel, *Women and Thomas Harrow* (1958), is partly autobiographical.

Marqués, René (b. Oct. 4, 1919, Arecibo, Puerto Rico—d. March 22, 1979, San Juan) Playwright, short-story writer, critic and Puerto Rican nationalist whose work shows deep social and artistic commitment.

Marqués graduated from the College of Agricultural Arts of Mayagüez. He studied at the University of Madrid and at Columbia University in New York City.

His best-known play, *La carreta* (1956); *The Oxcart*), concerns a rural Puerto Rican family that immigrates to New York City in search of its fortune but fails. In 1959 Marqués published three plays together in the collection *Teatro* ("Theater"): *La muerte no entrará en palacio* ("Death Will Not Enter the Palace"), a political allegorical play in which a governor betrays his youthful ideals; *Un niño azul para esa sombra* ("A Blue Child for That Shadow"); and *Los soles truncos* ("Maimed Suns"), one of his most successful plays.

Marqués also published the short-story collections *Otro día nuestro* (1955); "Another of Our Days"), *En una ciudad llamada San Juan* (1960); "In a City Called San Juan"), and *Inmersos en el silencio* (1976); "Immersed in Silence") and the novels *La víspera del hombre* (1959); "The Eve of Man") and *La mirada* (1975); "The Glance"). A collection of his essays, *Ensayos* (1966); some included in *El puertorriqueño dócil* [1967; *The Docile Puerto Rican*]), echoes his imaginative writing in examining the problem of national identity in Puerto Rico.

Marquis, Don, *in full* Donald Robert Perry Marquis (b. July 29, 1878, Walnut, Ill., U.S.—d. Dec. 29, 1937, New York, N.Y.) American newspaperman, poet, and playwright, creator of the literary characters Archy the cockroach and Mehitabel the cat—wry, down-and-out philosophers of the 1920s.

Marquis worked as a reporter on *The Atlanta Journal*. When in 1907 Joel Chandler Harris established *Uncle Remus's Magazine*, Marquis became his associate editor.

In 1912 Marquis left Atlanta for New York City, where he became one of the best known of literary journalists. He wrote his columns "The Sun Dial" for the *Evening Sun* and "The Lantern" for the *Herald Tribune*. Stories about Archy and Mehitabel, first published in "The Sun Dial," were later collected in ARCHY AND MEHITABEL (1927).

Among Marquis' published collections of humorous poetry, satirical prose, and plays are *Danny's Own Story* (1912), *Dreams and Dust* (1915),

Hermione (1916), *The Old Soak* (1916); made into a play, 1926), *Sonnets to a Red Haired Lady* (1922), *The Dark Hours* (1924), and *Out of the Sea* (1927). After Marquis' death *Archy and Mehitabel* was combined with several sequels into an omnibus, *the lives and times of archy and mehitabel* (1940).

Marshall, Paule, *original surname* Burke (b. April 9, 1929, Brooklyn, N.Y., U.S.) Novelist whose works emphasized the need for black Americans to reclaim their African heritage.

The Barbadian background of Marshall's parents was to inform all her work. After graduating from Brooklyn College, she worked briefly as a librarian before joining *Our World* magazine, where she worked from 1953 to 1956. Her autobiographical first novel, BROWN GIRL, BROWNSTONES (1959), tells of the American daughter of Barbadian parents who travels to their homeland as an adult; the book was critically acclaimed for its acute rendition of dialogue.

Soul Clap Hands and Sing, a 1961 collection of four novellas, presents four aging men who come to terms with their earlier refusal to affirm lasting values. Marshall's 1962 short story "Reena" was one of the first pieces of fiction to feature a college-educated, politically active black woman as its protagonist; frequently anthologized, it also was included in the author's 1983 collection *Reena and Other Stories. The Chosen Place, the Timeless People* (1969) is set on a fictional Caribbean island and concerns a philanthropic attempt to modernize an impoverished and oppressed society.

Marshall's most eloquent statement of her belief in African-Americans' need to rediscover their heritage was PRAISESONG FOR THE WIDOW, a highly regarded 1983 novel that established her reputation as a major writer. *Daughters* (1991) concerned a West Indian woman in New York who returns home to assist her father's reelection campaign. The protagonist, like those of Marshall's other works, has an epiphany after confronting her personal and cultural past.

Mason, Bobbie Ann (b. May 1, 1940, Mayfield, Ky., U.S.) Short-story writer and novelist known for her evocation of rural Kentucky life.

Mason was reared on a dairy farm. She graduated from the University of Kentucky and moved to New York City. She attended the State University of New York at Binghamton and the University of Connecticut; her dissertation on Vladimir Nabokov was published as *Nabokov's Garden: A Guide to Ada* (1974). After 1979, she began publishing stories in *The New Yorker*, the *Atlantic Monthly*, and elsewhere.

Mason received critical acclaim for *Shiloh and Other Stories* (1982), her first collection of stories, which described the lives of working-class people in a shifting rural society now dominated by chain stores, television, and superhighways. *In Country* (1985), her first novel, was also steeped in mass culture, leading one critic to speak of Mason's "Shopping Mall Realism." Many critics praised her realistic regional dialogue, although some compared the novel unfavorably to her shorter works. In 1988 Mason published *Spence + Lila*, the story of a long-married couple. *Love Life: Stories* appeared in 1989 and the novel *Feather Crowns* in 1993.

Masters, Edgar Lee (b. Aug. 23, 1869, Garnett, Kan., U.S.—d. March 5, 1950, Philadelphia, Pa.) American poet and novelist, best known as author of SPOON RIVER ANTHOLOGY (1915).

Masters grew up on his grandfather's farm near New Salem, Ill. A volume of his verses appeared in 1898, followed by *Maximilian*, a drama in blank verse (1902); *The New Star Chamber and Other Essays* (1904); *Blood of the Prophets* (1905); and a series of plays issued between 1907 (*Althea*) and 1911 (*The Bread of Idleness*).

In 1909 Masters was introduced to *Epigrams from the Greek Anthology*. He was seized by the idea of composing a similar series of free-verse epitaphs in the form of monologues. The result was *Spoon River Anthology*, in which the former inhabitants of the fictitious community of Spoon River speak from the grave of their bitter, unfulfilled lives in the dreary confines of a small town.

Though Masters continued to publish volumes of verse almost yearly, the quality of his work never again rose to the level of the *Spoon River Anthology*. Among his novels are *Mitch Miller* (1920) and *The Nuptial Flight* (1923). Masters wrote biographies of Abraham Lincoln, Walt Whitman (1937), and Mark Twain (1938). His best effort in this form is *Vachel Lindsay: A Poet in America* (1935), a study of his friend and fellow poet. Also notable are his autobiography, *Across Spoon River* (1936), and *The Sangamon* (1942), a volume in the "Rivers of America" series.

Matthews, Brander, *in full* James Brander Matthews (b. Feb. 21, 1852, New Orleans, La., U.S.—d. March 31, 1929, New York, N.Y.) Essayist, drama critic, novelist, and first American professor of dramatic literature.

Educated at Columbia University, Matthews was professor of literature at Columbia from 1892 to 1900 and of dramatic literature from 1900 to 1924. A prominent figure in New York literary groups, he was the founder of both the Authors' and Players' clubs. Matthews was the author of many short stories and critical essays, was a regular critic for *The New York Times* for a long period, and was the author or editor of more than 40 books. *A Confident Tomorrow* (1899) is considered his best novel. His sound scholarship was revealed in such works as *Molière: His Life and His Works* (1910), *Shakspere as a Playwright* (1913), and *French Dramatists of the 19th Century* (1881).

Matthiessen, Peter (b. May 22, 1927, New York, N.Y., U.S.) American novelist, naturalist, and wilderness writer whose work dealt with the destructive effects of encroaching technology on preindustrial cultures and the natural environment.

After serving in the U.S. Navy, Matthiessen attended the Sorbonne and Yale University. He moved to Paris, where he helped to found and edit the literary journal *The Paris Review*.

A dedicated naturalist, Matthiessen. He wrote more than 15 books of nonfiction, including *Wildlife in America* (1959), a history of the destruction of wildlife in North America; *The Cloud Forest: A Chronicle of the South American Wilderness* (1961); *Under the Mountain Wall: A Chronicle of Two Seasons of the Stone Age* (1962), about his experiences as a member of a scientific expedition to New Guinea; *Blue Meridian: The Search for the Great White Shark* (1971); *The Snow Leopard* (1978), set in remote regions of Nepal; and *African Silences* (1991). His book *In the Spirit of Crazy Horse* (1983), about the conflict between federal agents and the American Indian Movement at Wounded Knee, S.D., in 1973, was the subject of a prolonged libel suit that blocked all but an initial printing and was not settled until 1990; in 1991 the book was republished.

Matthiessen's novels include *Race Rock* (1954); the acclaimed *At Play in the Fields of the Lord* (1965; film, 1991), a surrealistic work involving missionaries, Indians, and an expatriate American pilot in the South American rain forest; *Far Tortuga* (1975), a complex work about events leading up to the death of the crew of a turtle-fishing boat in the Caribbean; and *Killing Mister Watson* (1990).

Peter Matthiessen

Maupin, Armistead (b. May 13, 1944, Washington, D.C., U.S.) Novelist known for his *Tales of the City* series.

Maupin's career as a fiction writer was launched when his *Tales of the City* was published as a serial in the *San Francisco Chronicle* in 1976–77, then as a book in 1978. The story, set in San Francisco, focuses on three characters—Mary Ann Singleton, a naive young woman from Cleveland; Michael "Mouse" Tolliver, her homosexual friend; and their motherly landlady, Anna Madrigal, a transsexual. The author's compassion for his characters and his lively, humorous style made *Tales of the City* a cult favorite. Five popular sequels followed: *More Tales of the City* (1980), *Further Tales of the City* (1982), *Baby cakes* (1984), *Significant Others* (1987), and *Sure of You* (1989), all but the last initially serialized in San Francisco newspapers. Although the tone of the books is generally light-hearted, throughout the series characters confront serious personal and political issues including loneliness, parenthood, and the loss of a partner to

AIDS. Maupin broke from the series to write *Maybe the Moon* (1992), the story of a dwarf actress.

Maxwell, William, *original name* William Maxwell Keepers, Jr. (b. Aug. 16, 1908, Lincoln, Ill., U.S.) American author of spare, evocative short stories and novels about small-town life in the American Midwest.

Maxwell taught English at the University of Illinois before joining the staff of *The New Yorker* magazine, where he worked from 1936 to 1976. His first novel, *Bright Center of Heaven*, was published in 1934. *They Came Like Swallows* (1937) tells how an epidemic of influenza affects a close family. *The Folded Leaf* (1945), perhaps Maxwell's best-known work, describes the friendship of two small-town boys through their adolescence and college years. In *Time Will Darken It* (1948) a long visit from relatives disrupts a family; in *The Château* (1961) American travelers encounter postwar French culture.

Maxwell's collections of short stories include *The Old Man at the Railroad Crossing and Other Tales* (1966), *Over by the River, and Other Stories* (1977), and *Billie Dyer and Other Stories* (1992). His 1980 novel *So Long, See You Tomorrow* returns to the subject of a friendship between two boys, this one disrupted by a parent's murder of his spouse, then suicide. In 1995 Maxwell's collected stories were published as *All the Days and Nights*.

McAlmon, Robert (Menzies) (b. March 9, 1896, Clifton, Kansas, U.S.— d. Feb. 2, 1956, Desert Hot Springs, Calif.) American author and publisher and an exemplar of the literary expatriate in Paris during the 1920s.

In 1920 McAlmon moved to Chicago and then to New York, where he and William Carlos Williams began the little magazine *Contact*. In 1921 McAlmon married the English writer Bryher (Annie Winifred Ellerman) and moved to Paris. After publishing a book of his short stories, *A Hasty Bunch* (1922), at his own expense, he founded his own publishing company; under the name Contact Editions, he published his short-story collection *A Companion Volume* (1923) and his autobiographical novel *Post-Adolescence* (1923), as well as works by Williams, Gertrude Stein, Ernest Hemingway, and Bryher.

McAlmon's best-received work was the novel *Village: As It Happened Through a Fifteen Year Period* (1924), a bleak portrait of the inhabitants of an American town. His later books include *Distinguished Air (Grim Fairy Tales)* (1925), the poetry collection *The Portrait of a Generation* (1926), the epic poem *North America, Continent of Conjecture* (1929), and *Being Geniuses Together: An Autobiography* (1938), a Paris memoir. *McAlmon and the Lost Generation: A Self-Portrait* (1962) is a collection of his autobiographical writings.

McBain, Ed. Pseudonym of Evan HUNTER.

McCarthy, Cormac, *byname of* Charles McCarthy, Jr. (b. July 20, 1933, Providence, R.I., U.S.) American writer in the Southern gothic tradition whose novels about wayward characters in the rural American South and Southwest are noted for their dark violence and dense prose.

Readers were introduced to McCarthy's difficult narrative style in the novel *The Orchard Keeper* (1965). Later works include *Outer Dark* (1968), about two incestuous siblings; *Child of God* (1974), which tells of a lonely man's descent into depravity; and *Suttree* (1979), about a man who overcomes his fixation on death. After *Blood Meridian* (1985), a violent frontier tale, McCarthy achieved popular fame with *All the Pretty Horses* (1992), winner of the National Book Award. The first volume of "The Border Trilogy," it is the coming-of-age story of two Texans who travel to Mexico. The second installment, *The Crossing* (1994), follows a pair of teenage brothers in southwestern New Mexico.

McCarthy, Mary (Therese) (b. June 21, 1912, Seattle, Wash., U.S.—d. Oct. 25, 1989, New York, N.Y.) American novelist and critic noted for bitingly satiric commentaries on marriage, the impotence of intellectuals, and the role of women in contemporary urban America.

McCarthy began her career writing book reviews. She served on the editorial staff of the *Partisan Review* from 1937 to 1948. She married four times, the second time, in 1938, to the noted American critic Edmund Wilson, who encouraged her to begin writing fiction.

Her first novel, THE COMPANY SHE KEEPS (1942), concerns a fashionable woman who experiences divorce and psychoanalysis. *The Oasis* (1949) is about the failure of a utopian community of intellectuals. *The Groves of Academe* (1952) is a satiric examination of American higher education during the era of the anticommunist "witch hunts." THE GROUP (1963), her most popular novel, follows the lives of eight Vassar graduates. *Birds of America* (1971) is a post-World War II version of the 19th-century novel in which American innocence is confronted with European sophistication. CANNIBALS AND MISSIONARIES (1979) is about the hijacking of a committee flying to Iran to investigate the shah's atrocities. She also wrote two autobiographies, MEMORIES OF A CATHOLIC GIRLHOOD (1957) and *How I Grew* (1987).

Mary McCarthy

McCullers, Carson, *original name* Lula Carson Smith (b. Feb. 19, 1917, Columbus, Ga., U.S.—d. Sept. 29, 1967, Nyack, N.Y.) American writer of novels and stories that depict the inner lives of lonely people.

McCullers' first novel, and in the opinion of many her finest work, THE HEART IS A LONELY HUNTER, appeared in 1940. The book concerns five inhabitants of a small town in Georgia—an adolescent girl with a passion to

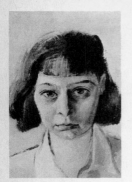

Carson McCullers

study music, an unsuccessful socialist agitator, a black physician struggling to maintain his personal dignity, a widower who owns a café, and John Singer, the work's protagonist. In the novel THE MEMBER OF THE WEDDING (1946), a 12-year-old motherless girl yearns to go on her brother's honeymoon. McCullers adapted the latter work into a successful stage play in 1950, and it was made into a film in 1952. Another novel, REFLECTIONS IN A GOLDEN EYE (1941), a highly colored psychological horror story set in a peacetime Southern army camp, was also made into a film, and THE BALLAD OF THE SAD CAFÉ, a novelette published with short stories in 1951, was dramatized by Edward Albee in 1963.

McCutcheon, George Barr (b. July 26, 1866, near Lafayette, Ind., U.S.— d. Oct. 23, 1928, New York, N.Y.) American novelist whose best-known works were GRAUSTARK (1901), a popular novel set in a mythical middle European kingdom, and *Brewster's Millions* (1902), a comic fantasy.

McCutcheon attended Purdue University briefly, leaving to become a newspaper reporter. City editor of the *Lafayette Daily Courier* from 1893 to 1901, he resigned after *Graustark* achieved popular success. Altogether, McCutcheon published some 40 works of fiction, including more swashbuckling tales of Graustark.

McElroy, Joseph (Prince) (b. Aug. 21, 1930, New York, N.Y., U.S.) American novelist and short-story writer who was known for intricate, lengthy, and technically complex fiction.

McElroy's first novel, *A Smuggler's Bible* (1966), is made up of eight disconnected chapters that are separated by authorial commentary. *Lookout Cartridge* (1974), perhaps McElroy's best work, is a political thriller about a filmmaker who searches London and New York City in an effort to recover movie footage that may have recorded a crime. *Plus* (1976) is about a rebellious, disembodied brain that operates a computer in outer space. In 1986 McElroy published *Women and Men*, a 1,191-page novel about a journalist and a feminist who live in the same apartment building in New York City but never meet. More accessible is *The Letter Left to Me* (1988), which centers on a letter of advice written by the late father of a 15-year-old boy.

McGee, Thomas D'Arcy (b. April 13, 1825, Carlingford, County Louth, Ire.—d. April 7, 1868, Ottawa, Ont., Can.) Irish-Canadian writer known for his nationalism.

An Irish patriot, McGee was associated with *The Nation* (1846–48), the literary organ of the Young Ireland political movement (which called for the study of Irish history and the revival of the Irish language). He was implicated in the abortive Irish rebellion of 1848 and fled to the United States, where he established two newspapers, the New York *Nation* and the *American Celt*. He came to advocate peaceful reforms for Ireland rather than revolution, and in 1857 he moved to Canada. He was elected to the Legislative Assembly of Canada in 1858 and served there until his death. According to his belief that literary and cultural nationalism must go along with political involvement, he encouraged the development of a Canadian culture and wrote nationalist poetry. He was assassinated in Ottawa, presumably by Irish nationalists in Canada. Selections from McGee's writings appear in two edited collections: *The Poems of Thomas D'Arcy McGee* (1869) and *D'Arcy McGee: A Collection of Speeches and Addresses* (1937).

McGinley, Phyllis (b. March 21, 1905, Ontario, Ore., U.S.—d. Feb. 22, 1978, New York, N.Y.) American poet and author of books for juveniles, best known for her light verse celebrating suburban home life.

Starting in the 1920s, McGinley wrote poetry for such magazines as *The New Yorker* and *The Atlantic*. Although her verse is often dismissed as being merely light, it is serious as well as witty. In 1961 she won the Pulitzer Prize in poetry for *Times Three: Selected Verse from Three Decades* (1960). McGinley also wrote a popular series of autobiographical essays about being a wife in the suburbs, titled *Sixpence in Her Shoe* (1964). Her works for juveniles include *The Horse Who Lived Upstairs* (1944) and *The Make-Believe Twins* (1953).

McGuane, Thomas, *in full* Thomas Francis McGuane III (b. Dec. 11, 1939, Wyandotte, Mich., U.S.) American author noted for his novels of violent action.

McGuane's first novels, *The Sporting Club* (1969), *The Bushwhacked Piano* (1971), and *Ninety-two in the Shade* (1973), presented the central plot and theme of his fiction: a man, usually from a secure family, exiles himself from American society and removes himself to an isolated locale; he then finds a reason—alienation, attraction to a woman, rights to territory—to oppose another man in a succession of acts of escalating violence and revenge.

The locales of his novels—Key West, Fla., northern Michigan, Montana—and his scenes of fishing and personal combat suggest the influence of Ernest Hemingway. While McGuane's early novels were noted for their stylistic extravagance, a growing plainness of style developed in his later novels. They include *Panama* (1978), *Nobody's Angel* (1981), *Something To Be Desired* (1984), *Keep the Change* (1989), and *Nothing But Blue Skies* (1992). *An Outside Chance* (1980); rev. ed., 1990) is a collection of his essays on sports.

Claude McKay

McKay, Claude (b. Sept. 15, 1890, Jamaica, British West Indies—d. May 22, 1948, Chicago, Ill., U.S.) Jamaican-born poet and novelist whose HOME TO HARLEM (1928) was the most popular novel written by an American black to that time.

Before moving to the United States in 1912, McKay wrote two volumes of Jamaican dialect verse, *Songs of Jamaica* and *Constab Ballads* (1912). After attending Tuskegee (Ala.) Institute and Kansas State Teachers College, he went to New York in 1914, where he contributed to the *Liberator*, then a leading journal of avant-garde politics and art. With the publication of two volumes of poetry, *Spring in New Hampshire* (1920) and *Harlem Shadows* (1922), McKay emerged as the first and most militant voice of the Harlem Renaissance. After 1922 McKay lived abroad, successively in the Soviet Union, France, Spain, and Morocco. In both *Home to Harlem* and *Banjo* (1929) he attempted to capture the vitality of the black vagabonds of urban America and Europe. There followed a collection of short stories, *Gingertown* (1932), and another novel, *Banana Bottom* (1933). In all these works McKay searched among the common folk for a distinctive black identity.

After returning to America in 1934, McKay wrote for various magazines and newspapers, including the *New Leader* and the New York *Amsterdam News*. He also wrote an autobiography, *A Long Way from Home* (1937), and the study *Harlem: Negro Metropolis* (1940). His *Selected Poems* (1953) was issued posthumously.

McMillan, Terry (b. Oct. 18, 1951, Port Huron, Mich., U.S.) African-American novelist whose work often portrays feisty, independent black women and their attempts to find fulfilling relationships with black men.

In McMillan's first novel, *Mama* (1987), a black woman manages to raise five children alone after she forces her drunken husband to leave. *Disappearing Acts* (1989) concerns two dissimilar people who begin an intimate relationship. *Waiting to Exhale* (1992) follows four black middle-class women, each of whom is looking for the love of a worthy man. McMillan edited *Breaking Ice: An Anthology of Contemporary African-American Fiction* (1990).

McMurtry, Larry (Jeff) (b. June 3, 1936, Wichita Falls, Tex., U.S.) American writer noted for his novels set on the frontier, in contemporary small towns, and in increasingly urbanized and industrial areas of Texas.

McMurtry's first novel, *Horseman, Pass By* (1961; filmed as *Hud*, 1963), is set in the Texas ranching country. The isolation and claustrophobia of small-town life are examined in *The Last Picture Show* (1966; film, 1971). McMurtry's frontier epic, *Lonesome Dove* (1985), won a Pulitzer Prize in 1986. A sequel, *Streets of Laredo*, appeared in 1993. Urban Houstonites appear in

Moving On (1970), *All My Friends Are Going to Be Strangers* (1972), and *Terms of Endearment* (1975; film, 1983). Other novels include *Leaving Cheyenne* (1963; filmed as *Lovin' Molly*, 1974), *Cadillac Jack* (1982), *The Desert Rose* (1983), *Buffalo Girls* (1990), and *The Evening Star* (1992).

McPhee, John (Angus) (b. March 8, 1931, Princeton, N.J.) American journalist who wrote accessible, informative books on a wide variety of topics—particularly profiles of figures in sports, science, and the environment.

McPhee was educated at Princeton University. He became an associate editor at *Time* (1957–64) and a staff writer at *The New Yorker* (from 1965). His first book, *A Sense of Where You Are* (1965), was based on an article he wrote for *The New Yorker* on basketball player and Rhodes scholar Bill Bradley. Subjects of his subsequent profiles include tennis players in *Levels of the Game* (1969) and *Arthur Ashe Remembered* (1993); a conservationist in *Encounters with the Archdruid* (1971); and a boat craftsman in *The Survival of the Bark Canoe* (1975).

McPhee focused on central New Jersey in *The Pine Barrens* (1968), the Scottish Highlands in *The Crofter and the Laird* (1970), and Switzerland in *La Place de la Concorde Suisse* (1984). He wrote a series of books on the geology of the western United States, which included *Basin and Range* (1981), *Rising From the Plains* (1986), and *Assembling California* (1993), and he examined the citrus industry in *Oranges* (1967), aeronautical engineering in *The Deltoid Pumpkin Seed* (1973), and nuclear terrorism in *The Curve of Binding Energy* (1974). Among his collections of essays are *A Roomful of Hovings and Other Profiles* (1968), *The John McPhee Reader* (1976), *Giving Good Weight* (1979), and *Table of Contents* (1985).

McPherson, James Alan (b. Sept. 16, 1943, Savannah, Ga., U.S.) African-American short-story writer whose realistic, character-driven fiction examines racial tension, the mysteries of love, and the pain of isolation.

McPherson's short story "Gold Coast" which won a contest in the *Atlantic Monthly* in 1968, and he became a contributing editor of the magazine in 1969.

In 1968 McPherson published his first volume of short fiction, *Hue and Cry*. His next collection, *Elbow Room* (1977), won a Pulitzer Prize in 1978. The stories in this book—among them "Elbow Room," "A Loaf of Bread," and "Widows and Orphans"—balance bitterness with hope.

Melville, Herman, *surname originally spelled* Melvill (b. Aug. 1, 1819, New York, N.Y., U.S.—d. Sept. 28, 1891, New York City) American author best known for his novels of the sea, including his masterpiece, MOBY-DICK (1851).

Herman Melville

A bout of scarlet fever in 1826 left Melville with permanently weakened eyesight. He attended Albany (N.Y.) Classical School in 1835. In 1839 he shipped out as cabin boy on the *St. Lawrence*, a merchant ship bound for Liverpool. In 1841, after a grinding search for work and a brief teaching job, he sailed on the whaler *Acushnet* to the South Seas. In June 1842 the *Acushnet* anchored in the Marquesas Islands, in present-day French Polynesia. Melville's adventures here, somewhat romanticized, became the subject of his first novel, TYPEE (1846). The voyage was unproductive, and Melville joined an uprising that landed the mutineers in a Tahitian jail, from which he escaped without difficulty. His carefree roving through the islands after his escape confirmed his bitterness against colonial and, especially, missionary debasement of the native Polynesian peoples. Melville based his second book, OMOO (1847), on these events.

In 1847 Melville began MARDI (1849) and became a regular contributor of reviews and other pieces to a literary journal. *Typee* and *Omoo* had provoked immediate enthusiasm and outrage, but when *Mardi* appeared, the public and critics alike found its wild, allegorical fantasy and medley of styles incomprehensible. Concealing his disappointment, Melville quickly wrote REDBURN (1849) and WHITE-JACKET (1850) in the manner expected of him. In 1850 he bought a farm, "Arrowhead," near Nathaniel Hawthorne's home at Pittsfield, Mass. Their relationship at first was close and reanimated Melville's creative energies. On his side, it was dependent, almost mystically intense, but to the cooler, withdrawn Hawthorne, such depth of feeling so persistently and openly declared was uncongenial. The two men gradually drew apart.

Moby-Dick was published in London in October 1851 and a month later in America. It brought its author neither acclaim nor reward. Increasingly a recluse, Melville embarked almost at once on PIERRE (1852). When published, however, it was another critical and financial disaster. ISRAEL POTTER was published in 1855 and enjoyed a modest success. Meanwhile, Melville had published important stories in *Putnam's Monthly Magazine*—BARTLEBY THE SCRIVENER (1853), THE ENCANTADAS (1854), and BENITO CERENO (1855)—reflecting the despair and the contempt for human hypocrisy and materialism that increasingly possessed him. Similar in theme was THE CONFIDENCE-MAN (1857), the last of his novels to be published in his lifetime.

The Civil War furnished the subject of his first volume of verse, *Battle-Pieces and Aspects of the War* (1866), published privately. Four months after it appeared, an appointment as a customs inspector on the New York docks finally brought him a secure income. His second collection of verse, *John Marr, and Other Sailors; With Some Sea-Pieces*, appeared in 1888, again privately published. By then he had been in retirement for three years, assisted by legacies from friends and relatives. *Timoleon* (1891) was his final verse collection. More significant was the return to prose that culminated in his last work, the novel BILLY BUDD, FORETOPMAN, which remained unpublished until 1924. Although by the end of the 1840s he had been among the most celebrated of American writers, his death evoked but a single obituary notice. Only after years of neglect did modern criticism finally secure his reputation with that of the great American writers.

Mencken, H.L., *in full* Henry Louis (b. Sept. 12, 1880, Baltimore, Md., U.S.—d. Jan. 29, 1956, Baltimore) Controversialist, humorous journalist, and pungent critic of American life.

H.L. Mencken

Mencken became a reporter for the *Baltimore Morning Herald* and later joined the staff of the Baltimore *Sun*, for which he worked throughout most of his life. From 1914 to 1923 he coedited (with George Jean Nathan) *The Smart Set*, then the magazine most influential in the growth of American literature. In 1924 he helped found (with Nathan) the AMERICAN MERCURY, and he edited it until 1933.

Mencken was probably the most influential American literary critic in the 1920s, and he often used literary criticism as a point of departure to jab at American weaknesses. His reviews and miscellaneous essays filled six volumes, aptly titled *Prejudices* (1919–27). He fought against writers whom he regarded as fraudulently successful and worked for the recognition of such outstanding newcomers as Theodore Dreiser and Sinclair Lewis. He jeered at American sham, pretension, provincialism, and prudery, and he ridiculed organized religion, business, and the middle class (which he called the "booboisie").

In 1919 Mencken published *The American Language*, an attempt to bring together examples of American expressions and idioms. The book grew with each reissue through the years, and in 1945 and 1948 Mencken published substantial supplements. By the time of his death, he was perhaps the leading authority on the language of his country.

Mencken's autobiographical trilogy, *Happy Days* (1940), *Newspaper Days* (1941), and *Heathen Days* (1943), is devoted to his experiences in journalism. A further volume, *My Life as Author and Editor*, was published in 1993.

Merrill, James (Ingram) (b. March 3, 1926, New York, N.Y., U.S.—d. Feb. 6, 1995, Tucson, Ariz.) American poet known for the fine craftsmanship and wit of his lyric and epic poems.

Merrill attended Amherst College. His first book, *Jim's Book: A Collection of Poems and Short Stories* (1942), and the early books that followed revealed his mastery of poetic form and technique, though they have been called restrained, rigid, and artificial. With the publication of *Water Street* (1962), critics noted a growing ease and the development of a personal vision in his writing. The interactions between art and life and between memory and experience became the major motifs of the transitional stage in his writing.

It was not until the publication of the epic poetry in *Divine Comedies* (1976), *Mirabell: Books of Number* (1978), and *Scripts for the Pageant* (1980)—a trilogy later published in *The Changing Light at Sandover* (1982)—that Merrill achieved a measure of wider public appreciation. He used a Ouija board in composing some of the poetry in the trilogy, which is a serious yet witty summation of his lifelong concerns. A selection of his poetry, *From the First Nine: Poems 1946–1976*, was published in 1982 and *Selected Poems, 1946–1985* in 1992. Merrill also wrote a memoir entitled *A Different Person* (1994). His last volume of poetry, *A Scattering of Salts* (1995), was posthumously published.

Merton, Thomas, *original name of* Father M. Louis (b. Jan. 31, 1915, Prades, Fr.—d. Dec. 10, 1968, Bangkok, Thai.) Roman Catholic monk known for his prolific writings on spiritual and social themes.

Merton was educated at Cambridge University and Columbia University. After teaching English at Columbia and at St. Bonaventure University near Olean, N.Y., he entered the Cistercian Abbey of Gethsemani (near Louisville, Ky.), housing a contemplative Trappist order. He was ordained a priest in 1949.

Merton's first published works were collections of poems—*Thirty Poems* (1944), *A Man in the Divided Sea* (1946), and *Figures for an Apocalypse* (1948). With the publication of the autobiographical *Seven Storey Mountain* (1948), he gained an international reputation. His early works were strictly spiritual, but in the early 1960s his writings tended toward social criticism, while many of his later works reveal an insight into Oriental philosophy and mysticism unusual in a Westerner. His only novel, *My Argument with the Gestapo*, written in 1941, was published posthumously in 1969. Merton's other writings include *The Waters of Siloe* (1949), a history of the Trappists; *Seeds of Contemplation* (1949); *The Living Bread* (1956), a meditation on the Eucharist; *Contemplation in a World of Action* (1971), an insightful book of essays; and *The Asian Journal of Thomas Merton* (1973).

Merwin, W.S., *in full* William Stanley (b. Sept. 30, 1927, New York, N.Y., U.S.) American poet and translator known for the spare style of his poetry in which he expressed his concerns about the alienation of humans from their environment.

After graduating from Princeton University, Merwin worked as a tutor in Europe and freelance translator. Later he was playwright-in-residence at the

Poet's Theatre, Cambridge, Mass., from 1956 to 1957 and poetry editor of *The Nation* (1962).

Critical acclaim for Merwin began with his first collection of poetry, *A Mask for Janus* (1952). His early poems include both lyrical works and philosophical narratives based on myth and folk tales. Subsequent collections include *Green with Beasts* (1956), *The Drunk in the Furnace* (1960), and *The Moving Target* (1963). The poems of *The Lice* (1967) reflect the poet's despair over human mistreatment of the rest of creation. Merwin won a Pulitzer Prize for *The Carrier of Ladders* (1970). Among his later poetic works are *The Compass Flower* (1977), *Finding the Islands* (1982), *The Rain in the Trees* (1988), *Travels* (1993), and *The Vixen* (1995). Merwin's translations, often done in collaboration with others, range from plays of Euripides and Federico García Lorca to the epics *The Poem of the Cid* and *The Song of Roland* to ancient and modern works from Chinese, Sanskrit, and Japanese.

Michener, James Albert (b. Feb. 3, 1907?) American novelist and short-story writer best known for his novels, epic and detailed works classified as fictional documentaries.

Michener served as a naval historian in the South Pacific from 1944 to 1946, and his early fiction is based on this area. He won a Pulitzer Prize in 1948 for the collection *Tales of the South Pacific* (1947), and his *Hawaii* (1959) was a popular success.

Michener's novels were typically detailed and massive in scope, and he researched them extensively, as he did in Spain for *Iberia: Spanish Travels and Reflections* (1968). In his later years, Michener turned his interest to American landscapes in such books as *Centennial* (1974), *Chesapeake* (1978), and *Alaska* (1988). *Space* (1982), a fictional chronicle of the U.S. space program, was another massive opus. His later works include the novels *Poland* (1983) and *Mexico* (1992) and a memoir entitled *The World Is My Home* (1992).

Millay, Edna St. Vincent (b. Feb. 22, 1892, Rockland, Maine, U.S.—d. Oct. 19, 1950, Austerlitz, N.Y.) American poet and dramatist who came to personify romantic rebellion and bravado in the 1920s.

Millay's earliest poems were published in the children's magazine *St. Nicholas*. She grew up in Camden, Maine, and her work is filled with the imagery of coast and countryside. Her first acclaim came when RENASCENCE was included in *The Lyric Year* in 1912; the poem brought Millay to the attention of a benefactor who made it possible for her to attend Vassar. For a time she supported herself in New York City by writing short stories under a pseudonym and as an actress and playwright. In 1923 she married, and she lived thereafter on a farm in the Berkshires.

Edna St. Vincent Millay

Her first book, *Renascence and Other Poems* (1917), was full of the romantic and independent temper of youth. The line "My candle burns at both ends," from a poem in *A Few Figs from Thistles* (1920), was taken up as the watchword of the "flaming youth" of the era and brought her a renown she came to despise. In 1921 she published *Second April* as well as three verse plays: *Two Slatterns and a King*, *The Lamp and the Bell*, and *Aria da Capo*. The title poem of *The Harp Weaver and Other Poems* (1923) is thought to have been inspired by her mother. She also wrote the libretto for Deems Taylor's opera *The King's Henchman*, first presented at the Metropolitan in 1927. Her major later works include *The Buck in the Snow* (1928), *Fatal Interview* (1931), and *Wine from These Grapes* (1934). Her letters, edited by A.R. Macdougall, were published in 1952.

Arthur Miller

Miller, Arthur (b. Oct. 17, 1915, New York, N.Y., U.S.) American playwright who combined social awareness with a searching concern for his characters' inner lives. He is best known for DEATH OF A SALESMAN (1949).

Miller's first public success was with *Focus* (1945), a novel about anti-Semitism. ALL MY SONS (1947), a drama about a manufacturer of faulty war materials, was his first important play. *Death of a Salesman*, his next major play, is the tragedy of a small man destroyed by false values that are in large part the values of his society.

THE CRUCIBLE (1953) was based on the witchcraft trials in Salem, Mass., in 1692, a period Miller considered relevant to the 1950s, when investigation of subversive activities was widespread. *A Memory of Two Mondays* and another short play, *A View from the Bridge* were staged on the same bill in 1955. AFTER THE FALL (1964) is concerned with failure in human relationships and its consequences. *The Price* (1968) continued Miller's exploration of the theme of guilt and responsibility by examining the strained relationship between two brothers. *The Archbishop's Ceiling*, produced in 1977, dealt with the Soviet treatment of dissident writers. *The American Clock*, a series of dramatic vignettes about the Great Depression, was produced in 1980. Miller produced several one-act plays in the 1980s, including two—*I Can't Remember Anything* and *Clara*—that were published together as *Danger, Memory! Two Plays* (1986). Later full-length plays include *The Ride Down Mount Morgan* and *The Last Yankee* (both 1991).

Miller, Henry (Valentine) (b. Dec. 26, 1891, New York, N.Y., U.S.—d. June 7, 1980, Pacific Palisades, Calif.) American writer and perennial bohemian whose autobiographical novels had a liberating influence on mid-20th-century literature. Because of their sexual frankness, his major works were banned as obscene in Britain and the United States until the 1960s, but they were widely known earlier from copies smuggled in from France.

Miller was brought up in Brooklyn, and he wrote about his childhood experiences there in *Black Spring* (1936). In 1930 he went to France. TROPIC OF CANCER (French edition, 1934; U.S. edition, 1961) is based on his hand-to-mouth existence in depression-ridden Paris. *Tropic of Capricorn* (France, 1939; U.S., 1961) draws on his earlier New York phase. In 1964 the U.S. Supreme Court rejected earlier state court findings that the "Tropics" books were obscene.

Miller's visit to Greece in 1939 inspired *The Colossus of Maroussi* (1941). THE AIR-CONDITIONED NIGHTMARE (1945) is a sharply critical account of a tour of the United States. After settling in Big Sur on the California coast, Miller produced his Rosy Crucifixion trilogy, made up of *Sexus*, *Plexus*, and *Nexus* (U.S. edition published as a whole in 1965). It traces the stages by which the hero-narrator becomes a writer.

Henry Miller

Other important books by Miller are the collections of essays *The Cosmological Eye* (1939) and *The Wisdom of the Heart* (1941). Various volumes of his correspondence have been published: with Lawrence Durrell (1963), to Anaïs Nin (1965), and with Wallace Fowlie (1975).

Miller, J. Hillis, *in full* Joseph (b. March 5, 1928, Newport News, Va., U.S.) American literary critic who was associated with the Geneva group of critics and, later, with deconstruction.

Miller graduated from Oberlin College in 1948. He received an M.A. and Ph.D. from Harvard University in 1949 and 1952, respectively. After teaching English at Williams College for one year, he held positions at Johns Hopkins University from 1953 to 1972, at Yale University from 1972 to 1986, and from 1986 at the University of California at Irvine.

Like the Geneva group of critics, Miller argued that literature is a tool for understanding the mind of the writer. His criticism emphasized theological concerns, as in *Poets of Reality: Six Twentieth-Century Writers* (1965), *The Form of Victorian Fiction: Thackeray, Dickens, Trollope, George Eliot, Meredith, and Hardy* (1968), and *The Disappearance of God: Five Nineteenth-Century Writers* (1963). By 1970, however, he had joined the deconstructionist critics at Yale, and his subsequent scholarship was steeped in arcane language and expressed the belief that language itself is a work's sole reality. Miller's criticism in this vein includes *Fiction and Repetition* (1982) and *The Linguistic Moment* (1985).

Miller, Joaquin, *pseudonym of* Cincinnatus Hiner Miller, Hiner *also spelled* Heine (b. Sept. 8, 1837, near Liberty, Ind., U.S.—d. Feb. 17, 1913, Oakland, Calif.) American poet and journalist whose best work conveys a sense of the majesty and excitement of the Old West. His best-known poem is "Columbus," with its refrain, "On, sail on!" once familiar to millions of American schoolchildren.

Miller led a picaresque early life in California among miners and gamblers. In Oregon he owned a newspaper (the *Eugene Democratic Register*) and was a county judge. His first books of poems, *Specimens* (1868) and *Joaquin et al.* (1869), attracted little attention.

In 1870 he traveled to England, where *Pacific Poems* (1871) was privately printed. *Songs of the Sierras* (1871), upon which his reputation mainly rests, was loudly acclaimed in England, while generally derided in the United States for its excessive romanticism. His other books of poetry include *Songs of the Sunlands* (1873), *The Ship in the Desert* (1875), *The Baroness of New York* (1877), *Memorie and Rime* (1884), and the *Complete Poetical Works* (1897).

Miller, May, *married surname* Sullivan (b. Jan. 26, 1899, Washington, D.C., U.S.) African-American playwright and poet associated with the Harlem Renaissance in New York City during the 1920s.

Miller graduated from Howard University in 1920, earning an award for her one-act play *Within the Shadows*. Afterwards she taught secondary school and continued to write. A prizewinning play, *The Bog Guide* (1925), helped establish Miller in the black cultural scene, and she became the most widely published woman playwright of the Harlem Renaissance. She openly addressed racial issues in plays such as *Scratches* (1929), *Stragglers in the Dust* (1930), and *Nails and Thorns* (1933). She also wrote many historical plays, four of which (including *Harriet Tubman* and *Sojourner Truth*) were anthologized in *Negro History in Thirteen Plays* (1935). Miller retired from teaching in 1943 and became a prolific poet, publishing seven volumes that included *Into the Clearing* (1959) and *Dust of Uncertain Journey* (1975).

Mitchell, Donald Grant, *pseudonym* Ik Marvel (b. April 12, 1822, Norwich, Conn., U.S.—d. Dec. 15, 1908) American farmer and writer known for nostalgic, sentimental books on American life, especially *Reveries of a Bachelor* (1850).

Mitchell graduated from Yale in 1841 and then returned home to farm his ancestral land. In 1844 he was appointed clerk to the U.S. consul at Liverpool, but poor health forced him to resign. Once back in America in 1846, he wrote newspaper articles for the *Morning Courier* and *New York Enquirer* under the pseudonym Ik Marvel, also editing *Lorgnette* (1850), a satirical magazine. His earliest books, *Fresh Gleanings* (1847) and *The Battle Summer* (1850), record incidents of his travels in Europe and the French revolution of 1848. With the publication of *Reveries of a Bachelor* he gained immediate fame, and in 1851 another volume, *Dream Life*, was published. His style is quiet, simple, and archaic, and he has been compared to Jerome K. Jerome, the English author of sentimental works.

In 1853 Mitchell married, and in 1855, with his wife, he bought Edgewood, an estate near New Haven, Conn., intending to farm full-time. He always considered his agricultural projects more important than his writing, and he tried to build a model farm. He wrote several more volumes of essays, mostly on farming life.

Mitchell, Margaret (b. 1900, Atlanta, Ga., U.S.—d. Aug. 16, 1949, Atlanta) American author of the enormously popular novel GONE WITH THE WIND (1936).

Mitchell wrote for *The Atlanta Journal*. After leaving the newspaper she spent 10 years writing her one book, *Gone with the Wind*, a novel about the American Civil War and Reconstruction as seen from the Southern point of view.

Gone with the Wind was almost certainly the largest selling novel in the history of U.S. publishing to that time. In the first six months after publication 1,000,000 copies were sold, 50,000 of them in one day. Before the author's death sales had totaled 8,000,000 in 40 countries.

Mitchell, S. Weir, *in full* Silas (b. Feb. 15, 1829, Philadelphia, Pa., U.S.— d. Jan. 4, 1914, Philadelphia) American physician and author who excelled in novels of psychology and historical romance.

Mitchell served as an army surgeon during the American Civil War, and his experiences were the basis for "The Case of George Dedlow" (1866), a story about an amputee notable for its psychological insights and realistic war scenes. *Wear and Tear* (1871) and *Fat and Blood* (1877), both medical popularizations, were best-sellers. Mitchell also published short stories, poems, and children's stories anonymously. Of later novels perhaps his most notable are *Roland Blake* (1886), *Hugh Wynne* (1898), *Circumstance* (1901), *Constance Trescott* (1905), and *The Red City* (1908). Mitchell's poetry, which lacks the psychological insight and contemporaneity of his novels, appears in several collections, including the volumes *The Hill of Stones* (1882) and *The Wager* (1900).

Mitchell, W.O., *in full* William Ormond (b. March 13, 1914, Weyburn, Sask., Can.) Writer of stories that deal humorously with the hardships of western Canadian prairie life.

Mitchell received favorable notice for his first novel, *Who Has Seen the Wind* (1947), a sensitive picture of a grim prairie town as seen from the point of view of a small boy. From 1950 to 1958, he wrote weekly scripts for the radio series "Jake and the Kid," which had originated as short stories. Thirteen of these scripts were published as *Jake and the Kid* (1961). His novel *The Kite* (1962) is about a newsman's interview with the oldest and wisest man in western Canada. Another novel, *The Vanishing Point* (1973), deals with a teacher's involvement with Indians in southwestern Alberta. His later novels include *How I Spent My Summer Holidays* (1981), *Ladybug, Ladybug* (1988), and *Roses Are Difficult Here* (1990).

Momaday, N. Scott, *in full* Navarre (b. Feb. 27, 1934, Lawton, Okla., U.S.) Native-American author of many works centered on his Kiowa Indian heritage.

Momaday grew up on an Oklahoma farm and on Southwestern reservations. He attended the University of New Mexico and Stanford University. His first novel, *House Made of Dawn* (1968), is his best-known work. It narrates, from several different points of view, the dilemma of a young man returning home to his Kiowa pueblo after a stint in the U.S. Army. The book won the 1969 Pulitzer Prize for fiction.

Momaday's limited-edition collection of Kiowa Indian folktales entitled *The Journey of Tai-me* (1967) was enlarged as *The Way to Rainy Mountain* (1969), illustrated by his father, Alfred Momaday. His poetry is collected in *Angle of Geese and Other Poems* (1974) and *The Gourd Dancer* (1976). *The Names: A Memoir* (1976) tells of his early life and of his respect for his Kiowa ancestors. In 1989 he published his second novel, *The Ancient Child. In the Presence of the Sun: Stories and Poems, 1961–1991* appeared in 1992.

Monroe, Harriet (b. Dec. 23, 1860, Chicago, Ill., U.S.—d. Sept. 26, 1936, Arequipa, Peru) American founder and longtime editor of POETRY magazine, which, in the first decade of its existence, became the principal organ for modern poetry of the English-speaking world.

Monroe worked on various Chicago newspapers as an art and drama critic while privately writing verse and verse plays. Her poem "Cantata" celebrates Chicago history, and her heroic "Columbian Ode" (1892) was recited at the dedication of Chicago's World's Columbian Exposition. In founding *Poetry* she secured the backing of wealthy Chicago patrons and invited contributions from a wide range of contemporary poets. Monroe served as the magazine's editor, and her open-minded, inclusive editorial policy and her awareness of the importance of the poetic revolution of the early years of the century made her a major influence in the development of modern poetry. Her autobiography, *A Poet's Life: Seventy Years in a Changing World*, was published posthumously in 1938.

Montgomery, L.M., *in full* Lucy Maud (b. Nov. 30, 1874, Clifton [now New London], P.E.I., Can.—d. April 24, 1942, Toronto, Ont.) Canadian regional novelist, known for *Anne of Green Gables* (1908), a sentimentalized story of a spirited, unconventional orphan girl who finds a home with an elderly brother and sister.

Montgomery was reared by her maternal grandparents. She taught school for several years and was briefly a journalist. While caring for her grandmother, she wrote *Anne of Green Gables*, which drew on her girlhood experiences and on the rural life and traditions of Prince Edward Island. The book brought her an international following. Six sequels, taking Anne from girlhood to motherhood, were less successful. Montgomery also produced another series of juvenile books, several collections of stories, and two books for adults.

Moore, Brian (b. Aug. 25, 1921, Belfast, N.Ire.) Irish novelist who immigrated to Canada and is best known for his first novel, THE LONELY PASSION OF JUDITH HEARNE (1955).

Moore arrived in Canada in 1948 and wrote for the *Montreal Gazette* from 1952. The novel *Judith Hearne* deals with an aging spinster whose crumbling pretensions to gentility are gradually dissolved in alcoholism. *The Feast of Lupercal* (1957) concerns a bachelor schoolteacher, THE LUCK OF GINGER COFFEY (1960) portrays a middle-aged Irish failure who immigrates to Canada to charm his way to fortune, and *The Emperor of Ice Cream* (1965) deals with a boy who is shocked into manhood by the bombing of Belfast in World War II. Among the more impressive of his later novels are *The Doctor's Wife* (1976), *The Color of Blood* (1987), and *Lies of Silence* (1990).

Moore, Clement Clarke (b. July 15, 1779, New York, N.Y., U.S.—d. July 10, 1863, Newport, R.I.) American scholar, now chiefly remembered for the ballad that begins " 'Twas the night before Christmas."

Moore, who was professor of Oriental and Greek literature at the General Theological Seminary, is said to have composed A VISIT FROM ST. NICHOLAS to amuse his children on Christmas 1822, but, unknown to him, a houseguest copied it and gave it to the press. It was first published anonymously in the *Troy* (N.Y.) *Sentinel*, Dec. 23, 1823.

Moore, Marianne, *in full* Marianne Craig Moore (b. Nov. 15, 1887, St. Louis, Mo., U.S.—d. Feb. 5, 1972, New York, N.Y.) American poet whose work distilled moral and intellectual insights from the close and accurate observation of objective detail. Extremely disciplined in her craft, Moore won the admiration of fellow poets throughout her long career.

Moore graduated in 1909 from Bryn Mawr College (in Pennsylvania). After 1919, living in Brooklyn, N.Y., she devoted herself to writing, contributing poetry and criticism to many journals in the United States and England.

In 1921 her first book, *Poems*, was published in London. Her first

Marianne Moore

American volume was titled *Observations* (1924). These initial collections exhibited Moore's conciseness and her creation of a mosaic of juxtaposed images leading unerringly to a conclusion that, at its best, is both surprising and inevitable. They contain some of her best-known poems, including "To a Steam Roller," "The Fish," "When I Buy Pictures," "Peter," "The Labors of Hercules," and POETRY. The last named is the source of her often-quoted admonition that poets should present imaginary gardens with real toads in them.

In 1925—already well known as one of the leading new poets—she became acting editor of *The Dial*, an influential American journal of literature and arts, and she served in the position until the journal was discontinued in 1929. Her *Collected Poems* appeared in 1951. She also published a translation of *The Fables of La Fontaine* (1954); a volume of critical papers, *Predilections* (1955); and *Idiosyncrasy and Technique: Two Lectures* (1958).

More, Paul Elmer (b. Dec. 12, 1864, St. Louis, Mo., U.S.—d. March 9, 1937, Princeton, N.J.) American scholar and conservative critic, one of the leading exponents of the New Humanism in literary criticism.

More was educated at Washington University, St. Louis, Mo., and at Harvard, where he met Irving Babbitt. He taught at Bryn Mawr College, Bryn Mawr, Pa., and was also a literary editor. Like Babbitt, his associate and fellow leader of the New Humanists, More was an uncompromising advocate of traditional critical standards and classical restraint.

More's best-known work is his *Shelburne Essays*, 11 vol. (1904–21), a collection of articles and reviews. Also notable are *Platonism* (1917), *The Religion of Plato* (1921), *Hellenistic Philosophies* (1923), *New Shelburne Essays* (1928–36), and his autobiography, *Pages from an Oxford Diary* (1937). His monumental *Greek Tradition*, 5 vol. (1924–31), is generally thought to be his finest work.

Morison, Samuel Eliot (b. July 9, 1887, Boston, Mass., U.S.—d. May 15, 1976, Boston) American biographer and historian who re-created in vivid prose notable maritime stories of modern history.

Morison was educated at Harvard University and, after further study abroad, returned to teach at Harvard for 40 years. To give authenticity to his writing, Morison undertook numerous voyages himself, sailed the ocean routes followed by Christopher Columbus, and during wartime served on 12 ships as a commissioned officer in the U.S. Naval Reserve.

Morison's writings include *Maritime History of Massachusetts* (1921); *Admiral of the Ocean Sea* (1942), a biography of Columbus for which he was awarded a Pulitzer Prize; *John Paul Jones* (1959), which also received a Pulitzer; the 15-volume *History of U.S. Naval Operations in World War II*

(1947–62); *The European Discovery of America: The Northern Voyages A.D. 500–1600* (1971); and *The European Discovery of America: The Southern Voyages A.D. 1492–1616* (1974).

Morley, Christopher (Darlington) (b. May 5, 1890, Haverford, Pa., U.S.— d. March 28, 1957, Roslyn Heights, Long Island, N.Y.) American writer whose versatile works are lighthearted, vigorous displays of the English language.

Morley gained popularity with his literary columns in the *New York Evening Post* and the *Saturday Review of Literature* and from collections of essays and columns such as *Shandygaff* (1918). His novels include the innovative *The Trojan Horse* (1937), a combination of prose, verse, and dramatic dialogue that satirizes human devotion to luxury, and the sentimental best-seller *Kitty Foyle* (1939). *The Old Mandarin* (1947) is a collection of witty free verse. Morley also edited Bartlett's *Familiar Quotations* (1937; 1948).

Morrison, Toni, *original name* Chloe Anthony Wofford (b. Feb. 18, 1931, Lorain, Ohio, U.S.) African-American writer and editor noted for her examination of the black experience, particularly the experience of women within the black community. She received the Nobel Prize for Literature in 1993.

Morrison grew up in the Midwest. She attended Howard University in Washington, D.C., and Cornell University in Ithaca, New York. After teaching at Texas Southern University for two years, she taught at Howard for several years. In 1965 she became an editor for a publishing house, also continuing to teach at two branches of the State University of New York.

Her first book, THE BLUEST EYE (1970), is a novel of initiation. In 1973 a second novel, SULA, was published; it examines (among other issues) the dynamics of friendship and the expectations for conformity within the black community. Morrison used a male narrator for the first time in *Song of Solomon* (1977); its publication brought Morrison to national attention. In 1981 *Tar Baby* was published, and the Pulitzer Prize-winning BELOVED appeared in 1987. Another novel, *Jazz*, and a work of criticism, *Playing in the Dark: Whiteness and the Literary Imagination*, were published in 1992. Morrison's use of fantasy and myth, mastery of ambiguity, and sinuous poetic style gave her works great strength and texture.

HELEN MARCUS

Toni Morrison

Morris, Wright (Marion) (b. Jan. 6, 1910, Central City, Neb., U.S.) American novelist who portrayed the frustration of contemporary life and sought to recapture the American past.

Morris' journeys to see America during the 1920s and '30s led to his first novel, *My Uncle Dudley* (1942), in which a group of people travel across country by car. Morris' other novels include *The Field of Vision* (1956) and *Ceremony in Lone Tree* (1960), books that describe the failed lives of a number of people from a small Midwestern town; the paired novels, *Fire Sermon* (1971) and *A Life* (1973); *The Fork River Space Project* (1977); and *Plains Song, for Female Voices* (1980). Morris also wrote books of nonfiction, including the essay collections *About Fiction* (1975) and *Earthly Delights, Unearthly Adornments* (1978), and several memoirs.

Mosley, Walter (b. 1952, Los Angeles, Calif., U.S.) African-American author of mystery stories noted for their realistic portrayals of segregated inner-city life.

Mosley attended Goddard College and Johnson State College, and he became a computer programmer before publishing his first novel, *Devil in a Blue Dress* (1990). Set in 1948, the novel introduces Ezekiel "Easy" Rawlins, an unwilling amateur detective from the Watts section of Los Angeles. Other novels featuring Rawlins include *A Red Death* (1991), *White Butterfly* (1992), and *Black Betty* (1994). In all of his novels Mosley used period detail and slang to create authentic settings and characters, especially the earnest, complex Rawlins, who continually is faced with personal, social, and moral dilemmas.

Moss, Howard (b. Jan. 22, 1922, New York, N.Y., U.S.—d. Sept. 16, 1987, New York City) American poet and editor who was the poetry editor of *The New Yorker* magazine for almost 40 years.

Moss graduated from the University of Wisconsin in 1943 and published the first of 12 volumes of his poetry, *The Wound and the Weather*, in 1946. He joined the staff of *The New Yorker* in 1948, and throughout his tenure there he showcased the works and helped establish the careers of such poets as Sylvia Plath, Richard Wilbur, and Elizabeth Bishop. He won the National Book Award for his *Selected Poems* (1971). Moss also published volumes of criticism and was an accomplished playwright. His plays include *The Folding Green* (1958), *The Oedipus Mah-Jongg Scandal* (1968), and *The Palace at 4 A.M.* (1972).

Mukherjee, Bharati (b. July 27, 1940, Calcutta, India) Indian-born American novelist and short-story writer whose work reflects Indian culture and immigrant experience.

Mukherjee attended the University of Calcutta, the University of Baroda, and the University of Iowa Writers' Workshop. From 1966 to 1980 she lived in Montreal, then moved to the United States and began teaching at the university level.

Mukherjee's work featured not only cultural clashes but undercurrents of violence. Her first novel, *The Tiger's Daughter* (1972), tells of a sheltered Indian woman jolted by immersion in American culture, then again shocked by her return to a violent Calcutta. *Wife* (1975) details the descent into madness of an Indian woman trapped in New York City by the fears and passivity resulting from her upbringing. Mukherjee's first book of short stories, *Darkness* (1985), includes many of the stories, including the acclaimed "The World According to Hsü." *The Middleman and Other Stories* (1988) feature third-world immigrants to America, also the subject of two later novels, *Jasmine* (1989) and *The Holder of the World* (1993).

Munro Alice, *original name* Alice Anne Laidlaw (b. July 10, 1931, Wingham, Ont., Can.) Canadian short-story writer who gained international recognition with her exquisitely drawn stories, usually set in rural Ontario and peopled by characters of Scotch-Irish stock.

Munro attended the University of Western Ontario. Her first collection of stories was published as *Dance of the Happy Shades* (1968). It is one of three collections—the other two being *Who Do You Think You Are?* (1978) and *The Progress of Love* (1986)—awarded the annual Governor General's Literary Award for fiction. Her second collection—*The Lives of Girls and Women* (1971), a group of coming-of-age stories—was followed by *Something I've Been Meaning to Tell You* (1974), *The Beggar Maid: Stories of Flo and Rose* (1978), *The Moons of Jupiter* (1982), *Friend of My Youth* (1986), *Open Secrets* (1994), and *A Wilderness Station* (1994).

Murray, Albert L. (b. May 12, 1916, Nokomis, Ala., U.S.) African-American essayist and critic whose writings assert the vitality and the powerful influence of black people in forming American traditions.

Murray attended Tuskegee Institute and New York University; he also taught at Tuskegee. In 1943 he entered the U.S. air force, from which he retired as a major in 1962. His collection of essays, *The Omni-Americans* (1970), used historical fact, literature, and music to attack false perceptions of black American life. *South to a Very Old Place* (1971) recorded his visit to scenes of his segregated boyhood during the 1920s. In *Stomping the Blues* (1976), he maintained that blues and jazz musical styles developed as affirmative responses to misery. He also co-wrote Count Basie's autobiography *Good Morning Blues* (1985) and wrote the novels *Train Whistle Guitar* (1974), *The Spyglass Tree* (1991), and *Seven League Boots* (1995). A collection of essays, *Blue Devils of Nada*, was also published in 1995.

Nabokov, Vladimir (Vladimirovich) (b. April 22, 1899, St. Petersburg, Russia—d. July 2, 1977, Montreux, Switz.) Russian-born American novelist and critic. He wrote in both Russian and English, and his best works, including LOLITA (1955), feature intricate, stylish literary effects.

Nabokov began his career as a poet, publishing two collections of verse before leaving Russia in 1919. He graduated from Trinity College, Cambridge, in 1922, and from then until 1940 he lived in Germany and France. By 1925 he had settled upon prose as his main genre. His first novel, *Mashenka (Mary)*, appeared in 1926; avowedly autobiographical, it contains descriptions of the young Nabokov's first serious romance as well as of the Nabokov family estate, both of which are also described in his autobiography, SPEAK, MEMORY (1951). Nabokov did not again draw so heavily upon personal experience until he wrote PNIN (1957), an episodic novel about an émigré professor in the United States that is partly based on his experiences while teaching at Cornell University, Ithaca, N.Y.

His second novel, *Korol, dama, valet* (1928); KING, QUEEN, KNAVE), marked a turn to the highly stylized form that characterized his art thereafter. The subject matter of Nabokov's novels is principally the problem of art itself presented in various figurative disguises. Thus, *Zashchita Luzhina* (1930); *The Defense*) seemingly is about chess, *Otchayaniye* (1936); *Despair*) about murder, and *Priglasheniye na kazn* (1938); INVITATION TO A BEHEADING) a political story, but all three works make statements about art that are central to understanding the book as a whole. Beginning with *Dar* (published serially 1937–38; THE GIFT), parody became another common feature of his novels.

His first novels in English, THE REAL LIFE OF SEBASTIAN KNIGHT (1941) and BEND SINISTER (1947), do not rank with his best Russian work, but PALE FIRE (1962) extends and completes Nabokov's mastery of unorthodox structure, first shown in *The Gift*. *Lolita* (1955) is another of Nabokov's subtle allegories, and ADA (1969) parodies the family chronicle.

Nabokov's major critical works are an irreverent book about Nikolay Gogol (1944) and a monumental four-volume translation of, and commentary on, Aleksandr Pushkin's *Eugene Onegin* (1964). He also produced a number of short stories and novellas, mostly written in Russian and translated into English.

Nasby, Petroleum V., *in full* Vesuvius, *pseudonym of* David Ross Locke (b. Sept. 20, 1833, Binghamton, N.Y., U.S.—d. Feb. 15, 1888, Toledo, Ohio) American humorist who had considerable influence on public issues during and after the American Civil War.

From an early age Locke worked for newspapers in New York and Ohio. In 1861, as editor of the *Findlay* (Ohio) *Jeffersonian*, he published the first of many satirical letters purporting to be written by one Petroleum V. Nasby. For more than 20 years Locke contributed "Nasby Letters" to the *Toledo Blade*, which under his editorship gained national circulation. Many of the letters appeared also in book form, including *The Nasby Papers* (1864) and *The Diary of an Office Seeker* (1881).

An ardent Unionist and foe of slavery, Locke vigorously supported the Northern cause. His chief weapon was a heavy irony, with his character Nasby, a coarse and vicious Copperhead, arguing illiterately the Southern position.

Nash, Ogden, *in full* Frederic Ogden Nash (b. Aug. 19, 1902, Rye, N.Y., U.S.—d. May 19, 1971, Baltimore, Md.) American writer of humorous poetry who won a large following for his audacious verse.

Nash sold his first verse (1930) to *The New Yorker*, on whose editorial staff he was employed for a time. With the publication of his first collection, *Hard Lines* (1931), Nash began a 40-year career during which he produced 20 volumes of verse with such titles as *The Bad Parents' Garden of Verse* (1936), *I'm a Stranger Here Myself* (1938), and *Everyone but Thee and Me* (1962). He wrote the lyrics for the musicals *One Touch of Venus* (1943) and *Two's Company* (1952), as well as several children's books.

His rhymes are jarringly off or disconcertingly exact, and his ragged stanzas vary from lines of one word to lines that meander the length of a paragraph, often interrupted by inapposite digressions. Nash said he learned his prosody from the unintentional blunders of poet Julia Moore, the "Sweet Singer of Michigan."

Nathan, George Jean (b. Feb. 14, 1882, Fort Wayne, Ind., U.S.—d. April 8, 1958, New York, N.Y.) American author, editor, and drama critic who is credited with raising the standards of producers and playgoers alike.

Beginning in 1906, Nathan was at various times drama critic for numerous magazines and newspapers, but his name is particularly associated with *The Smart Set*, of which he was coeditor (1914–23) with H.L. Mencken, and with the *American Mercury*, which, also with Mencken, he helped to found in 1924. As a critic Nathan championed the plays of Henrik Ibsen, August Strindberg, George Bernard Shaw, Eugene O'Neill, Sean O'Casey, and William Saroyan. He published the *Theatre Book of the Year* annually from 1943 through 1951, as well as more than 30 volumes of lively essays.

Naylor, Gloria (b. Jan. 25, 1950, New York, N.Y., U.S.) African-American novelist, known for her strong depictions of black women.

Naylor attended Brooklyn College of the City University of New York and Yale University. Her first novel, THE WOMEN OF BREWSTER PLACE (1982),

MARION ETTINGER

Gloria Naylor

won her instant recognition for its powerful dramatization of the struggles of seven women living in a blighted urban neighborhood. *Linden Hills* (1985) deals with the destructive materialism of upwardly mobile suburban blacks. *Mama Day* (1988) blends stories from William Shakespeare's *The Tempest* with black folklore, and *Bailey's Cafe* (1992) centers on a mythic Brooklyn diner that offers an oasis for the suffering.

Neihardt, John G., *in full* Gneisenau (b. Jan. 8, 1881, near Sharpsburg, Ill., U.S.—d. Nov. 3, 1973, Columbia, Mo.) American poet, novelist, and short-story writer whose works focus on the history of Native Americans, especially the Sioux.

Neihardt was a literary critic for various newspapers, worked for the Bureau of Indian Affairs, and taught at the University of Missouri, Columbia. Neihardt's early contact with both whites and Indians in Kansas and Nebraska led him to write such works as *The Lonesome Trail* (1907), a collection of short stories about pioneering heroes and the Omahas. The lyric sequence *A Bundle of Myrrh* (1908) established his reputation as a lyric poet. He also was instrumental in writing down the oral autobiography of Black Elk in BLACK ELK SPEAKS (1932).

Neihardt spent almost 30 years on his major work, *A Cycle of the West* (1949), which contains five book-length narrative poems. The work is a vital picture of the frontier and the people who battled for its control. The novel *When the Tree Flowered* (1951) was one of Neihardt's last works.

Nelligan, Émile (b. Dec. 24, 1879, Montreal, Can.—d. Nov. 18, 1941, Montreal) French-Canadian poet who was a major figure in the Montreal Literary School.

Nelligan attended the Collège Sainte-Marie in Montreal. His first poem, "Rêve fantasque" ("Whimsical Dream"), was published in the magazine *Le Samedi* ("Saturday") in 1896, and later that year he also published several poems in *Le Monde illustré* ("The Illustrated World"). Nelligan became a member of the Montreal Literary School (known as L'École Littéraire de Montréal), which attempted to modernize French-Canadian literature in both form and theme. The group was influenced by the French Parnassian and Symbolist poets. In 1899 Nelligan entered a mental institution and was eventually transferred to another hospital, where he remained until his death. The first collected edition of Nelligan's poems appeared in 1903, a complete English edition in 1983.

Nemerov, Howard (b. March 1, 1920, New York, N.Y., U.S.—d. July 5, 1991, University City, near St. Louis, Mo.) American poet, novelist, and critic whose poetry, marked by irony and self-deprecatory wit, is often about nature. In 1978 Nemerov received the Pulitzer Prize and the National Book Award for *The Collected Poems of Howard Nemerov*, which appeared in 1977.

After graduating from Harvard University, Nemerov served as a pilot in World War II. After the war he taught at various colleges, including Bennington College, Bennington, Vt., and Washington University, St. Louis, Mo. From 1963 to 1964 he was consultant in poetry to the Library of Congress. He was poet laureate of the United States in 1988–89 and again in 1989–90.

Nemerov's first book of verse, *The Image and the Law* (1947), was followed by a number of others, including *The Salt Garden* (1955), *Mirrors and Windows* (1958), *New and Selected Poems* (1960), *Blue Swallows* (1967), *Gnomes and Occasions* (1973), *Sentences* (1980), and *War Stories* (1987). Nemerov's fiction includes *The Melodramatists* (1949); *The Homecoming Game* (1957), a tale of a college professor who flunks a small college's football hero; and *A Commodity of Dreams and Other Stories* (1960). Among his considerable body of critical writing are *Journal of the Fictive Life* (1965), *Reflections on Poetry and Poetics* (1972), and *Figures of Thought: Speculations on the Meaning of Poetry and Other Essays* (1978).

Nevins, Allan (b. May 20, 1890, Camp Point, Ill., U.S.—d. March 5, 1971, Menlo Park, Calif.) American historian, known especially for his eight-volume history of the American Civil War and his biographies of American political and industrial figures. He also inaugurated the country's first oral history program.

Nevins was educated at the University of Illinois. His first book, *The Life of Robert Rogers* (1914), concerns a Colonial American soldier who fought on the Loyalist side. Nevins joined the New York *Evening Post* as an editorial writer and for nearly 20 years worked as a journalist. During this period he also compiled and edited a collection of documents entitled *American Social History as Recorded by British Travellers* (1923), wrote two works on U.S. history, and produced a biography of explorer John Charles Frémont.

In 1928 he accepted a post at Columbia University in New York City, where he remained for the next 30 years. While at Columbia, Nevins produced an impressive body of work, including two Pulitzer Prize-winning historical biographies: *Grover Cleveland, A Study in Courage* (1932) and *Hamilton Fish, The Inner History of the Grant Administration* (1936). In 1948 he established a project at Columbia for preserving on tape interviews with notable figures whose views of current affairs would interest future historians.

Nevins established himself as a leading authority on the American Civil War with his eight-volume work: *Ordeal of the Union*, 2 vol. (1947), *The Emergence of Lincoln*, 2 vol. (1950), and *The War for Union*, 4 vol.

(1959–71). He also wrote notable works on industrialists John D. Rockeller and Henry Ford.

Nin, Anaïs (b. Feb. 21, 1903, Neuilly, Fr.—d. Jan. 14, 1977, Los Angeles, Calif., U.S.) French-born author of novels and short stories whose literary reputation rests on the eight published volumes of her personal diaries. Her writing shows the influence of the Surrealist movement and her study of psychoanalysis.

Nin launched her literary career with the publication of *D.H. Lawrence: An Unprofessional Study* (1932). In the early 1940s, Nin went to New York City, where she printed and published her novels and short stories at her own expense. Not until 1966, with the appearance of the first volume of her diaries, did she win recognition as a writer. The success of the diary provoked interest in an earlier work entitled *Cities of the Interior* (1959), a five-volume *roman-fleuve*, or continuous novel, which consisted of *Ladders to Fire* (1946); *Children of the Albatross* (1947); *The Four-Chambered Heart* (1950); *A Spy in the House of Love* (1954); and *Solar Barque* (1958).

Nin's literary contribution was a subject of controversy in her lifetime and remained so after her death. Some critics admire her unique expression of femininity, her lyrical style, and her psychological insight, while others dismiss her concern with her own fulfillment as self-indulgent and narcissistic. Her other works of fiction include a collection of short stories, *Under a Glass Bell* (1944); the novels *House of Incest* (1936), *Seduction of the Minotaur* (1961), and *Collages* (1964); and three novelettes collected in *Winter of Artifice* (1939).

Niven, Frederick John (b. March 31, 1878, Valparaíso, Chile—d. Jan. 30, 1944, Vancouver, B.C., Can.) Regional novelist who wrote more than 30 novels, many of them historical romances, set in Scotland and Canada. Three of his best-known novels—*The Flying Years* (1935), *Mine Inheritance* (1940), and *The Transplanted* (1944)—form a trilogy dealing with the settlement of the Canadian west.

Niven went to Canada about 1900 and worked there in construction camps in the Canadian west. Returning to the British Isles, where he had been educated, he was a writer and journalist in England until after World War I, when he settled permanently in British Columbia. Niven also published two volumes of verse and an autobiography, *Coloured Spectacles* (1938), a collection of essays based on his personal experiences.

Norris, Frank, *in full* Benjamin Franklin Norris (b. March 5, 1870, Chicago, Ill., U.S.—d. Oct. 25, 1902, San Francisco, Calif.) Novelist and short-story writer who was the first important American author to embrace naturalism.

Norris' first important novel, MCTEAGUE (1899), tells the story of a dentist who murders his miserly wife and then meets his own end while fleeing through Death Valley. Norris' masterpiece, THE OCTOPUS (1901), was the first novel of a projected trilogy, *The Epic of the Wheat*. *The Octopus* pictures the struggle of California wheat growers against a monopolistic railway corporation. The second novel in the trilogy, *The Pit* (1903), deals with wheat speculation on the Chicago Board of Trade. A third novel was unwritten at Norris' death. *Vandover and the Brute*, published posthumously in 1914, is a study of degeneration.

Despite their romanticizing tendencies, Norris' novels present a vividly authentic and highly readable picture of life in California at the turn of the century. His writings were collected in 10 volumes and published in 1928.

Norton, Andre, *original name* Alice Mary Norton (b. Feb. 17, 1912, Cleveland, Ohio, U.S.) Prolific best-selling author of science-fiction and fantasy adventure novels for both juveniles and adults.

Norton spent 18 years as a children's librarian in the Cleveland Public Library, a job that enabled her to become familiar with children's literature. She legally changed her name to Andre Norton in 1934, when her historical fantasy *The Prince Commands* was published; it was the first of nine novels that she published during her librarian years. While working for the science-fiction publisher Gnome Press in the 1950s she wrote her first novel in the genre, *Star Man's Son, 2250 A.D.* (1952).

Norton's fast-moving science fiction and fantasy tales usually feature adolescents undergoing rites of passage—tests of physical, emotional, and moral strength. Her future Earth, distant planets, and fantasy lands are detailed, colorful, and extrapolated from her wide readings in history, biology, travel, archaeology, anthropology, mythology, folklore, and magic. Among her more than 100 books, the most noted include a series of 24 works, beginning with *Witch World* (1963), that are set on a matriarchal planet.

Norton, Charles Eliot (b. Nov. 16, 1827, Cambridge, Mass., U.S.—d. Oct. 21, 1908, Cambridge) American scholar and man of letters, an idealist and reformer.

Norton opened a night school in Cambridge, was director of a housing experiment in Boston, worked zealously as an editor for the Union cause, and was coeditor (1864–68) of *The North American Review* and one of the founders of *The Nation* (1865). A friend of many literary figures, including Thomas Carlyle, Ralph Waldo Emerson, John Ruskin, Henry Wadsworth Longfellow, and James Russell Lowell, he contributed valuable editions of their letters and other biographical material. Norton also wrote on art and edited collections of poetry, notably the poetry of John Donne (1895–1905).

Norton's best literary work probably was his prose translation of Dante's *The Divine Comedy* (1891–92). His letters were published in 1913.

Nugent, Richard (Bruce), *pseudonyms* Bruce Nugent, Richard Bruce (b. July 2, 1906, Washington, D.C., U.S.) African-American writer, artist, and actor associated with the Harlem Renaissance in New York City.

Nugent's introduction to Langston Hughes in 1925 signaled the beginning of his lifelong fascination with the arts and his contribution to the literary and political movements of the Harlem Renaissance. He explored issues of sexuality and black identity in his poems, short stories, and erotic drawings. "Shadows," Nugent's first published poem, was anthologized in Countee Cullen's 1927 work *Caroling Dusk: An Anthology of Verse by Negro Poets*. A one-act musical, "Sadhji: An African Ballet" (based on his earlier short story of the same name), was published in *Plays of Negro Life: A Source-book of Native American Drama* (1927) and produced in 1932. This African morality tale tells of the beautiful Sadhji, a chieftain's wife, beloved by Mrabo, her stepson, who, in turn, is loved by his male friend Numbo. In 1926 Nugent contributed two brush-and-ink drawings and the short story "Smoke, Lilies, and Jade" (published under the name Richard Bruce) to the only issue of *Fire!!* Controversial in its time, the story depicts a 19-year-old artist's sexual encounter with another man.

Nye, Bill, *pseudonym of* Edgar Wilson Nye (b. Aug. 25, 1850, Shirley, Maine, U.S.—d. Feb. 22, 1896, Arden, N.C.) Journalist and one of the major American humorists in the last half of the 19th century.

Settling in Laramie, Wyo., in 1876, Nye contributed to the *Denver Tribune* and *Cheyenne Sun*. His humorous squibs and tales in the *Laramie Boomerang*, which he helped found in 1881, were widely read and reprinted. Collected, they form the substance of numerous published volumes, from *Bill Nye and Boomerang* (1881) to *Bill Nye's History of the U.S.* (1894). Nye later returned to Wisconsin, where he had grown up, and for several years wrote for the *New York World*. In 1886 he lectured with the poet James Whitcomb Riley, the combination of Nye's wit and Riley's sentiment proving extremely popular.

O'Brien, Fitz-James (b. *c.* 1828, County Limerick, Ire.—d. April 6, 1862, Cumberland, Md., U.S.) Irish-American journalist, playwright, and author whose psychologically penetrating tales of pseudoscience and the uncanny made him one of the forerunners of modern science fiction.

O'Brien began to work in journalism in London. In 1852 he moved to New York City and soon became an important figure in that city's bohemia. But his work, though published in the leading periodicals of the day, won him neither the reputation he thought he merited nor the financial security he desired. He died from wounds received as a Union soldier during the first year of the American Civil War.

O'Brien's best-known stories include "The Diamond Lens," about a man who falls in love with a being he sees through a microscope in a drop of water; "What Was It?" in which a man is attacked by a thing he apprehends with every sense but sight; and "The Wondersmith," in which robots are fashioned only to turn upon their creators. These three stories appeared in periodicals in 1858 and 1859.

Oates, Joyce Carol (b. June 16, 1938, Lockport, N.Y., U.S.) Prolific American prose writer noted for her depictions of violence and evil in modern society.

Oates studied at Syracuse University and the University of Wisconsin. Her first collection of short stories, *By the North Gate*, was published in 1963, and her first novel, *With Shuddering Fall*, in 1964. She wrote prolifically thereafter, averaging about two books (chiefly short stories and novels) per year. Her more important novels include *A Garden of Earthly Delights* (1967), THEM (1969; winner of a National Book Award), and *Do with Me What You Will* (1973). Also significant is a parodic gothic series that includes *Bellefleur* (1980), *A Bloodsmoor Romance* (1982), and *Mysteries of Winterthurn* (1984). Some of her books are written under the pseudonym Rosamond Smith. She also wrote plays, essays, and literary criticism. She taught at the University of Detroit from 1961 to 1967, at the University of Windsor, Ontario, Can., from 1967 to 1978, and thereafter at Princeton University.

Oates typically portrays people whose intensely experienced lives often end in bloodshed and self-destruction owing to larger forces beyond their control.

O'Brien, Tim, *in full* William Timothy O'Brien (b. Oct. 1, 1946, Austin, Minn., U.S.) American novelist noted for his writings about American soldiers in the Vietnam War.

O'Brien fought in Vietnam, rising to the rank of sergeant. When he returned to the United States, he worked for the *Washington Post* (1971–74) as a reporter. He collected his newspaper and magazine articles about his war experiences in his first book, *If I Die in a Combat Zone, Box Me Up and Ship Me Home* (1973). By turns meditative and brutally realistic, it was praised for its honest portrayal of a soldier's emotions.

The Vietnam War is present in many of O'Brien's novels. One of the two protagonists in *Northern Lights* (1975) is a wounded war hero. A soldier abandons his platoon in Vietnam to try to walk to Paris in *Going after Cacciato* (1978). A man's lifelong fear of dying from a nuclear bombing is the subject of *The Nuclear Age* (1981), while *The Things They Carried* (1990) returns to the theme of Vietnam War experiences.

JOE MCTYRE

Flannery O'Connor

O'Connor, Flannery, *in full* Mary Flannery O'Connor (b. March 25, 1925, Savannah, Ga., U.S.—d. Aug. 3, 1964, Milledgeville, Ga.) American novelist and short-story writer whose works, usually set in the rural South and often depicting human alienation, are concerned with the relationship between the individual and God.

O'Connor's first published work, a short story, appeared in *Accent* in 1946. Her first novel, WISE BLOOD (1952), combines the keen ear for common speech, caustic religious imagination, and flair for the absurd that were to characterize her subsequent work. With the publication of further short stories, first collected in A GOOD MAN IS HARD TO FIND (1955), she came to be regarded as a master of the form. Her other works of fiction are a novel, THE VIOLENT BEAR IT AWAY (1960), and the short-story collection EVERYTHING THAT RISES MUST CONVERGE (1965). A collection of occasional prose pieces, *Mystery and Manners*, appeared in 1969. *The Complete Stories*, published posthumously in 1971, contained several stories that had not previously appeared in book form.

Crippled by lupus erythematosus, which eventually proved fatal, O'Connor lived modestly, writing and raising peafowl on her mother's ancestral farm. Her letters, which provided valuable insight into the role of Roman Catholicism in her life and art, were published as *The Habit of Being*, in (1979).

Clifford Odets

Odets, Clifford (b. July 18, 1906, Philadelphia, Pa., U.S.—d. Aug. 14, 1963, Hollywood, Calif.) Leading dramatist of the theater of social protest in the United States during the 1930s. As one of its original members, he contributed to the prestige of the Group Theatre from 1931.

Odets' WAITING FOR LEFTY (1935), his first great success, used both the auditorium and the stage for action and was an effective plea for labor unionism. *Awake and Sing!* (1935) was a naturalistic family drama, and GOLDEN BOY (1937) was about an Italian-American prizefighter. *Paradise Lost* (1935) deals with the tragic life of a middle-class family.

Odets moved to Hollywood in the late 1930s to write for motion pictures, and he became a successful director. His later plays include *The Big Knife* (1949), *The Country Girl* (1950); U.K. title, *Winter Journey*), and *The Flowering Peach* (1954).

O'Hara, Frank (b. June 27, 1926, Baltimore, Md., U.S.—d. July 25, 1966, Fire Island, N.Y.) American poet who gathered images from an urban environment to represent personal experience.

O'Hara was drawn to both poetry and the visual arts for much of his life. During the 1960s, as an assistant curator at the Museum of Modern Art in New York City, O'Hara sent his criticism of current painting and sculpture to such periodicals as *Art News*, and he wrote catalogs for the exhibits he arranged. Meanwhile, local theaters were producing many of his experimental one-act plays, including *Try! Try!* (1960), about a soldier's return to his wife and her new lover.

O'Hara, however, considered himself primarily a poet. His pieces, which mark him as a member of the New York school of poets, are a mixture of quotations, gossip, phone numbers, commercials—any mote of experience that he found appealing. He related what was happening to him rather than trying to clarify experiences for the reader. His first volume of poetry was *A City Winter, and Other Poems* (1952). *The Collected Poems of Frank O'Hara* (1971) was published posthumously.

O'Hara, John (Henry) (b. Jan. 31, 1905, Pottsville, Pa., U.S.—d. April 11, 1970, Princeton, N.J.) American novelist and short-story writer whose sparingly styled fiction stands as a social history of upwardly mobile Americans from the 1920s through the 1940s.

John O'Hara

O'Hara was raised in Pottsville, Pa., which appears in his fiction as Gibbsville, a typical small town in the United States. He worked as a critic and reporter in New York City. The influence of this journalistic experience is seen in the objective and nonexperimental style of his fiction.

O'Hara was fascinated by the effects of class, money, and sexuality on Americans, and his fictional representations of Hollywood and Broadway are thick with the snobbery of social structure. His highly acclaimed first novel, *Appointment in Samarra* (1934), explored the disintegration and death of an upper-class inhabitant of a small city. In 1956 he received a National Book Award for *Ten North Frederick* (1955; film, 1958). Many of his best-selling novels were adapted for stage and screen, including the popular *Butterfield 8* (1935; film, 1960) and *From the Terrace* (1958; film, 1960). O'Hara's short-story collections include *Waiting for Winter* (1966) and *And Other Stories* (1968).

Olds, Sharon (b. Nov. 19, 1942, San Francisco, Calif., U.S.) Poet best known for her powerful, often erotic, imagery of the body and the family.

Olds graduated from Stanford University and from Columbia University and then taught poetry at numerous schools and in workshops.

Olds's first collection, *Satan Says* (1980), described her early sexual life in frank language, making clear that the writer had no use for poetic politesse. *The Dead and the Living* (1984), which received several major poetry awards, refined her poetic voice. Her poems honoring the dead encompassed family members and victims of political violence; those addressed to the living continued her exploration of the life of the body, a theme she further developed in *The Gold Cell* (1987). *The Matter of This World: New and Selected Poems* (1987), *The Father* (1992), and *The Wellspring* (1995) continued her intimate exposition—free of bitterness and self-pity—of her own life.

Oliver, Mary (b. Sept. 10, 1935, Cleveland, Ohio, U.S.) American poet whose work reflected a deep communion with the natural world.

Oliver worked for a time as a secretary for Edna St. Vincent Millay's sister. Millay's influence is apparent in Oliver's first book of poetry, *No Voyage and Other Poems* (1963). Some of these lyrical nature poems are set in the Ohio of Oliver's youth. Her childhood plays a more central role in *The River Styx, Ohio, and Other Poems* (1972), in which she attempted to recreate the past through memory and myth. *The Night Traveler* (1978) explores the themes of birth, decay, and death through the conceit of a classical journey into the underworld.

Her volume *American Primitive* (1983), which won a Pulitzer Prize, glorifies the natural world, reflecting the American fascination with the ideal of the pastoral life. In *House of Light* (1990) Oliver explores the rewards of solitude in nature. *New and Selected Poems* (1992) and *White Pine: Poems and Prose Poems* (1994) are later collections. She also wrote *A Poetry Handbook* (1994).

Olsen, Tillie, *original surname* Lerner (b. Jan. 14, 1913, Omaha, Neb., U.S.) American author known for her powerful fiction about the inner lives of the working poor, women, and minorities.

Olsen's early adult life was devoted to political activism and to rearing a family. Her first novel, begun at the age of 19, was set aside for 35 years. Though she found it too painful to finish, Olsen eventually published the reconstructed manuscript as *Yonnondio: From the Thirties* in 1974. The novel tells the story of the Holbrook family, who struggle during the Depression era to survive as coal miners, tenant farmers, and meat packers. *Tell Me A Riddle: A Collection* (1961) contains three short stories and a novella, each a masterpiece in its own right. Olsen used rhythmic, metaphoric language to give a voice to otherwise inarticulate characters.

In her later works Olsen addressed feminist themes and concerns, especially as related to women writers. *Silences* (1978) contains, among other things, a long essay about the author Rebecca Harding Davis, whose career as a writer failed after she married. In 1984 Olsen edited *Mother to Daughter, Daughter to Mother: Mothers on Mothering.*

Olson, Charles (John) (b. Dec. 27, 1910, Worcester, Mass., U.S.—d. Jan. 10, 1970, New York, N.Y.) Avant-garde poet and literary theorist, notable for his influence on American poetry during the late 1950s.

Olson was educated at Wesleyan University (Conn.) and Harvard. He taught in Massachusetts at Clark University, Harvard, and Radcliffe College, but his real influence began in the late 1940s as an instructor and then as rector (1951–56) at Black Mountain College in North Carolina.

Olson first gained recognition for *Call Me Ishmael* (1947), a study of the literary influences on Herman Melville's *Moby-Dick*. His concepts of poetry, contained in his 1950 essay *Projective Verse* (published in book form, 1959), influenced such poets as Robert Creeley, Robert Duncan, and Denise Levertov. Olson's *The Maximus Poems* (1953, 1956, combined 1960) is a long sequence of poems continued in subsequent volumes, while *In Cold Hell, in Thicket* (1953) and *The Distances* (1960) contain some of his best-known shorter poems. *See also* BLACK MOUNTAIN POETS.

Olson, Elder (James) (b. March 9, 1909, Chicago, Ill., U.S.—d. July 25, 1992, Albuquerque, N.M.) American poet, playwright, and literary critic. He was a leading member of the Neo-Aristotelian school of critical theory that came to prominence in the 1940s at the University of Chicago.

After graduating from the University of Chicago, Olson taught for several years at the Armour Institute of Technology (now Illinois Institute of Technology) in Chicago. He returned to the University of Chicago in 1942 and taught there until his retirement in 1977. Along with his teachers and colleagues at Chicago, Richard McKeon, R.S. Crane, and Wayne Booth, Olson became known for his responses to the New Criticism. In *Critics and Criticism* (1952); the Neo-Aristotelian manifesto edited by Crane) and later works that included *Tragedy and the Theory of Drama* (1961) and *The Theory of Comedy* (1968), Olson argued for a systematic, comprehensive, and pluralistic approach to criticism based on the principles of Aristotle's *Poetics*. He attacked the New Critics for focusing on the diction of poetry and argued that criticism should concentrate on poetic wholes instead.

Although less widely known than his criticism, Olson's poetry is characterized by rich imagery, a serious and elegiac tone, sharp wit, technical dexterity, and metaphysical themes. His works include *Thing of Sorrow* (1934), *The Scarecrow Christ and Other Poems* (1954), *Plays and Poems* (1958), *Olson's Penny Arcade* (1975), and *Last Poems* (1984).

Eugene O'Neill

O'Neill, Eugene (Gladstone) (b. Oct. 16, 1888, New York, N.Y., U.S.— d. Nov. 27, 1953, Boston, Mass.) One of the greatest American playwrights and winner of the Nobel Prize for Literature in 1936.

O'Neill attended Princeton University for one year (1906–07), after which he shipped to sea, lived a derelict's existence on the waterfronts of Buenos Aires, Liverpool, and New York City, submerged himself in alcohol, and attempted suicide. While recovering from tuberculosis at a sanitarium in Wallingford, Conn., he began to write plays.

His first full-length play, *Beyond the Horizon*, was produced on Broadway in 1920. O'Neill's capacity for and commitment to work were staggering. Between 1920 and 1943 he completed 20 long plays and a number of shorter ones. His most distinguished short plays include four early sea dramas, *Bound East for Cardiff*, *In the Zone*, *The Long Voyage Home*, and *The Moon of the Caribbees*, which were written between 1913 and 1917 and produced in 1924 under the overall title *S.S. Glencairn*; THE EMPEROR JONES (1921); and THE HAIRY APE (1923).

O'Neill's plays were written from an intensely personal point of view, deriving directly from the scarring effects of his tragic relationships with his family—his mother and father, who loved and tormented each other; his older brother, who both loved and corrupted him and died of alcoholism in middle age; and O'Neill himself, caught and torn between love for and rage at all three.

Among his most celebrated long plays are ANNA CHRISTIE (1922); DESIRE UNDER THE ELMS (1925) and MOURNING BECOMES ELECTRA (1931), both of which evoked the starkness and inevitability of Greek tragedy that he felt in his own life; and THE GREAT GOD BROWN (1926) and STRANGE INTERLUDE (1928), in which O'Neill used experimental techniques such as expressionistic dialogue and spoken asides that have since become accepted on the stage but at the time were revolutionary. Following a long succession of tragic visions, O'Neill's only comedy, the lighthearted and nostalgic AH, WILDERNESS! (1933), appeared on Broadway. THE ICEMAN COMETH (1946), the most complex and perhaps the finest of the O'Neill tragedies, followed.

Even in his last writings, O'Neill's youth continued to absorb his attention. The posthumous production of LONG DAY'S JOURNEY INTO NIGHT in 1956 brought to light an agonizingly autobiographical play, one of O'Neill's greatest. Its sequel, A MOON FOR THE MISBEGOTTEN (1952), was produced the following year.

Oppen, George (b. April 24, 1908, New Rochelle, N.Y., U.S.—d. July 7, 1984, Sunnyvale, Calif.) American poet and political activist, one of the chief proponents of objectivism.

Oppen grew up in San Francisco and briefly attended Oregon State University, where he met his wife. From 1930 to 1933 Oppen and his wife ran the To Publishers press, which published *An "Objectivist" Anthology* (1932), a seminal work in the history of American poetry. The book was edited by Louis Zukofsky and contained work by Ezra Pound, T.S. Eliot, and William Carlos Williams, among others.

Oppen's own first book of poems, *Discrete Series*, was published in 1934. These spare, precisely written verses earned Oppen a reputation as one of the foremost objectivist poets, who celebrated simplicity over formal structure and rhyme and emphasized the poem as an object in itself, not as a vehicle of meaning or association. Oppen became active in the U.S. Communist Party in the mid-1930s. In 1950 he fled to Mexico City to avoid persecution because of his politics, but he returned in 1958 and began writing poetry again. *The Materials* (1962) was his first book of poetry in 28 years. Most critics agree that Oppen's best work is *Of Being Numerous* (1968), which won a Pulitzer Prize. *The Collected Poems of George Oppen* was published in 1975, and *Primitive*, his last volume of poetry, in 1978.

Ozick, Cynthia (b. April 17, 1928, New York, N.Y., U.S.) Novelist and short-story writer whose works seek to define the challenge of remaining Jewish in contemporary American life.

Ozick's first novel, *Trust* (1966), is the story of a woman's rejection of her wealthy American Jewish family and her search for her renegade father in Europe. In subsequent books, such as *Bloodshed and Three Novellas* (1976), Ozick struggled with the idea that the creation of art (a pagan activity) is in direct opposition to principles of Judaism, which forbids the creation of idols. The psychological aftermath of the Holocaust is another theme of Ozick's work, especially in *Levitation: Five Fictions* (1982) and the novel *The Cannibal Galaxy* (1983). Ozick often draws upon traditional Jewish mysticism to expand upon her themes, yet her later works turn away from the theme of the sacred and the profane. Her novel *The Messiah of Stockholm* (1987) is, in part, a meditation on the nature of writing. A collection of essays, *Metaphor and Memory*, was published in 1989.

P

Thomas Nelson Page

Page, Thomas Nelson (b. April 23, 1853, Oakland plantation, near Beaver Dam, Va., U.S.—d. Nov. 1, 1922, Oakland, Calif.) American author whose work fostered romantic legends of Southern plantation life.

Page attended Washington College (now Washington and Lee University), Va., and the University of Virginia. He practiced law until 1893, when he devoted himself to writing and lecturing. He first won notice with the story "Marse Chan" in the *Century Illustrated Magazine*. This and similar stories were collected in *In Ole Virginia, Marse Chan, and Other Stories* (1887). Among his essays and social studies are *Social Life in Old Virginia* (1897) and *The Old Dominion—Her Making and Her Manners* (1908). His other works include *Two Little Confederates* (1888), a children's tale; *The Burial of the Guns; and Other Stories* (1894); *The Old Gentlemen of the Black Stock* (1897); and *Red Rock* (1898).

Palés Matos, Luis (b. March 20, 1898, Guayama, P.R.—d. Feb. 23, 1959, San Juan) Writer considered by many to be Puerto Rico's most distinguished lyric poet, who enriched the vocabulary of Spanish verse with words, themes, symbols, images, and rhythms of African folklore and dance.

Palés Matos wrote his first poetry, which was collected in *Azaleas* (1915), in imitation of modernist trends, but he soon found his own direction in his personal interpretation (as a white man) of black culture. His poems on black themes gave impetus to the developing concern of Latin Americans with their African heritage.

Although he was best known and most influential for his "Negro" poetry, his reflective and introspective personality found expression in poetry of many other moods and themes. *Poesía, 1915–56* (1957), a collection of much of his poetry, reveals his more personal side as a lyric poet.

Paley, Grace, *original surname* Goodside (b. Dec. 11, 1922, New York, N.Y., U.S.) Poet and short-story writer known for her realistic seriocomic portrayals of working-class New Yorkers and for her political activism.

Paley attended Hunter College and the New School for Social Research, both in New York City. She joined the faculty of Sarah Lawrence College in Bronxville, N.Y., in 1966. During the 1960s she was actively involved in the opposition to the Vietnam War and continued her political activism after the war ended.

Her first volume of short stories, *The Little Disturbances of Man: Stories of Men and Women at Love* (1959), was noted for its realistic dialogue. It was followed by *Enormous Changes at the Last Minute* (1974) and *Later the Same Day* (1985), both of which continued her compassionate, often comic, exploration of ordinary individuals struggling against loneliness. All featured the character of Faith, Paley's reputed alter ego. She also published two volumes of poems, *Leaning Forward* (1985) and *Begin Again: New and Collected Poems* (1992).

Panneton, Philippe, *pseudonym* Ringuet (b. April 30, 1895, Trois-Rivières, Que., Can.—d. Dec. 29, 1960, Lisbon, Port.) French-Canadian novelist whose best-known works present the individual caught in the transition from primitive rural to modern urban life.

Panneton practiced medicine in Montreal and taught medicine at the University of Montreal. He was a cofounder of the French-Canadian Academy. From 1956 until his death, he served as Canadian ambassador to Portugal. *Trente Arpents* (1938); *Thirty Acres*), Panneton's major work, deals with the plight of the small French-Canadian farmer forced by the economic and social upheavals of the late 19th and early 20th centuries to migrate to the city. In other novels, such as *Fausse Monnaie* (1947); "False Money") and *Le Poids du jour* (1948); "The Heaviness of the Day"), he continued his examination of the lives of displaced peasants. He also published a volume of short stories and two historical sketches.

Paretsky, Sara (b. June 8, 1947, Ames, Iowa, U.S.) American mystery writer credited with breaking the gender barrier in detective fiction with her popular series of novels featuring V.I. Warshawski, a female private investigator.

Paretsky attended the University of Chicago and then worked for a large insurance company until she began to write full-time in 1985. Paretsky began her first book in 1979 and there the It was with *Indemnity Only* (1982) that her wisecracking, independent, passionate and compassionate female private detective was created.

V.I. uncovers an insurance scam involving shady insurance agents, a union leader, and a gangster. In Her other V.I. Warshawski novels are *Deadlock* (1984), *Killing Orders* (1985), V.I. becomes the target of violence and learns of conspiracies involving big business, organized crime, and (in Killing Orders) the Roman Catholic church. The author explores social issues in many of her books, including *Bitter Medicine* (1987), which deals with abortion rights and the medical community, *Blood Shot* (1988), *Burn Marks* (1990), *Guardian Angel* (1992), and *Tunnel Vision* (1994). which look critically at the treatment of the homeless and the elderly.

Many critics considered Blood Shot (1988) Paretsky's best novel. In the course of searching for an old friend's missing father, V.I. discovers that ruthless chemical company executives are poisoning her old neighborhood for material gain.

In the mid-1980s Paretsky helped found Sisters in Crime to promote the work of other women mystery writers and to challenge the publication of crime stories marred by gratuitous violence against women. She edited *A Woman's Eye* (1991), a collection of crime stories by women.

Parker, Dorothy, *original surname* Rothschild (b. Aug. 22, 1893, West End, N.J., U.S.—d. June 7, 1967, New York, N.Y.) American short-story writer and poet who is chiefly remembered for her witty remarks.

Parker became drama critic for *Vanity Fair* and with two other writers for the magazine—Robert Benchley and Robert Sherwood—formed the nucleus of the Algonquin Round Table, an informal luncheon club held at New York City's Algonquin Hotel. From 1927 until 1933 Parker contributed a personal kind of book review to *The New Yorker* magazine as "Constant Reader," and some of these reviews were collected in *A Month of Saturdays* (1971). Three books of her verse, *Enough Rope* (1926), *Sunset Gun* (1928), and *Death and Taxes* (1931), were collected in *Collected Poems: Not So Deep as a Well* (1936). *Laments for the Living* (1930) and *After Such Pleasures* (1933) were collections of her short stories, combined and augmented in 1939 as *Here Lies*. She also worked as a film writer, reported on the Spanish Civil War, and collaborated on several plays.

Parks, Gordon (b. Nov. 30, 1912, Fort Scott, Kan., U.S.) African-American author, photographer, and film director who documented black American life.

A high-school dropout, Parks worked odd jobs before becoming a photojournalist in the late 1930s. His first books were *Flash Photography* (1947) and *Camera Portraits* (1948). As a staff photographer for *Life* magazine (1948–72), he became known for his portrayals of ghetto life, black nationalists, and the civil-rights movement. A photo essay about a child from a Brazilian slum was expanded into a television documentary (1962) and a book with poetry (1978), both titled *Flavio*. His first work of fiction was *The Learning Tree* (1963).

Parks was noted for his forthright autobiographies, *A Choice of Weapons* (1966), *To Smile in Autumn* (1979), and *Voices in the Mirror* (1990). He combined poetry and photography in *A Poet and His Camera* (1968), *Whispers of Intimate Things* (1971), *In Love* (1971), and *Moments Without Proper Names* (1975). He also wrote *Born Black* (1971), a collection of essays, the novel *Shannon* (1981), and *Arias in Silence* (1994), and he directed several motion pictures.

Parrington, Vernon Louis (b. Aug. 3, 1871, Aurora, Ill., U.S.—d. June 16, 1929, Winchcombe, Gloucestershire, Eng.) American writer and teacher noted for his far-reaching appraisal of American literary history.

Parrington was educated at the College of Emporia, Kansas, and at Harvard University. He taught at the College of Emporia, the University of Oklahoma, Norman, and the University of Washington, Seattle. Parrington's major work on American literary history was published in *Main Currents in American Thought*, 2 vol. (1927), which won a Pulitzer Prize in 1928. A third volume with the subtitle *The Beginnings of Critical Realism in America*, incomplete at his death, was published in 1930. He also wrote *The Connecticut Wits* (1926) and *Sinclair Lewis, Our Own Diogenes* (1927).

Parton, Sara Payson Willis, *original name* Grata Payson Willis, *pseudonym* Fanny Fern (b. July 9, 1811, Portland, Maine, U.S.—d. Oct. 10, 1872, New York, N.Y.) One of the most popular American women writers in the 19th century.

Parton's sketches, often dealing with domestic life, were originally published in periodicals in Boston and New York City. They were first collected in *Fern Leaves from Fanny's Port-Folio* (1853), which sold a remarkable 100,000 copies its first year. The success of this and other books led to an offer by the *New York Ledger* that made Parton one of the first women newspaper columnists in America. from 1855 until her death, she reached an audience estimated at 500,000 readers weekly.

Parton's writings are considered valuable mostly as a source for social history and as a mirror of popular taste in the mid-19th century. In addition to her articles, Parton wrote a number of best-selling books, including *Ruth Hall* (1855) and *A New Story Book for Children* (1864).

Patchen, Kenneth (b. Dec. 13, 1911, Niles, Ohio, U.S.—d. Jan. 8, 1972, Palo Alto, Calif.) American experimental poet, novelist, painter, and graphic designer.

Patchen published many collections of verse from 1936 on, notably *Collected Poems* (1968), and several novels, including *The Journal of Albion Moonlight* (1941), *Memoirs of a Shy Pornographer* (1945), and *See You in the Morning* (1948). He also wrote plays and other works, all of which exhibit a combination of high idealism, abhorrence of violence, isolation from the mainstream of American thought, and shock at materialistic secularism. Patchen was one of the more successful practitioners of the poetry-and-jazz movement.

Paulding, James Kirke (b. Aug. 22, 1778, Dutchess County, N.Y., U.S.—d. April 6, 1860, Hyde Park, N.Y.) Dramatist and novelist, and public official chiefly remembered for his early advocacy and use of native American material in literature.

Together with the brothers William and Washington Irving, Paulding founded *Salmagundi* (1807–08), a periodical consisting mainly of light

James Kirke Paulding

satires on local subjects in New York City. He satirized England's conduct toward America during the War of 1812 in *The Diverting History of John Bull and Brother Jonathan* (1812) and in *The Lay of the Scottish Fiddle: A Tale of Havre de Grace* (1813), the latter a burlesque of Sir Walter Scott. He returned to this theme in two later satires: *A Sketch of Old England: By a New England Man* (1822) and *John Bull in America* (1825).

The advantages and hardships of western migration are the theme of "The Backwoodsman" (1818), a poem written to encourage American writers to find literary themes in their own country rather than in Europe. Novels such as *Koningsmarke, the Long Finne, a Story of the New World* (1823), *Westward Ho!* (1832), and *The Old Continental; or, the Price of Liberty* (1846) represent Paulding's attempts to employ the American scene in fiction. In the play *The Lion of the West* (performed 1831; published 1954), he introduced frontier humor to the stage and contributed to the growing legend of Davy Crockett.

John Howard Payne

Payne, John Howard (b. June 9, 1791, New York, N.Y., U.S.—d. April 9, 1852, Tunis, Tun.) American-born playwright and actor who followed the techniques and themes of the European Romantic blank-verse dramatists.

A precocious actor and writer, Payne wrote his first play, *Julia; or, The Wanderer*, when he was 15. In 1813 he left for England, where he triumphed onstage at Drury Lane in John Home's *Douglas*; he repeated his success in other European capitals. In Paris, Payne met the actor François-Joseph Talma, who introduced him to French drama (from which many of his more than 60 plays were adapted), and Washington Irving, with whom he was to collaborate on two of his best plays.

The finest play Payne wrote was *Brutus; or, The Fall of Tarquin* (produced 1818). The play remained popular for 70 years. Other important plays were *Clari; or, The Maid of Milan*, which included Payne's famous song "Home, Sweet Home"; *Charles the Second* (1824), written with Irving; and *Thérèse* (1821), a French adaptation.

Peabody, Elizabeth Palmer (b. May 16, 1804, Billerica, Mass., U.S.—d. Jan. 3, 1894, Jamaica Plain, Mass.) American educator and participant in the Transcendental movement.

After being educated at a small private school by her mother, Elizabeth Peabody started her own school in Boston in 1820. From 1825 to 1834 she was secretary to William Ellery Channing, the early leader of Unitarianism in the United States; she then began an association with Bronson Alcott in his Temple School, which she wrote about in *Record of a School* (1835). After two years at the school she became involved in adult education in Boston. In 1839 Peabody opened her West Street bookstore, which became a kind of club for the intellectual community of Boston. On her own printing press she published translations from German by Margaret Fuller and three of Nathaniel Hawthorne's earliest books. For two years she published and wrote articles for *The Dial*, the critical literary monthly and organ of the Transcendental movement; she also wrote for other periodicals.

Peabody's kindergarten, opened in 1860, marked the American adoption of what until then had been primarily a German institution. She devoted herself thereafter to organizing public and private kindergartens and to lecturing and writing in the field. A volume entitled *The Letters of Elizabeth Palmer Peabody*, was published in 1984.

Percy, Walker (b. May 28, 1916, Birmingham, Ala., U.S.—d. May 10, 1990, Covington, La.) American novelist who wrote of the search for faith and love in the New South, a place transformed by industry and technology.

NANCY CRAMPTON

Walker Percy

Percy studied at the University of North Carolina and Columbia University. While working at Bellevue Hospital, New York City, he contracted tuberculosis. During his recuperation he read widely (especially the works of European existentialists), decided on a career in writing, and converted to Roman Catholicism. His conversion and his interest in existentialism were both powerful influences on his works.

During the 1950s Percy wrote articles for philosophical, literary, and psychiatric journals. His first and best-known novel, THE MOVIEGOER (1961), won a National Book Award and introduced Percy's concept of "malaise," a disease of despair born of the rootless modern world. Other fiction includes *Love in the Ruins: The Adventures of a Bad Catholic at a Time Near the End of the World* (1971), *The Second Coming* (1980), and *The Thanatos Syndrome* (1987). He also wrote such nonfiction as *The Message in the Bottle* (1975), a sophisticated philosophical treatment of semantics.

Perelman, S.J., *in full* Sidney Joseph (b. Feb. 1, 1904, Brooklyn, N.Y., U.S.—d. Oct. 17, 1979, New York, N.Y.) American humorist who was a master of wordplay in books, movies, plays, and essays.

Perelman graduated from Brown University. He began writing for the early, frenetic Marx Brothers films and helped turn out the screenplays for such classics as *Monkey Business* (1931) and *Horse Feathers* (1932). He also regularly contributed essays to *The New Yorker* magazine under such absurd titles as *Beat Me, Post-Impressionist Daddy* and *No Starch in the Dhoti*. Perelman collaborated on the theatrical comedies *All Good Americans* (1934) and *One Touch of Venus* (1943), and for his collaboration on the film *Around the World in 80 Days* he shared an Academy Award for best screenwriter for 1956. His magazine pieces were collected in a long series of books, including *Strictly from Hunger* (1937), *Westward Ha!; or, Around the World in Eighty Clichés* (1948), and *The Road to Miltown; or, Under the Spreading Atrophy* (1957).

Perelman's humor is characterized by an exquisite sense of cliché and mimicry that is combined with a varied vocabulary to create effects of comic nihilism and literary parody.

Perry, Bliss (b. Nov. 25, 1860, Williamstown, Mass., U.S.—d. Feb. 13, 1954, Exeter, N.H.) American scholar and editor, especially noted for his work in American literature.

Perry was educated at Williams College, Williamstown, and the German universities of Berlin and Strassburg (now Strasbourg, Fr.). He taught at Williams (1886–93), Princeton University (1893–1900), and Harvard University (1907–30) and was Harvard lecturer at the University of Paris (1909–10). From 1899 to 1909 he edited *The Atlantic Monthly*.

Perry edited many volumes, including the works of Edmund Burke, Sir Walter Scott, and Ralph Waldo Emerson, and he was general editor (1905–09) of the Cambridge edition of the major American poets. He wrote a number of books, including works on Walt Whitman, John Greenleaf Whittier, Thomas Carlyle, Emerson, and others, as well as novels, short fiction, essays, an autobiography, studies of poetry, and collections of fiction and essays.

Petrakis, Harry Mark (b. June 5, 1923, St. Louis, Mo., U.S.) American novelist and short-story writer whose exuberant and sensitive works deal with the lives of Greek immigrants in urban America.

The son of an Eastern Orthodox priest, Petrakis attended the University of Illinois in 1940–41 and held a variety of jobs to support himself while writing. His novels and stories, usually set in Chicago, include *Lion at My Heart* (1959), *The Odyssey of Kostas Volakis* (1963), *A Dream of Kings* (1966), *The Hour of the Bell* (1976), *Nick the Greek* (1979), *Days of Vengeance* (1983), and *Ghost of the Sun* (1990), a sequel to *A Dream of Kings*. He also published collections of short stories, a biography, and an autobiography, *Stelmark: A Family Recollection* (1970).

Petry, Ann, *original surname* Lane (b. Oct. 12, 1908, Old Saybrook, Conn., U.S.) African-American novelist, journalist, and biographer whose works offered a unique perspective on black life in small-town New England.

Petry began her career as a journalist, writing for the *Amsterdam News* and the *Peoples' Voice* of Harlem, and then studied creative writing at Columbia University.

Her first novel, THE STREET (1946), became a best-seller and was critically acclaimed for its portrayal of a working-class black woman, Lutie Johnson, who dreams of getting out of Harlem but is inevitably thwarted by the pressures of poverty and racism. *Country Place* (1947) depicts the disillusionment and corruption among a group of white people in a small town in Connecticut. Her third novel, *The Narrows* (1953), is the story of Link Williams, a Dartmouth-educated black man who tends bar in the black section of Monmouth, Conn., and of his tragic love affair with a rich white woman. Petry's short stories were collected in *Miss Muriel and Other Stories* (1971). Petry also published several historical biographies for children, including *Harriet Tubman, Conductor on the Underground Railroad* (1955) and *Tituba of Salem Village* (1964).

Phelps, William Lyon (b. Jan. 2, 1865, New Haven, Conn., U.S.—d. Aug. 21, 1943, New Haven) American scholar and critic who did much to popularize the teaching of contemporary literature.

Phelps attended and taught at Yale and Harvard universities. In 1895, at Yale, he taught the first American college course in the modern novel. Both in this course and in his *Essays on Russian Novelists* (1911), he was influential in introducing Russian novelists to American readers.

Phelps was a popular lecturer and critic, and his literary essays that appeared in *Scribner's Magazine* and other periodicals, together with his syndicated newspaper column, "A Daily Thought," brought him an a wide audience. His *Autobiography with Letters* was published in 1939.

Pinsky, Robert (b. Oct. 20, 1940, Long Branch, N.J.) American poet and critic whose poems searched for the significance underlying everyday acts.

A graduate of Rutgers and Stanford universities, Pinsky taught at Wellesley College and at the University of California at Berkeley.

The title poem of his first collection, *Sadness and Happiness* (1975), comments on the poet's own life. His long poem *An Explanation of America* (1979) probes personal and national myths. Vivid imagery characterizes his other collections, which include *History of My Heart* (1984) and *The Want Bone* (1990). *Landor's Poetry* (1968) and *The Situation of Poetry: Contemporary Poetry and Its Tradition* (1976) are among his critical writings. He was poetry editor of *The New Republic* during the late 1970s. Pinsky cotranslated poems by Czesław Miłosz in *The Separate Notebooks* (1984). He devised and published an interactive quest romance called *Mindwheel* to be played on computers and published a critically acclaimed translation of Dante's *Inferno* in 1995.

Plath, Sylvia (b. Oct. 27, 1932, Boston, Mass., U.S.—d. Feb. 11, 1963, London, Eng.) American poet whose best-known poems are carefully crafted pieces noted for their personal imagery and intense focus. Many concern such themes as alienation, death, and self-destruction. She was little known at the time of her death by suicide, but by the mid-1970s she was considered a major contemporary poet.

Plath's first major publication was *The Colossus* (1960), a collection of poems written from 1956 to 1960. This was followed by her only novel, THE BELL JAR (1963), which first appeared under a pseudonym. Drawn from Plath's own experiences, the book describes the mental breakdown, attempted suicide, and eventual recovery of a young college girl. Works published posthumously include ARIEL (1965) and *Crossing the Water* (1971), both poetry collections, and *Johnny Panic and the Bible of Dreams* (1977), a book of short stories and other prose. *The Collected Poems*, which includes many previously unpublished poems, appeared in 1981 and was awarded a Pulitzer Prize.

Edgar Allen Poe

Poe, Edgar Allan (b. Jan. 19, 1809, Boston, Mass., U.S.—d. Oct. 7, 1849, Baltimore, Md.) American poet, critic, and short-story writer famous for his cultivation of mystery and the macabre in fiction.

After Poe's mother died in 1811, he was taken into the home of John Allan, a Richmond merchant. He briefly attended the University of Virginia, then went to Boston, where in 1827 he published a pamphlet containing TAMERLANE and other youthful Byronic poems. He then began to write stories, and in 1833 his MS. FOUND IN A BOTTLE won $50 from a Baltimore weekly. By 1835 he was in Richmond as editor of the *Southern Literary Messenger*, the first of several periodicals he was to edit or write for. There he married his cousin Virginia Clemm, who was only 13 years old.

In 1839 he became coeditor of *Burton's Gentleman's Magazine* in Philadelphia, for which he wrote some of his best-known stories of supernatural horror. His *Tales of the Grotesque and Arabesque* appeared later in 1839 (dated 1840). In addition to his stories Poe continued to write poetry, and his most famous poem, THE RAVEN, brought him national fame when it appeared in 1845. Several of his works, including the poem THE BELLS, were published posthumously.

Poe's writing is characterized by a strange duality. On the one hand, he was an idealist and a visionary. His sensitivity to women inspired his most touching lyrics, including ANNABEL LEE. More generally, in such verses as ULALUME and in his prose tales, his familiar mode of escape from the world was through eerie thoughts, impulses, or fears. From these materials he drew the startling effects of his tales of death (THE FALL OF THE HOUSE OF USHER, THE MASQUE OF THE RED DEATH, THE PREMATURE BURIAL), his tales of wickedness and crime (THE BLACK CAT, THE CASK OF AMONTILLADO, THE TELL-TALE HEART), and his tales of survival after dissolution (LIGEIA). Even when his characters are not actually in the clutch of mysterious forces or onto the untrodden paths of the beyond, he uses the anguish of imminent death as the means of causing the nerves to quiver (THE PIT AND THE PENDULUM).

On the other hand, Poe is conspicuous for his close observation of minute details, as in the long narratives (*The Narrative of Arthur Gordon Pym*) and in many of the descriptions that introduce the tales or constitute their settings. Closely connected with this is his power of ratiocination, as manifested in his analytical tales (THE GOLD BUG), detective stories (THE MURDERS IN THE RUE MORGUE), and science-fiction tales.

Poe's genius was early recognized abroad. No one did more to persuade the world and, in the long run, the United States of Poe's greatness than the French poets Charles Baudelaire and Stéphane Mallarmé. Indeed, his role in French literature was that of a poetic master model and guide to criticism. French Symbolism relied on his "The Philosophy of Composition," borrowed from his imagery, and used his examples to generate the modern theory of "pure poetry."

Pohl, Frederik (b. Nov. 26, 1919, New York, N.Y., U.S.) American science-fiction writer whose best work uses the genre as a mode of social criticism and as an exploration of the long-range consequences of technology in an ailing society.

By the late 1930s Pohl was working as an editor of science-fiction magazines. During World War II he served in the U.S. Army Air Forces and then worked briefly in an advertising agency before returning to writing and editing.

Pohl's most famous work, *The Space Merchants* (1953), was written in collaboration with C.M. Kornbluth. It tells the story of Mitchell Courtenay, a "copysmith star class" for a powerful advertising agency, who is made head of a project to colonize Venus in order to create consumers in space. This chilling portrait of a world dominated by the economic perspective of advertising executives made Pohl's reputation. Pohl wrote several other books with Kornbluth; some of their work can be found in *Our Best: The Best of Frederik Pohl and C.M. Kornbluth* (1987). Pohl's other novels include *The Age of the Pussyfoot* (1969), *Man Plus* (1976), and *Chernobyl* (1987). His numerous short-story collections include *The Best of Frederik Pohl* (1975), *Pohlstars* (1984), and *The Gateway Trip: Tales and Vignettes of the Heechee* (1990). Pohl published a memoir, *The Way the Future Was*, in 1978.

Porter, Katherine Anne (b. May 15, 1890, Indian Creek, Texas, U.S.—d. Sept. 18, 1980, Silver Spring, Md.) American novelist and short-story writer, a master stylist whose long short stories have a richness of texture and complexity of character delineation usually achieved only in the novel.

Porter worked as a journalist in Chicago and Denver, Colo., before leaving in 1920 for Mexico, the scene of several of her stories. "Maria Concepcion," her first published story (1922), was included in her first collection, FLOWERING JUDAS (1930), enlarged in 1935 by other stories.

The title story of her next collection, PALE HORSE, PALE RIDER (1939), is a poignant tale of youthful romance cruelly thwarted by the young man's death in the influenza epidemic of 1918. In it and the two other stories in the volume, "Noon Wine" and "Old Mortality," there appears for the first time her semiautobiographical heroine, Miranda, a spirited and independent woman. *The Leaning Tower* (1944) depicts in its title story a young Texas artist in Berlin during the rise of Nazism. The ascendancy of Nazism also haunts A SHIP OF FOOLS (1962), Porter's only novel.

Porter's *Collected Short Stories* (1965) won the National Book Award and the Pulitzer Prize for fiction. Her essays, articles, and book reviews were collected in *The Days Before* (1952); augmented 1970). Her last work, published in 1977, was *The Never-Ending Wrong*, dealing with the controversial murder trial (1920–27) of the anarchists Sacco and Vanzetti.

Porter, William Sydney. Real name of O. HENRY.

Potok, Chaim, *original name* Herman Harold Potok (b. Feb. 17, 1929, New York, N.Y., U.S.) Rabbi and author whose novels introduced to American fiction the spiritual and cultural life of Orthodox Jews.

The son of Polish immigrants, Potok was reared in an Orthodox home and attended religious schools. As a young man, he was drawn to the less restrictive Conservative doctrine; after attending Yeshiva University and the Jewish Theological Seminary, he was ordained a Conservative rabbi. He taught until he was named managing editor of *Conservative Judaism* in 1964. He further attended the University of Pennsylvania and in 1965 became editor in chief of the Jewish Publication Society. Throughout his publishing career Potok wrote scholarly and popular articles and reviews.

Potok's first novel was *The Chosen* (1967). was the first book from a major publisher to portray Orthodox Judaism in the United States. The author established his reputation with this story of the son of a Hasidic rabbi and his friend, whose humane Orthodox father encourages him to study secular subjects. *The Promise* (1969) followed the same characters to young adulthood. Potok again turned to the Hasidim in *My Name Is Asher Lev* (1972), which tells of a young artist in conflict with the traditions of his family and community.

Potok's next four novels, the autobiographical *In the Beginning* (1975), *The Book of Lights* (1981), *Davita's Harp* (1985), and *The Gift of Asher Lev* (1990), continued to explore the conflict between religious and secular interests. *I Am the Clay* appeared in 1992, and the illustrated *The Tree of Here* in

1993. Notable among Potok's nonfiction writings is *Wanderings: Chaim Potok's History of the Jews* (1978), in which the author combines impressive scholarship with dramatic narrative.

Pottle, Frederick Albert (b. Aug. 3, 1897, Lovell, Maine, U.S.—d. May 16, 1987, New Haven, Conn.) American scholar who became the foremost authority on the 18th-century British biographer James Boswell.

Pottle graduated from Colby College, Waterville, Maine. in 1917 He earned a Ph.D. from Yale University and taught there until his retirement in 1966. Almost all of Pottle's scholarly career was devoted to the editing and publication of Boswell's journals and letters, 13,000 pages of which were purchased by Yale in 1949. The publication of these materials under Pottle's guidance began in 1950 with *Boswell's London Journal, 1762–1763* and continued thereafter, with plans for a total of 30 to 35 volumes. Thirteen such volumes were published under Pottle's editorship. Among his other works are *James Boswell: The Earlier Years, 1740–1769* (1966); reissued 1985).

Pound, Ezra (Loomis) (b. Oct. 30, 1885, Hailey, Idaho, U.S.—d. Nov. 1, 1972, Venice, Italy) American-born poet and critic, often called the "poet's poet" because of his profound influence on 20th-century writing in English.

Ezra Pound

Pound graduated from Hamilton College, Clinton, N.Y., in 1905 and the following year received an M.A. degree from the University of Pennsylvania. After teaching briefly at a college in Indiana, he sailed for Europe. In Venice he published, at his own expense, his first book of poems, *A lume spento* (1908). He then went to England, where he published several books of poems, including *Personae* (1909). In 1912 Pound became European correspondent for *Poetry* magazine; he dwas soon a dominant figure in Anglo-American verse. He also became involved with IMAGISM, editing the first Imagist anthology, *Des Imagistes*, in 1914.

After World War I Pound published two of his most important poetical works, "Homage to Sextus Propertius," in the book *Quia Pauper Amavi* (1919), and HUGH SELWYN MAUBERLEY (1920), and he then moved to Europe. He lived for four years in Paris before moving to Rapallo, Italy, which was to be his home for the next 20 years. At about this time he began publishing volumes of THE CANTOS, a series of poems he was to continue to work on throughout his life, and his compendium volume PERSONAE (1926). He also developed interests outside of literature; his investigations in the areas of culture and history led to his brilliant but fragmentary prose work GUIDE TO KULCHUR (1938). Following the worldwide depression of the 1930s, he turned more and more to history, especially economic history. He became obsessed with monetary reform, involved himself in politics, and declared his admiration for the Italian dictator Benito Mussolini.

Between 1941 and 1943, after Italy and the United States were at war, he made several hundred broadcasts over Rome Radio, often openly condemning the U.S. war effort. He was arrested by U.S. forces in 1945 and spent six months in a prison camp near Pisa. Despite harsh conditions there, he wrote *The Pisan Cantos* (1948), the most moving section of his long poem-in-progress.

Returned to the United States to face trial for treason, he was pronounced "insane and mentally unfit for trial" by a panel of doctors and spent 12 years (1946–58) in Saint Elizabeth's Hospital for the criminally insane in Washington, D.C. After he was released, he returned to Italy, where he spent the rest of his life.

Pratt, E.J., *in full* Edwin John (b. Feb. 4, 1883, Western Bay, Nfd., Can.—d. April 26, 1964, Toronto, Ont.) The leading Canadian poet of his time.

Pratt was trained for the ministry as a youth and taught and preached before enrolling at Victoria College of the University of Toronto, where he went on to teach until his retirement in 1953. His earliest books of poetry were *Rachel* (privately printed 1917), *Newfoundland Verse* (1923), *The Witches' Brew* (1925), and *The Titans* (1926). The latter collection contains "The Cachalot," an account of a whale hunt and one of Pratt's most brilliant and widely read poems.

Pratt reached the pinnacle of his poetic career in *Brébeuf and His Brethren* (1940), a chronicle of the martyrdom of Jesuit missionaries. Later works include *Dunkirk* (1941), *Still Life and Other Verse* (1943), *Collected Poems* (1944), *They Are Returning* (1945), *Behind the Log* (1947), and *Towards the Last Spike* (1952). *E.J. Pratt: Complete Poems* was published in 1989.

Price, Reynolds, *in full* Edward Reynolds Price (b. Feb. 1, 1933, Macon, N.C., U.S.) American writer whose stories are set in his home state of North Carolina.

Price attended Duke University in Durham, N.C., and Merton College, Oxford, before he began his long teaching career at Duke. His first novel, *A Long and Happy Life* (1961), introduced his memorable young heroine, the naive, spirited Rosacoke Mustian. Rosacoke also appears in Price's short-story collection *The Names and Faces of Heroes* (1963), and in the novel *A Generous Man* (1966) her brother Milo experiences his sexual awakening. *Good Hearts* (1988) resumes the story of Rosacoke in her middle age. while searching the backwoods for a retarded brother, a dog, and an escaped python. Price's later novels include *Love and Work* (1968), *The Surface of the Earth* (1975), *The Source of Light* (1981), *Kate Vaiden* (1986), *The Tongues of Angels* (1990), and *Blue Calhoun* (1992). He also wrote poetry, plays, two books of memoirs, translations from the Bible, and essays. His

Collected Stories appeared in 1993 and the autobiographical *A Whole New Life* in 1994.

Prokosch, Frederic (b. May 17, 1908, Madison, Wis., U.S.—d. June 6, 1989, Plan-de-Grasse, Fr.) American writer who became famous for his early novels and whose literary stature subsequently rose as his fame declined.

By the age of 18 Prokosch he had received a master's degree from Haverford College (Pa.); he received a Ph.D. from Yale and a second M.A. from the University of Cambridge. Prokosch's first novel, *The Asiatics* (1935), was the picaresque story of a young American who travels from Beirut, Lebanon, across vivid Asian landscapes to China, encountering a variety of distinctive individuals along the way. His other novels of the 1930s, especially the travel adventure entitled *The Seven Who Fled* (1937) and *Night of the Poor* (1939), were also well received. Meanwhile, with his own press he published many of his own poems. His fourth novel, *The Skies of Europe* (1941), includes a portrait of Adolf Hitler as a failed artist.

During World War II Prokosch was cultural attaché of the American legation in Sweden, and he remained in Europe after the war. There he wrote several more novels, including two additional travel adventures, *Storm and Echo* (1948) and *Nine Days to Mukalla* (1953), and *The Missolonghi Manuscript* (1968), a fictional biography of Lord Byron. In addition to publishing four volumes of original poems, he also translated poetry of Euripides, Louise Labé, and Friedrich Hölderlin. His final work, *Voices* (1983), is a memoir of his encounters with leading 20th-century literary figures.

Proulx, E. Annie, *in full* Edna (b. Aug. 22, 1935, Norwich, Conn., U.S.) American writer whose darkly comic yet sad fiction was peopled with quirky, memorable individuals and unconventional families.

After publication of her first short-story collection, *Heart Songs and Other Stories* (1988), Proulx turned to writing novels, which better accommodated her dense plots and complex characterizations. *Postcards* (1992), her first novel, used the device of picture postcards mailed from the road over 40 years' time to illustrate changes in American life.

In *The Shipping News* (1993), the protagonist Quoyle and his dysfunctional family of two young daughters and a sensible old aunt leave the United States and settle in Newfoundland after the accidental death of his unfaithful wife. *The Shipping News* was awarded both the Pulitzer Prize and the National Book Award.

Purdy, Al, *in full* Alfred Wellington Purdy (b. Dec. 30, 1918, Wooler, Ont., Can.) Canadian poet whose erudite, colloquial verse, often dealt with the transitory nature of human life.

Purdy's early poetry, collected in *The Enchanted Echo* (1944), *Pressed on Sand* (1955), and *Emu, Remember!* (1956), was conventional and sentimental, but his maturation as a poet was evident in *The Crafte So Longe to Lerne* (1959), *Poems for All the Annettes* (1962), *The Blur in Between* (1962), and *The Cariboo Horses* (1965), a collection of allusive and energetic verse.

The influence of his extensive travels is reflected in many of the poems in the collections *North of Summer* (1967), *Wild Grape Wine* (1968), *Sex and Death* (1973), and *Birdwatching at the Equator* (1982). Poems about his native Ontario are featured in the collections *In Search of Owen Roblin* (1974), *Being Alive* (1978), and *Morning and It's Summer* (1983). His other books of poetry include *Hiroshima Poems* (1972), *Piling Blood* (1984), and *The Woman on the Shore* (1990). In 1990 he published his first novel, *A Splinter in the Heart*.

Purdy, James (b. July 17, 1923, Ohio, U.S.) American novelist and short-story writer whose works explore the American way of life and present a vision of human alienation, indifference, and cruelty.

Purdy's first two works—*Don't Call Me by My Right Name and Other Stories* (1956) and the novella *63: Dream Palace* (1956)—were initially rejected for publication and were privately printed, but later met with critical acclaim.

Purdy's fiction examines the relationships between individuals and the effects of family life. *Malcolm* (1959) is about a 15-year-old boy in a fruitless search for his identity. In *The Nephew* (1960) and *Cabot Wright Begins* (1964), Purdy further develops the bleak worldview that he first propounded in *Malcolm*. In the trilogy *Sleepers in Moon-Crowned Valleys*—consisting of *Jeremy's Vision* (1970), *The House of the Solitary Maggot* (1974), and *Mourners Below* (1981)—he explores small-town American life and destructive family relationships. Purdy also wrote the novels *I Am Elijah Thrush* (1972), *In a Shallow Grave* (1975), and *Candles of Your Eyes* (1986) and several collections of stories, plays, and poems.

Putnam, Samuel (Whitehall) (b. Oct. 10, 1892, Rossville, Ill., U.S.—d. Jan. 15, 1950, Lambertville, N.J.) American editor, publisher, and author best known for his translations of works by authors in Romance languages.

After incomplete studies at the University of Chicago, Putnam worked for various Chicago newspapers and became a literary and art critic for the Chicago *Evening Post* (1920–26). Moving to Europe in 1927, he financed his ventures as an editor and publisher by translating founded and edited the critical magazine *The New Review* (1931–32) and translated numerous works by French and Italian writers.

Returning to the United States in 1933, Putnam contributed regularly to such left-wing magazines as *Partisan Review*, the *New Masses*, and *The Daily Worker* until the mid-1940s, when his interests shifted to Latin-American and Spanish literature. His authoritative translation of Euclides da Cunha's Brazilian prose epic *Os sertões* appeared in 1944 under the title *Rebellion in the Backlands*, and in 1949 his translation of Miguel Cervantes' *Don Quixote*, on which he had spent 17 years, appeared to high praise. Putnam's survey of the history of Brazilian literature, entitled *Marvelous Journey*, was published in 1948. *Paris Was Our Mistress* (1947) depicts the American expatriate community in Paris in the during the late 1920s and early '30s.

Pyle, Howard (b. March 5, 1853, Wilmington, Del., U.S.—d. Nov. 9, 1911, Florence, Italy) American illustrator, painter, and author who is best known for his children's books.

Pyle's magazine and book illustrations are among the finest of the turn-of-the-century period in the Art Nouveau style. Many of his children's stories, illustrated by the author with vividness and historical accuracy, have become classics—most notably *The Merry Adventures of Robin Hood* (1883); *Otto of the Silver Hand* (1888); *Jack Ballister's Fortunes* (1895); and his own folktales, *Pepper & Salt* (1886), *The Wonder Clock* (1888), and *The Garden Behind the Moon* (1895).

Pynchon, Thomas (b. May 8, 1937, Glen Cove, Long Island, N.Y., U.S.) American novelist and short-story writer whose works combine black humor and fantasy to depict human alienation in the chaos of modern society.

Pynchon's first novel, V (1963), is a cynically absurd tale of a middle-aged Englishman's search for "V," an elusive, supernatural adventuress. In his next book, *The Crying of Lot 49* (1966), Pynchon described a woman's strange quest to discover the mysterious, conspiratorial Tristero System in a futuristic world of closed societies. Pynchon's masterpiece, GRAVITY'S RAINBOW (1973), another novel based on the idea of conspiracy, is filled with descriptions of paranoid fantasies, grotesque imagery, and esoteric mathematical language. Pynchon's next novel, *Vineland*, was not published until 1990.

Of his few short stories, most notable are "Entropy" (1960), a neatly structured tale in which Pynchon first used extensive technical language and scientific metaphors, and "The Secret Integration" (1964); collected in *Slow Learner*, 1984), which explores small-town bigotry and racism.

Queen, Ellery, *pseudonym of* Frederic Dannay and Manfred B. Lee, *original names, respectively*, Daniel Nathan and Manford Lepofsky (respectively b. Oct. 20, 1905, Brooklyn, N.Y., U.S.—d. Sept. 3, 1982, White Plains, N.Y.; b. Jan. 11, 1905, Brooklyn, N.Y.—d. April 3, 1971, near Waterbury, Conn.) American cousins who were coauthors of a series of more than 35 detective novels featuring a character named Ellery Queen.

Dannay and Lee first collaborated on an impulsive entry for a detective-story contest; the success of the result, *The Roman Hat Mystery* (1929), started Ellery Queen on his career. They took turns creating plots and writing stories about the sleuth Queen, whose adventures have been adapted for radio, television, and film. The pair also used the pseudonym Barnaby Ross when writing about their second detective creation, Drury Lane.

Other ventures of Dannay and Lee also cofounded *Ellery Queen's Mystery Magazine* in 1941; edited numerous anthologies, including *101 Years' Entertainment: Great Detective Stories, 1841–1941* (1945); and cofounded Mystery Writers of America.

Rabe, David (William) (b. March 10, 1940, Dubuque, Iowa, U.S.) American playwright whose experiences in a hospital-support unit in Vietnam were the basis for several acclaimed dramas. His work is known for its use of grotesque humor, satire, and surreal fantasy.

Rabe was educated at Loras College, Dubuque, and Villanova University, Pa. His plays about war include *The Basic Training of Pavlo Hummel* (1969), which depicts the ruthlessness of the Viet Cong and the brutalization of American troops; and shows the effects of the war on combatants and noncombatants alike. In *Sticks and Bones* (1972), in which a blinded, distraught veteran returns to his middle-American family; and *Streamers* (1975), which concerns violent racial and sexual tensions and prejudices in an army camp in Virginia. Other plays include *The Orphan* (1975), a reworking of the *Orestia*; *In the Boom Boom Room* (1975); *Hurlyburly* (1985) and *Those the River Keeps* (1991), a drama and its prequel about disillusionment in Hollywood; and *Recital of the Dog* (1993).

Raddall, Thomas Head (b. Nov. 13, 1903, Hythe, Kent, Eng.—d. April 1, 1994, Liverpool, N.S., Can.) English-Canadian novelist who accurately depicted the history, manners, and idiom of Nova Scotians.

Raddall immigrated with his parents to Nova Scotia in 1913. His first volume of short stories, *The Pied Piper of Dipper Creek* (1939), was followed by the novel *His Majesty's Yankees* (1942), set in Nova Scotia during the American Revolution. He also wrote several other carefully researched historical romances, including *Pride's Fancy* (1946), *The Governor's Lady* (1960), and *Hangman's Beach* (1966). In addition to historical novels he wrote *The Nymph and the Lamp* (1950), a story of contemporary life at a Canadian wireless station; *Halifax, Warden of the North* (1948), a history of Halifax; and several collections of short stories, including *At the Tide's Turn* (1959) and *The Dreamers* (1986). His autobiography, *In My Time*, appeared in 1976.

Rahv, Philip (b. March 10, 1908, Kupin, Ukraine, Russian Empire—d. Dec. 22, 1973, Cambridge, Mass., U.S.) Ukrainian-born American critic who was cofounder with William Phillips of *Partisan Review*, a journal of literature and social thought.

Rahv immigrated to the United States in 1922 and contributed to *The New Masses, The Nation, The New Republic*, and *The New Leader*. He wrote *Fourteen Essays on Literary Themes* (1949); enlarged, 1957). He also edited many books, including *The Partisan Reader* (1946, with Phillips), *The Discovery of Europe: The Story of the American Experience in the Old World* (1947), *Literature in America* (1958), *Modern Occasions* (1966), and collections of short novels by Henry James, Leo Tolstoy, and other writers.

Rand, Ayn, *original name* Alice *or* Alissa Rosenbaum (b. Feb. 2, 1905, St. Petersburg, Russia—d. March 6, 1982, New York, N.Y., U.S.) Russian-born American writer who, in novels noted for their commercial success, presented her philosophy of objectivism, which held that all real achievement is the product of individual ability and effort, that laissez-faire capitalism is most congenial to the exercise of talent, and that selfishness is a virtue, altruism a vice. Her reversal of the traditional Judeo-Christian ethic won her a cult of followers.

After graduating from the University of Petrograd in 1924, Rand immigrated to the United States in 1926 and worked as a screenwriter in Hollywood. THE FOUNTAINHEAD (1943), her first best-selling novel, depicts a highly romanticized architect-hero, a superior individual whose egoism and genius prevail over timid traditionalism and social conformism. The allegorical ATLAS SHRUGGED (1957), another best-seller, combines science fiction and a political message. Rand also wrote a number of nonfiction works expounding her beliefs, including *For the New Intellectual: The Philosophy of Ayn Rand* (1961), and she edited two journals propounding her ideas, *The Objectivist* (1962–71) and *The Ayn Rand Letter* (1971–76).

Ransom, John Crowe (b. April 30, 1888, Pulaski, Tenn., U.S.—d. July 4, 1974, Gambier, Ohio) American poet and critic, leading theorist of the Southern literary renaissance that began after World War I. Ransom's *The New Criticism* (1941) provided the name for the influential mid-20th-century school of criticism (*see* NEW CRITICISM).

Ransom was educated at Vanderbilt University, Nashville, Tenn., and from 1914 to 1937 he taught English there. At Vanderbilt he also was the leader of the Fugitives, a group of poets who published the influential literary magazine *The Fugitive* (1922–25) and shared a belief in the South and its regional traditions. He was among those Fugitives who became known as the Agrarians. Their *I'll Take My Stand* (1930) criticized the idea that industrialization was the answer to the needs of the South.

Ransom taught from 1937 until his retirement in 1958 at Kenyon College, Gambier, Ohio, where he founded and edited (1939–59) the literary magazine *The Kenyon Review*. Ransom's literary studies include *God Without Thunder* (1930); *The World's Body* (1938), in which he takes the position that poetry and science furnish different but equally valid knowledge about the world; *Poems and Essays* (1955); and *Beating the Bushes: Selected Essays, 1941–1970* (1972). Ransom's poetry is collected in *Chills and Fever* (1924) and *Two Gentlemen in Bonds* (1927).

Rawlings, Marjorie Kinnan (b. Aug. 8, 1896, Washington, D.C., U.S.—d. Dec. 14, 1953, St. Augustine, Fla.) American short-story writer and novelist who founded a regional literature of backwoods Florida.

After graduating from the University of Wisconsin in 1918, Rawlings worked as a journalist for 10 years, meanwhile trying, unsuccessfully, to write stories that would sell. While visiting Florida in 1926, she was enchanted by the landscape, and in 1928 she moved to Cross Creek, Hawthorn, Fla., where she devoted herself to writing fiction. She finally succeeded with her short story "Gal Young Un." Her first novel was *South Moon Under* (1933), followed by *Golden Apples* (1935) and the book for which she is best known, THE YEARLING (1938), which won the Pulitzer Prize for fiction in 1939.

Rawlings took her material from the people and land around her, and her books are less fiction than vivid factual reporting. Rawlings' books have been widely acclaimed for their magical description of the landscape, a quality that is evident in the minor classic *The Yearling*.

Other works include *Cross Creek* (1942), a mystical, autobiographical book describing her discovery of her Florida home, and *The Sojourner* (1953).

Read, Opie (Percival) (b. Dec. 22, 1852, Nashville, Tenn., U.S.—d. Nov. 2, 1939, Chicago, Ill.) American journalist, humorist, novelist, and lecturer. Read specialized in the homespun humor of life in Kentucky, Tennessee, and Arkansas.

Inspired by Benjamin Franklin's autobiography, Read became a printer, reporter, and editor. He later edited the Little Rock, Ark., *Gazette* (1878–81) and the *Arkansas Traveler* (1882), a weekly humor and literary journal. His books include *Len Gansett* (1888), a tale of the South; *Jucklins* (1895); *My Young Masters* (1896), about the American Civil War; and many others. His autobiography, *I Remember*, was published in 1930.

Opie Read

Reaney, James Crerar (b. Sept. 1, 1926, near Stratford, Ont., Can.) Canadian poet and playwright whose works, dealing with Ontario small-town life, transcend their manifest content to move into areas of symbol and dream.

Reaney graduated from the University of Toronto, in 1960 founding *Alphabet*, a literary magazine, and becoming professor of English at the University of Western Ontario. His works include *The Red Heart* (1949), lyric poems; *A Suit of Nettles* (1958), 12 pastoral eclogues; *The Killdeer, and Other Plays* (1962), verse plays; *The Dance of Death at London, Ontario* (1963), a poetic satire of that town; and *Poems* (1972). *Apple Butter and Other Plays* (1973) is a collection of plays for children. He later wrote *Fourteen Barrels from Sea to Sea* (1977), a commentary on Canadian theatrical life in the form of a travel diary.

Rechy, John (Francisco) (b. March 10, 1934, El Paso, Tex., U.S.) American novelist whose semiautobiographical works explore the worlds of sexual and social outsiders and occasionally draw on his Mexican-American heritage.

A graduate of Texas Western College, Rechy studied also at the New School for Social Research in New York. He taught creative writing at Occidental College, the University of Southern California, and the University of California at Los Angeles.

In *City of Night* (1963), his first and best-received novel, a young man working as a homosexual hustler makes his way to New Orleans for Mardi Gras. Rechy followed with *Numbers* (1967) and *This Day's Death* (1969), both of which deal with obsession and identity. *The Vampires* (1971) concerns the nature of evil, and *The Fourth Angel* (1972) records the adventures of four thrill-seeking adolescents. The nonfictional *The Sexual Outlaw* (1977) is Rechy's "prose documentary" of three days and nights in the sexual underground. His other novels include *Rushes* (1979), *Bodies and Souls* (1983), and *Marilyn's Daughter* (1988). In *The Miraculous Day of Amalia Gómez* (1991), set in the barrio of Los Angeles, Rechy makes use of the techniques of magic realism.

Reed, Ishmael (Scott) (b. Feb. 22, 1938, Chattanooga, Tenn., U.S.) African-American author of poetry, essays, and satiric novels.

Reed grew up in Buffalo, N.Y., and studied at the University of Buffalo. He moved to New York City, where he cofounded the *East Village Other* (1965), an underground newspaper that achieved a national reputation. His first novel, *The Free-Lance Pallbearers*, was published in 1967.

Reed's novels are marked by surrealism, satire, and political and racial commentary. They depict human history as a cycle of battles between oppressed people and their oppressors; the characters and actions are an antic mixture of inverted stereotypes, revisionist history, and prophecy. *Pallbearers* was followed by *Yellow Back Radio Broke-Down* (1969), *Mumbo Jumbo* (1972), *The Last Days of Louisiana Red* (1974), *Flight to Canada* (1976), *The Terrible Twos* (1982), its sequel *The Terrible Threes* (1989), and *Japanese By Spring* (1993). He also wrote several volumes of poetry and collections of essays.

Reed, John (b. Oct. 22, 1887, Portland, Ore., U.S.—d. Oct. 19, 1920, Moscow, Russian S.F.S.R., U.S.S.R.) American poet-adventurer whose short life as a revolutionary writer and activist made him the hero of a generation of radical intellectuals.

Reed, a member of a wealthy Portland family, graduated from Harvard, in 1910 and in 1913 he began writing for a socialist newspaper, *The Masses*. In 1914 he covered the revolutionary fighting in Mexico and recorded his impressions in *Insurgent Mexico* (1914). Frequently arrested for organizing and defending strikes, he rapidly became established as a radical leader and helped form the Communist Party in the United States.

John Reed

Reed covered World War I for *Metropolitan* magazine; out of this experience came *The War in Eastern Europe* (1916). He became a close friend of Vladimir Lenin and was an eyewitness to the 1917 Bolshevik revolution in Russia, recording this event in his best-known book, *Ten Days That Shook the World* (1919).

When the U.S. Communist Party and the Communist Labor Party split in 1919, Reed became the leader of the latter. Indicted for treason, he escaped to the Soviet Union and died of typhus; he was subsequently buried with other Bolshevik heroes beside the Kremlin wall.

Reese, Lizette Woodworth (b. Jan. 9, 1856, Baltimore county, Md., U.S.— d. Dec. 17, 1935, Baltimore, Md.) American poet whose work draws on the images of her rural childhood.

Reese's lyric talent was strikingly evident in her first book, *A Branch of May* (1887); it was followed by *A Handful of Lavendar* (1891). Her fresh images, condensed form, and sincerity of emotion broke with conventional sentimentality and foreshadowed 20th-century lyricism. Her best-known poem is the sonnet "Tears," published in 1899 in *Scribner's* magazine and widely anthologized. *The Selected Poems* (1926) was followed by several other volumes of verse and by two books of reminiscences, *A Victorian Village* (1929) and *The York Road* (1931), as well as a posthumous novel, *Worleys* (1936).

Rexroth, Kenneth (b. Dec. 22, 1905, South Bend, Ind., U.S.—d. June 6, 1982, Santa Barbara, Calif.) American painter, essayist, poet, and translator, an early champion of the Beat movement.

Rexroth's early poetry was experimental, influenced by Surrealism; his later work was praised for its tight form and its wit and humanistic passion. His *Complete Collected Shorter Poems* appeared in 1967 and *Complete Collected Longer Poems* in 1968. *New Poems* was published in 1974. His essays include *Bird in the Bush* (1959), *Assays* (1962), *The Alternative Society* (1970), and *With Eye and Ear* (1970). He wrote the literary history entitled *American Poetry in the Twentieth Century* (1971) and was also a prolific translator of Japanese, Chinese, Greek, Latin, and Spanish poetry. *An Autobiographical Novel* was published in 1966.

Rice, Alice Hegan, *in full* Alice Caldwell Hegan Rice (b. Jan. 11, 1870, Shelbyville, Ky., U.S.—d. Feb. 10, 1942, Louisville) American novelist and short-story writer most widely known for her 1901 best-seller *Mrs. Wiggs of the Cabbage Patch*. At the age of 16 Rice worked at a mission Sunday school in a Louisville slum known as the Cabbage Patch. With Louise Marshall, she later founded (1910) the Cabbage Patch Settlement House in Louisville. In addition to *Mrs. Wiggs of the Cabbage Patch*, Rice wrote many other novels noted for pathos and humor. Her autobiography, *The Inky Way*, appeared in 1940.

Elmer Rice

Rice, Elmer, *original surname* Reizenstein (b. Sept. 28, 1892, New York, N.Y., U.S.—d. May 8, 1967, Southampton, Hampshire, Eng.) American playwright, director, and novelist noted for his innovative and polemical plays.

Rice's first work, the melodramatic *On Trial* (1914), was the first play to employ on stage the motion-picture technique of flashbacks, in this case to present the recollections of witnesses at a trial. In *The Adding Machine* (1923), Rice adapted techniques from German Expressionist theater. His most important play, STREET SCENE (1929), won a Pulitzer Prize and was adapted into a highly popular musical. *Counsellor-at-Law* (1931) was a rather critical look at the legal profession. In *We, the People* (1933), *Judgment Day* (1934), and several other polemical plays of the 1930s, Rice treated the evils of Nazism, the poverty of the Great Depression, and racism. Rice also wrote several novels and an autobiography, entitled *Minority Report* (1963).

Adrienne Rich

Rich, Adrienne (Cecile) (b. May 16, 1929, Baltimore, Md., U.S.) American poet, scholar, teacher, and critic whose many volumes of poetry trace a stylistic transformation from formal, well-crafted but imitative poetry to a more personal and powerful style.

Rich attended Radcliffe College, and before her graduation her poetry was chosen by W.H. Auden for publication in the Yale Younger Poets series. The resulting volume, *A Change of World* (1951), reflected her mastery of the formal elements of poetry. *The Diamond Cutters and Other Poems* (1955) was followed by *Snapshots of a Daughter-in-Law* (1963), which exhibited a movement away from the restrained and formal to a looser, more personal form. Her fourth collection, *Necessities of Life* (1966), was written almost entirely in free verse. Throughout the 1960s and '70s her increasing commitment to the women's movement and to a lesbian/feminist aesthetic politicized much of her poetry. Among her later volumes of verse are *Leaflets* (1969), *Diving into the Wreck* (1973), *The Dream of a Common Language* (1978), *A Wild Patience Has Taken Me This Far* (1981), and *An Atlas of the Difficult World* (1991). Her Collected Early Poems 1950–1970 was published in 1993. Rich also wrote a number of books of criticism, including *Of Woman Born: Motherhood as Experience and Institution* (1976), *On Lies, Secrets, and Silence* (1979), and *What Is Found There: Notebooks on Poetry and Politics* (1993).

Richardson, John (b. Oct. 4, 1796, probably Fort George, Upper Canada [now Niagara-on-the-Lake, Ont., Can.]—d. May 12, 1852, New York, N.Y., U.S.) Canadian writer of historical and autobiographical romantic novels.

Richardson was a British volunteer in the War of 1812 and a British officer in England, Barbados, and Spain. He returned to Canada in 1838 and remained there in a variety of positions until 1849, when he moved to New York.

Richardson's first publication was the "metrical romance" *Tecumseh; or, The Warrior of the West* (1828). He wrote his first novel, *Écarté; or, The Salons of Paris*, 3 vol. (1829), in a realistic but somewhat sensational style. Its sequel was *Frascati's; or, Scenes in Paris* (1830). His third novel, *Wacousta; or, The Prophecy*, 2 vol. (1832), a gothic story about Pontiac's War (the Indian uprising of 1763–64), brought him popular acclaim. Its sequel, *The Canadian Brothers; or, The Prophecy Fulfilled*, 2 vol. (1840); U.S. edition, *Matilda Montgomerie*), was less successful. Among his significant works of nonfiction are *Personal Memoirs of Major Richardson* (1838), *War of 1812* (1842), and *Eight Years in Canada* (1847). He also wrote many short stories. His later novels include *The Monk Knight of St. John; A Tale of the Crusades* (1850), *Hardscrabble; or, The Fall of Chicago* (1851), *Wau-nangee; or, The Massacre at Chicago* (1852), and *Westbrook, the Outlaw* (1853).

Richler, Mordecai (b. Jan. 27, 1931, Montreal, Can.) Prominent Canadian novelist whose incisive and penetrating works explore fundamental human dilemmas and values.

In 1951–52 Richler lived in Paris, where he was influenced and stimulated by existentialist authors. Returning to Canada (1952), Richler, he published the novel *The Acrobats* (1954), about a young Canadian painter in Spain with a group of disillusioned expatriates and revolutionaries. Both *Son of a Smaller Hero* (1955) and *A Choice of Enemies* (1957) deal with angry, confused modern heroes. *The Apprenticeship of Duddy Kravitz* (1959) is a bawdy account of a Jewish boy in Montreal and his transformation into a ruthless and amoral businessman. Amusing descriptions of the leaders of the communications industries are the subject of *The Incomparable Atuk* (1963). *Cocksure* (1968) and *St. Urbain's Horseman* (1971) both examine North Americans in England. concerns a Canadian director's trial for sodomy and assault in London. Other works include a collection of humorous essays, *Notes on an Endangered Species and Others* (1974); a children's book, *Jacob Two-Two Meets the Hooded Fang* (1975); and two novels, *Joshua Then and Now* (1980) and *Solomon Gursky Was Here* (1989).

Richter, Conrad (Michael) (b. Oct. 13, 1890, Pine Grove, Pa., U.S.—d. Oct. 30, 1968, Pottsville, Pa.) American short-story writer and novelist known for his lyrical fiction about early America.

Richter became the editor of the Patton (Pa.) *Courier* at age 19. He then worked as a reporter and founded a juvenile magazine that he liquidated before moving to New Mexico in 1928. In an era when many American writers steeped themselves in European culture, Richter was fascinated with American history, and he spent years researching frontier life. He is best known for THE SEA OF GRASS (1936) and his trilogy of pioneer life, *The Trees* (1940), *The Fields* (1946), and THE TOWN (1950), the final volume of which won the Pulitzer Prize for fiction in 1951. Richter's stories are usually told through a contemporary narrator, allowing the reader to see the present and past as a continuum. An autobiographical novel, *The Waters of Kronos* (1960), won the National Book Award in 1961.

Riding, Laura, *original surname* Reichenthal, *married name* Jackson, *pseudonyms* Barbara Rich, Madeleine Vara, *and* Laura Riding Gottschalk (b. Jan. 16, 1901, New York, N.Y., U.S.—d. Sept. 2, 1991, Sebastian, Fla.) American poet, critic, and prose writer who was influential among the literary avant-garde during the 1920s and '30s.

Riding attended Cornell University, Ithaca, N.Y. Early on she came to be associated with the Fugitives, a prominent group of Southern writers. Riding lived abroad from 1926 to 1939, much of the time with the poet and critic Robert Graves; together they established the Seizin Press (1927–38) and published the journal *Epilogue* (1935–38). Their book *A Survey of Modernist Poetry* (1927, reprinted 1977) developed ideas of close textual analysis that influenced New Criticism.

In 1941 Riding married the critic Schuyler B. Jackson, and until his death in 1968 they worked together on lexicographical studies. She completed their "Rational Meaning: A New Foundation for the Definition of Words" in 1974, but it was not published. During this time Riding ceased to write poetry, which she renounced as being "inadequate," but her other writings continued to interest a select audience and her late philosophical work *The Telling* (1972) was highly esteemed among a small readership. Her *Collected Poems*, which was originally published in 1938, was issued in a revised edition in 1980, and *First Awakenings: The Early Poems* was published in 1992.

Riley, James Whitcomb (b. Oct. 7, 1849, Greenfield, Ind., U.S.—d. July 22, 1916, Indianapolis, Ind.) Poet remembered for nostalgic dialect verse and often called "the poet of the common people."

Riley's reputation was first gained by a series of poems in Hoosier dialect ostensibly written by a farmer (Benj. F. Johnson, of Boone) and contributed to the *Indianapolis Daily Journal*. They were later published as *The Old Swimmin' Hole and 'Leven More Poems* (1883). Riley was briefly local editor of the *Anderson* (Ind.) *Democrat*.

James Whitcomb Riley

Among Riley's numerous volumes of verse are *Pipes o' Pan at Zekesbury* (1888), *Old-Fashioned Roses* (1888), *The Flying Islands of the Night* (1891), *A Child-World* (1896), and *Home Folks* (1900). His best-known poems include "When the Frost Is on the Punkin," LITTLE ORPHANT ANNIE, "The Raggedy Man," and "An Old Sweetheart of Mine." His poems were collected in *Complete Works*, 10 vol. (1916).

Rinehart, Mary Roberts, *original surname* Roberts (b. Aug. 12, 1876, Pittsburgh, Pa., U.S.—d. Sept. 22, 1958, New York, N.Y.) American novelist and playwright best known for her mystery stories.

Rinehart's *The Man in Lower Ten*, serialized in 1907, was followed by her first book, *The Circular Staircase* (1908). In addition to mysteries, she wrote a long series of comic tales about a dauntless spinster named Tish and her adventures with two friends; these appeared in *The Saturday Evening Post* through many years. Of her plays, mostly written in collaboration with Avery Hopwood, the most successful was *The Bat* (1920). She also wrote romances and several books of travel, some of which reflected her experiences as a war correspondent during World War I.

Ripley, George (b. Oct. 3, 1802, Greenfield, Mass., U.S.—d. July 4, 1880, New York, N.Y.) Journalist and reformer who was the leading promoter and director of Brook Farm, the celebrated utopian community at West Roxbury, Mass., and a spokesman for the utopian socialist ideas of the French social reformer Charles Fourier. Later, as literary critic for the *New York Tribune*, he was an arbiter of taste and culture for much of the reading public.

Ripley entered the Unitarian ministry after graduating from Harvard Divinity School in 1826. While pastor of Boston's Purchase Street Church, he was a member of the Transcendental Club and an editor of *The Dial*, the prototypical little magazine. In 1841 Ripley left the pulpit to found the Brook Farm community. Brook Farm closed in 1847, and to pay off the community's debts, Ripley took a job with Horace Greeley's *New York Tribune* as book reviewer, city news writer, and translator of foreign news dispatches. His financial position remained precarious until the publication of *The Cyclopedia* (1862), a widely acclaimed reference book that he coedited.

George Ripley

Robbins, Tom, *in full* Thomas Eugene Robbins (b. July 22, 1936, Blowing Rock, N.C., U.S.) American countercultural novelist noted for his eccentric characters, playful optimism, and self-conscious wordplay.

Robbins served in the U.S. Air Force, hitchhiked across the United States, and worked as a journalist and art critic. His first two novels became popular only when they were released in paperback editions. *Another Roadside Attraction* (1971) is about a native of rural Washington who steals the mummy of Jesus Christ. *Even Cowgirls Get the Blues* (1976; film, 1994) is the story of a female hitchhiker with an enormous thumb who visits a woman's spa in South Dakota. Robbins' later novels include *Still Life with Woodpecker* (1980), *Jitterbug Perfume* (1984), and *Skinny Legs and All* (1990).

Roberts, Charles G.D., *in full* Sir Charles George Douglas Roberts (b. Jan. 10, 1860, Douglas, New Brunswick [Canada]—d. Nov. 26, 1943, Toronto, Ont.) Poet who was the first to express the new national feeling aroused by the Canadian confederation of 1867.

Roberts taught school, edited the influential Toronto magazine *The Week*, and for 10 years was a professor of English at King's College in Windsor, N.S. In 1897 he moved to New York City, where he worked as a journalist, and in 1911 he established residence in London. Returning to Canada 14 years later, Roberts embarked on a cross-Canada lecture tour and later settled in Toronto. He was knighted in 1935.

Roberts published some 12 volumes of verse beginning with *Orion, and Other Poems* (1880). He wrote of nature, love, and nationalism, but his best-remembered poems are simple descriptive lyrics about the scenery and rural life of New Brunswick and Nova Scotia. Outstanding among his poetic works are *In Divers Tones* (1887), *Songs of the Common Day* (1893), *The Vagrant of Time* (1927), and *The Iceberg, and Other Poems* (1934).

Roberts' most famous prose works are short stories in which his intimate knowledge of the woods and their animal inhabitants is displayed—*e.g.*, *Earth's Enigmas* (1896), *The Kindred of the Wild* (1902), *Red Fox* (1905), and *Neighbours Unknown* (1911). His other prose includes the pioneer *History of Canada* (1897) and several novels dealing with the Maritime Provinces.

Roberts, Elizabeth Madox (b. Oct. 30, 1886, Perryville, Ky., U.S.—d. March 13, 1941, Orlando, Fla.) American novelist, poet, and short-story writer noted especially for her vivid, impressionistic depiction of her protagonists' inner life and for her accurate portrayal of life in Kentucky.

Roberts' first novel, *The Time of Man* (1926), concerns a poor white woman living in Kentucky. Its rich texture, which contrasts inner growth with outward hardship, and its account of life in Kentucky brought her international acclaim. *The Great Meadow* (1930), her best-known novel, describes a woman's spiritual return to the wilderness. Her subsequent books generally dealt with similar themes and settings, but her fame declined in the 1930s. In addition to a number of lesser-known novels, Roberts wrote two books of short stories, *The Haunted Mirror* (1932) and *Not By Strange Gods* (1941), and two books of poetry, *Under the Tree* (1922); enlarged 1930) and *Song in the Meadow* (1940).

Roberts, Kenneth (Lewis) (b. Dec. 8, 1885, Kennebunk, Maine, U.S.— d. July 21, 1957, Kennebunkport) American journalist and novelist who wrote fictional reconstructions of the American Revolution.

Roberts was staff correspondent of *The Saturday Evening Post* from 1919 until 1928, when he devoted himself to writing fiction. Believing that the past is only poorly understood through historical accounts, he wrote *Arundel* (1930), a fictional treatment of the Revolutionary War. He is best known for *Northwest Passage* (1937), dealing with the career of the American frontier soldier Major Robert Rogers, and *Rabble in Arms* (1933), a celebration of Revolutionary War heroes who fought the British under conditions of great hardship. *Oliver Wiswell* (1940), another novel of the American Revolution, was written from the Loyalist point of view. Other works include *The Lively Lady* (1931), *Lydia Bailey* (1947), and *Boon Island* (1956). Roberts researched his books carefully and was devoted to arguing over minute points of American history. He considered his home state a last outpost of rugged individualism, and several of his books are set there.

Robinson, Edwin Arlington (b. Dec. 22, 1869, Head Tide, Maine, U.S.— d. April 6, 1935, New York, N.Y.) American poet who is best known for his short dramatic poems concerning the people in a small New England village.

After his family suffered financial reverses, Robinson cut short his attendance at Harvard and went to live in New York City, where he worked as a timekeeper on subway construction. From *The Children of the Night* (1897) to *The Man Against the Sky* (1916), his best poetic form was the dramatic lyric, as exemplified in the title poem of *The Man Against the Sky*. Among his best poems of this period are RICHARD CORY, MINIVER CHEEVY, "For a Dead Lady," "Flammonde," and "Eros Turannos." Robinson's work attracted the attention of President Theodore Roosevelt, who gave him a sinecure at the U.S. Customs House in New York (held from 1905 to 1909).

Edward Arlington Robinson

Merlin (1917) was the first of his long blank-verse narrative poems based on the King Arthur legends, followed by *Lancelot* (1920) and *Tristram* (1927). Robinson's *Collected Poems* appeared in 1921. *The Man Who Died Twice* (1924) and *Amaranth* (1934) are perhaps the most often acclaimed of his later narrative poems; later short poems include MR. FLOOD'S PARTY, "Many Are Called," and "The Sheaves."

Roethke, Theodore (b. May 25, 1908, Saginaw, Mich., U.S.—d. Aug. 1, 1963, Bainbridge Island, Wash.) American poet whose verse is characterized by introspection and intense lyricism.

Roethke was educated at the University of Michigan and Harvard University. He taught at several colleges and universities, notably the University of

Washington. His later career was interrupted by hospitalizations for manic depression.

His first book of poetry, *Open House*, which W.H. Auden called "completely successful," was published in 1941. It was followed by *The Lost Son and Other Poems* (1948) and *Praise to the End!* (1951). *The Waking: Poems 1933–1953* (1953), was awarded a Pulitzer Prize; *Words for the Wind* (1957) won a Bollingen Prize and a National Book Award. Roethke won a second National Book Award for *The Far Field* (1964). His *Collected Poems* were published in 1966. His essays and lectures are collected in his *On the Poet and His Craft* (1965).

Rølvaag, O.E., *in full* Ole Edvart (b. April 22, 1876, Dönna Island, Helgeland, Nor.—d. Nov. 5, 1931, Northfield, Minn., U.S.) Norwegian-American novelist and educator noted for his realistic portrayals of Norwegian settlers on the Dakota prairies and of the clash between transplanted and native cultures in the United States.

Rølvaag immigrated to the United States in 1896 and was naturalized in 1908. Educated at St. Olaf College, Northfield, Minn., and the University of Oslo, Norway, he spent most of his life at St. Olaf as a teacher of Norwegian language and literature and the history of Norwegian immigration. He wrote in Norwegian, the language in which his works were originally published, and worked closely with the translators of the English versions.

Two novels, *I de dage* ("In Those Days," 1924) and *Riket grundlæges* ("The Kingdom Is Founded," 1925), were translated as GIANTS IN THE EARTH (1927). It was his best work, representing the positive aspects of pioneering in the character Per Hansa, the negative aspects in his wife Beret. *Peder Victorious* (1929) and *Their Fathers' God* (1931) continued the story to the second generation.

Rosten, Leo (Calvin), *pseudonym* Leonard Q. Ross (b. April 11, 1908, Łódź [Poland]) Polish-born American author and social scientist best known for his popular books on Yiddish and for his comic novels concerning the immigrant night-school student Hyman Kaplan.

At age three Rosten immigrated with his parents to Chicago. After working as a screenwriter and having a series of wartime government-information jobs, he joined the staff of *Look* magazine in New York in 1949, where he worked until 1971; he also lectured at Columbia University.

In 1937 Rosten (as Leonard Q. Ross) published *The Education of H*Y*M*A*N K*A*P*L*A*N*; the book, based on the author's experiences teaching English to immigrants, is full of puns and malapropisms based on the fractured English of the cherubic, naive Kaplan, for whom the plural of "sandwich" is "delicatessen." It was acclaimed for its high spirits and its comic mastery of Yiddish-inflected English. Two sequels, *The Return of*

*H*Y*M*A*N*   *K*A*P*L*A*N* (1959) and *O   K*A*P*L*A*N! My K*A*P*L*A*N!* (1976), were not as well received.

While at *Look*, Rosten edited a series of articles that formed the basis of *A Guide to the Religions of America* (1955), noted for its readability and scholarly accuracy. *The Story Behind the Painting* (1962), a respected popular art-history book, also grew from a magazine assignment. Rosten enjoyed instant success with *The Joys of Yiddish* (1968), a comic dictionary of Yiddish words and their many nuances, which he expanded in *The Joys of Yinglish* (1989).

Roth, Henry (b. Feb. 8, 1906, Tysmenica, Galicia, Austria-Hungary [now Tismenitsya, Ukraine]—d. Oct. 13, 1995, Albuquerque, N.M., U.S.) American teacher and author whose novel CALL IT SLEEP (1934) is considered one of the neglected masterpieces of American literature of the 1930s.

Roth graduated from the City College of New York. *Call It Sleep* appeared in 1934 to laudatory reviews and sold 4,000 copies before it went out of print and was apparently forgotten. In the late 1950s and '60s, however, Alfred Kazin, Irving Howe, and other American literary figures revived public interest in the book, which came to be recognized as a classic of Jewish-American literature and as an important proletarian novel of the 1930s. Although he attempted to write a second novel shortly after finishing the first and several of his short stories were printed in *The New Yorker*, Roth published no more novels until 1994. He began writing again in the late 1960s, and *Shifting Landscape: A Composite, 1925–87*, a collection of short stories and essays, appeared in 1987. He began a projected six-volume series that returned to the themes of *Call It Sleep*, but only the first three volumes of *Mercy of a Rude Stream—A Star Shines Over Mt. Morris Park* (1994), *A Diving Rock on the Hudson* (1995), and *From Bondage* (1996)—were completed before his death.

Roth, Philip (Milton) (b. March 19, 1933, Newark, N.J., U.S.) American novelist and short-story writer whose works are characterized by an acute ear for dialogue, a concern with Jewish middle-class life, and the painful entanglements of sexual and familial love.

Roth attended the University of Chicago. He first achieved fame with *Goodbye Columbus* (1959), whose title story candidly depicts the boorish materialism of a Jewish middle-class suburban family. Roth's first novel, *Letting Go* (1962), was followed in 1967 by *When She Was Good*, but he did not recapture the success of his first book until PORTNOY'S COMPLAINT (1969). Several minor works, including *The Breast* (1972) and *The Professor of Desire* (1977), were followed by one of Roth's most important novels, *The Ghost Writer* (1979), centering on an aspiring young writer named Nathan Zuckerman. Roth's two subsequent novels, *Zuckerman Unbound* (1981) and

The Anatomy Lesson (1983), trace his writer-protagonist's subsequent life and career. The three novels were republished together with the novella *The Prague Orgy* under the title *Zuckerman Bound* (1985). A fourth novel in the series, *The Counterlife*, was published in 1986. In 1993 Roth published *Operation Shylock*, a book in which a narrator named Philip Roth has several adventures, including meeting his double (who also calls himself Philip Roth) in Jerusalem. In 1995 Roth's *Sabbath Theater* won the National Book Award.

Rowson, Susanna, *original surname* Haswell (b. *c.* 1762, Portsmouth, Hampshire, Eng.—d. March 2, 1824, Boston, Mass., U.S.) English-born American actress, educator, and author of the first American best-seller, *Charlotte Temple*. The novel, a conventional, sentimental story of seduction and remorse, was immensely popular after its publication in 1791 and went through more than 200 editions.

In 1792 she went on the stage with her husband, William Rowson. They performed in Scotland and in Philadelphia, Baltimore, and Boston. Rowson also wrote numerous plays and musicals, promoting the development of the performing arts in the United States.

Among her other works are novels, including *Rebecca, or the Fille de Chambre* (1792); theatrical works, such as *Slaves in Algiers* (1794); and textbooks, such as *A Spelling Dictionary* (1807) and *Biblical Dialogues Between a Father and His Family* (1822).

Roy, Camille, *in full* Joseph Camille Roy (b. Oct. 22, 1870, Berthier-en-Bas, Que., Can.—d. June 24, 1943, Quebec) Critic and literary historian, noted as an authority on the development of French-Canadian literature.

Ordained a Roman Catholic priest in 1894, Roy received a doctorate from Catholic University in Paris (1900). He taught French literature at Laval University in Quebec and then became a professor of Canadian literature. His many significant studies were based on the premise that the purpose of Canadian literature is to preserve the Christian heritage of 18th-century France while remaining untouched by contemporary French influence. These works include *Nos origines littéraires* (1909); "Our Literary Origins") and the standard text *Manuel d'histoire de la littérature canadienne-française* (1918); 10th edition, 1945; "Handbook of the History of French-Canadian Literature").

Roy, Gabrielle, *married name* Charbotte (b. March 22, 1909, St. Boniface, Man., Can.—d. July 13, 1983, Quebec, Que.) French-Canadian novelist praised for her skill in depicting the hopes and frustrations of the poor.

Roy taught school for a time, studied drama in Europe (1937–39), then returned to Canada and began her writing career. Her studies of poverty-stricken working-class people in cities include *Bonheur d'occasion* (1945); *The Tin Flute*) and *Alexandre Chenevert* (1954); *The Cashier*). Some of her novels, such as *La Petite Poule d'eau* (1950); *Where Nests the Water-Hen*) and *Rue Deschambault* (1955); *Street of Riches*), deal with isolated rural life in Manitoba. She also wrote a book of semiautobiographical stories, *La Route d'Altamont* (1966); *The Road Past Altamont*), and a novel based on her experiences as a schoolteacher, *Ces enfants de ma vie* (1977); *Children of My Heart*).

Rukeyser, Muriel (b. Dec. 15, 1913, New York, N.Y., U.S.—d. Feb. 12, 1980, New York City) American poet and activist best known for her poems concerning social and political issues.

While at college, Rukeyser contributed poems of a personal nature to *Poetry* magazine. Her *Theory of Flight* (1935) won the Yale Series of Younger Poets award. She broadened her experience by active involvement in the issues of the day. She attended the Scottsboro trials (a major civil-rights case) and witnessed the opening events of the Spanish Civil War, and the scope of her poetry widened accordingly. *U.S. 1* (1938) describes the oppressed poor along the industrial Atlantic seaboard. The work includes "The Book of the Dead," which tells of miners dying of silicosis in West Virginia, a piece considered one of Rukeyser's best works. Her use of fragmented, emotional imagery is sometimes thought lavish, but her poetry is praised for its power and acuity. *The Collected Poems of Muriel Rukeyser* was published in 1978. *Out of Silence* (1992) is a selection of Rukeyser's poetry edited by Kate Daniels.

Rukeyser wrote 14 volumes of poetry. In addition to her verse, she wrote a well-received biography of the mathematician and physicist Willard Gibbs, books for juveniles, and criticism. She also translated the poetry of Octavio Paz, Gunnar Ekelöf, and others.

Rule, Jane (b. March 28, 1931, Plainfield, N.J., U.S.) Novelist, essayist, and short-story writer known for her exploration of lesbian themes.

Upon graduation from Mills College, Oakland, Calif., in 1952, Rule studied briefly at University College, London, and Stanford University. She taught in Massachusetts before moving to Vancouver, where she joined the staff of the University of British Columbia. She began to write full-time in 1974.

Rule's characters are usually rewarded for following their hearts and punished for emotional cowardice. *Desert of the Heart* (1964; filmed as *Desert Hearts*, 1984), Rule's first, best-known novel, is considered a classic of lesbian literature; it traces the lives of two women, separated by age and background, who meet at a boardinghouse and fall in love. In contrast, *This Is*

Not for You (1970) is written as an (unmailed) letter to the narrator's best friend, whose love she denies at the cost of her own happiness. *Against the Season* (1971) explores the interwoven lives of several people in a small town. Other novels include *The Young in One Another's Arms* (1977), *Contract with the World* (1980), *Memory Board* (1987), and *After the Fire* (1989).

Rule published three volumes of short stories: *Theme for Diverse Instruments* (1975); *Outlander* (1981), which includes essays; and *Inland Passage and Other Stories* (1985).

In *Lesbian Images* (1975) Rule discussed her own sexuality and the history of lesbianism; the bulk of the book addresses the work of 12 women writers, including Colette, Willa Cather, and Elizabeth Bowen, and the ways in which they projected lesbian experience in their work. Other essays are collected in *A Hot-Eyed Moderate* (1985).

Rumaker, Michael (b. March 5, 1932, Philadelphia, Pa., U.S.) American author whose early fiction reflected the disaffection of the Beat generation.

Rumaker graduated with honors from Black Mountain College in North Carolina. In an unfinished memoir, "Robert Duncan in San Francisco," he described the new vitality the Beat movement brought to all the arts. In 1958 he suffered an emotional breakdown, for which he was hospitalized until 1960. He later attended Columbia University. (1969).

From the late 1950s Rumaker's short stories, such as "The Desert" (1957), were frequently anthologized. His semiautobiographical novel *The Butterfly* (1962) tells of a young man's struggles to gain control of his life following an emotional breakdown. *Exit 3, and Other Stories* (1966); U.S. title, *Gringos and Other Stories*) contains short fictions rife with marginal characters and random violence. *A Day and a Night at the Baths* (1979) and *My First Satyrnalia* (1981) are semiautobiographical accounts of initiation into New York's homosexual community. His later works include *3 × 3* (1989) and *To Kill a Cardinal* (1992).

Runyon, Damon, *in full* Alfred Damon Runyon (b. Oct. 4, 1884, Manhattan, Kan., U.S.—d. Dec. 10, 1946, New York, N.Y.) American journalist and short-story writer, best known for his book *Guys and Dolls*, written in the regional slang that became his trademark.

At age 14 Runyon enlisted in the U.S. Army and was sent to the Philippines in the Spanish-American War (1898). After the war he wrote for western newspapers for 10 years. Although Runyon gained a reputation as a political and feature reporter, his passion for sports was paramount. In 1911 he moved to New York City, where he became a reporter for the *New York American*. He covered the New York baseball clubs for many years, as well as various other sports topics, and along the way he developed his style of focusing on human interest rather than strictly reporting facts. He began writing stories about a racy section of Broadway, and these were collected in *Guys and Dolls* (1931). The book is representative of Runyon's style in its use of an exaggerated version of local idiom to portray a particular class of characters—gamblers, promoters, fight managers, racetrack bookies, and other habitués of the street. The stories were the basis for a successful stage play.

In the 1930s Runyon began writing columns, and his popular feature "As I See It" was syndicated in the Hearst newspapers across the country.

Said, Edward W., *in full* William (b. Nov. 1, 1935, Jerusalem) Palestinian-American literary critic who studied literature in light of social and cultural politics and was an outspoken proponent of Arab issues.

Said attended Princeton University and Harvard University before joining the faculty of Columbia University in 1963. His first book, *Joseph Conrad and the Fiction of Autobiography* (1966), was an expansion of his doctoral thesis. In *Orientalism* (1978), perhaps his best-known work, Said examines Western stereotypes about the Orient, specifically the Islāmic world and argues that Orientalist scholarship is based on Western imperialism. His books about the Middle East include *The Question of Palestine* (1979), *Blaming the Victims: Spurious Scholarship and the Palestinian Question* (1988); coedited with Christopher Hitchens), and *The Politics of Dispossession* (1994). Among his other books are *Beginnings: Intention and Method* (1975), *The World, the Text, and the Critic* (1983), *Nationalism, Colonialism, and Literature: Yeats and Decolonization* (1988), *Musical Elaborations* (1991), and *Culture and Imperialism* (1993).

Salinger, J.D., *in full* Jerome David (b. Jan. 1, 1919, New York, N.Y., U.S.) American writer whose novel THE CATCHER IN THE RYE (1951) won critical acclaim and devoted admirers, especially among the post-World War II generation of college students. His entire corpus of published works consists of one novel and 13 short stories.

Salinger's stories began to appear in periodicals in 1940. He served in the army from 1942 to 1946. Salinger's name and writing style became increasingly associated with *The New Yorker* magazine, which published almost all of his later stories. Some of the best of these made use of his wartime experiences: "For Esmé—With Love and Squalor" (1950) describes a U.S. soldier's poignant encounter with two British children; "A Perfect Day for Bananafish" (1948) concerns the suicide of the sensitive, despairing veteran Seymour Glass.

Major critical and popular recognition came with the publication of *The Catcher in the Rye*. Its humor and colorful language place it in the tradition of Mark Twain's *The Adventures of Huckleberry Finn* and the stories of Ring Lardner, but its hero, like most of Salinger's child characters, views his life with an added dimension of precocious self-consciousness. *Nine Stories* (1953), a selection of Salinger's best work, added to his reputation.

The reclusive habits of Salinger in his later years made his personal life a matter of speculation among devotees, while his small literary output was a subject of controversy among critics. FRANNY AND ZOOEY (1961) brought together two earlier *New Yorker* stories; both deal with the Glass family, as do the two stories in *Raise High the Roof Beam, Carpenters; and Seymour: An Introduction* (1963).

Saltus, Edgar Evertson (b. Oct. 8, 1855, New York, N.Y., U.S.—d. July 31, 1921, New York City) One of the few American novelists who adopted the sophisticated cynicism, art-for-art's-sake credo, and mannerisms of the European school of Decadents. In his time his novels were popular for their wit and for their shocking, erotic incidents.

Educated at Yale and abroad, Saltus received a law degree at Columbia College in 1880 but never practiced. He wrote popularized histories of the Roman emperors and of the Russian czars, titled, respectively, *Imperial Purple* (1893) and *Imperial Orgy* (1920). In addition, he published books on Honoré de Balzac and the German philosopher Arthur Schopenhauer and wrote *The Anatomy of Negation* (1886), a study of antitheistic philosophies from earliest times.

Sanchez, Sonia (Benita), *original name* Wilsonia Driver (b. Sept. 9, 1934, Birmingham, Ala., U.S.) African-American poet, playwright, and educator noted for her activism.

Sanchez graduated from Hunter College in Manhattan and briefly studied poetry writing at New York University. From 1966 she taught in a succession of universities, including Temple University in Philadelphia.

In the 1960s Sanchez published poetry in such journals as *Liberator*, *Journal of Black Poetry*, *Black Dialogue*, and *Negro Digest*. Her first book, *Homecoming* (1969), contained much invective against "white America" and "white violence"; thereafter she continued to write on what she called "neoslavery," the social and psychological enslavement of blacks. Much of her verse is written in American black speech patterns, eschewing traditional English grammar and pronunciations. Some of her later works are *I've Been a Woman: New and Selected Poems* (1978), *Homegirls & Handgrenades* (1984), and *Under a Soprano Sky* (1986).

Sandburg, Carl (b. Jan. 6, 1878, Galesburg, Ill., U.S.—d. July 22, 1967, Flat Rock, N.C.) American poet, historian, novelist, and folklorist.

When the Spanish-American War broke out in 1898, Sandburg enlisted in the 6th Illinois Infantry. These early years he later described in his autobiography, *Always the Young Strangers* (1953).

From 1910 to 1912 he acted as an organizer for the Social Democratic Party and secretary to the mayor of Milwaukee. Moving to Chicago in 1913, he became an editor of *System*, a business magazine, and later joined the staff of the *Chicago Daily News*.

In 1914 a group of his poems, including the well-known CHICAGO, appeared in *Poetry* magazine (they were issued as *Chicago Poems* in 1916). Sandburg's poetry made an instant and favorable impression. In Whitmanesque free verse, he eulogized American workers: "Pittsburgh,

Carl Sandburg

Youngstown, Gary, they make their steel with men" (*Smoke and Steel*, 1920).

In *Good Morning, America* (1928) Sandburg seemed to have lost some of his faith in democracy, but from the depths of the Great Depression he wrote *The People, Yes* (1936), a poetic testament to the power of the people to go forward. The folk songs he sang before delighted audiences were issued in two collections, *The American Songbag* (1927) and *New American Songbag* (1950). He also wrote the popular biography *Abraham Lincoln: The Prairie Years*, 2 vol. (1926). Its sequel, ABRAHAM LINCOLN: THE WAR YEARS, 4 vol. (1939), won the Pulitzer Prize in history in 1940.

Another biography, *Steichen, the Photographer*, the life of his famous brother-in-law, Edward Steichen, appeared in 1929. In 1948 Sandburg published a long novel, REMEMBRANCE ROCK, that recapitulates the American experience from Plymouth Rock to World War II. *Complete Poems* appeared in 1950. He wrote four books for children—ROOTABAGA STORIES (1922), *Rootabaga Pigeons* (1923), *Rootabaga Country* (1929), and *Potato Face* (1930).

Sandoz, Mari Susette (b. 1901, Sheridan county, Neb., U.S.—d. March 10, 1966, New York, N.Y.) American biographer and novelist known for her scrupulously researched books portraying the early American West.

Sandoz' life as a student and teacher in rural Nebraska—a rigorous life that left her blind in one eye at age 13—prepared her to depict pioneer and Indian life realistically. She wrote almost 80 stories while in college, but her first success came when she was in her mid-30s, with *Old Jules* (1935), a story of her father's hard farm life.

Sandoz' books include *Crazy Horse* (1942), a biography of the Sioux chief; *Cheyenne Autumn* (1953), which concerns Native Americans leaving a reservation to return home; *The Buffalo Hunters* (1954), which tells of the white settlers' slaughter of bison and its social impact on the West; and *The Battle of the Little Bighorn* (1966).

Santayana, George, *original name* Jorge Augustín Nicolás Ruiz de Santayana (b. Dec. 16, 1863, Madrid, Spain—d. Sept. 26, 1952, Rome, Italy) Spanish-American philosopher, poet, and humanist who made important contributions to aesthetics, speculative philosophy, and literary criticism.

Santayana was born of Spanish parents. He never relinquished his Spanish citizenship, and, although he was to write in English with subtlety and poise, he did not begin to learn the language until taken to join his mother in Boston in 1872. He graduated from Harvard College and studied at the University of Berlin before returning to Harvard to complete his doctoral thesis. He joined the faculty of philosophy in 1889, forming with William James and the idealist Josiah Royce a brilliant triumvirate of philosophers.

At Harvard Santayana began to write. His *The Sense of Beauty* (1896), an important work on aesthetics, is concerned with the nature and elements of aesthetic feelings. The vital affinity between aesthetic and moral faculties is illustrated in Santayana's next book, *Interpretations of Poetry and Religion* (1900), particularly in the discussion of the poetry of Robert Browning. His five-volume *The Life of Reason* (1905–06) is a major theoretical work. A number of his essays are gathered into two volumes: *Three Philosophical Poets: Lucretius, Dante, and Goethe* (1910) and *Winds of Doctrine* (1913), in which the poetry of Percy Bysshe Shelley and the philosophies of Henri Bergson, a French evolutionary philosopher, and of Bertrand Russell are trenchantly discussed.

Santayana was in Europe when his mother died in 1912; he retired from teaching and never returned to America. He continued to write, and in 1924 he settled permanently in Rome. There he produced additional works that consolidated his reputation as a humanist critic and man of letters, an aspect of his writing that was brought to perfect expression in a novel, *The Last Puritan* (1935).

The bulk of Santayana's energies in his later years went into speculative philosophy. He also wrote a three-volume autobiography, *Persons and Places* (1944, 1945, 1953), and he was at work on a translation of Lorenzo de' Medici's love poem "Ambra" when he died.

Saroyan, William (b. Aug. 31, 1908, Fresno, Calif., U.S.—d. May 18, 1981, Fresno) American writer who made his initial impact during the Great Depression with a deluge of brash, original, and irreverent stories celebrating the joy of living in spite of poverty, hunger, and insecurity.

The son of an Armenian immigrant, Saroyan left school at 15 and continued his education by reading and writing on his own. His first collection of stories, *The Daring Young Man on the Flying Trapeze* (1934), was soon followed by another collection, *Inhale and Exhale* (1936). His first play, *My Heart's in the Highlands*, was produced by the Group Theatre in 1939. In 1940 Saroyan refused the Pulitzer Prize for his play *The Time of Your Life* (performed 1939) because he felt that it was no better than anything else he had written.

William Saroyan

Saroyan was concerned with the basic goodness of all people, especially the obscure and naive, and with the value of life. His mastery of the vernacular makes his characters vibrantly alive. Most of his stories are based on his childhood and family, notably the collection MY NAME IS ARAM (1940) and the novel THE HUMAN COMEDY (1943). Novels such as *Rock Wagram* (1951) and *The Laughing Matter* (1953) were inspired by his own marriage, fatherhood, and divorce.

Although the autobiographical element was strong in all his fiction, some of his later memoirs—including *Here Comes, There Goes You Know Who* (1961), *Not Dying* (1963), *Days of Life and Death and Escape to the Moon* (1971), and *Places Where I've Done Time* (1975)—have their own enduring value.

Sarton, May, *original name* Eleanore Marie Sarton (b. May 3, 1912, Wondelgem, Belg.—d. July 16, 1995, York, Maine, U.S.) American poet, novelist, and essayist whose works were informed by themes of love, mind-body conflict, creativity, lesbianism, and the trials of age and illness.

Sarton began to write full-time after 1945. Her writing often earned greater acclaim from the public than from critics. Her novels increasingly reflected the concerns of her own life. Her early fiction, such as *The Single Hound* (1938) and *A Shower of Summer Days* (1952), was set in Europe and showed the merest glimpse of autobiography. *Mrs. Stevens Hears the Mermaids Singing* (1965), considered by many to be her most important novel, addressed issues of artistic expression. Her other novels include *As We Are Now* (1973), *A Reckoning* (1978), *The Magnificent Spinster* (1985), and *The Education of Harriet Hatfield* (1989).

Sarton preferred the writing of poetry to prose. Of her many volumes of poetry, *The Land of Silence* (1953), *In Time Like Air* (1958), and *A Private Mythology* (1966) are cited as among her best, the last for its varied forms and invocation of Japanese, Indian, and Greek cultures. Her *Collected Poems, 1930–1993* (1993) demonstrated her range of subjects and styles. Sarton's late autobiographical writings, such as *After the Stroke: A Journal* (1989) and *Encore: A Journal of the Eightieth Year* (1993), offered meditations on illness and aging.

Savard, Félix-Antoine (b. Aug. 31, 1896, Quebec, Que., Can.—d. Aug. 24, 1982, Quebec) French-Canadian priest, poet, novelist, and folklorist whose works show a strong French-nationalist bias and a love of the Canadian landscape.

Savard was ordained a Roman Catholic priest in 1922. He began to lecture in the faculty of arts at Laval University in Quebec in 1943 and was dean of arts there from 1950 to 1957. His works, which have been called both prose poems and novels, display a firsthand knowledge of Canadian logging and pioneering—e.g., *Menaud, maître-draveur* (1937); *The Boss of the River*), for which Savard received the literature prize both from the Académie Française in 1945 and from the Grand Jury of Letters in 1961; *L'Abatis* (1943); "The Slaughter"); and *La Minuit* (1948); "Midnight"). He also wrote *Martin et le pauvre* (1959); "Martin and the Beggar"), the story of St.

Martin of Tours, and *La Folle* (1960); "The Madwoman"), a drama in free verse. Among Savard's later works are *La Roche Ursule* (1972); "The Ursula Stone"), a volume of poems entitled *Aux marges du silence* (1975); "At the Borders of Silence"), and *Discours* (1975); "Speeches").

Schulberg, Budd (Wilson) (b. March 27, 1914, New York, N.Y., U.S.) American novelist, screenwriter, and journalist.

The son of a Hollywood motion-picture producer, Schulberg grew up in Hollywood and became a reader and then a screenwriter. His first novel, *What Makes Sammy Run* (1941), about an unprincipled motion-picture studio mogul, was a great success.

During and after World War II, Schulberg served in the military and was commended for collecting visual evidence of Nazi war crimes for the Nürnberg trials. In 1947 he published his second novel, *The Harder They Fall*, a fictional exposé of corrupt practices in professional boxing. In 1950 his novel *The Disenchanted* won an American Library Award for fiction. In 1954 his screenplay for the widely acclaimed *On the Waterfront* won an Academy Award for best story and screenplay. In the 1960s Schulberg helped establish the Douglass House Watts Writers Workshop in the Watts district of Los Angeles after riots there, and in 1971 he founded the Frederick Douglass Creative Arts Center in New York City. In *Moving Pictures: Memories of a Hollywood Prince* (1981), Schulberg described his childhood spent in the center of the American motion-picture industry; *Love, Action, Laughter, and Other Sad Tales* was published in 1989.

Schuyler, James (Marcus) (b. Nov. 9, 1923, Chicago, Ill., U.S.—d. April 12, 1991, New York, N.Y.) American poet, playwright, and novelist, often associated with the New York school of poets, which included Frank O'Hara, John Ashbery, and Kenneth Koch. An acute observer of natural landscapes, Schuyler described common experiences with familiar images in compact lines of varied rhythm.

Schuyler settled in New York City and began writing for the magazine *Art News*, where he met other poets of the New York school. His best-known volumes of poetry are *Freely Espousing* (1969), *The Crystal Lithium* (1972), and *Hymn to Life* (1974). The title poem of *The Crystal Lithium* examines the variability of experience while describing a beach in winter.

Among his other verse collections are *Salute* (1960), *May 24th or So* (1966), *A Sun Cab* (1972), *Song* (1976), *The Fireproof Floors of Witley Court* (1976), *The Home Book* (1977), *The Morning of the Poem* (1980), *A Few Days* (1985), *Selected Poems* (1988), and *Collected Poems* (1993). He also wrote plays and novels.

Delmore Schwartz

Schwartz, Delmore (b. Dec. 8, 1913, Brooklyn, N.Y., U.S.—d. July 11, 1966, New York City) American poet, short-story writer, and literary critic noted for his lyrical descriptions of cultural alienation and the search for identity.

Educated at the University of Wisconsin, New York University, and Harvard University, Schwartz later taught at Harvard and at a number of other schools. His first book, *In Dreams Begin Responsibilities* (1939), which brought him immediate fame, included the short story of the title and a group of lyrical and imaginative poems. Subsequent publications included *Shenandoah* (1941), a verse play; *Genesis, Book I* (1943), a long introspective poem; and *The World Is a Wedding* (1948) and *Successful Love, and Other Stories* (1961), short stories dealing primarily with middle-class Jewish family life.

Schwartz's lucid literary criticism was published in various periodicals. *New and Selected Poems, 1938–1958* appeared in 1959. Schwartz served as an editor for *Partisan Review* (1943–55) and *The New Republic* (1955–57). The brilliant but mentally unstable Schwartz was the model for the title character in Saul Bellow's novel *Humboldt's Gift* (1975).

Scott, Duncan Campbell (b. Aug. 2, 1862, Ottawa, Canada West [Ontario, Can.]—d. Dec. 19, 1947, Ottawa) Canadian regionalist poet who wrote of the untamed aspects of nature in the northern wilderness and of Indian life.

An administrator for more than 50 years in the Department of Indian Affairs (1879–1932), Scott had a conscientious and sincere concern for Indians. His poetry was influenced by that of his close friend, the Ottawa poet Archibald Lampman, whose work he edited on Lampman's death (1899). Scott produced several volumes of verse of uneven quality from 1893 (*The Magic House, and Other Poems*) to 1947 (*The Circle of Affection*). He also published two volumes of stories, *In the Village of Viger* (1896) and *The Witching of Elspie* (1923).

Scott, Francis Reginald, *byname* Frank *or* F.R. (b. Aug. 1, 1899, Quebec, Que., Can.—d. Jan. 31, 1985, Montreal) Member of the Montreal group of poets in the 1920s and an influential promoter of the cause of Canadian poetry.

Scott helped found various literary magazines and also edited poetry anthologies. As a poet, he is at his best as a satirist and social critic. His *Overture* (1945), *Events and Signals* (1954), and *The Eye of the Needle* (1957) are written in a colloquial, conversational style. His *Selected Poems* appeared in 1966 and *The Dance Is One* in 1973. He also wrote nonfiction concerning socialism and constitutional law and served as a UN representative in Burma (now Myanmar).

Seers, Eugène, *pseudonym* Louis Dantin (b. 1865, Beauharnois, Que. [Canada]—d. Jan. 17, 1945, Boston, Mass., U.S.) French-Canadian poet and critic who is regarded as the first major literary critic of Quebec.

While a member of the religious order Congrégation de Très Saint-Sacrement, Seers wrote religious poetry, short stories, and critical articles, especially on the poetry of the French-Canadian Émile Nelligan. He left the order in 1903. His criticism, at first in the form of correspondence with French-Canadian authors, achieved recognition in Montreal in the 1920s. In his *Poètes de l'Amérique française* (2 series, 1928 and 1934; "Poets of French America") and *Gloses critiques* (2 series, 1931 and 1935; "Critical Comments"), Seers stated his views that a work of art should exist for the sake of art alone and not for the promotion of any cause. He was also the author of *Le Coffret de Crusoé* (1932); "Crusoe's Chest"), a volume of poems dealing with his loss of faith, and *Les Enfances de Fanny* (1951), a semiautobiographical novel.

Selvon, Sam, *in full* Samuel Dickson Selvon (b. May 20, 1923, Trinidad—d. April 16, 1994, Port of Spain) Trinidad-born Canadian novelist and short-story writer known for his vivid evocation of the life of East Indian immigrants in the West Indies.

Selvon's first novel, *A Brighter Sun* (1952), describes Trinidadians and Creoles in Trinidad, their prejudices and mutual distrusts, and the effect of this animosity on a young man. Its sequel, *Turn Again Tiger* (1958), follows the protagonist on a journey to his ancestral home. Perhaps the best of his novels, *The Lonely Londoners* (1956) describes apparently naive immigrants living by their wits in a hostile city. In this novel Selvon, who drew heavily on oral tradition, made extensive and striking use of dialect.

His later works include a collection of short stories, *Ways of Sunlight* (1958); a collection of one-act plays, *Eldorado West One* (1988); and the novels *I Hear Thunder* (1963), *The Plains of Caroni* (1970), and *Moses Ascending* (1975) and *Moses Migrating* (1983), both sequels to *The Lonely Londoners*.

Sendak, Maurice (Bernard) (b. June 10, 1928, New York, N.Y., U.S.) American artist and author of children's books.

Sendak was the son of Polish immigrants and received his formal art training at the Art Students' League in New York City. The first children's books he illustrated were Marcel Aymé's *The Wonderful Farm* (1951) and Ruth Krauss's *A Hole Is To Dig* (1952). Both were successful, and Sendak went on to illustrate more than 80 children's books by a number of writers, including Meindert De Jong, Else Holmelund Minarik, and Randall Jarrell. With *Kenny's Window* (1956), he began both writing and illustrating stories.

Maurice Sendak

These include the miniature four-volume *Nutshell Library* (1962) and his innovative trilogy composed of *Where the Wild Things Are* (1963); winner of the 1964 Caldecott Medal), *In the Night Kitchen* (1970), and *Outside Over There* (1981).

In 1975 Sendak wrote and directed *Really Rosie*, an animated television special based on some of the children in his stories. It was expanded into a musical play in 1978. In addition to creating opera versions of some of his own stories—including *Where the Wild Things Are*—Sendak designed a number of other works for the stage, notably a production of W.A. Mozart's *The Magic Flute* in 1980.

Service, Robert William (b. Jan. 16, 1874, Preston, Lancashire, Eng.—d. Sept. 11, 1958, Lancieux, Fr.) Popular verse writer called "the Canadian Kipling" for rollicking ballads of the "frozen North," notably "The Shooting of Dan McGrew" and THE CREMATION OF SAM MCGEE.

Service immigrated to Canada in 1894 and lived for eight years in the Yukon. He was a correspondent for the Toronto *Star* during the Balkan Wars of 1912–13 and an ambulance driver and correspondent during World War I.

Service's first verse collections, *Songs of a Sourdough* (1907) and *Ballads of a Cheechako* (1909), describing life in the Canadian north, were enormously popular. Among his later volumes of verse are *Rhymes of a Red Cross Man* (1916) and *Bar Room Ballads* (1940). *The Trail of '98* (1910) is a vivid novel of men and conditions in the Alaskan Klondike. Service also wrote two autobiographical works, *Ploughman of the Moon* (1945) and *Harper of Heaven* (1948).

Seton, Anya, *original name* Ann Seton (b. 1904?, New York, N.Y., U.S.—d. Nov. 8, 1990, Old Greenwich, Conn.) American author of best-selling, exhaustively researched, romantic historical and biographical novels.

Seton was the daughter of Ernest Thompson Seton, the English naturalist, writer, and cofounder of the Boy Scouts of America, and Grace Gallatin, an American travel writer. She traveled extensively with her parents and used these and later travels as inspirations for her books. In 1941 she published her first book, *My Theodosia*, a novel about the daughter of Aaron Burr.

Seton's gothic romance *Dragonwyck* (1944) and her novel *Foxfire* (1950) were adapted for motion pictures. Among her many other novels are *The Turquoise* (1946), *The Hearth and Eagle* (1948), *The Winthrop Woman* (1958), and a number of dark romances with English settings, including *Devil Water* (1962), *Avalon* (1965), and *Green Darkness* (1972).

Seton, Ernest Thompson, *original name* Ernest Evan Thompson, *also called* Ernest Seton-Thompson (b. Aug. 14, 1860, South Shields, Durham,

Eng.—d. Oct. 23, 1946, Seton Village, Santa Fe, N.M., U.S.) Naturalist and writer best known for his animal stories.

Seton was raised in North America, his family having immigrated to Canada in 1866. He gained experience as a naturalist by trailing and hunting in the prairie country of Manitoba, using this knowledge as the basis for his animal stories. His most popular book, *Wild Animals I Have Known* (1898), is a collection of those stories.

Deeply concerned with the future of the prairie, Seton fought to establish reservations for Native Americans and parks for animals threatened by extinction. To provide children with the opportunities for nature study, he founded the Woodcraft Indians organization in 1902 and later was chairman of the committee that established the Boy Scouts of America.

Ernest Thompson Seton

Seuss, Dr. Pseudonym of Theodor Seuss GEISEL.

Sexton, Anne, *original surname* Harvey (b. Nov. 9, 1928, Newton, Mass., U.S.—d. Oct. 4, 1974, Weston, Mass.) American poet whose work is noted for its confessional intensity.

A lifelong resident of New England, Sexton studied poetry under Robert Lowell at Boston University and also worked as a model and as a librarian. She taught briefly at a high school and also at several universities.

Her first book of poetry, *To Bedlam and Part Way Back* (1960), is an intense examination of her mental breakdowns and subsequent recoveries. In both *All My Pretty Ones* (1962) and *Live or Die* (1966) Sexton continues this probing treatment of her personal life, especially of her continuing emotional illness. The poet's later volumes include *Love Poems* (1969), *Transformations* (1971), and *The Book of Folly* (1972). Her last poems were published posthumously in *The Awful Rowing Toward God* (1975), *45 Mercy Street* (1976), and *Uncollected Poems with Three Stories* (1978). *No Evil Star: Selected Essays, Interviews, and Prose* was published in 1985. Sexton died a suicide.

Shange, Ntozake, *original name* Paulette Williams (b. Oct. 18, 1948, Trenton, N.J., U.S.) African-American author of plays, poetry, and fiction noted for their feminist themes and racial and sexual anger.

Shange taught at California colleges from 1972 to 1975. Her 1975 theater piece *For Colored Girls Who Have Considered Suicide/When the Rainbow Is Enuf* quickly brought her fame. *For Colored Girls* is a group of 20 poems for seven actors on the power of black women to survive in the face of despair and pain. It ran for seven months Off-Broadway in New York, then moved to Broadway and was subsequently produced throughout the United States and on television.

Shange created a number of other theater works that employed poetry, dance, and music while abandoning conventions of plot and character development. The most popular of these was her 1980 adaptation of Bertolt Brecht's *Mother Courage*, featuring a black family in the time of the American Civil War.

Shange's poetry collections include *Nappy Edges* (1978) and *Ridin' the Moon in Texas* (1987). She later published the novel *Sassafrass, Cypress & Indigo* (1982), and the autobiographical novel *Betsey Brown* (1985); and *Liliane: Resurrection of the Daughter* (1994).

Shapiro, Karl Jay (b. Nov. 10, 1913, Baltimore, Md., U.S.) American poet and critic whose verse ranges from passionately physical love lyrics to sharp social satire.

Shapiro came to critical attention in 1942 with the collection *Person, Place and Thing*. He served in the U.S. Army during World War II, and his *V-Letter and Other Poems* (1944) won the Pulitzer Prize for Poetry in 1945. His later works include other volumes of poetry—notably *Poems of a Jew* (1958), *White-Haired Lover* (1968), and *Adult Bookstore* (1976)—and works of literary criticism such as *Beyond Criticism* (1953), *In Defense of Ignorance* (1960), and *The Poetry Wreck* (1975). Shapiro was consultant in poetry to the Library of Congress (1946–47) and editor of *Poetry* magazine (1950–56). From 1956 he taught at the universities of Nebraska, Illinois, and California. *Collected Poems, 1948–1978* was published in 1978 and *New & Selected Poems, 1940–86* in 1987. *Poet: An Autobiography in Three Parts* appeared in 1988.

Shaw, Irwin, *original name* Irwin Gilbert Shamforoff (b. Feb. 27, 1913, New York, N.Y., U.S.—d. May 16, 1984, Davos, Switz.) Prolific playwright, screenwriter, and author of critically acclaimed short stories and best-selling novels.

Shaw began his career at age 21 by writing scripts for radio shows. He wrote his antiwar one-act play *Bury the Dead* for a 1935 contest; though it lost, it was produced the next year. He wrote his first screenplay, *The Big Game*, in 1936. His stories, which appeared in such magazines as *The New Yorker* and *Esquire* beginning in the late 1930s, were praised for their plotting, naturalness of narration, and characterization.

Shaw's experiences in the U.S. Army in Europe during World War II led to his writing *The Young Lions* (1948), a novel about three young soldiers in wartime; it became a best-seller, and thereafter Shaw devoted most of the rest of his career to writing novels. Among the best-known of his 12 novels are *Two Weeks in Another Town* (1960), *Evening in Byzantium* (1973), and *Beggarman, Thief* (1977). Probably his most popular novel, though it was derided by critics, was *Rich Man, Poor Man* (1970).

Sheed, Wilfrid (John Joseph) (b. Dec. 27, 1930, London, Eng.) American author of essays, biographies, and other nonfiction works and of satirical fiction that contrasts transient modern values with steadfast traditional values.

Sheed's parents, authors themselves, founded Sheed & Ward, a leading Roman Catholic publishing firm. The family immigrated to the United States in 1940, and Sheed returned to England to study at Oxford University. In 1959 he began writing film, drama, and book criticism for magazines and newspapers in New York City.

The lives of individuals working in mass media are the subjects of most of his comic novels. Journalists battle over the editorial pecking order in *Office Politics* (1966), while compulsive analysis and perfectionism destroy the life of a critic in *Max Jamison* (1970). A reporter views the moral hypocrisy of a candidate in *People Will Always Be Kind* (1973).

Sheed's other novels include *The Hack* (1963), *Transatlantic Blues* (1978), and *The Boys of Winter* (1987). Among his nonfiction books are *Frank and Maisie: A Memoir with Parents* (1985), the biographies *Muhammad Ali* (1975) and *Clare Boothe Luce* (1982), the essay collections *The Good Word & Other Words* (1978) and *Essays in Disguise* (1990), and *Baseball and Lesser Sports* (1991).

Shepard, Sam, *in full* Samuel Shepard Rogers (b. Nov. 5, 1943, Fort Sheridan, Ill., U.S.) American playwright and actor whose plays adroitly blend images of the American West, pop motifs, science fiction, and other elements of popular and youth culture.

After a year of college, Shepard joined a touring company of actors and, in 1963, moved to New York City to pursue his theatrical interests. His earliest attempts at playwriting, a rapid succession of one-act dramas, found a receptive audience in Off-Off Broadway productions. In the 1965–66 season, Shepard won Obie awards (presented by New York's *Village Voice* newspaper) for his plays *Chicago*, *Icarus's Mother*, and *Red Cross*.

Shepard lived in England from 1971 to 1974, and two notable plays of this period—*The Tooth of Crime* (1972) and *Geography of a Horse Dreamer* (1974)—premiered in London. In late 1974, he became playwright-in-residence at the Magic Theatre in San Francisco, where most of his subsequent plays were first produced.

Shepard's works of the mid-1970s showed a heightening of earlier techniques and themes. In *Killer's Head* (1975), for example, the rambling monologue—a Shepard stock-in-trade—blends horror and banality in a murderer's last thoughts before electrocution. *Angel City* (1976) depicts the destructive machinery of the Hollywood entertainment industry, and

Suicide in B-Flat (1976) exploits the potentials of music as an expression of character.

In the late 1970s, Shepard wrote *Curse of the Starving Class* (1976), the Pulitzer Prize-winning BURIED CHILD (1979), and TRUE WEST (1981), plays linked thematically in their examination of troubled and tempestuous blood relationships in a fragmented society. His other plays include *La Turista* (1966), *Operation Sidewinder* (1970), *The Unseen Hand* (1970), *Seduced* (1979), FOOL FOR LOVE (1983; film, 1985), *Paris, Texas* (1984; film, 1984), and *A Lie of the Mind* (1985). Shepard also wrote several screenplays and acted in a number of motion pictures.

Sherwood, Robert Emmet (b. April 4, 1896, New Rochelle, N.Y., U.S.—d. Nov. 14, 1955, New York City) American playwright whose works reflect involvement in human problems, both social and political.

Sherwood served as drama editor of *Vanity Fair* (1919–20) and was a member of the Algonquin Round Table, the center of a New York literary coterie. He then worked as associate editor (1920–24) and editor (1924–28) of the humor magazine *Life*. His first play, *The Road to Rome* (1927), criticizes the pointlessness of war, a recurring theme in his work. The heroes of THE PETRIFIED FOREST (1935) and *Idiot's Delight* (1936) begin as detached cynics but recognize their own moral bankruptcy and sacrifice themselves for their fellowmen. In ABE LINCOLN IN ILLINOIS (1939) and *There Shall Be No Night* (1941), in which his pacifist heroes decide to fight, Sherwood suggests that a person can make his own life significant only by losing it for others. In 1938 Sherwood formed, with Maxwell Anderson, Sidney Howard, Elmer Rice, and S.N. Behrman, the Playwrights' Company, which became a major producing company.

The Lincoln play led to Sherwood's introduction to Eleanor Roosevelt and ultimately to his working for President Franklin D. Roosevelt as speechwriter and adviser. From his association with Roosevelt came much of the material for *Roosevelt and Hopkins: An Intimate History* (1948). Sherwood wrote the Academy Award-winning screenplay for the film *The Best Years of Our Lives* (1946), but otherwise his theatrical work after World War II was negligible.

Shirer, William Lawrence (b. Feb. 23, 1904, Chicago, Ill., U.S.—d. Dec. 28, 1993, Boston, Mass.) American journalist, historian, and novelist who is best known for his massive study *The Rise and Fall of the Third Reich: A History of Nazi Germany* (1960).

In the 1920s, '30s, and '40s, Shirer was stationed in Europe and in India as a foreign correspondent for the *Chicago Tribune* and the Universal News Service. In addition, he served from 1937 to 1941 as radio broadcaster for CBS, relaying to North America news of the European crises leading to

World War II. His impassioned statements alerting Americans to the Nazi danger earned him several journalistic awards.

Shirer collected his impressions of European political events in *Berlin Diary: The Journal of a Foreign Correspondent, 1934–1941* (1941), which gained an international audience for its simple documentation of survival amidst horror. In the 1950s he began his research for *The Rise and Fall of the Third Reich*, which won a National Book Award in 1961. The book is a comprehensive and readable study of the Nazis' rise to power under Adolf Hitler, their rule, and their eventual demise. Shirer's other major historical work is *The Collapse of the Third Republic: An Inquiry into the Fall of France in 1940* (1960). The book is considered by some to be the best one-volume study of France during the period between the world wars. In 1980 Shirer published *Gandhi: A Memoir*, in which he recalled a series of interviews he had conducted with Mahatma Gandhi during the early 1930s. Shirer's three-volume set of memoirs is collectively entitled *Twentieth-Century Journey* (1976, 1984, 1990). He also wrote *Love and Hatred: The Troubled Marriage of Leo and Sonya Tolstoy*, published posthumously in 1994.

Showalter, Elaine (b. Jan. 21, 1941, Boston, Mass., U.S.) American literary critic and teacher, founder of gynocritics, a school of feminist criticism that is concerned with "woman as writer . . . with the history, themes, genres, and structures of literature by women."

Showalter studied English at Bryn Mawr College, Brandeis University, and the University of California at Davis (Ph.D., 1970). She joined the faculty of Douglass College, the women's division of Rutgers University, in 1969, where she developed women's studies courses and began editing and contributing articles to books and periodicals about women's literature.

Showalter developed her doctoral thesis into her first book, *A Literature of Their Own: British Women Novelists from Brontë to Lessing* (1977), a pioneering study in which she created a critical framework for analyzing literature by women. As a result of the book, gynocritics became the leaders of feminist criticism in the United States. Her next book, *The Female Malady: Women, Madness, and English Culture, 1830–1980* (1985), was a historical examination of women and the practice of psychiatry. She also wrote *Sexual Anarchy: Gender and Culture at the Fin de Siècle* (1990) and *Sister's Choice: Tradition and Change in American Women's Writing* (1991) and edited several volumes, including *The New Feminist Criticism* (1985) and *Daughters of Decadence: Women Writers of the Fin de Siècle* (1993).

Sigourney, L.H., *in full* Lydia Howard, *original surname* Huntley (b. Sept. 1, 1791, Norwich, Conn., U.S.—d. June 10, 1865, Hartford, Conn.) Popular writer, educator, and one of few American women of her time to succeed at a literary career. She was sometimes known as "the sweet singer of Hartford."

Huntley's first work, *Moral Pieces in Prose and Verse*, was published in 1815. She wrote more than 60 books and more than a thousand articles during her career. Her writing relied on sentimental conventions of moral and religious themes; death and piety were her most popular subjects. Her best-known prose work was *Letters to Young Ladies* (1833). Although she remained popular until the end of her life, she was not respected by contemporary American writers.

Silko, Leslie Marmon (b. 1948, Albuquerque, N.M., U.S.) Native American poet and novelist.

While growing up on the Laguna Pueblo reservation in New Mexico, Silko learned Laguna traditions and myths from senior family members. After attending Bureau of Indian Affairs schools and the University of New Mexico (B.A., 1969), she published several short stories and the 1974 poetry collection *Laguna Woman*. Her novel *Ceremony* (1977) was the first novel by a Native American woman to be published. It follows half-Laguna, half-white protagonist Tayo home to his reservation after his service in World War II; his future bleak, he learns Laguna folklore and ceremonies that restore him. Apart from Silko's close observation of human nature, *Ceremony* was also noted for its nonchronological narrative method.

Storyteller (1981) is a collection of poetry, tribal stories, fiction, and photographs, and *The Delicacy and Strength of Lace* (1986) is a collection of letters between Silko and writer James A. Wright. In her second novel, *Almanac of the Dead* (1991), Native Americans whose lives and values are in tune with nature retake America from the environmentally destructive, personally perverse, and brutal whites.

Simic, Charles (b. May 9, 1938, Belgrade, Ygos. [now in Serbia]) Poet who evoked his eastern European heritage and his childhood experiences to comment on the dearth of spirituality in contemporary life.

When he was 15, Simic and his mother moved to Paris, and after a year they immigrated to the United States, where they were reunited with Simic's father. After graduating from New York University, he translated the works of Yugoslavian poets into English. From 1974 he taught at the University of New Hampshire.

Simic's first volume of poetry, *What the Grass Says* (1967), was well received; critics commented on the poem's imagery, which was rural and European, rather than urban and American. Among Simic's many subsequent poetry collections were *Somewhere Among Us a Stone Is Taking Notes* (1969), *Dismantling the Silence* (1971), *School for Dark Thoughts* (1978),

Unending Blues (1986), *The Book of Gods and Devils* (1990), and *Hotel Insomnia* (1993). He received a Pulitzer Prize for poetry for *The World Doesn't End* (1989). His *Dime-store Alchemy* (1992) was a collection of miscellaneous prose pieces written as a tribute to the artist Joseph Cornell.

Simms, William Gilmore (b. April 17, 1806, Charleston, S.C., U.S.— d. June 11, 1870, Charleston) Outstanding Southern man of letters known especially for his historical novels.

Simms, who was a child prodigy, began publishing poetry in Charleston newspapers at age 16. He edited a magazine and published a volume of poetry at 19. As state legislator and magazine and newspaper editor, he became embroiled in political and literary quarrels, but he was admired in both the South and the North.

Simms was at his best in employing a racy and masculine English prose style and in dealing humorously with rowdy frontier characters. His gift as a teller of tales in the oral tradition and the care he took in preparing historical materials are evident in his works. Notable among them are *Pelayo* (1838), with its 8th-century setting; *Vasconselos* (1853), set in the 16th century; *The Yemassee* (1835), set in colonial times and his most popular work; and the series set during the Revolution that includes *The Partisan* (1835), *The Kinsmen* (1841), *Katherine Walton* (1851), *Woodcraft* (1854), *Eutaw* (1856), and *Joscelyn* (1867). He also wrote two noteworthy romances about frontier life in the South, *Richard Hurdis* (1838) and *Border Beagles* (1840); a short-story collection, *The Wigwam and the Cabin* (1845); and the *History of South Carolina* (1840). Of 19 volumes of poetry, the collected *Poems* (1853) deserves mention. Most popular of his biographies were *The Life of Francis Marion* (1844) and *The Life of Chevalier Bayard* (1847). His literary criticism is represented in *Views and Reviews of American Literature* (1845).

Simon, Kate, *original name* Kaila Grobsmith (b. Dec. 5, 1912, Warsaw, Pol.—d. Feb. 4, 1990, New York, N.Y., U.S.) Memoirist and travel writer whose work was noted for its readability and its wit.

Simon's family immigrated to the United States in 1917 and settled in New York. She held various editorial positions, including jobs at *Publisher's Weekly* and *The New Republic*. Her first guidebook, *New York Places and Pleasures*, was published in 1959 and was well received. She won praise for similar guides to Italy, London, Mexico, and Paris, which combined carefully researched, up-to-date information with little-known facts and were written with elegance and verve.

Simon's three memoirs, BRONX PRIMITIVE: PORTRAITS IN A CHILDHOOD (1982), *A Wider World: Portraits in an Adolescence* (1986), and *Etchings in an Hourglass* (1990), won acclaim for their unsentimental evocation of her working-class immigrant Jewish family life.

Simon, Neil, *in full* Marvin Neil Simon (b. July 4, 1927, New York, N.Y., U.S.) Playwright, screenwriter, television writer, and librettist who was one of the most popular playwrights in the history of theater.

Simon studied at New York University before working as a comedy writer for various television shows in the late 1940s and throughout the 1950s, an experience he later portrayed in the play *Laughter on the 23rd Floor* (1994). His autobiographical play *Come Blow Your Horn* was a great success on Broadway and ran for two years after opening in 1961. The plays that followed proved extremely popular with audiences and usually had very long runs on Broadway. They include *Barefoot in the Park* (1963), *The Odd Couple* (1965), *The Star-Spangled Girl* (1966), *Plaza Suite* (1968), *Last of the Red Hot Lovers* (1969), *The Prisoner of Second Avenue* (1971), *The Sunshine Boys* (1972), *California Suite* (1976), *Chapter Two* (1977), *I Ought to Be in Pictures* (1980), a trilogy of autobiographical plays consisting of *Brighton Beach Memoirs* (1983), *Biloxi Blues* (1985), and *Broadway Bound* (1986), and *Lost in Yonkers* (1991). Simon wrote the screenplays for motion-picture adaptations of many of his plays as well as screenplays for a number of original motion pictures. He also wrote the books for the musicals *Little Me* (1962), *Sweet Charity* (1966), *Promises, Promises* (1968), and *They're Playing Our Song* (1979).

Simon's plays deal with the everyday lives and domestic problems of ordinary middle-class people. He examines his characters' marital and other dilemmas and, for comic effect, plays up the incongruity of their situations.

Simpson, Louis (Aston Marantz) (b. March 27, 1923, Jamaica) Jamaican-born American poet and critic, notable for his marked development in poetic style. In 1964 he won the Pulitzer Prize in poetry for his volume *At The End of the Open Road, Poems* (1963).

Simpson moved from Jamaica to New York City at age 17. He graduated from Columbia University. During the 1950s he worked as a book editor and taught at Columbia and at the University of California at Berkeley. From 1967 he taught at the State University of New York at Stony Brook.

Simpson's conventional early poetry—that of *The Arrivistes: Poems 1940–1949* (1949) and *Good News of Death and Other Poems* (1955)—gave way to experimental free verse in *A Dream of Governors* (1959). Simpson came to believe that poetry springs from the inner life of the poet and that its expression should be original and natural. By the publication of his next book of poetry, *At the End of the Open Road* (1963), he had abandoned the use of poetic conventions. Simpson's later collections of poetry include *Adventures of the Letter I* (1971), *Searching for the Ox* (1976), *Caviare at the Funeral* (1980), *The Best Hour of the Night* (1983), and *In the Room We Share* (1990). In addition to writing poetry, Simpson produced several critical studies of other poets and an autobiography, *North of Jamaica* (1972); U.K. title, *Air with Armed Men*).

Sinclair, Upton (Beall) (b. Sept. 20, 1878, Baltimore, Md., U.S.—d. Nov. 25, 1968, Bound Brook, N.J.) American novelist and polemicist for socialism and other causes; his THE JUNGLE (1906) is a landmark among naturalistic, proletarian novels.

Sinclair supported himself by journalistic writing. It was a newspaper assignment that led him to write *The Jungle*, his sixth novel and first popular success. Published at Sinclair's own expense after several publishers rejected it, it became a best-seller, and Sinclair used the proceeds to open Helicon Hall, the site of a cooperative-living venture in Englewood, N.J. The building was destroyed by fire in 1907 and the project abandoned.

A long series of other topical novels—among them *Oil!* (1927), based on the Teapot Dome Scandal of the early 1920s, and *Boston* (1928), based on the controversial trial of the anarchists Sacco and Vanzetti—followed, but none achieved the popularity of *The Jungle*. Sinclair again reached a wide audience with the Lanny Budd series, 11 contemporary historical novels beginning with *World's End* (1940) that are constructed around an implausible antifascist hero.

During the economic crisis of the 1930s, Sinclair organized the EPIC (End Poverty in California) socialist reform movement; in 1934 he was defeated as Democratic candidate for governor. His autobiographical *American Outpost: A Book of Reminiscences* (1932); U.K. title, *Candid Reminiscences: My First Thirty Years*) was reworked and extended in *The Autobiography of Upton Sinclair* (1962).

Singer, Isaac Bashevis, *Yiddish* Yitskhok Bashevis Zinger (b. July 14?, 1904, Radzymin, Poland, Russian Empire—d. July 24, 1991, Miami, Fla., U.S.) Polish-born American writer of novels, short stories, and essays in Yiddish. He was the recipient in 1978 of the Nobel Prize for Literature. His fiction, depicting Jewish life in Poland and the United States, is remarkable for its rich blending of irony, wit, and wisdom, flavored distinctively with the occult and the grotesque.

Coming from a family of Ḥasidic rabbis, Singer received a traditional Jewish education at the Warsaw Rabbinical Seminary. His first novel, *Der Sotn in Goray* (*Satan in Goray*), was published in installments in Poland shortly before he immigrated to the United States in 1935. Settling in New York City, he initially worked for the Yiddish-language daily newspaper

Isaac Bashevis Singer

JERRY BAUER

Forverts, and as a journalist he signed his articles with the pseudonym Varshavski. In 1943 he became a U.S. citizen.

Although Singer's works became most widely known in their English versions, he continued to write almost exclusively in Yiddish, personally supervising the translations. Among his most important novels are THE FAMILY MOSKAT (1950), THE MAGICIAN OF LUBLIN (1960), *The Slave* (1962), *The Manor* (1967), *The Estate* (1969), *Enemies, a Love Story* (1972), *Shosha* (1978), and *The Penitent* (1983). His short stories, including the well-known GIMPEL THE FOOL and THE SPINOZA OF MARKET STREET, were also popular. Titles of the collections include *Gimpel the Fool* (1957), *The Spinoza of Market Street* (1961), *Short Friday* (1964), *The Seance* (1968), *A Crown of Feathers* (1973); National Book Award), *Old Love* (1979), and *The Image and Other Stories* (1985). *The Collected Stories of Isaac Bashevis Singer* was published in 1982.

Singer's most ambitious narratives, *The Family Moskat* and the continuous story spun out in *The Manor* and *The Estate*, chronicle the changes in and the eventual breakup of large Jewish families during the late 19th and early 20th centuries as their members are differently affected by the secularism and assimilationist opportunities of the modern era. Singer's shorter novels examine characters who are tempted by evil in various forms. His short stories are saturated with Jewish folklore, legends, and mysticism and display his incisive understanding of the weaknesses inherent in human nature.

Singer, I.J., *in full* Israel Joshua (b. Nov. 30, 1893, Biłgoraj, Poland, Russian Empire—d. Feb. 10, 1944, New York, N.Y., U.S.) Polish-born writer in Yiddish, noted for his realistic historical novels.

Singer was the son of a Ḥasidic rabbi and was the older brother of the writer Isaac Bashevis Singer. He began writing tales of Ḥasidic life in 1915 and then worked as a journalist in Warsaw during the 1920s and early 1930s. Several collections of his short stories were published during this time, including the short story "Perl" ("The Pearl"), which was his first international success. His novel *Yoshe Kalb*, a description of Ḥasidic life in Galicia, appeared in 1932, and the next year he immigrated to the United States. His subsequent writings appeared in serialized form in *Forverts* in New York City.

Like his brother, Singer wrote multigenerational family novels, but, unlike his brother, he firmly linked his vivid characters with a larger historical and socioeconomic setting. *Di Brider Ashkenazi* (1936); *The Brothers Ashkenazi*), which is considered to be Singer's masterpiece, examines the rivalry of two very different brothers whose fortunes parallel that of their birthplace, the Polish industrial city of Łódź. *Di Mishpokhe Karnovski* (1943); *The Family Carnovsky*) traces an assimilated German-Jewish family for several decades until its members must immigrate to the United States after the Nazi takeover. Singer also wrote short stories and plays.

Skinner, Cornelia Otis (b. May 30, 1901, Chicago, Ill., U.S.—d. July 9, 1979, New York, N.Y.) American actress and author who, with satirical wit, wrote light verse, monologues, anecdotes, sketches, and monodramas in which she displayed her versatile and distinctive acting skills.

Cornelia Otis Skinner

Skinner made her first professional stage appearance with her father, the tragedian Otis Skinner, in *Blood and Sand* (1921), and she collaborated with him in writing her first play, *Captain Fury* (1925). During the 1930s she wrote and staged her own monodramas, including *The Loves of Charles II*, *The Empress Eugénie*, *The Mansions on the Hudson*, and *The Wives of Henry VIII*. In 1939, performing in *Candida*, Skinner established a reputation as a fine actress, and she confirmed her excellence as a dramatic actress in *Theatre* (1941). Other performances that won critical acclaim included her roles in *Lady Windermere's Fan* (1946), *Paris '90* (1952), and *The Pleasure of His Company* (1958), which she wrote with Samuel Taylor.

Skinner's diverse writing ability was evident in her 1942 best-seller *Our Hearts Were Young and Gay*, written with Emily Kimbrough, and in the moving *Madame Sarah* (1966), which chronicled the life of the French actress Sarah Bernhardt.

Smith, A.J.M., *in full* Arthur James Marshall (b. Nov. 8, 1902, Montreal, Ont., Can.—d. Nov. 21, 1980, East Lansing, Mich., U.S.) Canadian poet, anthologist, and critic who was a member of the Montreal group, which precipitated a revival of Canadian poetry in the 1920s.

As an undergraduate at McGill University in Montreal, Smith founded and edited the *McGill Fortnightly Review* (1925–27), a literary magazine dedicated to freeing Canadian literature from its narrow provincialism. He encouraged other young Canadian writers to broaden their outlook and to set high literary standards. After receiving his Ph.D. from the University of Edinburgh in 1932, he taught in the United States.

In a series of anthologies beginning with *The Book of Canadian Poetry* (1943), Smith approached Canadian literature in a scholarly manner that set the tone for modern Canadian criticism. His later anthologies include *The Blasted Pine* (1957), a collection of Canadian satiric and invective verse, *Modern Canadian Verse in English and French* (1967), and *The Colonial Century: English-Canadian Writing Before Confederation* (1973). In his own poetry, collected in such volumes as *News of the Phoenix* (1943), *Collected Poems* (1962), and *Poems: New and Collected* (1967), Smith displayed careful craftsmanship.

Smith, Lee (b. Nov. 1, 1944, Grundy, Va., U.S.) American author of fiction about her native southeastern United States.

Smith's first novel, *The Last Day the Dogbushes Bloomed* (1968), was written while she was in college. Her stories are set in the contemporary South and, eschewing the gothic and grotesque, are filled with the details of everyday life. Her widely admired fourth novel, *Black Mountain Breakdown*, and her short-story collection *Cakewalk* were both published in 1980. Critics noted her powerful characterizations of rural Southerners in the novel *Oral History* (1983), a history of a family over the course of 100 years. Her later books include *Family Linens* (1985), *Fair and Tender Ladies* (1988), *Me and My Baby View the Eclipse* (1990), and *The Devil's Dream* (1992).

Smith, Seba (b. Sept. 14, 1792, Buckfield, Maine, U.S.—d. July 28, 1868, Patchogue, N.Y.) American editor and humorist, creator of the fictional Major Jack Downing.

Smith founded (1829) the *Portland Courier*, in which the major's fictional letters first appeared in January 1830, continuing later in the *National Intelligencer* until July 1853. Major Jack was a common man magnified as oracle, a Yankee full of horse sense and wise saws, and a threadbare office seeker exposing follies in a "mobocracy." Shameless pirating of Smith's invention led to the author's collection of the letters in book form, the last volume being published in 1859 under the title *My Thirty Years Out of the Senate*. He further portrays New England character in *Way Down East* (1854).

Smith, William Jay (b. April 22, 1918, Winnfield, La., U.S.) American lyric poet who wrote for both adults and children.

The son of an army officer, Smith spent much of his early life on a U.S. Army post, a period he recalled in *Army Brat: A Memoir* (1980). Educated at Washington University, St. Louis, Mo. (B.A., 1939; M.A., 1941), he served in the U.S. Navy from 1941 to 1945, then attended Columbia University and the universities of Oxford and Florence. He taught at several colleges and universities, served in the Vermont House of Representatives from 1960 to 1962, and in 1968–70 was consultant in poetry to the U.S. Library of Congress.

Smith's first collections of poems, *Poems* (1947) and *Celebration at Dark* (1950), revealed the breadth of his narrative range, and with *The Tin Can and Other Poems* (1966) he began to experiment with free verse. His *Collected Poems: 1939–1989* was published in 1990.

Smith began collecting his whimsical and nonsense poems for children in *Laughing Time* (1955) and *Boy Blue's Book of Beasts* (1957); his later children's poetry included *Typewriter Town* (1960), *Ho for a Hat!* (1964); rev. ed., 1989), and *Laughing Time: Collected Nonsense* (1990). He also edited several volumes of children's poetry. He made a reputation as a translator with versions of *Poems of a Multimillionaire* by Valéry Larbaud (1955) and *Selected Writings of Jules Laforgue* (1956), and he edited and translated other poetry from several languages. He also wrote *The Spectra House* (1961), a study of well-known literary hoaxes and lampoons.

Snodgrass, W.D., *in full* William De Witt, *pseudonym* S.S. Gardons (b. Jan. 5, 1926, Wilkinsburg, Pa., U.S.) American poet whose powerful early work is described as formalist and confessional.

Snodgrass's first collection, *Heart's Needle* (1959), which won the Pulitzer Prize, is marked by careful formal control and a sensitive and solemn delineation of his experience of losing his daughter through divorce. The collection *After Experience* (1968) continues these formal and thematic concerns. His later work—including *Remains* (1970), *If Birds Build with Your Hair* (1979), *D.D. Byrde Calling Jennie Wrenn* (1984), and *The Death of Cock Robin* (1989)—employs free verse. Other writing by Snodgrass includes several volumes of translations of European ballads and *In Radical Pursuit* (1975), a volume of criticism.

Snyder, Gary (Sherman) (b. May 8, 1930, San Francisco, Calif., U.S.) American poet early identified with the Beat movement and, from the late 1960s, an important spokesman for the concerns of communal living and ecological activism. Snyder received the Pulitzer Prize for poetry in 1975.

Snyder's poetry is rooted in ancient, natural, and mythic experience. His style exhibits a variety of influences, from Walt Whitman to Ezra Pound to Japanese haiku. Prominent in his first two books of poems, *Riprap* (1959) and *Myths and Texts* (1960), are images and experiences drawn from his work as a logger and ranger in the Pacific Northwest. In *Six Sections from Mountains and Rivers Without End, Plus One* (excerpts from an ongoing cycle of poems, 1965), *The Back Country* (1967), and *Regarding Wave* (1969), the fusion of religion into everyday life reflects the author's increasing interest in Eastern philosophies. Later volumes include *Turtle Island* (1974), for which Snyder won the Pulitzer, and *Axe Handles* (1983). His alternatives to routine city life are presented in *Earth House Hold* (1969), a book of journal fragments and essays, and *The Real Work: Interviews and Talks 1964–1979* (1980).

Snyder's later publications include *The Old Ways* (1977), a selection of essays on aspects of tribal life; *He Who Hunted Birds in His Father's Village* (1979), an examination of Haida Indian myth *Passage Through India* (1984), an account of an Asian pilgrimage; the essays found in *The Practice of the Wild* (1990); and *No Nature: New and Selected Poems* (1992).

Sontag, Susan (b. Jan. 16, 1933, New York, N.Y., U.S.) American intellectual and writer best known for her essays on modern culture.

Sontag attended the University of California at Berkeley and the University of Chicago, from which she graduated in 1951. She studied English literature and philosophy at Harvard University, teaching philosophy at several colleges and universities before the publication of her first novel, *The Benefactor* (1963). During the early 1960s she also wrote a number of essays and reviews, most of which were published in such periodicals as *The New York Review of Books*, *Commentary*, and *Partisan Review*. Some of these short pieces were collected in *Against Interpretation and Other Essays* (1968). Her second novel, *Death Kit* (1967), was followed by another collection of essays, *Styles of Radical Will* (1969). Her later critical works include *On Photography* (1977), *Illness as Metaphor* (1977), *Under the Sign of Saturn* (1980), and *AIDS and Its Metaphors* (1988). In 1992 her historical romance *The Volcano Lover* was published.

Sontag's essays are characterized by a serious philosophical approach to various aspects and personalities of modern culture. She first came to national attention in 1964 with an essay entitled "Notes on 'Camp'." In addition to criticism and fiction, she wrote screenplays and edited selected writings of Roland Barthes and Antonin Artaud.

Sorrentino, Gilbert (b. April 27, 1929, Brooklyn, N.Y., U.S.) American poet and experimental novelist whose use of devices such as nonchronological structure illustrated his dictum that "form not only determines content but form *invents* content."

From 1956 to 1960 Sorrentino was editor and publisher of *Neon*, a magazine that featured works by Beat writers; he was also book editor (1961–65) for *Kulchur*. His poetry collections include *The Darkness Surrounds Us* (1960), *The Perfect Fiction* (1968), and *The Orangery* (1978).

Among his avant-garde novels are *The Sky Changes* (1966), each chapter of which is named for a town the protagonists visit; *Imaginative Qualities of Actual Things* (1971), a plotless, digressive satire of the New York art scene of the 1960s; *Splendide-Hôtel* (1973), a novelistic defense of poetry arranged in 26 alphabetical sections; *Mulligan Stew* (1979), considered by some critics to be the apotheosis of avant-garde fiction, a multilevel mélange of Joycean proportions that satirizes creativity; *Odd Number* (1985), which deals with unanswered questions; *Rose Theatre* (1987), each chapter of which is written in a different narrative style; *Misterioso* (1989), an exhaustive, alphabetical catalog of everything discussed in *Odd Number* and *Rose Theatre*; and *Under the Shadow* (1991), a series of 59 vignettes with recurring characters and images.

Southern, Terry (b. May 1, 1924, Alvarado, Texas, U.S.—d. Oct. 29, 1995, New York, N.Y.) American writer of satirical novels and screenplays.

Southern was educated at Southern Methodist University, the University of Chicago, Northwestern University, and the Sorbonne. His first novel, *Flash and Filigree* (1958), satirizes the institutions of medicine and law. *Candy* (1958), written with Mason Hoffenberg under the pseudonym Maxwell Kenton, tells the tale of a libidinous young woman in a parody of pornography. His other novels include *The Magic Christian* (1959), *Blue Movie* (1970), and *Texas Summer* (1991). His *Red-Dirt Marijuana, and Other Tastes* (1967) is a collection of short stories and essays.

Southern also collaborated on screenplays for several popular movies of the 1960s.

Southworth, Emma, *original name in full* Emma Dorothy Eliza Nevitte, *also called* Mrs. E.D.E.N. Southworth (b. Dec. 26, 1819, Washington, D.C., U.S.—d. June 30, 1899, Georgetown, Washington, D.C.) One of the most popular of the 19th-century American sentimental novelists. For more than 50 years her domestic novels reached a wide audience in the United States and Europe.

After teaching school for five years, Nevitte married Frederick Southworth, an itinerant inventor. When the couple separated in 1844, she turned to writing to support her family. Her first novel, *Retribution* (1849), sold 200,000 copies. Southworth went on to write 66 more novels, many of them first published serially in such magazines as the *The Saturday Evening Post* and the *New York Ledger*. Her stories contributed two new character types to American fiction: the self-made man and the independent woman. Her works also relied on sentimental plots of the gothic genre that reflected prevailing values of piety and domesticity.

Southworth's *Ishmael* and *Self-Raised* (both 1876) were huge successes. Among her other successful novels were *The Curse of Clifton* (1852), *The Hidden Hand* (1859), and *The Fatal Marriage* (1863).

Spillane, Mickey, *original name* Frank Morrison Spillane (b. March 9, 1918, Brooklyn, N.Y., U.S.) American writer of pulp detective fiction, whose popular work is characterized by violence and sexual licentiousness.

Spillane began his career by writing for pulp magazines and comic books in order to pay for his schooling. His first novel—*I, The Jury* (1947)—introduced detective Mike Hammer, who appeared in other works, such as *My Gun Is Quick* (1950), *The Big Kill* (1951), and *Kiss Me Deadly* (1952). In the early 1950s Spillane retired from writing. Ten years later he resumed his career with *The Deep* (1961). Spillane wrote the script and played the role of Hammer for the 1963 film version of *The Girl Hunters* (1962). *Day of the*

Guns (1964) initiated another series, with the international agent Tiger Mann. Among Spillane's later books were *The Erection Set* (1972), *The Last Cop Out* (1973), and *The Killing Man* (1989). He also wrote two books for children and a book of short stories.

Stafford, Jean (b. July 1, 1915, Covina, Calif., U.S.—d. March 26, 1979, White Plains, N.Y.) American short-story writer and novelist noted for her deft development of fictional characters.

Stafford's first novel, *Boston Adventure* (1944), became a best-seller, reaching 400,000 copies. Its publication launched her career and guaranteed her a position of prominence in literary circles. She later wrote two more novels, *The Mountain Lion* (1947) and *The Catherine Wheel* (1952), as well as children's books. *The Collected Stories of Jean Stafford* (1969) won a Pulitzer Prize, and she contributed frequently to such journals as *The New Yorker*, *Kenyon Review*, *Partisan Review*, and *Harper's Bazaar*.

Stafford's personal life was marked by bouts of alcoholism and illnesses and by three troubled marriages (to the writers Robert Lowell, Oliver Jensen, and A.J. Liebling).

Stedman, Edmund Clarence (b. Oct. 8, 1833, Hartford, Conn., U.S.—d. Jan. 18, 1908, New York, N.Y.) Poet, critic, and editor whose writing was popular in the United States during the late 19th century.

As a critic Stedman wrote of contemporary authors in *Victorian Poets* (1875) and *Poets of America* (1885); he also edited the works of Edgar Allan Poe and Walter Savage Landor and was an important figure in the New York literary world. His *Poetical Works* appeared in 1875, *Hawthorne and Other Poems* in 1877, *Lyrics and Idylls, with Other Poems* in 1879, and *Mater Coronata* in 1900.

Steffens, Lincoln, *in full* Joseph Lincoln Steffens (b. April 6, 1866, San Francisco, Calif., U.S.—d. Aug. 9, 1936, Carmel, Calif.) American journalist, lecturer, and political philosopher, a leading figure among the writers whom Theodore Roosevelt called muckrakers.

During nine years of New York City newspaper work ending in 1901, Steffens discovered abundant evidence of the corruption of politicians by businessmen seeking special privileges. In 1901, after he became managing editor of *McClure's Magazine*, he began to publish the influential articles later collected as *The Shame of the Cities* (1906).

His many nationwide lecture tours won him recognition. Using comic irony, he jolted his audience into awareness of the ethical paradox of private interest in public affairs. He revealed the shortcomings of the popular dogmas that connected economic success with moral worth and national progress with individual self-interest.

Political events in Mexico and Russia turned Steffens' attention from reform to revolution. After a trip to Petrograd (St. Petersburg) in 1919 he wrote a friend, "I have seen the future; and it works." His unorthodoxy lost him his American audience during the 1920s, but he continued to study revolutionary politics in Europe and became something of a legendary character for the younger expatriates. His *Autobiography* (1931) was a great success.

Stegner, Wallace (Earle) (b. Feb. 18, 1909, Lake Mills, Iowa, U.S.—d. April 13, 1993, Santa Fe, N.M.) American author of fiction and historical nonfiction set mainly in the western United States. All of his writings are informed by a deep sense of the American experience and the potential, which he termed "the geography of promise," that the West symbolizes.

Stegner graduated from the University of Utah and the University of Iowa. He taught at several universities, notably Stanford University, where from 1945 to 1971 he directed the creative-writing program. His first novel, *Remembering Laughter* (1937), like his next three novels, was a relatively short work. His fifth novel, *The Big Rock Candy Mountain* (1943), the story of an American family moving from place to place in the West, seeking their fortune, was his first critical and popular success. Among his later novels are *The Preacher and the Slave* (1950; later titled *Joe Hill: A Biographical Novel*), the best-selling *A Shooting Star* (1961), the Pulitzer Prize-winning *Angle of Repose* (1971), and *The Spectator Bird* (1976), which won a National Book Award.

Stegner's nonfiction includes two histories of the Mormon settlement of Utah, *Mormon Country* (1942) and *The Gathering of Zion: The Story of the Mormon Trail* (1964), and a biography of Western explorer-naturalist John Wesley Powell, *Beyond the Hundredth Meridian: John Wesley Powell and the Second Opening of the West* (1954). A book of essays, *Where the Bluebird Sings to the Lemonade Springs: Living and Writing in the West*, was published in 1992.

Steinbeck, John Ernst (b. Feb. 27, 1902, Salinas, Calif., U.S.—d. Dec. 20, 1968, New York, N.Y.) American novelist, best known for THE GRAPES OF WRATH (1939), one of several naturalistic novels with proletarian themes that he wrote in the 1930s. These works, with their rich symbolic structures, effectively convey the mythopoetic and symbolic qualities of his characters. He received the Nobel Prize for Literature in 1962.

Steinbeck attended Stanford University intermittently between 1920 and 1926 but did not earn a degree. He worked as a manual laborer while

John Steinbeck

writing, and his experiences lent authenticity to his depictions of the lives of the workers in his stories. He spent much of his life in Monterey county, Calif.

Steinbeck's first three novels—*Cup of Gold* (1929), *The Pastures of Heaven* (1932), and *To a God Unknown* (1933)—were unsuccessful. He first achieved popularity with TORTILLA FLAT (1935), an affectionately told story of Mexican-Americans. His next novel, *In Dubious Battle* (1936), is a classic account of a strike by farm workers. The novella OF MICE AND MEN (1937), is a tragic story about the strange, complex bond between two migrant laborers. A Pulitzer Prize and a National Book Award were granted to Steinbeck for his next work, *The Grapes of Wrath*. The novel is about the migration of a dispossessed family from the Oklahoma Dust Bowl to California and describes their subsequent exploitation by a ruthless system of agricultural economics. Another notable achievement of this period was THE RED PONY (1937), which contains four stories of initiation.

During World War II Steinbeck wrote several effective pieces of government propaganda, among them *The Moon Is Down* (1942), a novel of Norwegians under the Nazis, and he also served as a war correspondent. His immediate postwar work—CANNERY ROW (1945), THE PEARL (1947), *The Wayward Bus* (1947)—contained the familiar elements of his social criticism but were more relaxed in approach and sentimental in tone.

Steinbeck's later writings were comparatively slight works of entertainment and journalism interspersed with three attempts to reassert his stature as a major novelist: *Burning Bright* (1950), EAST OF EDEN (1952), and *The Winter of Our Discontent* (1961). In critical opinion, none equaled his earlier achievement. Steinbeck also wrote the scripts for the film versions of *The Pearl* and *The Red Pony*. Outstanding among the scripts he wrote directly for motion pictures were *Forgotten Village* (1941) and *Viva Zapata!* (1952).

Steiner, George, *in full* Francis George Steiner (b. April 23, 1929, Paris, France) Influential European-born American literary critic who studied the relationship between literature and society, particularly in light of modern history. His writings on language and the Holocaust reached a wide, nonacademic audience.

Steiner was born in Paris of émigré Austrian parents and educated at the Sorbonne, the University of Chicago, Harvard University, and Oxford University. He became an American citizen in 1944 but spent much of his time in Europe. He was a member of the editorial staff of the *Economist* (1952–56) and worked at the Institute for Advanced Study at Princeton University (1956–58) before teaching at Churchill College, Cambridge University, and the University of Geneva, Switzerland.

His first book, *Tolstoy or Dostoevsky* (1959), compares the two authors on the basis of historical, biographical, and philosophical data. *Language and Silence* (1967) is a collection of essays that examines the dehumanizing effect that World War II and the Holocaust had on literature. Steiner explores the intersection of culture and linguistics that underlies translation and multilingualism in *Extraterritorial* (1971) and *After Babel: Aspects of Language and Translation* (1975).

Among his other critical works are *The Death of Tragedy* (1961), *In Bluebeard's Castle: Some Notes Towards the Redefinition of Culture* (1971), *On Difficulty and Other Essays* (1978), *Martin Heidegger* (1979), *Antigones* (1984), and *Real Presences* (1989). His fiction includes *Anno Domini* (1964), *The Portage to San Cristóbal of A.H.* (1981), and *Proofs and Three Parables* (1992).

Stein, Gertrude (b. Feb. 3, 1874, Allegheny, Pa., U.S.—d. July 27, 1946, Neuilly-sur-Seine, Fr.) Avant-garde American writer, eccentric, and self-styled genius, whose Paris home was a salon for the leading artists and writers of the period between World Wars I and II.

Stein spent her infancy in Vienna and Passy, Fr., and her girlhood in Oakland, Calif. After studying at Radcliffe College in Cambridge, Mass., and at Johns Hopkins medical school, she went to Paris. From 1903 to 1909 she lived solely with her brother Leo, who became an accomplished art critic. In 1909 Alice B. Toklas, whom she had met in 1907, moved in with Gertrude and Leo, and Leo moved out in 1914.

Gertrude Stein

Stein and her brother were among the first collectors of works by the Cubists and other experimental painters of the period, including Pablo Picasso (who painted her portrait), Henri Matisse, and Georges Braque, several of whom became her friends. At her salon they mingled with expatriate American writers, such as Sherwood Anderson and Ernest Hemingway, and other visitors drawn by her literary reputation (and Toklas' cooking). Stein's literary and artistic judgments were revered, and her chance remarks could make or destroy reputations. In her own work, she attempted to parallel the theories of Cubism, specifically in her concentration on the illumination of the present moment and her use of slightly varied repetitions and extreme simplification and fragmentation. The best explanation of her theory of writing is found in the essay *Composition as Explanation*, which was based on lectures that she gave at the universities of Oxford and Cambridge and was issued as a book in 1926. TENDER BUTTONS (1914) is a Cubist-inspired work that carries fragmentation and abstraction to an extreme.

Stein's first published book, *Three Lives* (1909), the stories of three working-class women, has been called a minor masterpiece. THE MAKING OF

AMERICANS, a long composition written in 1906–11 but not published until 1925, was too convoluted and obscure for general readers, for whom she remained essentially the author of such lines as "Rose is a rose is a rose is a rose." Her only book to reach a wide public was THE AUTOBIOGRAPHY OF ALICE B. TOKLAS (1933), actually Stein's own autobiography. The performance in the United States of her FOUR SAINTS IN THREE ACTS (1934), which the composer Virgil Thomson had made into an opera, led to a triumphal American lecture tour in 1934–35. Thomson also wrote the music for her second opera, THE MOTHER OF US ALL (1947), based on the life of feminist Susan B. Anthony. One of Stein's early short stories, Q.E.D., was first published in *Things as They Are* (1950).

Stein became a legend in Paris, especially after surviving the German occupation of France and befriending the many young American servicemen who visited her. She wrote about these soldiers in *Brewsie and Willie* (1946).

Sterling, Bruce (b. April 14, 1954, Brownsville, Tex., U.S.) American author of science fiction who in the mid-1980s emerged as a proponent of the subgenre known as cyberpunk, notably as the editor of *Mirrorshades: The Cyberpunk Anthology* (1986).

In 1976 Sterling graduated from the University of Texas at Austin and published his first story, "Man-Made Self," in the anthology *Lone Star Universe*. His first novel, *Involution Ocean* (1977), describes a dystopian planet where inhabitants escape their confusing lives through drug abuse. The characters in *The Artificial Kid* (1980) struggle to gain stability in a world of fast-paced change.

Sterling's novel *Schismatrix* (1985) and the short-story collection *Crystal Express* (1989) examine the contrasting philosophies of the Shapers, who alter themselves genetically, and the Mechanists, who alter themselves with prosthetic devices. In *Islands in the Net* (1988) heroine Laura Webster is drawn into the geopolitics of a vast information network. In *The Difference Engine* (1990); written with William Gibson), Sterling imagined the ascent of the computer age during the 19th century. In 1992 he published *Globalhead*, a volume of short fiction, and *The Hacker Crackdown: Law and Disorder on the Electronic Frontier*, an exposé of computer crime.

Stern, Richard G., *in full* Gustave (b. Feb. 25, 1928, New York, N.Y., U.S.) American author and teacher whose literate fiction examines the intricacies of marital difficulties and family relationships.

Stern was educated at the University of North Carolina, Harvard University, and the University of Iowa. From 1955 he taught at the University of Chicago.

His novels include *Golk* (1960), a humorous examination of the television industry; *Europe: or, Up and Down with Schreiber and Baggish* (1961), concerning two middle-aged American men in postwar Germany; *Stitch* (1965), about an expatriate American sculptor, modeled after Ezra Pound; *Other Men's Daughters* (1973), an autobiographical account of a middle-aged professor in love with a young female student; *Natural Shocks* (1978), in which a journalist must deal with the deaths of those close to him; and *A Father's Words* (1986), about a divorced father and his relationship with his grown children. *Teeth, Dying, and Other Matters* (1964) is a collection of short fiction, a play, and an essay. *The Books in Fred Hampton's Apartment* (1973) contains essays and miscellaneous pieces. Stern's other compilations include *Noble Rot: Stories 1949–1988* (1989), *Shares and Other Fictions* (1992), and *One Person and Another: On Writers and Writing* (1993).

Stevens, Wallace (b. Oct. 2, 1879, Reading, Pa., U.S.—d. Aug. 2, 1955, Hartford, Conn.) American poet whose work explores the interaction of reality and the human interpretation of reality.

Stevens attended Harvard University, worked briefly for the New York *Herald Tribune*, and then earned a degree (1904) at the New York Law School and practiced law in New York City. His first published poems, aside from college verse, appeared in *Poetry* in 1914, and thereafter he was a frequent contributor to literary magazines. In 1916 he joined an insurance firm in Hartford, rising in 1934 to vice president, a position he held until his death.

Harmonium (1923), his first book, sold fewer than 100 copies but received favorable critical notices; it was reissued in 1931 and in 1947. In the work, he introduced the imagination-reality theme that occupied his creative lifetime, making his work so unified that three decades later he considered calling his collected poems "The Whole of Harmonium."

Stevens displayed his most dazzling verbal brilliance in his first book; he later tended to relinquish surface luster for philosophical rigor. *Harmonium* contained such poems as "Le Monocle de Mon Oncle," "Sunday Morning," "Peter Quince at the Clavier," and Stevens' own favorites, "Domination of Black" and "The Emperor of Ice-Cream"; all were frequently republished in anthologies. *Harmonium* also contained "Sea Surface Full of Clouds"—in which waves are described in terms of such unlikely equivalents as umbrellas, French phrases, and varieties of chocolate—and "The Comedian as the Letter C," in which he examines the relation of the poet, or person of imagination, to society.

In the 1930s and early 1940s, this theme was to reappear, although not to the exclusion of others, in Stevens' *Ideas of Order* (1935), *The Man with the Blue Guitar* (1937), and *Parts of a World* (1942). *Transport to Summer* (1947) incorporated two long sequences that had appeared earlier: "Notes Towards a Supreme Fiction" and "Esthétique du Mal" ("Aesthetic of Evil"), in which he argued that beauty is inextricably linked with evil. *The Auroras of Autumn* (1950) was followed by his *Collected Poems* (1954), which earned him the Pulitzer Prize for poetry. It was not until late in life that Stevens was widely read at all or recognized as a major poet by more than a few. A volume of his critical essays, *The Necessary Angel*, appeared in 1951.

Stewart, Donald Ogden (b. Nov. 30, 1894, Columbus, Ohio, U.S.—d. Aug. 2, 1980, London, Eng.) American humorist, actor, playwright, and screenwriter who won a 1940 Academy Award for his screenplay adaptation of *The Philadelphia Story*.

After graduation from Yale University (1916), Stewart served in the U.S. Naval Reserve Force during World War I and worked briefly in private business before taking up humorous writing in 1921. His *A Parody Outline of History* (1921) was an instant success, and he quickly was received into the literary circle known as the Algonquin Round Table, famous for the witty repartee of members Dorothy Parker, Robert Benchley, and others. In 1928 Stewart made his New York City acting debut as Nick Potter in *Holiday* and subsequently wrote his first play, *Rebound*, in which he also appeared (1930).

It was, however, as a screenwriter, usually of adaptations of plays or novels, that Stewart achieved his most enduring success; his screenplays were notable for witty dialogue and for their fidelity to the original work. He fell victim to the anticommunist mania of the 1950s and was one of many Hollywood figures to be blacklisted. Thereafter, he retired to England. His autobiography, *By a Stroke of Luck*, was published in 1975.

Stockton, Frank R., *in full* Francis Richard Stockton, *pseudonyms* Paul Fort, John Lewees (b. April 5, 1834, Philadelphia, Pa., U.S.—d. April 20, 1902, Washington, D.C.) American popular novelist and short-story writer of mainly humorous fiction, best known as the author of the title story of a collection called *The Lady, or the Tiger?* (1884).

Stockton contributed to and was on the staff of *Hearth and Home* and in 1873 became assistant editor of the *St. Nicholas Magazine*. His earliest fiction was written for children. Among his most popular children's stories were those collected in *Ting-a-Ling Tales* (1870) and *The Floating Prince, and Other Fairy Tales* (1881). "The Griffin and the Minor Canon" and the title story of the collection *The Bee-Man of Orn, and Other Fanciful Tales* (1887) were both republished in the 1960s with illustrations by Maurice Sendak.

His adult novel *Rudder Grange* (1879), originally serialized in *Scribner's Monthly*, recounted the whimsically fantastic and amusing adventures of a family living on a canal boat. Its success encouraged two sequels, *Rudder*

Grangers Abroad (1891) and *Pomona's Travels* (1894). *The Casting Away of Mrs. Lecks and Mrs. Aleshine* (1886) tells of two middle-aged women on a sea voyage to Japan who become castaways on a deserted island. A sequel appeared in 1888 as *The Dussantes*. After 1887 Stockton wrote mostly for adults.

Stoddard, Richard Henry (b. July 2, 1825, Hingham, Mass., U.S.—d. May 12, 1903, New York, N.Y.) American poet, critic, and editor, more important as a late 19th-century literary figure than as a poet.

In 1849 Stoddard gave up his trade and began writing for a living. He served as a literary reviewer and editor for a number of New York newspapers and magazines. His house was a leading gathering place for writers and artists in the last 30 years of the 19th century. Some of Stoddard's work—*Abraham Lincoln, An Horatian Ode* (1865) and parts of *Songs of Summer* (1857) and *The Book of the East* (1867)—can still be read with interest. Stoddard's autobiography, *Recollections Personal and Literary*, was published in 1903.

Stone, Irving, *original surname* Tennenbaum (b. July 14, 1903, San Francisco, Calif., U.S.—d. Aug. 26, 1989, Los Angeles, Calif.) American writer of popular historical biographies. Stone first came to prominence with the publication of *Lust for Life* (1934), a fictionalized biography of the painter Vincent van Gogh.

Stone termed his work "bio-history." Through meticulous and exhaustive research, he verified and expanded his preconception of a selected historical character. Then, by immersing himself in the subject's native environment and reading all available original documents, from letters and diaries to research notes and household accounts, he acquired the basis for imaginary or reconstructed dialogue.

In addition to *Lust for Life*, Stone's many popular works include *Clarence Darrow for the Defense* (1941); *They Also Ran* (1943), biographies of 19 defeated presidential candidates; *President's Lady* (1951), based on the life of Rachel Jackson, wife of the seventh U.S. president; *Love Is Eternal* (1954), a fictionalized account of the marriage of Mary Todd and Abraham Lincoln; *The Agony and the Ecstasy* (1961), a life of the Renaissance artist Michelangelo; *The Passions of the Mind* (1971), about Sigmund Freud; and *The Origin* (1980), a life of Charles Darwin centered on the voyage of the *Beagle* and its aftermath.

Stone, Robert (Anthony) (b. Aug. 21, 1937, New York, N.Y., U.S.) American author of fiction about individuals in conflict with the decaying, late 20th-century Western societies in which they live.

Stone served in the U.S. Navy before attending New York and Stanford universities. *A Hall of Mirrors* (1967), his first novel, was set in New Orleans and revolved around a right-wing radio station and its chaotic "Patriotic Revival"; Stone adapted his novel for the screenplay of the film *WUSA* (1970). His second novel, *Dog Soldiers* (1974), brought the corruption of the Vietnam War home to the United States. The novel won the 1975 National Book Award, and Stone cowrote the screenplay for the film based on it, *Who'll Stop the Rain?* (1978).

In the late 1970s Stone visited Central America, the setting of his novel *A Flag for Sunrise* (1981), about four individuals in a corrupt, poverty-stricken country ripe for revolution. His novel *Children of Light* (1986) features a debauched screenwriter and a schizophrenic actress, both in decline. Stone's fifth novel, *Outerbridge Reach* (1992), was a well-received story of a foundering marriage and an around-the-world sailboat race.

Stout, Rex (Todhunter) (b. Dec. 1, 1886, Noblesville, Ind., U.S.—d. Oct. 27, 1975, Danbury, Conn.) American author who wrote genteel mystery stories (both novelettes and novels), many of which revolve around the elegantly eccentric and reclusive detective Nero Wolfe and his wisecracking aide, Archie Goodwin.

Stout worked odd jobs until 1912, when he began to write sporadically for magazines. After writing four moderately successful novels, he turned to the form of the detective story. From 1927 Stout earned his living exclusively by writing. In *Fer-de-Lance* (1934) he introduced Nero Wolfe, the obese, brilliant aesthete who solves crimes without leaving his New York City apartment. Stout had a passion for gourmet foods and was obsessed with the growing of orchids, both of which characteristics he gave his detective. The Nero Wolfe mysteries are narrated by Archie Goodwin, a private detective and Wolfe's link to the outside world. Stout wrote 46 Wolfe mysteries, all of which were very popular.

Stowe, Harriet Beecher, *original name* Harriet Elizabeth Beecher (b. June 14, 1811, Litchfield, Conn., U.S.—d. July 1, 1896, Hartford, Conn.) American writer and philanthropist best known as the author of the powerful antislavery novel UNCLE TOM'S CABIN (1852).

Stowe was the daughter of a famous Congregationalist minister, Lyman Beecher. After 1832 she taught in Cincinnati, where she took an active part in literary and school life, contributing stories and sketches to local journals and compiling a school geography. She continued to write after the school closed in 1836 and after her marriage that year to Calvin Ellis Stowe. In 1843 she published *The Mayflower; or, Sketches of Scenes and Characters Among the Descendants of the Pilgrims.*

Harriet Beecher Stowe

In Cincinnati, Stowe was separated only by the Ohio River from a slave-holding community; she came in contact with fugitive slaves and learned about life in the South from friends and from her own visits there. These experiences prompted her to write *Uncle Tom's Cabin*, which was published serially in the *National Era*, an antislavery paper of Washington, D.C. Stowe reinforced her story with *The Key to Uncle Tom's Cabin* (1853), in which she accumulated a large number of documents and testimonies against slavery.

In 1853, when Stowe made a journey to Europe, she was lionized in England. Later, however, British public opinion turned against her with publication in 1869 of the magazine article "The True Story of Lord Byron's Life," detailing her charge that the poet had had an incestuous love for his half sister. In 1856 she published *Dred: A Tale of the Great Dismal Swamp*, in which she depicted the deterioration of a society resting on a slave basis. When *The Atlantic Monthly* was established the following year, she found a ready vehicle for her writings; she also found outlets in the *Independent* of New York and later the *Christian Union*, of which papers her brother, Henry Ward Beecher, was editor.

Stowe thereafter led the life of a woman of letters, writing novels, of which *The Minister's Wooing* (1859) is best known, and many studies of social life in both fiction and essay. She also published a small volume of religious poems.

Strand, Mark (b. April 11, 1934, Summerside, P.E.I., Can.) Poet, writer of short fiction, and translator whose poetry, noted for its surreal quality, explores the boundaries of the self and the external world.

Educated at Antioch College, Yale University, and the University of Iowa, Strand later taught at several American universities. He was named American poet laureate in 1990.

Strand was influenced stylistically by Latin-American surrealism and European writers such as Franz Kafka, and his poetry, especially his earliest works, was known for its symbolic imagery and its minimalist sensibility. Collections of Strand's poetry include *Sleeping with One Eye Open* (1964), *Reasons for Moving* (1968), *Darker* (1970), *The Story of Our Lives* (1973), *The Late Hour* (1978), *Selected Poems* (1980), *The Continuous Life* (1990), and *Dark Harbor* (1993), the latter a book-length poem. A collection of prose pieces, *Mr. and Mrs. Baby and Other Stories*, was published in 1985. Among his translations of poetry by South American writers are *18 Poems from the Quechua* (1971) and Rafael Alberti's *The Owl's Insomnia* (1973). Strand edited *The Contemporary American Poets* (1969), *New Poetry of Mexico* (1970), and, with Charles Simic, *Another Republic: 17 European and South American Writers* (1976). He also wrote several children's books and works of art criticism.

Stratemeyer, Edward (b. Oct. 4, 1862, Elizabeth, N.J., U.S.—d. May 10, 1930, Newark, N.J.) American writer of popular juvenile fiction, whose Stratemeyer Literary Syndicate (1906–84) produced such books as the *Rover Boys* series, the *Hardy Boys* series, the *Tom Swift* series, the *Bobbsey Twins* series, and the *Nancy Drew* series.

Stratemeyer began writing stories in imitation of those of Horatio Alger, Jr., and other popular adventure writers. He sold his first magazine story in 1888. In 1893 he became editor of *Good News*, for which he wrote boys' stories, and in 1896 he added the editorship of *Bright Days*. His first book, *Richard Dare's Venture*, appeared in 1894, the first in a series, and about 1896 he began writing concurrently several series, such as the *Rover Boys' Series for Young Americans*, beginning in 1899, and the *Boy Hunters Series*, beginning in 1906. Over the years he wrote hundreds of books and stories.

In 1906 he founded the Stratemeyer Literary Syndicate, which published various juvenile series, written by himself and others. (Any one series might have had several authors, all using the same pseudonym.) After his death in 1930, his company was largely directed by his daughter, Harriet Stratemeyer Adams (1893?-1982), who under pseudonyms wrote many of the novels in the *Nancy Drew*, *Dana Girls*, *Hardy Boys*, and *Bobbsey Twins* series. In 1984 the publisher Simon & Schuster acquired all rights to the Stratemeyer Literary Syndicate.

Sturgeon, Theodore, *original name* Edward Hamilton Waldo, *pseudonyms* Frederick R. Ewing, E. Waldo Hunter, and E. Hunter Waldo (b. Feb. 26, 1918, Staten Island, N.Y., U.S.—d. May 8, 1985, Eugene, Ore.) American science-fiction writer who emphasized romantic and sexual themes in his stories.

Sturgeon sold his first short story in 1937 and began to publish in science-fiction magazines under several pseudonyms. He was especially prolific in the period between 1946 and 1958. His most noted work is *More Than Human* (1953), about six outcast children with extrasensory powers. In *Venus Plus X* (1960), he envisioned a utopia achieved by the elimination of all sexual differences. Sturgeon's other science-fiction and fantasy novels include *The Dreaming Jewels* (1950); also published as *The Synthetic Man*), *The Cosmic Rape* (1958), and *Some of Your Blood* (1961). He also wrote western, historical, and mystery novels.

Sturgeon was unusual among his peers in writing about loneliness, love, and sex. His stories were considered daring for featuring the problems of hermaphrodites, exiled lovers, and homosexuals.

Styron, William (b. June 11, 1925, Newport News, Va., U.S.) American novelist noted for his treatment of tragic themes and his use of a rich, classical prose style.

Styron's first novel, *Lie Down in Darkness* (1951), set in his native tidewater Virginia, tells of a disturbed young woman from a loveless middle-class family who fights unsuccessfully for her sanity before committing suicide. His next work, the novella *The Long March* (1956), chronicles a brutal forced march undertaken by the recruits in a Marine training camp. The novel *Set This House on Fire* appeared in 1960. Styron's fourth novel, THE CONFESSIONS OF NAT TURNER (1967), is a tour de force of complex psychological presentation and a vivid evocation of slavery in the United States. It was awarded a Pulitzer Prize in 1968.

Styron's subsequent works include a play, *In the Clap Shack* (1972); the novel SOPHIE'S CHOICE (1979; film, 1982); *This Quiet Dust* (1982), a collection of essays that treat the dominant themes of Styron's fiction; *Darkness Visible* (1990), a nonfiction account of Styron's struggle against depression; and *A Tidewater Morning* (1993), a collection of three previously published stories.

Swenson, May (b. May 28, 1919, Logan, Utah, U.S.—d. Dec. 4, 1989, Ocean View, Del.) American poet whose work was noted for its engaging imagery, intricate wordplay, and eccentric use of typography.

Swenson was educated at Utah State University. She later moved to New York City and worked for New Directions press. She was writer-in-residence at several North American universities.

Her first published volume of poetry, *Another Animal* (1954), also appeared in *Poets of Today* in 1954. Swenson's other verse collections include *A Cage of Spines* (1958), *To Mix with Time* (1963), *Poems to Solve* (1966), *Iconographs* (1970), *More Poems to Solve* (1971), *New & Selected Things Taking Place* (1978), and *In Other Words* (1987). *Half Sun, Half Sleep* (1967) contained new work and her translations of poetry by six Swedish authors. With Leif Sjoberg, Swenson translated from the Swedish *Windows and Stones, Selected Poems of Tomas Transtromer* (1972). Her own poetry was widely anthologized, and a collection entitled *Nature: Poems Old and New* (1994) was published posthumously.

Ida M. Tarbell

Booth Tarkington

Tan, Amy (b. Feb. 19, 1952, Oakland, Calif., U.S.) American author of novels about Chinese-American women that contrast the hardships the immigrant women experienced in China with the very different lives of their American daughters. She is best known for her two semiautobiographical novels, *The Joy Luck Club* (1989; film, 1993) and *The Kitchen God's Wife* (1991). Tan also wrote two children's stories, *The Moon Lady* (1992) and *The Chinese Siamese Cat* (1994).

Tarbell, Ida M., *in full* Minerva (b. Nov. 5, 1857, Erie county, Pa., U.S.—d. Jan. 6, 1944, Bridgeport, Conn.) Investigative journalist, lecturer, and chronicler of American industry, best known for her classic *The History of the Standard Oil Company* (1904). Tarbell was one of the journalists characterized by President Theodore Roosevelt as a muckraker.

The History of the Standard Oil Company, originally a serial in *McClure's*, is one of the most thorough accounts of the rise of a business monopoly and its use of unfair practices. Tarbell's association with *McClure's* lasted until 1906. She also wrote for *American Magazine*, which she also co-owned and coedited for several years. In addition, she penned several popular biographies, including eight books on Abraham Lincoln. Her autobiography, *All in the Day's Work*, was published in 1939.

Tarkington, Booth, *in full* Newton Booth Tarkington (b. July 29, 1869, Indianapolis, Ind., U.S.—d. May 19, 1946, Indianapolis) American novelist and dramatist, best known for his satirical and sometimes romanticized pictures of American Midwesterners.

Tarkington studied at Purdue University, Ind., and at Princeton but took no degree. He won early recognition with the melodramatic novel *The Gentleman from Indiana* (1899), reflecting his disillusionment with the corruption in the lawmaking process. His humorous portrayals of boyhood and adolescence, PENROD (1914), *Penrod and Sam* (1916), SEVENTEEN (1916), and *Gentle Julia* (1922), became young-people's classics. He was equally successful with his portrayals of Midwestern life and character: *The Turmoil* (1915), THE MAGNIFICENT AMBERSONS (1918; film, 1942), and *The Midlander* (1923), combined as the trilogy *Growth* (1927), and *The Plutocrat* (1927). ALICE ADAMS (1921), a searching character study, is perhaps his most finished novel. He continued his delineations of female character in *Claire Ambler* (1928), *Mirthful Haven* (1930), and *Presenting Lily Mars* (1933) and wrote several domestic novels in his later years. He also wrote many plays, including an adaptation of his immensely popular romance *Monsieur Beaucaire* (1901).

Tate, Allen, *in full* John Orley Allen Tate (b. Nov. 19, 1899, Winchester, Ky., U.S.—d. Feb. 9, 1979, Nashville, Tenn.) American poet, teacher, and novelist, and a leading exponent of the New Criticism. In both his criticism and his poetry, he emphasized the writer's need for a tradition to adhere to; he found his own tradition in the culture of the conservative, agrarian South and, later, in Roman Catholicism, to which he was converted in 1950.

Tate entered Vanderbilt University, Nashville, Tenn., in 1918, where he helped found *The Fugitive* (1922–25), a poetry magazine. Along with several other Fugitive poets, Tate contributed to the symposium *I'll Take My Stand* (1930), a manifesto defending the traditional agrarian society of the South.

From 1934 Tate taught at several schools, including Princeton University and the University of Minnesota (1951–68). He also edited *The Sewanee Review* in the mid-1940s, during which time it acquired wide importance as a literary magazine.

Allen Tate

In his best-known poem, "Ode to the Confederate Dead" (1926); revised 1930), the dead symbolize the emotions he is no longer able to feel. The poems written from about 1930 to 1939 broaden the theme of disjointedness by showing its effect on society, as in the sadly ironical "The Mediterranean" (1932). In his later poems Tate suggested that only through the subjective wholeness of the individual can society itself be whole. The view emerged tentatively in "Seasons of the Soul" (1943) and confidently in "The Buried Lake" (1953), both devotional poems.

Tate's only novel, *The Fathers* (1938), refashions the Jason-Medea myth to promulgate agrarian beliefs. His *Collected Poems* was issued in 1977; *Essays of Four Decades* appeared in 1969. *See also* FUGITIVE.

Taylor, Bayard, *in full* James Bayard Taylor (b. Jan. 11, 1825, Kennett Square, Pa., U.S.—d. Dec. 19, 1878, Berlin, Ger.) American author known primarily for his lively travel narratives and for his translation of J.W. von Goethe's *Faust*.

In 1844 Taylor's first volume of verse, *Ximena*, was published. He then arranged with *The Saturday Evening Post* and the *United States Gazette* to finance a trip abroad in return for publication rights to travel letters, which were compiled in the extremely popular *Views Afoot* (1846). In 1847 he began a career in journalism in New York. He continued his trips—to the Orient, Africa, and Russia—and became renowned as something of a modern Marco Polo. In 1862 he became secretary of the U.S. legation at St. Petersburg, Russia, and in 1878, U.S. minister to Germany. Of his works in this later period, the translation of *Faust* (1870–71) remains his best known. His *Poems of the Orient* appeared in 1855.

Bayard Taylor

Taylor, Edward (b. 1645?, in or near Coventry, Warwickshire, Eng.—d. June 24, 1729, Westfield, Mass. [U.S.]) One of the foremost poets in colonial British North America.

Unwilling to subscribe to a required oath of conformity because of his staunch adherence to Congregational principles, Taylor gave up schoolteaching in England, immigrated to New England, and entered Harvard College (later University). After his graduation in 1671, he became minister in the frontier village of Westfield, Mass., where he remained until his death.

Taylor's manuscript, *Poetical Works*, came into the possession of Yale in 1883 by the gift of a descendant, but it was not until 1939 that any of his poetry was published. The important poems fall into two broad divisions. "God's Determinations Touching His Elect" is an extended verse sequence setting forth the grace and majesty of God as a drama of sin and redemption. The "Sacramental Meditations," about 200 in number, were described by Taylor as "Preparatory Meditations Before My Approach to the Lord's Supper."

Taylor, Peter (Hillsman) (b. Jan. 8, 1917, Trenton, Tenn., U.S.—d. Nov. 2, 1994, Charlottesville, Va.) American short-story writer, novelist, and playwright known for his portraits of Tennessee gentry caught in a changing society.

From 1936 to 1937 Taylor attended Vanderbilt University, Nashville, Tenn., then the center of a Southern literary renaissance led by poets Allen Tate, Robert Penn Warren, and John Crowe Ransom. He transferred to Southwestern College in Memphis to study with Tate in 1937, then completed his B.A. in 1940 under Ransom at Kenyon College, Ohio. Taylor taught at a number of schools until 1967, when he joined the faculty of the University of Virginia in Charlottesville.

Taylor was best known for his short stories, which are usually set in his contemporary Tennessee and which reveal conflicts between old rural society and the rough, industrialized "New South." His first collection, *A Long Fourth, and Other Stories* (1948), was praised for its subtle depictions of family disintegration. In his 1950 novella *A Woman of Means*, regarded by many as his finest work, a young narrator recalls his wealthy stepmother's nervous collapse and reveals the tension between her city ways and his father's rural values.

The Widows of Thornton (1954), *Happy Families Are All Alike* (1959), and *Miss Leonora When Last Seen and Fifteen Other Stories* (1963) secured the author's reputation as a master of short fiction. Later works include *In the Miro District and Other Stories* (1977); THE OLD FOREST, published in *The Old Forest and Other Stories* (1985); the Pulitzer Prize-winning novel *A Summons to Memphis* (1986); and *The Oracle at Stoneleigh Court* (1993), a collection of several short stories and three plays.

Teasdale, Sara (b. Aug. 8, 1884, St. Louis, Mo., U.S.—d. Jan. 29, 1933, New York, N.Y.) American poet whose short, personal lyrics were noted for their classical simplicity and quiet intensity.

Teasdale made frequent trips to Chicago, where she eventually became part of Harriet Monroe's *Poetry* magazine circle. After rejecting the poet Vachel Lindsay as a suitor, she married a St. Louis businessman, Ernst Filsinger, in 1914. In 1929 she divorced him and moved to New York City, where she lived in virtual retirement until her suicide.

Her first book, *Sonnets to Duse and Other Poems*, was printed privately in 1907. From the beginning, her work was well received. With *Rivers to the Sea* (1915) she was established as a popular poet; she won the Pulitzer Prize in poetry in 1918 for *Love Songs* (1917). Her familiar "Let It Be Forgotten" is included in *Flame and Shadow* (1920). Gradually, as her technical competence increased, her poetry became simpler and more austere—*e.g.*, the haunting "An End" (in *Dark of the Moon*, 1926). In her last book, *Strange Victory* (1933), many of the poems foreshadow her own death.

Sara Teasdale

Terhune, Albert Payson (b. Dec. 21, 1872, Newark, N.J., U.S.—d. Feb. 18, 1942, near Pompton Lakes, N.J.) American novelist and short-story writer who became famous for his popular stories about dogs.

Terhune graduated from Columbia University (N.Y.), traveled in Egypt and Syria, and in 1894 joined the staff of the *New York Evening World*. His first book was *Syria from the Saddle* (1896); his first novel, *Dr. Dale* (1900), was written in collaboration with his mother. He published more than 12 books before he left the *Evening World* in 1916.

In 1919 appeared the first of his popular dog stories, *Lad, a Dog*. He wrote more than 25 books after 1919, nearly all of them novels in which dogs played conspicuous parts, including *Bruce* (1920), *The Heart of a Dog* (1924), *Lad of Sunnybank* (1928), and *A Book of Famous Dogs* (1937). He also wrote two autobiographical books, *Now That I'm Fifty* (1925) and *To the Best of My Memory* (1930).

Albert Payson Terhune

Terry, Lucy, *married name* Prince, *also called* Bijah's (Abijah's) Luce *or* Luce (Lucy) Abijah (b. 1730, West Africa—d. 1821, Vermont, U.S.) American poet, storyteller, and activist of the colonial and postcolonial period. Her only surviving work, the poem "Bars Fight" (1746), is the earliest existing poem by an African-American; it was transmitted orally for over 100 years, first appearing in print in 1855. The poem commemorates white settlers who were killed in an encounter with Indians in 1746.

Born in Africa, Terry was taken by slave traders to Rhode Island at a very young age. She was baptized a Christian at age five, with the approval of her owner, Ebenezer Wells of Deerfield, Mass. She remained a slave in the Wells household until 1756, when she married Abijah Prince, a free black. In 1764 the Princes settled in Guilford, Vermont, where all six of their children were born.

Terry was considered a born storyteller and poet. She was also a persuasive orator, successfully negotiating a land case before the Supreme Court of Vermont. She delivered a three-hour address to the board of trustees of Williams College in a vain attempt to gain admittance for one of her sons.

Thériault, Yves (b. Nov. 28, 1916, Quebec City, Que., Can.—d. Oct. 20, 1983, Montreal?, Que.) One of the most prolific writers in Canada, with some 1,300 radio and television scripts and some 50 books to his credit. He was hailed as a literary genius after the publication of *Agaguk* (1958), a poignant tale about an Inuit family faced with a European-based code of law.

Thériault, who dropped out of school at the age of 15, held a variety of jobs before becoming a professional writer. His other works include *Aaron* (1954), which explores the problems faced by a Jewish family in a Gentile world; *Ashini* (1960), a lyrical tale of the last chief of the Montagnais to live by ancestral customs; and *N'Tsuk* (1968), the life story of a 100-year-old native woman. Thériault's works were widely translated.

Theroux, Paul (Edward) (b. April 10, 1941, Medford, Mass., U.S.) American novelist and travel writer known for the exotic settings of his works, in which he often describes a clash between two cultures.

Theroux graduated from the University of Massachusetts. in 1963. He then taught English in Malawi, Uganda, and Singapore; thereafter, he lived in England and devoted all his time to writing. Several of his early novels— including *Girls at Play* (1969), and *Saint Jack* (1973)—focus on the social and cultural dislocation of Westerners in postcolonial Africa and Southeast Asia. His later novels include *The Family Arsenal* (1976), *The Mosquito Coast* (1981), and *Millroy the Magician* (1993).

Theroux first achieved commercial success with a best-selling travel book, *The Great Railway Bazaar* (1975), describing his four-month train journey through Asia. He wrote several more travel books, including *The Old Patagonian Express* (1979) and *The Happy Isles of Oceania* (1992).

Thomas, Audrey (Grace), *original surname* Callahan (b. Nov. 17, 1935, Binghamton, N.Y., U.S.) American-born Canadian author known for her autobiographical novels, short stories, and radio plays.

Thomas graduated from Smith College and settled in Canada. After receiving an M.A. from the University of British Columbia in 1963, she lived in Ghana from 1964 to 1966 and then returned to British Columbia.

Thomas wrote about domestic life, women's search for independence, and conflicts between men and women. She often threw her characters' inner conflicts into relief by transplanting them to foreign lands. Thomas' experimental style involved incorporating into her works word play and fragments of popular culture.

The stories of *Ten Green Bottles* (1967) are told by an unhappy female narrator of varying circumstances but consistent character. Thomas' alter ego Isobel Cleary narrates the novels *Mrs. Blood* (1970); *Songs My Mother Taught Me* (1973), based on Thomas's childhood memories; and *Blown Figures* (1974), set in Ghana and using Africa as a metaphor for the unconscious. Her later works include the story collections *Goodbye Harold, Good Luck* (1986) and *The Wild Blue Yonder* (1990) and the novel *Graven Images* (1993).

Thomas, Lewis (b. Nov. 25, 1913, Flushing, N.Y., U.S.—d. Dec. 3, 1993, New York, N.Y.) American physician, researcher, author, teacher, and administrator best known for his collections of essays, which are meditations and reflections on the larger truths invoked by the study of biology.

Thomas was the son of a physician and a nurse. He attended Princeton University and Harvard Medical School (M.D., 1937). He served in the U.S. Navy Medical Corps and taught at Johns Hopkins and Tulane universities and at the University of Minnesota Medical School. In 1954 he moved to New York University School of Medicine, which he left as dean to teach in the pathology department at Yale. In 1973 he took the presidency of the Memorial Sloan-Kettering Cancer Center, becoming president emeritus in 1984.

Thomas' first book, *The Lives of a Cell: Notes of a Biology Watcher* (1974), was a collection of 29 essays originally written for the *New England Journal of Medicine*. His later books include *The Medusa and the Snail* (1979), *Late Night Thoughts on Listening to Mahler's Ninth Symphony* (1983), and *The Fragile Species* (1992).

Thomas, Lowell (Jackson) (b. April 6, 1892, Woodington, Ohio, U.S.—d. Aug. 29, 1981, Pawling, N.Y.) Preeminent American radio commentator and an explorer, lecturer, author, and journalist. He is especially remembered for his association with T.E. Lawrence (Lawrence of Arabia).

Thomas attended Valparaiso University, the University of Denver, and Princeton University. During his early 20s he worked as a war correspondent in Europe and the Middle East, eventually following Lawrence into the Arabian Desert and filing the exclusive story and pictures that helped make Lawrence legendary. Thomas became renowned as a globetrotter and his films and written records of his expeditions established his reputation as an adventurer and a reporter. He wrote more than 50 books, including *With Lawrence in Arabia* (1924), *Kabluk of the Eskimo* (1932), *Back to Mandalay* (1951), and *The Seven Wonders of the World* (1956).

Probably best known for his radio work, Thomas made nightly news broadcasts for nearly two generations. Volume one of his autobiography was entitled *Good Evening, Everybody* (1976); his sign-off—"So long, until tomorrow!"—became the title of the second volume (1977).

Thompson, Dorothy (b. July 9, 1894, Lancaster, N.Y., U.S.—d. Jan. 30, 1961, Lisbon, Port.) American newspaperwoman and writer, one of the most famous journalists of the 20th century.

Dorothy Thompson

The daughter of a Methodist minister, Thompson attended the Lewis Institute in Chicago and Syracuse (New York) University. After World War I she went to Europe as a freelance correspondent and became famous for an exclusive interview with Empress Zita of Austria after Emperor Charles' unsuccessful attempt in 1921 to regain the throne of Hungary. She was married to novelist Sinclair Lewis from 1928 to 1942 and for a time led a domestic life. She returned to Europe, however, and began reporting on the Nazi movement, for which she became the first American correspondent to be expelled from Germany. In 1936, for the *New York Herald Tribune*, she began her newspaper column "On the Record," which eventually was syndicated to as many as 170 daily papers.

Thompson wrote many books, including *New Russia* (1928), *I Saw Hitler!* (1932), *Refugees: Anarchy or Organization* (1938), *Let the Record Speak* (1939), and *The Courage to Be Happy* (1957).

Thompson, Jim, *in full* James Myers Thompson (b. Sept. 27, 1906, Anadarko, Okla., U.S.—d. April 7, 1977, Los Angeles, Calif.) Novelist and screenwriter best known for his paperback pulp novels narrated by seemingly normal men who are revealed to be psychopathic.

Thompson worked in a number of odd jobs before becoming affiliated with the Federal Writers Project in the 1930s. He later worked as a journalist for the New York *Daily News* and the Los Angeles *Times Mirror*. Blacklisted for leftist politics during the anti-communist scare of the early 1950s, Thompson was later summoned to Hollywood by director Stanley Kubrick to co-write screenplays for *The Killing* (1956) and *Paths of Glory* (1957).

Thompson's reputation rested on his ability to enter the minds of the criminally insane. *The Killer Inside Me* (1952) was admired as a chilling depiction of a criminally warped mind; its narrator, like most Thompson narrators, speaks directly and colloquially to the reader. *After Dark, My Sweet* (1955), considered one of Thompson's best works, presented a mentally imbalanced narrator who becomes embroiled in a kidnapping scheme with his lover but kills himself rather than harm her.

The posthumous publication of two Thompson omnibuses—*Hardcore* (1986) and *More Hardcore* (1987)—and a short-story collection, *Fireworks:*

The Lost Writings of Jim Thompson (1988) revived interest in his work as classic hard-boiled crime fiction.

Thompson, William Tappan (b. Aug. 31, 1812, Ravenna, Ohio, U.S.— d. March 24, 1882, Savannah, Ga.) American humorist remembered for his character sketches of Georgia-Florida backwoodsmen.

Thompson worked briefly on a Philadelphia newspaper. He moved to Georgia in the early 1830s, and in 1838 he founded the *Augusta Mirror*, the first of several literary magazines he developed. Discovering that the South would not support literary periodicals, in 1850 he founded the *Savannah (Ga.) Morning News* and continued as its editor until his death. Influenced by jurist and sometime humorist Augustus Baldwin Longstreet, Thompson wrote amusing dialect letters from a Georgia Cracker known as Major Jones; these were collected in 1843 as *Major Jones's Courtship*, which achieved nationwide popularity. Other volumes followed.

Thoreau, Henry David (b. July 12, 1817, Concord, Mass., U.S.—d. May 6, 1862, Concord) American essayist, poet, and practical philosopher who is best known for having lived the doctrines of Transcendentalism, recording his experience in his masterwork, WALDEN (1854).

Henry David Thoreau

Thoreau graduated from Harvard University and taught for a few years in a school he started with his brother John. A canoe trip along the Concord and Merrimack rivers in 1839 confirmed him in the opinion that he ought to be not a schoolmaster but a poet of nature. By chance he met the essayist and poet Ralph Waldo Emerson, who had settled in Concord. With his magnetism Emerson attracted others to Concord. Out of their heady speculations and affirmatives came New England Transcendentalism, one of the most significant literary movements of 19th-century America. Late in 1837, at Emerson's suggestion, Thoreau began keeping a journal that would eventually cover thousands of pages. The Transcendentalist magazine *The Dial* published many of Thoreau's writings on the outdoors.

Thoreau grew restless, and in 1842 he tried unsuccessfully to cultivate the New York literary market. Confirmed in his distaste for city life and disappointed by his failure, he returned home to Concord in late 1843.

Early in the spring of 1845, Thoreau, then 27 years old, began to build a home on the shores of Walden Pond, a lake two miles south of Concord on land Emerson owned. From the outset the move gave him profound satisfaction. When not busy weeding his bean rows and trying to protect them from hungry woodchucks or occupied with fishing, swimming, or rowing, he spent long hours observing and recording the local flora and fauna, reading, writing A WEEK ON THE CONCORD AND MERRIMACK RIVERS (1849), and making entries in his journals, which later he would polish and include in *Walden*, a series of 18 essays describing his experiment in basic living. Thoreau stayed for two years at Walden Pond.

Midway in his Walden sojourn Thoreau had spent a night in jail, an event that he reflected on in his most famous essay, CIVIL DISOBEDIENCE (1849). When Thoreau left Walden, his life lost much of its illumination. Slowly his Transcendentalism drained away as he turned to a variety of tasks to support himself. In this period he made excursions, producing three magazine articles collected posthumously in THE MAINE WOODS (1864). He became a dedicated abolitionist and, as much as anyone in Concord, he helped to speed fleeing slaves north on the Underground Railroad. He lectured and wrote against slavery, with "Slavery in Massachusetts," a lecture delivered in 1854, his harshest indictment.

Thomas Bangs Thorpe

Thorpe or **Thorp, Thomas Bangs** (b. March 1, 1815, Westfield, Mass., U.S.—d. Sept. 20, 1878, New York, N.Y.) American humorist and one of the most effective portrayers of American frontier life before Mark Twain.

Thorpe studied painting and at age 18 exhibited his "Ichabod Crane" at the American Academy of Fine Arts, New York City. In 1836 he moved to Louisiana, where he published a succession of newspapers. Thorpe's "The Big Bear of Arkansas" (published in 1841 in the New York City magazine *Spirit of the Times*), was so outstanding a tall tale that some historians have named certain southwestern contemporaries of Thorpe the Big Bear school of humorists.

Following a political defeat, Thorpe moved in 1854 to New York City and published his finest sketches as *The Hive of the Bee Hunter*. During the U.S. Civil War he saw service in New Orleans; afterward he returned to New York City and spent his remaining years painting, working at the customhouse, and writing for *Harper's*, *Appleton's*, and other magazines.

Thurber, James (Grover) (b. Dec. 8, 1894, Columbus, Ohio, U.S.—d. Nov. 2, 1961, New York, N.Y.) American writer and cartoonist noted for his vision of the urban man as one who escapes into fantasy because he is befuddled and beset by a world that he neither created nor understands. Thurber's best-known portrait of this character is probably Walter Mitty. Thurber's stock characters—the snarling wife, her timid, hapless husband, and a roster of serene, silently observing animals—have become classics of urban mythology.

Thurber held several newspaper jobs before going in 1926 to New York City, where he was a reporter for the *Evening Post*. In 1927 he joined Harold Ross's newly established magazine, *The New Yorker*, as managing editor and staff writer, making a substantial contribution to its urbane tone. He was later to write an account of his associates there in *The Years with Ross* (1959).

Thurber, who considered himself primarily a writer, first published a drawing in *The New Yorker* in 1931, though his drawings had been used earlier—at the behest of his colleague E.B. White—to illustrate their jointly written *Is Sex Necessary?* (1929).

After Thurber left *The New Yorker* staff in 1933, he remained a leading contributor. In 1940 failing eyesight forced him to curtail his drawing, and by 1952 he had to give it up altogether as his blindness became nearly total.

His collections of stories include *My Life and Hard Times* (1933), a whimsical group of autobiographical pieces; *Fables for Our Time* (1940), a stylistically simple and charming, yet unflinchingly clear-sighted appraisal of human foibles; a play, *The Male Animal* (1941); with Elliott Nugent), a serious but humorously written plea for academic freedom; and *The Thurber Album* (1952), a second collection of family sketches. His fantasies for children, *The 13 Clocks* (1950) and *The Wonderful O* (1957), are among the most successful modern fairy tales.

Thurman, Wallace Henry (b. Aug. 16, 1902, Salt Lake City, Utah, U.S.— d. Dec. 22, 1934, New York, N.Y.) African-American editor, critic, novelist, and playwright associated with the Harlem Renaissance of the 1920s.

Thurman moved to Harlem in 1925, and by the time he became managing editor of the black periodical *Messenger* in 1926 he had immersed himself in the Harlem literary scene and encouraged such writers as Langston Hughes and Zora Neale Hurston to contribute to his publication. That summer, Hughes asked Thurman to edit *Fire!!*, a literary magazine conceived as a forum for young black writers and artists. Despite outstanding contributors, who included Hughes, Hurston, and Gwendolyn Bennett, the publication folded after one issue. Two years later Thurman published *Harlem*, again with work by the younger writers of the Harlem Renaissance, but it too survived only one issue.

In 1929 Thurman's play *Harlem*, written with William Rapp, opened to mixed reviews, although its bawdy treatment of Harlem life made it a popular success. His first novel, *The Blacker the Berry: A Novel of Negro Life*, also appeared that year. Like his unfinished play *Black Cinderella*, it dealt with color prejudice within the black community. Thurman is perhaps best known for his novel *Infants of the Spring* (1932), a satire of what he believed were the overrated creative figures of the Harlem scene. Some reviewers welcomed Thurman's bold insight, while others vilified him as a racial traitor. Thurman never again wrote on African-American subjects.

Timrod, Henry (b. Dec. 8, 1828, Charleston, S.C., U.S.—d. Oct. 6, 1867, Columbia, S.C.) American poet who was called "the laureate of the Confederacy."

The son of a bookbinder, Timrod attended Franklin College (later the University of Georgia), Athens, and for a short time read law in Charleston. In 1860 a collection of his poems was published. In his best-known essay, "Literature in the South" (1859), he criticized the lack of respect accorded Southern writers in both the North and the South. During the American Civil War he enlisted in the Confederate army but was soon discharged for reasons of health. Later he was an editor and part owner of the *South Carolinian* in Columbia. After the city was burned by Union forces, however, he suffered from poverty and chronic ill health. He died of tuberculosis.

In 1873 the Southern poet Paul Hamilton Hayne, who was Timrod's lifelong friend, edited *The Poems of Henry Timrod*. Among Timrod's poems supporting the South are "Ode Sung at the Occasion of Decorating the Graves of the Confederate Dead," "The Cotton Boll," and "Ethnogenesis." *Katie*, a lyric poem to his wife, was published in 1884 and *Complete Poems* in 1899.

Tolson, Melvin (Beaunorus) (b. Feb 6, 1898, Moberly, Mo., U.S.—d. Aug. 29, 1966, Dallas, Tex.?) African-American poet who worked within the modernist tradition to explore African-American issues. His concern with poetic form and his abiding optimism set him apart from many of his contemporaries. Writing after the Harlem Renaissance but adhering to its ideals, Tolson was hopeful of a better political and economic future for African-Americans.

Tolson's first collection of poetry, *Rendezvous with America* (1944), includes one of his most popular works, "Dark Symphony," a poem in six "movements" that contrasts European-American history with African-American history. The success of this collection led to Tolson's appointment as poet laureate of Liberia in 1947. The last of his works to be published during his lifetime was *Harlem Gallery: Book I, The Curator* (1965), planned as the first of a projected five-volume history of African-Americans.

Tolson's most important work is the posthumous collection *A Gallery of Harlem Portraits* (1979). Modeled on Edgar Lee Masters' *Spoon River Anthology*, this collection is an epic portrait of a culturally and racially diverse community. The lives and emotions of its characters are portrayed in blues lyrics, dramatic monologues, and free verse.

Toomer, Jean (b. Dec. 26, 1894, Washington, D.C., U.S.—d. March 30, 1967) African-American poet and novelist who was associated with the Harlem Renaissance.

After attending the University of Wisconsin and the City College of New York, Toomer taught briefly and then turned to lecturing and writing. CANE (1923); reprinted 1967), considered his best work, is an experimental novel, made up of poems, short stories, and a play, which depicts the experience of being black in America. Toomer also wrote extensively for *The Dial* and other little magazines and was the author of several experimental plays. In 1926 he attended the Gurdjieff Institute in France, dedicated to the expansion of consciousness and meditation, and upon his return led Gurdjieff groups in Harlem (N.Y.) and Chicago in the late 1920s and early 1930s. He began a similar institution in Portage, Wis., in 1931. Although he influenced other black writers, only after his death was he recognized as a writer of note, primarily for *Cane*.

Traill, Catherine Parr, *original surname* Strickland (b. Jan. 9, 1802, London, Eng.—d. Aug. 29, 1899, Lakefield, Ont., Can.) Nature writer who, in richly detailed descriptions of frontier life, was one of the first to praise the beauties of the Canadian landscape.

A writer of children's books in England, Traill immigrated to the wilderness of Upper Canada (now Ontario) in 1832. *The Backwoods of Canada* (1836), which was based on a series of letters written to her mother in England, was the forerunner of the Canadian nature essay. This book was followed by *The Female Emigrant's Guide, and Hints on Canadian Housekeeping* (1854) and *The Canadian Settlers' Guide* (1860), entertaining and practical narratives of frontier life. Also a naturalist, Traill wrote *Canadian Wild Flowers* (1869), *Studies of Plant Life in Canada* (1885), and *Pearls and Pebbles* (1895), on birds and animals. She introduced the animal story for children into Canadian literature with the publication of *Afar in the Forest* (1869).

Trilling, Lionel (b. July 4, 1905, New York, N.Y., U.S.—d. Nov. 5, 1975, New York City) American literary critic and teacher whose criticism was informed by psychological, sociological, and philosophical methods and insights.

Educated at Columbia University (Ph.D., 1938), Trilling taught briefly at the University of Wisconsin and at Hunter College in New York City before joining the faculty of Columbia in 1931.

Trilling's critical writings include studies of Matthew Arnold (1939) and E.M. Forster (1943), as well as collections of literary essays: *The Liberal Imagination* (1950), *Beyond Culture: Essays on Literature and Learning* (1965), and *Sincerity and Authenticity* and *Mind in the Modern World* (both 1972). He also wrote *Freud and the Crisis of Our Culture* (1955) and *The Life and Work of Sigmund Freud* (1962). His single novel, *The Middle of the Journey* (1947), concerns the moral and political developments of the liberal mind in America in the 1930s and '40s.

Trumbull, John (b. April 24, 1750, Westbury, Conn. [U.S.]—d. May 11, 1831, Detroit, Michigan Territory) American poet and jurist, known for his political satire, who was a leader of the Hartford wits.

While a student at Yale College (now Yale University), Trumbull wrote two kinds of poetry: "correct" but undistinguished elegies of the Neoclassical school and brilliant comic verse that he circulated among friends. His burlesque "Epithalamium" (1769) combined wit and scholarship, and his essays in the style of Joseph Addison were published in *The Boston Chronicle* in 1770. While a tutor at Yale he wrote *The Progress of Dulness* (1772–73), an attack on educational methods. His major work was the comic epic *M'Fingal* (1776–82), which acquired an exaggerated reputation as anti-Tory (anti-royalist) propaganda. His literary importance declined after 1782, as he became increasingly interested in law and politics.

Tuchman, Barbara, *original surname* Wertheim (b. Jan. 30, 1912, New York, N.Y., U.S.—d. Feb. 6, 1989, Greenwich, Conn.) American writer whose popular histories are marked by masterful literary style and a clear and powerful understanding.

Educated at Radcliffe College, Tuchman worked as a research assistant for the Institute of Pacific Relations and then was a writer and correspondent for *The Nation* magazine and other publications. Although she had published two earlier books, she first gained notice with *The Zimmerman Telegram* (1958), a study of the World War I document in which Germany promised Mexico parts of the American Southwest in return for support of the German cause. *The Guns of August* (1962); also published as *August 1914*) was released to widespread critical and popular acclaim and was awarded a Pulitzer Prize in 1963. A detailed account of the first month of World War I, it describes the military errors and miscalculations that led to the stalemate of trench warfare.

Tuchman's next book, *The Proud Tower* (1966), was a survey of European and American society, culture, and politics in the 1890s. She was awarded a second Pulitzer Prize for *Stilwell and the American Experience in China, 1911–45* (1970), a study of the United States' relationship with 20th-century China as epitomized in the wartime experiences of General Joseph Stilwell. *A Distant Mirror: The Calamitous 14th Century* (1978), presents a vivid picture of the events, personalities, and texture of life in 14th-century France. Later works include *The March of Folly: From Troy to Vietnam* (1984) and *The First Salute* (1988).

Turow, Scott (b. April 12, 1949, Chicago, Ill., U.S.) Best-selling American novelist, the creator of a genre of legal crime and suspense novels written by lawyers.

Turow, a practicing attorney, published a nonfiction work, *One L: What They Really Teach You at Harvard Law School* (1977), that is considered a classic for law students. His first novel, *Presumed Innocent* (1987; film, 1990), was written while he was an assistant U.S. attorney in Chicago. The story of Rusty Sabich, a deputy prosecutor assigned to investigate the murder of a female colleague with whom he has had an affair, is a well-crafted tale of suspense. *The Burden of Proof* (1990) and *Pleading Guilty* (1993) continue in the vein of legal drama.

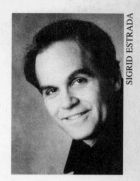

Scott Turow

Twain, Mark, *pseudonym of* Samuel Langhorne Clemens (b. Nov. 30, 1835, Florida, Mo., U.S.—d. April 21, 1910, Redding, Conn.) American humorist, writer, and lecturer who won a worldwide audience for his stories of youthful adventures, especially TOM SAWYER (1876), LIFE ON THE MISSISSIPPI (1883), and HUCKLEBERRY FINN (1884).

Clemens grew up in Hannibal, Mo., on the west bank of the Mississippi. At the age of 13 he became a full-time apprentice to a local printer. When his older brother Orion established the *Hannibal Journal*, Samuel became a compositor for that paper. After working for a time as an itinerant printer, he rejoined Orion in Keokuk, Iowa, until the fall of 1856. He then began another period of wandering with a commission to write some comic travel letters for the Keokuk *Daily Post*. Only five letters appeared, for on the way down the Mississippi, Clemens signed on as an apprentice to a steamboat pilot. For almost four years he plied the Mississippi. After 1859 he was a licensed pilot in his own right, but two years later the Civil War put an end to the steamboat traffic.

Mark Twain

In 1861 Clemens joined Orion in a trip to the Nevada Territory. Samuel became a writer for the Virginia City *Territorial Enterprise*, and there, on Feb. 3, 1863, "Mark Twain" was born when Clemens signed a humorous travel account with that pseudonym. The name was a riverman's term for water "two fathoms deep" and thus just barely safe for navigation. In 1864 Twain left Nevada for California. While at a mining camp Twain heard the story he would make famous as THE CELEBRATED JUMPING FROG OF CALAVERAS COUNTY, which was an immediate success.

In 1866 Twain visited Hawaii as a correspondent for *The Sacramento Union*, publishing letters on his trip and later giving popular lectures. He then set out on a world tour for California's largest paper, the *Alta California*. The letters that he wrote during the next five months for the *Alta California* and for Horace Greeley's *New York Tribune* caught the public fancy and, when revised for publication in 1869 as THE INNOCENTS ABROAD, established Twain as a popular favorite. Twain married in 1870 and moved with his wife to Hartford, Conn., in 1871.

In 1872 he published ROUGHING IT, a chronicle of an overland stagecoach journey and of Twain's adventures in the Pacific islands. Meanwhile, he collaborated with his neighbor Charles Dudley Warner on *The Gilded Age* (1873), a satire on financial and political malfeasance that gave a name to the expansive post-Civil War era.

Twain continued to lecture with great success in the United States and, in 1872 and 1873, in England. In 1876 he published *Tom Sawyer*, a narrative of youthful escapades, followed in 1880 by *A Tramp Abroad*, in 1881 by THE PRINCE AND THE PAUPER, and in 1883 by the autobiographical *Life on the Mississippi*. Twain's next novel, *Huckleberry Finn*, is generally considered his finest and one of the masterpieces of American fiction. In 1889 he published A CONNECTICUT YANKEE IN KING ARTHUR'S COURT, in which a commonsensical Yankee is transported back in time to medieval Britain.

Various unsuccessful financial speculations, including his own publishing firm, left Twain bankrupt; however, the returns from PUDD'NHEAD WILSON (1894), *Personal Recollections of Joan of Arc* (1895), a lecture tour around the world, and *Following the Equator* (1897), in which he described the tour, made him solvent again. THE MAN THAT CORRUPTED HADLEYBURG was published with other stories and sketches in 1900.

In the fall of 1903 Twain and his family settled near Florence, Italy. His wife died six months later, and he expressed his grief, his loneliness, and his pessimism about the human character in several late works, including LETTERS FROM THE EARTH.

HELEN MARCUS

Anne Tyler

Tyler, Anne (b. Oct. 25, 1941, Minneapolis, Minn., U.S.) American novelist and short-story writer whose comedies of manners are marked by compassionate wit and precise details of domestic life.

Tyler spent much of her youth in North Carolina and at age 16 entered Duke University (Raleigh, N.C.). She worked as a bibliographer at Duke and as a librarian at McGill University (Montreal, Que.) for several years before settling in Baltimore, Md., in 1967 and turning to writing full-time.

Tyler's first published novel, *If Morning Ever Comes* (1964), is typical of her work in its polished prose and its understated examination of personal isolation and the difficulties of communication between people. Her subsequent novels include *The Clock Winder* (1972), *Celestial Navigation* (1974), *Searching for Caleb* (1975), *Dinner at the Homesick Restaurant* (1982), *The Accidental Tourist* (1985), *Breathing Lessons* (1988), and *Saint Maybe* (1991). Several of Tyler's best novels focus on eccentric middle-class people living in chaotic, disunited families.

Tyler, Royall, *original name* William Clark Tyler (b. July 18, 1757, Boston, Mass. [U.S.]—d. Aug. 26, 1826, Brattleboro, Vt.) American lawyer, teacher, and dramatist and author of the first American comedy, *The Contrast* (1787).

With Joseph Dennie, Tyler formed a literary partnership; using the pseudonyms Colon and Spondee, they contributed satirical pieces to local newspapers.

A meeting with Thomas Wignell, the star comedian of New York City's American Company, led Tyler to write *The Contrast*, which premiered in New York in 1787. The play is a light comedy echoing the English playwrights Oliver Goldsmith and Richard Brinsley Sheridan (especially Sheridan's *The School for Scandal*). It contains a Yankee character, the predecessor of many such in years to follow, who was notable as a distinctly American type. His other plays, some no longer extant, did not equal *The Contrast*.

Underwood, Francis Henry (b. Jan. 12, 1825, Enfield, Mass., U.S.—d. Aug. 7, 1894, Edinburgh, Scot.) American author and lawyer who became a founder of *The Atlantic Monthly* (later *The Atlantic*) in order to further the antislavery cause.

Underwood attended Amherst (Mass.) College and the University of Kentucky. He joined the publishing house of Phillips, Sampson and Company as assistant editor in the early 1850s. The antislavery atmosphere of the Northeast and his close observation of slavery in Kentucky led him to the idea of publishing a literary magazine to oppose slavery. By 1857, after several years of editorial experience, he had gained the support of such liberal writers as Harriet Beecher Stowe, Oliver Wendell Holmes, Ralph Waldo Emerson, Henry David Thoreau, Henry Wadsworth Longfellow, and James Russell Lowell and persuaded his firm to publish a magazine. Edited by Lowell, with Underwood as assistant editor, *The Atlantic Monthly* began publication in November 1857. Underwood left the magazine in 1859 after it was purchased by another firm. He wrote biographies of Lowell, Longfellow, and John Greenleaf Whittier, as well as several short stories and novels. His best-known book is *Quabbin: The Story of a Small Town* (1893), an account of his boyhood in Enfield.

Updike, John (Hoyer) (b. March 18, 1932, Shillington, Pa., U.S.) American writer of novels, short stories, and poetry, known for his careful craftsmanship and realistic but subtle depiction of "American, Protestant, small-town, middle-class" life.

In 1955 Updike began an association with *The New Yorker* magazine, to which he contributed editorials, poetry, stories, and criticism throughout his prolific career. His poetry—intellectual, witty pieces on the absurdities of modern life—was gathered in his first book, *The Carpentered Hen and Other Tame Creatures* (1958), which was followed by his first novel, *The Poorhouse Fair* (1958). RABBIT, RUN (1960), which is considered to be one of his best novels, concerns a former star athlete, Harry "Rabbit" Angstrom, who is unable to recapture success when bound by marriage and small-town life. Three subsequent novels, *Rabbit Redux* (1971), *Rabbit Is Rich* (1981), and *Rabbit at Rest* (1990)—the latter two winning Pulitzer Prizes—follow the same character during later periods of his life. *The Centaur* (1963) and *Of the Farm* (1965) are notable among his novels set in his native Pennsylvania. Most of his later fiction is set in New England, where he lived (in Ipswich, Mass.) from the 1960s.

His later novels include *Couples* (1968), *Bech: A Book* (1970), *Marry Me* (1976), *The Coup* (1976), and *The Witches of Eastwick* (1984). His several collections of short stories include *The Same Door* (1959), PIGEON FEATHERS

(1962), *Museums and Women* (1972), *Problems* (1979), and *Trust Me* (1987). His nonfiction was collected in *Assorted Prose* (1965), *Picked-Up Pieces* (1975), *Hugging the Shore* (1983), *Just Looking* (1989), and *Odd Jobs* (1991).

Uris, Leon (Marcus) (b. Aug. 3, 1924, Baltimore, Md., U.S.) American novelist known for such panoramic, action-filled works as *Battle Cry* (1953), a story about a battalion of Marines during World War II, and *Exodus* (1958), which deals with the struggle to establish and defend the state of Israel.

Uris also wrote *The Angry Hills* (1955), an account of the Jewish brigade from Palestine that fought with the British army in Greece; *Mila 18* (1961), a novel about the Jewish uprising against the Nazis in the Warsaw ghetto in 1943; *QB VII* (1970), dealing with Nazi war crimes; *Trinity* (1976), a chronicle of a Northern Irish farm family from the 1840s to 1916; *The Haj* (1984), depicting the lives of Palestinian Arabs from World War I to the Suez war of 1956; and *Mitla Pass* (1988), an account of the Sinai campaign of 1956.

Van Dine, S.S., *pseudonym of* Willard Huntington Wright (b. Oct. 15, 1888, Charlottesville, Va., U.S.—d. April 11, 1939, New York, N.Y.) American critic, editor, and author of a series of best-selling detective novels featuring the brilliant but arrogant sleuth Philo Vance.

Pursuing a career as a writer, Wright became literary editor of the *Los Angeles Times* in 1907 and in 1912 moved to New York to become editor of *Town Topics* and *The Smart Set*, where he remained until 1914. With H.L. Mencken and George Jean Nathan he published a book of travel essays called *Europe After 8:15* (1914). He also wrote the poetry collection *Songs of Youth* (1913), the novel *The Man of Promise* (1916), and several critical works on art and philosophy, including *Modern Painting* (1915) and *What Nietzsche Taught* (1915).

While convalescing from an illness, Wright studied thousands of detective stories. As S.S. Van Dine, he eventually wrote a dozen Vance novels in that genre. Among them were *The Benson Murder Case* (1926), *The Bishop Murder Case* (1929), *The Kennel Murder Case* (1933), and *The Winter Murder Case* (1939). The successful series inspired numerous films and radio programs. Wright also edited the anthology *The Great Detective Stories* (1927) and wrote the essays "Twenty Rules for Writing Detective Stories," which appeared in *American Magazine* (1928), and *I Used to Be a Highbrow But Look at Me Now* (1929).

Van Doren, Carl (Clinton) (b. Sept. 10, 1885, Hope, Ill., U.S.—d. July 18, 1950, Torrington, Conn.) American author and teacher whose writings range through surveys of literature to novels, biography, and criticism.

Educated at Columbia University (Ph.D., 1911), Van Doren taught there until 1930. In that period he was one of a group of academicians who helped to establish American literature and history as an integral part of university programs. He also served as managing editor of the *Cambridge History of American Literature* (1917–21) and literary editor of *The Nation* (1919–22) and *Century Magazine* (1922–25).

For his discerning biography *Benjamin Franklin* (1938), Van Doren won a Pulitzer Prize. His other works include *The American Novel* (1921); revised 1940); *Contemporary American Novelists* (1922); *American and British Literature Since 1890* (1925), in collaboration with his brother, Mark Van Doren, and revised in 1939; and *What Is American Literature?* (1935). His autobiography, *Three Worlds,* appeared in 1936.

Van Doren, Mark (b. June 13, 1894, Hope, Ill., U.S.—d. Dec. 10, 1972, Torrington, Conn.) American poet, writer, and eminent teacher. He upheld the writing of verse in traditional forms throughout a lengthy period of experiment in poetry. As a teacher at Columbia University (N.Y.) for 39 years (1920–59), he exercised a profound influence on generations of students.

Like his older brother Carl, Van Doren attended Columbia University, from which he received a Ph.D. in 1920, and worked as literary editor (1924–28) and film critic (1935–38) of *The Nation* in New York City.

Van Doren's literary criticism includes *The Poetry of John Dryden* (1920); rev. ed., 1946); *Shakespeare* (1939); *Nathaniel Hawthorne* (1949); and *The Happy Critic* (1961), a book of essays. In *The Noble Voice* (1946); reprinted as *Mark Van Doren on Great Poems of Western Literature*, 1962) he considers 10 long poems by authors ranging from Homer and Virgil through William Wordsworth and Lord Byron. His *Introduction to Poetry* (1951); rev. ed., 1966) examines shorter classic poems of English and American literature.

The author of more than 20 volumes of verse, Van Doren published his first, *Spring Thunder*, in 1924. In 1940 he won the Pulitzer Prize for his *Collected Poems (1922–38)* (1939), a work that was later followed by *Collected and New Poems, 1924–1963* (1963). His poetry includes the verse play *The Last Days of Lincoln* (1959) and three book-length narrative poems, *Jonathan Gentry* (1931), *Winter Diary* (1935), and *The Mayfield Deer* (1941). Van Doren was the author of three novels—*The Transients* (1935), *Windless Cabins* (1940), and *Tilda* (1943)—and several volumes of short stories; he also edited a number of anthologies. In 1922 he married Dorothy Graffe, author of five novels and the memoir *The Professor and I*.

Van Duyn, Mona (Jane) (b. May 9, 1921, Waterloo, Iowa, U.S.) American poet noted for her examination of the daily lives of ordinary people, for mixing the prosaic with the unusual, the simple with the sophisticated. She is frequently described as a "domestic poet" who celebrates married love.

Van Duyn attended Iowa State Teachers College (now the University of Northern Iowa) and the University of Iowa. In 1947, with her husband, Jarvis Thurston, she founded *Perspective: A Quarterly of Literature and the Arts*, which she coedited until 1967. Her first volume of poetry, *Valentines to the Wide World*, was published in 1959. She won recognition following the publication of *To See, To Take* (1970), receiving the 1970 Bollingen Prize for achievement in American poetry and the 1971 National Book Award. Her other works include *A Time of Bees* (1964), *Merciful Disguises* (1973), and *Near Changes* (1990), for which she was awarded the 1991 Pulitzer Prize for poetry. *Firefall* and *If It Be Not I: Collected Poems 1959–1982* were published in 1993.

Van Duyn used wry humor, insight, irony, and technical skill to find meaning and possibility in a merciless world. She found in love and art the possibility of redemption—"but against that rage slowly may learn to pit/ love and art, which are compassionate."

Van Dyke, Henry (b. Nov. 10, 1852, Germantown, Pa., U.S.—d. April 10, 1933, Princeton, N.J.) American short-story writer, poet, and essayist.

Educated at Princeton, Van Dyke graduated from its theological seminary in 1877 and became a Presbyterian minister. His early works, "The Story of the Other Wise Man" (1896) and "The First Christmas Tree" (1897), were first read aloud to his congregation in New York as sermons. These quickly brought him recognition. His other stories and anecdotal tales were gathered at regular intervals into volumes. Among these collections were *The Ruling Passion* (1901), *The Blue Flower* (1902), *The Unknown Quantity* (1912), *The Valley of Vision* (1919), and *The Golden Key* (1926). Van Dyke's popularity also extended to his verse, collected in *Poems* (1920).

Van Vechten, Carl (b. June 17, 1880, Cedar Rapids, Iowa, U.S.—d. Dec. 21, 1964, New York, N.Y.) American novelist and music and drama critic, an influential figure in New York literary circles in the 1920s; he was an early enthusiast of American black culture.

Carl Van Vechten

Van Vechten worked as assistant music critic for *The New York Times* (1906–08) and later as that paper's Paris correspondent. His elegant, sophisticated novels, *Peter Whiffle, His Life and Works* (1922), *The Tattooed Countess* (1924), and *Nigger Heaven* (1926), were very popular. He also wrote extensively on music and published an autobiography, *Sacred and Profane Memories* (1932), following which he vowed to write no more and to devote his time to photography. His extensive collection of books on black Americana, the James Weldon Johnson Memorial Collection of Negro Arts and Letters, is now at Yale University. He also established the Carl Van Vechten Collection at the New York City Public Library and the George Gershwin Memorial Collection of Music and Musical Literature at Fisk University, Nashville, Tenn.

Van Vogt, A.E., *in full* Alfred Elton (b. April 26, 1912, near Winnipeg, Man., Can.) Canadian author of science fiction who emerged as one of the leading writers of the genre in the mid-20th century.

Van Vogt published his first story, "Black Destroyer," in the July 1939 issue of *Astounding Science Fiction.* He became a regular contributor to the magazine, which serialized his first novel, *Slan* (1946), from September to December of 1940. A story of mutants with superhuman powers, *Slan* was followed by *The Weapon Makers* (1947), which was first serialized in 1943. Other works first serialized in the 1940s were *The World of Ā* (1948); later published as *The World of Null-A*), a mysterious story about a developing superhero, and *The Weapon Shops of Isher* (1951), a sequel to *The Weapon Makers.*

Van Vogt took a break from science-fiction writing in the 1950s to help develop Dianetics, a form of psychotherapy that was later incorporated into Scientology. He resumed his writing career in the 1960s, but was unable to achieve his earlier fame. His later novels included *The Silkie* (1969), *Renaissance* (1979), and *The Cosmic Encounter* (1980).

Very, Jones (b. Aug. 28, 1813, Salem, Mass., U.S.—d. May 8, 1880, Salem) American Transcendentalist poet and Christian mystic.

Very was descended from a seafaring family. He was educated at Harvard College and Harvard Divinity School. At Harvard he became a Greek tutor, but his faculty colleagues ultimately forced his resignation after he began to relate his mystic beliefs and his "visions."

Very first came to notice for his critical essays. He began writing religious sonnets as early as 1837, insisting that they were all "communicated" to him. Contemporary authors, including Ralph Waldo Emerson, praised his work for its beauty and simplicity. His *Essays and Poems* was published in 1839. In 1843 Very was licensed to preach as a Unitarian minister.

Vidal, Gore, *original name* Eugene Luther Vidal (b. Oct. 3, 1925, West Point, N.Y., U.S.) Prolific American novelist, playwright, and essayist, noted for his irreverent and intellectually adroit novels.

Vidal graduated from Philips Exeter Academy in New Hampshire in 1943 and served in the U.S. Army in World War II. Thereafter he resided in many parts of the world—the east and west coasts of the United States, Europe, North Africa, and Central America. His first novel, *Williwaw* (1946), which was based on his wartime experiences, was praised by the critics, and his third novel, *The City and the Pillar* (1948), shocked the public with its direct and unadorned examination of a homosexual main character. Vidal's next five novels, including *Messiah* (1954), were received coolly by critics and were commercial failures. Abandoning novels, he turned to writing plays for the stage, television, and motion pictures and was successful in all three media. His best-known dramatic works from the next decade were *Visit to a Small Planet* (produced for television, 1955; on Broadway, 1957; for film, 1960), and *The Best Man* (play, 1960; film, 1964).

Vidal returned to writing novels with *Julian* (1964), a sympathetic fictional portrait of Julian the Apostate, the 4th-century pagan Roman emperor who opposed Christianity. *Washington, D.C.* (1967), an ironic examination of political morality in the U.S. capital, was followed by several popular novels that vividly re-created prominent figures and events in American history— *Burr* (1974), *1876* (1976), and *Lincoln* (1984). *Lincoln* presents a compelling portrait of President Abraham Lincoln's complex personality as viewed through the eyes of some of his closest associates during the American Civil War. Another success was the comedy *Myra Breckenridge* (1968), in which

Vidal lampooned both transsexuality and contemporary American culture. In *Rocking the Boat* (1962), *Reflections upon a Sinking Ship* (1969), *The Second American Revolution* (1982), *A View from the Diners Club* (1991), and other essay collections, he incisively analyzed contemporary American politics and government.

Vonnegut, Kurt, Jr. (b. Nov. 11, 1922, Indianapolis, Ind., U.S.) American novelist noted for his pessimistic and satirical novels that use fantasy and science fiction to highlight the horrors and ironies of 20th-century civilization.

Vonnegut's first novel, PLAYER PIANO (1952), visualizes a completely mechanized and automated society whose dehumanizing effects are unsuccessfully resisted by the scientists and workers in a New York factory town. *The Sirens of Titan* (1959) is a quasi-science-fiction novel in which the entire history of the human race is considered an accident attendant on an alien planet's search for a spare part for a spaceship. This he followed with CAT'S CRADLE (1963) and SLAUGHTERHOUSE-FIVE (1969).

Vonnegut also wrote several plays, including *Happy Birthday, Wanda June* (1970); several works of nonfiction; and several collections of short stories, chief among which was *Welcome to the Monkey House* (1968). His other novels include *Mother Night* (1961), *God Bless You, Mr. Rosewater* (1965), *Breakfast of Champions* (1973), *Slapstick* (1976), *Jailbird* (1979), *Deadeye Dick* (1983), *Galápagos* (1985), *Bluebeard* (1987), and *Hocus Pocus* (1990).

Wakoski, Diane (b. Aug. 3, 1937, Whittier, Calif., U.S.) American poet known for her personal verses that examine loss, pain, and sexual desire and that frequently reproduce incidents and fantasies from her own turbulent life. Her poetry probes the difficulties that the individual encounters in relationships with others, with the natural world, and with the cultural and popular ideas by which personal lives are structured.

Wakoski studied at the University of California, Berkeley, where she published her first poetry. The collection *Coins & Coffins* (1962), the first of more than 60 published volumes, contains the poem "Justice Is Reason Enough," about the suicide of an imaginary twin brother. In *The George Washington Poems* (1967) Wakoski addresses Washington as an archetypal figure. *Waiting for the King of Spain* (1976) concerns an imaginary monarch. *The Collected Greed: Parts 1–13* (1984), in which "greed" is defined as "failing to choose," contains previously published as well as unpublished poetry. Later collections include *Emerald Ice: Selected Poems 1962–1987* (1988) and *Medea the Sorceress* (1991).

Walker, Alice (Malsenior) (b. Feb. 9, 1944, Eatonton, Ga., U.S.) American writer whose novels, short stories, and poems were noted for their insightful treatment of black American culture. Her novels focused particularly on women, most notably THE COLOR PURPLE (1982; film, 1985), which won a Pulitzer Prize in 1983.

Alice Walker

After college Walker moved to Mississippi and became involved with the civil rights movement. She also began teaching and publishing short stories and essays and her first book of poetry, *Once* (1968). Her first novel, *The Third Life of Grange Copeland* (1970), traces a family's attempt to conquer a kind of emotional slavery that exists across three generations. In 1973 she published *In Love & Trouble: Stories of Black Women* and *Revolutionary Petunias & Other Poems*, before moving to New York to complete *Meridian* (1976), a novel about a young woman in the civil rights movement.

Walker later moved to California, where she wrote her most popular novel, *The Color Purple*. Written in epistolary form and in black English vernacular, the book depicts a black woman's struggle for racial and sexual equality. After releasing a collection of essays, *In Search of Our Mothers' Gardens* (1983), and a collection of poetry, *Horses Make a Landscape Look More Beautiful* (1984), she cofounded Wild Trees Press (1984–88). Her later novels include *The Temple of My Familiar* (1989) and *Possessing the Secret of Joy* (1992). Walker also wrote juvenile literature and critical essays on such women writers as Flannery O'Connor and Zora Neale Hurston.

Walker, Margaret (Abigail), *married name* Alexander (b. July 7, 1915, Birmingham, Ala., U.S.) American novelist and poet, one of the leading black woman writers of the mid-20th century.

After graduating from Northwestern University in Evanston, Ill., Walker joined the Federal Writers' Project in Chicago, where she began a brief literary relationship with novelist Richard Wright. She attended the University of Iowa and wrote *For My People* (1942), a critically acclaimed volume of poetry that celebrates black American culture. In the title poem, originally published in *Poetry* magazine in 1937, she recounts black American history and calls for a racial awakening.

Walker began teaching in the 1940s and joined the faculty at Jackson State College (now Jackson State University) at Jackson, Miss., in 1949. She completed her first novel, *Jubilee* (1966), as her doctoral dissertation for the University of Iowa. Based on the life of Walker's maternal great-grandmother, *Jubilee* chronicles the progress of a slave family from the mid to late 19th century. In *How I Wrote Jubilee* (1972), Walker traced her development of the story from her grandmother's oral family history through her extensive historical research. Her second volume of poetry, *Prophets for a New Day* (1970), makes comparisons between the prophets of the Bible and the black leaders of the civil rights movement. *October Journey* (1973) consists mostly of poems commemorating her personal heroes, such as Harriet Tubman, Gwendolyn Brooks, and her father. After she retired from teaching in 1979, Walker published *Richard Wright: Daemonic Genius* (1988) and a volume of poetry entitled *This Is My Century* (1989).

Wallace, Lewis, *byname* Lew Wallace (b. April 10, 1827, Brookville, Ind., U.S.—d. Feb. 15, 1905, Crawfordsville, Ind.) American soldier, lawyer, diplomat, and author, principally known for his historical novel BEN-HUR (1880).

Son of an Indiana governor, Wallace left school at 16 and became a copyist in the county clerk's office, reading in his leisure time. He began his study of law in his father's office but left to recruit volunteers for the Mexican War, in which he served from 1846 to 1847. In 1849, already a practicing attorney in Indianapolis, he was admitted to the bar. In the American Civil War he served with the Union forces and attained the rank of major general of volunteers. In 1865 Wallace resigned from the army and returned to law practice. He later held two diplomatic positions by presidential appointment.

Though he also wrote poetry and a play, Wallace's literary reputation rests upon three historical novels: *The Fair God* (1873), a story of the Spanish conquest of Mexico; *The Prince of India* (1893), dealing with the Byzantine Empire; and above all *Ben-Hur*, a romantic tale set in the Roman Empire

Lewis Wallace

during the time of Christ. *Lew Wallace: An Autobiography* was published in 1906.

Walrond, Eric (Derwent) (b. 1898, Georgetown, British Guiana [now Guyana]—d. 1966, London, Eng.) Caribbean writer who was associated with the Harlem Renaissance literary movement in New York City.

Walrond grew up in Guiana, Barbados, and Panama. From 1916 to 1918 he worked in the Panama Canal Zone as a clerk for the government and as a reporter for the Panama *Star-Herald*. In 1918 he immigrated to New York City, where he attended City College of New York and Columbia University.

Walrond was an editor and writer with the *Brooklyn and Long Island Informer* (1921–23), *Weekly Review* (1921–23), *Negro World* (1923–25), and *Opportunity* (1925–27). His articles and short fiction presented realistic examinations of racism in the United States, notably in the stories "On Being Black" (1922), "Cynthia Goes to the Prom" (1923), and "The Voodoo's Revenge" (1925), and in the article "The New Negro Faces America" (1923). His only book, *Tropic Death* (1926), a collection of short stories set against a lush Caribbean backdrop, juxtaposed impressionistic images of natural beauty with terse descriptions of misery and death in such stories as "The Yellow One," "The Palm Porch," and "Subjection." Walrond left the United States in 1927 and traveled throughout Europe before his death.

Ward, Artemus, *pseudonym of* Charles Farrar Browne (b. April 26, 1834, Waterford, Maine, U.S.—d. March 6, 1867, Southampton, Hampshire, Eng.) One of the most popular 19th-century American humorists, whose lecture techniques exercised much influence on such humorists as Mark Twain.

Starting as a printer's apprentice, Browne went to Boston to work as a compositor for *The Carpet-Bag*, a humor magazine. In 1860, after several years as local editor for the Toledo (Ohio) *Commercial* and the Cleveland *Plain Dealer*, he became staff writer for *Vanity Fair* in New York.

While working on the *Plain Dealer*, Browne created the character Artemus Ward, the manager of an itinerant sideshow who "commented" on a variety of subjects in letters to the *Plain Dealer*, *Punch*, and *Vanity Fair*. The most obvious features of his humor are puns and gross misspellings. In 1861 Browne turned to lecturing under the pseudonym Artemus Ward. Though his books were popular, it was his lecturing, delivered with deadpan expression, that brought him fame. His works include *Artemus Ward: His Book* (1862), *Artemus Ward: His Travels* (1865), and *Artemus Ward in London* (1867).

Artemas Ward

Ward, Elizabeth Stuart Phelps, *original name* Mary Gray Phelps (b. Aug. 31, 1844, Boston, Mass., U.S.—d. Jan. 28, 1911, Newton, Mass.) Popular 19th-century American author and feminist.

Mary Phelps assumed her mother's name, Elizabeth Stuart Phelps, after the latter's death in 1852. From the age of 13 she wrote juvenile fiction. In 1868 *The Gates Ajar*, her greatest success, was published. It is the story of a girl's struggle to renew her faith despite the death of a beloved brother. The novel was immediately popular, selling 80,000 copies in the United States and 100,000 in England; it was translated into at least four languages.

Phelps subsequently wrote 56 more books, in addition to poetry, pamphlets, and short articles. Her later work was often concerned with the domestic status of women. *The Story of Avis* (1877) and *Doctor Zay* (1882), for example, focus on the problems of women facing the demands of both career and marriage. Phelps also advocated the causes of labor, temperance, and antivivisection in her novels. Her autobiography, *Chapters From a Life*, was published in 1896.

Warren, Robert Penn (b. April 24, 1905, Guthrie, Ky., U.S.—d. Sept. 15, 1989, Stratton, Vt.) American novelist, poet, critic, and teacher, best known for his treatment of moral dilemmas in a South beset by the erosion of its traditional rural values. He won the Pulitzer Prize for fiction in 1947 and for poetry in 1958 and 1979, and he became the first poet laureate of the United States in 1986.

In 1921 Warren entered Vanderbilt University, Nashville, Tenn., where he joined a group of poets who called themselves the Fugitives. Warren was among several of the Fugitives who joined with other Southerners to publish the anthology of essays *I'll Take My Stand* (1930), a plea for the agrarian way of life in the South. After graduation from Vanderbilt, he studied at the University of California, Berkeley, and at Yale. He later served on the faculties of several colleges and universities—including Vanderbilt, the University of Minnesota, and Yale. With Cleanth Brooks and Charles W. Pipkin he founded and edited *The Southern Review* (1935–42), one of the most influential American literary magazines of the time.

Warren's first novel, *Night Rider* (1939), is based on the tobacco war (1905–08) between the independent growers in Kentucky and the large tobacco companies. It anticipates much of his later fiction in the way it treats a historical event with tragic irony, emphasizes violence, and portrays individuals caught in moral quandaries. His best-known novel is ALL THE KING'S MEN (1946), based on the career of the Louisiana demagogue Huey Long. Warren's other novels include *At Heaven's Gate* (1943), *World Enough and Time* (1950), *Band of Angels* (1956), and *The Cave* (1959). His long narrative poem *Brother to Dragons* (1953), dealing with the brutal murder of a slave by two nephews of Thomas Jefferson, is essentially a versified novel, and his poetry generally exhibits many of the concerns of his fiction. His other volumes of poetry include *Promises: Poems, 1954–1956* (1957); *You, Emperors, and Others* (1960); *Audubon: A Vision* (1969); *Now and Then: Poems, 1976–1978* (1978); *Rumor Verified* (1981); *Chief Joseph* (1983); and *New and Selected Poems, 1923–1985* (1985). *The Circus in the Attic* (1948), which included "Blackberry Winter," considered by some critics to be one of Warren's supreme achievements, is a volume of short stories, and *Selected Essays* (1958) is a collection of some of his critical writings.

Wasserstein, Wendy (b. Oct. 18, 1950, Brooklyn, N.Y., U.S.) Playwright whose work probes, with humor and sensibility, the situation of college-educated women and their responses to their own aspirations and to the feminism of the late 1960s. Her drama *The Heidi Chronicles* (1989) was awarded both a Pulitzer Prize and an Antoinette Perry award in 1989.

Wasserstein was educated at Mount Holyoke College, City College of the City University of New York, and Yale University. Her first play, *Any Woman Can't* (1973), is a cutting farce on one of her major themes—a woman's attempts to succeed in an environment traditionally dominated by men. Two other early works were *Uncommon Women and Others* (1978) and *Isn't It Romantic* (1984), which explore women's attitudes toward marriage and society's expectations of women. In *The Heidi Chronicles*, a successful art historian discovers that her independent life choices have alienated her from men as well as women. *The Sisters Rosenzweig* (1993) continues the theme into middle age.

Other works include an adaptation for television of the John Cheever short story "The Sorrows of Gin" (1979); the play "When Dinah Shore Ruled the Earth" (produced 1975; with Christopher Durang); "The Man in Case," an adaptation of Anton Chekhov's short story, published in the anthology *Orchards* (1986); and a musical, "Miami" (produced in 1986).

Welty, Eudora (b. April 13, 1909, Jackson, Miss., U.S.) American short-story writer and novelist whose work is focused with great precision on the regional manners of people inhabiting a small Mississippi town that resembles her own birthplace and the Delta country.

Welty was educated at the Mississippi State College for Women in Columbus, the University of Wisconsin, and the Columbia University School of Advertising in New York City. During the Great Depression she worked as a photographer on the Works Progress Administration's guide to Mississippi, and photography remained a lifelong interest. She also worked as a writer for a Jackson radio station and newspaper before her fiction won critical acclaim. Her readership grew steadily after the publication of *A Curtain of Green* (1941); enlarged 1979), a volume of short stories that contained two of her most anthologized stories—"Petrified Man" and WHY I LIVE AT THE P.O. Her novels include *The Robber Bridegroom* (1942), DELTA WEDDING (1946), THE PONDER HEART (1954), *Losing Battles* (1970), and THE OPTIMIST'S DAUGHTER (1972), which won a Pulitzer Prize. THE WIDE NET (1943), THE GOLDEN APPLES (1949), and THE BRIDE OF THE INNISFALLEN (1955) are collections of short stories, and *The Eye of the Story* (1978) is a volume of essays. *The Collected Stories of Eudora Welty* was published in 1980.

Welty's main subject is the intricacies of human relationships, particularly as revealed through her characters' interactions in intimate social encounters. Among her themes are the subjectivity and ambiguity of people's perception of character and the presence of virtue hidden beneath an obscuring surface of convention, insensitivity, and social prejudice. Welty's outlook is hopeful, and love is viewed as a redeeming presence in the midst of isolation and indifference. Her works combine humor and psychological acuity with a sharp ear for regional speech patterns.

One Writer's Beginnings, an autobiographical work, was published in 1984. Originating in a series of three lectures given at Harvard, it beautifully evoked what Welty styled her "sheltered life" in Jackson, Miss., and how her early fiction grew out of it.

Westcott, Edward Noyes (b. Sept. 27, 1846, Syracuse, N.Y., U.S.— d. March 31, 1898, Syracuse) American novelist and banker whose posthumously published novel *David Harum: A Story of American Life* (1898) proved to be immensely popular.

Westcott attended schools in Syracuse until age 16, when he became a junior clerk in a local bank. He devoted the next 30 years of his life to the banking business. In the summer of 1895 Westcott began to write *David Harum* while recuperating in the Adirondacks from tuberculosis. He continued writing the book in Italy and finished it in late 1896 after returning to the United States.

Westcott died six months before the publication of *David Harum*, which became a best-seller. More than 1,000,000 copies of the book were sold in the next four decades. *David Harum* is the story of a shrewd, crusty small-town banker in upstate New York who has an abundant fund of humor, an obvious talent for horse trading, and a strong streak of Yankee decency.

West, Nathanael, *original name* Nathan Weinstein (b. Oct. 17, 1903, New York, N.Y., U.S.—d. Dec. 22, 1940, near El Centro, Calif.) American writer best known for satiric novels of the 1930s.

Of middle-class Jewish immigrant parentage, West graduated from Brown University, Providence, R.I. During a 15-month stay in Paris he completed his first novel, *The Dream Life of Balso Snell*, which tells the story of an odd assortment of grotesque characters inside the Trojan horse. It was published in 1931 in an edition of only 500 copies. After his return to New York, West supported himself by working as a hotel manager, giving free or low-rent rooms to such struggling fellow writers as Dashiell Hammett, James T. Farrell, and Erskine Caldwell. His second novel, MISS LONELYHEARTS (1933), deals with an advice columnist whose manipulative attempts to solace his correspondents end in ironic defeat.

In *A Cool Million* (1934), West effectively mocks the American success dream popularized by Horatio Alger by portraying a hero who slides from bad to worse while doing what he supposes to be the right thing. In his last years West worked as a screenwriter in Hollywood. THE DAY OF THE LOCUST (1939) is, in the opinion of many, the best novel written about Hollywood. It dramatizes the false world and people on the fringes of the movie industry.

Nathaniel West

West was killed in an automobile accident with his wife, Eileen McKenney, who was the subject of Ruth McKenney's popular book *My Sister Eileen* (1938). Never widely read during his lifetime, West attracted attention after World War II, at first in France, where a successful translation of *Miss Lonelyhearts* appeared in 1946. Publication in 1957 of *The Complete Works of Nathanael West* sparked new interest in West's work in the United States.

Whalen, Philip (Glenn) (b. Oct. 20, 1923, Portland, Ore., U.S.) American poet who emerged from the Beat movement of the mid-20th century, known for his wry and innovative poetry.

Whalen served in the U.S. Army from 1943 to 1946 and attended Reed College, Portland, before joining the West Coast's nascent Beat movement. Like other Beats, he was contemptuous of structured, academic writing and was interested in Asian religions, personal freedom, and literary experimentation. Unlike the Beats, however, his poetry was often apolitical, whimsical, and steeped in the quotidian. In 1960 he published *Like I Say* and *Memoirs of an Interglacial Age*, both candid reflections of his "beatnik" life of the late 1950s. His poetry of the 1960s culminated in *Every Day* (1965) and *On Bear's Head* (1969), both of which include thoughtful observations of everyday life. He became an ordained Zen Buddhist priest in 1973, serving at centers in San Francisco and New Mexico. His later collections of poetry include *Decompressions* (1978), *Enough Said* (1980), and *Heavy Breathing* (1983). He also wrote the novels *You Didn't Even Try* (1967) and *Imaginary Speeches for a Brazen Head* (1972).

Wharton, Edith (Newbold), *original surname* Jones (b. Jan. 24, 1862, New York, N.Y., U.S.—d. Aug. 11, 1937, St.-Brice-sous-Forêt, Fr.) American author best known for her stories and novels about the upper-class society into which she was born.

Wharton was educated privately at home and in Europe. In 1885 she

Edith Wharton

married Edward Wharton, a Boston banker, and a few years later resumed the literary career she had begun tentatively as a young girl. Her major literary model was Henry James, whom she knew, and her work reveals James's concern for form and ethical issues.

The best of her early tales were collected in *The Greater Inclination* (1899). Her novel *The Valley of Decision* was published in 1902, followed in 1905 by the critical and popular success of her novel THE HOUSE OF MIRTH, which established her as a leading writer. After 1907 Wharton lived in France, visiting the United States only at rare intervals. In 1913 she was divorced from her husband.

In the two decades following the publication of *The House of Mirth*—before the quality of her work began to decline under the demands of writing for women's magazines—she wrote such novels as *The Reef* (1912), THE CUSTOM OF THE COUNTRY (1913), *Summer* (1917), and the Pulitzer Prize-winning AGE OF INNOCENCE (1920).

Her best-known work, however, was the long tale ETHAN FROME (1911), exploiting the grimmer possibilities of the New England farm life she had observed from her home in Lenox, Mass. She also wrote many short stories and poems, several books of travel reflecting her interest in architecture and landscape gardening, and a manual, *The Writing of Fiction* (1925). Her novel *Twilight Sleep* was a best-seller in 1927.

The most ambitious project of her later years was the novel *Hudson River Bracketed* (1929) and its sequel, *The Gods Arrive* (1932), books comparing the cultures of Europe and the sections of the United States she knew. Her best writing of that period was in the posthumous *The Buccaneers* (1938). Her autobiography, *A Backward Glance*, appeared in 1934.

Wharton, William (b. Philadelphia, Pa.) Pseudonymous novelist best known for his innovative first novel *Birdy* (1979; film, 1984), a critical and popular success.

Wharton wrote under that pseudonym to protect his privacy. Trained as a painter at the University of California at Los Angeles, he worked as an artist for almost 25 years before *Birdy*'s publication. During that time he and his family settled permanently in France.

Autobiographical elements and fantastic characters blend in Wharton's novels. *Birdy* tells of a man with a lifelong obsession with birds. Hospitalized as a result of his service in World War II, Birdy seems to want only to become a bird. Al, another scarred veteran and childhood friend, tries to help him. Wharton's second novel, *Dad* (1981), is about a middle-aged painter living in France who returns to the United States to care for his ailing parents. Further novels include the World War II story *A Midnight Clear* (1982; film, 1992);

Scumbler (1984), about an American artist in Paris; *Pride* (1985), a story of the Depression; *Tidings* (1987); and *Last Loves* (1991). Wharton also illustrated his seventh novel, *Franky Furbo* (1989).

Wheatley, Phillis (b. *c.* 1753, Senegal?—d. Dec. 5, 1784, Boston, Mass., U.S.) The first black woman poet and, after Anne Bradstreet, the second woman poet of note in the United States.

Phillis Wheatley

Wheatley, who is believed to have been of Fulani origin, is assumed to have been born in or near what is now Senegal or The Gambia. Transported on the slaver *Phillis*, she was sold in 1761 (at the age of about seven) to John Wheatley, a Boston merchant. The Wheatleys soon recognized her talents and gave her privileges unusual for a slave, including teaching her to read and write not only English but Latin as well. She read poetry and at the age of about 14 began to write it, taking Pope and other Neoclassical writers as models. Her elegy on the death of the famous Church of England evangelist George Whitefield, published in 1770, attracted much attention. To a surprising degree, she was accepted in Boston society. In 1773 her *Poems on Various Subjects, Religious and Moral*, consisting of 39 poems, was published in England under the sponsorship of the Countess of Huntingdon, and Wheatley's reputation spread in Europe as well as in America; the volume was issued more than a decade later in the United States. Upon her return from a trip to England in 1773 she was manumitted.

Mrs. Wheatley died in 1774 (her illness had prompted the poet's return from England), but Phillis remained with the family until the death of John Wheatley in 1778. In April of that year she married John Peters, a free black man who later failed in business and was sent to debtors' prison. At the end of her life Wheatley was working as a servant, and she died in poverty.

Wheatley's poetry, largely of the occasional type, was written in Neoclassical style. It reflected her own Christian concerns with morality and piety, and in that sense it was conventional. Until the later part of the 20th century many critics contended that her significance stemmed from the attention that she drew to her successful education, but later critical reevaluations were less patronizing and brought attention to bear on her mastery of style and suggested evidence of African influences on her work.

White, Edmund (Valentine) (b. Jan. 13, 1940, Cincinnati, Ohio, U.S.) Writer of novels, short fiction, and nonfiction whose critically acclaimed work focuses on male homosexual society in America. His studies of evolving attitudes toward homosexuality and of the impact of AIDS on homosexual communities in the United States were significant contributions to contemporary sociological and social history.

Educated at the University of Michigan, White taught writing seminars and creative writing at Columbia, Yale, New York, and George Mason universities. He was a frequent contributor of articles, reviews, and commentary to periodicals such as *New York Times Book Review*, *Mother Jones*, and *Architectural Digest*.

White's nonfiction includes *The Joy of Gay Sex* (1977); with Charles Silverstein), *States of Desire: Travels in Gay America* (1980), and a biography of Jean Genet (1993). Among White's novels are *Forgetting Elena* (1973), *Nocturnes for the King of Naples* (1978), *A Boy's Own Story* (1982), *Caracole* (1985), and *The Beautiful Room Is Empty* (1988). His play *Blue Boy in Black* was produced Off-Broadway in 1963.

White, E.B., *in full* Elwyn Brooks (b. July 11, 1899, Mount Vernon, N.Y., U.S.—d. Oct. 1, 1985, North Brooklin, Maine) Leading American essayist and literary stylist of his time.

White, who graduated from Cornell University, Ithaca, N.Y., in 1921, was a reporter and free-lance writer before joining *The New Yorker* magazine as a writer and contributing editor in 1927. He married Katherine Sergeant Angell, *The New Yorker*'s first fiction editor, in 1929 (he remained with the weekly magazine for the rest of his career). White collaborated with James Thurber on *Is Sex Necessary?* (1929), a spoof of the then-current sex manuals. From 1938 to 1943 he also contributed a monthly column to *Harper's* magazine. In 1959 White revised and published *The Elements of Style*, a manual originally written by William Strunk, Jr., whose student White had been; the book became a standard style manual for writing in the English language. In 1941 he edited with his wife *A Subtreasury of American Humor*. His three books for children—STUART LITTLE (1945), CHARLOTTE'S WEB (1952), and THE TRUMPET OF THE SWAN (1970)—are considered classics. His other works include *The Second Tree from the Corner* (1954) and *Points of My Compass* (1962). *Letters of E.B. White*, edited by D.L. Guth, appeared in 1976, his collected essays in 1977, and *Poems and Sketches of E.B. White* in 1981. He was awarded a Pulitzer Prize special citation in 1978.

White, Theodore Harold (b. May 6, 1915, Boston, Mass., U.S.—d. May 15, 1986, New York, N.Y.) American journalist, historian, and novelist, best known for his astute, suspenseful accounts of the 1960 and 1964 presidential elections.

After graduating from Harvard in 1938, White served as one of *Time* magazine's first foreign correspondents, being stationed in East Asia from 1939 to 1945. He then served as European correspondent for the Overseas News Agency (1948–50) and for *The Reporter* (1950–53). With this extensive background in analyzing other cultures, White was well equipped to tackle the American scene in *The Making of the President, 1960* (1961) and

The Making of the President, 1964 (1965). Accepted as standard histories of presidential campaigns, these books present their subjects by intelligently juxtaposing events and treating politicians as personalities rather than as symbols. White's approach elevated this type of history to an art form and won him the 1962 Pulitzer Prize for general nonfiction for *The Making of the President, 1960*. He went on to analyze the elections of 1968 and 1972 in similar books.

White was the coauthor (with Annalee Jacoby) of *Thunder Out of China* (1946) and also wrote *Fire in the Ashes* (1953), *The Mountain Road* (1958), *Breach of Faith: The Fall of Richard Nixon* (1975), the autobiographical *In Search of History: A Personal Adventure* (1978), and *America in Search of Itself: The Making of the President, 1956–1980* (1982). His books convey a genuine excitement about American institutions and politics.

Whitman, Walt, *in full* Walter Whitman (b. May 31, 1819, West Hills, Long Island, N.Y., U.S.—d. March 26, 1892, Camden, N.J.) American journalist, essayist, and poet whose style of writing in such works as LEAVES OF GRASS (first edition, 1855) revolutionized American literature. Such poems as I SING THE BODY ELECTRIC and SONG OF MYSELF asserted the beauty of the human body, physical health, and sexuality.

Whitman started work as a journeyman printer in 1835. A year later he began teaching and thereafter he held a great variety of jobs while writing and editing for several periodicals. He spent a great deal of his time walking and observing in New York City and Long Island; he visited the theater frequently; he developed a strong love of music, especially opera, and he read widely.

Walt Whitman

No publisher's or author's name appeared on the first edition of *Leaves of Grass* in 1855. But the cover had a portrait of Walt Whitman, "broad shouldered, rouge fleshed, Bacchus-browed, bearded like a satyr." The poems in *Leaves of Grass* addressed the citizens of the United States, urging them to be large and generous in spirit, a new race of races nurtured in political liberty. Whitman had been practicing his own style of writing in his private notebooks, and in 1856, after much rewriting, the second edition of *Leaves of Grass* appeared. This collection contained revisions of the poems of the first edition and several new ones, including the "Sun-down Poem" (later to become CROSSING BROOKLYN FERRY). All his later volumes of new poems were to be incorporated into successive editions of *Leaves of Grass*

From 1857 to 1859 Whitman edited the *Brooklyn Times*, and his way of life became bohemian. This period up to 1860, when the third edition of *Leaves of Grass* was published, was that of the "I" who was "turbulent, fleshy, sensual, eating, drinking and breeding." Notable in the 1860 volume were the

"Calamus" poems, which record a personal crisis of some intensity in his life, apparently a homosexual love affair; "Premonition" (later entitled "Starting from Paumanok"), which records the violent emotions that often drained the poet's strength; and "A Word Out of the Sea" (later entitled OUT OF THE CRADLE ENDLESSLY ROCKING).

When his brother was wounded at Fredericksburg, Whitman went there in 1862 to care for him. For the rest of the Civil War he spent much time cheering and caring for both Union and Confederate soldiers. In May 1865 DRUM-TAPS showed Whitman's readers a new kind of poetry, ranging from his early oratorical excitement to his later awareness of the horrors of war. The *Sequel to Drum-Taps*, published in the autumn of 1865, contained his great elegy on Lincoln, WHEN LILACS LAST IN THE DOORYARD BLOOM'D. The war had had its effect on Whitman's larger views, some of which emerged in the prose of DEMOCRATIC VISTAS (1871). His last works, aside from the ninth (authorized) edition of *Leaves of Grass* (1891–92), were the prose *Specimen Days & Collect* (1882–83) and a collection of 62 new poems entitled *November Boughs* (1888).

Whittemore, Reed, *in full* Edward Reed Whittemore II (b. Sept. 11, 1919, New Haven, Conn., U.S.) American teacher and poet noted for his free-flowing ironic verse.

Whittemore cofounded the literary magazine *Furioso* while he was a student at Yale University. He served in the U.S. Army Air Forces during World War II and afterwards revived and edited *Furioso* and its successor, *The Carleton Miscellany*, while a professor of English at Carleton College in Northfield, Minn. From 1968 to 1984 he taught at the University of Maryland, and he revived the magazine *Delos* in Maryland in 1988. Characters and quotes from literature inspired many of the whimsical poems in his first collection, *Heroes & Heroines* (1946). Daily life, the seasons, nature, and modern culture are the subjects of his verses in *An American Takes a Walk* (1956) and *The Self-Made Man* (1959).

In the 1960s, while his humorous tone remained, a note of sadness also began to make itself felt in such collections as *The Boy from Iowa* (1962) and *Poems, New and Selected* (1967); in *Fifty Poems Fifty* (1970) and *The Mother's Breast and the Father's House* (1974) the poet's bitterness emerges also. Whittemore's later collections include *The Past, the Future, the Present: Poems Selected and New* (1990). Among his prose writings are the biography *William Carlos Williams: Poet from Jersey* (1975) and a group portrait entitled *Six Literary Lives* (1993).

Whittier, John Greenleaf (b. Dec. 17, 1807, near Haverhill, Mass., U.S.— d. Sept. 7, 1892, Hampton Falls, Mass.) American author and Abolitionist noted for his vivid and deeply truthful portrayals of rural New England life.

Born on a farm, of Puritan and Quaker ancestry, Whittier had limited formal education, but he became acquainted with poetry at an early age. William Wordsworth, Samuel Taylor Coleridge, and Charles Lamb were lasting favorites, but his deepest admiration was for John Milton, whose role as apostle of freedom and goad to righteous living he sought to imitate.

Encouraged by the Abolitionist William Lloyd Garrison, Whittier wrote copiously and enthusiastically. When his father convinced him of the impracticality of poetry as a vocation, he turned to journalism. He edited newspapers in Boston and Haverhill and by 1830 had become editor of the *New England Weekly Review* in Hartford, Conn., the most important Whig journal in New England. During this period Whittier was also writing verse, sketches, and tales of New England, and he published his first volume of poems, *Legends of New England* (1831).

John Greenleaf
Whittier

By 1843 Whittier had broken with Garrison, but he continued actively to support humanitarian causes. He also became more active in literature. In the next two decades he published eight additional volumes of poems, which included "Songs of Labor" (1850), "Maud Muller" (1854), "The Barefoot Boy" (1855), and "Barbara Frietchie" (1863). Most of his literary prose, including his one novel, *Leaves from Margaret Smith's Journal* (1849), was also published during this period.

The American Civil War encompassed the deaths of several friends as well as his beloved younger sister Elizabeth, who with their mother had influenced him greatly. But national and personal grief furthered his literary maturity. The publication in 1866 of his best-known poem, SNOW-BOUND, in a collection of the same name, was followed by other triumphs in *The Tent on the Beach* (1867), *Among the Hills* (1868), and *The Pennsylvania Pilgrim* (1872).

Wideman, John Edgar (b. June 14, 1941, Washington, D.C., U.S.) American writer regarded for his intricate literary style in novels about the experiences of black men in contemporary urban America.

Until the age of 10, Wideman lived in Homewood, a black section of Pittsburgh, Pa., which later became the setting of many of his novels. An outstanding scholar and athlete at the University of Pennsylvania, he became the second black American to receive a Rhodes scholarship to Oxford University. He joined the faculty of the University of Pennsylvania in 1966, and the following year he published his first novel, *A Glance Away*, about a day in the lives of a reformed drug addict and a homosexual English professor. His second novel, *Hurry Home* (1970), is the story of an intellectual alienated from his black ancestry and the black community. *The Lynchers* (1973) was his first novel to focus on interracial issues.

Wideman left Pennsylvania to become a professor at the University of Wyoming (1975–85). The so-called *Homewood Trilogy*, an historical exploration of family and community, comprised two novels, *Hiding Place* (1981) and *Sent for You Yesterday* (1983), and a collection of short stories, *Damballah* (1981). In *Brothers and Keepers* (1984), his first nonfiction book, he contemplated the role of the black intellectual by studying his relationship with his brother, who was serving a life sentence in prison. After joining the faculty at the University of Massachusetts in 1985, Wideman published the short-story collection *Fever* (1989) and the novel *Philadelphia Fire* (1990). *The Stories of John Edgar Wideman* was published in 1992.

Wiesel, Elie, *in full* Elizer (b. Sept. 30, 1928, Sighet, Romania) Romanian-born American novelist whose works provide a sober yet passionate testament of the destruction of European Jewry during World War II. He was awarded the Nobel Prize for Peace in 1986.

Wiesel's early life, spent in a small Ḥasidic community in the town of Sighet, was a rather hermetic existence of prayer and contemplation and was barely touched by the war. In 1944, however, all the Jews of the town (annexed by Hungary in 1940), including Wiesel and the other members of his family, were deported to Auschwitz, where his mother and younger sister were killed. He was then sent as a slave laborer to Buchenwald, where his father was killed. After the war he settled in France, studied at the Sorbonne, and wrote for French and Israeli newspapers. He moved to the United States in 1956 and was naturalized in 1963. Wiesel taught at City College of New York and at Boston University.

While living in France, he was urged by the novelist François Mauriac to bear witness to what he had experienced in the concentration camps. The outcome was Wiesel's first book, his only work in Yiddish, *Un di velt hot geshvign* (1956; "And the World Remained Silent"), abridged as *La Nuit* (1958; *Night*). It is a semiautobiographical account of a young boy's spiritual reaction to Auschwitz and is one of the most powerful literary expressions of the Holocaust. All of Wiesel's works concern, in some manner, his wartime experiences and his reflections on their broader significance. They include *La Ville de la chance* (1962; *The Town Beyond the Wall*), a novel examining human apathy; *Le Mendiant de Jérusalem* (1968; *A Beggar in Jerusalem*), which ponders why people kill; *Célébration hassidique* (1972; *Souls on Fire*), a critically acclaimed collection of Ḥasidic tales; *Le Testament d'un poète juif assassiné* (1980; *The Testament*); *Le Cinquième fils* (1983; *The Fifth Son*); *Le Crépuscule, au loin* (1987; *Twilight*); and *L'Oublié* (1989; *The Forgotten*), in which a Holocaust survivor develops Alzheimer's disease and begins to lose his memories.

Wigglesworth, Michael (b. Oct. 18, 1631, Yorkshire?, Eng.—d. June 10, 1705, Malden, Mass. [U.S.]) British-American clergyman, physician, and author of rhymed treatises expounding Puritan doctrines.

Wigglesworth immigrated to America in 1638 with his family and settled in New Haven, Conn. In 1651 he graduated from Harvard College [later University], where he was a tutor and a fellow. He preached at Charlestown, Mass., in 1653–54 and was pastor at Malden from 1656 until his death. In addition to his clerical duties, Wigglesworth practiced medicine and wrote numerous poems, including "A Short Discourse on Eternity," "Vanity of Vanities," and *God's Controversy with New England* (published 1871). The first two were appended to *The Day of Doom: or a Poetical Description of the Great and Last Judgment* (1662), a long poem in ballad measure using horrific imagery to describe the Last Judgment. Once the most widely read poet of early New England, Wigglesworth declined in popularity together with Puritanism and has since been considered a writer of doggerel verse. A modern edition of *The Day of Doom* prepared by Kenneth B. Murdock was published in 1929.

Wilbur, Richard (Purdy) (b. March 1, 1921, New York, N.Y., U.S.) American poet, critic, editor, and translator noted for his urbane and well-crafted verse.

Wilbur was educated at Amherst College and Harvard University. With *The Beautiful Changes and Other Poems* (1947) and *Ceremony and Other Poems* (1950), he established himself as an important young writer. These early poems are technically exquisite and formal in their adherence to the convention of rhyme and other devices.

Wilbur next tried translating and in 1955 produced a version of Molière's play *Le Misanthrope*, later followed by Molière's *Tartuffe* (1963), *The School for Wives* (1971), *The Learned Ladies* (1977), and *The School for Husbands; and Sganarelle, or, the Imaginary Cuckold* (1994). He also translated Racine's *Andromache* (1982). In 1957 he won a Pulitzer Prize for poetry for *Things of This World: Poems* (1956). Wilbur wrote within the poetic tradition established by T.S. Eliot, using irony and intellect to create tension in his poems. His other collections include *Advice to a Prophet and Other Poems* (1961), *Walking to Sleep* (1969), and *The Mind Reader: New Poems* (1976). He also wrote the lyrics for Leonard Bernstein's musical comedy version of Voltaire's *Candide* (1957), children's books such as *Loudmouse* (1963) and *Opposites* (1973), and criticism, collected as *Responses: Prose Pieces 1953–1976* (1976). He was poet laureate of the United States in 1987–88, and in 1988 he published *New and Collected Poems*.

Wilder, Laura Ingalls (b. Feb. 7, 1867, Lake Pepin, Wis., U.S.—d. Feb. 10, 1957, Mansfield, Mo.) American author of children's fiction based on her own youth as a pioneer in the American Midwest.

Wilder spent 12 years editing the *Missouri Ruralist* before she began to write fiction. Her stories centered on the unrest of the men and patience of the women who were pioneers in the mid-1800s. She celebrated their peculiarly American spirit and independence. Her novels included *Little House in the Big Woods* (1932), *Farmer Boy* (1933), *Little House on the Prairie* (1935), *On the Banks of Plum Creek* (1937), *By the Shores of Silver Lake* (1939), *The Long Winter* (1940), *Little Town on the Prairie* (1941), and *These Happy Golden Years* (1943).

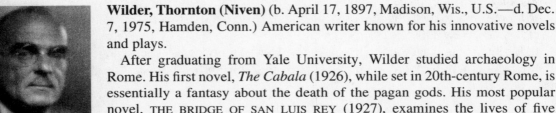
Thornton Wilder

Wilder, Thornton (Niven) (b. April 17, 1897, Madison, Wis., U.S.—d. Dec. 7, 1975, Hamden, Conn.) American writer known for his innovative novels and plays.

After graduating from Yale University, Wilder studied archaeology in Rome. His first novel, *The Cabala* (1926), while set in 20th-century Rome, is essentially a fantasy about the death of the pagan gods. His most popular novel, THE BRIDGE OF SAN LUIS REY (1927), examines the lives of five persons who died in the collapse of a bridge in Peru in the 18th century. *The Woman of Andros* (1930) is an interpretation of Terence's *Andria. Heaven's My Destination* (1934) is about a quixotically good hero in a contemporary setting. His later novels are *The Ides of March* (1948), *The Eighth Day* (1967), and THEOPHILUS NORTH (1973).

Wilder's plays, which are much better known than his novels, engage the audience in make-believe by having the actors address the spectators directly, by discarding props and scenery, and by treating time in an unrealistic manner through such devices as having the same characters appear in different historical periods and using deliberate anachronisms. Notable among them are OUR TOWN (1938), THE SKIN OF OUR TEETH (1942), and THE MATCHMAKER (1954). Wilder won Pulitzer Prizes for *The Bridge of San Luis Rey, Our Town,* and *The Skin of Our Teeth.*

Williams, C.K., *in full* Charles Kenneth (b. Nov. 4, 1936, Newark, N.J., U.S.) American poet whose early work is characterized by short lines and an acid tone, but who later altered both the form and content of his poetry.

Educated at Bucknell University (Lewisburg, Pa.) and the University of Pennsylvania, Williams was a contributing editor for *American Poetry Review* from 1972. His first collection of verse, *Lies* (1969), contains lyrical yet vituperative poems railing against human callousness and dishonesty. *I Am the Bitter Name* (1972), an overtly political collection, inveighs against the American military-industrial complex and the complacency of governments.

A stylistic and thematic departure is evident in *With Ignorance* (1977). It is an exploration of the American psyche rather than a diatribe, and its long-lined, conversational poems have a dramatic and investigative quality. His later works include *Tar* (1983), *Flesh and Blood* (1987), and *A Dream of Mind* (1992).

Williams, Tennessee, *original name* Thomas Lanier Williams (b. March 26, 1911, Columbus, Miss., U.S.—d. Feb. 25, 1983, New York, N.Y.) American dramatist whose plays reveal a world of human frustration in which sex and violence often underlie a pervasive atmosphere of romantic gentility.

FRED OHRINGER

Tennessee Williams

Williams became interested in playwriting while at the University of Missouri at Columbia and Washington University, St. Louis, Mo. Little theater groups produced some of his work, encouraging him to study dramatic writing at the University of Iowa. His first recognition came when *American Blues* (1939), a group of one-act plays, won a Group Theatre award.

Success came with THE GLASS MENAGERIE (1945), which portrays a declassed Southern family living in a tenement. Williams' next major play, A STREETCAR NAMED DESIRE (1947), is the story of the ruin of one member of a once-genteel Southern family. The play won a Pulitzer Prize. In 1953 *Camino Real*, a complex and bizarre work set in a mythical, microcosmic town whose inhabitants include Lord Byron and Don Quixote, was a commercial failure, but CAT ON A HOT TIN ROOF (1955) was awarded a Pulitzer Prize and was successfully filmed, as was THE NIGHT OF THE IGUANA (1961). In SUDDENLY LAST SUMMER (1958) Williams deals with lobotomy, pederasty, and cannibalism, and in SWEET BIRD OF YOUTH (1959) the gigolo hero is castrated for having infected a Southern politician's daughter with venereal disease.

Williams was in ill health frequently during the 1960s, culminating in a severe mental and physical breakdown in 1969. His later plays were unsuccessful. They include *Vieux Carré* (1977), *A Lovely Sunday for Crève Coeur* (1978–79), and *Clothes for a Summer Hotel* (1980). Williams also wrote two novels, *The Roman Spring of Mrs. Stone* (1950) and *Moise and the World of Reason* (1975), essays, poetry, film scripts, short stories, and an autobiography, *Memoirs* (1975). His works won four Drama Critics' awards and were widely translated and performed around the world.

Williams, William Carlos (b. Sept. 17, 1883, Rutherford, N.J., U.S.— d. March 4, 1963, Rutherford) American poet who succeeded in making the ordinary appear extraordinary through the clarity and discreteness of his imagery. Williams, trained as a pediatrician, devoted himself to a lifetime of poetry writing and medical practice in his hometown. In *Al Que Quiere!* (1917), roughly translated "To Him Who Wants It," his style is distinctly his own. Characteristic poems that express Williams' fresh, direct impression of the sensuous world are the frequently anthologized "Lighthearted William" and "By the Road to the Contagious Hospital" and "The Red Wheelbarrow," both of the latter published in SPRING AND ALL (1923).

In the 1930s, during the Depression, his images became less a celebration of the world and more a catalog of its wrongs. Such poems as "Proletarian Portrait" and "The Yachts" reveal his skill in conveying attitudes by presentation rather than explanation. The five-volume PATERSON (1946–58) is based on an examination of the industrial city in New Jersey and evokes a complex vision of America and modern life.

A prolific writer of prose, Williams analyzed the American character and culture through essays on historical figures in *In the American Grain* (1925). He also wrote a trilogy of novels about a family—*White Mule* (1937), *In the Money* (1940), and *The Build-Up* (1952). Among his notable short stories are "Jean Beicke," "A Face of Stone," and "The Farmers' Daughters." He also published the play *A Dream of Love* (1948) and his *Autobiography* (1951). In 1963 he was posthumously awarded the Pulitzer Prize in poetry for his PICTURES FROM BRUEGHEL (1962).

Wilson, August (b. April 27, 1945, Pittsburgh, Pa., U.S.) American playwright, author of a cycle of plays, each set in a different decade of the 20th century, about black American life. He won Pulitzer Prizes for FENCES (1986) and for THE PIANO LESSON (1990).

Largely self-educated, Wilson grew up in poverty and quit school at age 15. He joined the black aesthetic movement in the late 1960s, became the cofounder and director of Black Horizons Theatre in Pittsburgh (1968), and published poetry in such journals as *Black World* (1971) and *Black Lines* (1972). In the early 1980s he wrote several unpublished plays, including *Jitney* and *Fullerton Street*.

Wilson's first major play, MA RAINEY'S BLACK BOTTOM (1985), opened on Broadway in 1984. Set in Chicago in 1927, the play centers upon a verbally abusive blues singer, her fellow black musicians, and their white manager. *Fences*, first produced in 1985, is about a conflict between a father and son in the 1950s. Wilson's chronicle of the black American experience continued with JOE TURNER'S COME AND GONE (1988), a play about neighbors in a Pittsburgh boardinghouse in 1911; *The Piano Lesson*, set in the 1930s and concerning a family's ambivalence about selling an heirloom; and *Two Trains Running* (1992), whose action takes place in a Pittsburgh coffeehouse in the 1960s. His next play, *Seven Guitars*, was first produced in 1995.

Wilson, Edmund (b. May 8, 1895, Red Bank, N.J., U.S.—d. June 12, 1972, Talcottville, N.Y.) American critic and essayist recognized as the leading critic of his time.

Educated at Princeton, Wilson worked first as a newspaper reporter in New York before becoming managing editor of *Vanity Fair* (1920–21) and associate editor of *The New Republic* (1926–31). His first critical work, AXEL'S CASTLE (1931), was an important international survey of the Symbolist poets. During this period Wilson was married to writer Mary McCarthy. His next major book, TO THE FINLAND STATION (1940), was a historical study of the thinkers who laid the groundwork for the Russian Revolution. Until late in 1940 he was a contributor to *The New Republic*, and much of his work for it was collected in *Travels in Two Democracies* (1936), *The Triple Thinkers* (1938), and THE WOUND AND THE BOW (1941).

After World War II Wilson wrote *The Scrolls from the Dead Sea* (1955), for which he learned to read Hebrew; *Red, Black, Blond and Olive: Studies in Four Civilizations: Zuni, Haiti, Soviet Russia, Israel* (1956); *Apologies to the Iroquois* (1960); PATRIOTIC GORE (1962), an analysis of American Civil War literature; and *O Canada: An American's Notes on Canadian Culture* (1965).

In other works Wilson gave evidence of his crotchety character: *A Piece of My Mind: Reflections at Sixty* (1956), *The Cold War and the Income Tax* (1963), and *The Fruits of the MLA* (1968), a lengthy attack on the Modern Language Association's editions of American authors, which he felt buried their subjects in pedantry. His plays are in part collected in *Five Plays* (1954) and in *The Duke of Palermo and Other Plays with an Open Letter to Mike Nichols* (1969). His poems appear in *Notebooks of Night* (1942) and in *Night Thoughts* (1961); an early collection, *Poets, Farewell*, appeared in 1929. MEMOIRS OF HECATE COUNTY (1946) is a collection of short stories that encountered censorship problems when it first appeared. Wilson edited the posthumous papers and notebooks of his friend F. Scott Fitzgerald, published as *The Crack-Up* (1945), and also edited the novel *The Last Tycoon* (1941), which Fitzgerald had left uncompleted at his death. Wilson wrote one novel himself, *I Thought of Daisy* (1929). Wilson's journals were published posthumously in five volumes, each of which covers a decade.

Wilson, Harriet E., *original surname* Adams (b. 1828?, Milford, New Hampshire?, U.S.—d. 1863?, Boston, Mass?) Probably the first African-American to publish a novel in English in the United States. Her work, entitled *Our Nig; or, Sketches from the Life of a Free Black, in a Two-Story White House, North. Showing that Slavery's Shadows Fall Even There. By "Our Nig."* (1859), treated racism in the pre-Civil War North.

Almost nothing is known of Wilson's personal history until 1850. She may have been an indentured servant living with a family in Milford before she left to work as a domestic in Massachusetts, marrying Thomas Wilson, a fugitive slave, in 1851. He ran off to sea before the birth of their son, George.

The abandoned wife eventually left the baby in a white foster home in New Hampshire so that she could find work. In the preface to *Our Nig*, Wilson states that she wrote the novel to make money to reclaim her son. Unfortunately, George died of a fever in 1860. After 1863 Wilson disappeared from official public records.

Our Nig is largely autobiographical. Its protagonist, Frado, is of mixed race. Abandoned by her white mother, she is mistreated by the bigoted white family who employ her as an indentured servant. She eventually marries but is deserted by her husband.

DIANE GORODNITZKI

Lanford Wilson

Wilson, Lanford (Eugene) (b. April 13, 1937, Lebanon, Mo., U.S.) American playwright, a pioneer of the Off-Off Broadway and regional theater movements. His plays are known for experimental staging, simultaneous dialogue, and deferred character exposition. He won a 1980 Pulitzer Prize for *Talley's Folly* (1979).

From 1963 his plays were produced regularly at Off-Off-Broadway theaters. *Home Free!*, and *The Madness of Lady Bright* (published together in 1968) are two one-act plays first performed in 1964; the former involves a pair of incestuous siblings, and the latter features an aging transvestite. *Balm in Gilead* (1965), Wilson's first full-length play, is set in a crowded world of hustlers and junkies. *The Rimers of Eldritch* (1967) examines life in a small town.

In 1969, along with long-time associate Marshall W. Mason and others, he founded the Circle Theatre (later Circle Repertory Company), a regional theater in New York City. Wilson achieved commercial success with *The Great Nebula in Orion* (1971), *The Hot l Baltimore* (1973), and *The Mound Builders* (1975). He also wrote a cycle of plays about the effects of war on a family from Missouri; these included *The 5th of July* (1978), *Talley's Folly*, *A Tale Told* (1981), and *Talley and Son* (1985). His other plays include *The Gingham Dog* (1969), *Lemon Sky* (1970), *Burn This* (1987), and *Redwood Curtain* (1993).

Winters, Yvor, *in full* Arthur Yvor Winters (b. Oct. 17, 1900, Chicago, Ill., U.S.—d. Jan. 25, 1968, Palo Alto, Calif.) American poet, critic, and teacher who held that literature should be evaluated for its moral and intellectual content as well as its aesthetic appeal.

Educated at the University of Chicago, University of Colorado, and Stanford University, Winters taught at the University of Idaho from 1925 to 1927 and at Stanford from 1928 to 1966. He wrote one book of short stories and several books of poetry. His *Collected Poems* were published in 1952 (rev. ed., 1960).

Winters is probably best known for his literary criticism. His attacks on such contemporary literary idols as T.S. Eliot and Henry James aroused much controversy. His major critical works, including *Primitivism and Decadence: A Study of American Experimental Poetry* (1937), *Maule's Curse: Seven Studies in the History of American Obscurantism* (1938), and *The Anatomy of Nonsense* (1943), were collected as *In Defense of Reason* (1947); rev. ed., 1960). *Forms of Discovery: Critical and Historical Essays on the Forms of the Short Poem in English* appeared in 1967.

Wister, Owen (b. July 14, 1860, Philadelphia, Pa., U.S.—d. July 21, 1938, North Kingstown, R.I.) Novelist whose THE VIRGINIAN (1902) helped establish the cowboy as an American folk hero and stock fictional character.

Owen Wister

Wister graduated from Harvard Law School in 1888 and practiced for two years in Philadelphia. He spent his summers in the West, and in 1891, after the enthusiastic acceptance by *Harper's* of two of his Western sketches, he devoted himself to a literary career.

The Virginian is the story of a cowboy ranch foreman and was a great popular success. Wister's other major work was *Roosevelt: The Story of a Friendship, 1880–1919* (1930), detailing his long acquaintance with Theodore Roosevelt, a Harvard classmate. He also wrote a number of books for children. Wister's collected writings were published in 11 volumes in 1928. His journals and letters from 1885 to 1895 were published in *Owen Wister Out West* (1958), edited by his daughter, Fanny Kemble Wister.

Woiwode, Larry (Alfred) (b. Oct. 30, 1941, Carrington, North Dakota, U.S.) American writer whose fiction reflects his early childhood in a tiny town on the western North Dakota plains where five generations of his family had lived.

Woiwode first published fiction while at the University of Illinois, which he attended from 1959 to 1964. His short stories and poetry later appeared in such magazines as *Harper's*, *Partisan Review*, *The Atlantic*, and *The New Yorker*. Woiwode taught and led writing workshops at Dartmouth College and various universities, including the State University of New York at Binghamton.

Woiwode's critically acclaimed first novel, *What I'm Going to Do, I Think* (1969), is a study of a newly married couple. *Beyond the Bedroom Wall: A Family Album* (1975) is a multigenerational saga of a North Dakota family; *Born Brothers* (1988) continues the story of Charles and Jerome Neumiller, characters from *Beyond the Bedroom Wall*, who also appear in *The Neumiller Stories* (1989). *Poppa John* (1981) concerns an out-of-work television actor. *Indian Affairs* (1992) is a sequel to *What I'm Going to Do*. In 1977 Woiwode's collected poems were published under the title *Even Tide*, and a volume of short stories, *Silent Passengers*, appeared in 1993.

Thomas Wolfe

Wolfe, Thomas (Clayton) (b. Oct. 3, 1900, Asheville, N.C., U.S.—d. Sept. 15, 1938, Baltimore, Md.) American writer best known for his first novel, LOOK HOMEWARD, ANGEL (1929).

Educated privately, Wolfe entered the University of North Carolina in 1916, where he wrote and acted in several one-act plays. In 1920 he enrolled in George Pierce Baker's 47 Workshop at Harvard, intending to become a dramatist. Several of his works were produced at Harvard, including *Welcome to Our City* (1923), in which the town of Altamont (Asheville) first appeared. There, too, he began the play *Mannerhouse* (published 1948; never produced during his lifetime).

In 1923 Wolfe left Harvard for New York City where, except for trips to Europe and elsewhere, he resided most of his life. Some of his stories, notably "Only the Dead Know Brooklyn," contain observations of city life. Still intending to be a playwright, he taught at the Washington Square College of New York University, described in several of his novels. In 1926, while abroad, he began work on what eventually became *Look Homeward, Angel*, in which he recounted the growth of an autobiographical protagonist, Eugene Gant, in the mountain town of Altamont.

After publication of *Look Homeward, Angel*, Wolfe quit teaching to write full time. OF TIME AND THE RIVER (1935) is perhaps the most turbulent of his books. In his memoir *The Story of a Novel* (1936) he describes his close working relation with the editor Maxwell Perkins to bring the enormous manuscripts of these two works into manageable novelistic proportions.

Wolfe did not publish another novel before his death, though he left a prodigious quantity of manuscript, from which the editor Edward Aswell extracted two more novels, THE WEB AND THE ROCK (1939) and YOU CAN'T GO HOME AGAIN (1940), and a collection of shorter pieces and chapters of an uncompleted novel, *The Hills Beyond* (1941). Wolfe's *Letters to His Mother* (1943) were also published, as well as his *Selected Letters* (1956).

Wolfe, Tom, *in full* Thomas Kennerly Wolfe, Jr. (b. March 2, 1930, Richmond, Va., U.S.) American novelist, journalist, and social commentator who is known as a leading critic of contemporary life and as a proponent of New Journalism (the application of fiction-writing techniques to journalism).

After studying at Washington and Lee University and Yale University, Wolfe wrote for several newspapers, including the *Springfield Union* in Massachusetts and the *Washington Post*. He later worked as an editor on such magazines as *New York* and *Esquire* (from 1977) and as an artist for *Harper's*.

His first book, *The Kandy-Kolored Tangerine-Flake Streamline Baby* (1964), is a collection of essays satirizing American trends and celebrities of the 1960s. *The Electric Kool-Aid Acid Test* (1968) chronicles the psychedelic drug culture of the 1960s. His other works include *The Pump House Gang* (1968), *Radical Chic & Mau-Mauing the Flak Catchers* (1970), *The Painted Word* (1975), *Mauve Gloves & Madmen, Clutter & Vine* (1976), and *From Bauhaus to Our House* (1981). *The Right Stuff* (1979), which examines aspects of the first U.S. astronaut program, and *The Bonfire of the Vanities* (1987), a novel of urban greed and corruption, were best-sellers.

Wolff, Tobias (Jonathan Ansell) (b. June 19, 1945, Birmingham, Ala., U.S.) Writer primarily known for his short stories, in which many voices and a wide range of emotions are skillfully depicted.

Wolff's parents divorced when he was a child; from age 10 until he joined the U.S. Army, he traveled with his mother, who relocated frequently and finally settled in Seattle, Wash., where she remarried. Wolff wrote about his childhood in the 1950s, including his relationship with his abusive stepfather, in *This Boy's Life: A Memoir* (1989; film, 1993). His older brother, the novelist Geoffrey Wolff, was brought up by their father and wrote about his childhood in *The Duke of Deception: Memories of My Father* (1979). The brothers were reunited when Tobias was a young teenager.

Wolff served in Vietnam, after which he was educated at Oxford University and Stanford University. His first published collection of short stories was *In the Garden of the North American Martyrs* (1981); U.K. title, *Hunters in the Snow*). He also wrote a novella, *The Barracks Thief* (1984), and *Back in the World* (1985), a collection of short stories.

Woodcock, George (b. May 8, 1912, Winnipeg, Man., Can.—d. Jan. 28, 1995, Vancouver, B.C. Canadian poet, critic, historian, travel writer, playwright, scriptwriter, and editor whose work, particularly his poetry, reflects his belief that revolutionary changes would take place in society.

Woodcock published dozens of books. His poetry, particularly that published before World War II, expresses his anarchistic, rather than communistic, expectation of revolutionary changes in society. His poetry includes *The White Island* (1940), *The Centre Cannot Hold* (1943), *Imagine the South* (1947), *Selected Poems* (1967), *Notes on Visitations: Poems 1936–1975* (1975), *The Mountain Road* (1980), and *Collected Poems* (1983). Among his other works are travel books, including *To the City of the Dead* (1956) and *Incas and Other Men* (1959); collections of essays, such as *The Rejection of Politics* (1972); and biographies of Mordecai Richler (1970) and Sir Herbert Read (1972). *Letter to the Past*, an autobiography, appeared in 1982.

Woolf, Douglas (b. March 23, 1922, New York, N.Y., U.S.—d. Jan. 18, 1992, Urbana, Ill.) American author of gently comic fiction about people unassimilated into materialistic, technological society.

Woolf's short stories were published in literary periodicals beginning in the 1940s, and his first novel, *The Hypocritic Days*, was published in 1955. Most of Woolf's longer works concern cross-country journeys. In his most popular novel, *Fade Out* (1959), an elderly man rejected by his offspring makes a comic odyssey to an Arizona ghost town. *Wall to Wall* (1962), the story of a car salesman's son traveling from Los Angeles to New England, is often considered Woolf's finest work. The travels of the protagonist in *On Us* (1977) are interrupted by a meeting with a movie producer, and *The Timing Chain* (1985) relates events that occur on a car trip from the Rocky Mountains to Boston. Woolf's short novels *Ya!* and *John-Juan* were published together in 1971, and some of his short fiction was published in *Hypocritic Days & Other Tales* (1993).

Woollcott, Alexander (Humphreys) (b. Jan. 19, 1887, Phalanx, N.J., U.S.—d. Jan. 23, 1943, New York, N.Y.) American author, critic, and actor known for his acerbic wit. He was the self-appointed leader of the Algonquin Round Table, an informal luncheon club at New York City's Algonquin Hotel in the 1920s and '30s.

After graduating from Hamilton College, Clinton, N.Y., in 1909, Woollcott joined the staff of *The New York Times* as cub reporter and succeeded to the post of drama critic in 1914. After a brief stint in the U.S. Army, reporting for *The Stars and Stripes*, he returned to the *Times* and subsequently worked for the *New York Herald* and the *New York World*. He also wrote for *The New Yorker*, and beginning in 1929 he appeared on radio, establishing a nationwide reputation as raconteur, gossip, conversationalist, wit, and man-about-town. As a literary critic Woollcott wielded great influence. He was the author of *Mrs. Fiske, Her Views on Actors, Acting, and the Problems of Production* (1917), *Two Gentlemen and a Lady* (1928), and *While Rome Burns* (1934) and the publisher of two anthologies, *The Woollcott Reader* (1935) and *Woollcott's Second Reader* (1937).

Wouk, Herman (b. May 27, 1915, New York, N.Y., U.S.) American novelist best known for his epic war novels.

During World War II Wouk served in the Pacific aboard the destroyer-minesweeper *Zane*. One of his best-known novels, THE CAINE MUTINY (1951), was based on that experience. This drama of naval tradition presented the unforgettable character Captain Queeg and won the Pulitzer Prize for fiction in 1952.

Wouk's novels are all meticulously researched, and they provide an accurate and in-depth portrait of a particular slice of the world. They are built on a belief in the goodness of man or, in the case of MARJORIE MORNINGSTAR (1955), the purity of women, and revolve around moral dilemmas. Wouk wrote with little technical innovation, but his novels have been tremendously popular. Most have been made into screenplays. Popular television mini-series were based on his expansive two-volume historical novel set in World War II: *The Winds of War* (1971) and *War and Remembrance* (1978). A later novel was *Inside, Outside* (1985).

Wright, James (Arlington) (b. Dec. 13, 1927, Martin's Ferry, Ohio, U.S.— d. March 25, 1980, New York, N.Y.) American poet of the postmodern era who wrote about sorrow, salvation, and self-revelation, often drawing on his native Ohio River valley for images of nature and industry. In 1972 he won the Pulitzer Prize for *Collected Poems* (1971).

Wright studied under John Crowe Ransom at Kenyon College (Gambier, Ohio), attended the University of Vienna, and continued his studies under Theodore Roethke at the University of Washington. Wright taught at the University of Minnesota, Macalester College, St. Paul, Minn., and Hunter College, New York City. His first two books, *The Green Wall* (1957) and *Saint Judas* (1959), were influenced by the poetry of Edwin Arlington Robinson, Georg Trakl, and Robert Frost.

The Branch Will Not Break (1963), the watershed of Wright's career, is characterized by free verse, simple diction, and a casual mix of objective and subjective imagery, as illustrated by the poem "Lying in a Hammock at William Duffy's Farm in Pine Island, Minnesota." The successful *Collected Poems* was followed by *Two Citizens* (1973), *Shall We Gather at the River* (1968), *To a Blossoming Pear Tree* (1977), and *This Journey* (1982). Wright also translated the works of Trakl, César Vallejo, Hermann Hesse, and Pablo Neruda, often in collaboration with Robert Bly.

Wright, Richard (b. Sept. 4, 1908, near Natchez, Miss., U.S.—d. Nov. 28, 1960, Paris, Fr.) Novelist and short-story writer who was among the first American black writers to protest white treatment of blacks, notably in his novel NATIVE SON (1940).

Richard Wright

Wright's grandparents had been slaves. His father left home when he was five, and the boy, who grew up in poverty, was often shifted from one relative to another. He worked at a number of jobs before joining the northward migration, first to Memphis, Tenn., and then to Chicago. There, after working in unskilled jobs, he was given an opportunity to write through the Federal Writers' Project. In 1932 he became a member of the Communist Party and was executive secretary of the local John Reed Club of leftist writers and artists of Chicago. In 1937 he went to New York City, where he became Harlem editor of the communist *Daily Worker* and, later, vice president of the League for American Writers.

Wright first came to the general public's attention with a volume of novellas, UNCLE TOM'S CHILDREN (1938). His fictional scene shifted to Chicago in *Native Son*. It presents the story of Bigger Thomas, whose accidental killing of a white girl makes clear and immediate his hitherto vague awareness of antagonism from a white world.

Early versions of Wright's best novella, "The Man Who Lived Underground" (collected in its final version in a posthumous volume of stories, *Eight Men*, 1961), appeared in 1942 and 1944. The absurd, isolated subterranean life of its black hero foreshadows the existentialism that guided Wright's later works.

In 1944 Wright left the Communist Party because of political and personal differences. The autobiographical BLACK BOY, a moving account of his childhood and young manhood, appeared in 1945. Soon thereafter he settled in Paris as a permanent expatriate. *The Outsider* (1953), acclaimed as the first American existential novel, warned that blacks had awakened in a disintegrating society not ready to include them. Three later novels were not well-received. Among his polemical writings of that period was *White Man, Listen!* (1957), which was originally a series of lectures given in Europe. The autobiographical *American Hunger* was published posthumously in 1977.

Elinor Wylie

Wylie, Elinor, *original name* Elinor Morton Hoyt (b. Sept. 7, 1885, Somerville, N.J., U.S.—d. Dec. 16, 1928, New York, N.Y.) American poet and novelist whose work, written from an aristocratic and traditionalist point of view, reflected changing American attitudes in the aftermath of World War I.

Wylie came from a prominent Philadelphia family. Her work included four volumes of poetry and four novels. Her poetry, carefully structured and sensuous in mood, shows the influence of 16th- and 17th-century English verse. Her novels combine gentle fantasy and classical formality with thoroughly researched historical settings. *The Orphan Angel* (1926) imagines the life of the English poet Percy Bysshe Shelley if he had been rescued from drowning and taken to America. Her third husband, William Rose Benét, edited Wylie's *Collected Poems* (1932), *Collected Prose* (1933), and *Last Poems* (1943).

Yerby, Frank (Garvin) (b. Sept. 5, 1916, Augusta, Ga., U.S.—d. Nov. 29, 1991, Madrid, Spain) African-American author of popular historical fiction.

Yerby's story "Health Card" won the O. Henry award for best first published short story in 1944. In 1946 his first novel, *The Foxes of Harrow*, was an immediate success. His novels are action-packed, usually featuring a strong hero in an earlier period. The stories unfold in colorful language and include characters of all ethnic backgrounds, enmeshed in complex story lines laced with romantic intrigue and violence. His best work may be his novel *The Dahomean* (1971).

Young, Marguerite (Vivian) (b. 1909, Indianapolis, Ind., U.S.—d. Nov. 17, 1995, Indianapolis) Writer best known for *Miss MacIntosh, My Darling* (1965), a mammoth, many-layered novel of illusion and reality.

Young's first published works were two books of poetry, *Prismatic Ground* (1937) and *Moderate Fable* (1944). *Angel in the Forest: A Fairy Tale of Two Utopias* (1945) examines the foundation of two utopian communities of New Harmony, Ind. *Miss MacIntosh, My Darling*, the project that occupied virtually the next two decades of Young's life, is an exploration of myth and the mythmaking impulse. The book's protagonist, Vera Cartwheel, rejects her mother's opium-induced vagueness and searches for her long-lost nursemaid, Miss MacIntosh, who represents common sense and reality. Cartwheel's journey ends in disillusionment.

The author's later works include a collection of short stories entitled *Below the City* (1975) and *Inviting the Muses: Stories, Essays, Reviews* (1994).

Paul Zindel

Zindel, Paul (b. May 15, 1936, Staten Island, N.Y., U.S.) American playwright and novelist whose largely autobiographical work features poignant, alienated characters who deal with life's difficulties in pragmatic and straightforward ways.

Zindel attended Wagner College, Staten Island, N.Y., and taught high school chemistry for several years before becoming a full-time writer in 1972. In most of Zindel's dramas the main tension is between a nonconformist, domineering mother and an impressionable, bewildered young person. His plays include the Pulitzer Prize-winning THE EFFECT OF GAMMA RAYS ON MAN-IN-THE-MOON MARIGOLDS (1971), *And Miss Reardon Drinks a Little* (1971), *The Secret Affairs of Mildred Wild* (1973), *Let Me Hear You Whisper* (1970), *The Ladies Should Be in Bed* (1973), *A Destiny with Half Moon Street* (produced 1983; published 1992), and *Amulets Against the Dragon Forces* (1989); based partly on his novel *Confessions of a Teenage Baboon*). Among his novels for young adults are *The Pigman* (1968), *My Darling, My Hamburger* (1969), *Harry and Hortense at Hormone High* (1984), and *A Begonia for Miss Applebaum* (1989).

Zukofsky, Louis (b. Jan. 23, 1904, New York, N.Y., U.S.—d. May 12, 1978, Port Jefferson, N.Y.) American poet, the founder of Objectivist poetry and author of the massive poem *"A"*.

The son of Jewish immigrants from Russia, Zukofsky grew up in New York, attended Columbia University, and taught for several years at Polytechnic Institute of Brooklyn. By the 1930s he had begun the ill-defined Objectivist movement, and poets as radically different as William Carlos Williams, T.S. Eliot, and Ezra Pound contributed to the special Objectivist issue of *Poetry* magazine (1931) and to *An "Objectivist" Anthology* (1932), which Zukofsky edited.

Meanwhile, in 1928 he had embarked upon *"A"*, the great work of his life, which treats subjects as diverse as history, politics, aesthetics, science, and life in general. The poem was organized in a mosaic structure and planned in 24 parts. The complete poem, 826 pages long, beginning with the word "A" and ending with "Zion," was published in 1978. Zukofsky described himself as a comic poet, and punning is the characteristic medium of his and his wife Celia's *Catullus Fragmenta* (1969), a translation of the Roman poet Catullus' works into an obscure English that attempts to reproduce the sounds of the original Latin. His several volumes of prose include the critical study *Bottom: On Shakespeare* (1963) and *Little: A Fragment For Careenagers* (1967), which is a short novel about a youthful violin prodigy. *All: The Collected Short Poems, 1923–1964* was published in 1971.

Major Works of American Literature

Abe Lincoln in Illinois Drama in 12 scenes by Robert E. SHERWOOD, produced in 1938 and published in 1939.

The play, which in 1939 was awarded the Pulitzer Prize for drama, concerns Lincoln's life and career—from his early, unsuccessful days as a postmaster in New Salem, Ill., through his initial forays into local politics, his relationship with Mary Todd, and his debates with Stephen Douglas, and culminates with his election to the presidency and imminent departure for Washington, D.C., 30 years later.

Abraham Lincoln: The War Years Four-volume biography by Carl SANDBURG, published in 1939. It was awarded the 1940 Pulitzer Prize for history.

After the success of his 1926 biography, *Abraham Lincoln: The Prairie Years*, Sandburg turned to Lincoln's life after 1861, devoting 11 years to research and writing. The biography is informed not only by the author's journalistic style but also by his unwavering admiration for Franklin D. Roosevelt's liberal New Deal politics. Sandburg believed that both presidents were representative of the voice of the American people, and in many respects the biography expresses his faith in the workings of democracy through the office of a compassionate, gifted leader.

Absalom, Absalom! Novel by William FAULKNER, published in 1936.

The principal narrative, set in 19th-century Mississippi, concerns the efforts of Thomas Sutpen to transcend his lowly origins by establishing and maintaining a slave-driven empire—"Sutpen's Hundred"—on the frontier. Sutpen's consuming notion of racial superiority undermines his closest relationships and proves his undoing. By the novel's end his plantation is in ruins and his only living heir is a mentally deficient great-grandson of mixed blood.

Bracketing this mythic story is the struggle of Quentin Compson, a young Mississippian at Harvard decades later (and the grandson of a Sutpen

acquaintance), to come to terms with the story's implications for his native region. Criticized by contemporary critics for its turgid style and convoluted, redundant narration, the book later came to be considered one of the finest in American literature.

Ada (*in full* Ada; or, Ardor: A Family Chronicle) Novel by Vladimir NABOKOV, written in English and published in 1969. In its prodigious length and with the family tree on its frontispiece the book recalls the great 19th-century novels of the author's native Russia, but *Ada* boldly turns its predecessors on their heads. For his rich, sweeping saga of the Veen-Durmanov clan, Nabokov invented an incestuous pair of "cousins" (actually siblings, Van and Ada), a hybrid country (Amerussia), a familiar but strange planet (Antiterra), and a dimension of malleable time. The novel follows the lovers from their childhood idylls through impassioned estrangements and reunions to a tenderly shared old age. The work's rich narrative style incorporates untranslated foreign phrases, esoteric data, and countless literary allusions.

Adventures of Augie March, The Novel by Saul BELLOW, published in 1953. It is a picaresque story of a poor Jewish youth from Chicago, his progress, sometimes highly comic, through the world of the 20th century, and his attempts to make sense of it. *The Adventures of Augie March* won the National Book Award in 1954.

After the Fall A play in two acts by Arthur MILLER, produced and published in 1964.

The play presents retrospectively a series of encounters that have occurred over a 25-year span between the protagonist, Quentin, a lawyer about the age of 50, and his intimate associates. His first wife, Louise, accuses him of failing to acknowledge her personhood. A friend from his days as a Communist Party member appears now as an informer before congressional investigators. Another former "fellow traveler" commits suicide before Quentin has the opportunity to defend him. The second act traces the downward course of Maggie, Quentin's second wife, from popular entertainer to bitter neurotic to suicide. As the play ends, Quentin appears poised to marry Holga, whose struggle against Nazism in Germany embodies his own desire to confront evil. Thematic issues of ethical ambiguity and personal integrity help to unify the work's somewhat disjointed dramatic structure.

Age of Innocence, The Novel by Edith WHARTON, published in 1920. The work presents a picture of upper-class New York society in the late 19th century. The story is presented as a kind of anthropological study of this society through references to the families and their activities as tribal. In the story Newland Archer, though engaged to May Welland, a beautiful and proper fellow member of elite society, is attracted to Ellen Olenska, a former member of their circle who has been living in Europe but who has left her husband under mysterious circumstances and returned to her family's New York milieu. May prevails by subtly adhering to the conventions of that world. The novel was awarded a Pulitzer Prize.

Ah, Wilderness! Comedy in four acts by Eugene O'NEILL, published and first performed in 1933. Perhaps the most atypical of the author's works, the play presents a sentimental tale of youthful indiscretion in a turn-of-the-century New England town. Richard, adolescent son of the local newspaper publisher, Nat Miller, exhibits the wayward tendencies of his maternal uncle, Sid Davis. Forbidden to court the neighbor girl, Muriel, by her father, Richard goes on a bender and falls under the influence of Belle, whom he tries to impress but whose worldly ways frighten him. It is the dissolute Sid who handles the situation upon the prodigal's drunken return, and with the aid of warmhearted Nat and the forgiving Muriel everything is put to right. The play has since become a staple of the community-theater repertoire.

Air-Conditioned Nightmare, The Nonfiction account of Henry MILLER's travels through the United States, published in 1945. Miller undertook these travels in 1940 and 1941 after returning from a lengthy stay in Europe. Miller comments, mostly negatively, on America's physical landscape as well as on the mood and spirit of the American people. Among other things, he contrasts the ideals of the original founders with contemporary Americans' love of making money. Miller commented further on these themes in the sequel *Remember to Remember* (1947).

Alice Adams Novel by Booth TARKINGTON, published in 1921. The story of the disintegration of a lower middle-class family in a small Midwestern town, *Alice Adams* was awarded the Pulitzer Prize for best novel in 1922.

A social climber, the title character is ashamed of her unsuccessful family. Hoping to attract a wealthy husband, she lies about her background, but she is found out and is shunned by those whom she sought to attract. At the novel's end, she knows her chances for happiness and a successful marriage are bleak, but she remains unbowed.

All My Sons Drama in three acts by Arthur MILLER, performed and published in 1947.

All My Sons was considered Miller's first significant play. With an underlying theme of guilt and responsibility, the drama centers on Joe Keller, a manufacturer of substandard and defective war materials, whose faulty airplane parts cause the death of his son and other fliers during World War II.

All the King's Men Novel by Robert Penn WARREN, published in 1946. The story concerns the rise and fall of Willie Stark, a character modeled on Huey Long, the governor of Louisiana during the time frame of the novel (late 1920s to early 1930s). The book won the Pulitzer Prize in 1947.

Stark comes from a poor background, becomes a lawyer, and is elected governor. A self-styled man of the people, he soon learns to use such tactics as bribery and intimidation to assure passage of his populist programs such as the building of new rural roads and hospitals. These methods account for his power, but at the same time are responsible for his downfall.

Ambassadors, The Novel by Henry JAMES, published in 1903. The "eye" of the story, Lambert Strether, is a Massachusetts editor engaged to the widowed Mrs. Newsome. Disturbed by reports concerning her son Chadwick's love life in Paris, Mrs. Newsome presses Strether to engineer the young man's return to his mother's sphere of influence. The Chad that Strether finds is, to his mind, an improvement over the former one, although the nature of his relationship with Marie de Vionnet, a few years his senior, and her young daughter Jeanne remains indeterminate. Strether's "investigations" proceed slowly with the aid of Miss Gostrey, an expatriate friend of the Vionnets. By the time the impatient Mrs. Newsome sends the Pococks (her daughter, son-in-law, and his sister Mamie, Chad's fiancée) as reinforcements, her son has voiced compliance, but Strether has now fallen under the Vionnets' spell. His discovery of Chad and Marie's affair is considered one of the sublime revelations in American literature. The Pococks eventually defer to Chad regarding the direction of his own future. He heeds Strether's advice to remain in Paris.

American Buffalo Two-act play by David MAMET, produced in 1975 and published in 1976. With sparse action and vivid dialogue, it examines mistrust and dishonesty among the conspirators in an aborted burglary.

Don Dubrow, the owner of a junk shop where the action takes place, decides to steal a customer's coin collection when he feels that he has been bested in a transaction involving a buffalo nickel. He enlists the help of a young junkie named Bobby, but is convinced by a manipulative friend that Bobby is incompetent. Unable to trust either, Don invites a third person to join him. Bobby becomes a scapegoat as the burglary plot unravels and tensions build into suspicion, anger, and violence.

American Dream, The One-act drama by Edward ALBEE, published in 1959 (with *The Zoo Story*) and first produced in 1961. This brief absurdist drama established the playwright as an astute, acerbic critic of American values.

The American Dream addresses issues of childlessness and adoption. The play's central figures, Mommy and Daddy, represent banal American life. Clubwoman Mrs. Barker visits and Grandma reminds her of an earlier visit, when she brought an infant. This child did not turn out as Mommy and Daddy expected and so was abused by them until it died. When a handsome but emotionless young man—the American Dream—later arrives, Grandma suggests Mommy and Daddy adopt him, since his emptiness seems what they desire.

American, The Novel by Henry JAMES, published serially in 1876 in *The Atlantic Monthly* and in book form a year later, and produced as a four-act play in 1891. *The American* is the story of a self-made American millionaire, Christopher Newman, whose guilelessness and forthrightness contrast him with a family of arrogant and cunning French aristocrats, the Bellegardes, whose daughter he unsuccessfully seeks to marry.

In 1868 Newman travels to Paris to submerge himself in European culture and to find himself a wife. He courts Claire de Cintré, an aristocratic young widow, but he is deemed socially unacceptable by Claire's older brother and by her mother. Newman befriends Claire's younger brother, Valentin, who, on his deathbed, tells Newman how he can blackmail the family into approving the marriage with Claire, who has since joined a convent. Newman decides not to carry out his threat of blackmail, which nevertheless had failed to sway the Bellegardes' uncompromising allegiance to social class and family tradition.

American Tragedy, An Novel by Theodore DREISER, published in 1925. It is a complex and compassionate account of the life and death of a young antihero named Clyde Griffiths. The novel begins with Clyde's blighted background, recounts his path to success, and culminates in his apprehension, trial, and execution for murder. The book was called by one influential critic "the worst-written great novel in the world," but its questionable grammar and style are transcended by its narrative power. Dreiser's intricate speculations on the extent of Clyde's guilt are countered by his searing indictment of materialism and the American dream of success.

Dreiser's intricate speculations on the extent of Clyde's guilt are countered by his searing indictment of materialism and the American dream of success.

Anatomy of Criticism: Four Essays Work of literary criticism by Northrop FRYE, published in 1957 and generally considered the author's most important work. In his introduction, Frye explains that his initial intention to examine the poetry of Edmund Spenser had given way in the process to a broader survey of the ordering principles of literary theory. The four essays address modes, symbols, myths, and genres, corresponding respectively to what Frye sees as the historical, ethical, archetypal, and rhetorical dimensions of literary expression. In his view, the task of evaluating a particular poem or novel falls to the reviewer, while the critic brings to light those aspects of a work that situate it within the body of literature.

Annabel Lee Lyric poem by Edgar Allan POE, published in the *New York Tribune* on Oct. 9, 1849, two days after his death. Thought to be written in memory of his young wife and cousin, Virginia, who died in 1847, the poem expresses one of Poe's recurrent themes—the death of a young, beautiful, and dearly beloved woman.

Anna Christie Four-act play by Eugene O'NEILL, produced in 1921 and published in 1922, during which year it was also awarded the Pulitzer Prize.

The title character, long separated from her bargemaster father, is reunited with him in adulthood. Not realizing that she has become a prostitute, her sentimental father comes to blows with a seaman who has been smitten by her. When Anna reveals her sordid past, both men abandon her, go their separate ways, get drunk, and unwittingly sign on for the same distant voyage. At the play's end, Anna has agreed to wait for their return.

Another Country Novel by James BALDWIN, published in 1962. The novel is renowned for its graphic portrayal of bisexuality and interracial relations. Shortly after the action begins, Rufus Scott, a black jazz musician, commits suicide, impelling his friends to search for the meaning of his death and, consequently, for a deeper understanding of their own identities. Employing a loose, episodic structure, this work traces the affairs—heterosexual and homosexual as well as interracial—among Scott's friends. In its language and structure, the novel is a departure from Baldwin's earlier work.

Anthony Adverse Historical novel by Hervey ALLEN, published in 1933. A long, rambling work set in Europe, Africa, and the Americas during the Napoleonic era, *Anthony Adverse* relates the many adventures of the eponymous hero. These include slave trading in Africa, his experiences as a plantation owner in New Orleans, and his imprisonment and eventual death in Mexico.

Archy and Mehitabel Collection of humorous stories by Don MARQUIS, originally published from 1916 in Marquis's newspaper columns "The Sun Dial" in the New York *Evening Sun* and "The Lantern" in the New York *Herald Tribune* and published in book form in 1927. The stories center on Archy, a philosophical cockroach who types messages to the author in lowercase letters (being unable to activate the shift mechanism), and Mehitabel, a free-spirited alley cat whose motto is "toujours gai." After initial publication, the work and its sequels were usually published without capital letters.

Archy and Mehitabel consists mostly of free-verse poems on such concerns of Archy's as transmigration of souls, social injustice, life in

New York City, and death. Sequels included *Archys Life of Mehitabel* (1933) and *Archy Does His Part* (1935), both of which were included in *the lives and times of archy and mehitabel* (1940; illustrated by George Herriman), a posthumously published compendium of the previous books.

Ariel Collection of poetry by Sylvia PLATH, published posthumously in 1965. Most of the poems were written during the last five months of the author's life, which ended by suicide in 1963. Although the poems range in subject from pastoral chores ("The Bee Meeting") to medical trauma ("Tulips"), each contributes to an impression of the inevitability of the author's self-destruction. The collection contains "Daddy," one of Plath's best-known poems.

Arrowsmith Novel by Sinclair LEWIS, published in 1925. The author declined to accept a Pulitzer Prize for the work because he had not been awarded the prize for his *Main Street* in 1921.

The narrative concerns the personal and professional travails of Martin Arrowsmith, a Midwestern physician. Disheartened successively by rural practice, the state of public health care, and the elitism of an urban clinic, Martin accepts a research position at an institute in New York that leads him, along with his wife, Leora, a nurse, to an epidemic-ravaged island. Leora dies there, and Martin abandons his scientific principles in order to make an experimental serum more widely available. Returning to the institute, he marries a wealthy widow and finds her social demands a distraction. In a final move—and in realization of his ambitions—he leaves institutional medicine, as well as his wife, and sets up his own laboratory on a New England farm.

Art of Fiction, The Critical essay by Henry JAMES, published in 1884 in *Longman's Magazine*. It was written as a rebuttal to "Fiction as One of the Fine Arts," a lecture given by Sir Walter Besant in 1884, and is a manifesto of literary realism that decries the popular demand for novels that are saturated with sentimentality or pessimism. It was published separately in 1885.

In *The Art of Fiction*, James disagrees with Besant's assertions that plot is more important than characterization, that fiction must have a "conscious moral purpose," and that experience and observation outweigh imagination as creative tools. James argues against these restrictive rules for writing fiction, responding that "no good novel will ever proceed from a superficial mind."

Ash Wednesday Long poem by T.S. ELIOT, first published as *Ash-Wednesday* in 1930; three of the poem's six sections had previously been published separately. Published after Eliot's confirmation in the Church of England (1927), *Ash Wednesday* expresses the pangs and the strain involved in the acceptance of religious belief and religious discipline.

The first section introduces the irony of the modern man whose intellectual dithering prevents him from achieving spiritual renewal. The second section is an allegory about rebirth, based on a prophecy by Ezekiel, with a famous image of devouring leopards. The following two sections discuss spiritual journeys such as the one described in Dante's *Purgatorio*. In the fifth section, Eliot plays on the many religious and philosophical connotations of the word "word." The final section details the tension between meditation and distraction.

As I Lay Dying Novel by William FAULKNER, published in 1930. It is one of the many novels that Faulkner set in the fictional Yoknapatawpha County, Miss. The story unfolds by means of fragmented and intercut narration by each of the characters. These include Addie Bundren; her husband, Anse; their sons, Cash, Darl, and Vardaman, and daughter, Dewey Dell; and Addie's illegitimate son, Jewel. Addie watches from her deathbed as Cash builds her coffin. Upon her death, the family, under the direction of small-minded and ineffectual Anse, endeavors for once to respect Addie's wishes and transport her to her hometown for burial. The rest of the novel is an account of the family's journey and of the fates of the individual members of the family.

Aspern Papers, The Novelette by Henry JAMES, published in 1888, first in *The Atlantic Monthly* (March-May) and then in the collection *The Aspern Papers, Louisa Pallant, The Modern Warning*.

In "The Aspern Papers," an unnamed American editor rents a room in Venice in the home of Juliana Bordereau, the elderly mistress of Jeffrey Aspern, a deceased Romantic poet, in order to procure from her the poet's papers. Bordereau, a stingy, domineering woman, lives with her timid, middle-aged niece, Tina. (The niece was named Tita until James revised the text in 1908.) The manipulative editor, obsessed with possessing the Aspern papers, exhibits progressively unscrupulous behavior, such as assuming an alias, making false romantic overtures to Tina, and attempting burglary. When Bordereau dies, Tina offers the editor the coveted documents on the condition that he marry her. He initially refuses but returns to negotiate, only to find that Tina, in a display of newfound dignity, has burned the papers.

The novelette was inspired by an actual incident involving Claire Clairmont, once the mistress of Lord Byron.

Assistant, The Novel by Bernard MALAMUD, published in 1957. Set in Brooklyn, the novel portrays the complex relationship that develops between Morris Bober, a worn-out Jewish grocer, and Frank Alpine, a young Italian-American who first robs Morris and then comes to his aid after wounding him. In the course of the novel, Frank becomes Morris's assistant, falls in love with his high-minded daughter, Helen, and challenges the old man's expectations of life. Morris pursues various schemes for unburdening himself of the store. Religious differences undermine Frank's amorous intentions, and Morris fires him for petty theft. After Morris's death, Frank comes back to revive the store and converts to Judaism.

Atlas Shrugged Novel by Ayn RAND, published in 1957. The book's female protagonist, Dagny Taggart, struggles to manage a transcontinental railroad amid the pressures and restrictions of massive bureaucracy. Her antagonistic reaction to a libertarian group seeking an end to government regulation is later echoed and modified in her encounter with a utopian community, Galt's Gulch, whose members regard self-determination rather than collective responsibility as the highest ideal. The novel contains the most complete presentation of Rand's personal philosophy, known as objectivism, in fictional form.

Autobiography of Alice B. Toklas, The Autobiography by Gertrude STEIN, written as if it were the autobiography of her lifelong companion, Alice B. Toklas. Published in 1933, the work ostensibly contains Toklas' first-person account not of her own life, but of Stein's, written from Toklas's viewpoint and replete with Toklas' sensibilities, observations, and mannerisms. *The Autobiography* was originally published in an abridged version in *The Atlantic Monthly* magazine.

The book describes the life that Toklas and Stein lead in Paris, including their at-homes with such artists, literary lions, and intellectuals as Pablo Picasso, Ernest Hemingway, Henri Matisse, and Georges Braque. While Stein exchanges ideas with men of genius, Toklas sits with their wives. Its droll premise, masterful execution, and witty insights concerning the writers and artists then living in France make clear Stein's ability to write for a general public.

Autobiography of an Ex-Colored Man, The Novel by James Weldon JOHNSON, published in 1912. This fictional autobiography, originally issued anonymously in order to suggest authenticity, explores the intricacies of racial identity through the eventful life of its mixed-race (and unnamed) narrator.

Born in Georgia, the narrator tells of his childhood in Connecticut, where his mulatto mother, aided by monthly checks from the boy's white father, is able to provide a secure and cultured environment. Learning of his black heritage only by accident, the narrator experiences the first of several identity shifts that will eventually find him opting for membership in white society. Throughout the work, Johnson employs characters, locales, incidents, and motifs from his own life, but the narrator is less a conscious self-portrait than a representative of the author's own ambivalence.

Autobiography of Malcolm X, The Biography, published in 1965, of the American black militant religious leader and activist who was born Malcolm Little. Written by Alex HALEY, who had conducted extensive audiotaped interviews with Malcolm X just before his assassination in 1965, the book gained renown as a classic work on black American experience.

The *Autobiography* recounts the life of Malcolm X from his traumatic childhood plagued by racism to his years as a drug dealer and pimp, his conversion to the Black Muslim sect (Nation of Islam) while in prison for burglary, his subsequent years of militant activism, and the turn late in his life to more orthodox Islām.

Autobiography of Miss Jane Pittman, The Novel by Ernest J. GAINES, published in 1971. Set in rural southern Louisiana, the novel spans 100 years of American history—from the early 1860s to the onset of the civil rights movement in the 1960s—in following the life of the elderly Jane Pittman, who witnessed those years.

A child at the end of the Civil War, Jane survives a massacre by former Confederate soldiers. She serves as a steadying influence for several black men who work hard to achieve dignity and economic as well as political equality. After the death of her husband, Joe Pittman, Jane becomes a committed Christian and a spiritual guide in her community. Spurred on by the violent death of a young community leader, Jane finally confronts a plantation owner who represents the white power structure to which she has always been subservient.

Awakening, The Novel by Kate CHOPIN, published

in 1899. When first published, the novel was considered controversial because of its frank treatment of both adulterous love between a married woman, Edna Pontellier, and an unmarried younger man, Robert LeGrun, and the subject of female sexuality.

Awkward Age, The Novel by Henry JAMES, published in 1899. Written mostly in dialogue with limited narrative explanation, *The Awkward Age* is the story of Nanda Brookenham, a young society woman whose attempts at marriage are foiled by various members of her mother's social circle.

Nanda's manipulative mother, Fernanda, is the hostess of a fashionable London salon. The two women both appear to love Gustavus Vanderbank, a young government employee, who becomes alienated from them. Nanda is befriended by the elderly Mr. Longdon, who once courted her grandmother, and by the young Mr. Mitchett, who unhappily marries Little Aggie, a naive young woman steered into the marriage by her conniving aunt, the Duchess.

Axel's Castle Book of critical essays by Edmund WILSON, published in 1931. Subtitled "A Study in the Imaginative Literature of 1870–1930," the book traced the origins of specific trends in contemporary literature, which, Wilson held, was largely concerned with Symbolism and its relationship to naturalism.

Wilson followed his introductory essay on Symbolism with essays that trace the development of these trends in the works of W.B. Yeats, Paul Valéry, T.S. Eliot, Marcel Proust, James Joyce, Gertrude Stein, and Arthur Rimbaud and Auguste Villiers de l'Isle-Adam.

Babbitt Novel by Sinclair LEWIS, published in 1922. The novel's scathing indictment of middle-class American values made Babbittry a synonym for adherence to a conformist, materialistic, anti-intellectual way of life.

In the novel, George F. Babbitt is a prosperous real-estate broker in the Midwestern town of Zenith. He is a pillar of his community, a civic booster, and a believer in achieving success for its own sake. When his best friend is arrested for shooting his own wife, Babbitt begins to question and rebel against some of the values that he has always upheld. But Babbitt's rebellion is brief because he lacks inner strength. When his wife becomes ill he returns to her and to his former way of life.

Ballad of the Sad Café, The   Long novella by Carson MCCULLERS, the title work in a collection of short stories, published in 1951. Peopled with bizarre and grotesque characters, the novella has a folkloric quality and is considered one of the author's best works.

Amelia Evans, a tall and lonely woman, falls passionately in love with her cousin Lymon, a malevolent dwarf. Amelia opens a café that serves as a much-needed social outlet for their tiny Southern town. Lymon falls in love with Amelia's estranged husband, Marvin Macy, who has just been released from prison. Lymon and Macy overpower Amelia physically and wreck her café, after which they disappear together, leaving Amelia and the townspeople without hope.

Bartleby the Scrivener (*in full* Bartleby the Scrivener: A Story of Wall Street)   Short story by Herman MELVILLE, published anonymously in 1853 in *Putnam's Monthly Magazine*. It was collected in his 1856 volume *The Piazza Tales*.

Melville wrote "Bartleby" at a time when his career seemed to be in ruins, and the story reflects his pessimism. The narrator, a successful Wall Street lawyer, hires a scrivener named Bartleby to copy legal documents. Though Bartleby is initially a hard worker, one day, when asked to proofread, he responds, "I would prefer not to." As time progresses, Bartleby increasingly "prefers not to" do anything asked of him. Eventually he dies of self-neglect, refusing offers of help, while jailed for vagrancy.

Bear, The   Novelette by William FAULKNER, early versions of which first appeared as "Lion" in *Harper's Magazine* of December 1935 and as

"The Bear" in *Saturday Evening Post* in 1942, before it was published as one of the chapters in the novel GO DOWN, MOSES. Critical interpretations of the story vary depending upon whether it is judged as an independent work or as a chapter in the larger novel.

"The Bear," set in the late 19th century, is a hunting story told from the perspective of Isaac ("Ike") McCaslin, a young man from an old family in Yoknapatawpha county. In the first three parts of the novelette, Ike trains under the expert tracker Sam Fathers and hunts down the legendary bear Old Ben. The fourth part (omitted in some publications) comprises a long, convoluted dialogue between Ike and his cousin Carothers ("Cass") Edmonds, in which Ike repudiates his inheritance after he discovers incest and miscegenation in the family history. The final part concerns Ike's affinity for nature and his dismay at its gradual destruction.

Beast in the Jungle, The   Short story by Henry JAMES that first appeared in *The Better Sort* (1903). Despite its sluggish pace, implausible dialogue, and excessively ornate style, it is a suspenseful story of despair, with powerful images of fire, ice, and hunting.

"The Beast in the Jungle" concerns John Marcher, a neurotic egoist obsessed with the lurking feeling that something incredible is to happen to him. This impending fate has a predatory quality, like "a crouching beast in the jungle." Consumed with anticipation and dread, Marcher is unable to reciprocate the love of his long-suffering companion, May Bartram. She comes to see his fate but is unable to make him understand it before she dies. While visiting her grave one year later, Marcher suddenly realizes that his terrible fate was precisely his inability to comprehend her love for him.

Beautiful and Damned, The   Novel by F. Scott FITZGERALD, published in 1922. Fitzgerald's second novel, it concerns a handsome young married couple who choose to wait for an expected inheritance rather than involve themselves in productive, meaningful lives.

Anthony Patch pursues and wins the beautiful and sought-after Gloria Gilbert. He decides that they can survive on his limited income until he comes into a large fortune he stands to inherit from his grandfather. Through the ensuing years, their lives deteriorate into mindless alcoholic ennui. Anthony's grandfather makes a surprise appearance at one of their wild parties and, in disgust, disinherits him. After his grandfather's death, Anthony institutes a lawsuit that takes years to settle. Although the Patches eventually win, by then Anthony's spirit is broken, he and Gloria have grown apart, and they care about nothing.

Bell for Adano, A Novel by John HERSEY, published in 1944 and awarded a Pulitzer Prize in 1945.

The novel's action takes place during World War II after the occupation of Sicily by Allied forces. Major Victor Joppolo, an American army officer of Italian descent, is part of the Allied military government ruling the town of Adano. In his attempts to reform the town and bring democracy to the people by treating them with respect and decency, Joppolo comes into conflict with his commanding officer, a hard-nosed general who eventually has Joppolo transferred because of his refusal to follow orders. Joppolo's concern for the town is epitomized by his efforts to replace a bell that the fascists had melted down to use for ammunition.

Bell Jar, The Novel by Sylvia PLATH, first published in January 1963 under the pseudonym Victoria Lucas, and later published under her real name. Plath committed suicide one month after the publication of *The Bell Jar*, her only novel. This thinly veiled autobiography details the life of Esther Greenwood, a college woman who struggles through a mental breakdown in the 1950s. Plath examines coming of age in a hypocritical world in this painfully introspective novel, which is noted for its symbolic use of bottles and jars and black and white colors and its symbols of imprisonment and death.

Bells, The Poem by Edgar Allan POE, published posthumously in the magazine *Sartain's Union* (November 1849). This incantatory poem examines bell sounds as symbols of four milestones of human experience—childhood, youth, maturity, and death.

Composed of four stanzas of increasing length, "The Bells" is a showcase of onomatopoeia, alliteration, repetition, and assonance. The first stanza, a study of merry sleigh bells, is followed by a depiction of joyous wedding bells. The third stanza is a cacophony of roaring alarm bells, while the final stanza dwells upon the sullen, rhythmic tolling of funeral bells.

Beloved Novel by Toni MORRISON, published in 1987, and winner of the 1988 Pulitzer Prize for fiction. The work examines the destructive legacy of slavery, as it chronicles the life of a black woman named Sethe, following her from her pre-Civil War life as a slave in Kentucky to her life in Cincinnati, Ohio, in 1873; she is a free woman but is held prisoner by memories of the trauma of her life as a slave. During her escape Sethe gives birth to her fourth child. She attempts to kill her children rather than return with them to slavery. Only one of them, her firstborn, dies. It is the spirit of this child, called Beloved, that returns to Sethe in her new life.

Bend Sinister Novel by Vladimir NABOKOV, published in 1947. It is the second novel the Russian-born author wrote in English. It tells the story of Adam Krug, a philosopher who disregards his country's totalitarian regime until his son David is killed by the forces he has attempted to ignore.

Ben-Hur Historical novel by Lewis WALLACE, published in 1880 and widely translated. It depicts the oppressive Roman occupation of ancient Palestine and the origins of Christianity.

The Jew Judah Ben-Hur is wrongly accused by his former friend, the Roman Messala, of attempting to kill a Roman official. He is sent to be a slave and his mother and sister are imprisoned.

Years later he returns, wins a chariot race against Messala, and is reunited with his now leprous mother and sister. Mother and daughter are cured on the day of the Crucifixion, and the family is converted to Christianity.

Benito Cereno Short story by Herman MELVILLE, published in *Putnam's Monthly Magazine* in 1855 and later included in the collection *The Piazza Tales* (1856). It is a chilling story narrated by Amasa Delano, the captain of a seal-hunting ship who encounters off the coast of Chile a slave ship whose human cargo has revolted. Although it takes Delano some time to unravel the situation, eventually he saves the title character, who is the captain of the slaver, and his remaining crew, and the leaders of the insurrection are slaughtered.

Berlin Stories, The Collection of two previously published novels written by Christopher ISHERWOOD, published in 1946. Set in pre-World War II Germany, the semiautobiographical work consists of *Mr. Norris Changes Trains* (1935; U.S. title, *The Last of Mr. Norris*) and *Goodbye to Berlin* (1939).

The Berlin Stories merge fact and fiction and contain ostensibly objective, frequently comic tales of marginal characters who live shabby and tenuous existences as expatriates in Berlin; the threat of the political horrors to come serves as subtext. In *Goodbye to Berlin* the character Isherwood uses the phrase "I am a camera with its shutter open" to claim that he is simply a passive recorder of events. The two novels that comprise *The Berlin Stories* made Isherwood's literary reputation; they later became the basis for the play *I Am a Camera* (1951; film, 1955) and the musical *Cabaret* (1966; film, 1972).

Biglow Papers Satirical poetry in Yankee dialect by James Russell LOWELL. The first series of *Biglow Papers* was published in *The Boston Courier* newspaper in 1846–48 and collected in book form in 1848. The second series was published in *The Atlantic Monthly* during the American Civil War and collected in a book published in 1867.

Lowell opposed the Mexican War, regarding it as an attempt to extend slavery. The first series of poems expressed his opposition to the war, using the voice of rustic poet Hosea Biglow. Birdofredum Sawin, one of Lowell's most inspired inventions, is a Massachusetts wastrel who reports on the war in several letters. He loses an arm, a leg, and an eye in the fighting. The radical fires in Lowell had cooled somewhat by the time he issued the second series of *Biglow Papers*, which contain less effective satire of the wartime South.

Billy Budd, Foretopman *also called* Billy Budd, Sailor. Novel by Herman MELVILLE, written in 1891 and left unfinished at his death. It was first published in 1924, and the definitive edition was issued in 1962.

Provoked by a false charge, the sailor Billy Budd accidentally kills John Claggert, the satanic master-at-arms. In a time of threatened mutiny, he is hanged, and he goes willingly to his fate.

Melville's story is particularly noted for its powerful symbolic characterizations—with, for example, Billy Budd as both innocent (Adam) and Christ figure—and for its sympathetic treatment of the ambivalence of Captain Vere toward Billy's death.

Black Boy Autobiography by Richard WRIGHT, published in 1945 and considered to be one of his finest works. The book is sometimes considered a fictionalized autobiography or an autobiographical novel because of its use of novelistic techniques. *Black Boy* describes vividly Wright's often harsh, hardscrabble boyhood and youth in rural Mississippi and in Memphis, Tenn. When the work was first published, many white critics viewed *Black Boy* primarily as an attack on racist Southern white society. From the 1960s the work came to be understood as the story of Wright's coming of age and development as a writer whose race, though a primary component of his life, was but one of many that formed him as an artist.

Black Cat, The Short story by Edgar Allan POE,

first published in the *Saturday Evening Post* in August 1843 and included in the collection *Tales by Edgar Allen Poe* (1845). The story's narrator is an animal lover who, as he descends into alcoholism and perverse violence, begins mistreating his wife and his black cat Pluto. When Pluto attacks him in self-defense one night, he seizes the cat in a fury, cuts out one of its eyes, and hangs it. That night a fire destroys his house, leaving him in dire poverty. He later adopts a one-eyed black cat that he finds at a low-life tavern, but after he nearly trips on the cat, he attempts to kill it, too. When his wife intervenes he kills her instead and calmly conceals her in a wall. In the end the black cat reveals the narrator's crime to the police.

Black Elk Speaks Subtitled *Being the Life Story of a Holy Man of the Oglala Sioux as Told to John G. Neihardt (Flaming Rainbow)*, the work is the autobiography of Black Elk. It was dictated by Black Elk in Sioux, translated into English by his son Ben Black Elk, written by John G. Neihardt, and published in 1932. The work became a major source of information about 19th-century Plains Indian culture.

Black Elk, a member of the Oglala Lakota branch of the Sioux nation, tells of his boyhood participation in battles with the U.S. Army, his becoming a medicine man, and his joining Buffalo Bill's Wild West Show in 1886. Upon his return from a European tour, he found his tribe living on the bleak Pine Ridge reservation in South Dakota, starving, diseased, and hopeless, and with many fellow Sioux he joined the Ghost Dance movement. The book concludes with a description of the infamous massacre at Wounded Knee.

Black Thunder Historical novel by Arna BONTEMPS, published in 1936. One of Bontemps' most popular works, this tale of a doomed early 19th-century slave revolt in Virginia was noted for its detailed portrait of a slave community and its skillful use of dialect. Virtually unnoticed when it was first published, a second printing in 1968 attracted much critical attention.

Blithedale Romance, The Minor novel by Nathaniel HAWTHORNE, published in 1852. The novel, about a group of people living in an experimental community, was based in part on Hawthorne's disillusionment with the Brook Farm utopian community near Boston in the 1840s.

Blue Hotel, The Short story by Stephen CRANE, published serially in *Collier's Weekly* (Nov. 26-Dec. 3, 1898), and then in the collection *The Monster and Other Stories* (1899). Combining symbolic imagery with naturalistic detail, it is an existential tale about human vanities and delusions.

As the story opens, three visitors find shelter from a blizzard at Pat Scully's hotel in Fort Romper, Neb.: a nervous New Yorker known as the Swede, a rambunctious Westerner named Bill, and a reserved Easterner called Mr. Blanc. The Swede becomes increasingly drunk, defensive, and reckless. He beats Scully's son, Johnnie, in a fight after accusing him of cheating at cards. When the Swede accosts a patron of a bar, he is stabbed and killed. The story ends ambiguously at a point several months later, when timid Mr. Blanc confesses to Bill that he feels somewhat responsible for the Swede's death because he failed to act when he saw that Johnnie was indeed cheating at cards.

Blues for Mister Charlie Tragedy in three acts by James BALDWIN, produced and published in 1964. A denunciation of racial bigotry and hatred, the play was based on a murder trial that took place in Mississippi in 1955. "Mister Charlie" is a slang term for a white man.

The story concerns Richard Henry, a black man who returns to the Southern town of his birth to begin a new life and recover from drug addiction. Lyle Britten, a white bigot who kills him for "not knowing his place," is acquitted by an all-white jury. Racism scars both black and white members of the community who attempt to intervene.

Bluest Eye, The First novel by Toni MORRISON, published in 1970. This tragic study of a black adolescent girl's struggle to achieve white ideals of beauty and her consequent descent into madness was acclaimed as an eloquent indictment of some of the more subtle forms of racism in American society. Pecola Breedlove longs to have "the bluest eye" and thus to be acceptable to her family, schoolmates, and neighbors, all of whom have convinced her that she is ugly.

Bostonians, The Satirical novel by Henry JAMES, published serially in *Century Illustrated Magazine* in 1885–86 and in book form in three volumes in 1886. It was one of the earliest American novels to deal—even obliquely—with lesbianism.

Olive Chancellor, a Boston feminist in the 1870s, thinks she has found a kindred spirit in Verena Tarrant, a beautiful young woman who, though passive and indecisive, is a spellbinding orator for women's rights. Olive vies for Verena's attention and affections with Basil Ransom, a gracious but reactionary Confederate army veteran. Verena marries Basil and leaves Boston.

The Bostonians is based on Alphonse Daudet's novel *Lévangéliste* (1883); James transposed the work to Boston and to the milieu of the rising feminist movement.

Bride Comes to Yellow Sky, The Short story by Stephen CRANE, published in *The Open Boat and Other Stories* in London and a smaller collection, *The Open Boat and Other Tales of Adventure*, in New York in 1898.

Set at the end of the 19th century in a town called Yellow Sky, the story concerns the marshal, Jack Potter, and his unnamed bride and the effect their marriage has on the town. The drunken, belligerent Scratchy Wilson, a cowboy who represents the Old West, tries to effect a showdown with Jack, his nemesis. When Jack refuses to fight, responding to the cowpoke's taunts with "I'm married," Scratchy leaves without fighting, bewildered that the old rules have changed.

Bride of the Innisfallen, The Collection of short stories by Eudora WELTY, published in 1955. The seven stories, focused largely on female characters, elaborate upon tenuous relationships of the heart in a difficult world and upon the importance of place; they share a more experimental, allusive style than the rest of her work.

Bridge of San Luis Rey, The Pulitzer prize-winning novel by Thornton WILDER, published in 1927. Wilder's career was established with this book, in which he first made use of historical subject matter as a background for his interwoven themes of the search for justice, the possibility of altruism, and the role of Christianity in human relationships.

The plot centers on five travelers in 18th-century Peru who are killed when a bridge across a canyon collapses; a priest interprets the story of each victim in an attempt to explain the workings of divine providence.

Bronx Primitive: Portraits in a Childhood Memoir by Kate SIMON, published in 1982. It evokes working-class Jewish immigrant life in the Bronx during the early 20th century. *A Wider World: Portraits in an Adolescence* (1986) and *Etchings in an Hourglass* (1990) were later installments in Simon's autobiography.

Brown Girl, Brownstones First novel by Paule MARSHALL, originally published in 1959. Somewhat autobiographical, this groundbreaking work describes the coming of age of Selina Boyce, a Caribbean-American girl in New York City in the mid-20th century. Although the book did not gain widespread recognition until it was reprinted in 1981, it was initially noted for its expressive dialogue.

Buried Child Three-act tragedy by Sam SHEPARD, performed in 1978 and published in 1979. The play was awarded the 1979 Pulitzer Prize for drama.

Shepard had his first critical and commercial success with this corrosive study of American family life. The play, set on an Illinois farm, centers on the homecoming of Vince and his girlfriend, Shelly. Vince cherishes a romantic, bucolic vision of the home he left six years earlier, but the actual family turns out to be a collection of twisted grotesques.

Shepard considered the work to be part of a family trilogy with *Curse of the Starving Class* (1976) and *True West* (1981), both of which also portrayed destructive blood relationships.

Burnt Norton Poem by T.S. ELIOT, the first of the four poems that make up THE FOUR QUARTETS. "Burnt Norton" was published in *Collected Poems 1909–1935* (1936); it was published with the remaining three poems of the *The Four Quartets* in 1943.

Burnt Norton is a country house in the Cotswold Hills of Gloucestershire that Eliot visited in the summer of 1934. Set in the rose garden of the house, the poem addresses the pervasive theme of cyclical patterns in time. The opening lines, taken from a passage deleted from *Murder in the Cathedral* (1935), resonate with contradiction and ambiguity:

> Time present and time past
> Are both perhaps present in time future,
> And time future contained in time past.

Bus Stop Romantic comedy in three acts by William INGE, performed and published in 1955. An expansion of *People in the Wind*, a one-act play, *Bus Stop* is set in a small town in Kansas. The story concerns the passengers of a cross-country bus who are stranded overnight by a blizzard and congregate in Grace's restaurant. The passengers include Cherie, a flighty blonde bar singer, cowboys Bo and Virgil, and a drunken doctor, and they are joined by the sheriff, the bus driver, and a waitress. The passengers devise entertainments for themselves, and the men vie for Cherie's attention. When Bo eventually confesses his love to Cherie and tells her she is his first girl, she agrees to go to Montana with him.

Caine Mutiny, The Novel by Herman WOUK, published in 1951. The novel was awarded the 1952 Pulitzer Prize for fiction.

The Caine Mutiny grew out of Wouk's experiences aboard a destroyer-minesweeper in the Pacific in World War II. The novel focuses on Willie Keith, a rich New Yorker assigned to the USS *Caine*, who gradually matures during the course of the book. But the work is best known for its portrayal of the neurotic Captain Queeg, who becomes obsessed with petty infractions at the expense of the safety of ship and crew. Cynical, intellectual Lieutenant Tom Keefer persuades loyal Lieutenant Steve Maryk that Queeg's bizarre behavior is endangering the ship; Maryk reluctantly relieves Queeg of command. Much of the book describes Maryk's court-martial and its aftermath. The unstable Queeg eventually breaks down completely.

Call It Sleep Novel by Henry ROTH, published in 1934. It centers on the character and perceptions of a young boy, the son of Yiddish-speaking Jewish immigrants in a ghetto in New York City. Roth uses stream-of-consciousness techniques to trace the boy's psychological development and to explore his perceptions of his family and of the larger world around him. The book powerfully evokes the terrors and anxieties the child experiences in his anguished relations with his father and realistically describes the squalid urban environment in which the family lives.

The novel was rediscovered in the late 1950s and early '60s and came to be viewed both as an important proletarian novel of the 1930s and as a classic of Jewish-American literature.

Call of the Wild, The Novel by Jack LONDON, published in 1903 and often considered to be his masterpiece. London's version of the classic quest story using a dog as the protagonist has sometimes been erroneously categorized as a children's novel.

Buck, who is shipped to the Klondike to be trained as a sled dog, eventually reverts to his primitive, wolflike ancestry. He then undertakes an almost mythical journey, abandoning the safety of his familiar world to encounter danger, adventure, and fantasy. When he is transformed into the legendary "Ghost Dog" of the Klondike, he has become a true hero.

Cane Experimental novel by Jean TOOMER, published in 1923 and reprinted in 1967, about the black experience in the United States. This symbolic, poetic work comprises a variety of literary forms, including poems and short stories, and incorporates elements from both Southern black folk culture and the contemporary white avant-garde. Some literary critics associated the title with the Old Testament figure of Cain, the exiled son of Adam.

Cane is divided into three sections, the first focusing on the rural Southern past and sexuality. The characters in this section are unable to find success and are constantly frustrated by what life offers them. The second section deals with people moving from the agrarian South to the urban North and the spiritual quest of those who abandon their rural roots in hopes of finding a new life. The final section, "Kabnis," is a prose work that synthesizes the preceding sections. Kabnis is a black teacher and writer who struggles with the dilemma of race, with his ambivalent feelings about his African heritage and Southern enslavement, and with his difficulties in being a creative artist.

Cannery Row Novel by John STEINBECK, published in 1945. Like most of Steinbeck's postwar work, *Cannery Row* is sentimental in tone while retaining the author's characteristic social criticism. Peopled by stereotypical good-natured bums and warm-hearted prostitutes living on the fringes of Monterey, Calif., the picaresque novel celebrates lowlifes who are poor but happy.

Cannibals and Missionaries Novel of ideas that probes the psychology of terrorism, by Mary MCCARTHY, published in 1979.

The action of the novel begins when a plane carrying Americans bound for Iran is hijacked by terrorists. Some passengers are rich art collectors; others are politicians and activists planning to investigate allegations that Savak, the shah's secret police, is using torture against political dissidents. At first the terrorists intend to use the politicians and activists as hostages, but they soon realize that masterworks of art are of more value than any human being and decide to trade the art collectors for their artworks.

Cantos, The Collection of poems by Ezra POUND, who began writing these more or less philosophical reveries in 1915. The first were published in *Poetry* magazine in 1917; through the decades the writing of cantos gradually became Pound's major poetic occupation, and the last were published in 1968. The complete edition of *The Cantos* (1970) consists of 117 sections.

In his early cantos Pound offered personal, lyrical reactions to such writers as Homer, Ovid, Dante, and Rémy de Gourmont, as well as to sundry politicians and economists. The early verses include memories of his teenage trips to Europe. *The Pisan Cantos* (1948), written while Pound was incarcerated—first in a prison camp for war criminals and later in a hospital for the criminally insane—were among the most admired sections of the poem; they won a Bollingen Prize in 1949.

Cask of Amontillado, The Short story by Edgar Allan POE, first published in *Godey's Lady's Book* in November 1846. The narrator of this tale of horror is the aristocrat Montresor, who, having endured, as he claims, a thousand injuries at the hand of the connoisseur Fortunato, is finally driven by yet another insult to seek revenge. Amid the carnival celebrations Montresor encounters the drunken Fortunato and, on the pretext of seeking his judgment of a newly purchased cask of amontillado sherry, takes him to his palazzo.

While keeping up a conversation heavy with irony, Montresor leads Fortunato into the cellar to the deepest crypt. There Montresor chains the unlucky Fortunato in a small chamber and, brick by brick, walls him in.

Catcher in the Rye Novel by J.D. SALINGER, published in 1951. The influential and widely acclaimed story details the two days in the life of 16-year-old Holden Caulfield after he has been expelled from prep school. Confused and disillusioned, he searches for truth and rails against the "phoniness" of the adult world. He ends up exhausted and emotionally ill, in a psychiatrist's office. After he recovers from his breakdown, Holden relates his experiences to the reader.

Catch-22 Satirical novel by Joseph HELLER, first published in 1961. The plot of the novel centers on the antihero Captain John Yossarian, stationed at an airstrip on a Mediterranean island in World War II, and portrays his desperate attempts to stay alive. The "catch" in *Catch-22* involves a mysterious Air Force regulation which asserts that a man is considered insane if he willingly continues to fly dangerous combat missions, but that if he makes the necessary formal request to be relieved of such missions, the very act of making the request proves that he is sane and therefore ineligible to be relieved. The term catch-22 thereafter entered the English language with the meaning "a problematic situation for which the only solution is denied by a circumstance inherent in the problem" and later developed several additional senses.

In 1994 Heller published a sequel entitled *Closing Time*, which details the current lives of the characters established in *Catch-22*.

Cat on a Hot Tin Roof Play by Tennessee WILLIAMS, published and produced in 1955. It won a Pulitzer Prize. The play exposes the emotional lies governing relationships in the family of a wealthy Southern planter of humble origins. The patriarch, Big Daddy, is about to celebrate his 65th birthday. His two married sons, Gooper (Brother Man) and Brick, have returned for the occasion, the former with his pregnant wife and five children, the latter with his wife Margaret (Maggie). Gooper seeks by virtue of his progeny to inherit the plantation. The interactions between Big Daddy, Brick, and Maggie form the substance of the play.

Cat's Cradle Science-fiction novel by Kurt VONNEGUT, Jr., published in 1963. Notable for its black humor, it is considered one of the author's major early works.

The novel features two notable inventions: Bokononism, a religion of lies "that make you brave and kind and healthy and happy," and ice-nine, a type of ice that forms at any temperature up to 114.4 degrees and continues freezing all of the liquid it contacts in a kind of chain reaction. The story's two principal figures are Bokonon, the religion's founder, and Dr. Felix Hoenikker, inventor of ice-nine. The narrator, a journalist who calls himself Jonah, confronts the opposing forces of rationality and irrationality. The novel concludes with the inevitable end of the world caused by the release of ice-nine (as transmitted by a frozen body to the ocean).

Celebrated Jumping Frog of Calaveras County, The Short story by Mark TWAIN, first published in *The Saturday Press* in 1865.

The narrator of the story, who is searching for a Reverend Leonidas Smiley, visits the long-winded Simon Wheeler, a miner, in hopes of learning his whereabouts. Wheeler instead relates an elaborate story of a different man named Jim Smiley who was a compulsive and imaginative gambler and who once spent three months training a frog named Daniel Webster to jump and then won money by betting on the frog. The gambler, Wheeler reveals, was eventually duped by a quick-thinking stranger.

Celestial Railroad, The Allegorical short story by Nathaniel HAWTHORNE, published in 1843 and included in his short-story collection *Mosses from an Old Manse* (1846).

Following the path of Christian in John Bunyan's *The Pilgrim's Progress*, the narrator travels from the City of Destruction to the Celestial City—not on foot as had the original pilgrim but as a passenger on the Celestial Railroad. Mr. Smooth-it-away, a friendly fellow traveler, comments contemptuously about the arduous trip the old-fashioned pilgrims had to undergo. At the journey's end, Mr. Smooth-it-away leaves the other passengers and divulges his true identity by breathing fire and brimstone. The narrator awakens and realizes, with great relief, that it has all been a dream.

Chambered Nautilus, The Poem by Oliver Wendell HOLMES, first published in the February 1858 issue of *The Atlantic Monthly* in his "Breakfast-Table" column. Written in five seven-line stanzas, the poem later appeared in collections of poems by Holmes. The poem takes as its central metaphor the sea creature of the title, which constructs its shell in an ever-widening coil of chambers.

Charlotte's Web Children's novel by E.B. WHITE, published in 1952, with illustrations by Garth Williams. One of the classics of children's literature, this widely read tale takes place on a farm in Maine and concerns a pig named Wilbur and his devoted friend Charlotte, the spider who manages to save his life by writing words in her web.

Chicago Poem by Carl SANDBURG, first published in *Poetry* magazine in March 1914 and later in the book *Chicago Poems* (1916). An ode to the city in which Sandburg lived, "Chicago" is perhaps his best-known poem. Reminiscent of the poetry of Walt Whitman, the work celebrates ordinary life with strong affirmation.

In "Chicago" Sandburg used apostrophe to describe the city, notably in the terse epithets of the opening and closing lines of the poem, where the city is personified with the qualities of its leading industries:

> Hog Butcher for the World,
> Tool Maker, Stacker of Wheat,
> Player with Railroads and the Nation's
>   Freight Handler;
> Stormy, husky, brawling,
> City of the Big Shoulders

Children's Hour, The Drama in three acts about the tragic repercussions of a schoolgirl's malicious gossip by Lillian HELLMAN, performed and published in 1934. Hellman based the plot on an actual case in 19th-century Edinburgh that was detailed in the essay "Closed Doors, or The Great Drumsheugh Case" in *Bad Companions* (1931) by William Roughead.

The story concerns an attempt by Mary Tilford, a student at a New England boarding school, to explain to her rich, indulgent grandmother why she has run away from school. Angry over her mild altercation with Karen Wright and Martha Dobie, the women who own and run the school, Mary says that she knows the women to be lesbians, and she successfully blackmails another student into corroborating her accusation. Dr. Joe Cardin, Karen's fiancé, exposes Mary as a liar, but the school is forced to close. After Karen and Martha lose a libel suit, Karen realizes that Cardin's trust in her is altered and ends their relationship. Martha confesses her self-doubt to Karen and commits suicide.

Civil Disobedience Essay by Henry David THOREAU, originally delivered as a lecture at the Concord Lyceum in January-February 1848 and published in the only issue of the magazine *Aesthetic Papers* in May 1849 as "Resistance to Civil Government"; it was retitled "Civil Disobedience" in the posthumous collection *A Yankee in Canada, with Anti-Slavery and Reform Papers* (1866).

The essay is a defense of the private, individual conscience against the expediency of the majority and as such it contains Thoreau's defiantly anarchistic views of government. To Thoreau, moral law is superior to civil law, even if a penalty ensues, because "under a government which imprisons any unjustly, the true place for a just man is also a prison." The essay remains an important treatise on American individualism.

Clean, Well-Lighted Place, A Much-anthologized short story by Ernest HEMINGWAY, first published in *Scribner's Magazine* in March 1933 and later that year in the collection *Winner Take Nothing*. Late one night two waiters in a café wait for their last customer, an old man who has recently attempted suicide, to leave. The younger waiter, eager to get home to his wife, turns the old man out, but the older waiter is sympathetic to the human need for a clean, well-lighted place, an outpost in the darkness.

The story is a powerful existential statement about the insufficiency of religion as a source of comfort, and it contains an often cited version of the Lord's Prayer that substitutes the Spanish word *nada* ("nothing") for most of the prayer's nouns.

Clotel (*in full* Clotel; or, The President's Daughter: A Narrative of Slave Life in the United States) Novel by William Wells BROWN, first published in England in 1853. Brown revised it three times for publication in the United States—serially and in book form—each time changing the plot, the title, and the names of characters. The book was first published in the United States in 1864 as *Clotelle: A Tale of Southern States*. It was the first novel written by an African-American, but it was published in the United States after Harriet Wilson's *Our Nig*. It is a melodramatic tale of three generations of black women who struggle with the constrictions of slavery, miscegenation, and concubinage. Although criticized for its cluttered narrative and its stiff characters, the novel provides insight into the antebellum slave culture.

Cocktail Party, The Verse drama in three acts by T.S. ELIOT, produced in 1949 and published in 1950. Based on *Alcestis* by Euripides, it is a morality play presented as a comedy of manners. Eliot's most commercially successful play, it was more conventional and less poetic than his earlier dramatic works.

The marital problems of Edward and Lavinia Chamberlayne are of special interest to an unidentified guest at their dismal cocktail party. The guest is later identified as Sir Henry Harcourt-Reilly, a prescient psychiatrist who helps heal the Chamberlaynes' marriage. He also counsels Celia Coplestone, Edward's mistress and the main moral figure of the piece, to work out her salvation.

Color Purple, The Novel by Alice WALKER, published in 1982. It won a Pulitzer Prize in 1983. A feminist novel about an abused and uneducated black woman's struggle for empowerment, the novel was praised for the depth of its female characters and for its eloquent use of black English vernacular.

Come Back, Little Sheba Drama in two acts by William INGE, published in 1949 and first performed in 1950.

The play centers on the frustrated lives of Doc and Lola. Trapped in a barren 20-year-old marriage, Doc drowns his disappointment in alcohol and fantasizes about Marie, their young boarder. Lola sublimates her pain over her empty life in pining for Sheba, her lost dog. When in a drunken outburst Doc wrecks their home and nearly kills Lola, the couple are forced to see their lives clearly and to realize their mutual dependence.

Company She Keeps, The First novel by Mary MCCARTHY. Originally published as six separate short stories, the novel appeared in 1942.

Protagonist Margaret Sargent, a young student at a women's college, "a princess among the trolls," is based upon the author herself. The stories are barely disguised and acutely observed accounts of the author's own years as a young New Yorker and describe the failure of a marriage, random love affairs, and a passing flirtation with Trotskyism. Margaret's search for personal identity and her need for honesty and for distinguishing appearance from reality are the themes of the stories.

Confessions of Nat Turner, The Novel by William STYRON, published in 1967 and awarded the Pulitzer Prize for fiction in 1968. A fictional account of the Virginia slave revolt of 1831, the novel is narrated by the leader of the rebellion. Styron based *The Confessions of Nat Turner* on a pamphlet of the same title published in Virginia shortly after the revolt, but he took many liberties in developing Turner's character. Styron's Turner is a man of moral depth and farseeing vision who is nevertheless a bitter, self-denying, sexually repressed man who cannot attain either physical or spiritual freedom. Not surprisingly, the book generated controversy, primarily among black critics who objected to the white author's attempt to speak in the voice of a black slave. These critics also accused Styron of falsifying historical facts and misrepresenting Turner himself, and in 1968 a book of essays appeared called *William Styron's Nat Turner: Ten Black Writers Respond*. Styron answered in his own defense and was supported by several eminent historians.

Confidence-Man, The (*in full* The Confidence-Man: His Masquerade) Satirical allegory by Herman MELVILLE, published in 1857. The last novel to be published during Melville's lifetime, it reveals the author's pessimistic view of an America grown tawdry through greed, self-delusion, and lack of charity.

Set on a steamboat traveling on the Mississippi River, the work is an episodic series of vignettes of various passengers—some dupes, some tricksters—who represent a gullible American public that can be deceived by charlatans and by the lure of easy money.

Conjure Woman, The The first collection of stories by Charles W. CHESNUTT. The seven stories began appearing in magazines in 1887 and were first collected in a book in 1899.

The narrator of *The Conjure Woman* is a white male Northerner living in the southern United States who passes along the stories told him by ex-slave Julius McAdoo. Unusual for dialect tales of the period, the stories give a realistic picture of the pre-Civil War South, including descriptions of penurious, brutish masters. Conjuration—magic effected by hoodoo practitioners—helps slaves to overcome difficulties; thus, spells are cast and humans are transformed into birds and mammals in the course of these tales.

The relationships between the patronizing narrator, his wife, who sometimes glimpses the stories' deeper meanings, and the crafty, sometimes manipulative Uncle Julius—each of whom is subtly characterized—develop over the course of the book.

Connecticut Yankee in King Arthur's Court, A Satirical novel by Mark TWAIN, published in 1889. It is the tale of a commonsensical Yankee who is carried back in time to Britain in the Dark Ages, and it celebrates homespun ingenuity and democratic values in contrast to the superstitious ineptitude of a feudal monarchy. Twain wrote it after reading Sir Thomas Malory's *Le Morte Darthur*.

Hank Morgan, a mechanic at a gun factory, is knocked unconscious and awakens in England in the year 528. He is captured and taken to Camelot, where he is put on exhibit before the knights of King Arthur's Round Table. He is condemned to death, but remembering having read of an eclipse on the day of his execution, he amazes the court by predicting the eclipse. It is decided that he is a sorcerer like Merlin, and he is made minister to the ineffectual king. In an effort to bring democratic principles and mechanical knowledge to the kingdom, he strings telephone wire, starts schools, trains mechanics, and teaches journalism. He also falls in love and marries.

But when Hank tries to better the lot of the peasants, he meets opposition from many quarters. He and Arthur, in disguise, travel among the miserable common folk, are taken captive and sold as slaves, and only at the last second are rescued by 500 knights on bicycles. Hank and his family briefly retire to the seaside. When they return they find the kingdom engulfed in civil war, Arthur killed, and Hank's innovations abandoned. Hank is wounded, and Merlin, pretending to nurse him, casts a spell that puts him to sleep until the 19th century.

Contending Forces (*in full* Contending Forces: A Romance Illustrative of Negro Life North and South) Novel by Pauline HOPKINS, published in 1900.

The complicated plot of *Contending Forces* follows a mixed-race family from early 19th-century slavery in the West Indies and the southern United States to early 20th-century Massachusetts. The story centers on Will and his sister Dora as each works to improve the social and political situations faced by African-Americans. Their marriages to ideological opposites suggest Hopkins' hopes for reconciling the contrary philosophies of Booker T. Washington and W.E.B. Du Bois. Other characters are used to depict the horrors of rape, lynching, racism, and sexism. *Contending Forces* is especially notable as one of the earliest novels by an African-American woman.

Country of the Pointed Firs, The Collection of sketches about life in a fictional coastal village in Maine by Sarah Orne JEWETT; published in 1896, it is an acclaimed example of local color.

Highly regarded for its sympathetic yet unsentimental portrayal of the town of Dunnet Landing and its residents, this episodic book is narrated by a nameless summer visitor who relates the life stories of various inhabitants, capturing the idiomatic language, customs, mannerisms, and humor peculiar to Down-Easters. Among the villagers are the narrator's landlady, Mrs. Almira Todd, a widow of great inner strength; a former seaman, Captain Littlepage, who scorns modern ways; Mrs. Todd's gracious mother, Mrs. Blackett; Mrs. Todd's brother, William; and a former fisherman, Elijah Tilley, an old widower.

The book evokes both the isolation and the sense of community of this small, dying town, whose inhabitants live chiefly to preserve memory and affirm and maintain values of the past.

Crack-Up, The Essay by F. Scott FITZGERALD, published serially in *Esquire* magazine in 1936 and posthumously, in book form, in *The Crack-Up: With Other Uncollected Pieces, Note-Books, and Unpublished Letters* (1945). This confessional essay documents the spiritual and physical deterioration of Fitzgerald in the mid-1930s.

Cream of the Jest, The Novel by James Branch CABELL, published in 1917 and revised in 1920. It is the 16th book of the 18-volume series called *The Works of James Branch Cabell* (1927–30), also known as *The Biography of the Life of Manuel.* The comic novel blends contemporary realism and historical romance.

Cremation of Sam McGee, The Ballad by Robert SERVICE, published in Canada in 1907 in *Songs of a Sourdough* (U.S. title, *The Spell of the Yukon, and Other Verses*). A popular success upon publication, this exaggerated folktale about a pair of a Yukon gold miners was reprinted 15 times in its first year.

In the ballad, set in the icy wilds of northwestern Canada, the title character dies after asking the narrator to cremate his body rather than bury it. After placing the body in a blazing furnace, the narrator takes a last look into the fire and hears McGee urge him to close the door before the heat escapes. The ballad has remained a favorite recitation piece because of its internal rhymes, driving rhythms, and macabre irony.

Crimes of the Heart Drama in three acts by Beth HENLEY, produced in 1979 and published in 1982. It won the Pulitzer Prize in 1981.

Set in a small Mississippi town, the play examines the lives of three quirky sisters who have gathered at the home of the youngest. During the course of the work the sisters unearth grudges, criticize each other, reminisce about their family life, and attempt to understand their mother's suicide years earlier.

Crossing Brooklyn Ferry Poem by Walt WHITMAN, published as "Sun-Down Poem" in the second edition of *Leaves of Grass* in 1856 and revised and retitled in later editions. It is a sensitive, detailed record of the poet's thoughts and observations about the continuity of nature and of brotherhood while aboard a ferry between Brooklyn and Manhattan. His panoramic description of the harbor includes rich images of sunlight on the water, the flight of seagulls, and the commerce of ships. Through the use of repetition, exclamation, and apostrophe, Whitman conveys his joyful belief in world solidarity.

Crucible, The A four-act play by Arthur MILLER, performed and published in 1953. Set in 1692 during the Salem witch trials, *The Crucible* is an examination of contemporary events in American politics during the era of fear and desire for conformity brought on by Senator Joseph Mc-Carthy's sensational allegations of communist subversion in high places.

Custom of the Country, The A novel of manners by Edith WHARTON, published in 1913.

The Custom of the Country is the story of Undine Spragg, a young woman with social aspirations who convinces her nouveau riche parents to leave the Midwest and settle in New York. There she captures and marries a young man from New York's high society. This and each subsequent relationship she engineers prove unsatisfactory, chiefly because of her greed and great ambition.

Daddy Poem by Sylvia PLATH, published posthumously in 1965 in the collection ARIEL. One of Plath's most famous poems, "Daddy" was completed during a brief prolific period of writing before her suicide in February 1963. In images that progress from domestic to demonic, the poem confronts a woman's conflicting feelings about her father's death when she was a child.

Daisy Miller Novel by Henry JAMES, published in *Cornhill Magazine* in 1878 and published in book form in 1879.

The book's title character is a young American woman traveling in Europe with her mother. There she is courted by Frederick Forsyth Winterbourne, an American living abroad. In her innocence, Daisy is compromised by her friendship with an Italian man. Her behavior shocks Winterbourne and the other Americans living in Italy, and they shun her. Only after she dies does Winterbourne recognize that her actions reflected her spontaneous, genuine, and unaffected nature and that his suspicions of her were unwarranted. Like others of James's works, *Daisy Miller* uses the contrast between American innocence and European sophistication as a powerful tool with which to examine social conventions.

Day of the Locust, The Novel by Nathanael WEST about the savagery lurking beneath the Hollywood dream. Published in 1939, it is one of the most striking examples of the "Hollywood novel" in American fiction.

Tod Hackett, a set designer, becomes involved in the lives of several individuals who have been warped by their proximity to the artificial world of Hollywood. Hackett's completion of his painting "The Burning of Los Angeles" coincides with the explosion of the other characters' unfulfilled dreams in a conflagration of riot and murder.

Dead Lecturer, The Collection of verse by Amiri BARAKA, published in 1964 under the name LeRoi Jones. The collection marked a separation for Baraka from the style and literary philosophy of the Beats, with whom he had previously been associated. In the poem "Rhythm & Blues" he uses the structures of jazz and blues to forge a new, distinctly African-American voice. Poems such as "Black Dada Nihilismus" and "An Agony. As Now." reveal the anger and despair of a black man trapped in a white, middle-class society. The collection is notable for its strong imagery and lyrical treatment of violence.

Deal in Wheat, A Short story by Frank NORRIS, first published serially in 1902 and then in the book *A Deal in Wheat and Other Stories of the New and Old West*, published posthumously in 1903. Employing the techniques of naturalism, the five-part story examines the business of wheat speculation at the Chicago Board of Trade at the turn of the 20th century. Norris was concurrently working on the unfinished trilogy *The Epic of Wheat*, comprising *The Octopus* (1901) and *The Pit* (1903).

The first episode of "A Deal in Wheat" features Sam Lewiston, who loses his Kansas farm as a result of low wheat prices. The middle three episodes detail the economic warfare of two wealthy speculators, Mr. Hornung of the bull market and Mr. Truslow of the bear market. In the last episode Lewiston is denied free bread in Chicago because of high wheat prices.

Death Comes for the Archbishop Novel by Willa CATHER, published in 1927. The novel is based on the lives of Bishop Jean Baptiste L'Amy and his vicar Father Joseph Machebeut and is considered emblematic of the author's moral and spiritual concerns.

Death Comes for the Archbishop traces the friendship and adventures of Bishop Jean Latour and vicar Father Joseph Vaillant as they organize the new Roman Catholic diocese of New Mexico. Latour is patrician, intellectual, introverted; Vaillant, practical, outgoing, sanguine. Friends since their childhood in France, the clerics triumph over corrupt Spanish priests, natural adversity, and the indifference of the Hopi and Navajo to establish their church and build a cathedral in the wilderness.

The novel, essentially a study of character, explores Latour's inner conflicts and his relationship with the land, which through the author's powerful description becomes an imposing, unyielding character in its own right.

Death in the Family, A Novel by James AGEE about a family's reactions to the accidental death of the father. Published in 1957, the novel was praised as one of the best examples of American autobiographical fiction, and it won a Pulitzer Prize in 1958.

As told through the eyes of six-year-old Rufus Follet, the story emerges as an exploration of conflicts both among members of the family and in society. The differences between black and white, rich and poor, country life and city life, and, ultimately, life and death are richly depicted. Agee used contrasting narratives as a structural device to link the past and present; italicized passages describing the family's life before the fatal automobile accident are incorporated into the primary narrative of the crash and its immediate effects.

Death of a Salesman A play in "two acts and a requiem" by Arthur MILLER, written in 1948 and produced in 1949. Miller won a Pulitzer Prize for the work, which he described as "the tragedy of a man who gave his life, or sold it" in pursuit of the American Dream.

After many years on the road as a traveling salesman, Willy Loman realizes he has been a failure as a father and husband. His sons, Happy and Biff, are not successful—on his terms (being "well-liked") or any others. His career fading, Willy escapes into reminiscences of an idealized past. In the play's climactic scene, Biff prepares to leave home, starts arguing with Willy, confesses that he has spent three months in jail, and mocks his father's belief in "a smile and a shoeshine." Willy, bitter and broken, his illusions shattered, commits suicide.

Death of the Hired Man, The Narrative poem by Robert FROST, published in *North of Boston* in 1914. The poem, written in blank verse, consists of a conversation between the farmer Warren and his wife Mary about their former farmhand Silas, an elderly man who has come "home" to their farm to die. Silas' plight is poignantly presented, and the characterizations of home as "where, when you have to go there,/They have to take you in" and "Something you somehow haven't to deserve" are well known.

Deerslayer, The (*in full* The Deerslayer; or, The First War-Path) The fifth of five novels in the series THE LEATHER-STOCKING TALES by James Fenimore COOPER, published in two volumes in 1841.

In *The Deerslayer*, Cooper returns to Natty Bumppo's youth at Lake Oswego, N.Y. (called Glimmerglass in the novel), in the 1740s, at the time of the French and Indian War. Known as "Deerslayer" among the Delaware Indians with whom he lives, young Bumppo and the giant Hurry Harry help the trapper Thomas Hutter to resist an attack by the Iroquois, who are allied with the French. The Iroquois capture Hutter and Hurry Harry; Bumppo and his friend, the Mohican chief Chingachgook, secure their release, but in an attempt to rescue Chingachgook's bride, Bumppo himself is captured. Hutter is killed. His daughter, Judith, confesses her love to Bumppo and manages to delay his execution until Chingachgook arrives with a troop of British soldiers to effect a rescue.

Delicate Balance, A Drama in three acts by Edward ALBEE, published and produced in 1966. Winner of a Pulitzer Prize in 1967, the play, about a middle-aged couple's struggle to restore the "balance" of their routine after it has been threatened by intruding friends, is representative of the playwright's concerns with the hidden terrors of everyday life.

The drama is set in the living room of an upper-middle-class home in suburbia. Using a relatively simple story of a frightened couple who ask their friends for refuge, Albee examines illusion and loss in American families. Although the play was criticized for repeating the structure and thematic content of his *Who's Afraid of Virginia Woolf*, it stood as a dark comic portrait of modern angst.

Delta Wedding Novel by Eudora WELTY, published in 1946. It was Welty's first full-length novel, presenting a comprehensive and insightful portrait of a Southern plantation family in 1923.

Set in the context of the wedding of one of the daughters, the novel explores the relationships among members of the Fairchild family, most of whom have been sheltered from any contact with the world outside the Mississippi Delta. Although they quarrel among themselves, they also unite against any threats to the family's status, honoring the belief in the family as a sacred and unchanging entity. Only Ellen Fairchild, who has married into the family, has a more worldly perspective; her clear-sightedness allows her to work toward family harmony without being defeated by the internal bickering.

Democratic Vistas Prose pamphlet by Walt WHITMAN, published in 1871. The work comprises three essays that outline the author's ideas about the role of democracy in establishing a new cultural foundation for America.

Writing a few years after the American Civil War, Whitman suggested that some notion of heroism and honor had been lost by Americans. He particularly criticized the materialism and the preoccupation with business he observed in soci-ety. The antidote, he felt, was a return to the Jeffersonian-Jacksonian brand of democracy and the cultivation of spiritual fellowship. Often criticized for its optimistic belief in progress and its naive dismissal of history as a factor in human development, the pamphlet remains an important supplement to Whitman's poetry as well as an example of his philosophy of government.

Deptford Trilogy, The A series of three novels by Robertson DAVIES, consisting of *Fifth Business* (1970), *The Manticore* (1972), and *World of Wonders* (1975). Throughout the trilogy, Davies interweaves moral concerns and bits of arcane lore.

The novels trace the lives of three men from the small town of Deptford, Ont., connected and transformed by a single childhood event: Percy "Boy" Staunton throws a snowball containing a stone at Dunstable (later Dunstan) Ramsay. Ramsay dodges the snowball and it hits Mary Dempster, who gives birth prematurely to a son, Paul, and slides into dementia.

Fifth Business is an autobiographical letter written by Dunstan upon his retirement as headmaster of a boys' school; he has been tormented by guilt throughout his life. Boy Staunton lies at the bottom of Lake Ontario at the opening of *The Manticore*; the stone that hit Mrs. Dempster some 60 years earlier is found in his mouth. Much of the book describes the course of Jungian analysis undertaken by Boy's son David. *World of Wonders* tells the story of Paul Dempster. Kidnapped as a boy by a magician, he learns the trade and eventually becomes Magnus Eisengrim, one of the most successful acts on the European continent.

Désirée's Baby Short story by Kate CHOPIN, published in her collection *A Night in Acadie* in 1897. A widely acclaimed, frequently anthologized story, it is set in antebellum New Orleans and deals with slavery, the Southern social system, Creole culture, and the ambiguity of racial identity.

Désirée and her husband Armand are happily

married. But when Désirée gives birth to a child who is obviously of mixed racial ancestry, Armand forces her and the child into exile and to a tragic end and becomes more brutal toward his slaves. Only when it is too late does Armand discover that it is he, and not Désirée, who is part black.

Desire Under the Elms Tragedy in three parts by Eugene O'NEILL, produced in 1924 and published in 1925. The last of O'Neill's naturalistic plays and the first in which he re-created the starkness of Greek tragedy, *Desire Under the Elms* draws from Euripides' *Hippolytus* and Jean Racine's *Phèdre*, both of which feature a father returning home with a new wife who falls in love with her stepson.

In this play Ephraim Cabot abandons his farm and his three sons, who hate him. The youngest son, Eben, buys out his brothers, who head off to California. Shortly after this, Ephraim returns with his young new wife, Abbie. Abbie becomes pregnant by Eben; she lets Ephraim believe that the child is his, but she later kills the infant when she sees it as an obstacle between herself and Eben. Eben, enraged, turns Abbie over to the sheriff, but not before he realizes his love for her and confesses his complicity.

One of O'Neill's most admired works, *Desire Under the Elms* invokes the playwright's own family conflicts and Freudian treatment of sexual themes. Although the play is now considered a classic of 20th-century American drama, it scandalized some early audiences for its treatment of infanticide, alcoholism, vengeance, and incest; the first Los Angeles cast was arrested for performing an obscene work.

Devil and Daniel Webster, The Often-anthologized short story by Stephen Vincent BE-NÉT, published in 1937. Two years later it reappeared as a one-act folk opera by Benét and composer Douglas Moore.

Jabez Stone, a New Hampshire farmer, receives a decade of material wealth in return for selling his soul to the Devil—Mr. Scratch. When the Devil comes to claim Stone's soul, the farmer has the statesman and orator Daniel Webster argue his case at midnight before a jury of historic American villains. The Faust legend, gentle satire of New England eccentricities, patriotism, and faith in humanity's higher aspirations are all elements of this tall tale; Benét's prose style, colloquial yet flexible, is important to the story's success.

Devil and Tom Walker, The Short story by Washington IRVING, published as part of the collection *Tales of a Traveller* in 1824. This all-but-forgotten tall tale is considered by some to be one of Irving's finest short stories. Set in Massachusetts, the plot is a retelling of the Faust legend, with a Yankee twist. The story is especially notable for Irving's mastery of narrative technique.

Devil's Dictionary, The Satiric lexicon by Ambrose BIERCE, first compiled as *The Cynic's Word Book* in 1906 and reissued under the author's preferred title five years later. The barbed definitions that Bierce began publishing in the *Wasp*, a weekly journal he edited in San Francisco from 1881 to 1886, brought this 19th-century stock form to a new level of artistry. Employing a terse, aphoristic style, Bierce lampooned social, professional, and religious convention, as in his definitions for *bore*—"A person who talks when you wish him to listen"; *architect*—"One who drafts a plan of your house, and plans a draft of your money"; and *saint*—"A dead sinner revised and edited." Many of the entries include "authenticating" citations from spurious scholarly sources.

Dharma Bums, The Autobiographical novel by Jack KEROUAC, published in 1958. The story's narrator, Raymond Smith, is based on Kerouac himself, and the poet-woodsman-Buddhist, Japhy Ryder, is a thinly disguised portrait of the poet Gary Synder. The book contains a number of other characters who are drawn from actual poets and writers.

The plot unfolds when Smith, who is suffering

spiritual conflicts amid the emptiness of middle-class American life, meets Ryder, whom he immediately recognizes as a spiritual model. The novel tells of the growth of their friendship and Smith's groping toward personal understanding. Much of the story occurs on the American West Coast.

Diamond as Big as the Ritz, The Allegorical short story about lost illusions, by F. Scott FITZGERALD, published in 1922 in *Tales of the Jazz Age*.

John T. Unger is a student at an exclusive Massachusetts prep school. He befriends Percy Washington, a new classmate who boasts that his father is "the richest man in the world" and who invites John to spend the summer at his family's home in the Montana Rockies. The Washington mansion is built upon a secret diamond mine that contains a single diamond one cubic mile in size; the site is well hidden and visible only from the air.

After a squadron of government aircraft locates the diamond mine, military climbers begin to scale the mountain. Rather than allow his private empire to be invaded and appropriated by the government, Percy's father blows up the diamond mountain, killing himself and his wife, the invaders, and Percy, as John and the Washington sisters watch helplessly, horror-struck.

Dodsworth Novel by Sinclair LEWIS, published in 1929. The book's protagonist, Sam Dodsworth, is an American automobile manufacturer who sells his company and takes an extended European vacation with his wife, Fran. *Dodsworth* recounts their reactions to Europeans and European values, their various relationships with others, their estrangement, and their brief reconciliation.

Dolphin, The Book of confessional poetry by Robert LOWELL, published in 1973. It was awarded a Pulitzer Prize in 1974. The poems concern the author's third marriage, the son it produced, and the response to these matters by his previous wife of 20 years. The poems are unrhymed sonnets,

and in subject matter and narrative content they recall late Victorian love sonnets.

Dream Songs, The Masterwork of John BERRYMAN, published in 1969 as a compilation of his earlier works *77 Dream Songs* (1964) and *His Toy, His Dream, His Rest* (1968).

Dream Variation *also called* Dream Variations. Poem by Langston HUGHES, published in 1926 in *The Weary Blues*, his first poetry collection. The poem articulates the dream of African-Americans as the speaker yearns for freedom and for acceptance in American society. It ends with the well-known lines: "Night coming tenderly/ Black like me."

Dr. Heidegger's Experiment Story by Nathaniel HAWTHORNE, published in *Twice-Told Tales* (1837).

Elderly Dr. Heidegger and four of his contemporaries participate in his scientific experiment on aging. Dr. Heidegger applies water from the Fountain of Youth to a faded rose; the flower regains its freshness and beauty. After drinking some of the fabled water, each of the three male participants gradually revert to young manhood and woo the sole female subject, whose youthful beauty has been revived. After the vial of water is spilled accidentally, the rose and the experimenters wither and become old. The experiment has taught Dr. Heidegger not to desire the transient headiness of youth. However, his four friends intend to search for the Fountain of Youth.

Driving Miss Daisy One-act play by Alfred Uhry, produced and published in 1987. The play won the 1988 Pulitzer Prize for drama. It is the story of a friendship that develops over a 25-year period between Daisy Werthan, an elderly Jewish widow living in Atlanta, and Hoke Coleburn, the African-American chauffeur her son hires for her. Set during the years of the civil-rights movement, the drama was hailed for its quiet, unsentimental examination of its elderly characters and for its balanced depiction of gradually changing political sensibilities in the South.

Uhry won an Academy Award for his screenplay adaptation of *Driving Miss Daisy*, produced in 1989.

Drums at Dusk Historical novel by Arna BONTEMPS, published in 1939.

Set in Haiti in the late 18th century, the work is based on the uprising of black slaves that occurred at the time of the French Revolution of 1789, securing independence for their country. A young Frenchman living in Haiti is sympathetic to the plight of the blacks but is nonetheless marked for revenge. Aided by his black friend Toussaint l'Ouverture, he escapes from Haiti with the girl he loves.

Drum-Taps Collection of poems in free verse, most on the subject of the American Civil War, by Walt WHITMAN, published in May 1865. The mood of the poetry moves from excitement at the falling-in and arming of the young soldiers at the beginning of the war to the troubled realization of the war's true significance. The disillusion of the Battle of Bull Run is reflected in "Beat! Beat! Drums!" while an understanding of the depth of suffering of the wounded informs "Vigil Strange I Kept on the Field One Night."

Sequel to Drum-Taps, published in the fall of 1865 (the title page reads 1865–66), includes "Pioneers! O Pioneers!" and Whitman's poems on the death of Abraham Lincoln, O CAPTAIN! MY CAPTAIN! and the elegy WHEN LILACS LAST IN THE DOORYARD BLOOM'D. Both *Drum-Taps* and *Sequel to Drum-Taps* were incorporated into the fourth (1867) edition of LEAVES OF GRASS.

Dry Salvages, The Poem by T.S. ELIOT, first published in 1941 in the *New English Weekly* and in pamphlet form. The third of the four poems in THE FOUR QUARTETS, it was written in strong-stress "native" meter and divided into five sections. "The Dry Salvages" (pronounced to rhyme with *assuages*) resumes the themes of time and history set forth in "Burnt Norton" and "East Coker."

The title of the poem refers to a formation of rocks near Cape Ann, Mass., which Eliot visited as a child. In addition to its images of the Atlantic Ocean, the work describes the continuous power of the Mississippi River, another memory from Eliot's childhood in St. Louis.

The poem is primarily concerned with experience and the human response to Christian doctrines, particularly the Incarnation. Like the other three poems, "The Dry Salvages" struggles with what it acknowledges are difficult, often contradictory concepts that can only be partially understood:

> But to apprehend
> The point of intersection of the timeless
> With time, is an occupation for the saint.

Dust Tracks on a Road Autobiography of Zora Neale HURSTON, published in 1942.

Controversial for its refusal to examine the effects of racism or segregation, *Dust Tracks on a Road* opens with the author's childhood in Eatonville, Fla., the site of the first organized African-American effort at self-government. It follows her through an expanding world of experience and intellectual growth to Howard University, where the writer Charles S. Johnson discovers her work and publishes two stories. The most notable of her patrons thereafter are Fannie Hurst, a white writer for whom she works as a secretary, and anthropologist Franz Boas, who encourages and arranges a fellowship for her research of black folklore. This research formed the basis of her well-received book *Mules and Men* (1935).

Hurston maintains a sunny, invincible attitude throughout the book. White readers seemed to like her lack of comment on racial problems; black critics, however, found this unconscionable and accused her of playing up to whites. In fact, critical comments on U.S. race relations and U.S. foreign policy had been excised by the book's editors.

Dutchman One-act drama by Amiri BARAKA, produced and published in 1964 under the playwright's original name LeRoi Jones. *Dutchman* presents a stylized encounter that illustrates hatred between blacks and whites in America as well as the political and psychological conflicts facing black American men in the 1960s. The play won an Obie Award as best American off-Broadway play of 1964; it was made into a film in 1967. Set in a New York City subway car, the play involves Clay, a young, middle-class black man who is approached seductively by Lula, a white fellow passenger. Lula provokes Clay to anger and finally murders him.

East Coker Poem by T.S. ELIOT, originally appearing in 1940, first in the *New English Weekly* and then in pamphlet form. It is the second of the four poems in THE FOUR QUARTETS. Like the other three poems, "East Coker" was written in strong-stress meter and organized into five sections. Continuing the study of cyclical patterns begun in "Burnt Norton," it examines the nature of history and spiritual renewal.

"East Coker" is named after the hamlet in Somersetshire where Eliot's ancestors lived before immigrating to America in the 1660s. The poem is bleak in tone, with images of deserted streets, subterranean shelters, and hospitals. It closes with the determination that "For us, there is only the trying. The rest is not our business."

East of Eden Novel by John STEINBECK, published in 1952. It is a symbolic recreation of the biblical story of Cain and Abel woven into a history of California's Salinas Valley. With *East of Eden* Steinbeck hoped to reclaim his standing as a major novelist, but his broad depictions of good and evil come at the expense of subtlety in characterization and plot and it was not a critical success.

Spanning the period between the American Civil War and the end of World War I, the novel highlights the conflicts of two generations of brothers; the first being the kind, gentle Adam Trask and his wild brother Charles. Adam eventually marries Cathy Ames, an evil, manipulative, and beautiful prostitute; she betrays him, joining Charles on the very night of their wedding. Later, after giving birth to twin boys, she

shoots Adam and leaves him to return to her former profession. In the shadow of this heritage Adam raises their sons, the fair-haired, winning, yet intractable Aron, and the dark, clever Caleb. This second generation of brothers vie for their father's approval. In bitterness Caleb reveals the truth about their mother to Aron, who then joins the army and is killed in France.

Education of Henry Adams, The Autobiographical work by Henry ADAMS that was privately printed in 1906 and published in 1918. Considered to be one of the most distinguished examples of the genre, the *Education* combines autobiography, bildungsroman, and critical evaluation of an age. Its chapter entitled "The Dynamo and the Virgin" contrasts the Virgin Mary, the unifying force acting on the European Middle Ages, with the dynamo, as representative of the forces of technology and industry acting upon civilization in the early 20th century. Adams marks the destruction of the human values that supported the achievements of his forebears and fears a future age driven by corruption and greed.

Effect of Gamma Rays on Man-in-the-Moon Marigolds, The Naturalistic drama in two acts by Paul ZINDEL, produced in 1965. It won the Pulitzer Prize when it was published in 1971. Largely autobiographical, the play is noted for its sympathetic characterizations.

The story centers on Beatrice Hunsdorfer, an impractical, embittered widow living with her two awkward teenage daughters in a ramshackle house where she makes a living by nursing an elderly invalid. Alternately charming and abrasive, Beatrice is generally selfish like her elder daughter, Ruth, who suffers from convulsions brought on by a childhood trauma. The younger daughter, Tillie, is an eccentric outcast who earns respect by winning her school science project.

Elmer Gantry Novel by Sinclair LEWIS, a satiric indictment of fundamentalist religion that caused an uproar upon its publication in 1927.

The title character of *Elmer Gantry* starts out as a greedy, shallow, philandering Baptist minister, turns to evangelism, and eventually becomes the leader of a large Methodist congregation. Throughout the novel Gantry encounters fellow religious hypocrites, including Mrs. Evans Riddle, Judson Roberts, and Sharon Falconer, with whom he becomes romantically involved. Although he is often exposed as a fraud, Gantry is never fully discredited.

Emperor Jones, The Drama in eight scenes by Eugene O'NEILL, produced in 1920 and published in 1921. *The Emperor Jones* was the playwright's first foray into Expressionist writing.

Based loosely on an event in Haitian history, the play shows the decline of a former Pullman porter, Brutus Jones, who has escaped from prison to an unnamed Caribbean island. With help from a Cockney adventurer, Jones persuades the superstitious natives that he is a magician, and they crown him emperor. He abuses and exploits his subjects and boasts of his power, insisting that only a silver bullet can kill him. Advised that an uprising is in the offing, Jones flees into the jungle. There he is forced to confront his internal demons; scenes show his private past, as images of his victims assail him. More scenes depict bizarre racial memories, including the sale at a slave auction and the earlier capture in the Congo of his ancestors. Terrified, Jones fires all his ammunition at his ghostly tormentors. In the final scene, the rebels find Jones and shoot him.

While not considered one of O'Neill's finest plays, the work was a sensation and remains a staple of small theater groups.

Encantadas, The Ten fictional sketches by Herman MELVILLE, published in 1854 in *Putnam's Monthly Magazine* as "The Encantadas, or Enchanted Isles," under the pseudonym Salvator R. Tarnmoor.

Seven of the sketches describe the Galapagos Islands in the eastern Pacific Ocean, which Melville had seen when he was a working sailor and about which he had read in Charles Darwin's *The Voyage of the Beagle*. Sailors believed that these islands were enchanted. The other three pieces are sketches of people who reside for a time in the Encantadas, mostly renegades and castaways.

Ethan Frome Tragic novel by Edith WHARTON, published in 1911. Wharton's original style and her use of hard-edged irony and the flashback technique set *Ethan Frome* apart from the work of her contemporaries.

The main characters are Ethan Frome, his wife Zenobia, called Zeena, and her young cousin Mattie Silver. Frome and Zeena marry after she nurses his mother in her last illness. Although Frome seems ambitious and intelligent, Zeena holds him back. When her young cousin Mattie comes to stay on their New England farm, Frome falls in love with her. But the social conventions of the day doom their love and their hopes. The story forcefully conveys Wharton's abhorrence of society's unbending standards of loyalty. Written while Wharton lived in France but before her divorce (1913), *Ethan Frome* became one of the best known and most popular of her works.

Evangeline (*in full* Evangeline, A Tale of Acadie) Narrative poem by Henry Wadsworth LONGFELLOW, published in 1847. The poem tells a sentimental tale of two lovers separated when British soldiers expel the Acadians (French colonists) from what is now Nova Scotia. The lovers, Evangeline and Gabriel, are reunited years later as Gabriel is dying. After both die, they are finally buried together.

Written in classical hexameters, the poem intentionally echoes such epics as Homer's *Odyssey*. Although it is considered overly sentimental by many critics, *Evangeline* is respected for its sense of the vast North American landscape and its evocation of an earlier time.

Everything That Rises Must Converge Collection of nine short stories by Flannery O'CONNOR, published posthumously in 1965. The flawed characters of each story are fully revealed in apocalyptic moments of conflict and violence that are presented with comic detachment.

The title story is a tragicomedy about social pride, racial bigotry, generational conflict, false liberalism, and filial dependence. The protagonist Julian Chestny is hypocritically disdainful of his mother's prejudices. His smug selfishness is replaced with childish fear when she suffers a fatal stroke after being struck by a black woman she has insulted out of oblivious ignorance rather than malice. Similarly, "The Comforts of Home" is about an intellectual son with an Oedipus complex. Driven by the voice of his dead father, the son accidentally kills his sentimental mother in an attempt to murder a harlot.

The other stories are "A View of the Woods," "Parker's Back," "The Enduring Chill," "Greenleaf," "The Lame Shall Enter First," "Revelation," and "Judgment Day."

Fall of the House of Usher, The Story of supernatural horror by Edgar Allan POE, published in 1839 in *Burton's Gentleman's Magazine* and issued in *Tales* (1845). One of Poe's most terrifying tales, "The Fall of the House of Usher" is narrated by a man who has been invited to visit his childhood friend Roderick Usher. Usher gradually makes clear that his twin sister Madeline has been placed in the family vault not quite dead. When she reappears in her blood-stained shroud, the visitor rushes to leave as the entire house splits and sinks into a lake.

Family Moskat, The Novel by Isaac Bashevis SINGER, first published in installments from 1945 to 1948 in the Yiddish-language daily newspaper *Forverts* and in book form (two volumes) as *Di familye Mushkat* in 1950. A one-volume English translation was published in 1950.

Panoramic in sweep, the novel follows many characters and story lines in depicting Jewish life in Warsaw from 1911 to the late 1930s. Singer examines Hasidism, Orthodoxy, the rise of secularism, the breakdown of 19th-century traditions, assimilation, Marxism, and Zionism.

Fanshawe First novel by Nathaniel HAWTHORNE, published in 1828 at his own expense. Hawthorne wrote *Fanshawe* while a student at Bow-

doin College in Brunswick, Maine. Soon after he deemed the work to be of such derivative and mediocre quality that he attempted, unsuccessfully, to destroy all existing copies. The book's treatment of plot and character development were derived chiefly from the conventions of gothic novels and the works of Sir Walter Scott.

Farewell to Arms, A Novel by Ernest HEMINGWAY, published in 1929. Like his early short stories and his novel *The Sun Also Rises*, the work is full of the disillusionment of the "lost generation" expatriates. While serving with the Italian ambulance service during World War I, the American lieutenant Frederick Henry falls in love with the English nurse Catherine Barkley, who tends him after he is wounded. She becomes pregnant but refuses to marry him, and he returns to his post. Henry deserts during the Italians' retreat after the Battle of Caporetto, and the reunited couple flee to Switzerland. There, however, Catherine and her baby die during childbirth, leaving Henry desolate.

Fences Play in two acts by August WILSON, performed in 1985 and published in 1986. It won the Pulitzer Prize for drama in 1987. Set in 1957, it is the second in Wilson's projected series of plays depicting African-American life in the 20th century.

The protagonist of *Fences* is Troy Maxson, who had been an outstanding baseball player at a time when the major leagues were closed to black players; he bitterly resents his lost opportunities. An ex-convict as well, Troy is now a garbage collector. He is married to Rose and is the father of teenaged Cory. An emotional, hard-drinking man, Troy ranges from tyrannical fury to delicacy as his preconceived ideas are challenged.

Fields, The Novel by Conrad Richter, published in 1946. It was the second novel in a trilogy published collectively as *The Awakening Land*. The other novels in the trilogy are *The Trees* and THE TOWN.

Fifth Business First of a series of novels known collectively as THE DEPTFORD TRILOGY by Robertson Davies.

Financier, The Novel by Theodore DREISER, published in 1912, the first book of an epic trilogy that Dreiser intended to call the Trilogy of Desire, based on the life of Charles T. Yerkes, an American transportation magnate. The other two volumes were *The Titan* (1914) and *The Stoic*, which was completed by Dreiser's wife after his death and published posthumously in 1947.

The Financier begins the saga of Frank Algernon Cowperwood. Driven, vital, and unscrupulous, he sees himself bound for greatness. The novel describes his career in the brokerage business, his advantageous but ultimately doomed marriage, his deals with corrupt politicians, and his relationship with his mistress, whose father eventually uses political influence to ruin Cowperwood and send him to prison. Out of prison in little more than a year, Cowperwood recoups his fortune during the panic of 1873 and moves to Chicago.

The remaining two novels follow Cowperwood to Chicago and London through a series of shady deals, love affairs, and intrigues until, after his death, his empire collapses and his life is seen to have been meaningless.

Fire Next Time, The Nonfiction book, published in 1963, comprising two previously published essays in letter form by James BALDWIN. In these essays Baldwin warned that, if white America did not change its attitudes and policies toward black Americans and alter the conditions under which blacks were forced to live, violence would result.

In the brief first essay, "My Dungeon Shook: Letter to My Nephew on the One Hundredth Anniversary of the Emancipation," the author attacks the idea that blacks are inferior to whites and emphasizes the intrinsic dignity of black people. In the second essay, "Down at the Cross: Letter from a Region in My Mind," Baldwin recounts his coming-of-age in Harlem, appraises the Black Muslim (Nation of Islam) movement, and gives a statement of his personal beliefs.

Fixer, The Novel by Bernard MALAMUD, published in 1966. It received the Pulitzer Prize in 1967.

Considered by some to be the author's finest novel, *The Fixer* is the story of a Jewish handyman, or fixer, who discovers that there is no rational reason for human cruelty; he also learns that freedom requires constant vigilance. As in Malamud's other works, the condition of the Jews serves as a metaphor for the condition of humanity.

The novel, set in czarist Russia in the early 20th century, tells the story of Yakov Bok. Bok says of himself that he fixes what's broken—except in the heart. His tinkering includes altruistic acts of kindness to others, but his generosity is repaid with misfortune and vilification. Most of the novel takes place while Bok is imprisoned awaiting trial for a murder he did not commit.

Flags in the Dust *see* SARTORIS.

Flowering Judas Short story by Katherine Anne PORTER, published in *Hound and Horn* magazine in 1930. It is the title story of Porter's first and most popular collection, which was published in the same year. When the collection was reissued in 1935, four stories were added to make a total of 10.

Set in Mexico in 1920 during the Mexican Revolution, "Flowering Judas" concerns the attempts of Laura, a beautiful, young American teacher of Indian children and a clandestine worker for the revolutionary cause, to rationalize her actions as she faces the loss of her ideals.

Fool for Love One-act play by Sam SHEPARD, produced in San Francisco and published in 1983. It is a romantic tragedy about the tumultuous love between a rodeo performer and his half sister. The father they have in common, a character called Old Man, acts as narrator and chorus.

For the Union Dead Title poem of a collection by Robert LOWELL, published in 1964. Lowell originally titled the poem "Colonel Shaw and the Massachusetts 54th" to commemorate Robert

Gould Shaw, a white Bostonian who had commanded a battalion of black Union troops during the American Civil War, and published it in the 1960 edition of *Life Studies*.

The poem alludes to three significant incidents of the previous 100 years: Shaw's death and anonymous burial; the dedication, in Boston in the 1890s, of a memorial to Shaw and others who died for the Union; and the violent resistance to school integration in contemporary America.

For Whom the Bell Tolls Novel by Ernest HEMINGWAY, published in 1940.

Set near Segovia, Spain, in 1937, the novel tells the story of American teacher Robert Jordan, who has joined the antifascist Loyalist army. Jordan has been sent to make contact with a guerrilla band and blow up a bridge to advance a Loyalist offensive. The action takes place during Jordan's 72 hours at the guerrilla camp. During this period he falls in love with Maria, and he befriends the shrewd but cowardly guerrilla leader Pablo and his courageous wife Pilar. Jordan manages to destroy the bridge; Pablo, Pilar, Maria, and two other guerrillas escape, but Jordan is injured. Proclaiming his love to Maria once more, he awaits the fascist troops and certain death.

The title is from a sermon by John Donne containing the famous words "No man is an Iland, intire of it selfe; every man is a peece of the Continent. . . . And therefore never send to know for whom the bell tolls; it tolls for thee."

Fountainhead, The Novel by Ayn RAND, published in 1943. An exposition of the author's anticommunist philosophy of "objectivism," *The Fountainhead* tells of the struggle of genius architect Howard Roark—said to be based on Frank Lloyd Wright—as he confronts conformist mediocrity.

In Rand's world, suppression of individual creativity is the greatest evil. Roark is expelled from architectural school for his nonconformist ideas, but he pursues his vision undaunted.

Four Quartets, The Series of four poems by

T.S. ELIOT, published individually from 1936 to 1942, and in book form in 1943; the work is considered to be Eliot's masterpiece.

Each of the quartets has five "movements" and each is titled by a place name—BURNT NORTON (1936), EAST COKER (1940), THE DRY SALVAGES (1941), and LITTLE GIDDING (1942). Eliot's insights into the cyclical nature of life are revealed through themes and images deftly woven throughout the four poems. The work addresses the connections of the personal and historical present and past, spiritual renewal, and the very nature of experience; it is considered the poet's clearest exposition of his Christian beliefs.

Four Saints in Three Acts Opera consisting of a prologue and four acts, with libretto by Gertrude STEIN and music by Virgil Thomson. Stein completed the libretto in 1927, the score was published in 1934, and the opera was first performed in 1934.

Thomson divided Stein's libretto into scenes and acts, and added two figures representing the laity to the cast of characters. The plotless opera, set in 16th-century Spain, treats the Spaniards St. Theresa of Avila, St. Ignatius of Loyola, and two fictional figures, St. Settlement and St. Chavez.

Franny and Zooey Volume containing two interrelated stories by J.D. SALINGER, published in book form in 1961. The stories, originally published in *The New Yorker* magazine, concern Franny and Zooey Glass, two members of the family that was the subject of most of Salinger's short fiction.

Franny is an intellectually precocious late adolescent who tries to attain spiritual purification by obsessively reiterating the "Jesus prayer" as an antidote to the perceived superficiality and corruptness of life. She subsequently suffers a nervous breakdown. In the second story, her next older brother, Zooey, attempts to heal Franny by pointing out that her constant repetition of the "Jesus prayer" is as self-involved and egotistical as the egotism against which she rails.

Furnished Room, The Short story by O. HENRY, published serially in 1904 and then collected in

The Four Million (1906). Set in New York City, it is a melodramatic tale about a young man who, after a futile search for his missing girlfriend, commits suicide in his rented room, not knowing that it is the same room in which his girlfriend had killed herself one week earlier.

Geography III Collection of poetry by Elizabeth BISHOP, published in 1976. The poems offer meditations on the need for self-exploration, on the significance of art, especially poetry, to human life, and on human responsibility in a chaotic world. The collection includes some of Bishop's best-known poems, among them "In the Waiting Room," "Crusoe in England," and the villanelle "One Art." The book won the 1976 National Critics' Circle Award.

Giant Novel about two generations of wealthy Texans by Edna FERBER, published in 1952.

The story unfolds as Leslie Lynnton, a patrician Virginian, marries Bick Benedict, a Texas cattle baron. The reader experiences Texas from Leslie's point of view, as she attemps to understand and to adapt to the customs and expansive way of life of Texans. Alongside her vivid descriptions of the crudeness of the newly rich oil men and cattle barons, Ferber observes their exploitation of the impoverished Mexicans who work for them.

Giants in the Earth (*in full* Giants in the Earth: A Saga of the Prairie) Novel by O.E. RØLVAAG that chronicles the struggles of Norwegian immigrant settlers in the Dakota territory in the 1870s. First published in Norway in two volumes as *I de Dage* (1924; "In Those Days") and *Riket grundlæges* (1925; "The Kingdom Is Founded"), the novel was published in English as a single volume in 1927 as *Giants in the Earth*. It had two sequels, *Peder Seier* (1928; *Peder Victorious*) and *Den signede dag* (1931; *Their Fathers' God*).

The book's indomitable protagonist, Per Hansa, his wife Beret, their children, and three other Norwegian immigrant families settle at Spring Creek, living in makeshift sod huts. Surviving the winters' fierce blizzards, they see their crops destroyed by locusts in summer. They nonetheless persist; new settlers arrive, and the community grows. Beret, who cannot adapt to life on the prairie, almost dies giving birth to the son Per names Peder Victorious. Cheered when a traveling minister baptizes Peder, Beret eventually becomes obsessively religious. When another settler lies dying, Beret insists that Per find a minister for him, but Per is caught in a fierce snowstorm and dies.

Gift of the Magi, The Short story by O. HENRY, published in the *New York Sunday World* in 1905 and then collected in *The Four Million* (1906).

The story concerns James and Della Dillingham Young, a young couple who, despite their poverty, individually resolve to give each other an elegant gift on Christmas Eve. Della sells her beautiful long hair in order to buy a platinum fob chain for Jim's antique gold watch. Meanwhile, Jim pawns his treasured watch to purchase jeweled tortoiseshell combs for Della's precious tresses. The tale concludes with the exchange of gifts and the couple's recognition of the irony of their sacrifices.

Gift, The Novel by Vladimir NABOKOV, originally published serially (in expurgated form in Russian) as *Dar* in 1937–38. It was published in its complete form as a book in 1952. *The Gift* was set in post-World War I Berlin, where Nabokov himself had been an émigré. Steeped in satiric detail about the Russian émigré community, the novel tells parallel stories of the protagonist Fyodor's maturation as a gifted young writer and of his love affair with Zina, a fellow émigré.

Giles Goat-Boy (*in full* Giles Goat-Boy; or, The Revised New Syllabus) Satiric allegorical novel by John BARTH, published in 1966. The book is set in a vast university that is a symbol for the world.

The novel's protagonist, Billy Bockfuss (also called George Giles, the goat-boy), was raised with herds of goats on a university farm after being found as a baby in the bowels of the giant West Campus Automatic Computer (WESCAC).

The WESCAC plans to create a being called GILES (Grand-Tutorial Ideal, Laboratory Eugenical Specimen) that would possess superhuman abilities. Billy's foster father, who tends the herd, suspects Billy of being GILES but tries to groom him to be humanity's savior and to stop WESCAC's domination over humans.

Gimpel the Fool Short story by Isaac Bashevis SINGER, published in 1945 in Yiddish as "Gimpl tam." It was later published in Singer's collection *Gimpel the Fool and Other Stories* (1957). Set in a bygone era in an eastern European shtetl (Jewish small town), the tale concerns Gimpel, a gullible man who responds to a lifetime of betrayal, heckling, and deception with childlike acceptance and complete faith.

Gin Game, The Two-act play by American dramatist D.L. Coburn, produced in 1976. Coburn's first play, it won the Pulitzer Prize for Drama in 1978, the year it was published.

The Gin Game centers on two lonely residents of a retirement home. While playing a series of gin rummy games, they undergo a painful review of their lives. Their four card games are marked by violent exchanges that intensify until ultimately their friendship is ruined.

Giovanni's Room Novel by James BALDWIN, published in 1956, about the conflict in the sexual identity of a young expatriate American in Paris.

After a single homosexual experience in adolescence, David represses his unacceptable impulses. In Paris, he meets Hella Lincoln. He is determined to live the life that he thinks is expected of a male in white, middle-class Western culture. He and Hella have an affair, and David proposes marriage.

While Hella is in Spain considering his proposal, David has an affair lasting several months with Giovanni, an Italian bartender. Still unable to reconcile homosexuality with the life he envisions for himself, David rejects Giovanni. David and Hella go to the south of France. She finds him in a homosexual bar with a sailor and realizes what David's relationship with Giovanni had been. David is left alone, abandoned by Hella, and still in conflict over his sexuality.

Glass Menagerie, The One-act drama by Tennessee WILLIAMS, produced in 1944 and published in 1945. Considered by some critics to be Williams' finest drama, *The Glass Menagerie* launched his career.

Amanda Wingfield lives in a St. Louis tenement, clinging to the myth of her early years as a Southern belle. Her daughter Laura, who wears a leg brace, is painfully shy and often seeks solace in her collection of small glass animals. Amanda's son Tom is desperate to escape his stifling home life and his warehouse job. Amanda encourages him to bring "gentleman callers" home to his sister. When Tom brings Jim O'Connor for dinner, Amanda believes that her prayers have been answered. Laura blossoms during Jim's visit, flattered by his attention. After kissing her, however, he confesses that he is engaged. Laura retreats to her shell, and Amanda blames Tom, who leaves home for good after a final fight with his mother.

Glengarry Glen Ross Play in two acts by David MAMET, originally produced in London in 1983 and published in 1984, when it won the Pulitzer Prize for drama. The play concerns a group of ruthless real-estate salesmen who compete to sell lots in Florida developments known as Glengarry Highlands and Glen Ross Farms. Built on the strength of its explosive and often profane dialogue, *Glengarry Glen Ross* depicts the real-estate industry as seedy and unscrupulous.

Go Down, Moses A collection of seven stories by William FAULKNER, first published in 1942 as a novel under the inaccurate title *Go Down, Moses, and Other Stories*; the title was corrected for the second printing. Set in Faulkner's fictional Yoknapatawpha County, the book contains some of the author's best writing.

The voices of Faulkner's South—black and white, comic and tragic—ring through this sprawling tale of the McCaslin clan. The tone ranges from the farcical to the profound. As the title suggests, the stories are rife with biblical themes. Although the seven stories were originally published separately, *Go Down, Moses* is best read as a novel of interconnecting generations, races, and dreams.

The first story, "Was," is considered a comic masterpiece. It opens with a raucous fox chase that suggests the theme and action of the story. Buck and Buddy, twin sons of Carothers McCaslin, chase their slave and half-brother, Turl; Turl chases his girlfriend Tennie, slave of Hubert and his sister Sibbey Beauchamp; and Sibbey, the only white woman in the countryside, pursues Buck. A poker game decides the fate of the couples and ownership of the slaves. "The Fire and the Hearth" establishes the dignity of Lucas Beauchamp, son of Turl and Tennie. "Pantaloon in Black," the story of a black man lynched for killing a deceitful white, has little relation to the other stories, but echoes their themes of love, loss, and racial tension. "The Old People" and THE BEAR feature Ike McCaslin's confrontations with nature. In "Delta Autumn," Ike, at age 79, is forced to confront his role in perpetuating the exploitation of his own black relatives. In the final story, "Go Down, Moses," Faulkner focuses not on inner family struggles but on the entire community.

God's Trombones (*in full* God's Trombones: Seven Negro Sermons in Verse) Volume of poetry by James Weldon JOHNSON, published in 1927. The work represents what the author called an "art-governed expression" of the traditional black preaching style. The constituent poems are an introductory prayer, "Listen, Lord—A Prayer," and seven verse sermons entitled "The Creation," "The Prodigal Son," "Go Down Death—A Funeral Sermon," "Noah Built the Ark," "The Crucifixion," "Let My People Go," and "The Judgment Day." Although he identified himself as an agnostic, Johnson drew heavily throughout his career from the oral tradition and biblical poetry of his Christian upbringing. In *God's Trombones*, he conveys the raw power of fire-and-brimstone oratory while avoiding the hackneyed devices of dialectal transcription that had marred previous literature in the black idiom.

Gold Bug, The Mystery story by Edgar Allan POE, published in 1843 in the Philadelphia *Dollar Magazine*; it was later published in the collection *Tales* (1845). The central character, William Legrand, has sequestered himself on Sullivan's Island, South Carolina, after a series of economic setbacks. With his servant Jupiter he finds a golden beetle. The parchment in which he captured it is later revealed to be inscribed with cryptic writing and an emblem similar to the death's-head marking on the insect. Legrand deciphers the message and follows its strange instructions, which lead him to uncover the buried treasure of Captain Kidd.

Golden Apples, The Collection of short stories by Eudora WELTY, published in 1949. The stories had all been published previously, and Welty added one novella-length story, "Main Families in Morgana."

Symbolism from Greek mythology unifies the stories, all of which are set in the Mississippi Delta town of Morgana over a 40-year period. The hero of "Moon Lake" and the guitarist in "Music from Spain" are Perseus figures. King MacLain, the protagonist of "Shower of Gold," is a sexually adventurous Zeus figure.

Golden Bowl, The Novel by Henry JAMES, published in 1904.

Wealthy American widower Adam Verver and his daughter Maggie live in Europe, where they collect art and relish each other's company. Through the efforts of the manipulative Fanny Assingham, Maggie becomes engaged to Amerigo, an Italian prince in reduced circumstances, but remains blind to his rekindled affair with her longtime friend Charlotte Stant. Maggie and Amerigo marry, and later, after Charlotte and Adam have also wed, both spouses learn of the ongoing affair, though neither seeks a confrontation. Not until Maggie buys the gilded crystal bowl of the title as a birthday present for Adam does truth crack the veneer of propriety.

Golden Boy Drama in three acts by Clifford ODETS, produced and published in 1937. It traces the downfall of Joe Bonaparte, a gifted young musician who becomes corrupted by money and brutality when he chooses to become a prize-fighter rather than a classical violinist.

Gone With the Wind Novel by Margaret MITCHELL, published in 1936. *Gone With the Wind* is a sweeping, romantic story about the American Civil War from the point of view of the Confederacy. In particular it is the story of Scarlett O'Hara, a headstrong Southern belle who survives the hardships of the war and afterwards manages to establish a successful business by capitalizing on the struggle to rebuild the South. Throughout the book she is motivated by her unfulfilled love for Ashley Wilkes, an honorable man who is happily married. After a series of marriages and failed relationships with other men, notably the dashing Rhett Butler, she has a change of heart and determines to win Rhett back.

Good Earth, The Novel by Pearl BUCK, published in 1931. The novel, about peasant life in China in the 1920s, was awarded the Pulitzer Prize for fiction in 1932.

The Good Earth follows the life of Wang Lung, from his beginnings as an impoverished peasant to his eventual position as a prosperous landowner. He is aided immeasurably by his equally humble wife, O-Lan, with whom he shares a devotion to the land, to duty, and to survival. Buck combines descriptions of marriage, parenthood, and complex human emotions with depictions of Chinese reverence for the land and for a specific way of life.

Good Man Is Hard to Find, A Volume of short stories by Flannery O'CONNOR, published in 1955. Like much of the author's work, the collection presents vivid, hidebound characters seemingly hounded by a redemption that they often successfully elude. Several of the stories are gen-

erally considered masterpieces of the form. These include "The Artificial Nigger," in which the strange sight of a black lawn statue causes a bigoted grandfather to realize a truth about injustice; "Good Country People," in which a young woman's sense of moral superiority proves her downfall; and the title story, whose demonic character the Misfit becomes an instrument of revelation for his most formidable victim.

Grapes of Wrath, The Novel by John STEINBECK, published in 1939. Set during the Great Depression, it traces the migration of an Oklahoma Dust Bowl family to California and their subsequent hardships as migrant farm workers. It won a Pulitzer Prize in 1940. The work did much to publicize the injustices of migrant labor.

The narrative, interrupted by prose-poem interludes, chronicles the struggles of the Joad family's life on a failing Oklahoma farm, their difficult journey to California, and their disillusionment once they arrive there and fall prey to a parasitic economic system. The insularity of the Joads—Ma's obsession with family togetherness, son Tom's self-centeredness, and daughter Rose of Sharon's materialism—ultimately gives way to a sense of universal community.

Graustark Romantic quasi-historical novel subtitled *The Story of a Love Behind a Throne*, by George Barr MCCUTCHEON, first published in 1901. Modeled on Anthony Hope's popular novel *The Prisoner of Zenda* (1894), *Graustark* is set in the mythical middle-European kingdom of Graustark and is suffused with derring-do, court intrigues, and passionate romance. McCutcheon's further novels about the imaginary principality include *Beverly of Graustark* (1904) and *The Prince of Graustark* (1914).

In its extended senses, the word Graustark is used to refer to an imaginary land of high romance or to a highly romantic piece of writing.

Gravity's Rainbow Novel by Thomas PYNCHON, published in 1973. The sprawling narrative comprises numerous threads having to do either directly or tangentially with the secret development and deployment of a rocket by the Nazis near the end of World War II. Lieutenant Tyrone Slothrop is an American working for Allied Intelligence in London. Agents of the Firm, a clandestine military organization, are investigating an apparent connection between Slothrop's erections and the targeting of incoming V-2 rockets. As a child, Slothrop was the subject of experiments conducted by a Harvard professor who is now a Nazi rocket scientist. Slothrop's quest for the truth behind these implications leads him on a nightmarish journey of either historic discovery or profound paranoia, depending on his own and the reader's interpretation. The novel won the National Book Award for fiction in 1974.

Great Gatsby, The Novel by F. Scott FITZGERALD, published in 1925. The narrator, Nick Carraway, is a young Princeton man who works as a bond broker in Manhattan. His neighbor at West Egg, Long Island, is Jay Gatsby, a self-made Midwesterner of considerable wealth. Nick watches as Gatsby is betrayed by his own dreams, which have been nurtured by a meretricious society.

Great God Brown, The Drama in four acts and a prologue by Eugene O'NEILL, produced and published in 1926. An example of O'Neill's pioneering experiments with Expressionistic theater, the play makes use of multiple masks to illustrate the private and public personas of the characters, as well as the changing tenor of their interior lives.

The action juxtaposes its two central characters, William "Billy" Brown, a mediocre architect, and Dion Anthony, a talented but dissolute artist. Both characters are in love with Margaret, who chooses Dion because she is in love with the sensual, cynical mask he presents to the world. But when he removes his mask to reveal the spiritual, artistic side of his nature, she is repulsed. Frustrated at being unable to realize his artistic promise, Dion sinks deeper into his self-destructive habits and soon dies. Billy, who has always been jealous of Dion's talent, steals Dion's mask and takes on his persona. He marries Margaret, who believes that he is Dion. Billy

eventually is accused of the murder of his "old" self and is shot by the police. Margaret continues to worship Dion's mask.

Group, The Novel by Mary MCCARTHY, published in 1963, that chronicles the lives of eight Vassar College friends from their graduation in 1933 to the funeral of Kay Strong, the protagonist, in 1940.

The women believe that their superior education has given them control over their lives and the ability to break down existing taboos and limitations. They all believe in progress, modernity, marrying well, and accumulating wealth and possessions. The novel is the story of their subsequent loss of illusion as they discover that both bohemia and high society have their hypocrisies and that resistance to change is universal.

The Group interweaves the stories of the eight group members—Kay Strong, Helena Davison, Dottie Renfrew, Elinor Eastlake, Mary "Pokey" Prothero, Libby MacAusland, Polly Andrews, and Priss Hartshorn—as they encounter the realities of sex, marriage, motherhood, and careers.

Guide to Kulchur Prose work by Ezra POUND, published in 1938. A brilliant but fragmentary work, it consists of a series of apparently unrelated essays reflecting his thoughts on various aspects of culture and history.

Hairy Ape, The Drama in eight scenes by Eugene O'NEILL, produced in 1922 and published the following year. It is considered one of the prime achievements of expressionism on stage.

Yank Smith, a brutish stoker on a transatlantic liner, bullies and despises everyone around him, considering himself superior. He is devastated when a millionaire's daughter is repulsed by his simian ways, and he vows to get even with her. Ashore in New York, Yank schemes to destroy the factory owned by the woman's father, but his plans fail. Yank wanders into a zoo. There, feeling alienated from humanity, he releases an ape (for whom he feels some kinship), and the ape kills him.

Hamlet, The Novel by William FAULKNER, published in 1940, the first volume of a trilogy including *The Town* (1957) and *The Mansion* (1959). Set in the late 19th century, the narrative depicts the early years of the crude and contemptible Flem Snopes and his clan who by the trilogy's end supplant the dispirited gentry class (represented by the Sartoris family) of Frenchman's Bend, Miss.

Hans Brinker (*in full* Hans Brinker; or, The Silver Skates) Novel for children by Mary Mapes DODGE, published in 1865.

The story is set in The Netherlands and concerns the fortunes of the impoverished Brinker family. The good deeds of the Brinker children (Hans and Gretel) help to restore their father's health and bring about their own good fortune. The plot of the novel, however, is secondary to informative details about Dutch family life and to considerable history and geography of the country, which Dodge had never visited.

Harlem *also called* A Dream Deferred. Poem by Langston HUGHES, published in 1951 as part of his *Montage of a Dream Deferred*, an extended poem cycle about life in Harlem. The 11-line poem speculates about the consequences of white society's withholding of equal opportunity. After listing several relatively benign possibilities, the poet suggests that a dream deferred may explode.

Harvey Comedy in three acts by Mary Chase, performed and published in 1944. The play, which was awarded a Pulitzer Prize in 1945, features Elwood P. Dowd, a kindly, alcoholic middle-aged man whose constant companion is a six-foot tall pooka (an imaginary creature) named Harvey. Though his sister attempts to have him committed to a sanatorium, in the end she changes her mind when she realizes that the treatment he would be given would change his personality.

Heart Is a Lonely Hunter, The Novel by Carson MCCULLERS, published in 1940. With its profound sense of moral isolation and its sensitive glimpses into the inner lives of lonely people, it is considered McCullers' finest work.

The focus of the work is on John Singer, a deaf-mute in a Georgia mill town during the 1930s, and on his effect on the people who confide in him. When Singer's mute Greek companion of 10 years goes insane, Singer is left alone and isolated. He takes a room with the Kelly family, where he is visited by the town's misfits, who turn to him for understanding but have no knowledge of his inner life. When Singer discovers that his Greek friend has died, he realizes that he can communicate with no one and shoots himself.

Henderson the Rain King Seriocomic novel by Saul BELLOW, published in 1959. The novel examines the midlife crisis of Eugene Henderson, an unhappy millionaire.

The story concerns Henderson's search for meaning. A larger-than-life 55-year-old who has accumulated money, position, and a large family, he nonetheless feels unfulfilled. He makes a spiritual journey to Africa, where he draws emotional sustenance from experiences with African tribes. Deciding that his true destiny is as a healer, Henderson returns home, planning to enter medical school.

Hero Ain't Nothin' but a Sandwich, A Novel for young adults by Alice CHILDRESS, published in 1973. Presented in 23 short narratives, it is the story of an arrogant black teenager whose fragmented domestic life and addiction to heroin lead him into delinquency.

Herzog Novel by Saul BELLOW, published in 1964. The work was awarded the National Book Award for fiction in 1965.

Moses Herzog, like many of Bellow's heroes, is a Jewish intellectual who confronts a world peopled by sanguine, incorrigible realists. Much of the action of the novel takes place within the hero's disturbed consciousness, including a series of flashbacks, many of which involve his sexual and marital past.

Like much of Bellow's work, *Herzog* was

praised for its combination of erudition and street smarts, for its lively, Yiddish-influenced prose, and for its narrative drive, though some critics felt Herzog's wives and lovers were not fully realized.

Hiawatha (*in full* The Song of Hiawatha) Long narrative poem by Henry Wadsworth LONG-FELLOW, published in 1855. It is especially notable for its relentless use of trochaic meter, which Longfellow adapted from the meter of the Finnish epic *Kalevala*.

As background for the work, Longfellow consulted two books on the Indian tribes of North America by Henry Rowe Schoolcraft. He perpetuated an error of Schoolcraft's that placed Hiawatha among the forest tribes of the northern Midwest; the historical Hiawatha was chief (*c.* 1450) of the Onondaga tribe, who lived well to the east.

Longfellow's Hiawatha is an Ojibwa Indian, raised by Nokomis, his wrinkled and wise grandmother, "daughter of the Moon." When he grows up, Hiawatha wants to avenge the wrong done by his father, the West Wind, to his mother, Wenonah. Father and son eventually reconcile. Hiawatha becomes his people's leader and marries Minnehaha, of the former enemy Dakota tribe. An era of peace and enlightenment ensues under his reign. Later, disease and famine afflict the tribe and Minnehaha dies. Before Hiawatha takes his leave of the tribe to go to the Isles of the Blessed, he tells his people to heed those who will come with a new religion.

Some of the poem's lines are among the best known of American poetry: "By the shores of Gitche Gumee, / By the shining Big-Sea-Water, / Stood the wigwam of Nokomis, / Daughter of the Moon, Nokomis." The poem, and its sing-song meter, have been frequent objects of parody.

Hills Like White Elephants Short story by Ernest HEMINGWAY, published in 1927 in the periodical *transition* and later that year in the collection *Men Without Women*. The themes of this sparsely written vignette about an American couple wait-ing for a train in Spain are almost entirely implicit. Largely devoid of plot, the story is notable for its use of irony, symbolism, and repetition.

Hiroshima Report by John HERSEY of the explosion of an atomic bomb over Hiroshima, Japan, by the U.S. Army Air Forces on August 6, 1945, and of the aftermath of the explosion. First published in *The New Yorker* magazine as the entire editorial content of its issue of August 31, 1946, the account was objective rather than sensational, focusing on six survivors of the atomic blast and on the horrors they witnessed and endured. Hersey's article was published in book form in November 1946.

History of New York, A (*in full* A History of New York from the Beginning of the World to the End of the Dutch Dynasty, by Diedrich Knickerbocker) A satirical history by Washington IRVING, published in 1809 and revised in 1812, 1819, and 1848. Originally intended as a burlesque of historical methodology and heroic styles of epic poetry, the work became more serious as the author proceeded.

Diedrich Knickerbocker, the putative narrator, begins with a mock-pedantic cosmogony and proceeds to a history of New Netherlands, often ignoring or altering facts. Descriptions of early New Amsterdam landmarks and old Dutch-American legends are included in the history, as are the discovery of America, the voyage of Henry Hudson, the founding of New Amsterdam, and the hostility of the British, who were based in nearby Connecticut. The book's portrait of the overeducated, belligerent governor William the Testy (Willem Kieft) is actually a Federalist satire of Thomas Jefferson. The history concludes with the rule of Peter the Headstrong (Peter Stuyvesant) and the fall of New Amsterdam to the British in 1664.

Homage to Mistress Bradstreet Long poem by John BERRYMAN, written in 1948–53 and published in 1956. Noted for its intensity, it is a tribute to colonial poet Anne Bradstreet that also reveals much about the author.

The poem examines the tension between Bradstreet's personal life and her artistic life, concluding in a spirit of fatalism. It shows throughout a loving and intimate grasp of the details of American history. The work primarily examines creative repression, religious apostasy, and the temptation to adultery.

Home to Harlem First novel by Claude MCKAY, published in 1928. In it and its sequel, *Banjo*, McKay attempted to capture the vitality of the black vagabonds of urban America and Europe.

Jake Brown, the protagonist of *Home to Harlem*, deserts the U.S. Army during World War I and lives in London until a race riot inspires him to return to Harlem. On his first night home he meets the prostitute Felice, for whom he spends much of the rest of the novel searching. Amid his adventures in Harlem, a gallery of rough, lusty, heavy-drinking characters appear to vivid effect. While working as a dining-car waiter Jake encounters another point of view in Ray, a pessimistic, college-educated Haitian immigrant who advocates behavior based on racial pride.

Hoosier School-Master, The Regional novel by Edward EGGLESTON, first serialized in *Hearth and Home* in 1871 and published in book form the same year.

The novel is primarily of interest for its naturalism, its setting in rural Indiana, and its extensive use of Hoosier dialect. Based partially on the experiences of the author's brother, the novel relates episodes in the lives of inhabitants of a backwoods Indiana town as well as the experiences of the young man who is hired to be the only teacher in the town's school.

House of Mirth, The Novel by Edith WHARTON, published in 1905.

The story concerns the tragic fate of the beautiful and well-connected but penniless Lily Bart, who at age 29 lacks a husband to secure her position in society. Maneuvering to correct this situation, she encounters both Simon Rosedale, a rich man outside her class, and Lawrence Selden, who is personally appealing and socially accept-

able but not wealthy. She becomes indebted to an unscrupulous man, has her reputation sullied by a promiscuous acquaintance, and slides into genteel poverty. Unable or unwilling to ally herself with either Rosedale or Selden, she finally despairs and takes an overdose of sleeping pills.

House of the Seven Gables, The Romance by Nathaniel HAWTHORNE, published in 1851. Set in mid-19th-century Salem, Mass., the work is a somber study in hereditary sin based on the legend of a curse pronounced on Hawthorne's own family by a woman condemned to death during the infamous Salem witchcraft trials. The greed and arrogant pride of the novel's Pyncheon family through the generations is mirrored in the gloomy decay of their seven-gabled mansion, in which the family's enfeebled and impoverished relations live. At the book's end the descendant of a family long ago defrauded by the Pyncheons lifts his ancestors' curse on the mansion and marries a young niece of the family.

Howl Poem in three sections by Allen GINSBERG, published in *Howl and Other Poems* in 1956. It is considered the foremost poetic expression of the Beat movement of the 1950s.

A denunciation of the weaknesses and failings of American society, *Howl* is a combination lamentation, jeremiad, and vision. The poem opens with a run-on sentence that describes the despair and frustration of American youths, beginning "I saw the best minds of my generation destroyed by madness, starving/hysterical naked,/dragging themselves through the negro streets at dawn looking for an/angry fix."

The poem was praised for its incantatory rhythms and raw emotion; critics noted the influences of Ginsberg's mentor William Carlos Williams (who wrote an introduction to the 1959 edition of the book), Walt Whitman, and William S. Burroughs. *Howl* also was an unabashed celebration and critique of the masculine. Its frank references to heterosexual and homosexual coupling landed its publisher, Lawrence Ferlinghetti, in court on charges of distributing obscene material, but he was acquitted in 1957 in a landmark decision.

Huckleberry Finn (*in full* The Adventures of Huckleberry Finn) Novel by Mark TWAIN, published in 1884. The book's narrator is Huckleberry Finn, a youngster whose artless vernacular speech is admirably adapted to detailed and poetic descriptions of scenes and narrative renditions that are both broadly comic and subtly ironic.

Huck runs away from his abusive father and, with his companion, the runaway slave Jim, makes a long and frequently interrupted voyage down the Mississippi River on a raft. During the journey Huck encounters a variety of characters and types in whom the book memorably portrays almost every class living on or along the river. As a result of these experiences Huck overcomes conventional racial prejudices and learns to respect and love Jim. The book's pages are dotted with idyllic descriptions of the great river and the surrounding forests, and Huck's good nature and unconscious humor permeate the whole. But a thread that runs through adventure after adventure is that of human cruelty, which shows itself both in the acts of individuals and in their unthinking acceptance of such institutions as slavery. The natural goodness of Huck is continually contrasted with the effects of a corrupt society.

Hugh Selwyn Mauberley Long dramatic poem by Ezra POUND, published in 1920, that provides a finely chiselled "portrait" of one aspect of British literary culture of the time.

Pound referred to *Mauberley* as an attempt "to condense a [Henry] James novel." The subject of the opening section is the gaudiness, corruption, and deterioration of culture in modern commercial society. The fictional Mauberley appears in the poem's second section. He represents the worst failings of contemporary artists and serves as the springboard for Pound's plea that form and style be reinstated as the bearers of authentic meaning.

Human Comedy, The Sentimental novel of life in a small California town by William SAROYAN, published in 1943.

The narrator of the story, 14-year-old Homer Macauley, lives with his widowed mother, his sister Bess, and his little brother Ulysses; his older brother has left home to fight in World War II. While family relationships and domestic situations are in the foreground, the events of the outside world, including the cataclysmic war, are never entirely out of the picture.

Humboldt's Gift Novel by Saul BELLOW, published in 1975. The novel, which won the Nobel Prize for Literature in 1976, is a self-described "comic book about death," whose title character is modeled on the self-destructive lyric poet Delmore Schwartz.

Charlie Citrine, an intellectual, middle-aged author of award-winning biographies and plays, contemplates two significant figures and philosophies in his life: Von Humboldt Fleisher, a dead poet who had been his mentor, and Rinaldo Cantabile, a very-much-alive minor mafioso who has been the bane of Humboldt's existence. Humboldt had taught Charlie that art is powerful and that one should be true to one's creative spirit. Rinaldo, Charlie's self-appointed financial adviser, has always urged Charlie to use his art to turn a profit. At the novel's end, Charlie has managed to set his own course.

Iceman Cometh, The Tragedy in four acts by Eugene O'NEILL, written in 1939 and produced and published in 1946. Considered by many to be his finest work, the drama exposes the human need for illusion and hope as antidotes to the natural condition of despair.

O'Neill mined the tragedies of his own life for this depiction of a ragged collection of alcoholics in a rundown New York tavern-hotel run by Harry Hope. The saloon regulars numb themselves with whiskey and make grandiose plans, but they do nothing. They await the arrival of big-spending Theodore Hickman ("Hickey"), who forces his cronies to pursue their much-discussed plans, hoping that real failure will make them face reality. Hickey finally confesses that he killed his long-suffering wife just hours before he arrived at Harry's, and he turns himself in to the police. The others slip back into an alcoholic haze, clinging to their dreams once more.

If He Hollers Let Him Go First novel by Chester HIMES, published in 1945, often considered to be his most powerful work.

Bob Jones, a sensitive black man, is driven to the brink by the humiliation he endures from the racism he encounters while working in a defense plant during World War II. Dishonesty and violence mark his relationship with his demanding fiancée; a greater threat is a white female co-worker who insults, then entices him.

Innocents Abroad, The (*in full* The Innocents Abroad; or, The New Pilgrims' Progress) A humorous travel narrative by Mark TWAIN, published in 1869 and based on Twain's letters to newspapers about his 1867 steamship voyage to Europe, Egypt, and the Holy Land.

The Innocents Abroad sharply satirized tourists who learn what they should see and feel by reading guidebooks. Assuming the role of a keen-eyed, shrewd Westerner, Twain was refreshingly honest and vivid in describing foreign scenes and his reactions to them. He alternated serious passages—history, statistics, description, explanation, argumentation—with risible ones. The humor itself was varied, sometimes in the vein of the Southwestern yarn spinners whom he had encountered as a young man, sometimes in that of contemporaneous humorists such as Artemus Ward and Josh Billings, who chiefly used burlesque and parody and other verbal devices.

Intruder in the Dust Novel by American author William FAULKNER, published in 1948. Set in Faulkner's fictional Yoknapatawpha County, the novel combines the solution of a murder mystery with an exploration of race relations in the South. Charles ("Chick") Mallison, a 16-year-old white boy, feels that he must repay a debt of honor to Lucas Beauchamp, an elderly black man who has helped him but spurns his offers of payment.

When Beauchamp is arrested for the murder of a white man, Chick searches for the real killer to save Beauchamp from being lynched.

Invisible Man A novel by Ralph ELLISON, published in 1952.

The narrator of *Invisible Man* is a nameless young black man who moves in a 20th-century America where reality is surreal and who can survive only through pretense. Because the people he encounters "see only my surroundings, themselves, or figments of their imagination," he is effectively invisible. He leaves the racist South for New York City, but his encounters continue to disgust him. Ultimately, he retreats to a hole in the ground, which he furnishes and makes his home.

Invitation to a Beheading Anti-utopian novel by Vladimir NABOKOV, published serially in Russian as *Priglasheniye na kazn* from 1935 to 1936 and in book form in 1938.

Set in a mythical totalitarian country, the novel presents the thoughts of Cincinnatus, a former teacher who has been convicted of "gnostic turpitude" for being different from his mediocre fellow countrymen. Sentenced to be executed at an unknown date, Cincinnatus sits in his prison cell and records in his diary his private thoughts and intuitions about an ideal world that he considers to be his "true" home. He sees the world around him as delusional and himself as the only "real" person in the universe. As the ax falls and he is executed, he, or his spirit, rises toward other beings like himself.

Iron Heel, The Novel by Jack LONDON, published in 1908, describing the fall of the United States to the cruel fascist dictatorship of the Iron Heel, a group of monopoly capitalists. Fearing the popularity of socialism, the plutocrats of the Iron Heel conspire to eliminate democracy and, with their secret police and military, terrorize the citizenry. They instigate a German attack on Hawaii on Dec. 4, 1912; as socialist revolutions topple capitalist governments around the world, the Iron Heel has 52 socialist members of the U.S. Congress imprisoned for treason. Elements of London's vision of fascism, civil war, and governmental oppression proved to be prophetic in the first half of the 20th century.

I Sing the Body Electric Poem by Walt WHITMAN, published without a title in *Leaves of Grass* (1855 edition), later appearing as "Poem of the Body," and acquiring its present title in 1867. The poem is a paean to the human form in all its manifestations of soundness. The respective vigors of male and female, youth and age are equally celebrated and ultimately equated with the soul.

Israel Potter (*in full* Israel Potter: His Fifty Years of Exile) Fictionalized story of an American who fought in the War of Independence and of his subsequent struggles for survival, by Herman MELVILLE. Published serially in 1854–55 in *Putnam's Monthly Magazine* and in 1855 in book form, this short picaresque novel was based on a historical Israel Potter, whose autobiographical narrative Melville had read.

Israel Potter lived a life of adventure, serving bravely as a regular soldier in the American Revolution. Later, he served under John Paul Jones in the new American navy and was a secret courier for Benjamin Franklin. In exile in Europe, Potter lived a poverty-stricken existence. Upon his return to the United States, his request for a pension was denied. He died forgotten and destitute. Melville turned Potter into a picaresque hero and embellished the facts of his life, satirizing his encounters with Franklin and adding a vignette about Ethan Allen.

It Can't Happen Here Novel by Sinclair LEWIS, published in 1935. It is a cautionary tale about the rise of fascism in the United States.

During the presidential election of 1936, Doremus Jessup, a newspaper editor, observes with dismay that many of the people he knows support the candidacy of a fascist, Berzelius Windrip. When Windrip wins the election, he forcibly gains control of Congress and the Supreme Court, and, with the aid of his personal paramilitary storm troopers, turns the United States into a totalitarian state. Jessup opposes him, is captured, and escapes to Canada.

Jennie Gerhardt Novel by Theodore DREISER, published in 1911. It exemplifies the naturalism of which Dreiser was a proponent, telling the unhappy story of a working-class woman who accepts all the adversity life visits on her and becomes the mistress of two wealthy and powerful men in order to help her impoverished family.

Joe Turner's Come and Gone Play in two acts by August WILSON, performed in 1986 and published in 1988. Set in 1911, it is the third in Wilson's projected series of plays depicting African-American life in each decade of the 20th century.

The play is set in a Pittsburgh boardinghouse whose inhabitants are all from the rural South, new to the industrial North, separated from their families and from their heritage. Each is engaged in a search for identity and equilibrium; all maintain links with African traditions as they try to find their places in post-Civil War society.

John Brown's Body Epic poem in eight sections about the American Civil War by Stephen Vincent BENÉT, published in 1928 and subsequently awarded a Pulitzer Prize.

The scrupulously researched narrative begins just before John Brown's raid on Harpers Ferry and ends after the assassination of President Abraham Lincoln. Benét's tone is one of reconciliation. From his viewpoint there are few villains and many heroes; the North and the South are afforded equal respect. Along with historical figures like Lincoln and Robert E. Lee, Benét presents Americans of many backgrounds, occupations, and opinions, from Southern aristocrats and their slaves to farm-boy soldiers from Pennsylvania and Illinois.

Jungle, The Novel by Upton SINCLAIR, published privately by Sinclair in 1906 after commercial publishers refused the manuscript. The most famous, influential, and enduring of all muckraking novels, *The Jungle* was an exposé of conditions in the Chicago stockyards. Because of public response, the U.S. Pure Food and Drug Act was passed and conditions in the slaughterhouses were improved.

The novel was written when Sinclair was sent by the socialist weekly newspaper *Appeal to Reason* to investigate working conditions in the meatpacking industry. Although Sinclair's chief goal was to expose abusive labor conditions, the American public was most horrified by the novel's descriptions of unsanitary conditions in the meat-processing plants.

Jurgen (*in full* Jurgen: A Comedy of Justice) Novel by James Branch CABELL, published in 1919. The New York Society for the Prevention of Vice declared *Jurgen* obscene and banned all displays and sales of the book. Both *Jurgen* and Cabell achieved considerable notoriety during the two years the book could not be sold legally; when the case came to trial, the judge recommended acquittal.

One of a series of novels Cabell wrote about the mythical medieval kingdom of Poictesme, the book chronicles the adventures of a pawnbroker named Jurgen who, motivated by guilt and gossip, sets off reluctantly in search of Dame Lisa, his loquacious, nagging wife who has been abducted by the Devil. Along the way, Jurgen encounters Dorothy, the love of his youth, who does not recognize him. Through the power granted him by the earth goddess, he relives one day with Dorothy. Jurgen and legendary women such as Guinevere share erotic experiences. Jurgen and his wife are ultimately reunited.

Kaddish Long poem in five parts by Allen GINSBERG, published in 1961 in *Kaddish and Other Poems: 1958–1960*. Taking the name of a Jewish hymn of praise to God that traditionally is recited by mourners, it is an emotionally driven, personal eulogy for Ginsberg's unstable mother, Naomi, who died insane in 1956. It was composed in the late 1950s under the influence of hallucinogenic drugs.

King, Queen, Knave Novel by Vladimir NABOKOV, first published in Russian in 1928 as *Korol, dama, valet*. With this novel, Nabokov began his career-long obsession with gamesmanship, word play in several languages, and multiple, surreal images and characterizations.

The image of a deck of playing cards is used throughout the novel. Franz, an unsophisticated young man, works in the department store of his rich uncle Dreyer. Out of boredom Martha, the uncle's young wife, seduces Franz. The lovers subsequently plot to drown Dreyer and marry each other. Martha changes her mind abruptly when she learns that an invention by Dreyer stands to increase his wealth, but she then dies suddenly from pneumonia. Her husband never discovers his late wife's duplicity.

Last Leaf, The Short story by O. HENRY, published in 1907 in his collection *The Trimmed Lamp and Other Stories*. "The Last Leaf" concerns Johnsy, a poor young woman who is seriously ill with pneumonia. She believes that when the ivy vine on the wall outside her window loses all its leaves she will also die. Her neighbor Behrman, an artist, tricks her by painting a leaf on the wall. Johnsy recovers, but Behrman, who caught pneumonia while painting the leaf, dies.

Last of the Mohicans, The (*in full* The Last of the Mohicans: A Narrative of 1757) The second and most popular novel in the series THE LEATHERSTOCKING TALES by James Fenimore COOPER, first published in two volumes in 1826. In terms of narrative order, it also is the second novel in the series, taking place in 1757, during the French and Indian War. Its principal character is Natty Bumppo, also called Hawkeye, now in middle life and at the height of his powers. The story tells of brutal battles with the Iroquois and their French allies, cruel captures, narrow escapes, and revenge. The beauty of the unspoiled wilderness and sorrow at its disappearance, symbolized in Hawkeye's Mohican Indian friends, the last of their tribe, are important themes of the novel.

Last Tycoon, The Unfinished novel by F. Scott FITZGERALD, published posthumously in 1941. As edited by Edmund Wilson, it contained six completed chapters, an abridged conclusion, and some of Fitzgerald's notes. The work is an indictment of the Hollywood film industry, where Fitzgerald had had a disappointing career as a screenwriter.

Monroe Stahr is a studio executive who has worked obsessively to produce high-quality films without regard to their financial prospects. He takes a personal interest in every aspect of the studio. At age 35 he is almost burned out, and the novel is the story of how he loses control of the studio and his life.

Leather-Stocking Tales, The Series of five novels by James Fenimore COOPER, published between 1823 and 1841. The novels constitute a saga of 18th-century life among Indians and white pioneers on the New York State frontier through their portrayal of the adventures of the main character, Natty Bumppo, who takes on various names throughout the series. The books cover his entire adult life, from young manhood to old age, though they were not written or published in chronological order. The individual novels are THE PIONEERS (1823), THE LAST OF THE MOHICANS (1826), THE PRAIRIE (1827), THE PATHFINDER (1840), and THE DEERSLAYER (1841).

The Pioneers is both the first and finest detailed portrait of frontier life in American literature; it is also the first truly original American novel. The main subject of the book is the conflict between two different views of the frontier—that of Natty Bumppo (here called Leather-Stocking), who sees the land as "God's Wilderness," and that of another main character who wants to tame and cultivate the land. *The Last of the Mohicans* takes the reader back to the French and Indian War of Natty's middle age, when he is at the height of his powers. This work was succeeded by *The Prairie*, in which, by now very old and philosophical, Leather-Stocking dies, facing the westering sun he has so long followed. Identified from the start with the vanishing wilderness and its natives, Leather-Stocking becomes an unalterably elegiac figure.

Cooper intended to bury Leather-Stocking with *The Prairie*, but many years later he resuscitated the character and portrayed his early maturity in *The Pathfinder* and his youth in *The Deerslayer*. While all of *The Leather-Stocking Tales* have been criticized as artless, some critics see *The Deerslayer* as the best of the five novels. Mark Twain mocked it (and *The Pathfinder*) in "Fenimore Cooper's Literary Offences."

Leaven of Malice Novel by Robertson Davies, the second in a series known collectively as the SALTERTON TRILOGY.

Leaves of Grass Collection of poetry by American author Walt WHITMAN, first presented as a group of 12 poems published anonymously in 1855. It was followed by five revised and three reissued editions during the author's lifetime. Poems not published in his lifetime were added in 1897. The unconventional language and subjects of the poems exerted strong influence on American and foreign literature but also led to the book's suppression on charges of indecency.

The first edition included noted poems such as SONG OF MYSELF and I SING THE BODY ELECTRIC, celebrating the beauty of the human body, physical health, and sexual passion. In a preface that was deleted from later editions, Whitman maintained that a poet's style should be simple and natural, without orthodox meter or rhyme, like an animal or tree in harmony with its environment.

Among the 122 new poems in the third edition (1860–61) were Whitman's "Calamus" poems, which record an intense homosexual love affair. His Civil War poems, DRUM-TAPS (1865) and *Sequel to Drum-Taps* (1865), were included in the fourth edition (1867). The seventh edition (1881–82) grouped the poems in their final order, and the eighth edition (1889) incorporated his *November Boughs* (1888).

Left Hand of Darkness, The Science-fiction novel by Ursula K. LE GUIN, published in 1969. The book, set on a planet called Gethen, or Winter, is a vehicle for Le Guin's Daoist view of the complementary nature of all relationships. Gethen is inhabited by a race of androgynous humans who may change sexual roles during monthly estrus periods, so that at different times any individual may be either a mother or a father. Interspersed with anthropological comments on the Gethenians as well as extracts from their own folklore and philosophy, the plot follows the exploits of Genly Ai, the first ambassador to Gethen from the Ekumen (the league of known worlds), who with the aid of Estraven, a sympathetic Gethenian, attempts to bring the peoples of Gethen into the Ekumen.

Legend of Sleepy Hollow, The Short story by Washington IRVING, first published in THE SKETCH BOOK in 1819–20.

The protagonist of the story, Ichabod Crane, is a Yankee schoolteacher who lives in Sleepy Hollow, a Dutch enclave on the Hudson River. A suggestible man, Crane believes the ghost stories he has heard and read. He is particularly impressed by the tale of a spectral headless horseman said to haunt the area. Crane is also mercenary; he courts Katrina Van Tassel mostly because she is expected to receive a large inheritance. Abraham Van Brunt (also called Brom Bones) is Crane's jealous rival, who often plays tricks on the schoolmaster. Late one night as Ichabod Crane rides home from a party at Katrina's home, he is suddenly frightened by a ghostlike headless horseman. The ghost pursues him and hurls at him a round object that might be a head but is later revealed to have been a pumpkin. Ichabod Crane is never seen in Sleepy Hollow again.

Letters from the Earth Miscellany of fiction, essays, and notes by Mark TWAIN, published posthumously in 1962. Written over a period of 40 years, the pieces in the anthology are characterized by a sense of ironic pessimism.

The title piece comprises letters written by Satan to his fellow angels about the shameless pride and foolishness of humans. "Papers of the Adam Family," a first-person family history of Adam and Eve, traces the first failed attempts at civilization. Other pieces include "A Cat-Tale,"

an amusing, alliterative bedtime story; "Fenimore Cooper's Literary Offenses," a critique of that author's style; and "The Damned Human Race," a collection of bitter satirical bits.

Let Us Now Praise Famous Men Nonfiction book on the daily lives of Depression-era tenant farmers, with text by James AGEE and black-and-white portraits by documentary photographer Walker Evans, published in 1941.

In 1936, at the request of *Fortune* magazine, Agee and Evans went to Alabama to report on the lives of tenant farmers. During the next five years the project evolved into a visually stunning, multilayered work that conveyed in the first person Agee's responses to his subjects as an involved observer, as well as his difficulties in chronicling their lives in this manner.

Life on the Mississippi Memoir of the steamboat era on the Mississippi River before the American Civil War by Mark TWAIN, published in 1883.

The book begins with a brief history of the river from its discovery by Hernando de Soto in 1541. Chapters 4–22 describe Twain's career as a Mississippi steamboat pilot, the fulfillment of a childhood dream.

The second half of *Life on the Mississippi* tells of Twain's return, many years after, to travel the river from St. Louis to New Orleans. By then the competition from railroads had made steamboats passé, in spite of improvements in navigation and boat construction. Twain sees new, large cities on the river and records his observations on greed, gullibility, tragedy, and bad architecture.

Life Studies A collection of poetry and prose by Robert LOWELL, published in 1959. The book marked a major turning point in Lowell's writing and also helped to initiate the 1960s trend to confessional poetry; it was awarded the National Book Award for poetry in 1960. The book is in four sections, including "91 Revere Street," an autobiographical sketch in prose of Lowell's youth amid stormy domestic tensions. The other sections include a series of poems in traditional forms, a group of poems about authors Ford

Madox Ford, George Santayana, Delmore Schwartz, and Hart Crane, and "Life Studies," which consists of 15 confessional poems, including the well-known SKUNK HOUR and *Waking in Blue.*

Ligeia Short story by Edgar Allan POE, published in the magazine *American Museum* in September 1838 and later included in the two-volume *Tales of the Grotesque and Arabesque* (1840).

In the first half of the story the aristocratic narrator describes the beauty and intelligence of his late wife, dark-haired Ligeia, and how she died convinced that a strong will could stave off death. Distraught after her death, the narrator leaves the Rhine valley for rural England, where he enters into an unhappy marriage with fair-haired Lady Rowena Trevanion, of Tremaine. He uses opium; she falls ill and dies. Sitting with the corpse, he watches in amazement as it rises and sheds the burial shroud, revealing dark-haired Ligeia, reborn.

Light in August Novel by William FAULKNER, published in 1932, the seventh in the series set in the fictional Yoknapatawpha County, Mississippi.

The central figure of *Light in August* is the orphan Joe Christmas, whose mixed blood condemns him to life as an outsider, hated or pitied. Joe is frequently whipped by Simon McEachern, the puritanical farmer who raises him, and, after savagely beating his adoptive father, Joe leaves home when he is 18. He then wanders for 15 years, eventually moving in with Joanna Burden, a white woman devoted to helping Negroes. Her evangelism comes to remind Joe of Simon's, and he murders her. Betrayed by his companion Lucas Burch, Joe is hunted down, killed, and castrated.

Little Foxes, The Drama in three acts by Lillian HELLMAN, a chronicle of greed and hate in a ruthless family in the American South, produced and published in 1939.

Set at the turn of the 20th century, the play concerns the manipulative Regina Giddens and her two brothers, Ben and Oscar Hubbard, who want to borrow money from Regina's rich, termi-nally ill husband Horace so that they can open the first cotton mill in town. When Horace discovers that they have arranged the theft of $80,000 in bonds, instead of prosecuting his brothers-in-law, he informs Regina that he will draw up a new will leaving her only $80,000. The threatened disin-heritance causes Regina to reveal all the loathing and disgust she feels for Horace. When he suffers an attack, Regina withholds his medication and cold-bloodedly watches him die.

Hellman's play *Another Part of the Forest* (1947) portrays the Hubbard family 20 years prior to the action in *The Little Foxes.*

Little Gidding Poem by T.S. ELIOT, originally appearing in 1942, both in the *New English Weekly* and in pamphlet form. The next year it was published in a volume with the previous three poems of THE FOUR QUARTETS. Written in five sections in strong-stress meter, "Little Gidding" concludes Eliot's study of human experience, Christian faith, and the nature of time and history.

The title is taken from the name of a village in Huntingdonshire where Nicholas Ferrar established an Anglican community in the 17th century. The poem, set at the Little Gidding chapel in winter and in London during World War II, addresses spiritual renewal.

Little Orphant Annie One of the best-known poems of James Whitcomb RILEY, first published under the pseudonym "Benj. F. Johnson, of Boone" in the popular collection *The Old Swimmin' Hole and 'Leven More Poems* (1883).

"Little Orphant Annie" was written in the Hoosier dialect of Riley's native Indiana. Sentimental and cheerfully philosophical, the poem concerns an orphaned girl who tells the children in whose house she lives scary stories about "the Gobble-un."

The cartoonist Harold Gray named his comic strip about a similarly plucky girl "Little Orphan Annie."

Little Women (*in full* Little Women, or Meg, Jo, Beth, and Amy) Novel for children by Louisa May ALCOTT, published in two parts in 1868 and

1869. It initiated a genre of family stories for children.

Meg, Jo, Beth, and Amy March are raised in genteel poverty by their loving mother Marmee in a quiet Massachusetts town while their father serves as an army chaplain during the American Civil War. They befriend Theodore Lawrence (Laurie), the lonely grandson of a rich old man next door. The vital force of the family is Jo, a headstrong tomboy who is the emotional center of the book. In the course of the novel beautiful, vain Meg marries Laurie's tutor John Brooke and starts her own family; quiet, sickly Beth dies from scarlet fever; artistic Amy marries Laurie after he is turned down by Jo; and Jo marries Professor Bhaer, whom she meets while living in a boardinghouse, and together they set up a school for boys.

The novel had two sequels: *Little Men: Life at Plumfield with Jo's Boys* (1871) and *Jo's Boys and How They Turned Out* (1886).

Lolita Novel by Vladimir NABOKOV, published in 1955 in France. Upon its American publication in 1958 *Lolita* created a cultural and literary sensation.

The novel is presented as the posthumously published memoirs of its antihero Humbert Humbert. A European intellectual and pedophile, Humbert lusts obsessively after 12-year-old nymphet Lolita (real name, Dolores Haze), who becomes his willing inamorata. The work examines love in the light of lechery.

Lonely Passion of Judith Hearne, The Novel by Brian MOORE, published in 1955 as *Judith Hearne*, about an aging Irish spinster's disillusionment and her subsequent descent into alcoholism. The U.S. version was published in 1956 as *The Lonely Passion of Judith Hearne*.

Set in Belfast in the early 1950s, the novel is the study of a Roman Catholic woman who tries to gain the affection of James Madden, an unscrupulous retired man she meets at a local pub. Madden sees her as a potential investor in a business scheme, but she mistakenly infers a romantic interest. She begins to drink heavily, and she finds no comfort in her confession to an indifferent priest. Her disintegration is rapid, and she eventually becomes a resident at a nursing home.

Long Day's Journey into Night Drama in four acts by Eugene O'NEILL, written 1939–41 and produced and published, posthumously, in 1956. The play, which is considered an American masterpiece, was awarded a Pulitzer Prize in 1957.

O'Neill's autobiographical play is a shattering depiction of a day in the dreary life of a couple and their two sons. James Tyrone, a semiretired actor, is vain and miserly; his wife Mary feels worthless and retreats into a morphine-induced haze. Jamie, their older son, is a bitter alcoholic. James refuses to acknowledge the illness of his consumptive younger son, Edmund. As Mary sinks into hallucination and madness, father and sons confront each other in searing scenes that reveal their hidden motives and interdependence.

O'Neill wrote *A Moon for the Misbegotten* (1952) as a sequel, charting the subsequent life of Jamie Tyrone.

Look Homeward, Angel (*in full* Look Homeward, Angel: A Story of the Buried Life) Novel by Thomas WOLFE, published in 1929. It is thinly veiled autobiography.

The novel traces the unhappy early years of the introspective protagonist, Eugene Gant, before he sets off for graduate study at Harvard. Wolfe employed a remarkable variety of literary styles in the novel, reflecting Gant's shifting feelings and attitudes: evocative description, acutely realistic dialogue, satire, fantasy, and meandering passages in which the author becomes intoxicated with his own prose. *Of Time and the River: A Legend of Man's Hunger in His Youth* (1935) continued Gant's story.

Lord Weary's Castle Collection of poems by Robert LOWELL, published in 1946. It was awarded the Pulitzer Prize in 1947. Some of the poems reflect Lowell's New England roots; others have Roman Catholic themes, and still others recall events that occurred during World War II.

Lost Lady, A Novel by Willa CATHER, published in 1923, depicting the decline of the American pioneer spirit and the aridity of small-town life.

The title character, Marian Forrester, is portrayed through the adoring eyes of young Niel Herbert. He initially views Marian, the gracious wife of an industrial magnate and Western pioneer, as the personification of ladylike propriety. In truth she is somewhat less perfect than she seems, and after her husband's death, she drinks too much and looks to other men for emotional and financial support. By the time Niel leaves home to start his adult life in Boston, he feels only a "weary contempt" for her. Niel learns much later, however, that she managed to escape and that she has married a suitable, wealthy man.

Lottery, The Short story by Shirley JACKSON, published in *The New Yorker* in June 1948 and included the following year in her collection *The Lottery; or, The Adventures of James Harris*. Much anthologized, the story is a powerful allegory of barbarism and social sacrifice.

Set in a small New England town, the story recounts the events on the day of the town's annual lottery. Mr. Summers and Mr. Graves conduct the lottery drawing, a festive event that, according to nostalgic Old Man Warner, has lost some of its traditional luster. Tessie Hutchinson is announced as the winner; she begins to protest but is silenced when the community surrounds her and stones her to death. The unemotional narrative voice underlines the horror of the final act.

Love Song of J. Alfred Prufrock, The Dramatic monologue by T.S. ELIOT, published in *Poetry* magazine in 1915 and in book form in *Prufrock and Other Observations* in 1917.

The poem consists of the musings of Prufrock, a weary middle-aged man haunted by the feeling that he has lost both youth and happiness: "I have measured out my life with coffee spoons."

"Prufrock" was both Eliot's first major publication and the first masterpiece of modernism in English. Eliot's experiment with poetic form, meter, rhyme, and voice was a radical departure from the restrictions of established forms and diction.

Luck of Ginger Coffey, The Novel by Brian MOORE, published in 1960. The story concerns an Irish-born Canadian immigrant whose self-deluded, irresponsible behavior nearly breaks up his family.

Luck of Roaring Camp, The Short story by Bret HARTE, published in 1868 in the *Overland Monthly*, which Harte edited.

"The Luck" is a baby boy born to Cherokee Sal, a fallen woman who dies in childbirth at Roaring Camp, a California gold rush settlement. The men of the camp decide to raise the child themselves, and his presence inspires them to stop fighting and gambling and to clean themselves and the camp. When they discover gold, they believe that the child has brought them the fortune. Tragedy strikes, however, when a flood sweeps the camp, killing both the Luck and his protector.

Lyre of Orpheus, The Novel by Robertson DAVIES, published in 1988. The book is the third in the so-called Cornish trilogy that also includes *The Rebel Angels* (1981) and *What's Bred in the Bone* (1985). This fable about the nature of artistic creation has two major plot lines. One thread concerns the production of an unfinished opera said to have been written by E.T.A. Hoffmann. The other concerns the discovery that the famous art collector Francis Cornish actually passed off one of his own paintings as a 16th-century masterpiece.

Magic Barrel, The Collection of 13 short stories by Bernard MALAMUD, published in 1958. Malamud's first published collection, *The Magic Barrel* won the 1959 National Book Award. The title story, first published in 1954, is considered one of Malamud's finest.

Most of the stories concern impoverished New York Jews. Reflecting the rhythm and style of Yiddish folktales, their settings are often bleak; the plots are ironic and humorous and show the influence of Hasidic tales.

Magician of Lublin, The Novel by Isaac Bashevis SINGER, published serially as *Der Kuntsnmakher fun Lublin* in the Yiddish-language daily newspaper *Forverts* in 1959 and published in book form in English in 1960. The entire novel did not appear in Yiddish in book form until 1971.

The novel is set in late 19th-century Poland. It concerns Yasha Mazur, an itinerant professional conjurer, tightrope walker, and hypnotist. He loves five women, including his barren and pious wife. To support himself, his assorted women, and his future plans to escape to Italy, he attempts a robbery and fails. Yasha has a crisis of conscience and returns to his wife, becoming a recluse. People begin to refer to him as Jacob the Penitent, and they flock to him as if to a holy man.

Magnificent Ambersons, The Novel by Booth TARKINGTON, published in 1918. The book, about life in a Midwestern American town, was awarded a Pulitzer Prize in 1919. It was the second volume in the author's trilogy *Growth*, which included *The Turmoil* (1915) and *The Midlander* (1923, later retitled *National Avenue*).

The novel traces the growth of the United States through the decline of the once-powerful, socially prominent Amberson family. Their fall is contrasted with the rise of new industrial tycoons and land developers, whose power comes not through family connections but through financial dealings and modern manufacturing.

Maine Woods, The Collection of three autobiographical narratives by Henry David THOREAU. Each of the essays recounts the details of an excursion in Maine. The collection, edited by Thoreau's friend and frequent touring companion, William Ellery Channing, was issued posthumously in 1864.

The three essays are "Ktaadn and the Maine Woods," "Chesuncook," and "The Allegash and East Branch." The essays describe Thoreau's guides and include detailed studies of the flora, fauna, and history of each geographic area.

Main Street Novel by Sinclair LEWIS, published in 1920. The story of *Main Street* is seen through the eyes of Carol Kennicott, a young woman married to a Midwestern doctor who settles in the Minnesota town of Gopher Prairie (modeled on Lewis' hometown of Sauk Center). The power of the book derives from Lewis' careful rendering of local speech, customs, and social amenities. The satire is double-edged—directed against both the townspeople and the superficial intellectualism of those who despise them.

Making of Americans, The Novel by Gertrude STEIN, completed in 1911. Considered to be one of Stein's major works, the novel was not published in book form until 1925 because of its lengthiness and experimental style. *The Making of Americans* lacks plot, dialogue, and action. Subtitled *Being a History of a Family's Progress*, the work is ostensibly a history of three generations of Stein's forebears. By generalizing from her own family, Stein claimed that the book was the history of all Americans. Fitting her prose to the sameness or very slight variations she found in human nature, Stein produced what many readers found to be a repetitious, prolix compilation of vignettes.

Maltese Falcon, The Mystery novel by Dashiell HAMMETT, generally considered his finest work. It originally appeared as a serial in *Black Mask* magazine in 1929 and was published in book form the next year.

The novel's sustained tension is created by vivid scenes and by the pace and spareness of the author's style. The other major attraction of *The Maltese Falcon* is its colorful cast of characters; they include the antiheroic detective Sam Spade; Brigid O'Shaughnessy, a deceptive beauty; Joel Cairo, an effete Levantine whose gun gives him courage; the very fat and jovial but sinister Casper Gutman; and Gutman's "gunsel" Wilmer, eager to be feared. All of them are looking for the Maltese falcon, a fabulously valuable 16th-century artifact.

Manchild in the Promised Land Autobiographical novel by Claude Brown, published in 1965. The work was noted for its realistic depiction of desperate poverty in Harlem.

Brown's tale of heroin addicts, pimps, and small-time criminals in New York slums shocked readers who were unfamiliar with ghetto life. The autobiographical hero, Sonny, narrates the story of his escape from the addiction and violence that defined his childhood. Sent to the Wiltwyck School for Boys at age nine, Sonny is encouraged to pursue an education. Back home, however, he steals and sells drugs. After more time in reform school, Sonny escapes the neighborhood and immerses himself in African and African-American culture. Brown's most vivid passages detail Sonny's return visit to Harlem, where he discovers his younger brother mired in a life of crime and both an old friend and a former sweetheart destroyed by heroin addiction.

Mansion, The Novel by William FAULKNER, first published in 1959 as the third volume of his Snopes trilogy.

The rapacious Snopes family meets its final dissolution in *The Mansion*. In *The Hamlet* (1940) and *The Town* (1957), Faulkner had described the ascent of ruthless Flem Snopes, who clawed his way to power in Jefferson, Miss. *The Mansion* focuses on Linda, Flem's stepdaughter, who is widowed and deafened while fighting for the Loyalists with her husband in the Spanish Civil War, and on her actions when she returns to Jefferson.

Man That Corrupted Hadleyburg, The Short story by Mark TWAIN satirizing the vanity of the virtuous. It was first published in *Harper's Magazine* in 1899 and collected in *The Man That Corrupted Hadleyburg and Other Stories and Sketches* in 1900. The story reflects Twain's disillusionment and pessimism after a period of financial reversals and sadness over the death of his daughter.

A grim tale of revenge, the story relates the downfall of the citizens of a town that boasts of its honesty with the motto "Lead us not into temptation." A mysterious stranger, however, exposes the townspeople's underlying greed and hypocrisy.

Manticore, The Second of a series of novels by Robertson Davies, known collectively as THE DEPTFORD TRILOGY.

Man with the Golden Arm, The Novel by Nelson ALGREN, published in 1949. It won the National Book Award for 1950.

Set in Chicago's West Side, the novel evokes the gritty street life of petty criminals and hustlers. Hero Frankie Machine is a shrewd poker dealer whose "golden arm" shakes as he relies on morphine to overcome the pain of a war injury and to numb the guilt he feels for a drunken spree that put his wife Sophie in a wheelchair. Much of the psychological action centers on Sophie's attempts to manipulate her husband. After Frankie kills his drug dealer and flees, he hangs himself in a seedy hotel.

Ma Rainey's Black Bottom Drama in two acts by August WILSON, performed in 1984 and published in 1985. It was the first of a series of plays in which Wilson portrayed African-American life in the 20th century.

The play features Ma Rainey, a popular blues singer, and the members of her band. Set in a recording studio in Chicago in 1927, *Ma Rainey* comments on the violence perpetrated by blacks against other blacks in their frustration over being excluded from white society.

Marble Faun, The (*in full* The Marble Faun; or, the Romance of Monte Beni) Novel by Nathaniel HAWTHORNE, published in 1860. The novel's central metaphor is a statue of a faun by Praxiteles that Hawthorne had seen in Florence. In the faun's fusing of animal and human characteristics he finds an allegory of the fall of man from amoral innocence to the knowledge of good and evil, a theme that had usually been assumed in his earlier works but that now received direct and philosophic treatment.

The faun of the novel is Donatello, a passionate young Italian who makes the acquaintance of three American artists, Miriam, Kenyon, and Hilda, who are spending time in Rome. When Donatello kills a man who has been shadowing

Miriam, he is wracked by guilt until he is arrested by the police and imprisoned. Both of the women are tainted by guilt.

Mardi Third novel by Herman MELVILLE, originally published in two volumes as *Mardi: And a Voyage Thither* in 1849. *Mardi* is an uneven and disjointed transitional book that uses allegory to comment on contemporary ideas—about nations, politics, institutions, literature, and religion. It was a dismal failure. The action involves two whaling-ship deserters—the American Taji and Norwegian Jarl—who meet up with a variety of characters, including Yillah, a blonde Pacific Islander who symbolizes Absolute Truth.

Marjorie Morningstar Novel by Herman WOUK, published in 1955, about a woman who rebels against the confining middle-class values of her industrious American-Jewish family. Her dream of being an actress ends in failure. She ultimately forfeits her illusions and marries a conventional man with whom she finds sufficient contentment as a suburban wife and mother, thus finally coming to accept her parents' values.

Martin Eden Semiautobiographical novel by Jack LONDON, published in 1909.

The title character becomes a writer, hoping to acquire the respectability sought by his society-girl sweetheart. She spurns him, however, when his writing is rejected by several magazines and when he is falsely accused of being a socialist. She tries to win him back after he achieves fame, but Eden realizes her love is false. Financially successful and robbed of connection to his own class, aware that his quest for bourgeois respectability was hollow, Eden travels to the South Seas, where he jumps from the ship and drowns.

Masque of the Red Death, The Allegorical short story by Edgar Allen POE, first published in *Graham's Magazine* in April 1842.

In a medieval land ravaged by the Red Death, a plague that causes swift, agonizing death, Prince Prospero retreats to his castle with 1,000 knights and ladies. There he welds the doors and windows shut, confident that he and his guests will escape death. Prospero gives a masquerade ball. At midnight, the grotesquely costumed courtiers find a fearful figure among them, costumed in shrouds and dried blood as the Red Death. Prospero orders the figure's execution, then raises his sword to stab it himself but falls dead. When others try to hold the specter, they find it has no body. They realize that it is the Red Death itself, and one by one they expire.

Matchmaker, The Comedy in four acts by Thornton WILDER, produced in 1954 and published in 1955.

The Matchmaker is more traditional than Wilder's earlier plays, although it does employ one of the playwright's favorite nontraditional devices of having the characters address the audience directly.

In the drama, wealthy merchant Horace Vandergelder, a widower, hopes to marry the milliner Irene Molloy. He turns to his late wife's friend Dolly Levi for help, but Dolly wants Horace herself. A series of comic misadventures follow.

In 1964 the play was adapted into the immensely successful musical *Hello Dolly!* (film, 1969).

McTeague Novel by Frank NORRIS, published in 1899. The work was considered to be the first great portrait in American literature of an acquisitive society.

In *McTeague*, Norris sought to describe the influence of heredity and environment on human life. The dentist McTeague marries Trina, whose acquisitiveness is revealed when she wins a lottery. McTeague, initially free of the destructive avarice that defines Trina and his friend and rival Schouler, is a bovine "natural man," brutalized by the more rapacious urban characters. The marriage disintegrates as Trina becomes more and more miserly with her fortune and McTeague drinks heavily. McTeague kills Trina and flees. He later strangles his rival in Death Valley, but not before Schouler handcuffs them together, condemning McTeague to die chained to the body of his enemy.

Member of the Wedding, The Novel by Carson

MCCULLERS, published in 1946. It depicts the inner life of 12-year-old Frankie Addams, a Georgia tomboy who imagines that she will be taken by the bride and groom (her brother) on their honeymoon. Frankie finds refuge in the company of two equally isolated characters, her ailing six-year-old cousin John Henry and her father's black housekeeper, Berenice, who serves as both mother figure and oracle. Much of the novel consists of a series of kitchen-table conversations among these three. The threesome is broken by the cousin's death and Berenice's own wedding.

Memoirs of Hecate County Collection of six loosely connected short stories by Edmund WILSON, first published in 1946. Because of the frankly sexual nature of the story "The Princess with the Golden Hair," the book was suppressed on obscenity charges until 1959, at which time Wilson published a revised edition.

Some of the stories are narrated by an upper-middle-class intellectual recollecting his past sexual relationships and friendships in Manhattan and in insular, suburban Hecate county. Each story portrays a different aspect of socially dysfunctional America, such as the vapid ritual of the cocktail hour, bogus artists, and the erosion of intellectual rigor by popular culture.

Memories of a Catholic Girlhood Autobiography of Mary MCCARTHY, published in 1957.

McCarthy wrote about her troubled childhood with detachment. Wanting to prove herself a "superior girl," McCarthy strove in her formative years for intellectual distinction. Critics noted that *Memories* was more searching, and considerably less acerbic, than her fiction; some considered it her best work.

Mending Wall Poem by Robert FROST, published in the collection *North of Boston* (1914). Written in blank verse, it depicts a pair of neighboring farmers working together on the annual chore of rebuilding their common wall. The wall serves as the symbolic fulcrum of their friendly antagonism; it balances their contrasting philosophies about brotherhood, represented by the senti-

ments "Good fences make good neighbors" and "Something there is that doesn't love a wall."

Miniver Cheevy A poem in iambic tetrameter quatrains by Edwin Arlington ROBINSON, published in the collection *The Town Down the River* (1910).

The poem portrays the melancholy Miniver Cheevy who lives in Tilbury Town, an imaginary small town in New England that was a frequent setting for Robinson's poetry. Cheevy has little insight into his personal deficiencies. With exaggerated romantic sadness, he wishes that he had lived in a more gracious era.

Miss Lonelyhearts Novel by Nathanael WEST, published in 1933. It concerns a male newspaper columnist whose attempts to give advice to the lovelorn end in tragedy. The protagonist, known only by his newspaper nom de plume, Miss Lonelyhearts, feels powerless to help his generally hopeless correspondents. His boss, Willie Shrike, relentlessly mocks him for taking his job seriously. When Lonelyhearts tries to become personally involved with one of his correspondents, he is killed.

Mixture of Frailties, A Novel by Robertson Davies, the third in a series known collectively as the SALTERTON TRILOGY.

Moby-Dick (*in full* Moby-Dick; or, The Whale) Novel by Herman MELVILLE, published in London in October 1851 and published a month later in the United States. *Moby-Dick* is generally regarded as its author's masterpiece and one of the greatest American novels.

The basic plot of *Moby-Dick* is simple. The narrator (who asks to be called "Ishmael") tells of the last voyage of the ship *Pequod* out of New Bedford, Mass. Captain Ahab is obsessed with the pursuit of the white whale Moby-Dick, which finally kills him. On that level, the work is an intense, superbly authentic narrative. Its theme and central figure, however, are reminiscent of Job in his search for justice and of Oedipus in his search for truth. The novel's richly symbolic language and tragic hero are indicative of Melville's deeper concerns: the equivocal defeats and triumphs of the human spirit and its fusion of creative and murderous urges.

Mont-Saint-Michel and Chartres Extended essay by Henry ADAMS, printed privately in 1904 and commercially in 1913. It is subtitled *A Study of Thirteenth-Century Unity.*

Mont-Saint-Michel and Chartres is best considered a companion to the author's autobiography, *The Education of Henry Adams* (1918). In *Chartres*, he described the medieval world view as reflected in its cathedrals, which he believed expressed "an emotion, the deepest man ever felt—the struggle of his own littleness to grasp the infinite." Adams was drawn to the ideological unity expressed in Roman Catholicism and symbolized by the Virgin Mary; he contrasted this coherence with the uncertainties of the 20th century.

Moon for the Misbegotten, A Drama in four acts by Eugene O'NEILL, written in 1943 and published in 1952. It was first performed in New York City posthumously in 1957.

This sequel to O'Neill's masterpiece, *Long Day's Journey into Night*, is set on the Tyrones' Connecticut farm, which has been leased to bullying widower Phil Hogan. Hogan's daughter Josie loves Jim Tyrone, Jr., an alcoholic actor who has come back to the farm after his mother's death. To secure his hold on the farm, Hogan convinces Josie that Jim intends to sell it; he encourages Josie to seduce Jim and force a marriage proposal. Jim spurns her advances, reassures her that he is not going to sell the farm, and confesses that he had been too drunk to attend his mother's funeral. They part, for Josie realizes that Jim lives in misery and that he longs for deliverance in death.

Mosses from an Old Manse Collection of short stories by Nathaniel HAWTHORNE, published in two volumes in 1846. Written while Hawthorne lived at the Old Manse in Concord, Mass., the home of Ralph Waldo Emerson's ancestors, the 25 tales and sketches include some of the author's finest short works. Many of the Romantic themes found in Hawthorne's longer fiction are addressed in the stories: for example, the conflict between reason and emotion in the gothic tales RAPPACCINI'S DAUGHTER and "The Birthmark," and between Puritan religion and the supernatural in YOUNG GOODMAN BROWN. Also noteworthy are the title essay describing the parsonage and ROGER MALVIN'S BURIAL, a historical tale.

Mother of Us All, The Opera in two acts with libretto by American writer Gertrude STEIN and music by American composer Virgil Thomson, first performed and published in 1947. The opera concerns the woman suffrage movement of 19th-century America, as exemplified in the life and work of American suffragist and feminist Susan B. Anthony.

Mourning Becomes Electra Trilogy of plays by Eugene O'NEILL, produced and published in 1931. The trilogy, consisting of *Homecoming*, *The Hunted*, and *The Haunted*, was modeled on the *Oresteia* trilogy of Aeschylus and represents O'Neill's most complete use of Greek forms, themes, and characters. O'Neill set his trilogy in the New England of the American Civil War period.

Moviegoer, The Novel by Walker PERCY, published in 1961. It won a National Book Award. A philosophical exploration of the problem of personal identity, the story is narrated by Binx Bolling, a successful but alienated businessman. Bolling undertakes a search for meaning in his life, first through an obsession with the movies and later through an affair.

Mr. Flood's Party Rhymed narrative poem by Edward Arlington ROBINSON, published in his *Collected Poems* (1921). Considered one of Robinson's finest works, the poem is set in Tilbury Town. The narrative concerns lonely, isolated Eben Flood, who climbs a hill above the town one moonlit night and walks down an empty road. Frequently drinking from a jug of liquor, "secure, with only two moons listening," he salutes the harvest moon, the bird on the wing, and old times.

Mr. Sammler's Planet Novel by Saul BELLOW,

published in 1970. It won the National Book Award for fiction in 1971.

The setting is New York City during the politically tumultuous late 1960s. Sammler, an elderly Polish Jewish survivor of the Holocaust, is an intellectual who has been injured both physically and psychologically; he has lost the vision in one eye and suffers from a sense of emotional and intellectual alienation. With his intact eye, he views the world, its people, and their insanities. With his blind eye, he internalizes current events, using his historical and philosophical training to analyze and synthesize.

MS. Found in a Bottle Short story by Edgar Allan POE, published in the Baltimore weekly *Saturday Visiter* (October 1833) as the winner of a contest held by the magazine. The story, one of Poe's first notable works, was later published in the two-volume *Tales of the Grotesque and Arabesque* (1840).

The story's narrator, whose journal entries initially reveal him to be a staunch rationalist, begins to accept supernaturalism when a hurricane throws him from his sinking boat onto a large, mystical ship. The crew, made up of extremely aged foreigners who busy themselves with ancient nautical instruments, are oblivious to the narrator, who walks unnoticed among them. The story concludes when the strange ship vanishes into a whirlpool in icy, uncharted waters.

Mule Bone (*in full* Mule Bone: A Comedy of Negro Life in Three Acts) Play about African-American rural life written collaboratively in 1931 by Zora Neale HURSTON and Langston HUGHES. Drawing on Southern black oral tradition and folklore, the play features such customs as "mule-talking," a type of verbal one-upmanship. (Hurston, an anthropologist as well as a writer, had collected examples of mule-talking in black communities.)

The play remained unfinished and unproduced during the authors' lifetimes; it was published in 1990.

Murder in the Cathedral Poetic drama in two parts, with a prose sermon interlude, the most successful play of T.S. ELIOT. The play was performed at Canterbury Cathedral in 1935 and published the same year. Set in December 1170, it is a modern miracle play on the martyrdom of St. Thomas Becket, archbishop of Canterbury.

The play's most striking feature is the use of a chorus in the classical Greek manner. The poor women of Canterbury who make up the chorus nervously await Thomas' return from his seven-year exile, fretting over his volatile relationship with King Henry II. Thomas arrives and must resist four temptations: worldly pleasures, lasting power as chancellor, recognition as a leader of the barons against the king, and eternal glory as a martyr. After Thomas delivers his Christmas morning sermon, four knights in the service of the king accost him and order him to leave the kingdom. When he refuses, they return to slay him in the cathedral.

Murders in the Rue Morgue, The Short story by Edgar Allan POE, first published in *Graham's* magazine in 1841. It is considered the world's first detective story.

The story opens with the discovery of the violent murder of an old woman and her daughter; no grisly detail is spared in the description of the crime scene as it is discovered by neighbors responding to the women's screams. The police are baffled by the fact that the murderer has managed to escape even though the women's apartment appears to have been completely sealed from the inside. The genteel but impoverished C. Auguste Dupin and his nameless friend—who narrates the story—offer their services to the police and, through a brilliant interpretation of the clues at the scene, identify the murderer—an escaped orangutan.

In its presentation of an amateur detective who uses "ratiocination" to solve a mystery, the story shaped a new genre of fiction. It influenced Sir Arthur Conan Doyle, Dame Agatha Christie, and dozens of writers who borrowed, knowingly or not, Poe's original conception of the detective story.

Mutiny on the Bounty Romantic novel by Charles Nordhoff and James Norman Hall, published in 1932.

The vivid narrative is based on the actual mutiny against Captain William Bligh of HMS *Bounty* in 1789. Narrated by Roger Byam, a former midshipman and linguist aboard the vessel, the novel describes how Fletcher Christian and 15 others revolted against the petty, tyrannical Bligh, setting him and a number of loyal men adrift in a small craft in the South Seas.

Nordhoff wrote the Polynesian chapters of the novel, Hall the English, although each assisted the other. They collaborated on two sequels, *Men Against the Sea* (1934) and *Pitcairn's Island* (1934), which addressed the fate of the *Bounty* crew.

My Ántonia Novel by Willa CATHER, published in 1918. Her best-known work, it honors the immigrant settlers of the American plains. Narrated by the protagonist's lifelong friend, Jim Burden, the novel recounts the history of Ántonia Shimerda, the daughter of Bohemian immigrants who settled on the Nebraska frontier. The book contains a number of poetic passages about the disappearing frontier and the spirit and courage of frontier people. Many critics consider *My Ántonia* to be Cather's finest achievement.

My Kinsman, Major Molineux Short story by Nathaniel HAWTHORNE, first published in 1832 in *The Token*, an annual Christmas gift book. The story was collected in *The Snow-Image, and Other Twice-Told Tales* (1851).

The story is set in New England before the American Revolution. Young Robin Molineux seeks out his kinsman, a major in the British army, with the hope of gaining access to power. He finds, however, that his kinsman is scorned, and he is advised to make his own way in the world.

On one level its theme is the loss of innocence. On a second level the story may be interpreted as a political allegory of nascent democratic self-government.

My Name Is Aram Book of 14 interconnected short stories by William SAROYAN, published in 1940. The book consists of exuberant, often whimsical episodes in the imaginative life of young Aram Garoghlanian, an Armenian-American boy who is the author's alter ego.

Naked and the Dead, The Novel by Norman MAILER. Published in 1948, the book was hailed as one of the finest American novels to come out of World War II. The story concerns a platoon of 13 American soldiers who are stationed on the Japanese-held island of Anopopei in the Pacific. With almost journalistic detail, Mailer records the lives of men at war, characterizing the soldiers individually in flashbacks that illuminate their past.

Native Son Novel by Richard WRIGHT, published in 1940. The novel addresses the issue of white American society's responsibility for the repression of blacks. The plot charts the decline of Bigger Thomas, a young African-American imprisoned for two murders—the accidental smothering of his white employer's daughter and the deliberate killing of his girlfriend to silence her. In his cell Thomas confronts his growing sense of injustice and concludes that violence is the only alternative to submission to white society.

Natural, The First novel by Bernard MALAMUD, published in 1952. The story of gifted athlete Roy Hobbs and his bat "Wonderboy" is counted among the finest baseball novels.

Hobbs's promising baseball career is cut short when he is shot by a mysterious woman. He turns up some 15 years later to play left field for the New York Knights, whose fortunes suddenly and miraculously improve. Off the playing field, Roy is torn between the dangerous affection of Memo Paris, the niece of team manager Pop Fisher, and Iris Lemon, whose love is genuine. After rejecting Iris for Memo, Hobbs agrees to throw a playoff game. During the game he regrets his decision and decides to play honestly, but Wonderboy is split asunder and Hobbs strikes out, losing the game.

Nature Book-length essay by Ralph Waldo EMERSON, published anonymously in 1836. It contains a formulation of his essential philosophy and helped initiate the Transcendentalism.

In the essay, Emerson reevalutes traditional views of God and Nature. He asserts the human ability to transcend the materialistic world of sense experience and facts and become conscious of the all-pervading spirit of the universe and the potentialities of human freedom. Although these concepts were not original, Emerson's polished style and breadth of vision lent them a particular vividness.

Negro Speaks of Rivers, The Poem in free verse by Langston HUGHES, published in the June 1921 issue of *The Crisis*. Hughes's first acclaimed poem, it is a panegyric to people of black African origin throughout history and is written in a style derived from Walt Whitman and Carl Sandburg as well as from African-American spirituals.

Night Before Christmas, The *see* A VISIT FROM ST. NICHOLAS.

Night of the Iguana, The Three-act drama by Tennessee WILLIAMS, produced and published in 1961. Williams turned from his usual Southern settings and themes in this tale of tourists at a seedy Mexican hotel. The play's first act was noted for its detailed evocation of a dank jungle; some critics found it, and the characters— among them a defrocked priest, a lusty widow, and a dying poet—overblown.

North & South (*in full* Poems: North & South: A Cold Spring) Collection of poetry by Elizabeth BISHOP, published in 1955. The book, which was awarded a Pulitzer Prize in 1956, was a revision of an earlier collection, *North & South* (1946), to which 17 poems were added. The spare, closely observed verses are marked by a firm grounding in reality, each being set in a recognizable geographic location, such as Nova Scotia, a farm in Maryland, Florida, Paris, and Brazil.

Notes Towards the Definition of Culture Critical treatise by T.S. ELIOT, originally appearing as a series of articles in *New England Weekly* in 1943, and published in book form in 1948. In the *Notes*, Eliot presents culture as an organic, shared system of beliefs that cannot be planned or artificially induced. Its chief means of transmission, he holds, is the family. The book has been viewed as a critique of postwar Europe and a defense of conservatism and Christianity.

O Captain! My Captain! Three-stanza poem by Walt WHITMAN, published in *Sequel to Drum-Taps* in 1865. From 1867 the poem was included in the 1867 and subsequent editions of *Leaves of Grass*.

An elegy on the death of President Abraham Lincoln, "O Captain! My Captain" is noted for its regular form, meter, and rhyme, though it is also known for its sentimentality verging on the maudlin. The poem, which was highly popular, portrays Lincoln as the captain of a sea-worn ship—the Union triumphant after the American Civil War. While "The ship is anchor'd safe and sound, its voyage closed and done," the Captain lies on the deck, "Fallen cold and dead."

Occurrence at Owl Creek Bridge, An Short story by Ambrose BIERCE, published in 1891 in *Tales of Soldiers and Civilians*, a collection that in 1898 was revised, enlarged, and retitled *In the Midst of Life*. The narrative concerns the final thoughts of a Southern planter as he is being hanged by Union soldiers. In the brief period between the tightening of the noose and the actual breaking of his neck, the man imagines his escape.

Octopus, The Novel by Frank NORRIS, published in 1901 and subtitled *A Story of California*. It was the first volume of *The Epic of the Wheat*, his unfinished trilogy about the production, distribution, and consumption of American wheat. *The Octopus* examines the struggle of California wheat farmers in the San Joaquin valley against the powerful Pacific and Southwestern Railroad monopoly. Norris employed the technique of literary naturalism in the novel to dramatize the issues of environmental determinism and social justice.

Of Mice and Men Novella by John STEINBECK, published in 1937. The tragic story, given poignancy by its objective narrative, is about the complex bond between two migrant laborers. The book, which was adapted by Steinbeck into a three-act play (produced 1937), earned him national renown.

The plot centers on George Milton and Lennie Small, itinerant ranch hands who dream of one day owning a small farm. George acts as a father figure to Lennie, who is large and simpleminded, calming him and helping to rein in his immense physical strength. When Lennie accidentally kills the ranch owner's flirtatious daughter-in-law, George shoots his friend rather than allow him to be captured by a vengeful lynch mob.

Of Time and the River (*in full* Of Time and the River: A Legend of Man's Hunger in His Youth) Novel by Thomas WOLFE, begun in 1931 and, after extensive editing by Wolfe and editor Maxwell Perkins, published in March 1935 as a sequel to *Look Homeward, Angel* (1929). The book chronicles the maturing of Eugene Gant as he leaves his Southern home for the wider world of Harvard University, New York City, and Europe.

Old Forest, The Title story of *The Old Forest and Other Stories* (1985) by Peter TAYLOR, a collection of 14 pieces representative of 50 years of the author's fiction. The stories are set in the American South from the 1930s to the middle 1950s; seven were originally published in *The New Yorker*.

"The Old Forest," like much of Taylor's fiction, concerns upper-middle-class Southerners whose privileged, semiagrarian way of life is vanishing because of the industrialization and urbanization of the South. The story is a memory piece in which the action is recalled by the narrator-protagonist after 50 years. On a snowbound day in 1937, one week prior to his marriage to the debutante Caroline Braxley, Nat Ramsey takes Lee Ann Deehart, a girl of "unknown origins," for an innocent ride in his car. The car is involved in an accident, and Lee Ann runs away, disappearing into the old forest. The Braxleys refuse to allow the wedding to take place until Lee Ann is located and any hint of scandal is dissipated.

Old Man and the Sea, The Short novel by Ernest HEMINGWAY, published in 1952 and awarded the 1953 Pulitzer Prize for fiction. Completed after a 10-year literary drought, it was his last major work of fiction.

The novel is written in Hemingway's characteristically spare prose. It concerns an old Cuban fisherman named Santiago who finally catches a magnificent fish after weeks of not catching anything. After three days of playing the fish, he finally manages to reel it in and lash it to his boat, only to have sharks eat it as he returns to the harbor. The other fishermen marvel at the size of the skeleton; Santiago is spent but triumphant.

Omoo (*in full* Omoo: A Narrative of Adventures in the South Seas) Novel by Herman MELVILLE, published in 1847 as a sequel to his novel *Typee*. Based on Melville's own experiences in the South Pacific, this episodic novel, in a more comical vein than that of *Typee*, tells of the narrator's participation in a mutiny on a whale ship and his subsequent wanderings in Tahiti with the former doctor of the ship.

One of Ours Novel by Willa CATHER, published in 1922. This story of a Nebraska farm boy who dies fighting in France in World War I took four years to write and was a best-seller in its time. It won a Pulitzer Prize in 1923. Cather based the plot on letters written by a cousin who had died in World War I.

On the Road Novel by Jack KEROUAC, published in 1957. A formless book, it describes a series of frenetic trips back and forth across the United States by a number of penniless young people who are in love with life, beauty, jazz, sex, drugs, speed, and mysticism. The book was one of the first novels associated with the Beat movement of the 1950s.

Open Boat, The Short story by Stephen CRANE, published in the collection *The Open Boat and*

Other Tales of Adventure in 1898. It recounts the efforts of four survivors of a shipwreck—a newspaper correspondent and the ship's cook, captain, and oiler—as they attempt to remain afloat in a dinghy on the rough seas. Told from a shifting point of view, the narrative reveals nature's indifference.

O Pioneers! Regional novel by American writer Willa CATHER, published in 1913. The work is known for its vivid re-creation of the hardships of prairie life and of the struggle of immigrant pioneer women. The novel was partially based on Cather's Nebraska childhood, and it reflected the author's belief in the primacy of spiritual and moral values over the purely material. Its heroine, Alexandra Bergson, exemplified the courage and purpose Cather felt were necessary to subdue the wild land. The title is taken from Walt Whitman's poem "Pioneers! O Pioneers!" which, like the novel, celebrated frontier virtues of strength and inner spirit.

Optimist's Daughter, The Pulitzer Prize-winning short novel by Eudora WELTY, published in 1972. This partially autobiographical story explores the subtle bonds between parent and child and the complexities of love and grief.

Our Town Pulitzer Prize-winning drama in three acts by Thornton WILDER, produced and published in 1938, considered a classic portrayal of small-town American life.

Set in Grover's Corners, N.H., the play features a narrator, the Stage Manager, who sits at the side of the unadorned stage and explains the action. Through flashbacks, dialogue, and direct monologues the other characters reveal themselves to the audience. The main characters are George Gibbs, a doctor's son, and Emily Webb, daughter of a newspaper editor. The play concerns their courtship and marriage and Emily's death in childbirth, after which she and other inhabitants of the graveyard describe their peace.

Considered enormously innovative for its lack of props and scenery and revered for its sentimental but at bottom realistic depictions of middle-class America, *Our Town* soon became a staple of American theater.

Outcasts of Poker Flat, The Short story by Bret HARTE, first published in the magazine *Overland Monthly* in 1869, later published in the collection *The Luck of Roaring Camp and Other Sketches* (1870); it has become a minor classic of American literature. One of the best examples of Harte's local-color fiction, this story about exiles from an 1850 California mining camp who are caught in a blizzard shows how even the "immoral" members of society are capable of acting unselfishly to help others who are in danger.

Out of the Cradle Endlessly Rocking Poem by Walt WHITMAN, first published as "A Word Out of the Sea" in the 1860 edition of his collection *Leaves of Grass* and later published in the 1871 version using the final title. This long poem, one of the most powerful in the collection, is written in lyrical free verse. A boy stands by the seashore at night listening to the song of a mockingbird mourning for his mate; at the same time he listens to the death song of the sea and realizes that "my own songs awaked from that hour." The lonely mockingbird, singing to relieve his solitude, is a metaphor for the poetic spirit, while the sea is a symbol of the spiritual world to which poetry is witness.

Ox-Bow Incident, The Novel by Walter van Tilburg CLARK, published in 1940. This psychological study of corrupt leadership and mob rule was read as a parable of fascism when it first appeared. Set in Nevada in 1885, the story concerns the brutal lynching of three characters falsely accused of murder and theft. The strong-willed leader of the lynch mob, Major Tetley, easily takes advantage of the mood of suppressed resentment and boredom of the townspeople.

Painted Bird, The Semiautobiographical novel by Jerzy KOSINSKI, published in 1965 and revised in 1976. The ordeals of the central character parallel Kosinski's own experiences during World War II. A dark-haired Polish child who is taken for either a Gypsy or a Jew loses his parents in the mayhem of war and wanders through the countryside at the mercy of the brutal, thick-headed peasants he meets in the villages. He learns how to stay alive at any cost, turning survival into a moral imperative. Full of graphic scenes depicting rape, torture, and bestiality, the novel portrays evil in all its manifestations and speaks of human isolation as inevitable.

Pale Fire Novel in English by Vladimir NABOKOV, published in 1962. It consists of a long poem and a commentary on it by an insane pedant. This brilliant parody of literary scholarship is also an experimental synthesis of Nabokov's talents for both poetry and prose. It extends and completes his mastery of unorthodox structure.

Pale Horse, Pale Rider A collection of three novellas by Katherine Anne PORTER, published in 1939. The collection consists of "Noon Wine," "Old Mortality," and the title story. For their stylistic grace and sense of life's ambiguity, these stories are considered some of the best Porter wrote.

Paterson Long poem by William Carlos WILLIAMS, published in five consecutive parts, each a separate book, in between 1946 and 1958. Fragments of a sixth volume were published posthumously in 1963.

According to Williams, "a man in himself is a city," and Paterson is both an industrial city in New Jersey and a character of that name. *Paterson* has a mosaic structure, with occasional passages of prose, including letters and a diary, integrated into the poem; it is written in Williams' "variable-foot" free verse.

Pathfinder, The (*in full* The Pathfinder; or, The Inland Sea) Novel by James Fenimore COOPER, published in two volumes in 1840, the fourth of five novels published as THE LEATHER-STOCKING TALES. In terms of the chronological narrative, *The Pathfinder* is third in the series.

Living near Lake Ontario during the French and Indian War, Natty Bumppo is a 40-year-old wilderness scout who comes to the aid of a British colonial garrison under attack. He dearly loves Mabel Dunham, daughter of a sergeant. Mabel refuses his offer of marriage; she loves his friend, Jasper Western, who is under suspicion of being a traitor, in large part because of his fluency in French. The actual traitor, Lieutenant Davy Muir, is eventually killed. At the novel's end Mabel and Jasper are married.

Patriotic Gore Collection of essays by Edmund WILSON, published in 1962. Subtitled *Studies in the Literature of the American Civil War*, the book contains 16 essays on contemporaries' attitudes toward the Civil War, the effect it had on their lives, and the effects of the postwar Reconstruction period.

Among the subjects of the essays are Oliver Wendell Holmes, Jr.; diaries of Southern women from various social strata; fiction such as *Poganuc People* by Harriet Beecher Stowe and *Old Creole Days* by George Washington Cable; and memoirs by Union commanders Ulysses S. Grant and William T. Sherman and their Confederate counterparts, Robert E. Lee and John S. Mosby.

Paul Revere's Ride Poem by Henry Wadsworth LONGFELLOW, published in 1861 and later collected in *Tales of a Wayside Inn* (1863). Written in anapestic tetrameter meant to suggest the galloping of a horse, this popular folk ballad about a hero of the American Revolution is narrated by the landlord of an inn who remembers the famous "midnight ride" to warn the Americans about the impending British invasion. Although the account of the ride is historically inaccurate, the poem created an American legend.

Paul's Case Short story by Willa CATHER, published in the collection *The Troll Garden* in 1905. It recounts the tragic results of a boy's desire to escape what he sees as a stifling environment.

The protagonist is a sensitive high-school student who despises his middle-class family and sees the art world as a glamorous alternative to that life. He frequents art galleries, concert halls, and theaters until is father pulls him out of school and sends him to work in an office. Paul steals money from the firm and runs away to New York, where he buys elegant clothes and rents a luxurious room in the Waldorf Hotel. When he learns that his father is coming to find him, Paul believes that his idyllic life is over, and he commits suicide.

Pearl, The Short story by John STEINBECK, published in 1947. It is a parable about a Mexican Indian pearl diver named Kino who finds a valuable pearl and is transformed by the evil it attracts.

Kino sees the pearl as his opportunity for a better life. When the townsfolk of La Paz learn of Kino's find, he is immediately set upon by the greedy priest, doctor, and businessmen. After a series of disasters, Kino throws the pearl back into the ocean. Thereafter his tragedy is legendary in the town.

Penrod Comic novel by Booth TARKINGTON, published in 1914. Its protagonist, Penrod Schofield, a 12-year-old boy who lives in a small Midwestern city, rebels against his parents and teachers, and experiences the baffling ups and downs of preadolescence. Tarkington expertly conveys the speech and behavior of his boyish characters and writes with charm and humor about Penrod's escapades. He wrote two sequels, *Penrod and Sam* (1916) and *Penrod Jashber* (1929).

Personae (*in full* Personae: The Collected Poems of Ezra Pound) Anthology of short verse by Ezra POUND, published in 1926. The work contains many of his shorter poems, including selections from the earlier collections *A lume spento* (1908), *A Quinzaine for this Yule* (1908), *Personae* (1909), *Exultations* (1909), *Canzoni* (1911), *Ripostes* (1912), and *Lustra* (1916), but the emphasis of the anthology was on his later verse.

Petrified Forest, The Drama in two acts by Robert SHERWOOD, published and produced in 1935. This melodramatic Depression-era tale of frustrated lives and spiritual emptiness is set in a gas station and lunchroom along an Arizona highway. Gabby, the daughter of the station's owner, is unhappy with her life in the desert and longs to go to Paris to paint. She falls in love with Alan Squier, a failed author who stops at the restaurant on his way to California and proposes elopement. Everything changes when the escaped criminal Duke Mantee arrives and holds them hostage. Though flawed by didacticism and romantic clichés, the play offers insight into the search for values in a decadent civilization.

Piano Lesson, The Drama in two acts by August WILSON, produced in 1987 and published in 1990. The play, which was awarded a Pulitzer Prize in 1990, is part of Wilson's cycle about African-American life in the 20th century.

The action takes place in Pittsburgh in 1936 at the house of a family of African-Americans who have migrated from Mississippi. The conflict centers around a piano that was once traded by the family's white master for two of the family's ancestors. Boy Willie and Berniece, the siblings who inherit the piano (carved to show family history), argue about whether or not to sell it. Berniece's climactic refusal to allow Boy Willie to move the piano exorcises both the literal and figurative ghost of the white slave owner who has been haunting the family.

Piazza, The First sketch in the collection *The Piazza Tales* published by Herman MELVILLE in 1856. The sketch describes Melville's farmhouse, "Arrowhead," in Pittsfield, Mass. Supposedly the other tales in the collection, including "Bartleby the Scrivener" and "Benito Cereno," were narrated on the piazza of the farmhouse.

Picnic Drama in three acts by William INGE, produced and published in 1953 and awarded a Pulitzer Prize in the same year. This popular play about a group of lonely women in a small Kansas town whose lives are disrupted by the appearance of a virile, charming drifter captures the frustrations and limitations of Midwestern life. Inge slightly rewrote the ending in a 1962 version called *Summer Brave*.

Pictures from Brueghel (*in full* Pictures from Brueghel, and Other Poems) Collection of poetry by William Carlos WILLIAMS, published in 1962 and awarded a Pulitzer Prize in 1963. In this volume Williams transcends the objectivist style of his earlier work, treating poetry as a medium for ideas as well as a means of depicting the physical world. Williams also explored new verse forms in the collection. Wanting to find a rhythm suited to American speech, he experimented with a version of free verse he termed *versos sueltos* ("loose verses"), which makes use of the triadic stanza and a "variable foot" measure.

Pierre (*in full* Pierre; or, The Ambiguities) Novel by Herman MELVILLE, published in 1852. An intensely personal work, it reveals the somber mythology of Melville's private life framed in terms of a story of an artist alienated from his society. The artist, Pierre Glendinning, is a well-to-do young man. When he discovers that he has an illegitimate half sister, he tries to provide for her by taking her to live in New York City, where they live in poverty as he attempts to make a living as a writer. He ultimately destroys both of their lives as well as that of his fiancée. The novel, a slightly veiled allegory of Melville's own dark imaginings, was rooted in his relationships with his own family.

An edition of the novel without its odd literary subplot was published in 1995.

Pigeon Feathers (*in full* Pigeon Feathers and Other Stories) Collection of short fiction by John UPDIKE, published in 1962 and comprising the stories "Pigeon Feathers," "Flight," and "Friends from Philadelphia." In these early stories Updike attempted to capture overlooked or unexpected beauty inherent in life. The title story, one of his best known, concerns 14-year-old David Kern's religious doubts, his fear of death, and his triumphant return to faith, the "unexpected gift" that he is granted while shooting pigeons in a barn.

Pilot, The (*in full* The Pilot; A Tale of the Sea)

Novel by James Fenimore COOPER, published in two volumes in 1823. Admired for its authentic portrayal of a seafaring life, the work, which takes place during the American Revolutionary War, launched a whole genre of maritime fiction. It features a mysterious and almost superhuman American sea pilot (based on the American hero John Paul Jones) who fights battles off the coast of England against the British and American loyalists. One of the book's themes is the ambiguous nature of loyalty. Although often complicated by nautical terminology and by intrusive philosophical dialogue, the novel is nevertheless noted for its spiritual and moral dimensions.

Pioneers, The (*in full* The Pioneers; or, The Sources of the Susquehanna) The first of five novels in the series THE LEATHER-STOCKING TALES by James Fenimore COOPER, first published in two volumes in 1823. It began the saga of frontiersman Natty Bumppo, also called Leather-Stocking. In this narrative, however, Bumppo is an old man, as is his Indian friend Chingachgook; together they have seen the frontier change from wilderness to settlement, and they know that their way of life is about to vanish.

Pit and the Pendulum, The Gothic horror story by Edgar Allan POE, first published in *The Gift* (an annual giftbook of occasional verse and stories) in 1843. The work helped secure its author's reputation as a master of lurid gothic suspense.

Like many of Poe's stories, "The Pit and the Pendulum" is a dramatic monologue. Sentenced to death by the Spanish Inquisition, the imprisoned narrator finds himself in absolute darkness, in danger of falling to his death into a pit in the center of the cell. After narrowly escaping the razor-edged blade of a swinging pendulum, he is forced toward the pit by the hot, metal dungeon walls that are closing in. Just as he begins to slip, the walls recede and he is rescued.

Player Piano First novel by Kurt VONNEGUT, published in 1952 and reissued in 1954 as *Utopia 14*. This anti-utopian novel employs the standard science-fiction formula of a futuristic world run by machines and of one man's futile rebellion against that world.

Pnin Novel written in English by Vladimir NABOKOV, published in 1957. It is an episodic story about Timofey Pnin, an older, exiled Russian professor of entomology at the fictional Waindell College in upstate New York. While not considered one of Nabokov's major works, the novel is a comic and tender portrait of a defenseless intellectual trying to deal with the complexities of American life. The character Pnin turns up again as a minor character in *Pale Fire*, another of Nabokov's novels about academic life.

Poetry Poem by Marianne MOORE, originally published in a 30-line version in 1921. Moore cut the poem to 13 lines in 1924, replaced most of the excised lines in 1935, and cut it drastically again in 1967. Most critics prefer the 1935 poem published in the collection *Selected Poems* (1935).

Beginning with the famous line "I, too, dislike it," Moore examines her ambivalent feelings toward poetry which, she feels, is not important in itself but can be "useful" if written properly. A "useful" poem, according to Moore, is one that has successfully merged the world of the imagination with the world of the senses; a poet's subject, she holds, should be based on firsthand experience.

Ponder Heart, The Comic novella by Eudora WELTY, published in 1954. Cast as a monologue, it is rich with colloquial speech and descriptive imagery.

The narrator of the story is Miss Edna Earle Ponder, one of the last living members of a once-prominent family, who manages the Beulah Hotel in Clay, Miss. She tells a traveling salesman the history of her family and fellow townsfolk.

Porgy Novel by DuBose HEYWARD, published in 1925. Based partially on Heyward's experiences working on the wharves in Charleston, S.C., this lyrical book records the adventures of Porgy, a crippled black beggar, and his mistress Bess. Narrated in a simple, straightforward style, the authentic rendering of black life on Catfish Row

led many readers to assume, mistakenly, that Heyward himself was black. In 1927, collaborating with his wife Dorothy, Heyward dramatized the book. It became the basis for the 1935 opera *Porgy and Bess*, with music by George Gershwin and libretto by Ira Gershwin and Heyward.

Portnoy's Complaint Novel by Philip ROTH, published in 1969. The book became a minor classic of Jewish-American literature. This comic novel is structured as a confession to a psychiatrist by Alexander Portnoy, who relates the details of his adolescent obsession with masturbation and his domination by his over-possessive mother, Sophie. Portnoy's "complaint" refers to the damage done to him by the culture that has shaped him; although he is successful, his achievements are marred by a nagging sense of guilt.

Portrait of a Lady, The Novel by Henry JAMES, published in three volumes in 1881. The masterpiece of the first phase of James's career, the novel is a study of Isabel Archer, a young American woman of great promise who travels to Europe and becomes a victim of her own provincialism. It offers a shrewd appraisal of the American character and embodies the national myth of freedom and equality hedged with historical blindness and pride.

Prairie, The Novel by James Fenimore COOPER, published in two volumes in 1827, the third of five novels published as THE LEATHER-STOCKING TALES. Chronologically, *The Prairie* is the fifth in the series, ending with the death of the frontiersman Natty Bumppo, or Hawkeye, now an octogenarian.

The Prairie extols the vanishing American wilderness, disappearing because of the westward expansion of the American frontier. It concerns Natty Bumppo's travels with a party of settlers across the unsettled prairie of the Great Plains. Bumppo ultimately rejects life with the settlers and goes to live out his days in a Pawnee village, away from the encroaching civilization he distrusts.

Praisesong for the Widow Novel by Paule

MARSHALL, published in 1983. Recently widowed Avey (Avatara) Johnson, a wealthy, middle-aged African-American woman, undergoes a spiritual rebirth and finds a vital connection to her past while visiting an island in the Caribbean. Marshall portrays the special anguish of certain blacks who, in their drive to achieve material success, have lost touch with their heritage. Well-received by critics, the work was often compared to the novels of Toni Morrison.

Premature Burial, The Short story by Edgar Allan POE, first published in *Dollar Newspaper* in July 1844.

As a frequent victim of catalepsy, the narrator has obsessive fears and horrible nightmares that he will be buried alive while comatose. As a precaution, he supplies his tomb with escape routes and provisions. Once, upon awakening, he feels trapped in a coffin not of his making. After realizing that he has fallen asleep in a ship's narrow berth, he conquers his morbid fears and suffers no further from catalepsy.

Prince and the Pauper, The Novel by Mark TWAIN, published in 1881. In it Twain satirizes social conventions, concluding that appearances often hide a person's true value. Despite its saccharine plot, the novel succeeds as a critique of legal and moral injustices.

On a lark two identical-looking boys, Prince Edward Tudor of Wales and street urchin Tom Canty, exchange clothes. In the ensuing mix-up, each is mistaken for the other and both are believed to be mad. Edward learns about the problems of commoners, while Tom learns to play the role of a prince and then a king.

Princess Casamassima, The Novel by Henry JAMES, published in three volumes in 1886. In the novel James examines the anarchist violence of the late 19th century by depicting the struggle of Hyacinth Robinson, a man who toys with revolution and is destroyed by it. James offers an interesting portrait of an upper-class reformer in the character of the Princess Casamassima, who has rejected the empty social life of her husband

and has become involved with reformers and proletarian groups in London.

Professor's House, The Novel by Willa CATHER, published in 1925, in which the protagonist, a university professor, confronts middle age and personal and professional loneliness.

Professor Godfrey St. Peter has completed his significant academic work on Spanish explorers in North America. His daughters have married, his favorite student has died in World War I, and his wife has moved into a new house. The professor prefers to work in his study in the garret of their old house, and there he is almost asphyxiated by a gas leak from a defective stove. He is ready to let go of life when he is saved by Augusta, an old sewing woman who shares his garret. Through Augusta's patience and friendship, he learns to accept life on its own terms.

Prophet, The Book of 26 poetic essays by Khalil GIBRAN, published in 1923. A best-selling book of popular mysticism, *The Prophet* was translated into more than a dozen languages. Gibran's narrative frame relates that the Prophet, about to board a ship that will take him home back to his homeland after 12 years in a foreign city, is stopped by a group of the city's inhabitants, who ask him to speak to them about the mysteries of life. He does so, discussing love, marriage, beauty, reason and passion, and death, among other topics. Although many critics thought Gibran's poetry mediocre, *The Prophet* achieved cult status among American youth for several generations.

Pudd'nhead Wilson (*in full* The Tragedy of Pudd'nhead Wilson, and the Comedy of Those Extraordinary Twins) Novel by Mark TWAIN, originally published as *Pudd'nhead Wilson, A Tale* (1894). A story about miscegenation in the antebellum South, the book is noted for its grim humor and its reflections on racism and responsibility.

Roxana, a light-skinned mixed-race slave, switches her baby with her white owner's baby. Her natural son, Tom Driscoll, grows up in a privileged household to become a criminal who finances his gambling debts by selling her to a slave trader and who later murders his putative uncle. Meanwhile, Roxy raises Valet de Chambre as a slave. David ("Pudd'nhead") Wilson, an eccentric lawyer, determines the true identities of Tom and Valet. As a result Roxy is exposed, Wilson is elected mayor, Tom is sold into slavery, and Valet, unfitted for his newly won freedom, becomes an illiterate, uncouth landholder.

Purloined Letter, The Short story by Edgar Allan POE, first published in an unauthorized version in 1844. An enlarged and authorized version was published in *The Gift* (an annually published gift book containing occasional verse and stories) in 1845 and was collected the same year in Poe's *Tales*.

The Paris police prefect approaches amateur detective C. Auguste Dupin with a puzzle: a cabinet minister has stolen a letter from a woman of royalty whom he is now blackmailing. Despite a painstaking search of the minister's rooms, the police find nothing. When the prefect returns a month later and mentions a large reward for the letter, Dupin casually produces the document. Dupin later explains to his assistant, the story's narrator, that by analyzing the personality and behavior of the minister, he correctly concluded that the letter would be hidden in plain sight.

While the story has been traditionally regarded as an early prototype of detective fiction, it has also been the subject of intense scholarly debate, notably between French philosopher Jacques Derrida, who upheld the story as a model of ambiguous narrative, and French psychoanalyst Jacques Lacan, who maintained that it was a sexual allegory.

Q.E.D. Short story by Gertrude STEIN, one of her earliest works. Written in 1903, it was published posthumously in 1950 in *Things As They Are*, a novel in three parts.

Q.E.D. is autobiographical, based on an ill-fated relationship between Adele (Stein), an exuberant young woman, and Helen, who seduces her. Helen eventually rejects Adele for Mabel, a manipulative, wealthy woman who uses her money and passionate nature to dominate Helen.

Quaker Graveyard in Nantucket, The Poem by Robert LOWELL, published in 1946 in the collection *Lord Weary's Castle*. This frequently anthologized elegy for a cousin who died at sea during World War II echoes both Herman Melville and Henry David Thoreau in its exploration of innocence, corruption, sin, and redemption. The poem is divided into seven parts and written in rhymed iambic pentameter with occasional trimeter lines.

Rabbit, Run Novel by John UPDIKE, published in 1960. The novel's hero is Harry ("Rabbit") Angstrom, a 26-year-old former high-school athletic star who is disillusioned with his present life and flees from his wife and child in a futile search for grace and order.

Three sequels—*Rabbit Redux* (1971), *Rabbit Is Rich* (1981), and *Rabbit at Rest* (1990)—continue the story of Rabbit in the succeeding decades of his life.

Ragged Dick Children's book by Horatio ALGER, Jr., published serially in 1867 and in book form in 1868. Alternately titled *Street Life in New York with the Bootblacks*, the popular though formulaic story chronicles the successful rise of the title character from rags to respectability. Like most of Alger's novels, *Ragged Dick* served a second purpose as a guide to proper behavior for city youth.

Raisin in the Sun, A Drama in three acts by Lorraine HANSBERRY, published and produced in 1959. The play's title is taken from "Harlem," a poem by Langston Hughes, which examines the question "What happens to a dream deferred? Does it dry up/like a raisin in the sun? . . ." This penetrating psychological study of a working-class black family on the south side of Chicago in the late 1940s reflected Hansberry's own experiences of racial harassment after her prosperous family moved into a white neighborhood.

Walter Lee Younger, a chauffeur, hopes to use

his father's life-insurance money to open a liquor store with two partners. His mother, with the support of Walter's pragmatic wife Ruth and independent sister Beneatha, instead uses part of the money as a down payment on a house in an all-white neighborhood. Mama gives the remaining money, including Beneatha's share (which is to be deposited in the bank), to Walter. After one of his partners absconds with the money, Walter despondently contacts Karl Lindner, a representative of the white neighborhood who had earlier tried to buy out the Youngers so as to avoid racial integration, intending to accept his offer. However, Walter finally rejects the proposal.

Ransom of Red Chief, The Short story by O. HENRY, published in the collection *Whirligigs* in 1910. In the story two kidnappers make off with the young son of a prominent man only to find that the child is more trouble than he is worth; in the end, they agree to pay the boy's father to take him back. This highly popular story reflects the influences of Mark Twain and Ambrose Bierce. Told in the first person in a humorous, energetic style, the story embodies the mischievous spirit of American boyhood.

Rappaccini's Daughter Allegorical short story by Nathaniel HAWTHORNE, first published in *United States Magazine and Democratic Review* (December 1844) and collected in *Mosses from an Old Manse* (1846).

Rappaccini, a scholar-scientist in Padua, grows only poisonous plants in his lush garden. His lovely daughter, Beatrice, has been nurtured on poison and is sustained by her father's toxic plants. Giovanni, a student who lives next door to Rappaccini, falls in love with Beatrice and himself becomes contaminated by the garden's poisonous aura. The antidote he is given cures him; when he gives it to Beatrice, however, she drinks it and dies.

Raven cycle A collection of oral trickster-transformer tales popular mainly among the Indians of the Northwest Pacific Coast from Alaska to northwestern Washington. The tales feature Raven as a culture hero, an alternately clever and stupid bird-human whose voracious appetite and eroticism give rise to violent and amorous adventures.

The cycle begins with a boy's birth and relates early adventures that include the seduction of his aunt (some versions substitute the daughter of the Sky Chief) and his flight to the sky to escape the ensuing flood. Raven, his child, falls to earth, where he is adopted by a chief; as an adult he transforms the earth from a dark and arid land inhabited by a variety of ferocious monsters into a land of rivers, lakes, and mountains inhabited by animals and human beings. He later travels about, changing aspects of the physical environment into their present form, often through deception.

Raven, The Best-known poem by Edgar Allan POE, published in 1845 and collected in *The Raven and Other Poems* the same year. Poe achieved instant national fame with the publication of this melancholy evocation of lost love.

On a stormy December midnight, a grieving student is visited by a raven who speaks but one word, "Nevermore." As the student laments his lost love Lenore, the raven's insistent repetition of the word becomes an increasingly harrowing response to the student's own fears and longing.

The poem consists of 18 six-line stanzas; the first five lines of each are written in trochaic octameter, the sixth in trochaic tetrameter. The rhyme pattern, *abcbbb*, enhances the gloom of the lyric; the *b* rhymes are, or rhyme with, "Lenore" and "Nevermore." Poe's 1846 essay "The Philosophy of Composition" describes his careful crafting of the poem.

Reality Sandwiches Fourth volume of collected poems by Allen GINSBERG, published in 1963. The poems in the collection are of interest mainly as a record of the Beat lifestyle and of Ginsberg's own experiences.

Real Life of Sebastian Knight, The Novel by Vladimir NABOKOV, published in 1941. It was his first prose narrative in English.

The work, which is a satire of literary biography and scholarship, purports to be the true biography of a great writer, the late and neglected Sebastian Knight; it is written by his half brother, V., in response to another biographer's belittling analysis of Sebastian. Before long, however, V.'s "biography" turns into a mystery story, as he searches for the true facts about Sebastian among Sebastian's acquaintances. Himself a mediocre writer, V. eventually has a crisis of identity and his search for the real Sebastian becomes a search for himself.

Rebel Angels, The Novel of ideas by Robertson DAVIES, published in 1981. The novel was the first in a trilogy that included *What's Bred in the Bone* (1985) and *The Lyre of Orpheus* (1988).

Set in a prominent Canadian university, the novel examines the dual themes of the distinction between knowledge and wisdom and the role of the university in contemporary society.

Red Badge of Courage, The Novel of the American Civil War by Stephen CRANE, published in 1895 and considered to be his masterwork for its perceptive depiction of warfare and of the psychological turmoil of the soldier. Crane had had no experience of war when he wrote the novel, which he based partly on a popular anthology, *Battles and Leaders of the Civil War*.

The Red Badge of Courage has been called the first modern war novel because, uniquely for its time, it tells of the experience of war from the point of view of an ordinary soldier. Henry Fleming is eager to demonstrate his patriotism in a glorious battle, but when the slaughter starts, he is overwhelmed with fear and flees the battlefield. Ironically, he receives his "red badge of courage" when he is slightly wounded by being struck on the head by a deserter. He witnesses a friend's gruesome death and becomes enraged at the injustice of war. The courage of common soldiers and the agonies of death cure him of his romantic notions. He returns to his regiment and continues to fight on with true courage and without illusions.

Redburn (*in full* Redburn: His First Voyage) Novel by Herman MELVILLE, published in 1849. Based on a trip Melville took to Liverpool, Eng., in June 1839, *Redburn* is a hastily written adventure about Wellingborough Redburn, a genteel but impoverished boy from New York City who endures a rough initiation into life as a sailor.

Red Pony, The Book of four related stories by John STEINBECK, published in 1937 and expanded in 1945. The stories chronicle a young boy's maturation.

In "The Gift," the best-known story, young Jody Tiflin is given a red pony by his rancher father. Under ranch hand Billy Buck's guidance, Jody learns to care for and train his pony, which he names Gabilan. Caught in an unexpected rain, Gabilan catches a cold and, despite Billy Buck's ministrations, dies. Jody watches the buzzards alight on the body of his beloved pony, and, distraught at his inability to control events, he kills one of them.

The other stories in *The Red Pony* are "The Great Mountains," "The Promise," and "The Leader of the People," in which Jody develops empathy and also learns from his grandfather about "westering," the migration of people to new places and the urge for new experiences.

Reflections in a Golden Eye Novel by Carson MCCULLERS, published in 1941. Set in the 1930s on a Southern army base, the novel concerns the relationships between self-destructive misfits whose lives end in tragedy and murder.

The cast of characters includes Captain Penderton, a sadomasochistic, latent homosexual officer; his wife, who is having an affair with Major Langdon; the major's wife, who responds to the trauma of her son's death with self-mutilation; Anacleto, a homosexual servant who is befriended by the major's wife; and an army private who engages in voyeurism.

Remembrance Rock Novel by Carl SANDBURG, published in 1948. Sandburg's only novel, the work is a massive chronicle that uses historical facts and both historical and fictional characters to depict American history from 1607 to 1945 in a mythic, passionate tribute to the American people.

Renascence Poem by Edna St. Vincent MILLAY, first published in 1912 in the anthology *The Lyric Year* and later included as the title poem of her first published collection, *Renascence and Other Poems* (1917).

"Renascence" consists of 214 lines written in octosyllabic couplets. Written when Millay was 20, the poem reflects in simple, direct language the poet's feelings of wonder at the magnitude of the universe and the concepts of God and death.

Richard Cory Poem by Edwin Arlington ROBINSON, published in the collection *The Children of the Night* (1897). Perhaps Robinson's best-known poem, it is one of several works set in Tilbury Town, a fictional New England village.

The Tilbury Town community, represented by the collective "we," narrates the four-stanza poem about Richard Cory, a mysterious fellow villager. The villagers admire him for his wealth, education, and manners. An object of their fascination and envy, he reminds them of royalty. Their ignorance of his troubled soul is underscored by the surprise ending, which reports his suicide with understatement.

Rip Van Winkle Short story by Washington IRVING, published in THE SKETCH BOOK in 1819–20. Though set in the Dutch culture of pre-Revolutionary War New York state, the story of Rip Van Winkle is based on a German folktale.

Rip Van Winkle is an amiable farmer who wanders into the Catskill Mountains, where he comes upon a group of dwarfs playing ninepins. Rip accepts their offer of a drink of liquor and promptly falls asleep. When he awakens, 20 years later, he is an old man with a long, white beard; the dwarfs are nowhere in sight. Rip goes into town and finds that everything is changed: his wife is dead, his children are grown, and George Washington's portrait hangs in place of King George III's. The old man entertains the townspeople with tales of the old days and of his encounter with the little men in the Catskill mountains.

Rise of Silas Lapham, The The best-known novel of William Dean HOWELLS, published in 1885.

The novel recounts the moral dilemma of Colonel Silas Lapham, a newly wealthy, self-made businessman who has climbed over his former partner on the ladder to success. After Lapham moves from Vermont to Boston, his family befriends the Coreys, a Brahmin family in financial difficulties. Tom Corey, the son, appears to return the romantic interest of the Laphams' younger daughter Irene, but he really loves her older sister Penelope. Lapham and his wife move awkwardly in Boston's highly stratified society, and he gets drunk at a party and reveals his common origins. Meanwhile, business reversals cause him to entertain an offer to sell a worthless property to an English syndicate. The resulting money would enable him to continue to rise in society, but after struggling with his conscience, Silas at last refuses to sell and bankruptcy results. Though Silas has fallen socially, he has risen morally. Penelope elopes to Mexico with Tom, thus escaping Boston's tedious social strictures.

Road Not Taken, The Poem by Robert FROST, published in *Atlantic Monthly* in August 1915, and used as the opening poem of his collection *Mountain Interval* (1916). Written in iambic tetrameter, it employs an *abaab* rhyme scheme in each of its four stanzas. One of its author's best-known poems, The poem presents a narrator recalling a journey through a woods, when he had to choose which of two diverging roads to travel. The work's meaning has long been disputed by readers; Frost himself claimed that it was a parody of the Georgian poet Edward Thomas.

Roderick Hudson First novel by Henry JAMES, serialized in *The Atlantic Monthly* in 1875 and published in book form in 1876. It was revised by the author in 1879 for publication in England. *Roderick Hudson* is the story of the conflict between art and the passions; the title character is an American sculptor in Italy. Faltering in both his artistic ambitions and his personal relationships, he travels to Switzerland and dies there.

Roger Malvin's Burial Short story by Nathaniel HAWTHORNE, first published in 1832 in the periodical *The Token* and collected in *Mosses from an Old Manse* (1846). Based on an actual occurrence, the story is less concerned with historical narrative than with real or obsessive guilt, a theme to which Hawthorne returned in much of his fiction.

Roger Malvin and Reuben Bourne make their way home after participating in a skirmish with Indians. Badly wounded, Roger urges Reuben to leave him and return home alone. Reuben agrees to go on, swearing that he will either send help or will return himself to give Roger a decent burial. Reuben never fulfills his oath, and for years he lives as if under a curse. His guilt is finally expiated through a tragic sacrifice. *See also* MOSSES FROM AN OLD MANSE.

Rootabaga Stories Collection of children's stories by Carl SANDBURG, published in 1922. These fanciful tales reflect Sandburg's interest in folk ballads and nonsense verse. He modeled his expansive fictional land on the American Midwest. The lighthearted stories, referred to as moral tales by Sandburg, feature such silly characters as Hot Dog the Tiger, Gimme the Ax, White Horse Girl, Blue Wind Boy, and Jason Squiff the Cistern Cleaner. Succeeding books in the same vein include *Rootabaga Pigeons* (1923), *Rootabaga Country* (1929), and *Potato Face* (1930).

Roots (*in full* Roots: The Saga of an American Family) Book combining history and fiction, by Alex HALEY, published in 1976 and awarded a special Pulitzer Prize.

Beginning with stories recounted by his grandmother Cynthia in Henning, Tenn., Haley spent 12 years tracing the saga of seven generations of his family, beginning with Kunta Kinte, his ancestor from Gambia who had been enslaved and brought to America in 1767. Through oral tradition, the descendants of Kunta Kinte kept alive the tales of their forebears through each generation.

Roots was a runaway best-seller. It was adapted for television in 1977, and the eight installments were some of television's most widely viewed programs. The success of *Roots* precipitated a nationwide resurgence of interest in all phases of genealogical research. African-Americans who had felt cut off from their origins and whose heritage seemed untraceable were inspired to attempt to fill in the gaps in their family history. However, later investigations of Haley's methods and attempts to duplicate his research cast serious doubts on the accuracy of his story. A pivotal character—the griot, or African oral historian, who knew the name Kunta Kinte—proved to be a fraud. Despite its faults, the book retains its emotional impact and its significance for African-American literature.

Roughing It Semiautobiographical novel by Mark TWAIN, published in 1872. This humorous travel book, based on Twain's stagecoach journey through the American West and his adventures in the Pacific islands, is full of colorful caricatures of outlandish locals and detailed sketches of frontier life.

Roughing It describes how the narrator, a polite greenhorn from the East, is initiated into the rough-and-tumble society of the frontier. He works his way through Nevada, California, and the Pacific islands as a prospector, journalist, and lecturer, and along the way he meets a number of colorful characters.

Sacred Wood, The Book of critical essays by T.S. ELIOT, published in 1920. In it, Eliot discusses several of the issues of modernist writings of the period.

The best-known essay of the collection, "Tradition and the Individual Talent," puts forth Eliot's theory of a literary tradition that comprises the whole of European literature from Homer to the present and of the relationship of the individual poet to that tradition. Another notable essay is "Hamlet and His Problems," in which Eliot expresses his theory of the Objective Correlative, a phrase he adapted from either George Santayana or Washington Allston.

Salterton trilogy Series of novels by Robertson DAVIES, consisting of *Tempest-Tost* (1951), *Leaven of Malice* (1954), and *A Mixture of Frailties* (1958).

The books are comedies of manners that are loosely connected by the fact that they are all set in Salterton, a provincial Canadian university town, and they feature recurring characters. *Tempest-Tost* concerns the efforts of a local theater company to put on a production of William Shakespeare's *The Tempest*. *Leaven of Malice* opens with the placement of a false notice of engagement in the local paper and examines the effects of the practical joke on those involved as they try to discover who placed the announcement. In *A Mixture of Frailties* a woman's will provides for the education in the arts of a young woman of the town. The book traces the young woman's experiences as she trains to be a singer.

Sanctuary Novel by William FAULKNER, published in 1931. The book's depictions of degraded sexuality generated both controversy and spectacular sales, making it the author's only popular success during his lifetime.

A vision of a decayed South, the novel pitted idealistic lawyer Horace Benbow against a cast of amoral fiends. The book's seething violence and despair were characteristic of Faulkner, although elsewhere less brutally displayed.

Faulkner's publisher balked at releasing this study of human evil, set in the author's fictional Yoknapatawpha County, Miss., and asked him to rewrite it in proof. Faulkner did so, refining its art without softening its horror.

Sandbox, The One-act play by Edward ALBEE, published in 1959 (with *The Death of Bessie Smith*) and produced in 1960. It is a trenchant satire on false values and the lack of love and empathy in the American family. For his expanded one-act play *The American Dream* (1961), Albee used the characters he created for *The Sandbox*—Mommy, Daddy, and Grandma— as well as some of the play's dramatic material.

Sapphira and the Slave Girl Novel by Willa CATHER, published in 1940. The novel is set in Virginia in the mid-1800s on the estate of a declining slaveholding family.

Sapphira and the Slave Girl centers on the family's matriarch, Sapphira Colbert, and her attempt to sell Nancy Till, a mixed-race slave girl. Sapphira's plot is foiled by her husband Henry and their widowed daughter Rachel Blake. A confident, strong-willed invalid, Sapphira has earned the respect of many of her slaves despite her subtle cruelty toward Nancy. Henry is a pious miller whose simple upbringing and passivity contrast with the aristocratic and manipulative nature of his wife. Henry's nephew Martin, a suave but lecherous ex-soldier, tries to seduce Nancy. Rachel, who helps Nancy flee to Canada, remains at odds with Sapphira over the issue of slavery until the death of Rachel's daughter reconciles the pair. Cather appears in the epilogue as a child who notes Nancy's triumphant return 25 years later.

Sartoris Novel by William FAULKNER, published in 1929 as a shortened version of a novel that was eventually published in its entirety in 1973 under the original title *Flags in the Dust*.

Disproportioned and sometimes emotionally overwrought, Faulkner's third novel was the last of his apprentice works but also the first set in his imagined community of Yoknapatawpha County, Miss. The novel concerns the Sartoris family, which revels in a mythical history of clan heroism and nobility that is belied by their current desperation and recklessness. The work addresses many of the themes Faulkner developed at length in his later novels: innate brutality, racial tension, the contrast between a romanticized Southern past and a tawdry present. It also introduces characters who featured prominently in his other Yoknapatawpha novels, including the crass Snopes family and lawyer Horace Benbow. The early history of the Sartoris family is told in *The Unvanquished* (1938).

Scarlet Letter, The Novel by Nathaniel HAWTHORNE, published in 1850. It is considered a masterpiece of American literature and a classic moral study.

The novel is set in a village in Puritan New England. The main character is Hester Prynne, a young woman who has borne an illegitimate child. Hester believes herself a widow, but her husband, Roger Chillingworth, returns to New England very much alive and conceals his identity. He finds his wife forced to wear the scarlet letter *A* on her dress as punishment for her adultery. Chillingworth becomes obsessed with finding the identity of his wife's former lover. When he learns that the father of Hester's child is Arthur Dimmesdale, a saintly young minister who is the leader of those exhorting her to name the child's father, Chillingworth proceeds to torment the guilt-stricken young man.

In the end Chillingworth is morally degraded by his monomaniacal pursuit of revenge; Dimmesdale is broken by his own sense of guilt, and he publicly confesses his adultery before dying in Hester's arms. Only Hester can face the future bravely, as she plans to take her daughter Pearl to Europe to begin a new life.

Sea of Grass, The Novel by Conrad RICHTER, published in 1936, presenting in epic scope the conflicts in the settling of the American Southwest.

Set in New Mexico in the late 19th century, the novel concerns the often violent clashes between the pioneering ranchers, whose cattle range freely through the vast sea of grass, and the farmers, or "nesters," who build fences and turn the sod. Against this background is set the triangle of rancher Colonel Jim Brewton, his unstable Eastern wife Lutie, and the ambitious Brice Chamberlain. Richter casts the story in Homeric terms, with the children caught up in the conflicts of their parents.

Seascape Drama in two acts by Edward ALBEE, produced and published in 1975; it won the Pulitzer Prize for drama.

The play presents Nancy and Charlie, a married couple. Picnicking by the ocean one day, they meet Leslie and Sarah, middle-aged giant lizards from beneath the sea who want to evolve. The witty dialogue between the couples affords the playwright an opportunity to examine humans as a species.

Sea-Wolf, The Novel by Jack LONDON, published in 1904. This highly popular novel combines elements of naturalism and romantic adventure.

The story concerns Humphrey Van Weyden, a refined castaway who is put to work on the motley schooner *Ghost*. The ship is run by brutal Wolf Larsen, who, despite his intelligence and strength, is antisocial and self-destructive. Hardened by his arduous experiences at sea, Humphrey develops strength of both body and will, protecting another castaway, Maud Brewster, and facing down the increasingly deranged Larsen.

Second Tree from the Corner, The Collection of literary miscellanea by E.B. WHITE, published in 1954. Most of these essays, poems, and stories originally appeared in *The New Yorker* magazine over a period of two decades. White treats modernity and progress with skepticism and nostalgia.

Secret Garden, The Novel for children by Frances Hodgson BURNETT, published in 1911. The book, considered Burnett's best, has become a classic of children's literature.

The novel's protagonist, Mary Lennox, a sickly and unpleasant orphan, is sent to England to live with a reclusive uncle she has never met. Her guardian's housekeeper takes charge of Mary, turning her into a healthy, delightful child. While exploring the estate, Mary discovers a secret garden that had been abandoned 10 years earlier, after the death of her uncle's wife. Mary brings the garden back to life and works a similar transformation on her guardian's spoiled, semi-invalid son.

Seize the Day Novella by American author Saul BELLOW, published in 1956. This short novel examines one day in the unhappy life of Tommy Wilhelm, who has fallen from marginal middle-management respectability to unemployment, divorce, and despair. Like many of Bellow's other novels, *Seize the Day* exhibits an ambivalent attitude toward worldly success, and it follows its sensitive, gullible protagonist's quest for meaning in a chaotic and hostile world.

Self-Reliance Essay by Ralph Waldo EMERSON, published in the first volume of his collected *Essays* (1841). Developed from his journals and from a series of lectures he gave in the winter of 1836–37, it exhorts the reader to consistently obey "the aboriginal self," or inner law, regardless of institutional rules, popular opinion, tradition, or other social regulators. Emerson's doctrine of self-sufficiency and self-reliance naturally arose from his view that the individual need only look inward for the spiritual guidance that was previously the province of the established churches.

Separate Peace, A Novel by John KNOWLES, published in 1959. It recalls with psychological insight the maturing of a 16-year-old student at a preparatory school during World War II.

Looking back to his youth, the adult Gene Forrester reflects on his life as a student at Devon School in New Hampshire in 1942. Although he is an excellent student, he envies the athleticism and vitality of his friend Phineas, or Finny. Unable to cope with this insecurity, Forrester causes Finny to break his leg, sabotaging his athletic career. When the incident is later examined in a mock trial, Finny runs away, reinjures himself, and dies during consequent surgery.

Seventeen Humorous novel by Booth TARKINGTON, published in 1916. The novel recalls the events of one summer in the life of William Sylvanus Baxter, his family, and his friends in a Midwestern town in the early 20th century. Seventeen-year-old Willie develops a crush on Lola Pratt, a baby-talking, flirtatious visitor. The novel presents an accurate picture of the emotional ups and downs of a self-absorbed, love-struck teenager.

77 Dream Songs Volume of verse by American poet John BERRYMAN, published in 1964. It was awarded a Pulitzer Prize in 1965 and was later published together with its sequel, *His Toy, His Dream, His Rest* (1968), as *The Dream Songs* (1969). The entire sequence of 385 verses, consisting of three six-line stanzas each, is the self-narrated, confessional story of the antihero Henry, Berryman's poetic persona.

Shadows on the Rock Novel by Willa CATHER, published in 1931. The novel is a detailed study of the lives of French colonists in the late 1600s on the "rock" that is Quebec city, Que., Can. Like many of Cather's novels, *Shadows on the Rock* evokes the pioneer spirit and emphasizes the importance of religious tradition.

Euclide Auclair is a widowed apothecary who initially desires to return to France but later accepts his frontier surroundings. Much of the story is presented from the perspective of Auclair's daughter, Cécile, who eventually marries the woodsman and fur trader Pierre Charron.

Sheltering Sky, The First novel by Paul BOWLES, published in 1948. Considered a model of existential fiction, it sold well and was a critical success. The novel was described by the author as "an adventure story in which the adventures take place on two planes simultaneously: in the actual desert, and in the inner desert of the spirit."

Bowles's cool, detached prose contrasts with the increasingly violent and irrational events of the novel. Port and Kit Moresby, an American couple of independent means, have been traveling aimlessly for 12 years. By the time they reach Morocco they have become disaffected and alienated. They take up with a series of unreliable, rootless wanderers. On a trip to the interior Port contracts typhoid fever—out of apathy he has neglected to be vaccinated—and dies. Kit has an affair with an Arab and joins his household, but their relationship soon falls apart. Kit is found and returned to Oran. She is teetering on the brink of insanity and finds an opportunity to disappear into the crowded bazaar.

Ship of Fools, A Novel by Katherine Anne PORTER, published in 1962. Porter used as a framework *Das Narrenschiff* (1494; *The Ship of Fools*), by Sebastian Brant, a satire in which the world is likened to a ship whose passengers, fools and deranged people all, are sailing toward eternity.

Porter's novel is set in 1931 aboard a German passenger ship returning to Bremerhaven, Germany, from Veracruz, Mexico. The ship carries a microcosm of peoples, including Germans, Americans, Spaniards, Gypsies, and Mexicans. Jews, anti-Semites, political reactionaries, revolutionaries, and neutrals coexist aboard ship, at the same time that jealousy, cruelty, and duplicity pervade their lives.

Short Happy Life of Francis Macomber, The Short story by Ernest HEMINGWAY, first published in *Cosmopolitan* in 1936, collected in *The Fifth Column and the First Forty-Nine Stories* (1938). Set on an African safari, the story contains some of the author's recurrent themes—"grace under pressure" and adherence to a manly code of behavior. It is also known for its ambiguous depiction of emotions and motivations.

The character Francis Macomber, a wealthy American, and his wife, Margot, are on safari with their English guide, Robert Wilson. Macomber wounds a lion and runs away in fear. The guide is horrified at his bad sportsmanship; his wife ridicules him for his cowardice. Margot seduces Wilson, taking care that Macomber is not unaware of her infidelity and contempt. The next day, Macomber redeems himself by killing a buffalo cleanly and bravely. He achieves a feeling of happiness he has never known before; standing his ground, unafraid, he faces another buffalo, a charging, badly wounded bull. From the car where she has been watching, Margot takes aim and shoots at the charging buffalo, apparently to save her husband's life. Her shot strikes her husband, killing him at his moment of triumph.

Show Boat Popular sentimental novel by Edna FERBER, published in 1926. The book chronicles three generations of a theatrical family who perform and live on a Mississippi River steamboat. It was the basis of a successful Broadway musical and has been produced several times for film and television.

Sign in Sidney Brustein's Window, The Drama in three acts by Lorraine HANSBERRY, produced in 1964 and published the following year. The play concerns the nature of personal commitment to an ideal.

The character Sidney Brustein is a disillusioned white intellectual. Alton Scales, a black activist who loves Sidney's sister-in-law, Gloria, persuades Sidney to support the candidacy of Wally O'Hara, a local reform politician. Sidney does so but eventually learns of O'Hara's corruption. Sidney's wife, Iris, is an aspiring actress who leaves him to act in television commercials. When Alton learns that Gloria is a prostitute and not a model, as she had claimed, he leaves her; Gloria kills herself. Her suicide effects a reconciliation between Sidney and Iris.

Sister Carrie First novel by Theodore DREISER, published in 1900, but suppressed until 1912.

Sister Carrie tells the story of a rudderless but pretty small-town girl who comes to the big city filled with vague ambitions. She is used by men and uses them in turn to become a successful Broadway actress, while George Hurstwood, the married man who has run away with her, loses his grip on life and descends into beggary and suicide. *Sister Carrie* was the first masterpiece of the American naturalistic movement in its grittily factual presentation of the vagaries of urban life and in its ingenuous heroine, who goes unpunished for her transgressions against conventional sexual morality. The book's strengths include a brooding but compassionate view of humanity, a memorable cast of characters, and a compelling narrative line. The emotional disintegration of Hurstwood is a much-praised triumph of psychological analysis. *Sister Carrie* is a work of pivotal importance in American literature, and it became a model for subsequent American writers of realism.

Sketch Book, The (*in full* The Sketch Book of Geoffrey Crayon, Gent.) Short-story collection by Washington IRVING, first published in 1819–20 in seven separate parts. Most of the book's 30-odd pieces concern Irving's impressions of England, but six chapters deal with American subjects. Of these, the tales THE LEGEND OF SLEEPY HOLLOW and RIP VAN WINKLE have been called the first American short stories, although both are actually Americanized versions of German folktales. In addition to the stories based on folklore, the collection contains travel sketches, literary essays, and miscellany. *The Sketch Book* was the first American work to gain international literary success and popularity. Its unprecedented success allowed Irving to devote himself to a career as a professional author.

Skin of Our Teeth, The Comedy in three acts by Thornton WILDER, performed and published in 1942. Known for its experimental representation of all of human history, it won Wilder one of his three Pulitzer Prizes.

With a cast of characters that includes a dinosaur and drum majorettes, *The Skin of Our Teeth* employs bizarre anachronisms and audience-involvement techniques to argue that human experience is much the same whatever the time or place. From their living room in New Jersey, George and Maggie Antrobus (from the Greek *anthropos*, "human"), their promiscuous daughter Gladys, hostile and destructive son Henry (who represents the biblical Cain), and maid Sabina (who represents Lilith, the eternal temptress) face the trials of humanity through the ages, from icy destruction to flood and war.

Skunk Hour Poem by Robert Lowell, published in LIFE STUDIES (1959). It is modeled on "The Armadillo," a poem by Elizabeth Bishop; both poets dedicated their respective poems to each other. Composed of eight six-line stanzas, "Skunk Hour" is one in a series of confessional poems that characterized Lowell's verse from the 1950s.

In the first four stanzas the narrator describes several residents of his coastal resort town in Maine. In the final four stanzas the narrator isolates himself from the other townspeople, focusing on his inner turmoil. His anguished reverie gives way to a concluding description of other inhabitants of the town, a bold family of hungry skunks in a single-minded and confident search for food.

Slaughterhouse-Five (*in full* Slaughterhouse-Five; or, The Children's Crusade: A Duty-Dance with Death) Novel by Kurt VONNEGUT, Jr., published in 1969. The book blends science fiction with historical facts, notably Vonnegut's own experience as a prisoner of war in Dresden, Ger., during the Allied firebombing of that city in early 1945.

While serving in the army during World War II Billy Pilgrim becomes "unstuck in time," and from that point on he lives concurrently on Earth and on the distant planet Tralfamadore. On Earth Billy preaches the fatalistic philosophy of the Tralfamadorians, who know the future of all things, including the inevitable demise of the universe. They are resigned to fate, unfailingly responding to events with their catchphrase "So it goes."

slave narrative American literary genre consisting of slave memoirs of daily plantation life, including the sufferings and humiliations borne and the eventual escape to freedom. The narratives contain humorous anecdotes of the deception and pretenses that the slave was forced to practice, expressions of religious fervor and superstition, and, above all, a pervasive longing for freedom, dignity, and self-respect.

A Narrative of the Uncommon Sufferings and Surprising Deliverance of Briton Hammon, a Negro Man, which is often considered the first slave narrative, was published in Boston in 1760.

(Some scholars cite *Adam Negro's Tryall* [1703] as the first slave narrative, but it is about Adam, not by him.) Other early examples, such as *A Narrative of the Lord's Wonderful Dealings with J. Murrant, a Black, Taken Down from His Own Relation* (1784) and *The Interesting Narrative of Olaudah Equiano, or Gustavus Vassa, the African* (1789), followed.

The major period of slave narratives was 1830–60. Their publication was encouraged by abolitionists, and during this period the narratives, many of them based on oral accounts, multiplied. Although some, such as *Scenes in the Life of Harriet Tubman* (1869), are factual autobiographies, many others were influenced or sensationalized by the writer's desire to arouse sympathy for the abolitionist cause. The reworkings and interpolations in such works are usually obvious. In some cases, such as *The Autobiography of a Female Slave* (1856) by Mattie Griffith and Richard Hildreth's *The Slave, or Memoirs of Archy Moore*, the accounts were entirely fictitious. The slave-narrative genre reached its height with Frederick Douglass' classic autobiography *Narrative of the Life of Frederick Douglass, an American Slave* (1845; revised 1882).

In the first half of the 20th century a number of folklorists and anthropologists compiled documentary narratives based on recorded interviews with former black slaves. Notable compilations of such narratives include the brief accounts in Charles S. Johnson's *Shadow of the Plantation* (1934) and the fuller narratives found in B.A. Botkin's *Lay My Burden Down* (1945), which was an extract from 17 volumes of slave narratives collected by black and white interviewers for the WPA Federal Writers' Project. In the second half of the 20th century the growth of black cultural consciousness stimulated a renewed interest in slave narratives.

Slave, The One-act play by Amiri BARAKA, performed and published in 1964. An examination of tension between blacks and whites in contemporary America, *The Slave* is the story of a visit by African-American Walker Vessles to the home of Grace, his white ex-wife, and Easley, her white husband. Baraka points up the black man's low status in American society but also stresses that he is victimized and enslaved by his own hatred and is thus unable to effect social change.

Snow-Bound Poem by John Greenleaf WHITTIER, published in 1866. Subtitled "A Winter Idyll," this nostalgic pastoral poem recalls the New England rural home and family of the poet's youth, where, despite the pummeling of the winter winds and snow, he and his family remained secure and comfortable inside the house.

Snows of Kilimanjaro, The Short story by Ernest HEMINGWAY, first published in *Esquire* magazine in 1936 and later collected in *The Fifth Column and the First Forty-Nine Stories* (1938). The stream-of-consciousness narrative relates the feelings of Harry, a novelist dying of gangrene poisoning while on an African safari. Hemingway considered *The Snows of Kilimanjaro* his finest story.

So Big Novel by Edna FERBER, published in 1924 and awarded the Pulitzer Prize for fiction in 1925. The book tells the story of Selina Peake DeJong, a gambler's daughter with a love of life and a nurturing spirit.

Soldier's Play, A Drama in two acts by Charles FULLER, produced and published in 1981 and awarded the Pulitzer Prize for drama in 1982.

Set on an army base in Louisiana during World War II, the play deals with the open and covert conflicts between whites and blacks that limit the possibility of personal growth and social progress. The work concerns an investigation into the murder of a black sergeant of an all-black company. By interviewing witnesses, the investigator discovers that the sergeant had been a tyrannical, sadistic man who had hated everyone, black and white. He eventually discovers that the murder was not committed by white soldiers, town bigots, or members of the Ku Klux Klan, but by a young black soldier whom the sergeant had goaded unmercifully.

Song of Myself Poem of 52 sections and some 1,300 lines by Walt Whitman, first published untitled in the collection LEAVES OF GRASS in 1855. The expansive, exuberant poem was given its current title in 1881. Considered Whitman's most important work, and certainly his best-known, the poem revolutionized American verse. It departed from traditional rhyme, meter, and form and introduced frank sexual imagery. Among its characteristic elements are repetition, exclamation, and an incantatory voice. Many sections, compelling in their unrelenting rhythm, are catalogs of individuals, locations, and actions that move the poet.

Song of the Lark Novel by Willa CATHER, published in 1915. The heroine, Thea Kronborg, overcomes many hardships to become a leading Wagnerian soprano at the Metropolitan Opera. The *Song of the Lark* is one of several works in which Cather displayed her lyrical powers and in which she presented a protagonist who, by virtue of talent and determination, is able to rise above small-town provincialism.

Song of the Open Road Poem by Walt Whitman, first published in the second edition of LEAVES OF GRASS in 1856. The 15-stanza poem is an optimistic paean to wanderlust.

Whitman exalts the carefree pleasures of traveling, encouraging others to break free from their stifling domestic attachments to join him. Inspired by the expansive American landscape, he exhorts the reader to become his fellow traveler. Written in free verse, the poem is noted for its use of apostrophe, repetition, and exclamation.

Sophie's Choice Novel by William STYRON, published in 1979, that examines the historical, moral, and psychological ramifications of the Holocaust through the tragic life of a Roman Catholic survivor of Auschwitz.

Set in the late 1940s, the novel is narrated by Stingo, a young Southern writer who is the author's thinly veiled alter ego. In a boardinghouse

in Brooklyn, N.Y., Stingo becomes friends with a pair of tormented lovers: Nathan Landau, a brilliant but unstable Jew, and Sophie Zawistowska, a beautiful and guilt-ridden Polish refugee. On a journey to the South, accompanied by Sophie, Stingo learns that while at Auschwitz, Sophie was forced to choose which of her two children would survive and which would die. Sophie leaves unexpectedly and Stingo trails her to the boardinghouse, where he discovers that Nathan and Sophie have committed suicide.

Sot-Weed Factor, The Picaresque novel by John BARTH, originally published in 1960 and revised in 1967. A parody of the historical novel, it is based on and takes its title from a satirical poem published in 1708 by Ebenezer Cooke, who is the protagonist of Barth's work. The novel's black humor is derived from its purposeful misuse of conventional literary devices.

Sound and the Fury, The The first major novel by William FAULKNER, published in 1929.

The novel is set in Faulkner's fictional Yoknapatawpha County, Miss., in the early 20th century. It describes the decay and fall of the aristocratic Compson family, and, implicitly, of an entire social order, from four different points of view. The first three sections are presented from the perspectives of the three Compson sons: Benjy, an "idiot"; Quentin, a suicidal Harvard freshman; and Jason, the eldest. Each section is focused primarily on a sister who has married and left home. The fourth section comments on the other three as the Compsons' black servants, whose chief virtue is their endurance, reveal the family's moral decline. With *The Sound and the Fury*, Faulkner for the first time incorporated several challenging and sophisticated stylistic techniques, including interior monologues and stream-of-consciousness narrative.

Speak, Memory Autobiographical memoir of his early life and European years by Vladimir NABOKOV. Fifteen chapters were published individually (1948–50), mainly in *The New Yorker*.

The book was originally published as *Conclusive Evidence: A Memoir* (1951); it was also published the same year as *Speak, Memory: A Memoir*. Nabokov translated into Russian and revised the original work as *Drugiye berega* ("Other Shores") in 1954; in 1966, he published a further revised and expanded English-language edition entitled *Speak, Memory: An Autobiography Revisited*, which contains family photographs and incorporates recollections and revisions by his sisters and cousins.

The memoir describes in the first 12 chapters Nabokov's happy childhood in an aristocratic family in St. Petersburg, Russia. The remaining three chapters cover his years as a university student at Cambridge and as an intellectual and fledgling writer in the Russian émigré communities of Berlin and Paris.

Spinoza of Market Street, The Title story of a short-story collection by Isaac Bashevis SINGER, published in Yiddish in 1944 as "Der Spinozist." The collection was published in English in 1961.

The story is set in Warsaw on the brink of World War I. There Dr. Nahum Fischelson lives a meager, isolated existence alone in an attic room overlooking teeming Market Street. He devotes his energies to explicating the philosophical works of the 17th-century Dutch-Jewish philosopher Benedict de Spinoza, descending to the street only once a week to buy food. Black Dobbe, an illiterate, ugly woman who lives in the attic room next to his, goes to the philosopher's room to have him read a letter she has received. When she discovers Fischelson unconscious and ill, she nurses him back to health. To the amusement of their neighbors, Fischelson and Black Dobbe are married. Fischelson discovers that he has the ardor and vigor of a young man. As he gazes at the stars, he silently asks Spinoza to forgive him his happiness and his acceptance of the world of passion and joy.

Spoils of Poynton, The Short novel by Henry JAMES, first published as a serial titled *The Old Things* in *The Atlantic Monthly* in 1896. Retitled *The Spoils of Poynton*, it was published as a book in 1897.

Poynton Park is the home of old Mrs. Gereth, an antique collector with impeccable taste who has filled her lodgings with splendid art objects and furniture. The possessive Mrs. Gereth wants her weak-willed son to marry a pleasant young woman who shares her refined tastes. Instead he becomes engaged to a vulgar, greedy woman, and the treasures of Poynton become the prize over which mother and fiancée battle. In the end Poynton and its spoils, which have destroyed all of the novel's relationships, are immolated in a fire of undetermined origin.

Spoon River Anthology Poetry collection, the major work of Edgar Lee MASTERS, published in 1915. It was inspired by the epigrams in the *Greek Anthology*.

The *Spoon River Anthology* is a collection of 245 free-verse epitaphs in the form of monologues. They are spoken from beyond the grave by former residents of a dreary, confining small town like the ones Masters himself had known during his Illinois boyhood. The speakers tell of their hopes and ambitions, and of their bitter, unrealized lives. The realistic poems contradicted the popular view of small towns as repositories of moral virtue and respectability. A theatrical version of *Spoon River Anthology* appeared on Broadway in 1963.

Spring and All Volume of poems and prose pieces by William Carlos WILLIAMS, published in 1923 in Paris in an edition of 300 copies. It contains Williams' attempts to articulate his beliefs about the role and form of art in a modern context. Included are some of Williams' best-known poems.

The prose portions of *Spring and All* were, according to the author, "a mixture of philosophy and nonsense" in a format that parodied contemporary experimentation with typography. The poetry, on the other hand, is straightforward and concerned with the matter of daily life. In "By the Road to the Contagious Hospital," the poet observes fragile signs of spring emerging from a blighted landscape, and the subject of awakening life recurs in many of the remaining 26 poems. Despite the harsh social criticism of "The Crowd at the Ball Game" and "The Pure Products of America," the dominant mood is hopeful, and the images, such as the often reprinted "The Red Wheelbarrow," are vivid and sensuous.

Stopping by Woods on a Snowy Evening Poem by Robert FROST, published in the collection *New Hampshire* (1923). One of his most frequently explicated works, it describes a solitary traveler in a carriage who is both driven by the business at hand and transfixed by a wintry woodland scene. The poem is composed of four iambic tetrameter quatrains, and the meditative lyric derives its incantatory tone from an interlocking rhyme scheme of *aaba bbcb ccdc dddd*.

Story of a Bad Boy, The Classic children's novel by Thomas Bailey ALDRICH, published serially in *Our Young Folks* (1869) and in book form in 1870. An autobiographical book about a happy boyhood, it was the first full-length work in which the protagonist was a realistic boy instead of a priggish paragon.

Strange Interlude Pulitzer Prize-winning drama in two parts and nine acts by Eugene O'NEILL. It was produced in 1928 in New York City and was published the same year. The work's complicated plot is the story of a woman in her roles as daughter, wife, mistress, mother, and friend. Its length was an innovation, for in its original production it began in the late afternoon, paused for a dinner intermission, and resumed at the hour when most plays begin. It also employed innovative (at least in 20th-century drama) stage techniques, such as stream-of-consciousness soliloquies and asides.

Streetcar Named Desire, A Play in three acts by Tennessee WILLIAMS, first produced and published in 1947 and winner of the Pulitzer Prize for drama for that year. One of the most admired plays of its time, it concerns the mental and moral disintegration and ultimate ruin of Blanche DuBois, a former Southern belle. Her neurotic, genteel pretensions are no match for the harsh realities symbolized by her brutish brother-in-law, Stanley Kowalski.

Street Scene Play in three acts by Elmer RICE, produced and published in 1929. The play is set in a New York City slum and offers a realistic portrayal of life in a tenement building. The story focuses particularly on the tragedy of one family, the Maurrants, which is destroyed when the husband shoots and kills his wife and her lover. *Street Scene* won a Pulitzer Prize and was adapted into a musical in 1947 with lyrics by Langston Hughes and music by Kurt Weill.

Street, The Naturalistic novel by Ann PETRY, published in 1946, that was one of the first novels by an African-American woman to receive widespread critical acclaim. Set in Long Island, New York, in suburban Connecticut, and in Harlem, *The Street* is the story of intelligent, ambitious Lutie Johnson, who strives to make a better life for herself and her son despite a constant struggle with sexual brutality and racism.

Stuart Little Children's book by E.B. WHITE, published in 1945. The episodic story of the title character, a two-inch-tall boy who resembles a mouse, is noted for its understated humor, graceful wit, and ironic juxtaposition of fantasy and possibility.

Despite his diminutive stature—his family is of normal size—Stuart is a dashing, picaresque hero who is confident and courageous. His daring escapades include racing a toy boat in a Central Park pond, retrieving his mother's ring from a drain, and crawling inside a piano to fix the keys for his brother. He embarks on a quest to find his beloved Margalo, a little bird who is frightened away by the ferocious family cat, Snowbell.

Studs Lonigan Trilogy of novels by James T. FARRELL about life among lower-middle-class Irish Roman Catholics in Chicago during the first third of the 20th century. The trilogy consists of *Young Lonigan: A Boyhood in Chicago Streets*

(1932), *The Young Manhood of Studs Lonigan* (1934), and *Judgment Day* (1935).

As a boy, William Lonigan (always referred to as "Studs") makes a slight effort to rise above his squalid urban environment. However, the combination of his own personality, unwholesome neighborhood friends, a small-minded family, and his schooling and religious training all condemn him to the life of futility and dissipation that are his inheritance.

Suddenly Last Summer Drama in two acts by Tennessee WILLIAMS, published in 1958 and produced the same year under the title *Garden District*. The play concerns the voraciousness of violence; lobotomy, pederasty, and cannibalism are some of the subject matter. In the play, a self-involved, sadistic homosexual with an overprotective mother is eventually murdered on an island and eaten by cannibals.

Sula Novel by Toni MORRISON, published in 1973. It is the story of two black women friends and of their community of Medallion, Ohio. The community has been stunted and turned inward by the racism of the larger society. The rage and disordered lives of the townspeople are seen as a reaction to their stifled hopes. The novel follows the lives of Sula and Nel from childhood to maturity to death.

Sun Also Rises, The Novel by Ernest HEMINGWAY, published in 1926. In England the book's title is *Fiesta*. Set in the 1920s, the novel deals with a group of aimless expatriates in France and Spain. They are members of the cynical and disillusioned post-World War I Lost Generation, many of whom suffer psychological and physical wounds as a result of the war. Two of the novel's main characters, Lady Brett Ashley and Jake Barnes, typify this generation. Lady Brett drifts through a series of affairs despite her love for Jake, who has been rendered impotent by a war wound. Friendship, stoicism, and natural grace under pressure are offered as the values that matter in an otherwise amoral and often senseless world.

Sweeney Agonistes Poetic drama in two scenes by T.S. ELIOT, published in two parts in the *New Criterion* as "Fragment of a Prologue" (October 1926) and "Fragment of an Agon" (January 1927), and together in book form as *Sweeney Agonistes: Fragments of an Aristophanic Melodrama* (1932). Cast in a music-hall format with scenes interspersed with songs, *Sweeney Agonistes* comments on the meaninglessness of contemporary life and the pettiness and sinfulness of humanity.

Sweet Bird of Youth Drama in three acts by Tennessee WILLIAMS, published and produced in 1959 as an expanded version of Williams' one-act play *The Enemy: Time* (1959). An aging movie star, Princess Kosmonopolis, and her kept lover, Chance Wayne, return to Chance's Southern hometown to avoid what the princess assumes will be a negative reception of her latest movie. Chance is also a failure, having wasted his youth in the pursuit of fame. When the actress learns that her movie is in fact a success, she makes plans to leave and asks Chance to go with her. Chance has learned, however, that on a previous visit home he infected a local politician's daughter with a venereal disease. He decides to stay and face his punishment, which he knows will be castration.

Swimmer, The Short story by John CHEEVER, published in *The New Yorker* (July 18, 1964) and collected in *The Brigadier and the Golf Widow* (1964). A masterful blend of fantasy and reality, it chronicles a middle-aged man's gradual acceptance of the truth that he has avoided facing—that his life is in ruins.

Tales of the Jazz Age Second collection of short works by F. Scott FITZGERALD, published in 1922. Although the title of the collection alludes to the 1920s and the flapper era, all but two pieces were written before 1920.

The best-known of the tales is the critically acclaimed short story THE DIAMOND AS BIG AS THE RITZ. Also included are the novella "May Day," several sketches Fitzgerald had written in college, and two minor short plays. The collection was published to coincide with release, also in 1922, of Fitzgerald's novel *The Beautiful and Damned*.

tall tale Narrative that depicts the extravagantly exaggerated wild adventures of North American folk heroes.

The tall tale is essentially an oral form of entertainment; the audience appreciates the imaginative invention rather than the literal meaning of the tales. Associated with the lore of the American frontier, tall tales often explain the origins of lakes, mountains, and canyons; they are spun around such legendary heroes as Paul Bunyan, the giant lumberjack of the Pacific Northwest; Mike Fink, the rowdy Mississippi River keelboatman; and Davy Crockett, the backwoods Tennessee marksman. Other tall tales recount the superhuman exploits of Western cowboy heroes such as William F. Cody and Annie Oakley. Native to the New England region are the tales of Captain Stormalong, whose ship was driven by a hurricane across the Isthmus of Panama, digging the Panama Canal, and Johnny Appleseed, who planted apple orchards from the East Coast to the Western frontier. Washington Irving, in the *History of New York* (1809), and later Mark Twain, in *Life on the Mississippi* (1883), made literary use of the tall tale.

One of the few examples of the tall tale not native to the United States is found in the German collection *Baron Munchausen's Narratives of His Marvellous Travels and Campaigns in Russia* (1785) by the German scholar and adventurer R.E. Raspe.

Tamerlane Dramatic monologue by Edgar Allan POE, published in *Tamerlane and Other Poems* (1827) and revised in later editions of the book. Like much of Poe's early verse, "Tamerlane" shows the influence of the Romantic poets, in particular Lord Byron, with its themes of youthful loss, idealistic longing, and universal truths; it also contains an underlying sense of melancholy.

The narrator of the poem is a dying Turkic conqueror who makes his confession to a friar. He tells of his return to his native village and his dismay upon discovering that his beautiful childhood sweetheart is now dead.

Tanglewood Tales for Girls and Boys Collection of children's stories by Nathaniel HAWTHORNE, published in 1853. The book comprises six Greek myths that Hawthorne bowdlerized.

Written as a sequel to *A Wonder-Book for Girls and Boys* (1851), *Tanglewood Tales* is more serious than its lighthearted predecessor. The tales are "The Minotaur," "The Pygmies," "The Dragon's Teeth," "Circe's Palace," "The Pomegranate Seeds," and "The Golden Fleece." Because Hawthorne considered the original myths to be impure and inappropriate for his readership, he altered such stories as the seduction of Ariadne by Theseus and the abduction of Proserpine by Pluto.

Teahouse of the August Moon Comedy in three acts by American playwright John Patrick, produced in 1953. Patrick satirized American good intentions in this lighthearted examination of an attempt by the military forces to Americanize a foreign culture. It was his most famous play and was based on a novel of the same name by Vern Sneider. The play was awarded the Pulitzer Prize for drama in 1954.

In the play, Colonel Purdy sends Captain Fisby to indoctrinate Okinawans in the virtues of American democracy. Fisby "goes native"; soon the islanders, inspired by American entrepreneurial techniques, are selling huge quantities of potato brandy, their only marketable product. They build a teahouse instead of the Americans' proposed schoolhouse. The U.S. government hails Fisby's work as a stellar example of American capitalism.

Tell-Tale Heart, The Short gothic horror story by Edgar Allan POE, published in *The Pioneer* in 1843.

Poe's tale of murder and terror, told by a nameless homicidal madman, influenced later stream-of-consciousness fiction and helped secure the author's reputation as master of the macabre. The narrator relates with relish his murder and dismemberment of an old man. Poe's revelation of the narrator's dementia is a classic study in psychopathology. Before killing the old man, the narrator is maddened by what he believes to be his victim's loud heartbeats. After he commits the murder the police arrive, having been summoned by a neighbor who heard a scream. While he is talking to the police, the narrator believes he can hear the corpse's heart still beating, and he hysterically confesses his crime.

Tempest-Tost Novel by Robertson Davies, the first in his series of books known as the SALTERTON TRILOGY.

Tender Buttons Book of poems by Gertrude STEIN, first published in 1914 as *Tender Buttons: Objects, Food, Rooms.*

Heavily influenced by Cubism, the poetry in this work was considered by some critics to have taken abstraction and fragmentation past the limits of comprehensibility. The poems are dense and obscure and are devoid of conventional logic, syntax, or grammar. Rather than using conventional ways of conveying meaning and impressions, Stein juggles the sequence of the sounds of words to make verbal still-lifes.

Tender Is the Night Semiautobiographical novel by F. Scott FITZGERALD, published in 1934. It is the story of a psychiatrist who marries one of his patients; as she slowly recovers, she exhausts his vitality until he is, in Fitzgerald's words, *un homme épuisé* ("a used-up man").

At first a charming success, Dick Diver disintegrates into drunkenness, failure, and anonymity as his wife Nicole recovers her strength and independence. Fitzgerald's portrayal of the Divers' life of lassitude was a reflection of his years spent among the American expatriate community in France; his insight into Nicole's madness came from his observations of his wife Zelda's nervous breakdowns. Diver is said to be based on the author's friend Gerald Mur-

phy, but the character reflects much of Fitzgerald as well.

A revised version, which appeared in 1948, abandons the original edition's flashbacks and relates the story in chronological order.

Thanatopsis Poem by William Cullen BRYANT, published in the *North American Review* in 1817 and then revised for the author's *Poems* (1821). The poem, written when Bryant was 17, was his best-known work.

In its musings on a magnificent, omnipresent Nature, the poem, whose Greek title means "view of death," shows the influence of deism, and it in turn influenced the Transcendentalist ideas of Ralph Waldo Emerson and Henry David Thoreau. The poem brought Bryant early fame and established him as a major nature poet. Bryant's colloquial voice and celebration of nature were considered poetic innovations.

Their Eyes Were Watching God Novel by Zora Neale HURSTON, published in 1937. It is considered her finest book.

In lyrical prose influenced by folk tales that the author heard while assembling her anthology of African-American folklore *Mules and Men* (1935), Janie Crawford tells of her three marriages, her growth to self-reliance, and her identity as a black woman. Much of the dialogue conveys psychological insight through plain speech written in dialect.

While her first two husbands are domineering, Janie's third husband, Tea Cake, is easy-going and reluctantly willing to accept Janie as an equal. Hurston manages to characterize these three very different men without resorting to caricature in the first two instances or idealization in the third. Janie is one of few fictional heroines of the period who is not punished for her sensual nature.

them Novel by Joyce Carol OATES, published in 1969 and granted a National Book Award in 1970. Violent and explosive in both incident and tone, the work is set in urban Detroit from 1937 to 1967 and chronicles the efforts of the Wendell family to break away from their destructive, crime-ridden background. Critics praised the novel for its detailed social observation and its bitter indictment of American society.

Theophilus North Novel by Thornton WILDER, published in 1973. The last work published during Wilder's lifetime, it has striking parallels to his own life experiences and may be considered a fictionalized memoir of Wilder's idealized artistic and philosophical life.

A first-person reminiscence of life among the rich at Newport, R.I., during the summer of 1926, the novel is narrated by the elderly North from a distance of 50 years.

Thin Man, The Novel by Dashiell HAMMETT, published in 1934. Hammett's portrayal of sophisticated New York cafe society during Prohibition and his witty protagonists Nick and Nora Charles made this the most popular of his works, if not the most successful critically.

Nick Charles is a detective who has given up his profession to manage his wife Nora's fortune, which allows the couple to lead an easy life of nonstop parties and cocktails. Yet when the secretary of a former client is murdered, Nick is drawn in, urged on by Nora, who loves a mystery. The couple's playful banter, rather than the crime, forms the actual center of the book.

This Side of Paradise First novel by F. Scott FITZGERALD, published in 1920. Immature though it seems today, the work when it was published was considered a revelation of the new morality of the young in the early Jazz Age; and it made Fitzgerald famous. The novel's hero, Amory Blaine, is a handsome, spoiled young man who attends Princeton, becomes involved in literary activities, and has several ill-fated romances. A portrait of the Lost Generation, the novel addresses Fitzgerald's later theme of love distorted by social climbing and greed.

To a Waterfowl Lyric poem by William Cullen BRYANT, published in 1818 and collected in *Poems* (1821). It is written in alternately rhymed quatrains. At the end of a difficult day filled with uncertainty and self-doubt, the poet is comforted by the sight of a solitary waterfowl on the horizon and realizes that everything in nature is guided by a protective divine providence.

Tobacco Road Novel by Erskine CALDWELL, published in 1932. A tale of violence and sex among rural poor in the American South, the novel was highly controversial in its time. It is the story of Georgia sharecropper Jeeter Lester and his family, who are trapped by the bleak economic conditions of the Depression as well as by their own limited intelligence and destructive sexuality. Its tragic ending is almost foreordained by the characters' inability to change their lives. Caldwell's skillful use of dialect and his plain style made the book one of the best examples of literary naturalism in contemporary American fiction. The novel was adapted as a successful play in 1933.

To Be Young, Gifted, and Black Collection of writings, some previously unpublished, by playwright Lorraine HANSBERRY, produced in a stage adaptation Off-Broadway in 1969 and published in book form in 1970. Robert Nemiroff, Hansberry's literary executor and ex-husband, edited and published this collection after Hansberry's death in 1965. Subtitled *Lorraine Hansberry in Her Own Words*, the autobiographical work contains material from her letters, journals, essays, memoirs, and poetry, as well as scenes from her dramas.

To Build a Fire Short story by Jack LONDON, published in *Century Magazine* in 1908, later reprinted in the 1910 collection *Lost Face*. (An earlier draft had been published in 1902 in *Youth's Companion*.) London's widely anthologized masterpiece illustrates in graphic terms the futility of human efforts to conquer nature. Set in the Klondike in winter, the story concerns a man who ignores warnings and attempts to travel a great distance in the extreme cold. Although even his dog senses the folly of the journey, the man stubbornly continues to believe in his own infallibility. His doom is sealed when, after getting his feet wet, he is unable to build the crucial fire that might save his life. London's stark, unadorned prose is a powerful vehicle for his grim message.

To Have and Have Not Minor novel by Ernest HEMINGWAY, published in 1937. Set in and near Key West, Florida, the novel is about a cynical boat owner whose concern for his rum-soaked sidekick and love for a reckless woman lead him to risk everything to aid gunrunners in a noble cause.

To Kill a Mockingbird Novel by Harper LEE, published in 1960. Winner of the Pulitzer Prize in 1961, the novel was praised for its sensitive treatment of a child's awakening to racism and prejudice in the American South. It takes place in a small Alabama town in the 1930s and is told from the point of view of six-year-old Jean Louise ("Scout") Finch. She is the daughter of Atticus Finch, a white lawyer hired to defend Tom Robinson, a black man accused of raping a white woman. By observing the townspeople's reactions to the trial, Scout becomes aware of the hypocrisy and prejudice that exist in the adult world.

Tom Sawyer (*in full* The Adventures of Tom Sawyer) Novel by Mark TWAIN, published in 1876.

Tom Sawyer, an enduring narrative of youthful escapades, is perhaps Twain's best book for a juvenile audience. The setting is a small Mississippi River town in the 1830s, and the characters are the grownups and the children of the town. The book's nostalgic attitude and its wistful re-creation of pre-Civil War life are humorously spiced by its main character, Tom Sawyer. Rather than the preternaturally "model boy" of Sunday-school stories, Tom is mischievous and irresponsible but goodhearted.

Although Thomas Bailey Aldrich's *Story of a Bad Boy* was published seven years before it, *Tom Sawyer* and *Huckleberry Finn* changed the course of American writing and gave the first deeply felt vision of boyhood in juvenile literature.

Tortilla Flat Novel by John STEINBECK, published in 1935. The first of his novels to be set in the Monterey peninsula of California, this episodic, humorous tale of the adventures of a group of pleasure-loving Mexican-Americans contains some of Steinbeck's most interesting characters. The men drink, steal, chase women, make music, and dance until they are eventually undone by a climactic fire.

To the Finland Station Critical and historical study of European writers and theorists of socialism who set the stage for the Russian Revolution of 1917, by Edmund WILSON. It was published in book form in 1940 although much of the material had previously appeared in *The New Republic*.

The work discusses European socialism, anarchism, and various theories of revolution from their origins to their implementation. It presents ideas and writings of political theorists representing all aspects of socialist, anarchist, and what would later be known as communist thought, among them Jules Michelet, Henri de Saint-Simon, Robert Owen, Mikhail Bakunin, Anatole France, Karl Marx, Friedrich Engels, Leon Trotsky, and Vladimir Ilich Lenin—who arrived at Petrograd's (St. Petersburg's) Finland Station in 1917 to lead the Bolshevik revolution.

Town, The Novel by William FAULKNER, published in 1957. It is the second work in the Snopes family trilogy, which includes *The Hamlet* (1940) and *The Mansion* (1959). A dramatization of Faulkner's vision of the disintegration of the South after the Civil War, *The Town* relates through three narrators of varying reliability the story of Flem Snopes' rise to prominence in the fictional Yoknapatawpha County. Flem's coldly calculated vengeance on his wife, Eula, and her lover culminates in Eula's suicide and Flem's rise to power in Jefferson, the county seat. Because Flem longs for respect as well as money, he turns against the clan of shiftless Snopes cousins who have followed him to town and forces them to leave Jefferson. In his hunger for social validation, he denies his own origins, and the book ends with a hint that the cousins' revenge will follow.

Town, The Novel by Conrad RICHTER, published in 1950. The third book in a trilogy that includes *The Trees* and *The Fields*, *The Town* was awarded the Pulitzer Prize for fiction in 1951. The three books were published in a single volume as *The Awakening Land* in 1966.

The trilogy, which is set in the Ohio River valley in the late 18th- through mid-19th century, offers a realistic portrayal of frontier life as it chronicles the development of the area from wilderness. The changing landscape provides the background for the story of Sayward Luckett Wheeler, who embodies the strength and perseverance of the pioneer spirit. The books follow her life as she matures from a young girl to a wife and mother of many children to an old woman.

Tragic Muse, The Novel by Henry JAMES, published serially in *The Atlantic Monthly* from 1889 to 1890 and in book form in 1890. This study of the conflict between the demands of art and those of the "real world" is set in London and Paris in the 1880s. Nicholas Dormer, an Englishman, gives up a career in Parliament and marriage to a beautiful, wealthy woman to become a portrait painter. He is encouraged by his actress friend Miriam Rooth, the "tragic muse" of the title. Although by the end of the novel Nicholas has still not achieved his goal, James implies that he made the right decision in choosing to live at a higher level of consciousness, whether or not he achieves material success. Written when James himself was suffering setbacks in his career as a playwright, the novel reflects many of the author's concerns about personal sacrifice for the sake of art.

Trees, The Novel by Conrad Richter, published in 1940. It was the first novel in a trilogy published collectively as *The Awakening Land*. The other novels in the trilogy are *The Fields* and THE TOWN.

Troll Garden, The First short-story collection by Willa CATHER, published in 1905. Publication of the collection, which contains some of her best-known work, led to Cather's appointment as managing editor of *McClure's Magazine*, a New York monthly.

The stories are linked thematically by their depiction of characters who seek the realm of beauty and imagination but are constantly assaulted by the vulgar and brutal outside world. The story "The Sculptor's Funeral," originally published in *McClure's* in 1905, concerns the reactions of the townspeople in a prairie village when the body of a famous sculptor is brought back to be buried there. The book's climactic story, now considered an American classic, is PAUL'S CASE.

Tropic of Cancer Autobiographical novel by Henry MILLER, published in France in 1934 and, because of censorship, not published in the United States until 1961. Written in the tradition of Walt Whitman and Henry David Thoreau, it is a monologue about Miller's picaresque life as an impoverished expatriate in France in the early 1930s. The book benefited from favorable early critical response and gained popular notoriety later as a result of obscenity trials.

Containing little plot on narrative, *Tropic of Cancer* is made up of anecdotes, philosophizing, and rambling celebrations of life. Despite his poverty, Miller extols his manner of living, unfettered as it is by moral and social conventions. He lives largely off the resources of his friends. In exuberant and sometimes preposterous passages of unusual sexual frankness, he chronicles numerous encounters with women, including his mysterious wife Mona, as he pursues a fascination with female sexuality.

Tropic of Cancer was the first of an autobiographical trilogy, followed by *Black Spring* (1936) and *Tropic of Capricorn* (1939).

True West Drama in two acts by Sam SHEPARD, produced in 1980 and published in 1981. The play concerns the struggle for power between two brothers—Lee, a drifter and petty thief, and Austin, a successful screenwriter—while they collaborate on a screenplay in their mother's southern California home. This savage and blackly humorous version of the Cain and Abel story also satirizes the modern West's exploitation of the romanticized cowboys-and-Indians West of American mythology.

Trumpet of the Swan, The Novel by E.B. WHITE, published in 1970. The book is considered a classic of children's literature. White's version of the ugly duckling story involves a mute swan named Louis who becomes a famous jazz trumpet player to compensate for his lack of a natural voice. Aided by his father, who steals a trumpet for him, and by Sam Beaver, an 11-year-old human friend, Louis is able to attract a mate and eventually to return to the wilderness.

Turn of the Screw, The Novella by Henry JAMES, published serially in *Collier's Weekly* in 1898 and published in book form later that year. One of the world's most famous ghost stories, the tale is told mostly through the journal of a governess and depicts her struggle to save her two young charges from the demonic influence of the eerie apparitions of two former servants in the household. The story inspired critical debate over the question of the "reality" of the ghosts and of James's intentions. James himself, in his preface to volume XII of *The Novels and Tales of Henry James*, called the tale a "fable" and said that he did not specify details of the ghosts' evil deeds because he wanted readers to supply their own vision of terror.

Twice-Told Tales Collection of previously published short stories by Nathaniel HAWTHORNE, issued in 1837 and revised and expanded in 1842. The 1837 edition consisted of 18 stories; the 1842 enlargement brought the total to 39.

Stories such as "The Gray Champion," "The May-pole of Marymount," "The Gentle Boy," and "Endicott and the Red Cross" reflect Hawthorne's moral insight and his lifelong interest in the history of Puritan New England. Among other tales are the allegorical "The Ambitious Guest"; "The Minister's Black Veil" and "Wakefield," psychological explorations of sin and guilt; "Howe's Masquerade," a ghostly leg-

end set in Boston just prior to the American Revolution; and "Dr. Heidegger's Experiment," an allegorical search for the Fountain of Youth.

Typee (*in full* Typee: A Peep at Polynesian Life) First novel by Herman MELVILLE, published in London in 1846 as *Narrative of a Four Months' Residence Among the Natives of a Valley of the Marquesas Islands*. Initially regarded as a travel narrative, the novel is based on Melville's month-long adventure as a guest-captive of the Typee people, natives of the Marquesas Islands in present-day French Polynesia, following his desertion from the whaler *Acushnet* along with shipmate Richard Tobias Greene in July 1842. Melville injured his leg in the escape from the *Acushnet*, and Greene was allowed to leave the Typees to find Melville a doctor, but he became sidetracked and never returned. Shortly thereafter, Melville was rescued by the Australian whaler *Lucy Ann*.

Typee is an anthropological study of an exotic and savage native culture that both impressed and frightened Melville (allegedly the Typees were cannibals). The protagonist of the novel, Tom (also known as Tommo), spends four months with his companion Toby in a Polynesian island paradise as prisoners of the Typees. Tom's opportunities for escape are limited by his disease-swollen leg and by his personal jailer-servant, the devoted Kory-Kory. He befriends several natives, notably the beautiful Fayaway. Tom is intrigued by the Typees' social and religious customs, but he is also disgusted by their indolence and cannibalism. Ultimately, he chooses civilization over idyllic island life.

Ulalume Poem by Edgar Allan POE, published in the magazine *American Review* in December 1847. It is about a man who wanders unconsciously to his lover's tomb, and it is noted for its gothic imagery and hypnotic rhythm.

In "Ulalume" the narrator, with the nighttime stars as his guide, wanders through an eerie woodland. His dreamy walk abruptly concludes at a tomb, which he recognizes with anguish as belonging to his lover, Ulalume. He had buried her there exactly one year before. Regarded by Poe as a ballad, this lyrical poem is written in anapestic trimeter with consistent end rhyme. It originally comprised 10 stanzas, but it often is printed without the final stanza.

Uncle Tom's Cabin (*in full* Uncle Tom's Cabin; or, Life Among the Lowly) Novel by Harriet Beecher STOWE, published in serialized form in 1851–52 and in book form in 1852. Dramatizing the plight of slaves, the novel had so great an impact that it is sometimes cited as one of the causes of the American Civil War.

While being transported by boat to a slave auction in New Orleans, the protagonist, a saintly, dignified slave named Uncle Tom, saves the life of Little Eva St. Clare, whose grateful father then purchases Tom. Little Eva and Tom soon become great friends. Always frail, Eva's health begins to decline rapidly, and on her deathbed she asks her father to free all his slaves. Mr. St. Clare makes plans to manumit his slaves but is killed before he can do so, and the brutal Simon Legree, Tom's new owner, has Tom whipped to death after he refuses to divulge the whereabouts of certain runaway slaves.

The dramatic adaptation of *Uncle Tom's Cabin* played to capacity audiences and was a staple of touring companies through the rest of the 19th century and into the 20th century.

Uncle Tom's Children Collection of four novellas by Richard WRIGHT, published in 1938. The collection, Wright's first published book, was awarded the 1938 *Story* magazine prize for the best book written by anyone involved in the WPA Federal Writers' Project.

Set in the American Deep South, each novella concerns an aspect of the lives of black people and explores their resistance to white racism and oppression. The stories are "Big Boy Leaves Home," "Down by the Riverside," "Long Black Song," and "Fire and Cloud." Thematically and stylistically they form a consistent whole.

In 1940 an enlarged edition of *Uncle Tom's Children* was published. Subtitled "Five Long Stories," it also contained a nonfiction essay, "The Ethics of Living Jim Crow," and a polemical short story, "Bright and Morning Star"; both additions were thought by critics to have damaged the literary integrity of the book.

U.S.A. Trilogy by John DOS PASSOS, comprising *The 42nd Parallel* (1930), covering the period from 1900 up to World War I; *1919* (1932), dealing with the war and the critical year of the Treaty of Versailles; and *The Big Money* (1936), which moves from the boom of the '20s to the bust of the '30s. Dos Passos reinforces the histories of his fictional characters with interpolated montages of newspaper headlines and popular songs. He also includes biographies that range from representative members of the establishment such as Henry Ford and Thomas Edison to such figures as labor organizer and socialist Eugene V. Debs and economist and social scientist Thorstein Veblen.

V Novel by Thomas PYNCHON, published in 1963 and granted the Faulkner Foundation award for a first novel. The complex and frequently whimsical narrative recounts the search of Benny Profane and Herbert Stencil for the mysterious and elusive V, a woman who surfaces in various incarnations and guises at crucial moments in the history of late 19th- and early 20th-century Europe.

Violent Bear It Away, The Southern gothic novel by Flannery O'CONNOR, published in 1960. It is the story of a young man's struggle to live with the burden of being a prophet and is representative of the author's fierce, powerful, and original vision of Christianity.

Young Francis Marion Tarwater has been reared by his fanatical, tyrannical grand-uncle Mason to be a prophet; when Mason dies, however, Francis rejects his mission and consequently suffers tortures of doubt and indecision. Although for a time he weighs the value of humanistic rationalism (as exemplified by his uncle George Rayber), Tarwater unexpectedly experiences a vision and comes to accept his calling.

Virginian, The (*in full* The Virginian: A Horseman of the Plains) Western novel by Owen WISTER, published in 1902. Its great popularity contributed to enshrining the American cowboy as an icon of American popular culture and a folk ideal.

A chivalrous and courageous but mysterious cowboy known only as "the Virginian" works as foreman of a cattle ranch in the Wyoming territory during the late 1870s and 1880s. The gunplay and violence that are inherent in his frontier code of behavior threaten the Virginian's relationship with a pretty schoolteacher from the East. The novel's climactic gun duel is the first "showdown" in fiction. It also introduced the now-classic phrase that the Virginian utters when pushed to the limit by an adversary, "When you call me that, *smile!*"

Vision of Sir Launfal, The Long verse parable by James Russell LOWELL, published in 1848. Lowell, who was influenced by Alfred, Lord Tennyson and Thomas Malory, offers his version of the Grail story in this tale of a knight who decides not to take a journey in search of the Holy Grail after he learns, during the course of a long dream, that the real meaning of the Grail is charity. The poem is written in iambic tetrameter and is divided into two parts, each with a prelude. Although set in the medieval era, the poem contains moving descriptions of the American landscape.

Visit from St. Nicholas, A *also called* The Night Before Christmas. Narrative poem by Clement Clarke MOORE, written for the enjoyment of Moore's own children for the Christmas of 1822 and first published anonymously in the *Troy* (N.Y.) *Sentinel* on Dec. 23, 1823. It was acknowledged as Moore's work when it was included in his collection entitled *Poems* (1844). The poem became an enduring part of Christmas tradition and because of its wide popularity, both Nicholas, the patron saint of Christmas, and the mythic American Santa Claus were permanently linked with the holiday.

Waiting for Lefty One-act play by Clifford ODETS, published and produced in 1935. One of the first examples of proletarian drama, the play takes place during the Depression, in a meeting hall of the taxi drivers' union. The union members are waiting for their representative, Lefty, to arrive so that they can vote on a strike. In a series of six vignettes, various drivers make a plea to strike, relating the stories of their lives as justification for their decision. Odets placed actors representing members of the union in the audience to increase audience involvement in the play.

Walden (*in full* Walden; or, Life in the Woods) Series of 18 essays by Henry David THOREAU, published in 1854. An important contribution to New England Transcendentalism, the book was a record of Thoreau's experiment in simple living on the northern shore of Walden Pond in eastern Massachusetts (1845–47). *Walden* is viewed not only as a philosophical treatise on labor, leisure, self-reliance, and individualism, but also as an influential piece of nature writing. It is considered Thoreau's masterwork.

Relatively neglected during Thoreau's lifetime, *Walden* achieved tremendous popularity in the 20th century. The physical act of living day by day at Walden Pond is what gave the book authority, while Thoreau's command of a clear, straightforward, but elegant style helped raise it to the level of a literary classic.

Walk on the Wild Side, A Novel by Nelson ALGREN, published in 1956. The book is a reworking of his earlier novel *Somebody in Boots* (1935). Dove Linkhorn (Cass McKay from the earlier book), a drifter in Depression-era New Orleans, gets involved with prostitutes, pimps, and con men and eventually ends up isolated and hopeless after he has been blinded by a man whose girl he tried to steal. Written with black humor in Algren's characteristic tough-guy style, the novel has been called an erotic epic of bohemianism.

Wall, The Novel by John HERSEY, published in 1950. Based on historical fact but using fictional characters and fictional diary entries, the work presents the background of the valiant but doomed uprising of Jews in the Warsaw ghetto against the Nazis.

The Wall is a powerful presentation, in human terms, of the tragedy of the annihilation of European Jews. The novel relates the lives and actions of many different characters against the background of the Holocaust.

Wapshot Chronicle, The Novel by John CHEEVER, published in 1957 and granted a National Book Award in 1958. Based in part on Cheever's adolescence in New England, the novel takes place in a small Massachusetts fishing village and relates the breakdown of both the Wapshot family and the town. Part One focuses on Leander, a gentle ferryboat operator harried by his tyrannical wife and his eccentric sister; he eventually swims out to sea and never returns. Part Two chronicles the disastrous lives of Leander's sons, Coverly and Moses. Told in a comic rather than a tragic vein, the novel uses experimental prose techniques to convey a nostalgic vision of a lost world. A sequel, *The Wapshot Scandal*, was published in 1964.

Washington Square Short novel by Henry JAMES, published in 1880 and praised for its depiction of the complicated relationship between a stubborn father and his daughter.

The novel's main character, Catherine Sloper, lives with her widowed aunt and her physician father in New York City's fashionable Washington Square district. A plain, rather stolid young woman, Catherine is a disappointment to her father. She is courted by Morris Townsend, who is interested only in her potential inheritance. When her father threatens to disinherit her if she marries the fortune hunter, Townsend abandons her. Many years later, after her father's death, Townsend reappears and attempts to renew his suit. Catherine rejects him and lives on as a confirmed spinster in her Washington Square house.

Waste Land, The Long poem by T.S. ELIOT, published in 1922, first in London in *The Criterion*

(October), next in New York City in *The Dial* (November), and finally in book form, with footnotes by Eliot. The 433-line, five-part poem was dedicated to fellow poet Ezra Pound, who helped condense the original manuscript to nearly half its size. It was one of the most influential works of the 20th century.

The Waste Land expresses with great power the disillusionment and disgust of the period after World War I. In a series of fragmentary vignettes, loosely linked by the legend of the search for the Grail, it portrays a sterile world of panicky fears and barren lusts, and of human beings waiting for some sign or promise of redemption. The depiction of spiritual emptiness in the secularized city—the decay of *urbs aeterna* (the "eternal city")—is not a simple contrast of the heroic past with the degraded present; it is rather a timeless, simultaneous awareness of moral grandeur and moral evil.

The poem initially met with controversy as its complex and erudite style was alternately denounced for its obscurity and praised for its modernism.

Watch on the Rhine Drama in three acts by Lillian HELLMAN, published and produced in 1941. Performed just eight months before the United States entered World War II, Hellman's play exposed the dangers of fascism in America, asserting that tyranny can also be battled on the home front. The play is set in 1940 in the Washington, D.C., home of the wealthy widow Fanny Farrelly, who is expecting the arrival of her daughter Sara, Sara's German husband Kurt, and their three children. A leader in the anti-Nazi resistance movement, Kurt has been forced to flee Europe. Count Teck de Brancovis, a Romanian houseguest in the Farrelly home and a Nazi supporter, discovers Kurt's identity and threatens to expose him to the German embassy. From a comedy of manners the play gradually evolves into a tense thriller.

Web and the Rock, The Novel by Thomas WOLFE, published posthumously in 1939 after being reworked by editor Edward Aswell from a larger manuscript. Like Wolfe's other novels, *The Web and the Rock* is an autobiographical account of a successful young writer from North Carolina living in New York City in the early 20th century.

The main character, George Webber, bears many similarities to Eugene Gant, the soul-searching protagonist of Wolfe's earlier novels *Look Homeward, Angel* (1929) and *Of Time and The River* (1935). Esther Jack, who first appeared in *Of Time and the River,* is an urban sophisticate who becomes Webber's lover and muse. *The Web and the Rock* has been criticized for its inconsistent style but praised for its poetry and passion. Its sequel is *You Can't Go Home Again* (1940).

Week on the Concord and Merrimack Rivers, A Autobiographical narrative by Henry David THOREAU, published in 1849. This Transcendental work is a philosophical treatise couched as a travel adventure.

Written mainly during the two years he lived in a cabin on the shores of Walden Pond in Massachusetts (1845–47), *A Week on the Concord and Merrimack Rivers* chronicles a boating trip Thoreau took with his brother John to the White Mountains in New Hampshire in 1839. Comprising both prose and poetry, the book includes romantic descriptions of the natural environment and thoughtful digressions on philosophy, literature, and history. Like *Walden* (1854), Thoreau's masterwork, *A Week on the Concord and Merrimack Rivers* achieved fame only after the author's death.

What Maisie Knew Novel by Henry JAMES, published in 1897.

Set mostly in England, the novel is related from the perspective of Maisie, a preadolescent whose parents were divorced when she was six years old and who spends six months of the year with each parent. The only emotional constant in Maisie's life is Mrs. Wix, a motherly old governess. Maisie's parents marry other partners, but neither marriage succeeds. Her new stepparents are attracted to each other, divorce Maisie's par-

ents, and marry. Maisie knows intuitively that she cannot depend on the adults in her life, and she chooses to live with Mrs. Wix, on whose unconditional love she can depend.

What's Bred in the Bone Novel by Robertson DAVIES, published in 1985 as the second volume of his so-called Cornish trilogy. The other books in the trilogy are *The Rebel Angels* (1981) and *The Lyre of Orpheus* (1988). Two angels narrate this story about the mysterious life of a famous art collector named Francis Cornish.

When Lilacs Last in the Dooryard Bloom'd Elegy in free verse by Walt WHITMAN mourning the death of President Abraham Lincoln. First published in Whitman's collection *Sequel to Drum-Taps* (1865) and later included in the 1867 edition of *Leaves of Grass*, the poem expresses revulsion at the assassination of the country's first "great martyr chief." Implicitly, it also condemns the brutality and waste of war. This elegy is notable for its use of pathetic fallacy in attributing grief to nature. Also included in the 1867 edition of *Leaves of Grass* was a second elegy Whitman wrote for Lincoln, "O Captain! My Captain!"

White Fang Novel by Jack LONDON, published in 1906. The novel was intended as a companion piece to *The Call of the Wild* (1903), in which a domesticated dog reverts to a wild state. *White Fang* is the story of a wolf dog that is rescued from its brutal owner and gradually becomes domesticated through the patience and kindness of its new owner, Weedon Scott. White Fang eventually defends Scott's father from attack by an escaped convict.

White-Jacket Novel by Herman MELVILLE, published in 1850. Based on the author's experiences in 1834–44 as an ordinary seaman aboard the U.S. frigate *United States*, the critically acclaimed novel won political support for its stand against the use of flogging as corporal punishment aboard naval vessels. It is not known if *White-Jacket* was directly responsible for the cessation of flogging; however, members of

Congress received copies of the novel during the Congressional debate over the issue, and flogging in the U.S. Navy was abolished that year.

Subtitled *The World in a Man-of-War*, the novel depicts life aboard a typical frigate, the *Neversink*, and describes the tyrannies to which ship's officers subject ordinary seamen and the appalling conditions under which the seamen live.

Who's Afraid of Virginia Woolf? Play in three acts by Edward ALBEE, published and produced in 1962. The action takes place in the living room of a middle-aged couple, George and Martha, who have come home from a faculty party drunk and quarrelsome. When Nick, a young biology professor, and his strange wife Honey stop by for a nightcap, they are enlisted as fellow fighters, and the battle begins. A long night of malicious games, insults, humiliations, betrayals, painful confrontations, and savage witticisms ensues. The secrets of both couples are laid bare and illusions are viciously exposed. When, in a climactic moment, George decides to "kill" the son they have invented to compensate for their childlessness, George and Martha finally face the truth and, in a quiet ending to a noisy play, stand together against the world, sharing their sorrow.

Why I Live at the P.O. Short story by Eudora WELTY, first published in the *Atlantic Monthly* in 1941 and collected in *A Curtain of Green* (1941).

This comic monologue by Sister, a young woman in a small Mississippi town who has set up housekeeping in the post office to escape from her eccentric family, is a prime example of Southern gothic writing. As Sister's story of betrayal and injustice unfolds, the reader gradually becomes aware that Sister's view of the world is as strange as that of the various members of her family. The narrow-minded and hostile characters are portrayed as cartoonish grotesques; at the same time, however, Welty's accurate depiction of small town Southern life lends an air of uncomfortable realism, and her perfectly nuanced dramatic monologue gives the story a wickedly

funny air that has made it a classic of American literature.

Wide Net, The Short-story collection by Eudora WELTY, published in 1943. In the title story, a man quarrels with his pregnant wife, leaves the house, and descends into a mysterious underwater kingdom where he meets "The King of the Snakes" who forces him to confront the darker mysteries of nature. He returns to his wife better capable of living a meaningful, fulfilling life. This blend of domestic realism with mythology and ancient fertility tales is characteristic of the entire collection.

Wieland (*in full* Wieland, or The Transformation) Gothic novel by Charles Brockden BROWN, published in 1798. The story concerns Theodore Wieland, whose father has died by spontaneous combustion apparently for violating a vow to God. The younger Wieland, also a religious enthusiast, misguidedly assumes that a ventriloquist's utterances are supernatural in origin; driven insane, he acts upon the prompting of this "inner voice" and murders his wife and children. He is eventually driven to kill himself.

Wings of the Dove, The Novel by Henry JAMES, published in 1902. It explores one of James's favorite themes: the cultural clash between naive Americans and sophisticated, often decadent Europeans.

The story is set in London and Venice. Kate Croy is a Londoner who encourages her secret fiancé, Merton Densher, to woo and marry Milly Theale, a wealthy young American who is dying of a mysterious malady. Thus, Kate reasons, although Milly will die soon, she will at least be happily in love, Merton will inherit her fortune, and Kate and Merton can marry and be rich. Shortly after Milly learns of Merton's and Kate's motives, she dies, leaving Merton a legacy that he is too guilt-ridden to accept. Kate is unwilling to forgo the inheritance, and she and Merton part forever, their relationship destroyed by Milly's unwittingly prescient gift.

Wise Blood First novel by Flannery O'CONNOR,

published in 1952. This darkly comic and disturbing novel about religious beliefs was noted for its witty characterizations, ironic symbolism, and use of Southern dialect.

Wise Blood centers on Hazel Motes, a discharged serviceman who abandons his fundamentalist faith to become a preacher of antireligion in a Tennessee city, establishing the "Church Without Christ." Motes is a ludicrous and tragic hero who meets a collection of equally grotesque characters. One of his young followers, Enoch Emery, worships a museum mummy. Hoover Shoats is a competing evangelist who creates the "Holy Church of Christ Without Christ." Asa Hawks is an itinerant preacher who pretends to have blinded himself to show his faith in redemption.

Women of Brewster Place, The Novel by Gloria NAYLOR, published in 1982. It chronicles the communal strength of seven diverse black women who live in decaying rented houses on a walled-off street of an urban neighborhood.

As the middle-aged matriarch of the group, Mattie Michael is a source of comfort and strength. She recalls her past tragedies in flashbacks. Her close friend, Etta Mae Johnson, is a restless free spirit who repeatedly attaches herself to disappointing men. Embracing racial pride, idealistic Kiswana Browne initially disparages her mother's middle-class values but later accepts them. Mattie saves the long-suffering Ciel Turner from self-destruction after she barely endures a series of personal disasters. Kiswana helps Cora Lee, a young unmarried mother, realize that her many children should not be treated like dolls. Lorraine seeks social acceptance, unlike her outspoken lesbian lover, Theresa. When she is gang-raped, Lorraine is deranged by the attack and murders one of her only supporters, Ben, the kind janitor of Brewster Place. At the novel's end the women angrily demolish the wall that separates them from the rest of the city.

Wonderful One-Hoss Shay, The (*in full* The Deacon's Masterpiece, or The Wonderful "One-Hoss Shay") Poem by Oliver Wendell HOLMES, published in his "Breakfast-Table" column in *The Atlantic Monthly* (September 1858).

Often interpreted as a satire on the breakdown of Calvinism in America, the poem concerns a "one-hoss shay" (*i.e.*, one-horse chaise) constructed logically and with all parts of equal strength by a New England deacon. Though it is meant to last forever, the vehicle spontaneously falls apart 100 years after it was built.

World of Wonders Third of a series of novels by Robertson Davies known collectively as THE DEPTFORD TRILOGY.

Wound and the Bow, The Book of literary criticism by Edmund G. WILSON, published in 1941. Employing psychological and historical analysis, Wilson examines the childhood psychological traumas experienced by such writers as Charles Dickens, Ernest Hemingway, James Joyce, Rudyard Kipling, and Edith Wharton and the effects of those experiences on their writing.

The title of the book comes from a myth retold by Wilson in which an injured, foul-smelling Greek warrior who has been banished because of his odor is sought out by his fellow Greeks because they need his prowess with the magic bow given to him by Apollo in order to win the Trojan War.

Wrinkle in Time, A Juvenile novel by Madeleine L'ENGLE, published in 1962. It won a Newbery Medal in 1963.

Combining theology, fantasy, and science, it is the story of travel through space and time to battle a cosmic evil. With their neighbor Calvin O'Keefe, young Meg Murry and her brother Charles Wallace embark on a cosmic journey to find their lost father, a scientist studying time travel. Assisted by three eccentric women—Mrs. Whatsit, Mrs. Who, and Mrs. Which—the children travel to the planet Camazotz where they encounter a repressed society controlled by IT, a disembodied brain that represents evil. Among the themes of the work are the dangers of unthinking conformity and scientific irresponsibility and the saving power of love. The sequels are *A Wind in the Door* (1973), *A Swiftly Tilting Planet* (1978), and *Many Waters* (1986).

Yearling, The Novel by Marjorie Kinnan RAWLINGS, published in 1938 and awarded the Pulitzer Prize in 1939.

Set in the backwoods of northern Florida, the story concerns the relationship between 12-year-old Jody Baxter and Flag, the fawn he adopts. When the fawn cannot be stopped from eating the family's crops, Jody's father forces Jody to shoot Flag. This tragedy propels Jody into greater maturity and a better understanding of his parents' hardscrabble life.

Yellow Wallpaper, The Short story by Charlotte Perkins GILMAN, published in *New England Magazine* in May 1892 and in book form in 1899.

The Yellow Wallpaper, initially interpreted as a gothic horror tale, was an autobiographical account fictionalized in the first person. It describes the gradual emotional and intellectual deterioration of a young wife and mother who, apparently suffering from postpartum depression, undergoes a "rest cure," involving strict bed rest and a complete absence of mental stimulation, under the care of her male neurologist.

Yet Do I Marvel Sonnet by Countee CULLEN, published in the collection *Color* in 1925. Reminiscent of the Romantic sonnets of William Wordsworth and William Blake, the poem is concerned with racial identity and injustice.

The poet ponders the nature of God, stating "I do not doubt God is good, well-meaning, kind." While he accepts God's wisdom in most puzzling matters of life and death, he is confounded by the contradiction of his own plight in a racist society: "Yet do I marvel at this curious thing: / To make a poet black, and bid him sing!"

You Can't Go Home Again Novel by Thomas WOLFE, published posthumously in 1940 after heavy editing by Edward Aswell. This novel, like Wolfe's other works, is largely autobiographical, reflecting details of his life in the 1930s.

As the sequel to *The Web and the Rock* (1939), *You Can't Go Home Again* continues the story of George Webber, a thoughtful author in search of meaning in his personal life and in American society. Leaving New York City, he is dismayed at the social decay he finds on his travels to England, Germany, and his small hometown in the Carolinas. Nonetheless, he is optimistic about the future of the United States.

Young Goodman Brown Allegorical short story by Nathaniel Hawthorne, published in 1835 in *New England Magazine* and collected in MOSSES FROM AN OLD MANSE (1846). Considered an outstanding tale of witchcraft, it concerns a young Puritan who ventures into the forest to meet with a stranger. It soon becomes clear that he is approaching a witches' Sabbath; he views with horror prominent members of his community participating in the ceremonies. Ultimately Brown is led to a flaming altar where he sees his wife, Faith. He cries out to her to "resist" and suddenly finds himself alone among the trees. He returns home but loses forever his faith in goodness or piety.

Youth and the Bright Medusa Collection of eight short stories about artists and the arts by Willa CATHER, published in 1920. Four of the stories were reprinted from Cather's first published collection, *The Troll Garden* (1905).

The stories include "Flavia and Her Artists," in which an artist exploits a benefactor; "The Garden Lodge," about a woman who suppresses her artistic impulses in exchange for a well-ordered life; "A Wagner Matinée," in which a nephew witnesses his aunt's communion with music; and PAUL'S CASE, Cather's most famous short story. The remaining four stories—"Coming, Aphrodite!," "The Diamond Mine," "A Gold Slipper," and "Scandal"—all concern opera singers.

Zoo Story, The One-act play by Edward ALBEE, produced and published in 1959, about an isolated young man desperate to interact with other people.

As the play opens, Peter (a publishing executive who is reading in New York City's Central Park) is approached by a stranger named Jerry. Announcing "I've been to the zoo!" Jerry proceeds to probe deep into Peter's life. He relates details from his own life—his stay in a rooming house with a bizarre landlady and her repulsive dog and his unsuccessful attempt to poison the dog. Peter grows increasingly agitated by this encounter. Jerry becomes abusive, tosses Peter a knife, provokes him into a fight, and impales himself on the knife.

Groups, Movements and Periodicals

Accent (*in full* Accent: A Quarterly of New Literature) Literary magazine published from 1940 to 1960 at the University of Illinois. Founded by Kerker Quinn and Charles Shattuck, the journal evolved from an earlier version called *Direction* that Quinn put out in his undergraduate days. *Accent* published some of the best examples of contemporary writing by both new and established authors, including Wallace Stevens, Katherine Anne Porter, William Gass, James T. Farrell, Eudora Welty, Thomas Mann, Bertolt Brecht, and Richard Wright.

Algonquin Round Table *also called* The Round Table. Informal group of American literary men and women who met daily for lunch on weekdays at a large round table in the Algonquin Hotel in New York City during the 1920s and '30s. The Algonquin Round Table began meeting in 1919, and within a few years its participants included many of the best-known writers, journalists, and artists in New York City. Among them were Dorothy Parker, Alexander Woollcott, Heywood Broun, Robert Benchley, Robert Sherwood, George S. Kaufman, Franklin P. Adams, Marc Connelly, Harold Ross, Harpo Marx, Edna Ferber, and Russel Crouse. The Round Table became celebrated in the 1920s for its members' lively, witty conversation and urbane sophistication. After 1925, many of them were closely associated with *The New Yorker*, whose editorial offices were established on the same block. The last meeting of the Round Table took place in 1943.

American Academy of Arts and Letters *also called* (1904–92) The American Academy and Institute of Arts and Letters, *original name* National Institute of Arts and Letters. Organization founded 1898 whose stated purpose is to "foster, assist and sustain an interest" in literature, art, and music. The New York-based academy has 250 members.

The academy was the inspiration of H. Holbrook Curtis, a medical doctor, and Simeon E. Baldwin, a judge. After they had organized the original 250 members, they decided (perhaps with an eye to the Académie Française's 40 "Immortals") that they had not been exclusive enough; they renamed the 250-member body an institute and from among its members were elected the academy—an elite membership of 50. The first seven members, who were elected to the academy in 1904, were the writers William Dean Howells, Mark Twain, and Edmund C. Stedman, sculptor Augustus Saint-Gaudens, painter John LaFarge, composer Edward MacDowell, and historian-statesman John Hay. The first female member of the institute was Julia Ward Howe (author of "The Battle Hymn of the Republic"), who was elected to the institute in 1907 and to the academy in 1908. She was followed by Edith Wharton in 1926. In 1992 members voted to return to a single form of membership of 250, and the merger was announced in 1993. Membership in the academy is for life. One member, Wilhelm Diederich, was expelled in 1947 for using official stationery to write anti-Semitic letters.

Committees of the organization award to selected struggling artists any of several annual monetary gifts, including the Mildred and Harold Strauss Livings (to two distinguished prose writers for a period of five consecutive years).

American Mercury American monthly literary magazine known for its often satiric commentary on American life, politics, and customs. It was founded in 1924 by H.L. Mencken and George Jean Nathan.

Under the editorship of Mencken, the periodical fast gained a reputation for Mencken's vitriolic articles directed at the American public (the "booboisie") and for Nathan's excellent theatrical criticism. Its fiction and other articles were the work of the most distinguished American authors and often the sharpest satiric minds of the day. Later, the magazine developed a militant anticommunist stand and a strident right-wing tone.

American Poetry Review, The Literary periodical founded in 1972 in Philadelphia by Stephen Berg and Stephen Parker. Issued bimonthly in a news-paper tabloid format, *The APR* sought a mass-market readership for its high-quality contribu-tors and content. *The APR* offered an eclectic collection of serious poetry and prose by out-standing English-language writers and critics as well as works in translation from Europe, the Middle East, Africa, Latin America, and Asia. Contributors included Richard Wilbur, David Ig-natow, Allen Ginsberg, Denise Levertov, Tess Gallagher, Adrienne Rich, Marge Piercy, May Swenson, William Stafford, Ntozake Shange, John Updike, Isaac Bashevis Singer, Vladimir Nabokov, Elie Wiesel, Octavio Paz, Czesław Miłosz, and Roland Barthes.

American Renaissance *also called* New England Renaissance. Period from the 1830s roughly un-til the end of the American Civil War in which American literature, in the wake of the Romantic movement, came of age as an expression of a national spirit.

The literary scene of the period was domi-nated by a group of New England writers, the BRAHMINS, notably Henry Wadsworth Long-fellow, Oliver Wendell Holmes, and James Russell Lowell. They were aristocrats, steeped in foreign culture, active as professors at Harvard College, and interested in creating an American literature based on foreign models. Longfellow adapted European methods of storytelling and versifying to narrative poems dealing with American history; Holmes, in his occasional poems and his "Breakfast Table" series (1858–91), brought touches of urbanity and jocosity to polite literature; and Lowell put much of his homeland's outlook and values into verse, espe-cially in his satirical *Biglow Papers* (1848–67).

One of the most important influences in the period was that of TRANSCENDENTALISM. This movement, centered in the village of Concord, Mass., and including among its members Ralph Waldo Emerson, Henry David Thoreau, Bronson Alcott, George Ripley, and Margaret Fuller, con-tributed to the founding of a new national cul-

ture based on native elements. The Transcenden-talists advocated reforms in church, state, and society, fostering the rise of Free Religion and the abolition movement and the formation of various utopian communities, such as Brook Farm. The abolition movement was also bol-stered by other New England writers, including the Quaker poet John Greenleaf Whittier and the novelist Harriet Beecher Stowe.

Apart from the Transcendentalists, there emerged during this period great imaginative writers—Nathaniel Hawthorne, Herman Melville, and Walt Whitman—whose novels and poetry left a permanent imprint on American literature. Contemporary with these writers but outside the New England circle was the Southern genius Edgar Allan Poe, who later in the century had a strong impact on European literature.

Atlantic, The *also called* (1857–1932, 1971–81) The Atlantic Monthly. Monthly journal of litera-ture and opinion, founded in 1857 by Moses Dresser Phillips and published in Boston. One of the oldest and most respected of American re-views, *The Atlantic Monthly* has long been noted for the quality of its contents. Its long line of distinguished editors and authors included James Russell Lowell, Ralph Waldo Emerson, Henry Wadsworth Longfellow, and Oliver Wendell Holmes.

In the early 1920s, *The Atlantic Monthly* ex-panded its scope to political affairs, featuring articles by such figures as Theodore Roosevelt, Woodrow Wilson, and Booker T. Washington. The high quality of its literature and its literary criticism have preserved the magazine's reputa-tion as a lively literary periodical with a moder-ate worldview.

Beat movement American social and literary movement originating in the 1950s and centered in the bohemian artists' communities of San Francisco's North Beach, southern California's Venice West, and New York City's Greenwich Village. Its adherents, self-styled as "beat" (originally meaning "weary," but later also connoting a musical sense, a "beatific" spirituality, and other meanings) and derisively called "beatniks," expressed their alienation from conventional, or "square," society by adopting an almost uniform style of seedy dress, "cool"—detached, ironic—manners, and "hip" vocabulary borrowed from jazz musicians. Generally apolitical and indifferent to social problems, they advocated personal release, purification, and illumination through the heightened sensory awareness that might be induced by drugs, jazz, sex, or the disciplines of Zen Buddhism.

Beat poets—including Gregory CORSO, Lawrence FERLINGHETTI, Allen GINSBERG, Gary SNYDER, and Philip WHALEN—sought to liberate poetry from academic preciosity and bring it "back to the streets." Their verse was frequently chaotic and liberally sprinkled with obscenities but was sometimes, as in the case of Ginsberg's *Howl* (1956), ruggedly powerful and moving. Ginsberg and other major figures of the movement, such as the novelist Jack KEROUAC, advocated a type of free, unstructured composition in which the writer put down thoughts and feelings without plan or revision—to convey the immediacy of experience—an approach that led to the production of much undisciplined and incoherent verbiage on the part of their imitators. By about 1960, the Beat movement had paved the way for acceptance of other unorthodox and previously ignored writers, such as the BLACK MOUNTAIN POETS and the novelist William Burroughs.

black aesthetic movement *also called* black arts movement. Period of artistic and literary development among black Americans in the 1960s and early '70s. Based on the cultural politics of black nationalism, the movement sought to create a populist art form to promote the idea of black separatism. Many adherents viewed the artist as an activist responsible for the formation of racially separate publishing houses, theater troupes, and study groups. The literature of the movement, generally written in black English vernacular and confrontational in tone, addressed such issues as interracial tension, sociopolitical awareness, and the relevance of African history and culture to blacks in the United States.

Leading theorists of the black aesthetic movement included Houston A. Baker, Jr.; Henry Louis Gates, Jr.; Addison Gayle, Jr., editor of the anthology *The Black Aesthetic* (1971); Hoyt W. Fuller, editor of the journal *Negro Digest* (which became *Black World* in 1970); and LeRoi Jones and Larry Neal, editors of *Black Fire: An Anthology of Afro-American Writing* (1968). Jones, later known as Amiri BARAKA, wrote the critically acclaimed play *Dutchman* (1964) and founded the Black Arts Repertory Theatre in Harlem (1965). Haki R. MADHUBUTI, known as Don L. Lee until 1973, became one of the movement's most popular writers with the publication of *Think Black* (1967) and *Black Pride* (1968). Characterized by an acute self-awareness, the movement produced such autobiographical works as *The Autobiography of Malcolm X* (1965) by Alex Haley, *Soul On Ice* (1968) by Eldridge Cleaver, and *Angela Davis: An Autobiography* (1974). Other notable writers were Toni Morrison, Ishmael Reed, Ntozake Shange, Sonia Sanchez, Alice Walker, and June Jordan.

Black Mountain poets A loosely associated group of poets that formed an important part of the advance guard of American poetry in the 1950s. They published innovative yet disciplined poetry in the *Black Mountain Review* (1954–57), which became a leading forum of experimental verse. The group grew up around the poets Robert Creeley, Robert Duncan, and Charles Olson while they were teaching at Black Mountain College in North Carolina.

Turning away from the poetic tradition espoused by T.S. Eliot, the Black Mountain poets emulated the freer style of William Carlos Williams. Charles Olson's essay *Projective Verse* (1950) became their manifesto. Olson emphasized the creative process, in which the poet's energy is transferred through the poem to the reader. Inherent in this new poetry was the reliance upon decidedly American conversational language.

Much of the group's early work was published in the magazine *Origin* (1951–56). Dissatisfied with the lack of critical material in that magazine, Creeley and Olson established the *Black Mountain Review*. It featured the work of Williams and Duncan, as well as Paul Blackburn, Denise Levertov, Gary Snyder, and many others who later helped shape poetry in America.

black theater In the United States, dramatic movement encompassing plays written by, for, and about blacks. The minstrel shows of the early 19th century are believed by some to be the roots of black theater, but initially they were written by whites, acted by whites in blackface, and performed for white audiences. After the American Civil War, blacks began to perform in minstrel shows, and by the turn of the century they were producing black musicals, many of which were written, produced, and acted entirely by blacks. The first known play by an American black was James Brown's *King Shotaway* (1823). William Wells Brown's *Escape; or, A Leap for Freedom* (1858) was the first black play published, but the first real success of a black dramatist was Angelina W. Grimké's *Rachel* (1916).

Black theater flourished during the HARLEM RENAISSANCE of the 1920s and '30s. Experimental groups and black theater companies emerged in Chicago, New York City, and Washington, D.C. Garland Anderson's play *Appearances* (1925) was the first play of black authorship to be produced on Broadway, but black theater did not experience a Broadway hit until Langston Hughes's *Mulatto* (1935) won wide acclaim. In the late 1930s, black community theaters began to appear, and by 1940 black theater was firmly grounded in the American Negro Theater and the Negro Playwrights' Company.

After World War II black theater grew more progressive, more radical, and more militant, seeking to establish a mythology and symbolism apart from white culture. Councils were organized to abolish the use of racial stereotypes in theater and to integrate black playwrights into the mainstream. Lorraine Hansberry's *A Raisin in the Sun* (1959) and other successful black plays of the 1950s portrayed the difficulty blacks had in maintaining an identity in a society that degraded them.

The 1960s saw the emergence of a new black theater, angrier and more defiant than its predecessors, with LeRoi Jones (later Amiri Baraka) as its strongest proponent. He established the Black Arts Repertory Theatre in Harlem in 1965 and inspired playwright Ed Bullins and others seeking to create a strong "black aesthetic" in American theater. Another playwright of this era was Ntozake Shange.

In the 1970s several black musicals were widely produced. In the early 1980s Charles Fuller's *A Soldier's Play* won a Pulitzer Prize, an award later given also to the powerful and prolific dramatist August Wilson.

Brook Farm *in full* The Brook Farm Institute of Agriculture and Education. A utopian experiment in communal living that lasted from 1841 to 1847. The farm itself was located in West Roxbury, Mass., near Boston. It was organized and virtually directed by George Ripley, editor of *The Dial* (a critical literary monthly) and a leader in the Transcendental Club, an informal gathering of intellectuals of the Boston area.

Among the original shareholders in the project were Charles A. Dana and Nathaniel Hawthorne. Ralph Waldo Emerson, Bronson Alcott, Margaret Fuller, Elizabeth Peabody, and Orestes A. Brownson were among its interested visitors.

For a while the project seemed to prosper. But disaster struck when the members put all available funds into the construction of a large central building that burned to the ground as its completion was being celebrated. Though the colony struggled on for a while, the enterprise gradually failed; the land and buildings were sold in 1849.

Hawthorne's *The Blithedale Romance* (1852)

is a fictional treatment of some aspects of the Brook Farm setting.

Chicago literary renaissance The flourishing of literary activity in Chicago during the period from approximately 1912 to 1925. The leading writers of this renaissance—Theodore DREISER, Sherwood ANDERSON, Edgar Lee MASTERS, and Carl SANDBURG—realistically depicted the contemporary urban environment, condemning the loss of traditional rural values in the increasingly industrialized and materialistic American society. They mourned the failure of the romantic promise that hard work would automatically bring material and spiritual rewards. Most of these writers were originally from small Midwestern towns and were deeply affected by the regional writing of the 1890s. The renaissance also encompassed the revitalization of journalism as a literary medium; writers such as Floyd Dell, Anderson, Dreiser, and Sandburg all were associated at one time with Chicago newspapers.

The Little Theatre, established in Chicago in 1912 by Maurice Browne, became an important outlet for the creative talents of young playwrights. The Little Room, a literary group that included both artists and patrons of the arts, encouraged literary activity. *The Dial* magazine, established in 1880, grew to be a respected literary organ. Henry Blake Fuller and Robert Herrick, who belonged to the genteel tradition, wrote several novels that foreshadowed the later realistic novels of Dreiser and Anderson. Hamlin Garland, already famous for novels on the bleakness of rural life in the Midwest, was associated briefly with the Little Room.

The appearance of Dreiser's naturalistic novel *Sister Carrie* (1900), Masters' collection of poetic epitaphs entitled *Spoon River Anthology* (1915), Sandburg's *Chicago Poems* (1916), and Anderson's *Winesburg, Ohio* (1919) marked the height of the Chicago renaissance. Two Chicago literary magazines—POETRY: *A Magazine of Verse*, founded in 1912 by Harriet Monroe, and THE LITTLE REVIEW (1914–29), founded by Mar-

garet Anderson—published exciting new verse by such local poets as Vachel Lindsay, Masters, and Sandburg. Dell, a journalist associated with the *Friday Literary Review* (1909–11), the weekly literary supplement to the *Chicago Evening Post,* was the center of a vital literary circle that included Dreiser, Sherwood Anderson, Margaret Anderson, and Monroe.

Confederation group Canadian English-language poets of the late 19th century whose work expressed the national consciousness inspired by the Confederation of 1867. Their transcendental and romantic view of the Canadian landscape dominated Canadian poetry until the 20th century. The Confederation group is also called the Maple Tree school because of the love characteristically shown for that dominant feature of the Canadian landscape. The group includes four poets: Charles G.D. Roberts, whose *Orion, and Other Poems* (1880) heralded the movement; Bliss Carman, who wrote lyric poems on nature, love, and the open road; Archibald Lampman, known for his vivid descriptions of nature; and Duncan Campbell Scott, who composed ballads and dramas of the northern Ontario wilderness.

Contact Literary magazine founded in 1920 by American author Robert McAlmon, aided by poet William Carlos Williams. Devoted to avant-garde writing of the period, it led to McAlmon's important Contact Editions book-publishing enterprise.

Contact began in New York as a mimeographed magazine and relocated to Paris in 1921 following McAlmon's marriage to English author Bryher (Annie Winifred Ellerman). Four issues were published in 1920–21 and a fifth in 1923. Contributors included Kay Boyle, H.D., Marianne Moore, Ezra Pound, Wallace Stevens, and Glenway Wescott. Meanwhile, in 1922 McAlmon had himself published his short-story collection *A Hasty Bunch*. This, his contacts with fellow expatriate writers in Paris, and a large gift of money from his father-in-law led McAlmon to establish a book-publishing venture. Contact

Editions books began to appear in 1923. Over the years McAlmon issued works by himself and Bryher; Williams' *Spring and All*; Ernest Hemingway's first book; *The Making of Americans* by Gertrude Stein; and *Contact Collection of Contemporary Writers*, an anthology including works by James Joyce and Ford Madox Ford. Nathanael West's novel *The Dream Life of Balso Snell* (1931) was the last Contact book. Williams and West revived *Contact* magazine for three issues in the United States in 1932, publishing prose by S.J. Perelman, James T. Farrell, and McAlmon and poetry by E.E. Cummings and Louis Zukofsky.

Crisis, The (*in full* The Crisis: A Record of the Darker Races) Monthly magazine published by the National Association for the Advancement of Colored People (NAACP). It was founded in 1910 and, for its first 24 years, edited by W.E.B. DU BOIS; by the end of its first decade it had achieved a monthly circulation of 100,000 copies. In its pages, Du Bois displayed the evolution of his thought from his early, hopeful insistence on racial justice to his resigned call for black separatism.

The Crisis was an important medium for the young black writers of the Harlem Renaissance, especially from 1919 to 1926, when Jessie Redmon Fauset was its literary editor. The writers she discovered or encouraged included the poets Arna Bontemps, Langston Hughes, and Countee Cullen and the novelist-poet Jean Toomer. After Fauset's departure *The Crisis* was unable to sustain its high literary standards.

Dial, The Quarterly journal published between July 1840 and April 1844 and associated with the New England Transcendentalist movement. Edited first by Margaret Fuller and later by Ralph Waldo Emerson, *The Dial* printed poems and essays by Emerson, Fuller, Henry David Thoreau, and Bronson Alcott, among others. Although the magazine often suffered from undeveloped material and a lack of consensus about its purpose, it was an important vehicle for Transcendental philosophy. *See also* TRANSCENDENTALISM.

Dial, The Literary magazine founded in Chicago by Francis F. Browne and published from 1880 to 1929. It moved to New York City in 1918. Intended as a forum in which to carry on the tradition of the Transcendentalist journal of the same name, *The Dial* became famous for introducing some of the best new writing and artwork of the early 20th century. In its heyday it published works by Thomas Mann, T.S. Eliot, Sherwood Anderson, Djuna Barnes, D.H. Lawrence, and E.E. Cummings, among others. Line drawings by Henri de Toulouse-Lautrec, Pablo Picasso, and Marc Chagall also appeared in its pages. The prestigious succession of its editors included Conrad Aiken, Van Wyck Brooks, Scofield Thayer, and Marianne Moore.

Double Dealer, The American literary magazine founded in New Orleans, La., and published from January 1921 until May 1926. From July 1921 it was subtitled *A National Magazine from the South*.

The Double Dealer, sometimes rendered *The Double-Dealer*, was named after a William Congreve play. Enjoying the support of H.L. Mencken and Sherwood Anderson, it was the first magazine to publish the fiction of Ernest Hemingway (May 1922) and the second magazine to publish William Faulkner's verse (June 1922). It also helped launch the careers of Hart Crane, Thornton Wilder, Jean Toomer, and Kenneth Fearing. Among the other writers it published were Robert Penn Warren, Edmund Wilson, Amy Lowell, John Crowe Ransom, Richard Aldington, Hilda Doolittle (H.D.), Joseph Campbell, Mary Austin, and Ben Hecht.

Epoch American literary journal founded in 1947. *Epoch* published fiction and poetry of high caliber by unknown as well as established writers. Its first issue contained works by E.E. Cummings and John Ciardi. Subsequent issues included the writings of, among others, Hayden Carruth, David Ignatow, Anne Sexton, May Swenson, Diane Ackerman, William Kennedy, Leslie Fiedler, Ray Bradbury, Joyce Carol Oates, Philip Roth, Richard Farina, and Thomas Pynchon.

Beginning with its Spring 1956 issue, when publication was taken over by Cornell University, *Epoch* published two or three times yearly. Later issues were devoted in large measure to special topics.

Esquire American monthly magazine, founded in 1933 by Arnold Gingrich, that began production as an oversized magazine for men, featuring drawings of scantily clad young women. It later abandoned its titillating role but continued to cultivate the image of refined taste. In 1943 the U.S. postmaster general attempted to withdraw *Esquire*'s second-class mailing privileges (an economy generally essential to a magazine's survival) because he did not believe the magazine made a "special contribution to the public welfare." Gingrich and his associates eventually won their case in the U.S. Supreme Court.

Esquire was a pioneer in the use of unconventional topics and feature stories. As it began to publish the work of Thomas Wolfe, Ernest Hemingway, William Faulkner, John Steinbeck, Truman Capote, and Norman Mailer, the magazine's risqué image gradually receded. It provided an outlet for new writers of fiction and nonfiction, and its topical features, satiric humor, and excellent book, movie, and music reviews filled a void between literary and opinion periodicals in the American market.

Evergreen Review Literary magazine published from 1957 to 1973 in the United States. Its editor, Barney Rosset, developed the progressive periodical into a forum for radical expression of ideas on topics from sex to politics. The magazine was known for publishing erotic—some said pornographic—material. Some of the more noteworthy contributors to the magazine included Che Guevara, Vladimir Nabokov, Jack Kerouac, Allen Ginsberg, Samuel Beckett, Henry Miller, and E.E. Cummings.

Federal Theatre Project *see* WPA FEDERAL THEATRE PROJECT.

Federal Writers' Project *see* WPA FEDERAL WRITERS' PROJECT.

Fire!! Magazine that exerted a marked impact on the Harlem Renaissance of the 1920s and early '30s despite its demise after the first issue (November 1926).

The idea for the experimental, apolitical Negro literary journal was conceived in Washington, D.C., by poet Langston Hughes and writer and graphic artist Richard Nugent. The two, along with an editorial board comprising Zora Neale Hurston, Gwendolyn Bennett, John Davis, and Aaron Douglas, selected the brilliant young critic and novelist Wallace Henry Thurman to edit the publication. Thurman solicited art, poetry, fiction, drama, and essays from his editorial advisers, as well as from such leading figures of the New Negro movement as Countee Cullen and Arna Bontemps. Responses to the magazine ranged from minimal notice in the white press to heated contention among African-American critics. *See also* HARLEM RENAISSANCE.

Forverts *also called* Jewish Daily Forward. Yiddish-language newspaper founded in 1897 and published in New York City.

The newspaper was established by Abraham Cahan and the Jewish Socialist Press Federation as a civic aid and a unifying device for Jewish immigrants from Europe. It carried socialist-oriented columns on government and politics and covered subjects intended to familiarize readers with American culture. It also published short stories and novels in serial form, most notably those of Isaac Bashevis Singer.

At the height of its influence, the *Forverts* had a daily circulation of some 200,000 in several regional editions, but by the late 20th century readership was greatly reduced. In 1984 the paper changed from a daily to a weekly, and in 1990 the editors began publishing an English-language version entitled *Forward*.

Fugitive Any of a group of young poets and critics

formed shortly after World War I at Vanderbilt University in Nashville, Tenn. The group, led by the poet and critic John Crowe RANSOM, published a bimonthly magazine, *The Fugitive* (1922–25), edited by poet Allen Tate. Other important members of the group were Donald Davidson and Robert Penn Warren. Outstanding selections from the magazine were collected in the *Fugitive Anthology* (1928).

Acutely aware of their Southern heritage, the Fugitives advocated a form of literary regionalism. Many of the Fugitives went on to become leaders in the Agrarian movement of the 1930s, which sought to resist the inroads of industrialism by a return to the agricultural economy of the Old South. Their views were published as a symposium in *I'll Take My Stand: The South and the Agrarian Tradition* (1930).

Godey's Lady's Book A magazine that was one of the most successful and influential periodicals in the United States for much of the 19th century. Founded by Louis Antoine Godey in Philadelphia in 1830, *Godey's Lady's Book* was an important arbiter of fashion and etiquette. The magazine also published works by such American authors as Ralph Waldo Emerson, Henry Wadsworth Longfellow, Edgar Allan Poe, Nathaniel Hawthorne, and Harriet Beecher Stowe.

Edited by Godey until 1836, the magazine was then edited by Sarah Josepha Hale until 1877. In 1892, *Godey's* was moved to New York City and renamed *Godey's Magazine*. It published fiction by popular writers of the period until it ceased publication in 1898.

Group Theatre Company of stage craftsmen founded in 1931 in New York City by Harold Clurman, Cheryl Crawford, and Lee Strasberg, for the purpose of presenting American plays of social significance. The characteristic Group production was a social protest play with a leftist viewpoint. After its first trial production of Sergey Tretyakov's *Roar China*, the Group staged Paul Green's *House of Connelly*, a play of the decadent Old South as reflected by the disintegrating gentry class. The Group then followed with two anticapitalist plays, *1931* and *Success Story*. Financial and artistic success came two years later with the production of Sidney Kingsley's *Men in White*, which was awarded a Pulitzer Prize.

In 1935 the Group Theatre staged *Waiting for Lefty* by one of its actors, Clifford Odets. The play, suggested by a taxicab drivers' strike of the previous year, used flashback techniques and "plants" in the audience to create the illusion that the strikers' meeting was occurring spontaneously. The Group also staged Odets' *Awake and Sing!*, *Till the Day I Die*, *Paradise Lost*, and *Golden Boy*; other productions included Paul Green's *Johnny Johnson*, Irwin Shaw's *Bury the Dead*, Robert Ardrey's *Thunder Rock*, and William Saroyan's *My Heart's in the Highlands*. The Group was disbanded in 1941.

hard-boiled fiction Of or relating to a tough, unsentimental style of American crime writing characterized by impersonal, matter-of-fact presentation of naturalistic or violent themes or incidents, by a generally unemotional or stoic tone, and often by a total absence of explicit or implied moral judgments. Hard-boiled fiction uses graphic sex and violence, vivid but often sordid urban backgrounds, and fast-paced, slangy dialogue.

The genre was popularized by Dashiell HAMMETT, whose first truly hard-boiled story, "Fly Paper," appeared in the pulp magazine *Black Mask* in 1929. Combining his own experiences with the realistic influence of writers such as Ernest Hemingway and John Dos Passos, Hammett developed a distinctly American type of detective fiction that differed considerably from the more genteel English mystery story.

Hammett's innovations were incorporated in the hard-boiled melodramas of James M. Cain, particularly in such early works as *The Postman Always Rings Twice* (1934) and *Double Indemnity* (1936). Successors included Raymond

Chandler, with novels such as *The Big Sleep* (1939), *Farewell, My Lovely* (1940), and *The Little Sister* (1949), and Jim Thompson, in such works as *The Killer Inside Me* (1952), *Savage Night* (1953), and *Pop. 1280* (1964). Other important writers of the hard-boiled school were George Harmon Coxe (1901–84), author of such thrillers as *Murder with Pictures* (1935) and *Eye Witness* (1950), and W.R. Burnett (1899–1982), who wrote *Little Caesar* (1929) and *The Asphalt Jungle* (1949). Hard-boiled fiction ultimately degenerated into the extreme sensationalism and undisguised sadism of what *Ellery Queen's Mystery Magazine* called the "guts-gore-and-gals-school," as found in the works of Mickey Spillane, writer of such phenomenal best-sellers as *I, the Jury* (1947).

Harlem Renaissance *also called* New Negro Movement. Period of outstanding literary vigor and creativity that took place in the United States during the 1920s. The Harlem Renaissance altered the character of literature created by many black American writers, moving from quaint dialect works and conventional imitations of white writers to sophisticated explorations of black life and culture that revealed and stimulated a new confidence and racial pride. The movement was centered in the vast black ghetto of Harlem, in New York City.

One of the leading figures and chief interpreters of the period was Alain Locke, a teacher, writer, and philosopher. Another leading figure was James Weldon Johnson, author of the pioneering novel *Autobiography of an Ex-Coloured Man* (1912) and *God's Trombones* (1927), a collection of seven sermons in free verse. Johnson acted as mentor to many of the young black writers who formed the core of the Harlem group. Claude McKay, an immigrant from Jamaica, produced an impressive volume of verse, *Harlem Shadows* (1922), and a best-selling novel, *Home to Harlem* (1928), about a young black man's return from World War I. Countee Cullen helped bring more Harlem poets to public notice by editing *Caroling Dusk: An Anthology of Verse by Negro Poets* in 1927. Langston Hughes published his first collection of verse, *The Weary Blues*, in 1926, and his novel *Not Without Laughter* appeared in 1930. He also collaborated on a play (*Mule Bone*, 1931) with Zora Neale Hurston, another writer associated with the movement. Wallace Thurman and William Jourden Rapp collaborated on a popular play, *Harlem*, in 1929. Thurman, one of the most individualistic talents of the period, also wrote a satirical novel, *The Blacker the Berry* (1929), that ridiculed elements of the movement. Another notable writer was Arna Bontemps, whose novel *God Sends Sunday* (1931) is considered the final work of the Harlem Renaissance. The movement was accelerated by philanthropic grants and scholarships and was supported by white writers such as Carl Van Vechten.

Harper's Magazine Monthly magazine published in New York City, one of the oldest and most prestigious literary and opinion journals in the United States. It was founded in 1850 as *Harper's New Monthly*, a literary journal, by the printing and publishing firm of the Harper brothers. *Harper's* was the first American magazine extensively to use woodcut illustrations. It was a leader in publishing the writings of the most illustrious British and American authors, and before 1865 it had become the most successful periodical in the United States. In the late 1920s the periodical changed its editorial format to that of a forum on public affairs, balanced with short stories by contemporary writers. Expenses exceeded revenues in the late 1960s, and the magazine's economic problems worsened. Its certain closing in 1980 was averted by grants by a philanthropic organization, the MacArthur Foundation.

Hartford wit *also called* Connecticut wit. Any of a group of federalist poets centered in Hartford, Conn., who collaborated to produce a considerable body of political satire just after the American Revolution. Employing burlesque verse modeled upon Samuel Butler's *Hudibras* and

Alexander Pope's *The Dunciad*, the wits advocated a strong, conservative central government and attacked such proponents of democratic liberalism as Thomas Jefferson. Leaders of the group, all graduates of Yale College, were John Trumbull, Timothy Dwight, and Joel Barlow, who later turned apostate and espoused Jeffersonian democracy.

The works that the wits produced are generally more notable for patriotic fervor than for literary excellence. Their most important effort was a satirical mock epic entitled *The Anarchiad: A Poem on the Restoration of Chaos and Substantial Night* (1786–87), which attacks states slow to ratify the American Constitution.

Home Journal One of the earliest general-circulation magazines in the United States, founded in 1846 by Nathaniel Parker Willis and George P. Morris. Intended for readers in high society, the magazine was an attempt to provide both society news and intellectual stimulation. In its early years it published works by such American authors as Edgar Allan Poe, James Fenimore Cooper, and Washington Irving; among the transatlantic authors it introduced were Honoré de Balzac, Victor Hugo, Thomas Carlyle, and Thomas de Quincey. In 1901 the journal's name was changed to *Town and Country*, and its emphasis became largely the lifestyle of the wealthy.

Hound and Horn American quarterly of the arts cofounded and edited by Lincoln Kirstein. It was published from 1927 to 1934. Initially published at Harvard University, *Hound and Horn* became a widely inclusive American arts review by its third issue (1928), and it moved to New York in 1930. The philosophical perspective of the *Hound and Horn* fluctuated drastically, from humanism to Southern agrarianism to Marxism, but it continued to publish works by leading modern poets, writers, and critics, including its staff editors R.P. Blackmur and Yvor Winters.

Imagism A movement of American and English poets whose verse was characterized by concrete language and figures of speech, modern subject matter, freedom in the use of meter, and avoidance of romantic or mystical themes.

Imagism was a successor to the French Symbolist movement. The Imagist credo was formulated about 1912 by Ezra Pound—in conjunction with fellow poets Hilda Doolittle (H.D.), Richard Aldington, and F.S. Flint—and was inspired by the critical views of T.E. Hulme.

The Imagists wrote succinct verse of dry clarity and hard outline in which an exact visual image made a total poetic statement. In 1914 Pound turned to Vorticism, and Amy Lowell largely took over the spiritual leadership of the group. Among others who wrote Imagist poetry were John Gould Fletcher and Harriet Monroe. The movement influenced the poetry of Conrad Aiken, Marianne Moore, Wallace Stevens, D.H. Lawrence, and T.S. Eliot.

The four anthologies (*Des Imagistes*, 1914; *Some Imagists*, 1915, 1916, 1917), and the magazines *Poetry* (from 1912) and *The Egoist* (from 1914), in the United States and England, respectively, published the work of a dozen Imagist poets. *Compare* SYMBOLISM.

Jewish Daily Forward Yiddish-language newspaper better known by its Yiddish name, FORVERTS.

kayak American literary magazine founded in San Francisco in 1964 by poet George Hitchcock as a forum for surrealist, imagist, and political poems. The magazine, which eventually published short fiction and essays as well, was known for its irreverence and its openness to experimentation, including found poems (verses made from other printed matter such as flyers or discarded letters). Attention was directed especially to the nature of poetry itself, which was addressed in a number of poems and essays throughout the magazine's history. The magazine moved its headquarters to Santa Cruz, Calif., in 1970. The last issue was produced in 1984. Regular contributors included W.S. Merwin, Wendell Berry, Robert Bly, David Ignatow,

James Tate, Margaret Atwood, Raymond Carver, Carolyn Kizer, Charles Simic, and Sharon Olds.

Kenyon Review, The American intellectual serial founded in 1939 as a quarterly magazine of literary criticism by faculty members of Kenyon College, Gambier, Ohio. John Crowe RANSOM was its first editor. Until 1958, *The Kenyon Review* was closely identified with the New Criticism, and as such it soon became one of the most influential magazines of its kind in the country. It attracted writers of international literary reputation, including Allen Tate, Robert Penn Warren, and Mark Van Doren. The *Review* published criticism by Ransom, William Empson, Yvor Winters, I.A. Richards, and Cleanth Brooks and poetry by Marianne Moore, Stephen Spender, Wallace Stevens, John Berryman, and Dylan Thomas.

In 1960, when Robie Macauley assumed the editorship, the *Review* began to publish more fiction, though the emphasis remained on criticism. The magazine ceased publication in 1970 but was revived in 1979.

Knickerbocker school Group of writers active in and around New York City during the first half of the 19th century. Taking its name from Washington Irving's *A History of New York* "by Diedrich Knickerbocker" (1809), the group sought to promote a genuinely American national culture and establish New York City as its literary center. The most important members of the group were Irving, his friend the novelist J.K. Paulding, James Fenimore Cooper, and William Cullen Bryant. *The Knickerbocker Magazine* (1833–65), a literary monthly edited by Lewis G. and Willis G. Clark, though not an official organ of the group, published members' work.

Kulchur A review of contemporary arts, important for the vital nature of its writing and for its role as the representative of the avant-garde arts community in New York City. It was published in New York from spring 1960 to winter 1965–66 and was named for Ezra Pound's *Guide to Kulchur*. Unlike other avant-garde "little" magazines of its time, *Kulchur* concentrated on presenting criticism rather than fiction. Poetry, painting and sculpture, experimental film and theater, dance, jazz and contemporary classical music, sex, and politics were among the subjects that fell within its scope, and the 12th issue was devoted to writings on the subject of civil rights.

Ladies' Home Journal American monthly magazine, one of the oldest in the country and long the trendsetter among women's magazines. It was founded in 1883 as a women's supplement to the *Tribune and Farmer* (1879–85) of Cyrus H.K. Curtis. The *Journal* began independent publication in 1884 with a pious and demure editorial posture and a sentimental literary diet. Edward W. Bok became editor in 1889, and under him the *Journal* attracted great writers from Europe and the United States—including such individuals as W.D. Howells, Hamlin Garland, Mark Twain, Bret Harte, Rudyard Kipling, Sarah Orne Jewett, and Arthur Conan Doyle.

Little Review, The Avant-garde American literary magazine founded in Chicago by Margaret ANDERSON, published from 1914 to 1929. Despite minimal financial support and numerous fights with censors, *The Little Review* managed to be the most influential arts magazine of its time. Its contributors included T.S. Eliot, Wyndham Lewis, Gertrude Stein, William Carlos Williams, Ezra Pound, and Wallace Stevens, but the magazine is probably best known for its serialization of James Joyce's novel *Ulysses*.

The first issue, published in March of 1914, featured work by Vachel Lindsay and essays on feminism, Friedrich Nietzsche, and psychoanalysis. In the May 1914 issue Anderson extolled the ideas of anarchist Emma Goldman and called for the abolition of private property; her few financial backers then abandoned her. In 1916 Anderson's companion, artist Jane Heap, joined her as associate editor. Anderson and Heap moved to New York's Greenwich Village in 1917. It was Pound, who was the European editor, who brought *Ulysses* to the magazine. The serialization of *Ulysses* began in the March 1918 issue; over the next three years the U.S. Post Office burned entire press runs of four issues for alleged obscenity.

Financially strapped and demoralized by the tepid response to *Ulysses*, in 1921 Anderson and Heap began to publish *The Little Review* as a quarterly rather than a monthly. In 1922 Anderson turned over the editorship to Heap, who in 1927 relocated the then irregularly published magazine to Paris. With Anderson, she drafted a questionnaire mailed to dozens of artists and writers, including questions such as "What is your attitude toward art today?" More than 50 responded, including Sherwood Anderson, Edith Sitwell, Jean Cocteau, Marianne Moore, and Bernard Russell, and their replies made up the last issue of *The Little Review*.

little theater Movement in American theater to free dramatic forms and methods of production from the limitations of large commercial theaters by establishing small experimental centers of drama. The movement was influenced by the vital European theater of the late 19th century, especially the revolutionary theories of the German director Max Reinhardt, the designing concepts of Adolphe Appia and Edward Gordon Craig, and the staging experiments at such theaters as the Théâtre-Libre of Paris, the Freie Bühne in Berlin, and the Moscow Art Theater. Community playhouses such as the Toy Theatre in Boston, the Little Theatre in Chicago, and the Little Theatre, New York City, all founded in 1912, were centers of the experimental activity. The little theaters provided a valuable early opportunity for such playwrights as Eugene O'Neill, George S. Kaufman, Elmer Rice, Maxwell Anderson, and Robert E. Sherwood.

Living Newspaper Theatrical production consisting of dramatizations of current events, social problems, and controversial issues, with appropriate suggestions for improvement. The technique was used for propaganda in the U.S.S.R. after the Revolution of 1917. It became part of the Epic Theater tradition initiated by Erwin Piscator and Bertolt Brecht in Germany in the 1920s.

The Living Newspaper was initiated in the United States in 1935 as part of the WPA FEDERAL THEATRE PROJECT. One of its major supporters was dramatist Elmer Rice. Outstanding productions included *Triple-A Plowed Under*, dealing with the Supreme Court's invalidation of the Agricultural Adjustment Administration (AAA), and *One-Third of a Nation*, dramatizing the plight of the poor. Criticism of the Living Newspaper for alleged communist leanings contributed to the cancellation of the Federal Theatre Project in 1939.

Living Theatre, The Theatrical repertory company known for its innovative production of experimental drama, often on radical themes, and for its confrontations with tradition, authority, and audiences. It was formed in New York City in 1951 by Julian Beck and Judith Malina. The group struggled during the 1950s, producing plays by Gertrude Stein, Luigi Pirandello, Alfred Jarry, T.S. Eliot, Jean Cocteau, August Strindberg, and others. Its first big success came with its 1959 production of *The Connection*, Jack Gelber's drama about drug addiction.

Members of the troupe tangled with the federal government over their political (nonviolent and anarchial) views and failure to pay income taxes. Beck and Malina were jailed briefly, and The Living Theatre was closed.

In 1964 the company took up "voluntary exile" in Europe. Influenced by Oriental mysticism, Gestalt psychology, and an Artaudian desire to abolish the distinction between art and life, The Living Theatre moved toward deliberately shocking and confronting its audiences. In 1970 the troupe split into several groups and dispersed.

local color Style of writing marked by the presentation of the features and peculiarities of a particular locality and its inhabitants. The name is given especially to a type of American literature that in its most characteristic form made its appearance just after the Civil War.

The frontier novels of James Fenimore Cooper have been cited as precursors of the local-color story, as have the New York Dutch tales of Washington Irving. Set during the California gold rush, Bret Harte's "The Luck of Roaring Camp" (1868), with its use of miners' dialect and western background, is among the early local-color stories. Many authors first achieved success with vivid descriptions of their own localities: Mark Twain described Mississippi River life; Harriet Beecher Stowe, Rose Terry Cooke, and Sarah Orne Jewett wrote of New England; George Washington Cable, Joel Chandler Harris, and Kate Chopin described the Deep South; T.N. Page did the same for Virginia; Edward Eggleston wrote of Indiana frontier days; Charles E. Craddock told stories of the Tennessee mountaineers; and O. Henry chronicled both the Texas frontier and the streets of New York City.

Lost Generation In general, the post-World War I generation, but specifically a group of American writers who came of age during the war and established their literary reputations in the 1920s. The term stems from a remark made by Gertrude Stein to Ernest Hemingway, "You are all a lost generation." Hemingway used the comment as an epigraph to *The Sun Also Rises* (1926). The generation was "lost" in the sense that its inherited values could no longer operate in the postwar world and because of its spiritual alienation from a country that seemed to its members to be hopelessly provincial and emotionally barren. The term embraces Hemingway, F. Scott Fitzgerald, John Dos Passos, E.E. Cummings, Archibald MacLeish, and Hart Crane, among others. The last representative works of the era were Fitzgerald's *Tender Is the Night* (1934) and Dos Passos' *The Big Money* (1936).

Midwestern Regionalism American literary movement of the late 19th century that is characterized by the realistic depiction of Midwestern small-town and rural life. The movement was an early stage in the development of American realistic writing. E.W. Howe's *The Story of a Country Town* (1883) and Joseph Kirkland's *Zury* (1887) and *The McVeys* (1888) foreshadowed the stories and novels of Hamlin Garland, the foremost representative of Midwestern Regionalism. Garland's *Main-Travelled Roads* (1891) and *A Son of the Middle Border* (1917) are works that deal with the poverty and hardship of Midwestern rural life and that explode the myth of the pioneer idyll. Chicago was the focal point of Midwestern realist activity; Garland lived in the city for a time, as did such others as Theodore Dreiser, Edgar Lee Masters, and Sherwood Anderson.

Montreal group Coterie of poets who during the 1920s and '30s advocated a break with the traditional picturesque landscape poetry that had dominated Canadian poetry since the late 19th century. They encouraged an emulation of the realistic themes, metaphysical complexity, and techniques of the American and British poets Ezra Pound, T.S. Eliot, and W.H. Auden. Based in Montreal, then Canada's most cosmopolitan city, the group included A.M. Klein, A.J.M. Smith, Leo Kennedy, and Francis Reginald Scott, as well as two kindred spirits from Toronto, E.J. Pratt and Robert Finch. First brought together at McGill University in Montreal, the poets founded the *Canadian Mercury* (1928–29), a literary organ for young writers, and subsequently founded, edited, and wrote for a number of other influential journals, including the *McGill Fortnightly Review* and *Canadian Forum*.

muckraker Any of a group of American writers identified with pre-World War I reform and exposé literature. The name was pejorative when used by President Theodore Roosevelt in his speech of April 14, 1906; he borrowed a passage from John Bunyan's *Pilgrim's Progress*, which referred to the man with the muckrake who "could look no way but downwards." But "muckraker" also came to take on favorable connotations of social concern and courageous exposure of injustice.

New Criticism *also called* formalism. A type of literary criticism that developed in England and the United States after World War I. New Criticism focused intensively upon the language, imagery, and emotional or intellectual tensions in particular literary works in an attempt to explain their total formal aesthetic organization. New Critics insisted on the intrinsic value of a work of art and focused attention on the work alone as an independent unit of meaning; they were opposed to the critical practice of bringing historical or biographical data to bear on interpretation. To the New Critics, poetry was a special type of discourse, a means of communicating feeling and thought that could not be expressed in any other kind of language. These critics set out to define and formalize the qualities of poetic thought and language, with special emphasis on the connotative and associative values of words and on the multiple functions of figurative language—symbol, metaphor, and image—in the work.

The primary technique employed in New Criticism was analytic (or "close") reading of the text. Seminal works in the tradition were those of the English critics I.A. Richards (*Principles of Literary Criticism*, 1924) and William Empson (*Seven Types of Ambiguity*, 1930), as well as John Crowe Ransom's *The New Criticism* (1941), which loosely organized the principles of this basically linguistic approach to literature. Other figures associated with the movement included Robert Penn Warren, Cleanth Brooks, and Allen Tate.

New Humanism Critical movement in the United States between 1910 and 1930, based on the literary and social theories of the English Victorian poet and critic Matthew Arnold, who sought to recapture the moral quality of past civilizations. Reacting against the scientifically oriented philosophies of literary realism and naturalism, New Humanists argued that: (1) human beings are

unique among nature's creatures; (2) the essence of experience is fundamentally moral and ethical; and (3) the human will, although subject to genetic laws and shaped by the environment, is essentially free. Among the New Humanists were Paul Elmer More, Irving Babbitt, Norman Foerster, and Robert Shafer. By the 1930s the New Humanists had come to be regarded as cultural elitists and advocates of social and aesthetic conservatism, and their influence became negligible.

New Yorker, The American weekly magazine, famous for its varied literary fare and humor. It was founded in 1925 by Harold Ross, who was its editor until his death in 1951. *The New Yorker*'s initial focus was on New York City's amusements and social and cultural life, but the magazine gradually acquired a broader scope that encompassed literature, current affairs, and other topics. *The New Yorker* became renowned for its short fiction, essays, foreign reportage, and probing biographical studies, as well as its comic drawings and its detailed reviews of cinema, books, theater, and other arts.

Contributors to the magazine included S.J. Perelman, Robert Benchley, Ogden Nash, E.B. White, John O'Hara, John Hersey, Edmund Wilson, J.D. Salinger, John Updike, Rebecca West, and Dorothy Parker. Among its great cartoonists were Charles Addams, James Thurber (a writer as well), and Rea Irvin, the creator of Eustace Tilley, the early American dandy who is the magazine's trademark.

In 1985 *The New Yorker* was sold to the publisher Samuel I. Newhouse, Jr., this being the first time in its history that the magazine's ownership had changed hands.

New York Intellectuals A group of literary critics who were active from the late 1930s through the 1970s in New York City. Characterized by their rejection of bourgeois culture, their adherence to democratic socialism, and their espousal of modernism in literature, the critics were famous for book reviews and essays published in such journals as *The Nation*, *Commentary*, and *Dissent*. The moniker "New York Intellectuals" was coined by Irving Howe in his 1968 essay of the same name. Some of the leading figures in the movement were Lionel Trilling, Philip Rahv, and Alfred Kazin.

North American Review, The American magazine first published in 1815 that became one of the country's leading literary journals of the 19th and 20th centuries. Founded in Boston as *The North American Review and Miscellaneous Journal* (a title it kept until mid-1821), the magazine followed the model of established English and Scottish literary journals. The work of J.W. von Goethe and Friedrich von Schiller first became known to American readers in its pages. It later moved to New York City and became a national periodical, providing an impartial forum in which current public affairs could be discussed. Noted for its outstanding writing on social and political issues, the magazine featured the work of numerous distinguished authors, including Henry George, David Dudley Field, Wendell Phillips, Walt Whitman, William Gladstone, Oliver Wendell Holmes, and H.G. Wells. In 1935 the magazine was sold to Joseph Hilton Smyth, under whose ignominious editorship it ceased publication in 1940. It was resurrected in 1964.

Open Theatre Experimental United States theater company founded in 1963 in New York City by Peter Feldman and Joseph Chaikan. The group—made up of actors, playwrights, musicians, and choreographers—sought to explore the possibilities of uniting improvisation, pantomime, music, and dance in new dramatic productions. Playwrights worked closely with the entire troupe, and they generated communal works that usually addressed subjects of current political or social relevance.

The best-known Open Theatre productions were *The Serpent* (1969), written by Jean-Claude Van Itallie, and *Terminal* (1969–70), from a text by Susan Yankowitz. The Open Theatre disbanded in 1973.

Opportunity (*in full* Opportunity: A Journal of Negro Life) African-American magazine associated with the Harlem Renaissance and published from 1923 to 1949. The editor, Charles S. Johnson, aimed to give voice to black culture, hitherto neglected by mainstream American publishing. Johnson sponsored three literary contests to encourage young writers to submit their work. The 1925 winners included Zora Neale Hurston, Langston Hughes, and Countee Cullen. *Ebony and Topaz, A Collectanea* (1927) was an anthology of the best works published in the magazine. *See also* HARLEM RENAISSANCE.

Origin (*in full* Origin: A Quarterly for the Creative) American literary magazine largely devoted to poetry, published and edited by poet Cid Corman as a 64-page quarterly in several intermittent series. The first series, published from 1951 to 1957, included works by such classic modern poets as Wallace Stevens and William Carlos Williams; its primary focus was on such younger postwar poets as Denise Levertov, Robert Duncan, and, especially, Robert Creeley, Charles Olson, and Corman himself. *Origin*'s second series (1961–64) included works by Louis Zukofsky, Gary Snyder, and Michael McClure, and Douglas Woolf's short novel *John-Juan* appeared in the third series (1966–71). In addition, the magazine published translations of troubadour poetry, Chinese and Japanese poetry, and works by 20th-century European and Latin-American poets, including César Vallejo. Corman's anthology *The Gist of Origin* (1975) includes selected works from the magazine.

Others (*in full* Others: A Magazine of New Verse) American literary magazine founded by Alfred Kreymborg and published monthly from July 1915 to July 1919. Created in response to the conservatism of *Poetry*, the most notable of the little magazines, *Others* featured experimental poetry and, from December 1918, prose and artwork. Though the mainstream press received the magazine with hostility, its success as an outlet for modernism resulted in three anthologies and a short-lived theater troupe.

Individual issues of *Others* were devoted to such themes as women writers and writers in Chicago and in Latin America. Its contributors included T.S. Eliot, Mina Loy, Max Bodenheim, Amy Lowell, Wallace Stevens, Marianne Moore, Ezra Pound, Hilda Doolittle (H.D.), Carl Sandburg, Richard Aldington, Conrad Aiken, and Sherwood Anderson.

Overland Monthly Literary magazine published in San Francisco from 1868 to 1875 and from 1883 to 1935. This ambitious venture, edited for the first two and a half years by Bret Harte, was begun in an attempt to establish Western literature as a legitimate genre. Harte's local-color parables such as "The Luck of Roaring Camp" and "The Outcasts of Poker Flat" first appeared in its pages and solidified his reputation.

Partisan Review American literary quarterly founded by William Phillips and Philip Rahv in 1933 as a vehicle for the communist John Reed Club. It was published irregularly from 1934 to 1962 and quarterly thereafter. During its first years the magazine sought to represent the fight for intellectual and political freedom and asked for contributions by revolutionary writers. Over the years, however, the magazine became more oriented toward literature and art criticism. Works by W.H. Auden, Saul Bellow, Robert Lowell, Mary McCarthy, Denise Levertov, and Susan Sontag among others have been published in its pages.

Poetry (*in full* Poetry: A Magazine of Verse) American poetry magazine founded in Chicago in 1912 by Harriet MONROE, who also served for many years as the magazine's editor.

The first issue of *Poetry: A Magazine of Verse* appeared in October 1912. Because its inception coincided with the Midwestern cultural ferment later known as the CHICAGO LITERARY RENAISSANCE, it is often thought of particularly as the vehicle for the raw, original, local-color poetry of Carl Sandburg, Edgar Lee Masters, Vachel Lind-

say, and Sherwood Anderson, but it also championed new formalistic movements in verse. The poet and critic Ezra Pound was European correspondent. Imagism, impressionism, and vers libre were expounded in its pages. "The Love Song of J. Alfred Prufrock" by the then-unknown T.S. Eliot appeared in *Poetry* (1915), as did the experimental poems of Wallace Stevens, Marianne Moore, D.H. Lawrence, and William Carlos Williams. *Poetry* survived the withering of the Chicago literary renaissance and World Wars I and II. It remained a highly respected journal even after Monroe's sudden death in 1936.

Prairie Schooner, The *also called* (after 1956) Prairie Schooner. Quarterly literary magazine founded in 1927 by Lowry Charles Wimberly and associated with the University of Nebraska. At first the journal published only literature and criticism relevant to the Midwest, but it later adopted a broader, more national perspective, publishing authors such as Randall Jarrell, Robert Penn Warren, and Tillie Olsen. The magazine was responsible for establishing Willa Cather's reputation as a serious writer.

Provincetown Players Theatrical organization that began performing in 1915 in Provincetown, Mass., U.S. It was founded by a nontheatrical group of writers and artists whose common aim was the production of new and experimental plays. Among the original Provincetowners who staged the first plays in members' homes were Mary Heaton Vorse, George Cram Cook, Susan Glaspell, Hutchins Hapgood, Wilbur Steele, and Robert Edmond Jones.

The group, which took up residence in New York City's Greenwich Village in 1916, discovered and developed the work of such noted writers as Eugene O'Neill, Floyd Dell, Edna St. Vincent Millay, and Paul Green. The Provincetown Players flourished as a noncommercial theater until its demise in 1929.

Salmagundi (*in full* Salmagundi; or, The Whim-Whams and Opinions of Launcelot Langstaff, Esq., and Others) Popular American periodical consisting of pamphlets containing humorous and satiric essays and poems, published from 1807 to 1808 and from 1819 to 1820.

Salmagundi was originally published by William Irving, James Kirke Paulding, and Washington Irving, all writing under such pseudonyms as Anthony Evergreen, Jeremy Cockloft the Younger, Will Wizard, Pindar Cockloft, Esq., and Mustapha Rub-a-Dub Keli Khan (a Tripolitan prisoner of war observing American society from his cell in New York). The 20 pamphlets (Jan. 24, 1807, to Jan. 25, 1808) were collected and published in book form in 1808. The periodical consisted of light verse and droll commentary, and caricatures of New York City tastemakers and society were included, along with essays on such topics as "the conduct of the world," politics, public mores and women's fashions, music, and theater. The best of the satirical magazines yet published in the United States, *Salmagundi* was an immediate success.

Paulding published a second series (May 1819 to September 1820) by himself, but it did not contain the heterogeneous mixture that constitutes an authentic salmagundi, and it was unsuccessful.

Saturday Club *also called* Magazine Club *or* Atlantic Club. American social club of New England literati that was founded in 1855 and that met monthly at the Parker House, a Boston hotel. Notable members included Oliver Wendell Holmes, Ralph Waldo Emerson, Henry Wadsworth Longfellow, James Russell Lowell, Richard Henry Dana, John Greenleaf Whittier, William Dean Howells, Nathaniel Hawthorne, Henry James, and Charles Sumner.

Saturday Review, The *also called* (until 1952) The Saturday Review of Literature. Literary periodical founded in New York by Henry Seidel Canby in 1924. It was originally devoted to the work of new writers, including many foreign writers in translation, as well as to that of earlier writers such as Walt Whitman and Ralph Waldo Emerson. Among the early contributors to the periodical were Mary Austin, Edgar Lee Masters, and G.K. Chesterton. The scope of the review was expanded by Norman Cousins, who edited the magazine for more than 30 years, and for a time the magazine was published as four separate reviews of the arts, society, education, and the sciences. It folded in 1986.

Sewanee Review, The Quarterly periodical of general culture with an emphasis on literature, founded at the University of the South in Sewanee, Tennessee, in 1892. In the early 1940s the review began publishing fiction, and the emphasis on criticism was also increased. *The Sewanee Review* became associated in particular with the New Criticism, though it published other views as well. Contributors included Cleanth Brooks, Robert Lowell, Wallace Stevens, Robert Penn Warren, Malcolm Cowley, W.H. Auden, Dylan Thomas, Louise Bogan, and George Woodcock.

Smart Set, The American literary magazine founded by William D'Alton Mann and published monthly in New York City from 1900 to 1930. Most notable among its editors were S.S. Van Dine and the team of H.L. Mencken and George Jean Nathan. It was a consciously fashionable magazine that featured novelettes, short stories in English and in French, essays, poems, plays, criticisms, and humorous sketches.

Among the American writers whose early work was published in *The Smart Set* were Eugene O'Neill, F. Scott Fitzgerald, and O. Henry; it also introduced the nation to the writings of James Joyce, D.H. Lawrence, Ford Madox Ford, and Gabriele D'Annunzio. Other notable contributors included W. Somerset Maugham, Frank Norris, Sinclair Lewis, Theodore Dreiser, Willa Cather, Sherwood Anderson, Ezra Pound, and James Branch Cabell.

Southern gothic A style of writing practiced by many writers of the American South whose stories set in that region are characterized by grotesque, macabre, or fantastic incidents. Flannery O'Connor, Tennessee Williams, Truman Capote,

William Faulkner, and Carson McCullers are among the best-known writers of Southern gothic. *See also* GOTHIC.

Theatre Guild A theatrical society founded in New York City in 1918 for the production of high-quality, noncommercial American and foreign plays. The guild, founded by Lawrence Langner, departed from the usual theater practice in that its board of directors shared the responsibility for choice of plays, management, and production. The first two seasons included plays by Jacinto Benavente y Martínez, Saint John Ervine, John Masefield, and August Strindberg.

Following the world premiere of George Bernard Shaw's *Heartbreak House* in 1920, the guild became Shaw's American agent, producing 15 of his plays, including world premieres of *Back to Methuselah* and *Saint Joan*. Eugene O'Neill's long association with the guild began with its production of *Marco Millions* in 1928. Other American authors whose works were produced by the guild included Sidney Howard, William Saroyan, Maxwell Anderson, and Robert Sherwood—all Pulitzer Prize winners. The Theatre Guild contributed to American musical theater by producing George Gershwin, Ira Gershwin, and DuBose Heyward's *Porgy and Bess* and by bringing Richard Rodgers and Oscar Hammerstein II together for such collaborations as *Oklahoma!* The "Theatre Guild of the Air" (1945–63) successfully produced plays for radio and television.

Transcendentalism Movement of writers and philosophers in 19th-century New England who were loosely bound together by adherence to an idealistic system of thought based on a belief in the essential unity of all creation, the innate goodness of humankind, and the supremacy of insight over logic and experience for the revelation of the deepest truths. The writings of the Transcendentalists represent the first flowering of the American artistic genius and introduced the American Renaissance in literature.

Sources to which the New England Transcendentalists turned in their search for a liberating philosophy were German transcendentalism, especially as it was refracted by Samuel Taylor Coleridge and Thomas Carlyle; Platonism and Neoplatonism; the Indian and Chinese scriptures; and the writings of such mystics as Emanuel Swedenborg and Jakob Böhme. Part of the Romantic movement, New England Transcendentalism originated in the area around Concord, Mass., and from 1830 to 1855 represented a battle between the younger and older generations and the emergence of a new national culture based on native materials. It attracted such diverse and highly individualistic figures as Ralph Waldo Emerson, Henry David Thoreau, Margaret Fuller, Orestes Brownson, Elizabeth Palmer Peabody, and James Freeman Clarke, as well as George Ripley, Bronson Alcott, the younger W.E. Channing, and W.H. Channing. Emerson and Fuller founded *The Dial* (1840–44), the prototypal "little magazine" wherein some of the best writings by minor Transcendentalists appeared.

western A genre of novels and short stories, motion pictures, and television and radio shows that are set in the American West, usually in the period from the 1850s to 1900 when the area was fully opened to white settlers. Though basically an American creation, the western has its counterparts in the gaucho literature of Argentina and even in tales of the settlement of the Australian outback.

The western has as its setting the immense plains, rugged tablelands, and mountain ranges of that portion of the United States lying west of the Mississippi River, in particular the Great Plains and the Southwest. The conflict between white pioneers and Indians and between cattle ranchers and fence-building farmers form two basic themes. Cowboys, the town sheriff, and the U.S. marshal are staple figures. Actual historical persons in the American West have figured prominently: Wild Bill Hickok, Wyatt Earp, and other lawmen, notorious outlaws such as Billy the Kid and Jesse James, and Indian leaders such as Sitting Bull and Geronimo.

In literature, the western story had its beginnings in the first adventure narratives, accounts of the western plainsmen, scouts, buffalo hunters, and trappers. Perhaps the earliest and finest work in this genre was James Fenimore Cooper's *The Prairie* (1827). E.Z.C. Judson (Ned Buntline) wrote dozens of western stories and was responsible for transforming Buffalo Bill into an archetype. Owen Wister wrote the first western that won critical praise, *The Virginian* (1902). By far the best-known and one of the most prolific writers of westerns was Zane Grey, an Ohio dentist who became famous with the classic *Riders of the Purple Sage* in 1912. Another prolific author of westerns was Louis L'Amour.

Notable among the authors of western short stories are A.H. Lewis, Stephen Crane, and Conrad Richter. Many western novels and short stories first appeared in pulp magazines, such as *Ace-High Western Stories* and *Double Action Western*.

Other western classics are Walter van Tilburg Clark's *The Ox-Bow Incident* (1940) and A.B. Guthrie, Jr.'s *The Big Sky* (1947) and *The Way West* (1949). Larry McMurtry's *Lonesome Dove* (1985) was a Pulitzer-Prize winning paean to the bygone cowboy.

WPA Federal Theatre Project National theater project sponsored and funded by the U.S. government as part of the Works Progress Administration (WPA). Its purpose was to create jobs for unemployed theatrical people in the Great Depression years of 1935–39.

While the project was in operation, some 10,000 professionals were employed in all facets of the theater. The four-year effort involved about 1,000 productions in 40 states; performances were often free to the public. These productions included classical and modern drama, children's plays, puppet shows, musical comedies, and documentary theater known as Living Newspaper. Other projects included the production of plays by young, unknown American playwrights, the promotion of black American theater, and the presentation of radio broadcasts of dramatic works. Following a series of controversial investigations by the House Committee on Un-American Activities and Subcommittee on Appropriations into leftist commentary on social and economic issues, the Federal Theatre Project was terminated in 1939 by congressional action.

WPA Federal Writers' Project A program established in 1935 by the Works Progress Administration (WPA) as part of the New Deal struggle against the Great Depression. It provided jobs for unemployed writers, editors, and research workers. Directed by Henry G. Alsberg, it operated in all states and at one time employed 6,600 individuals. The American Guide series, the project's most important achievement, included guidebooks to every state and territory (except Hawaii), as well as to Washington, D.C., New York City, Los Angeles, San Francisco, New Orleans, and Philadelphia; to several major highways (U.S. 1, Ocean Highway, Oregon Trail); and to scores of towns, villages, and counties. The project also produced ethnic studies, folklore collections, local histories, and nature studies— totaling more than 1,000 books and pamphlets.

In accordance with WPA regulations, most of the project's personnel came from the relief rolls. They included such already prominent authors as Conrad Aiken, Maxwell Bodenheim, and Claude McKay and such future luminaries as Richard Wright, Ralph Ellison, Nelson Algren, Frank Yerby, Saul Bellow, Loren Eiseley, and Weldon Kees. (Eudora Welty was a photographer for the Mississippi guide.) Congress ended federal sponsorship of the project in 1939 but allowed it to continue under state sponsorship until 1943.

Yale school A group of literary critics, specifically several English professors at Yale University, who became known in the 1970s and '80s for their deconstructionist theories. The Yale school's skeptical, relativistic brand of deconstruction expanded upon the groundwork of French philosopher Jacques Derrida and helped to popularize the deconstruction movement.

The most prominent members of the Yale school were Paul de Man and J. Hillis Miller. They contributed essays to the collection *Deconstructionism and Criticism* (1979), which analyzed the poem *The Triumph of Life* by P.B. Shelley. De Man, the most influential member, was closely allied to Derrida and based his theories on a system of rhetorical figures. The writings of Geoffrey H. Hartman and Harold Bloom (both of whom were also at Yale) were frequently critical of the Yale school, while Miller, whose work focused on textual opposites and differences, often defended charges that the Yale school was nihilistic. Other American deconstructionists included Barbara Johnson and Jonathan Culler.